Law and Philosophy Library

Volume 151

The Law and Philosophy Library, which has been in existence since 1985, aims to publish cutting edge works in the philosophy of law, and has a special history of publishing books that focus on legal reasoning and argumentation, including those that may involve somewhat formal methodologies. The series has published numerous important books on law and logic, law and artificial intelligence, law and language, and law and rhetoric. While continuing to stress these areas, the series has more recently expanded to include books on the intersection between law and the Continental philosophical tradition, consistent with the traditional openness of the series to books in the Continental jurisprudential tradition. The series is proud of the geographic diversity of its authors, and many have come from Latin America, Spain, Italy, the Netherlands, Germany, and Eastern Europe, as well, more obviously for an English-language series, from the United Kingdom, the United States, Australia and Canada.

Giorgio Maniaci

The Unbearable Lightness of Legal Antipaternalism

Springer

Giorgio Maniaci
Department of Law
University of Palermo
Palermo, Palermo, Italy

ISSN 1572-4395 ISSN 2215-0315 (electronic)
Law and Philosophy Library
ISBN 978-3-031-96843-3 ISBN 978-3-031-96844-0 (eBook)
https://doi.org/10.1007/978-3-031-96844-0

This Springer imprint is published by the registered company Springer Nature Switzerland AG
The registered company address is: Gewerbestrasse 11, 6330 Cham, Switzerland

Foreword: Pelagius or Augustine?

I am pleased to write these brief comments on this new book by Giorgio Maniaci.[1] It is an impassioned book, written from the heart, as writing against someone or something tends to be. This, however, in no way impedes the, sometimes obsessive, analytical rigour in the presentation of the various arguments and counter-arguments. Those of us who have known Giorgio for many years are well aware of this. I have academic and personal, fraternal ties with him, as with the whole legal philosophy group in Palermo, and Giorgio, when he was a young doctoral student, made two research stays at my university, in Barcelona, and he has visited us several times since then. In other words, this preface is another link in the long rope that binds our philosophical conversations, a rope braided with arguments and also with affection.

The legal paternalism that Giorgio attacks is the political-legal conception according to which it is justified to use state coercion, at least sometimes, to prevent some people from causing themselves some harm, even if they have consciously, deliberately, rationally, with adequate information, in the absence of threats, chosen the course of action or omission that causes that harm.

In the book there are many, usually controversial, examples of such use of coercion in our contemporary Western societies: the obligation to wear seat belts in cars or helmets on motorbikes, the prohibition in some countries of prostitution or surrogacy, the use of narcotics, the prohibition of euthanasia, etc. There are many more, however, which are widely accepted: the regulation of working hours, the establishment of a minimum wage, health and safety measures at work, and a host of labour law regulations which, while protecting the interests of workers, are characteristically *paternalistic*.

Then, Giorgio defends what he calls, at the beginning of the second chapter, *moderate legal antipaternalism*, defined as it follows:

> the state or an official acting under the state's authority may *not* [...] use coercion against the will of adult individuals if (a) the sole or primary purpose for doing so is to make sure

[1] On the occasion of the Spanish version of these ideas (Maniaci 2020) I published a comment I partially return to here (Moreso 2021).

> that the actions they take or fail to take (or otherwise attempt to take or to avoid) do not cause harm to themselves (or what is understood to be such) or put them at significant risk of harm, be it physical, psychophysical, economic, or of any other nature, and so do not undermine their own good, and if (b) it is clear or is reasonable to assume that these persons' intentions—to engage in a course of conduct that is considered harmful or dangerous to themselves—have been formed in a rational way, with full mental capacity and taking the relevant facts into account, and as long as the choices so made are stable over time and are sufficiently free of coercive pressures.

I think that all of us who consider that the most adequate conception of morality rests on the *autonomy* of moral agents must accept this position that Giorgio masterfully articulates. Only to prevent those decisions we make in conditions in which we are not rational, those conditions in which we are basic incompetent, are paternalistic decisions justified.

However, deciding when human beings act in a rational way, i.e. when we give consent in a vice-free, truly autonomous way, is more controversial. Perhaps here, to use an old theological polemic, there are two conceptions of rationality and human agency, a *Pelagian* and an *Augustinian* conception. It may be useful, in order to understand what I am saying, to turn to some reflections on the work of John Rawls, since Rawls' work embodies the contemporary version of Kantian autonomy and, on the other hand, I consider myself a Rawlsian.

In 2009, Thomas Nagel edited what had been, in 1942, the degree thesis of the young John Rawls at Princeton University; to it, he added an unpublished text written by Rawls in 1997, shortly before his death, "On My Religion."[2] In this text, Rawls explains how religion was enormously important to him at Princeton and that he was even considering entering a seminary to become an Episcopalian pastor. But then World War II broke out, and he was called up to fight for the US Army in its conflict with Japan in the Philippines. He goes on to explain that around 1945, he abandoned his religious beliefs as a consequence of his time in the army and describes three events that affected him deeply.[3] Firstly, the sermon of an Anglican pastor who told them that God aimed the Americans' bullets at the Japanese and protected them from theirs. Secondly, the death of one of his best friends who had volunteered with him for a double mission whereby one had to participate in a reconnaissance of the Japanese position, and the other had to give blood to a wounded man. By chance, Rawls' blood was compatible, and his friend died on the mission. Thirdly and most significantly, according to Rawls, was the knowledge, of which he had previously been completely unaware, of the monstrosities suffered by the Jewish people at the hands of the Nazis in the Holocaust.

In his thesis,[4] Rawls strongly criticized Pelagius' position that we can only achieve salvation through merit. Pelagius was that monk from Roman Britain, who at the beginning of the fifth century of our era came in for bitter criticism from Augustine of Hippo, who ultimately succeeded in having his ideas declared hereti-

---

[2] Rawls (2009).

[3] *Ibidem*, pp. 262–263.

[4] *Ibidem*, pp. 229–230.

cal by the Catholic Church. Pelagius had a somewhat optimistic conception of human rationality and action, believing that humans are fully responsible for their actions and that, to use his religious language, salvation is ours to obtain. Augustine of Hippo was more pessimistic: he saw excessive boasting in that position, believing instead that human nature is "violated, wounded, torn, ruined ..."[5]

And Rawls, in his youthful work, sided with Augustine:[6]

> There is no merit before God [...]. The authentic community does not count the merits of its members. Merit is a concept rooted in sin...'.

But there are other passages in which Rawls foreshadows what will be a fundamental aspect of his theory of justice, for example:[7]

> The human person, once perceiving that the Revelation of the Word is a condemnation of the self, casts away all thoughts of his own merit [...] The more he examines his life, the more he looks into himself with complete honesty, the more clearly he perceives that what he has is a gift. Suppose he was an upright man in the eyes of society, then he will now say to himself: 'So you were an educated man, yes, but who paid for your education; so you were a good man and upright, yes, but who taught you your good manners and so provided you with good fortune that you did not need to steal; so you were a man of a loving disposition and not like the hard-hearted, yes, but who raised you in a good family, who showed you care and affection when you were young so that you would grow up to appreciate kindness—must you not admit that what you have, you have received? Then be thankful and cease your boasting—."

As Joshua Cohen and Thomas Nagel say in the introduction to this Rawls book:[8]

> This brings us to a particularly striking continuity between this thesis and Rawls' later views: the rejection of merit. One of the famous and controversial assumptions in *A Theory of Justice* is that a just social order should not seek to distribute benefits on the basis of merit. Rawls is not interested in rejecting the ideal of the moral value of merit entirely, but he rejects its adequacy as a basis for determining how goods, or any other of people's titles, are distributed in a well-ordered society.

Rawls believes that merit should not be the measure of justice or the distribution of goods because our talents and capacities are the result of the natural lottery, and for this reason, they must be understood as "common assets."[9] In Rawls' mature theory, this most painful aspect of human nature is no longer remedied by divine grace but by sharing a common project under the principles of justice, and it is in this context that we develop our rationality and autonomy. Therefore, justice as fairness must provide everyone with access to primary goods, especially the primary good of self-respect.

---

[5] "Quid tantum de naturae possibilitate praesumitur? Vulnerata, sauciata, vexata, perdita est", Augustinus Hipponensis, *De natura et gratia* [413–417]. S. Aurelii Augustini, *Opera Omnia: Patrologiae Latinae*, https://www.augustinus.it/latino/natura_grazia/index.htm.

[6] Rawls (2009), p. 241.

[7] *Ibidem, p.* 240.

[8] Cohen and Nagel (2009), p. 18.

[9] Rawls (1999), sec. 48. Rawls (2001), p. 72-73.

It is my conjecture that this position of Rawls' makes room in his conception of justice as fairness for the acceptance of various measures of justified paternalism. Perhaps, in this way, Maniaci's moderate antipaternalism is also a way of vindicating a *justified legal paternalism.* In fact, I share many, though not all, of Giorgio's positions, in the sense that some measures that do not seem justified to him seem justified to me. The reason for this discrepancy, I think, is that I conceive of moral autonomy as embodied in beings who are *vulnerable*, and *vulnerability* makes it more plausible to accept some of these measures.

I shall end with an example that highlights this space for discrepancy: Manuel Wackemheim, a French national, performed in the early 1990s in a show called "dwarf tossing," which usually took place in discotheques, and which consisted of throwing extremely short people, dwarfs, suitably dressed to protect them, against padded walls. Obviously, with the consent of the people who starred in such attractions, the French municipalities of Morsang-sur-Orge and Aix-en-Provence banned such shows. The affected Mr. Wackenheim appealed to the Courts, which found in his favour, but the municipalities appealed to the French Council of State, which ruled in his favour, basically on this argument:[10]

> Le Conseil d'État a jugé que le respect de la dignité de la personne humaine est une composante de l'ordre public. Par conséquent, l'autorité investie du pouvoir de police municipale peut interdire une attraction qui y porte atteinte, même en l'absence de circonstances locales particulières, en faisant usage de son pouvoir de police générale.

I guess that my conception of human dignity is founded on an idea of *autonomy embodied in vulnerable beings*. To adequately develop this idea of vulnerability is a task that I consider very relevant.[11] Perhaps Giorgio can contribute, with his usual lucidity, to shed light also in this area.

Barcelona, 2nd November 2024.

Pompeu Fabra University J. J. Moreso
Barcelona, Spain
BIAP (Barcelona Institute of Analytic Philosophy),
María de Maeztu Unit of Excellence
Barcelona, Spain

[10] *Conseil d'Etat, 27 octobre 1995, Commune de Morsang-sur-Orange et Ville d'Aix-en Provence.* https://www.conseil-etat.fr/ressources/decisions-contentieuses/les-grandes-decisions-du-conseil-d-etat/conseil-d-etat-27-octobre-1995-commune-de-morsang-sur-orge-et-ville-d-aix-en-provence.

[11] A valuable reflection in Ricoeur (2001), pp. 85–105. The notion of vulnerability is crucial in some feminist literature, for instance, Mackenzie C et alii (eds) (2014). My first approach is in Moreso (2023), pp. 157–172.

References

Cohen J, Nagel T 'Introduction' to Rawls J (2009) Conseil d'Etat, 27 octobre 1995, Commune de Morsang-sur-Orange et Ville d'Aix-en Provence. https://www.conseil-etat.fr/ressources/decisions-contentieuses/les-grandes-decisions-du-conseil-d-etat/conseil-d-etat-27-octobre-1995-commune-de-morsang-sur-orge-et-ville-d-aix-en-provence.

Maniaci G (2020) Contra el paternalismo jurídico. trad. De M. Maldonado. Marcial Pons, Madrid

Moreso JJ (2021) Acerca del pelagianismo de Maniaci. Comentario a Contra el paternalismo jurídico (2021). Diritto e questioni pubbliche XXI(2):123–135.

Moreso JJ (2023) El semipelagianismo de Manuel Atienza. In: Díaz E, Laporta FJ (eds) Leer a Manuel Atienza. Madrid, Centro de Estudios Políticos y Constitucionales, pp 157–172

Rawls J (1999) A theory of justice, 2nd edn. Harvard University Press, Cambridge

Rawls J (2001) Justice as fairness. A restatement. In: Kelly E (ed) Harvard University Press, Cambridge

Rawls J (2009) A brief inquiry into the meaning of sin and faith, with 'On my Religion'. In: Nagel T (ed) Harvard University Press, Cambridge

Ricoeur P (2001) Autonomie et vulnérabilité. In: Ricoeur P, Le Juste 2, Paris, Éditions Esprit: 85–105. Mackenzie C et alii (2014) (eds) Vulnerability: New Essays in Ethics and Feminist Philosophy. Oxford University Press, New York

Preface

I will devote my first lecture to the opposition between lightness and weight and will uphold the values of lightness. This does not mean that I consider the virtues of weight any less compelling, but simply that I have more to say about lightness.

[...] the time has come for me to look for an overall definition of my work. I would suggest this: my working method has more often than not involved the subtraction of weight. I have tried to remove weight, sometimes from people, sometimes from heavenly bodies, sometimes from cities; above all I have tried to remove weight from the structure of stories and from language. —Italo Calvino, "Lightness," in *Six Memos for the Next Millennium* (Harvard University Press, 1988)

I still have to face the hours, and the hours after the party, and the hours after that. [...] I stay alive for you, but now you have to let me go [...]. You were so good to me, Mrs. Dalloway. I love you, I don't think two people could have been happier than we have been. —Dialogue between the poet (Ed Harris) and Mrs. Dalloway (Meryl Streep), *The Hours*, by Stephen Daldry (2002)

Antipaternalism is a *light* conception in the sense that it gives autonomous agents the legitimate power to pursue their happiness or well-being. This implies letting people go, as the Poet asserts in the epigraph quote from the movie *The Hours*, allowing them to be happy in the way they prefer, as long as they do not cause harm to others, letting them fulfil their true nature, a nature that depends on how the individual reacts during childhood, based on their genome, both consciously and unconsciously, to their family upbringing and the socio-cultural context. Paternalism is a heavy and dour conception. As Calvino says in the epigraph quotes, I have tried to remove weight from philosophical and ethical conceptions.

There are three main senses of *unbearable*: "that which cannot be resisted," "emotionally or psychologically untenable," or "a thesis that is absurd, false, devoid of empirical evidence." In this context the fundamental senses of *unbearable* are the first two. For the paternalists, the intolerant, or the weak, legal antipaternalism is emotionally or psychologically untenable. For the antipaternaists it is the opposite. Secondly, strictly speaking, an ethical and legal conception cannot be "false," but it is precisely legal paternalism and/or the criminalization of drugs that is untenable or unbearable, because it is based on false empirical premises and incoherencies.

Thirdly, the unbearable lightness of legal antipaternalism means that this conception cannot be resisted: it is like an unstoppable force or a driving passion. The reason why the argument of individual autonomy cannot be resisted is that there are no valid arguments against autonomy. The perfectionist and utilitarian-organicist arguments are based on false empirical premises, or they are incoherent, even if these errors are not explicit or easy to detect. As Oscar Wilde says, "I can resist anything, except temptations." I would say that I can resist anything except legal antipaternalism. It is only a matter of time: the principle of individual autonomy will prevail in West.

As I will discuss in the last chapter, legal provisions allowing the production and sale of cannabis for nonmedical use have been approved in Canada and Uruguay, as well as in twenty-one jurisdictions of the United States (eighteen states, two territories, and the District of Columbia). Other countries that have legalized the recreational use of cannabis are Georgia, Germany, Malta, Mexico, South Africa, and Thailand.

In 2002, at the time of the judgement of the European Court of Human Rights *Pretty v. United Kingdom*, only the Netherlands, Belgium, and Switzerland recognized euthanasia or assisted suicide. At present, euthanasia or assisted suicide is also legal in Luxembourg, Germany, Spain, Italy, and under very limited conditions Portugal. In May 2024, the French Government introduced a bill on medically assisted dying. Active voluntary euthanasia is also legal in non-European countries such as Canada, Colombia, Ecuador, New Zealand, and Australia. While active euthanasia is illegal across the United States, assisted suicide is legal in Colorado, Oregon, Hawaii, New Mexico, Washington State, Vermont, Maine, New Jersey, California, and the District of Columbia, and it is *de facto* legal in Montana.

As concerns the view expressed by Moreso in the Preface, I'd like to say that I do not believe in *libertarian free will*. There could be a liberal-egalitarian conception without strong free will, because conscious desires are formed by unconscious desires, which in turn depend, deterministically or probabilistically, on our Genome, family upbringing, culture background, and later experiences that may aggravate some childhood traumas. According to a compatibilist conception, an action is freely or voluntarily performed, essentially when there are neither internal compulsions, such as serious relevant psychopathologies or incapacities, nor external compulsions, such as threats of harm from a third party. Thus, like Moreso and Rawls, I don't believe in the ordinary concept of *merit*, which normally depends on the concept of a libertarian free will. As Moreso says, "Rawls believes that merit should not be the measure of justice or the distribution of goods because our talents and capacities are the result of the natural lottery, and for this reason, they must be understood as 'common assets.'" As Rawls says in *A Theory of Justice*, our ability to cultivate talents depends on the character, which in turn depends on the natural lottery. Be that as it may, I think that assassins, rapists, kidnappers, and the like should be criminally punished, as happens today, because they show that they are motivated by harmful or/and dangerous unconscious desires.

Secondly, contrary to what Moreso says, there are some coercive measures—such as "the regulation of working hours, the establishment of a minimum wage, health and safety measures at work, and a host of labour law regulations which, while protecting the interests of workers"—that are *not* characteristically *paternalistic*, and I agree with that. As I say in Chap. 5, Sect. 5.2.1:

Generally speaking, it can be argued that certain or many workers' rights, such as paid holidays, daily rest, minimum hourly wages, and safe working environments, are rights that protect the autonomous preferences of workers, i.e., the autonomous preference for no negotiating these terms with employers. If negotiation on these rights were possible, if there were no maximum set hours for work shifts and overtime, there could easily be a race to the bottom in the labour-supply market, where some, driven by extreme poverty and/or by slightly greater economic resources, might accept increasingly worse working conditions because of unjust threats to not hire workers or threats of layoffs, offshoring, or reduced production, such as fourteen-hour shifts, contracts without paid holidays, or unsafe work environments, against the autonomous wishes of the great majority of workers who do not want to work under these conditions and who can withstand two or three months of strike. In a short time, the market might only offer contracts with exhausting shifts, without paid holidays, or with unsafe work environments, harming the autonomy of those desiring not working under these conditions. On the labour-demand side, employers could exert unjust coercive pressures (threats to not hire workers or threats of layoffs, offshoring, or reduced production), which vitiate the consent, to induce workers to accept contracts with fewer protections and rights, such as fourteen-hour shifts.

And "sufficient freedom from coercive pressures" is one of the conditions of individual autonomy. But Moreso is right. As I say in Chap. 3, Sects. 3.8.1 and 3.9.1, I do not believe in the argument of vulnerability and dignity against the autonomy of people, as in the case of the French "dwarf tossing" show, in which dwarfs, suitably dressed with protective gear, are thrown against padded walls, and which a French court has found to be illegal.

Consider the argument that since seriously ill, or elderly patients, or people with childhood trauma are frail, vulnerable, and suggestible, they cannot, by definition, have the mental capacity or autonomy needed to make decisions form themselves when the stakes are so high. If that were the case, and if we were to act on that argument, we would fall into the paradox whereby the people sick, elderly or with childhood trauma are barred from making important personal decisions (some of them in a sense wholly or partially irreversible), such as getting married; having an abortion; having gender-affirming surgery; giving consent to life-threatening operations; refusing life saving treatment; determining whether, with whom, and how to raise children; or drawing up a will. There are many circumstances and events that can make someone fragile, vulnerable, or unhappy: betrayal, divorce, separation, a failing romantic relationship, bereavement, a family quarrel, being unable to reunite with one's own family, having possessive or unloving parents, getting uprooted from one's native land, not being able to have children, getting fired from one's job, a serious neurosis. And yet it would be absurd to legally qualify the vulnerability or anguish attendant on such circumstances as a condition barring someone from carrying out certain "acts in the law," particularly acts through which patients may consent to medical treatment of any kind. If vulnerability or emotional distress were in fact a disabling condition preventing someone from properly consenting to medical treatment, then in at least half of the cases in which a patient consents to such treatment, the authorization would have to be deemed invalid (Chap. 3, Sect. 3.8.1).

The same goes with "dwarf tossing." If the argument of dignity is used paternalistically against the value of individual autonomy, the moment we specify what human dignity consists of, we get an argument that is either circular (vitiated by *petitio principii*) or parasitic, because it is so vague and capacious as to be able to take any argument in its premises, including the theological argument, the utilitarian/organicist argument, and the perfectionist argument. In fact, this is most likely to be the case (Chap. 3, Sect. 3.9.1).

The discussion in the rest of this work will be organized as follows. I start out in Chap. 1 by diagramming two types of paternalists, the intolerant and the weak. I continue in Chap. 2 by framing the problem and defining the two views in question: legal paternalism and antipaternalism. Then, in Chap. 3, with that frame of reference in place, I will go through the arguments for and against the same two views. In so doing, I will put forward a conception of practical rationality, an idea I take to be part of the very definition of antipaternalism and an essential part of individual autonomy as I understand this notion. And it is this further idea of individual autonomy that, in turn, as I will argue, provides the main foundation on which legal antipaternalism rests. In Chap. 4, I will probe deeper into the idea of individual autonomy by using it as a benchmark in light of which to assess the cognitive errors that individuals can make. In Chap. 5, I will turn to some cases that have traditionally proved challenging for antipaternalism, as in the example of voluntary slavery contracts. In Chap. 6, I will elaborate the notion of harm according to a liberal ethics and Mill's thought. Finally, in Chap. 7, I will argue against criminalizing drugs and in favour of an antipaternalistic legalization of drugs.

And now four closing remarks. First, I do not pretend that the ideas set out in this book will be shared by any majority of people. I rather believe that the ethico-political theses expounded in this book are essentially a minority view, or, in other words, and if I may resort to Latin, the book is conceived not so much *de iure condendo* as *de iure utopico*. But I have a reasonable amount of faith in the future generations. Second, I should comment on the ability of faith in an ideal or utopia to put reason to sleep, or rather, I should comment on the *places* where this phenomenon, the sleep of reason, can easily find a home: I will list applied ethics, and bioethics in particular, as well as legal philosophy, criminal scholarship, and (it almost goes without saying) politics. And the point is not that these are necessarily places of unreason, but that they *enable* the phenomenon of slumbering reason by making it possible for language to be manipulated, principles to be held up without stating the reasons for doing so, and arguments to be advanced without taking care to address the obvious counterarguments: they are places, in other words, that might well post the sign "Abandon all hope, ye who enter," or, at the very least, "Do not come in with high expectations." Third, I like to consider this book as a tribute to the great philosopher and criminal law scholar Joel Feinberg, and even more specifically as a brief gloss on his *Harm to Self*, the third in his four-volume *The Moral*

Limits of the Criminal Law: I see myself as attempting to understand and refine this deeply insightful work, which in turn, like my own book, pays homage to John Stuart Mill's *On Liberty*. Finally, with this work I am also revisiting a book I wrote that came out in 2012, with Giappichelli, in the "Analisi e diritto" series, edited by Paolo Comanducci and Riccardo Guastini, titled *Contro il paternalismo giuridico*, which is here presented in a revised, updated, and corrected form, even with respect to the Spanish version, which contains a new chapter, the third one. The Spanish version is titled *Contra el paternalismo jurídico*, published with Marcial Pons in 2020 in the "Filosofía y Derecho" series, edited by Jordi Ferrer and José Juan Moreso, with a translation by Mauricio Maldonado. The English version is an entirely new book: it fully revises and updates the Italian and Spanish versions and has new sections and two new chapters, the sixth and the seventh. The sixth chapter fully revises, updates, and rewrites the article "Il concetto di danno nell'etica liberale e i suoi critici," *Rivista di filosofia del diritto*, VI, 2, 2017, and the seventh chapter fully revises, updates, and rewrites the article "Principio del danno, antipaternalismo e proibizionismo delle droghe," in *L'antipaternalismo liberale e la sfida della vulnerabilità*, edited by Nicola Riva (Carocci editore, 2020).

Palermo, Italy Giorgio Maniaci

Acknowledgements

As always, I find myself recognizing that there are too many people with whom I have incurred a debt of gratitude in writing this book. Some of them have painstakingly read and commented on parts of this book; others have discussed them with me in conversation. Some have made a much greater contribution than others, often much greater than I suspect they think, and sometimes even beyond what they themselves had intended. But I will not make any distinction in my appreciation for their input. I begin by thanking the mourned Fred Schauer and the series editors Francisco J. Laporta and Torben Spaak for having included this book in Springer's prestigious *Law and Philosophy Library*. I would like to thank Filippo Valente for translating and proof-reading this book and for offering to provide support on some of the subsequent rewriting. I wish to thank my friend José Jusn Moreso for the *Preface* and Manuela Schwietzer, Associate Editor of Springer, for the help. I also extend my thanks to all the participants in the seminar held in Palermo in April 2010 and the annual seminar for young students of legal philosophy organized by Stefano Fuselli and held at the Verona Law School on 25 and 26 June 2010, to which I add the seminar organized by Prof. Jordi Ferrer held at the University of Girona on 13 October 2010, as well as the seminars held on 28 February 2011 at the Université Paris Ouest Nanterre, on 28 October 2011 at the University of Girona, and on 12 March 2012 as part of the PhD programme "Diritti umani: Evoluzione, tutela, limiti", offered at the University of Palermo, and finally the seminar held at Bocconi University on 16 May 2012. Special thanks go to Federico Arena, Mauro Barberis, Damiano Canale, Clelia Bartoli, Marco Brigaglia, Pierre Brunet, Bruno Celano, Francesca Ciulla, Veronique Champeil-Desplats, Pietro Denaro, Enrico Diciotti, Isabel Fanlo, Francesco Ferraro, Jordi Ferrer, Giulio Itzcovich, Carlo Lottieri, Enrico Maestri, Realino Marra, Paola Molinatto, Nicola Muffato, Maribel Narvaez Mora, Diego Martin Papayannis, Giorgio Pino, Francesca Poggi, Veronica Rodriguez Blanco, Janaina Roland Matida, Giulia Sajeva, Maurilia Scamardo, Adrian Varjao Sgarbi, Aldo Schiavello, Alessandro Spena, Ninni Sucato, Alessandro Tesauro, Carmen Vazquez Rojas, Vito Velluzzi, Francesco Viola, Vittorio Villa, and Federico Zumpani. I am most grateful, finally, to my parents, who in one way or another have taught me to appreciate the value of autonomy.

Contents

Chapter 1
A Guide to Diagramming a Paternalist

The general problem that paternalists and antipaternalists debate is the extent to which one can legitimately make decisions about one's own body or life, or the extent to which this can cause harm to oneself (or what may be widely regarded as such). More specifically, paternalists and antipaternalists debate highly controversial moral and legal issues about the legitimacy or illegitimacy of practices such as prostitution, religious flagellation, the sale and use of hard drugs, euthanasia, assisted suicide, extreme sports, and practices at the far end of the spectrum, such as selling one's own body parts.

In very broad outline, legal paternalism argues that the state is justified in curtailing individual liberties coercively, as by criminal penalty, so as to protect individuals themselves—or what is understood to be their "good"—or to prevent them from doing (what is considered) harm to themselves even if they are not doing harm to others. Legal antipaternalism, by contrast, argues that the state *cannot* claim such a power: it is not justified in coercively limiting the ability of adult individuals to make uncoerced and rational choices, even when these choices bring (what is considered) harm to them, whether the harm is physical or psychophysical—so long as it is not harm that *others* stand to suffer. It is to legal paternalism and legal antipaternalism that this book is devoted, arguing the case against the former and in favour of the latter.

Legal paternalism is an ethico-political doctrine that has widespread appeal in the West. To see why, I would suggest breaking down the paternalist camp into two broad, albeit highly stylised, groups: in one group we can place those who fear others, in the other those who fear themselves. Those in the first group know who they are and what they want; they claim to know what a person's well-being, happiness, or salvation depends on, and they claim to know this about *everyone*. They so firmly believe their claim that they are willing to impose their idea of happiness or salvation on others, even by force. They could be described as true fundamentalists (even if they are rarely honest with themselves, and so rarely describe themselves that way), in that they do not tolerate diversity; they cannot countenance those who are

G. Maniaci, *The Unbearable Lightness of Legal Antipaternalism*, Law and Philosophy Library 151, https://doi.org/10.1007/978-3-031-96844-0_1

"other": consciously or otherwise, they fear that these others may alter, contaminate, "infect," or enfeeble them with ideologies, sexualities, cultures, or religions other than their own. Indeed, paternalists do not confine themselves to believing what others should do in order not to waste their life: they are not content to just counsel that we should strive to advance science rather play poker, find inner strength rather than drown our pain in alcohol or heroin, or work hard rather than idle away the hours. There are many of us who hold such convictions. Paternalists take these convictions one step further and argue that it is the task and calling of the state to coercively (by force) impose on everyone the ideal of happiness or salvation they believe in. It does not matter what god paternalists are devoted to, or whether they are devoted to any god at all. It does not matter what religious cult they practice or whether they practice a cult of self-devotion. They often know they are paternalists. And in this they at least need to be recognized for being honest with themselves. It is not easy today, in the West, to recognize oneself as a paternalist, especially if one accepts the idea that contemporary ethics is inevitably a godless ethics, not because God does not exist—this we don't know with any certainty—but because, from Grotius onward, we cannot but *proffer reasons* and set about *solving moral problems*, as if God did not exist (*etiamsi Deus non daretur*).[1]

It is even more difficult to be public and vocal about being a paternalist. Indeed, this means mustering the boldness needed to look someone in the eye and tell them that what they want—what they have freely and rationally determined to be the content of their desires—doesn't count for much or doesn't hold much value. This is indeed brash and brazen, for it involves the pretension that you can go up to a rational adult and tell them that others know better than they do what it is that achieves their own good. Indeed, not all those who know themselves to be paternalists are upfront and public about it. And that is not because they do not have what it takes to be that way, but because they appreciate that it is often politically and socially more expedient to declare themselves to be liberal minded and to invoke fuzzy concepts like human dignity, reasonableness, or the sacredness of human life as tools with which to impose paternalistic ideals on others, thereby restricting their liberty.[2]

[1] "A secular bioethics is a bioethics developed as if God did not exist!" Scarpelli (1998), p. 10, my translation.

[2] This means that the relation among deceit, manipulation, and paternalism can take various forms, and I should highlight three in particular. Some paternalists know perfectly well that they are so, but they would rather not disclose that fact, and so they resort to fallacious or rationally inadequate arguments—such as the argument from human dignity, reasonableness, or the sacredness of life—so as to limit the freedom of others. Other paternalists deceive themselves, that is, they do not admit to themselves that they are paternalist. And still others are perfectly aware that they are making an instrumental use of paternalist rhetoric—the idea that "this is for your own good"—to promote ecclesiastical, racist, or homophobic ideals, and so they know that these ideals do not protect the interests of those whose good these ideals are meant to protect. Indeed, homophobic or racist arguments cannot be used in the space of public reason, at least in the West. Those who take this route, then, sometimes prefer to be considered paternalists rather than racists.

Other paternalists are instead afraid of themselves. And they often do not see their own paternalism, their positions being clothed in a more liberal, and sometimes egalitarian, garb. They often even deceive themselves. Unlike fundamentalists, and regardless of whether or not they are aware of their own paternalism, they are essentially afraid of their own weaknesses and therefore want to be saved or redeemed. They are afraid of temptations they cannot resist. They are not afraid of others: they are afraid of losing what they take to be their self-control, afraid of what they might do in certain situations, afraid of crossing the line. They are unable to exercise full control over their own environment, their space, their time, themselves—a full control they believe they could and should have, and in which believe strongly. This is a fear that will be familiar to anyone who has had some addiction—to cocaine, alcohol, sex, gambling, shopping, the internet—especially if they have fallen into this addiction headlong and have felt the need for someone to save them from the abyss, someone who will keep them from getting lost, who will deliver them from temptation, before they even fall. If you cannot resist the temptation to do something you think you shouldn't do, and you hate yourself for not being able to so resist, you can reach a point where you will want one thing and one thing only: that someone should intervene to get rid of the temptation for you. If we cannot exercise what we take to be our full control over ourselves, we may even grow resentful, coming to hate those who, instead of keeping us from temptation, leave us exposed to danger. In fact, we will need someone who will save us from ourselves, from our own temptations, and who will punish us if we should transgress, crossing into the realm of the forbidden. It makes no difference what the object of the addiction is (gambling, marijuana, sex, alcohol): once we have grown up, and our parents are no longer there to protect us, and punish us for falling into temptation when we should have resisted, we are left with the protection and punishment of the state, the super-ego incarnate. Some of the paternalists who are afraid of themselves may not be afraid of yielding to temptations they cannot resist but may still be afraid of what they take to be the need for them to choose, to deal with the stress and anxiety, and even the angst, of some of the choices they need to make according to the libertarian free will they believe in. These paternalists, in other words, are gripped by the fear of what they understand to be the *freedom to choose*, and they would rather not have that freedom in which they believe: they would rather not have the ability to choose.

As will become clear in Chap. 2, what I am calling the paternalistic error is to be distinguished into two different kinds of error depending on the group we are looking at. The error of the first group—the paternalists I am calling fundamentalist, those whose fear is of others—can be described as *ontological*: it consists in failing to appreciate that the only thing which achieves someone's good or well-being—the only good or well-being that can empirically, concretely be known—is what they themselves understand to achieve that good or well-being, so long as they are sufficiently rational and free from coercive pressures, as well as aware of the relevant facts (and so long as their desires are stable over time). The rest is just an illusion, deceptiveness. And it is a dangerous illusion, too, for it forms the basis on which to proceed to suppress the wishes of others. Nor does it make much sense to subject others to ideals of *otherworldly* salvation, ideals based on metaphysico-transcendent propositions that are empirically unverified and unfalsified (undemonstrated) and quite likely impossible to empirically verify or falsify (demonstrate), such as "God is against euthanasia." Rather, and contrary to this understanding of a person's good, everyone is responsible for their *own* faith. Surely, even people who are sufficiently rational and uncoerced can be unhappy. But in this case their unhappiness depends not on an inability to know what they want (within the bounds of what is humanly possible to be known) but on the impossibility of achieving what they want.

Fundamentalist paternalists, those who fear others, impose on others an idea of the good, ostensibly based on an ideal conception of interests, a conception on which there exist so-called objective interests, meaning interests entirely independent of the desires or preferences of sufficiently rational individuals, that is, desires or preferences decoupled from any element in the individual's "motivational set." This ideal interests conception, I submit, is prescientific, premodern, deeply deceptive, and absurd. Indeed, on this conception, it might be claimed that Agent Cogito has an interest in doing X (say, going into prostitution)—but *where* does this interest lie except in connection with an element of the agent's self?—even if nowhere in the manifestations of that self (not even in its unconscious manifestations)—and so nowhere in the agent's desires, preferences, or sufficiently rational motivations—is there any *evidence* of such an interest. Likewise, an ideal interests theory might be used to support the claim that an escort has an interest in getting married even if this escort has no desire to do so—no such desire that is sufficiently free and rational (uncoerced and based on a knowledge of the relevant facts), much less a sufficiently uncoerced and rational desire that every human being should have an interest in chastity.[3]

So the only correct sense in which we can say that it is in someone's best interest or nature to do X, or that X achieves their good or well-being, or that it comports with their *true* nature, or fosters their flourishing (or that of the humanity inherent in them) is the sense in which, as noted, this good or well-being can normally be determined in an empirical way by the individual concerned (unless this person suffers from some debilitating incapacity, such as a serious neurosis or psychosis); that is, the thing X must be something that the individuals concerned determine to be good for them or to be conducive to their own well-being or happiness, so long as the usual conditions are met (they need to be adult, for example, as well as

[3] The idea here is that humans—in virtue of their nature or of a divine design, or indeed on any other basis—have certain ends whose achievement is necessary to their well-being, their happiness. But as will be further discussed at note 93 of Chap. 2, this idea makes sense only if we can proceed from an *empirical* theory of *subjective well-being*—a theory which (a) tells us what makes people happy (whether it is people in a specific group or, universally, all humans in a given historical period), and which (b) can be put to an empirical test (as far as that is feasible). Such an empirical test may well tell us that someone in flesh and blood is happy and satisfied even if they do not live up to the values of prudence, temperance, industriousness, or family, or even if they do not maximize collective utility, nor does this necessarily mean that they have corrupted their nature. It simply means that it is not always necessary to pursue temperance or any other canonical ideal in order to achieve well-being or happiness.

sufficiently rational, aware of the relevant facts, and sufficiently free from coercive pressures, and it must be the case that the desires they form are stable over time).[4] Crucially, in support of this claim, it must be considered that the concept of well-being is normally subjective. In ordinary language, well-being can be physical or moral, or it can be psychophysical, but moral well-being is not ordinarily understood as something that can only be achieved through the pursuit of ideal interests or aims (such as temperance or industriousness) that are posited to exist independently of an individual's rational desires and are to be pursued on the basis of an ideal interests theory, nor (on the flip side) is it ordinarily understood that only in the absence of moral corruption can there be any moral well-being. Rather, moral well-being is ordinarily understood as spiritual well-being, which is a kind of psychological well-being, and so is a subjective well-being that cannot exist independently of the individual (unless it is the well-being of that person's immortal soul): this is the well-being that someone achieves if *they* fulfil their fundamental desires, meaning the desires they so regard (as fundamental) given the standard conditions (adequate rationality, a knowledge of the relevant facts, and sufficient freedom from coercive pressures).

So it is possible that someone doesn't realize that satisfying certain interests would make them happier or would make for greater well-being, but in all likelihood this will happen only when the standard conditions are not met: when that person suffers from a deep neurosis, for example, or is unaware of the relevant facts. If, instead, the interests identified on the basis of an ideal theory (such as an interest in practicing temperance or industriousness) do not coincide with the interests that, under the standard conditions, we consider to be our individual interests, we would find ourselves looking at the absurdity of an ideal interests theory stating that someone has an objective interest in pursuing some ideal (such as temperance or industriousness) even if these interests are doubly misaligned: not only do these ideal or objective interests not coincide with that person's actual fundamental desires, but they also do nothing to sustain his or her psychophysical well-being or this-worldly happiness.

So the question arises, what nature can be ascribed to these objective interests if they are identified independently of an agent's psychophysical well-being? They must have a metaphysico-transcendent nature—mysterious and quite likely mystical or religious—whose existence would pose a serious ontological problem, in that we would not have a sufficiently solid empirical basis on which to determine whether or not they actually exist, precisely as is the case with the question of the

[4] Although instrumental rationality is normally part of psychophysical well-being—for if we cannot form correct beliefs about reality, we won't be able to achieve our desires—it is not always the case that if we are behaving irrationally, we must therefore be unhappy. As Griffin points out, a compulsive hand-washer (someone who washes their hands hundreds of times a day, for example) may well be behaving irrationally, and the desire this behaviour satisfies may well be irrational, but it is nonetheless part of this person's well-being to satisfy this desire by so behaving. Griffin (1986), p. 25.

existence of God or of an immortal soul.[5] And it would be contrary to the whole point of institutionalized public discourse, like the discourse of judges or jurists, to make decisions on metaphysico-transcendent grounds (reasoning from tenets such as "God is contrary to euthanasia") or ones based on objective interests—identified on metaphysico-transcendent, typically religious bases—for that would undermine the principle of the separation of church and state (and so also its stronger sibling, the principle of *laïcité*).

So we have three scenarios here, giving us three alternatives, only one of which can stand. In the first scenario, the ideal interests theory truly is committed to a factual, descriptive account of the uncoerced and rational desires that people actually form, an account of what individuals, on careful reflection, come to regard as their true interests—all under the standard conditions, namely, the same individuals are sufficiently rational, sufficiently free of coercive pressures, and aware of the relevant facts, and their desires are stable over time—in which case we would have no empirical warrant for statements of the kind that everyone has a desire to do X or an interest in doing X (such as prostituting oneself or getting married or having children) or that anyone who is seriously ill (whether physically or psychically) wants to live: such claims would turn out to be false, or they would be exposed to the fallacy of composition, or both. But it is clear that this is not the function of the ideal theory. Otherwise, we need to concede that the ideal interests theory is *not* committed to a factual account of human interests: it therefore reveals itself to be a normative theory disguised as a factual one, a deceitful theory, and that is the second scenario, or, in the third scenario, a theory resting on metaphysico-transcendent, typically religious, foundations, and so a theory that cannot be reconciled with the principle of the separation of church and state.

We can turn now to the error committed by paternalists in the second group, those who fear that they won't be able to exercise self-restraint or self-control, which they believe is possible and exists. This error is twofold. Just like the sailors ordered by Ulysses to tie him to the mast of his ship so that he could hear the sirens singing and not fall prey to the enchantment of their honeyed song, so a antipaternalistic state (and one that, in truth, is only moderately so) can introduce measures or restrictions designed to make it less likely for people to give in to certain temptations (the state, for example, could restrict the sale or consumption of certain goods by limiting the places and hours of sale, under a sales curfew, or it could prohibit the sale of addictive substances, such as heroin or cocaine at a drug store, or it could permit the sale of heroin and cocaine at a pharmacy so long as certain conditions are met, such as showing a prescription issued by a doctor who will explain what the risks are of using such substances, and the prescription might last for, say, ten years).

---

[5] In order to demonstrate that the well-being of an immortal soul coincides with the individual's psychophysical well-being, we would have to prove that people considered to be "bad" or wicked—corruptors, malfeasants, financial fraudsters, robbers, organized criminals, murderers, rapists, and the like—necessarily undergo psychological suffering as a result of their bad or wicked behaviour, something that contemporary psychology and criminology rule out (except for some sociopaths and serial killers affected by serious personality or mental disorders).

Even an antipaternalistic state can help those who fear their own weakness in protecting themselves from specific dangers or temptations.[6] If it then turns out that there is a limit beyond which someone can exercise what they take to be their control over themselves, over their impulses—because their first-order desires are contradicted by their second-order desires (i.e., their first-order desire do X is contradicted by their desire *not* to have the desire to do X)—then they cannot be said to have sufficient rationality. And if they do not have sufficient rationality (they might be affected by a polar disorder, for example), then there will be some cases in which they are not permitted to engage in certain activities that would cause serious injury to themselves. So the first error consists in assuming that only under a paternalistic state is it possible to solve the problem of self-harm resulting from weakness of will or other incapacity that prevents people from acting with sufficient rationality. The second error consists in assuming that not just a few individuals but the vast majority of them are so weak-willed, unhinged, and incapable of resisting temptation, or so apprehensive about the freedom to make certain choices that those who are not that way need to bear the burden of a system designed for those who are, for those who cannot resist their own temptations or who would rather not have the freedom to choose they believe they have.

There is, however, one fear that paternalists in both groups seem to have in common: the fear they have for the fate of their children. For paternalists in the fundamentalist camp, this is primarily the fear that their children—their own flesh and blood—may stray from the model they are meant to embody. On the other hand, for paternalists in the self-identified weak-willed camp—for whom life is a constant barrage of internal conflicts, of temptations they must not, but ultimately do, yield to, and for whom life is filled with remorse and regret—this fear is the fear that their children, like their parents, will be unable to exercise what they take to be their self-control. Hence, as the self-fearing paternalists see it, if they cannot control themselves, they can at least control their children. They want their children to *not* be like them, that is, weak-willed; they want their children to be "better," strong-willed, and they want the state to protect their children should they lapse, losing their fortitude and sliding into weakness; they want the state to be there to save their children from the very temptations that they themselves (the parents) cannot resist, and to punish their children if they should succumb and give in to temptation.[7] But in both groups, paternalists fear that their children should engage in some bad or awful behaviour,

[6] Also easy to solve is the problem of punishment for transgressions that have gone beyond temptation and have actually been committed. For an antipaternalistic state would permit various forms of help and flagellation received from others (even in exchange for payment).

[7] Even here, in reality, there is very much at work the idea that the relation between parents and children is properly to be construed as one of "possession." For even if, as parents, we feel ourselves to be weak-willed—and thus want our children to be stronger, less pliant, and free of remorse and inner conflict—we can still, at the same time, and without contradiction, want them to be free in the sense that they should be able to decide for themselves what is good for them, in light of their *own* values rather than the ones *we* happen to hold dear, whereas paternalistic parents posit their own values as the benchmark against which to decide which "temptations" their children ought to fight back and which ones they can instead indulge.

with consequences that may be irreparable, such as doing hard drugs (crack or cocaine, for example); what they ultimately both fear is that they will no longer be able to control their children once the child has become an adolescent or an adult: they fear "losing" their children.

As we will see, however, the problem this book is concerned with does not extend to the actions of minors or of persons affected by a debilitating mental disorder, one that makes them incapable of willing the consequences of some of their actions (as in some case of schizophrenia). As I will note in Chap. 2, this is just a drawing of boundaries, an *actio finium regundorum*. The antipaternalistic thesis I will be arguing is exclusively concerned with adults who can be considered to be sufficiently rational to decide about their own lives, and sufficiently uncoerced in making such decisions, for it is a different ontological framework that we have to take into account in solving the problem of what behaviour can legitimately be engaged in by minors or by psychopathic subjects whose actions are harmful to their own health or life (this is a thornier and much more complex question that will not be taken up here). And yet, even if the discussion will not be concerned with minors, I do believe that the state ought to bring the full force of its administrative and criminal law to bear on those who sell hard drugs to minors. And I would take the same view even if the consumption of hard drugs were to be legalized or decriminalized for adults. But that need not be a paternalistic argument. In fact there appears to me to be a fundamental error in the reasoning of some paternalists. This is the error of assuming that the state can effectively prevent dangerous temptations from being offered to the youth, as by eliminating or significantly reducing the consumption of psychoactive drugs among adolescents, which means that on any given day, at any party, nightclub, or pub, or during any field trip, student sit-in, or concert, the state will be there to prevent a friend or anyone from approaching a youth and lure this person into taking drugs.

The sobering truth, however, is that the factors which drive a youth to take up drugs (such as cocaine or heroin) by and large fall beyond the control of the state as an organized community: these are factors like peer pressure, a cultural vogue or trend, a failure of the education system, emotional disorder, rebellion to authority, or a desire for the forbidden fruit, and they are even more likely to fall outside the purview of the state as a repressive apparatus (unlike what happens, for example, in an educational setting). In fact a hundred years of prohibitionist policy in the West have amply demonstrated that only a totalitarian state, a police state, can, perhaps, have some chance of effectively preventing the sale and consumption of narcotics. Certainly, this is not within the range of possibilities of a constitutional state subject to the rule of law, much less one that is democratic, liberal (in the classic sense of limited government), and egalitarian. For if countless youths every day go down the street in search of drugs, the market will sooner or later find ways to meet that demand, and cannot but respond in any other way.[8]

[8] As the foregoing remarks suggest, the reasons for rejecting a paternalistic ethico-political doctrine are fundamentally reasons of principle: they are ethico-political reasons rooted in the need to protect individual autonomy. Even so, we cannot discount the fact that paternalistic policies, such as

So, if parents, in their desperate effort to keep their adolescent children from temptation, are willing to prohibit everyone, including adults, from having access to the market that delivers the goods which draw adolescents into temptation, they should recall that the state cannot fix the errors these parents themselves have made in raising their children (in fact, it wouldn't even be possible for the state to do so), nor can the state, through the use of repressive force, hope to exercise any significant control over such deep-rooted cultural phenomena as the consumption of psychoactive drugs (what the state can and ought to do, if anything, is provide psychological and financial support for parents and children in serious difficulty, and punish abusive parents).

In that regard, and this is particularly apparent when we look at the broad support for prohibiting the sale and consumption of narcotics, many paternalists—particularly parents, and even more so fathers, as well as siblings and close friends—seem unable or unwilling to accept certain simple truths. They seem unable or unwilling to accept the possibility that they have made serious mistakes in bringing up their children, nor do they seem capable of bearing the sense of guilt deriving from the errors they have made in bringing up their children (even if there are many environmental factors that may lead an adolescent to consume drugs). They seem unable or unwilling to accept the consequences of such errors (consequences such as seeing their children end up doing drugs). And, most especially, they seem unable or

those prohibiting the sale and consumption of narcotics, are for the most part ineffective: this is a practical consideration that reinforces the argument against paternalism next to its reasons of principle. Clearly, when it comes to minors, and especially adolescents, prohibitions may well be warranted for antipaternalistic reasons of principle (such as the immaturity of the potential drug-takers). As noted, however, I will not be going into the intricate question of the relation between a person's capacity to make decisions for themselves and their rationality and psychological maturity (whether in adulthood or adolescence). On the inability of national and international organisms to shut down or significantly reduce the market for narcotics, see Alldridge (1996), pp. 239–257. These data are borne out as well by Italian government agencies: "Only through an adequate effort to study, analyse, and assess the threat as a whole is it possible to develop a strategy for fighting multinational criminal organizations, whose main source of profit comes precisely from drug trafficking. In this way, it will be possible to effectively and intelligently clamp down on *a market that, for the time being, does not appear to be contracting*." "The massive inflow of heroin from Asia, cocaine from South America, cannabis from North Africa, and synthetic drugs from the European bases keeps growing. In this scenario, the global production of opium is seeing a slight uptrend. The same holds for coca leaves and cocaine [...]. In fact, despite a diminished output from Colombia as a result of the strategic Plan Colombia, that decrease has been more than made up for by increased production out of Peru and Bolivia. The production of cannabis, for its part, has seen a clear upsurge in comparison with previous years, owing to increased demand worldwide." Dipartimento della Pubblica Sicurezza, Direzione Centrale per i Servizi Antidroga del Ministero dell'Interno (2006), pp. 53–76, at 53–54 (my translation, italics added; the report is also available at http://www.dronet.org/pdf/1.3%20Cocaina.pdf, accessed October 23, 2021). Similar findings are reported in Husak (1992), p. 52, noting that 56 percent of adolescents in the United States between the ages of twelve and seventeen said that it was easy for them to obtain illegal drugs, and 60 percent of high-school students had tried drugs. Cf. Husak (2002), p. 67ff., 71ff., and the exhaustive data from the World Drug Report 2009, 2010, and 2011, published by the United Nations Office on Drugs and Crime (UNODC), http://www.unodc.org/unodc/data-and-analysis/WDR.html, accessed June 2021.

unwilling to accept what amounts to an inevitability, namely, that in a constitutional state subject to the rule of law in an ethnically, culturally, and religiously pluralistic community, they will no longer be able to exercise control (or at least not full control) over their children once the child has reached the age of majority or has become an adult. They seem unable or unwilling to accept that they may "lose" the huge investment they have poured into the childrearing enterprise—all the time, energy, emotions, and material resources they have devoted to their children. And they ask the state to work a *miracle*: they ask the state as an organized community to make possible that which is impossible, namely, to ensure that adolescents and youths will always be kept safely away from temptations that may do harm to them. And since this miracle cannot be realized, their purpose in advancing this demand can ultimately only be to shake off the torment and feeling of guilt for the errors they have made, to quell the distress that comes with losing control over their own children, or to punish the "fruit" of those errors.

Finally, I do not know what antipaternalists fear, nor do I know if they can be "diagrammed," or sorted into classes, probably yes. But they probably fear that someone might take control of their body and mind—that a doctor or government official may use the power of the law to dictate how they ought to think and what they may do with their own bodies. In other words, I would guess that what antipaternalists fear is, above all else, paternalists themselves.

References

Alldridge P (1996) Dealing with drug dealing. In: Simester AP, Smith ATH (eds) Harm and culpability. Clarendon Press, Oxford, pp 239–257

Dipartimento della Pubblica Sicurezza, Direzione Centrale per i Servizi Antidroga del Ministero dell'Interno (2006) Traffico di cocaina: L'attività di controllo e prevenzione delle forze dell'ordine. In: Serpelloni G et alii, Cocaina: Manuale di aggiornamento tecnico scientifico, Verona Progetto Start, Dipartimento Nazionale per le Politiche Antidroga

Griffin J (1986) Well-being: its meaning, measurement, and moral importance. Clarendon Press, Oxford

Husak DN (1992) Drugs and rights. Cambridge University Press, Cambridge

Husak DN (2002) Legalize This! the case for decriminalizing drugs. Verso, London

Scarpelli U (1998) Bioetica laica. Baldini & Castoldi, Milan

World Drug Report 2009, 2010, and 2011, published by the United Nations Office on Drugs and Crime (UNODC)

Chapter 2
What Is Legal Paternalism?

2.1 Distinguishing Between Legal Paternalism and Legal Antipaternalism

As we saw in the introduction, the debate between paternalists and antipaternalists concerns some highly controversial moral and legal issues about the legitimacy or legality (or lack thereof) of activities such as prostitution, religious flagellation, the sale and consumption of addictive drugs, euthanasia and assisted suicide, extreme sports, and, moving further into the fringes, selling one's own body parts or even selling oneself into servitude or enslavement. But, as with any major ethical debate, there is a range of questions that need to be addressed before we can move into the debate and take a position within it: philosophical questions,[1] as well as definitional, theoretico-empirical, and moral. Thus, for example, paternalism and antipaternalism themselves are defined in several different ways in the literature.

This therefore makes it necessary to frame the terms of the discussion by drawing its boundaries by an *actio finium regundorum*. So in this second chapter I will begin by laying out what I mean by legal paternalism and legal antipaternalism. As for the former, I will be defining legal paternalism in a similar manner to the way that Gerald Dworkin defines paternalism,[2] not necessarily because this is the best

[1] By "philosophical questions" I mean a residual class of problems that can be described as ontological or metaphysico-transcendent, and I call them "residual" because it seems doubtful that they can be classed as definitional, empirical, or ethical.

[2] See Dworkin (1983a), p. 20; Feinberg (1983), p. 3; Garzón Valdés (1988), p. 156; Atienza (1988); Alemany (2005). For a broader definition of paternalistic action or interference, see Gert and Culver (1976); and VanDeVeer (1986), p. 22. Gert and Culver, for example, correctly point out that even a lie told to protect someone's good can, in certain circumstances, be considered paternalistic, while VanDeVeer includes within the paternalistic range not only actions aimed at doing good to others, but also actions aimed at protecting others from harm. For a deep analysis of political and legal paternalism, see Alemany (2006), chap. 1, esp. pp. 343ff., and Diciotti (1986), pp. 557–86.

G. Maniaci, *The Unbearable Lightness of Legal Antipaternalism*, Law and Philosophy Library 151, https://doi.org/10.1007/978-3-031-96844-0_2

definition in every context, but because it circulates widely in the literature and does a better job than others at delimiting the scope of the discussion for the questions we will be considering in this work. As can be appreciated from the definition offered here, and as I will be clarifying in the next section and in Chap. 3, I will mostly be concerned with the problem of justifying the state's use of coercion, whose most paradigmatic case, though certainly not the only case, is the state's use of criminal punishment. In other words, we will be primarily focused on "coercive paternalism." This means that we will not be addressing the problem of the legitimacy or otherwise of acts of paternalistic interference between sovereign states, nor (save for some brief remarks in Chap. 4) will we be addressing the legitimacy or otherwise of acts of interference aimed at nudging citizens toward making certain choices (what some argue to be a form of paternalism)[3] rather than at using force to prevent them from making other choices.

Legal paternalism can be defined as the moral-political conception on which the state or an official acting under the state's authority may rightfully use coercion against the will of adult individuals even when these persons' choices meet a set of practical standards—such as being sufficiently coherent, based on a knowledge of the relevant facts, and free from coercion and compulsion—solely or mainly for the purpose of protecting what are deemed to be these persons' interests, or what is qualified as their good, and particularly for the purpose of making sure that these persons, through some act or failure to act, will not do harm to themselves or attempt to do so in a way that poses a significant risk of harm to themselves, where the harm may be physical, psychophysical, economic, or of some other sort.[4] From here on out, for convenience's sake, this legal paternalism will simply be referred to as *paternalism*. But what does "solely or mainly for the purpose" mean in speaking of the purpose of protecting what are deemed to be someone's interests, or what is qualified as their good? In determining whether the justification for a law is paternalistic or liberal, we have to look at whether the law has a basis or justification in the harm principle, to which end we cannot rely on the lawmakers' publicly offered reasons for enacting that law, since the lawmakers may have been disingenuous in proffering those purported reasons, nor can we rely on the actual or real reasons that led the lawmakers to enact the law, since these reasons may not have any justificatory weight. We instead have to identify the reasons the lawmakers would sincerely offer or be ready and willing to espouse once their reasoning—their justificatory argument—is stripped of all evident contradictions, fallacies, and false premises or beliefs. In this sense, what makes a law paternalistic is not so much its stated purpose or the psychology or frame of mind behind its enactment but the basis on which it can reasonably be justified. This justificatory basis certainly qualifies as liberal if it can be seen to ultimately come down to the harm principle—the principle

[3] See G. Dworkin (1983b), pp. 105–106. On methods for orienting individuals toward choices deemed to be more rational or reasonable than the ones they would otherwise make, and doing so in ways that are more or less disguised, but without being coercive, see Sunstein and Thaler (2003) and Thaler and Sunstein (2003).

[4] A similar definition can be found in Pope (2004), p. 683ff.

under which any action is legitimate so long as it does not do harm to any third parties—since this stands as the basic liberal principle in Western societies in a state subject to the rule of law. Take, for example, a scenario in which opposition is growing against the practice of ritual slaughter and lawmakers move to ban the practice: they could do so on a discriminatory or paternalist ideological basis, or both, and in either case illiberal; or the justification could be based on public health, in which case the harm principle can be said to govern, and the justification can accordingly be described as liberal.

That can be contrasted with what I will be calling *moderate legal antipaternalism*, understood as the moral-political conception on which the state or an official acting under the state's authority may *not* use coercion in that way, that is, may not use coercion against the will of adult individuals solely or mainly for the purpose of making sure that these persons, through some act or failure to act, will not bring about some result that is regarded as harmful to themselves or to make sure that they will not attempt any course of action that poses a significant risk of doing such harm to themselves, where the harm may be physical, psychophysical, economic, or of some other sort, and so will not act against their own good, if it is clear or is reasonable to assume that these persons' intentions—to engage in a course of conduct that is considered harmful to themselves—have been formed in a sufficient rational way,[5] with sufficient mental capacity and taking the relevant facts into account, and as long as the choices so made are stable over time and are sufficiently free of coercive pressures. All the more so, on this conception, the state clearly may not limit the freedom of individuals if the actions they intend to take are not considered to be harmful to themselves or to others. Indeed, on the moderate antipaternalism here defended, if someone's decision-making is not vitiated in the sense just outlined, their freedom of action can be limited by recourse to coercion only if it does harm to others.[6] This is essentially a statement of John Stuart Mill's famous *harm-to-*

[5]As I will argue in Chap. 3, Sects. 3.2 and 3.4.1, the conception of rationality that is needed to define and defend an antipaternalistic position is essentially a formal conception. And it is in this formal sense that rationality is to be understood in defining antipaternalism.

[6]See Alemany (2005), p. 112; Feinberg (1986), p. 10ff.; Feinberg (1984), p. 31ff.; and Mill [1859] (1971), pp. 213–310. In that sense, the antipaternalistic conception here defended can be said to contain two basic theses, partly independent of each other. According to the first of these, a view endorsed by Feinberg, doing harm to oneself—or acting in ways that others see as contrary to one's own good—is never in itself a basis on which the state may justifiably resort to coercion to prevent that harm, so long as the person concerned is uncoerced and acting rationally. The second thesis is the harm-to-others principle, according to which, in a nutshell, the only or the fundamental reason that may justify the state in using force against adult and rational individuals who are sufficiently free from coercive pressures is to prevent them from doing harm to others. This is a principle that Feinberg in reality complements with what he calls the offense principle, under which the state may legitimately intervene not only to prevent someone from doing harm to others (the harm principle just stated) but also to prevent that person from causing "serious offenses" to others. (On the way these two principles relate to each other, a question we cannot here enter into, see Feinberg (1984), pp. 26ff. and 45ff.) The concept of harm is quite complex, its meaning being to a significant extent indeterminate, thereby inevitably entailing an evaluative component, and it will be closely analyzed in Chap. 6. In broad outline, however, and without pretending to be exhaustive, there can

others principle. From here on out, for convenience's sake, this moderate legal antipaternalism will simply be referred to as *antipaternalism*.

With some authors, this antipaternalism—or something comparable to the moderate legal antipaternalism just introduced—is referred to by a different name: *moderate paternalism*, clearly in distinction to a kind of paternalism termed *hard*. This is the choice that Joel Feinberg makes, for example.[7] As noted, however, these are

---

be distinguished six types of harm: (1) bodily harm (Agent A physically harms Agent B); (2) psychophysical harm (as a result of A doing wilful injury to B, B suffers post-traumatic stress or depression); (3) economic or financial harm; (4) "personal" harm, consisting in a significant intrusion into a person's bodily or perceptive sphere or home or in harm done to their personal identity (including harm done by tarnishing their name, likeness, or reputation; by spreading falsehoods about them; or by breaching their confidentiality); also included in this fourth type of harm are acts that significantly curtail a person's freedom of movement, such as kidnapping, sexual harassment (and harassment generally, by any means, including by telephone), stalking, defamation, and violations of privacy); (5) social harm, in which one is denied recognition or esteem by one's peers or within one's social group; and (6) emotional harm, where A is made to feel an abiding anger or resentment for some behaviour of B or to feel otherwise distraught as a result; this can be understood to include moral injury, but it is doubtful that it can include what might be called moral harms, where A embarks on a course of moral perversion or lures B into such behaviour, especially if B is construed as a disapproving, third-party bystander simply *witnessing* the perversion.

Feinberg agrees that this latter scenario does not amount to harm to others (to the disapproving witness), and certainly the distinction between paternalism and antipaternalism will not make much sense if A's immoral behaviour (or what B regards as immoral) is made to fall within the range of what constitutes harm to others. Here I am in agreement with Waldron (1993), p. 126. It is also worth pointing out that emotional harm seems inconsistent with antipaternalism if taken *in itself* as a sufficient basis for criminal penalties (except when children need to be protected), for if emotional harm were to be used in that way, it could easily lead to some serious and intolerable restrictions on individual liberty; thus, for example, interreligious marriage between A and B might be prohibited on grounds of the emotional distress it could cause to their families. There is no shortage of literature on the nexus between emotional harm and the law, but see Alemany (2006), p. 381ff.; Del Bò (2007), p. 20ff.; Diciotti (2005), p. 100ff., 112; Dworkin (2000); Feinberg (1984), p. 31ff.; Feinberg (1986), p. 10ff.; Ferrajoli (1989), p. 468ff.; Fiandaca (2010), p. 225; Gardner (2007), chaps. 1, 4, and 5; Wertheimer (1977), p. 306ff.; Sartorius (1983), p. IXff.; Spena (2010), pp. 497–524.

[7] See Feinberg (1986), p. 12: "Soft paternalism holds that the state has the right to prevent self-regarding harmful conduct [...] *when but only when* that conduct is substantially nonvoluntary, or when temporary intervention is necessary to establish whether it is voluntary or not." In this statement, Feinberg's position aligns with the first of the two basic theses of antipaternalism here defended (as outlined in the previous n. 6). But there are differences, and the main one comes down to a matter of framing, in that Feinberg's definition is cast in terms of powers, rights, and permissions: the state has the *power*, the *right*, to interfere only when certain conditions are met. My definition, by contrast, is cast in terms of *non*-powers and prohibitions: the state does *not* have this power or right—it is *prohibited* from exercising such a power or right—unless certain conditions are met. There are three reasons for so framing the definition in the language of prohibition. First, by so framing the state—as subject to prohibitions rather than as endowed with powers—we can make sure that we keep within range of the underlying liberal idea of limited government: the idea that there exists a protected sphere within which individuals are sovereign and in which the state has no right to interfere. Not incidentally, a similar statement can be found in Mill, even if Mill does not explicitly describe his view as antipaternalistic. Second, a negative definition does not prejudge the problem, addressed in the next section, of extreme acts of self-harm carried out by

different names for the same broad idea, and for the most part they do not point to any substantive difference. I will not be going into the relative merits of each nomenclature: suffice it to say that even if Feinberg calls his conception *soft paternalism*, there is nothing paternalistic about that conception. Nor will I be making a direct argument against extreme or radical antipaternalism, a minority view and one that cannot be easily defended. According to radical antipaternalism, the state may not, under any circumstance, use force to limit the ability of adult individuals to do harm to themselves: the state, in other words, may not, to this end, use force against someone's will, and may not do so regardless of how this will was formed (whether rationally or irrationally, coercively or noncoercively), and so even if it was not freely formed. Unlike radical antipaternalists, I believe that in *some* (not all) cases, the state does have a right to intervene where someone is affected by serious personality or mental disorders that deprive them of the ability to understand the consequences of some of their actions, especially if this incapacity leads them to engage in behaviour that is likely to do great harm to them. I will not frontally address the question of what the specific cases are that might justify such intervention. But when, in Chap. 3, we turn to the requisites of agency—rationality, mental capacity, and a knowledge of the relevant facts—we will be able to see, even if only indirectly, why radical antipaternalism proves to be untenable. What I suspect, in reality, is that the disagreement between the two types of antipaternalism at issue is not moral. Indeed, in the view of many radical antipaternalists, the problem with moderate antipaternalism is rather that it is logically incoherent, for it posits requisites (such as the aforementioned rationality and knowledge of the relevant facts) that instead of empowering individuals, enabling them to achieve what they want to achieve, act to *restrict* their ability to do so as *limiting* criteria. For this reason, in Chap. 3, Sect. 3.8, I will challenge this thesis, arguing that, on the contrary, it is radical antipaternalism that is (at least in part) incoherent, for if someone lacks the

---

persons affected by serious personality or mental disorders (such as schizophrenia) or who fundamentally lack mental capacity (such as children). In capsule form, Feinberg's thesis would say: "The state only has the right to limit the freedom of individuals who are *not* rational or autonomous." My thesis, in capsule form, would instead say: "The state does *not* have the right to limit the freedom of rational and uncoerced adult individuals so as to do what is good for them." So my statement of the principle does not say anything about what powers the state might have with respect to persons affected by serious personality or mental disorders or who lack mental capacity and thus cannot understand the consequences of some of their actions. This is a deliberate "gap" in the definition because, as will be explained later, I do not want to tilt the argument toward the view that the state can *at will* limit the freedom of persons who suffer from a serious mental or personality disorder or from a neurodegenerative disease that in certain circumstances deprives them of the requisite mental capacity. I do believe that there are cases in which the state is justified in limiting the freedom of persons who lack full mental capacity, and that, within this limited set of cases, the state should therefore have the power to intervene to prevent these persons from doing harm to themselves, but I will not be pursuing that line of argument. And third, it seems too much of a stretch to argue that the state has the right to limit individual freedom in order to determine whether a course of conduct deemed to be harmful to the very individuals concerned is voluntary or not. In fact, it wouldn't be difficult to envision scenarios in which such a limitation would prove excessive (consider, for example, a law or regulation banning the consumption of junk food).

requisite rationality or mental capacity or is being coerced into doing something, and this something does serious harm to them, then we know, or at least can reasonably assume, that they were not truly acting on their own volition.

2.2 Delimiting the Field of Inquiry

In Chap. 3, we will be looking at the arguments commonly deployed in making the case for and against paternalism and antipaternalism. It goes without saying that these are broad-gauged arguments, serving as guideposts in thinking through a wide range of cases, such as euthanasia, riding a motorcycle without wearing a helmet, or doing drugs, even if each of these cases is peculiar to itself. But before we get to those arguments, we should be clear about the field of inquiry to which they apply (and by which this work itself is delimited): it is to this field of inquiry that we will now turn in this Section, drawing its boundaries on the basis of the definitions of paternalism and antipaternalism offered in Sect. 2.1.

To begin with, there is a long history to the antipaternalistic principle that the state is not justified in limiting the freedom of individuals who do harm to themselves, assuming that these individuals meet the standard criteria of agency (adult, rational, sufficiently uncoerced, and so on), and so long as they do not do harm to others. We cannot explore this history in any detail here, but I do want to quote two thinkers, one contemporary and one classic. First the contemporary, Luigi Ferrajoli:

> This principle, asserted by Enlightenment political thought in opposition to the premodern tradition of theological criminal law, forms a corollary of the [...] separation between law and morality and of the principle whereby there can be no criminally punishable harm where there is no legally protected interest. Worth recalling in this regard are the battles that Montesquieu, Voltaire, Beccaria, Bentham, and then John Stuart Mill waged against the punishment of "thought crimes," of vices and inclinations, attempted suicide, homosexuality, prostitution, and the like. It was this secularization of criminal law that gave rise to a good many of the structural elements of the modern state subject to the rule of law: the freedom to engage in action that is not harmful to others, the autonomy of persons and their sovereignty over their own body, legal tolerance for diversity, the firm limits on prohibitions and punishments, and the use that can be made of these measures exclusively to protect people against the violent acts of *others*.[8]

Striking very much the same note is the classic thinker, Immanuel Kant:

> "No one has a right to compel me to be happy in the peculiar way in which he may think of the well-being of other men; but everyone is entitled to seek his own happiness in the way that seems to him best, if it does not infringe the liberty of others in striving after a similar end for themselves when their Liberty is capable of consisting with the Right of Liberty in

[8] Ferrajoli (1991), pp. 133–157. "On the principle of 'penal utility,' as formulated by Grotius, Hobbes, Pufendorf, Thomasius, and Beccaria, and more extensively by Bentham, the only acts that can be made subject to criminal prohibition [...] are those that are deemed to be repugnant in view of the harm they do to *others*." Ferrajoli (1989), p. 466ff., my translation, italics added; cf. Pope (2004), p. 682.

> all others according to possible universal laws."—A Government founded upon the principle of Benevolence towards the people—after the analogy of a *father* to his children, and therefore called a *paternal Government* [*imperium paternale*]—would be one in which the Subjects would be regarded as children or minors unable to distinguish what is beneficial or injurious to them. These subjects would be thus compelled to act in a merely passive way; and they would be trained to expect solely from the Judgment of the Sovereign and just as he might will it, merely out of his goodness, all that ought to make them happy. Such a Government would be the greatest conceivable *Despotism*; for it would present a Constitution that would abolish all Liberty in the Subjects and leave them no Rights.[9]

In the second place, and as may have become clear by now, the antipaternalistic conception here defended is only concerned with a certain kind of agent: an independent agent that, in very short summary, can be described as an adult individual who is rational and sufficiently free of various coercive pressures. Save for a brief discussion in Chap. 3, Sect. 3.4.2, I will not be dealing with the problem of persons who cannot be described that way (such as minors, persons affected by serious senile dementia or serious personality or mental disorders) and whether there are certain things they should or shouldn't be allowed to do. But that is not to say that this problem can be set aside as somehow trivial or unimportant. On the contrary, it is a very difficult and complex problem, and very much worth considering. Nor am I setting this problem aside because I think that there are no cases in which we should respect the choices made by persons who fall outside the rubric of the stylized free and rational agent just described (as with small children or persons with schizophrenia or serious mental disabilities), or because I think they ought to be regarded as second-class citizens—rightless persons over whom the state can exercise the power to do what it chooses. That is not my thinking, even if it is what some people think who espouse political liberalism in one form or another. Thus, for example, I believe that freedom from pain (physical or psychophysical) is an inviolable right of the individual, and it remains so even if in exercising this right the individual is led to make extreme choices, such as assisted suicide, and even if the individual suffers from the most debilitating mental or personality disorder. But at the same time I also think that the concept of psychopathology—properly understood, that is, on the basis of a formal conception of rationality (as outlined in Chap. 3, Sect. 3.2)—cannot be dismissed as an ideological construct, and so as something through which society does violence to whoever does not fall within its standard.

Unfortunately, it is the methods for treating or "curing" such persons that have historically often been violent and criminal. But that is not true of the diagnosis, or at least not *necessarily*—"not necessarily" meaning that the diagnosis, too, has on occasion been violent and criminal, as with the "diagnosis" of homosexuality. I believe the way a paranoid schizophrenic person perceives reality and reasons and forms judgments and beliefs about reality differs *objectively* from the way a rational person does so, the former being in an objectively different situation, much like that of one who has lost a limb. This difference requires a "different treatment."

[9] Kant (1891), chap. II ("The Principles of Political Right: Considered in Connection with the Relation of Theory to Practice in the Right of the State," 1791), 36, italics in the original.

Therefore, in order to determine if and when someone affected by serious personality or mental disorders ought to be allowed to do things that are harmful to them or dangerous, we need to rely not on a concept of rational will but on one of psychophysical well-being (where the individual's will nonetheless remain fundamental). Indeed, *in some cases*, with persons affected by serious personality disorders, it seems right for the state to impose prohibitions preventing them from engaging in some kinds of conduct that do serious harm to them. What I understand "in some cases" to mean here can be clarified by way of a concrete example: on the one hand, as I see it, the state should not be able to prohibit a schizophrenic person from consuming heroin if they choose to do so; on the other hand, if someone who is hallucinating sees a sun-drenched beach with an emerald sea and decides to go for a swim, when in fact they are about to dive into the Tiber River in January, it only seems commonsensical that we should normally try to prevent them from doing so, considering that their desire is presumably *not* to lunge to their death. As mentioned, however, I will not be analytically distinguishing the different cases in which the state's intervention might be warranted, for this problem falls outside the scope of the present investigation.

In the third place, we will also not be concerned with the problem of the limits that administrative and criminal law places on private property, on the use of works of authorship, or generally on the freedom to use technology to bring about permanent changes affecting public lands or natural resources.

In the fourth place, and as mentioned already, in analyzing the arguments for and against legal paternalism, we will be taking as our frame of reference the problem of justifying the state's use of *force*: paradigmatic in this respect is the meting out of criminal punishments, even if this is not the only case exemplifying the state's use of force, which can come in the form of administrative rules restricting the consumption of certain goods or in the form of high taxes levied on such consumption. We will not, instead, be devoting any extensive analysis to the general problem of contracts or legal transactions between natural or legal persons, private or public, or to the very complex problem of noncontractual (or tort) liability.

There is a very important aspect that needs to be underscored in regard to the question of contracts or legal transactions entered into between natural or legal persons. Which is to say that there is a significant difference between the standard analysis of the dispute between paternalism and antipaternalism and the problem of the validity of consent in the making of a contract. The dispute between paternalism and antipaternalism is primarily concerned with the question of the limits within which it needs to be recognized that individuals can make decisions about their own body or life on the basis of their present wishes. We can posit the condition that their wishes be formed in a rational way on the basis of a knowledge of the relevant facts. But these will always be their *present* wishes. In a minority of cases, we will be looking at wishes formed *before* the individual concerned becomes mentally incapacitated. A case in point is the living will or advance directive for medical decisions, through which individuals make decisions for and about themselves that apply to a future time when they will no longer be able to make such decisions rationally—because they have gone into a reversible coma, for example, or have entered a persistent vegetative state or a state of deep senile dementia—and through that instrument they therefore leave oral or written instructions that others are to follow in case they should thus become incapacitated (instructions that, for example, might say whether or not they want to receive artificial nutrition and hydration).

In the case of contracts and legal transactions, there are further problems that seem to come up on top of those traditionally raised in the debate between paternalism and antipaternalism. To what extent should the intentions someone has expressed at an earlier time be recognized to prevail over their present wishes in the event that these wishes should, at the present time, reflect the rational will of a person with full mental capacity? To what extent can the legal limits placed on freedom of contract be justified under an antipaternalistic conception, or indeed under a paternalistic one? Supposing we have a jurisdiction where euthanasia is legal and a patient has authorized their doctor to administer it but then, at the last minute, came to regret that choice, wouldn't it be reasonable to say that their current wishes override their earlier ones? If someone enters into a contract of sale and then has a change of heart, why is it that in this case we instead recognize their *earlier* intent as the one by which they are bound? Some commentators of liberal persuasion, ones whose outlook is in fact more *libertarian* than liberal in the classic sense, will argue that when an individual's earlier wishes are found to prevail over their current wishes, this conclusion follows as a necessary consequence (a logical implication) of espousing an antipaternalistic conception. And they also believe that laws and court rulings are necessarily paternalistic, and therefore unjustified, when they restrict the freedom of employees, as by making it illegal for employment contracts to include terms requiring a ten-hour work day (without overtime), or to exclude paid vacation or rest days following a night shift), or to bar employees from striking, or to deny the right to a healthy workplace environment.[10] The same goes for employment contracts under which the employer is relieved of any liability for negligence, as well as for unconscionable clauses excluding warranties in a contract of sale or including arbitration clauses that accord a decisive advantage to one party over the other, or simply *mandating* arbitration. In Anglo-American law, such restrictions on freedom of contract find their basis in the so-called unconscionability doctrine.[11] What is interesting is that some commentators instead see these restrictions as *justified*, even while recognizing them to be paternalistic.[12]

But is that reconstruction correct? If Sue Seller signs a contract with Bob Buyer, agreeing to sell him an apartment she owns, and the state does not allow her to withdraw from the contract, especially once the agreed amount has been paid, it would not seem that we are protecting Sue Seller's current, valid, and rationally formed wishes, as would be called for on an antipaternalistic conception, considering that it

[10] See Burrows (1995), p. 489, 501; Shapiro (1988), pp. 535–37; Trebilcock (1993), pp. 162–163; West (1990), p. 695; and Zamir (1998), p. 230ff.

[11] "The unconscionability doctrine in contract law enables a court to decline to enforce a contract whose terms are seriously one-sided, overreaching, exploitative, or otherwise manifestly unfair" Shiffrin (2000), p. 205.

[12] See Kennedy (1982), pp. 563–658; Kennedy (1998), p. 472; and Kronman (1983), p. 764.

is Sue's current and rationally formed wish to withdraw from the same contract. Are we then protecting a market system, where goods and services can be bought and sold for a price determined by the intersection of supply and demand? Are we protecting Sue Seller's antecedent wish, the one she expressed when she entered into the contract, through which she chose to bind her own autonomy? Are we also protecting her *interest*, as a liberal or libertarian worldview would have it, considering that without a market system as just described, in a scenario where contracts could not be enforced, no one would be willing to sell anything to anybody (there would in effect be no buying or selling)—something that even our unreliable seller presumably would not want? Or are we, above all, protecting the interests of those who have a stake in that market system and stand to gain from it, and who set the bulk of its rules?

It is not our concern here to go through all the different moral-political justifications behind the institution of contract or the reasons why we think it proper that certain promises (contractual or otherwise) ought to be binding. But two fundamental arguments do merit attention, for it is not the case that all legal restrictions on freedom of contract are necessarily paternalistic. And, furthermore, these two arguments will enable us to delve deeper into different aspects of the debate between paternalism and antipaternalism. The first argument is distinguished by two features. Even if this argument stands on solid ground (its validity seems beyond doubt), it is narrower in scope than the second, for it shows that, in certain conditions, some of the limits placed on freedom of contract or on the legal enforceability of contracts are undoubtedly not paternalistic. The second argument, which we will be looking at in the next section, is broader in scope and places the opposing camp in a much more difficult position, but I cannot as firmly vouch for its validity. The first argument contends that there are certain background conditions under which the two potential contracting parties will be asymmetrically placed, one of them occupying a position of socioeconomic power that affords an undeniable negotiating advantage over the counterparty,[13] before the two even sign the contract, such that one party (the disfavoured one) is *unfairly* stuck in a situation of necessity that forces him or her to enter into a certain agreement. For example, if the right to paid vacation or to daily and weekly rest periods and the right to strike were all waivable, employees could face coercive measures (threatened layoff, offshoring, or downsizing) that would put pressure on them to waive such rights. How does this argument tie in with our definition of paternalism? In a nutshell, on the antipaternalistic view, the state does *not* have the right to limit the freedom of an adult individual if it is certain, or at least reasonable to assume, that this person's wishes have been formed in a way that is rational and (among other requisites) *sufficiently free of coercive pressures* (not under duress)—except, of course (under the harm principle previously discussed), when a decision to act on those wishes means that harm will come to others.

[13] On this idea of an unequal bargaining position, see Shiffrin (2000), p. 209, and Feinberg (1986), p. 249ff.

What does it mean to say that someone's will or wishes have been formed in a way that sufficiently uncoerced? This is a question I will be discussing extensively in Chap. 3, looking at three paradigmatic cases of coercion and compulsion (where compulsion is to be understood in the sense of being *compelled* to do something), namely, physical, psychological, and epistemic violence—but we can already lay out some groundwork, and I begin by marking the distinction between psychological coercion (coercive threats or offers) and physical coercion. As Alan Wertheimer observes, if A presses B's finger against a trigger, firing a gun that will kill B, who is fully incapacitated and unable to make any movement, there is no "will" that B can be said to have exercised, such that we can only speak of "involuntary movements" on B's part, and so none that B can be said to have "made." This first kind of coercion is physical. With psychological coercion, by contrast, someone can be said to have acted in a way that is involuntary or nonintentional, or else insufficiently voluntary, but these are still actions this person actually *carried out.*[14]

Let us suppose that a state legalizes euthanasia and that A, a gravely ill man, has requested the procedure because his brother, B, who would receive an inheritance from A if A should die, has threatened to kill their sister unless A requests the procedure. In this case, A's decision to undergo euthanasia would be considered rational and stable over time but would be made under an unacceptable condition of duress. It would therefore not count as a *validly* expressed decision, or a valid expression of will. This is a clear example of psychological coercion, since we have a specific individual making a specific and real threat to harm a specific other individual, and what is being threatened is something that everyone, including the victim, would regard as harm in a very real sense (a threat to life and limb made against oneself or against one's loved ones). As will be discussed in Chap. 3, Sect. 3.6, I will not analyse the meaning of the terms *coercion* and *compulsion* in every relevant aspect. In other words, I will not develop a comprehensive theory of coercion, and that is so in at least two respects.

First, we will not be concerned with the active (agential or performative) aspect of coercion, that is, with coercion from the standpoint of those who actually do the coercing or who make threats or coercive offers. As Wertheimer underscores, there is a normative, moralized (or morally laden) use of the terms *coercion* and *compulsion* and other like expressions ("He has been forced to do such and such a thing," "She made him do it," "She had no choice," "He acted under duress"), for in many contexts we use this kind of language to either (a) ascribe moral or legal responsibility to the *coercing* agent (the aggressor, the blackmailer, and the like) or (b) exclude such responsibility on the part of the *coerced* agent (the one on the receiving end of coercion, who is *being* coerced into doing something or forced to do it).

The moral or legal force of coercion, then, lies in that dual purpose it can be put to: in its enabling us to either (a) ascribe some kind or degree of responsibility to the *coercing* agent (and thus make this person liable to punishment for the threats or the blackmailing) or (b) ascribe a lesser responsibility to the *coerced* agent or to

[14] See Wertheimer (1987), p. 9ff., 171ff.; Lamond (1996), p. 218; and Frankfurt (1988), pp. 26–27.

altogether exclude the latter's responsibility (by showing, for example, that when this person contracted a marriage, made a will, entered into a contract, or committed a crime, these acts were done either *involuntarily* or in a way that was *not sufficiently voluntary*). Something to the same effect happens with the *moral* force of coercion. Thus, in ordinary language, we might say that a hurricane was "responsible" or "to blame" for something or that it "caused" some event or behaviour, in that it forced those in its path to flee to safety or evacuate their homes, and for that reason (on account of the hurricane) these people cannot be said to have acted in a sufficiently voluntary way (of their own volition). This explains why it is typically the case that the meaning of expressions like "A forced B to do X" seems to shift depending on the kind of responsibility we are trying to ascribe (moral or legal or, in the latter case, civil or criminal) and on what the act is that B has been "forced" into, and so has carried out in a way that, allegedly, is not sufficiently voluntary.

The degree of coercion required to exclude voluntariness or responsibility in forming a contract is normally lesser than the degree required to do so when a serious crime has been committed. For this reason, I will not be concerned with the active/performative side of coercion; that is, I will not be looking at coercion from the standpoint of those who engage in it (making threats or coercive offers). We will accordingly not be dealing with the circumstances under which someone might be held criminally responsible for a coercive act or with the distinction between a threat and a coercive offer, nor will we be considering the complex conceptions that have been developed to distinguish an offer from a threat,[15] nor will we be parsing

[15] In the philosophy of criminal law and in legal dogmatics, a distinction is usually drawn between threats and offers. As a rule of thumb, we have before us a threat when A conveys to B that A will do something that will make B worse off than if A did not act on that proposition in relation to B. In an offer, by contrast, what A conveys to B is a proposition that, if acted on, will make B *better* off than if the proposition is not accepted (or at least it will make B better off according to B's reasonable expectations). As is widely recognized, there is a whole range of challenges that a distinction so formulated comes up against. Can an offer be coercive? Can it conceal a threat? On what grounds can B's reasonable expectations be established? Should the criterion be moral, statistical, or of some other kind? These questions come up when the "offer" is particularly unfair or exploitative, in that it exploits B's predicament in a way that raises moral concerns. A famous case is that of the "lustful millionaire," who lusts after a young mother whose child needs a heart transplant without which he would not be able to survive: the millionaire thus offers to pay for the lifesaving operation if she agrees to give herself to him. Is this a coercive offer? If so, why? According to many authors, the main or decisive criterion for distinguishing an offer from a threat is an empirical, statistical criterion by which to determine B's expectations, so long as these expectations are rationally founded. According to Robert Nozick, we should accord greater weight to the moral or the empirical criterion depending on the case at hand. Nozick's view seems more problematic. Suppose that B has fallen overboard on the high seas, in waters where he knows he won't be able to survive for more than fifteen minutes, but he runs into A, who is sailing nearby, and A, knowing that B is one to always keep his promises, offers to take B aboard and rescue him if he promises to pay 100,000 euros. Is A's offer in fact a threat? Now suppose that B has committed theft and A tells B that he will report B to the police unless B splits the loot with A. Is A making an offer? Nozick argues that the answer to the question in both cases may be yes. The rescue offer can be considered a threat and the proposal to split the loot an offer because, in the former case, if we are in danger of drowning we have a morally legitimate expectation that others should rescue us if the cost to

the conditions under which a blackmailer or coercer can be deemed liable to criminal punishment. None of that falls within the purview of this work.

---

them is not unreasonable, whereas, in the latter case, we do *not* have a comparable morally legitimate expectation (we cannot morally expect others not to report us to the police for a theft we have committed). But that is not necessarily the correct way to analyse the two cases: the rescue can properly be characterized as an offer and the proposal to split the loot as a threat.

The case of the lustful millionaire is instead a case in which something is offered that will make the offeree better off than she could otherwise expect to be: she couldn't reasonably expect to be able to pay for her child's life-saving surgery, nor was it likely that a stranger should come up to her and offer to do so. At the same time, however, the offer is conditional: it is made on condition that the young mother accepts to give herself to him in exchange for the money, and since her situation is one of necessity that doesn't give her any other viable option, and the offeror uses that fact to his advantage, the conditional offer is certainly at the same time exploitative. Still, this does not yet answer the question, is it also a *coercive* offer? There is certainly a sense in which the young offeree can be said to have been forced to give the lustful offeror the sex he wants. But if we ask *who* or *what* is forcing her to accept money for sex, then the question becomes much more complex. It is the lustful offeror who is forcing her to so act, from an actively agential point of view? To be sure, he isn't giving her much of a choice, for even though he may have expanded the menu of options available to her by introducing a new option that wasn't previously there, this new option is really the *only* course of action she can take if she wants to save her child's life. But is his "forcing" her to take this offer, so framed, comparable to what a highwayman does in surprising his victim at gunpoint with the threat "Your money or your life!"? The answer to this question probably depends on what role the millionaire plays in the young mother's state of necessity. For, on the one hand, there is certainly an element of systemic coercion that describes her situation. But, on the other, there is a responsibility that can be ascribed to the millionaire, and to people like him, for bringing about, or otherwise not doing anything to change, the state of need or necessity of an entire class of individuals who are exploited by society, individuals like the young mother. That would be the case if, for example, the millionaire manages to avoid paying taxes, a portion of which goes toward funding programs aimed at supporting social rights, such as the right to universal health care, or if he does not make any charitable contributions to nongovernmental organizations devoted to fighting poverty or youth unemployment or to financing scholarships for talented youths from needy families. But, even then, his role, so described, would probably not be enough to support the claim that the young mother was *forced* by him to accept money for sex. But then, again, if that is the case, the criterion we need to use in determining whether an offer is coercive is one that, as Zimmerman argues, asks us to consider in what ways and to what extent the offeror's actions and intentions actually contribute to the offeree's state of need or necessity or to the general state of economic, legal, and social inferiority and subjection of individuals like the offeree. See Zimmerman (1981), p. 132ff. If the offeror has already acted in such a way as to put the offeree in a highly vulnerable situation of need or subjection, thereby setting the stage for the offeree to yield to the offer, then that offer certainly must be accounted as coercive, just like a threat. (The same conclusion is reached by Nozick in his discussion of a similar case in which a slave is daily beaten by a slavemaster who offers to stop beating him if he does X. See Nozick (1999), p. 27.) Suppose now that, through great sacrifice, the young mother manages to take out a bank loan for her child's operation and that this loan can be paid back in manageable monthly instalments, but then the millionaire, a malicious and well-connected man, intervenes specifically to have the loan cancelled or the terms of its payment plan altered, or even to have her fired from her job, so as to further aggravate her financial and social position. In this scenario, we probably couldn't say that we are looking at a threat proper—in part because the millionaire is acting behind the mother's back, rather than telling her up front that he is going to have her loan cancelled or have her fired—but his offer certainly does count as coercive, which makes him no less morally or legally responsible. Cf. Feinberg (1986), p. 216ff., 242ff.; Frankfurt (1988), p. 28ff.; Lamond (1996), p. 225ff.; Nozick (1999), p. 23ff.; Wertheimer (1987), p. 202ff.; and Zimmerman (1981).

In short, we will only be concerned with coercion and compulsion *from the receiving end* of what it is to be coerced or to be forced to do something, that is, we will be looking at things from the standpoint of those who are so coerced or forced. Indeed, the concept of someone being "sufficiently free from coercive pressures" (sufficiently uncoerced, for short) is useful to us simply as a gauge by which to judge when a decision one makes involving one's own body or person is sufficiently voluntary.

Second, I will not develop a full-fledged conception of what it means to be subject to pressure that is sufficiently coercive: I will not, in other words, be putting forward a conception that will resolve all borderline cases. In fact, that is not necessary. What matters, rather, is that we have some core features which can be extracted from some paradigmatic cases of coercion and compulsion, and which can be used as guiding criteria in identifying what counts as such. We have already briefly discussed the distinction between physical and psychological coercion. But we have also seen that there are forms of coercion—systemic coercion—in which we cannot easily identify an agent who has made a direct threat, but in which we do have someone in a situation of dire need (such as extreme poverty) that forces them, or others similarly situated, to do things they would not otherwise do. Thus, for example, even in ordinary language we might say that someone has been "forced" to go into prostitution or to steal in order to survive (or at least has felt "compelled" to so do).

This is not an uncommon problem, and in fact it exists on a spectrum, with many borderline cases, but there can be little doubt that the systemic coercion just mentioned exists in one form or another wherever there exists (unacceptable) exploitation in a free-market or capitalist system, and, as might also be argued, the stronger the system, or the less regulated it is, the greater its potential for systemic coercion, in the form of basic rights that are either not recognized or not protected, with the effects that are known to follow when such systems are in place. I am therefore going to say that in this agentless (but nonetheless very real) systemic coercion lies a first basic form of coercive pressure that crosses the threshold beyond which a decision one makes under such pressure can no longer be said to be properly voluntary. Systemic coercion can be so qualified (as systemic) in that it is difficult, if not impossible, to determine which or how many individuals or socioeconomic factors are involved in bringing about the state of need or necessity of those who are subjected to it. In fact, up to a point this question may even be irrelevant, but with this caveat: while systemic coercion does not depend on any single agent doing any specific action—the action that brings it about is that of the *system* within which agents act—and so the agent doesn't necessarily matter and the phenomenon is therefore not specifically commissive, it may (within such a system) be specifically *omissive*, a case in point being the (systemic) coercion that, to a greater or lesser extent, results from failure of the state to protect rights: this may come in the form of legislatures failing to pass legislation that will protect constitutionally protected rights or of judges failing to recognize and apply those rights even if they are constitutionally protected. Squarely nonsystemic, by contrast, is the kind of coercion we have when a specific person makes specific threats against another, especially when such threats are credible (the person making the threats, for example, may be known to act on them if the person receiving the threats does not comply with the demand embedded in them).

So one core feature of coercion lies in its ability to coerce without there being any specifically identifiable coercing agents. I am calling this kind of coercion systemic. A second core feature (applying especially to systemic coercion, but also to nonsystemic coercion) is that the concept of coercion or compulsion I will be relying on in this investigation is a hybrid concept, for it is in part *subjective* (relating to the subjective experience of those who undergo coercion) and in part *objective*, since it always involves some kind of recognizable harm or injury that makes those being coerced (objectively) worse off than they would be if the coercive pressure at issue were not brought to bear on them).

2.3 Two Conceptions of Coercion and Compulsion

> My team! My team! That son of a bitch got my team.
>
> What kind of pressure did he use, Milt?
>
> I said, 'I want sixty-seven million.' And he said, 'okay.'
>
> Ruthless bastard.—*Heaven Can Wait*, starring and codirected by Warren Beatty, 1978

There are at least two conceptions of coercion and compulsion (see Anderson (2021) and Wertheimer (1987), p. 3ff.). A theory of coercion and compulsion is a theory about the meaning of a family of words that come up in sentences where it is said that someone was "*coerced* into doing such and such a thing" or was "*compelled, forced*, or *made to* do it," or that they "had *no choice*" or "acted *under duress, unwillingly*, or *nonvoluntarily*" or "under *sufficient coercive pressures*," or that they were "*not sufficiently free* from such pressures." When I say that someone "was not free (or was insufficiently free) from coercive pressures," I mean something like what Wertheimer calls "coercion claims," understood as subjective statements in which someone says that what they did was forced on them by somebody or something ("I have been coerced by so-and-so" or "what I did was dictated by circumstances"). As we will see, a coercion claim (being subjective) is not in itself conclusive: just *saying* that we were forced to do something, in other words, doesn't mean that we were thus coerced, for the coercive pressure we are claiming to have forced our hand may well be *insufficient* to make the action itself involuntary or sufficiently involuntary. A theory of coercion, then, is a theory of what it is to be under sufficient coercive pressures, sufficient to make the act in question insufficiently voluntary. Clearly, coercion can be either justified (if it is coming from, say, a police officer acting within the rules of the profession) or it can be unjustified (from, say, a mafia boss extracting some "pledge" from someone), and as is suggested by the two examples just made, the justification always involves a judgment call or some kind of moral judgment that is often implicit in the context. Coercion is normally used when there is someone, a coercer, who coerces someone else, a coercee, into doing something under threat of violence. Furthermore, as we just saw, someone can be said to be been forced or compelled not only by a specifically identifiable individual but also by circumstances or external factors, as is the case with people who flee their homes when threatened by an oncoming hurricane or who flee their home country under the pressure of a humanitarian crisis or of extreme poverty. So the threat that makes for coercion can be personal (an individual threat of violence) or it can come from an external force, which in turn may be "natural" (force majeure) or manmade and to a greater or lesser degree systemic, that is, not attributable to the agency of any specific individual, as with displacement under the pressure of forces that can range from the geopolitical to the economic (the poverty to which one can be reduced under a free-market or capitalist system).

We thus have a subjective, "internalistic," or formal conception of coercion and compulsion and an objective or substantive one that may also be described as a "moralized" conception.[16] On the subjective conception, coercion or compulsion obtains whenever we have plans, intentions, or desires that we cannot act on or fully realize because of factors external to us that limit the options available to us in that regard. So, whenever there are no available options or whenever the options we have are insufficient to enable us to do what we want to do or to do it in the way we want to do it—and yet the thing we want to do matters to us: we see it as contributing or as central to our well-being or happiness—then we can, from a subjective point of view, use expressions like "I had to do it" or "I have been compelled to do it" or "I was forced to so act." We are in the mode described by the subjective conception when we say, for example, that we *had to* sell our old motorcycle *in order to buy a new one*. This case is distinguished by four characteristics that make it what it is (a case of subjective coercion): (a) the *sacrifice* involved in selling something that was dear to us (our old motorcycle), and so the unhappiness or sense of loss we feel as a result of having had to make that decision—an aspect of the situation implicit in which is the fact that (b) we wanted *both* motorcycles, the old one and the new one, or we didn't want to part with the old one as a condition for getting the new one, and yet (c) our desire to buy the new motorcycle was stronger than our desire not to sell the old one—and (d) the lack of any alternative options we regarded as worthwhile or acceptable, as would have been the case if buying the new motorcycle (without selling the old one) had meant working two jobs for long hours (say, eighteen a hours day), while cutting back on basic necessities, such as food or heating.[17]

[16] What I am calling the formal conception is described by Wertheimer (1987) as "empirical" or "value-free."

[17] Wertheimer argues that there is no set of necessary and sufficient conditions which need to be satisfied in order for us to be justified in using the term *coercion* or *compulsion*, for the term is used in different ways in different moral, legal, or ordinary contexts. I will concede that, from the standpoint of linguistic or psycholinguistic analysis, it is important to investigate all the uses of a term, and Wertheimer may well be correct in making that claim about context, but that is not what matters most when it comes to working out a conception of coercion that applies in the moral and legal domains. Rather, and this is my contention, if the account of coercion we want to arrive at is *explicative*—which a philosophical account necessarily has to be—and if we are reasoning within a

Now, on an unqualifiedly and strictly subjective conception, it makes perfect sense to say that blue collar worker Factory Joe is *forced* to do his job, and we can sensibly say so even if, by hypothesis, he is protected under a constitution that grants a full spectrum of rights, including social rights (the right to health care, to occupational safety and a healthy workplace environment, to a living wage, and to unemployment benefits, as well as the right to unionize and go on strike). In this picture, Factory Joe can be said to be properly *forced* to do his job—in the sense that he *has to* do it—if we assume that he very much wants to have the leisure time needed to devote himself to his hobbies and personal pursuits, and yet, absent any other viable alternative, he would rather clock in the hours he does on the factory floor than not work at all or be underpaid or underemployed. In other words, there are no other options available to him that he deems reasonable or worthwhile, and he would be more than willing to quit his job at a moment's notice if an opportunity came up that enabled him to make a comparable salary working half the hours he worked on his previous job (cf. Nozick (1999), p. 24).

On closer inspection, however, such an unqualifiedly subjective conception of coercion and compulsion will reveal itself to be quite problematic. One problem is that the conception, so described, is not always consistent with the way the term *coercion* or compulsion is used in ordinary language. Indeed, the conception no longer seems to hold up once we factor in preferences that can be considered unconventional relative to criteria over which there is broad consensus in the relevant community. For example—and this case offers just one clue among several signalling that something is amiss—let us suppose that Leisurely Larry often lapses into boredom and that, as an escape, he likes to seek the companionship Opportunistic Olivia. Sensing an opportunity, Olivia threatens not to speak to Larry any longer unless he turns over one-fifth of his paycheck to her every month. Few in a Western community would qualify this as extortion, and it would be quite odd to say that Larry has been "coerced" into handing over a fifth of his paycheck to Olivia or that he has been "forced" to do so. That is because the situation could also be framed as a deliberative problem, a calculation involving a balancing of pros and cons: Larry prefers to surrender a fifth of his paycheck to Olivia (or has chosen or decided to do so) rather than lose her company; he has resolved that he would rather have event A take place (forfeiting a fifth of his paycheck) than have event B take place (losing Olivia's company). In ordinary language, the concept of coercion usually hinges on what most people would regard as basic or essential goods, meaning that in order for a threat to be credible or effective, and thus recognizable as such, it needs to put at stake a good that would drive someone to act in ways they would not otherwise do, or to feel *compelled* to so act. Now, to be sure, there is nothing inherently wrong with moving away from established usage, that is, from the stable and settled uses a term has acquired over time. But examples such as the one just considered

formal conception of coercion, then we do have to consider the use of the term as subject to necessary conditions, the only exception being when the term is understood to mean "physical coercion," where somebody is literally using physical force against me to make me do something against my will. Cf. Wertheimer (1987), p. 184ff.

nonetheless stand as clues suggesting that an unqualifiedly subjective conception is inadequate. Indeed, just about anyone, on this conception, could account themselves as "coerced" into a broad array of actions, or as "forced" to do such actions.[18]

And here is another example. The notion of sexual violence or harassment assumes that the victim did not consent to the act or behaviour (to the physical assault or other coercive tactic) or that whatever consent there might have been was signalled under conditions of psychological duress, as when the aggressor threatens some kind of retaliation or makes it known to the victim that a refusal to comply comes with (bad) consequences. It is clear that an unqualifiedly subjective, or formal, conception will not, on its own, help us determine whether someone's actions or conduct amounted to rape. Thus, suppose that Lustful Lou moves in with Committed Chloe, who owns the house in which they live and is also financially independent, and Lou announces that he will leave Chloe if she should decide she no longer wants to have sex with Lou: if (a) Chloe agreed to Lou's terms, reasoning that she would rather have sex with him than part with him forever, and if (b) she thinks it a great sacrifice to have sex with him (she wants to be in an *affective* but not a *sexual* relationship with him), then, on a strictly *formal* conception, we would in fact be looking at a case of coercion or compulsion. And yet, outside the frame of such a conception, we couldn't reasonably say that Lou is guilty of rape, nor would we be able to say, without further qualifying Lou's behaviour, that Chloe has been forced or coerced into a sexual relationship, even if she acted under pressure from Lou and would not otherwise have acted as she did.[19] *A fortiori*, it makes no sense

[18] For such a line of criticism, see Anderson (2021), sec. 2.5. Cf. Lamond (1996), p. 223.

[19] More to the point, while it would in this case be absurd to suggest that Lou had "coerced" or "forced" Chloe into a sexual relationship she didn't want, it could well be said that Chloe, given the predicament of her wishes, outlook, and preferences, didn't have any other reasonable choice: what she faced was in effect blackmail, which Lou perpetrated and which she succumbed to. Chloe could even be said to have been *forced* to have a sexual relationship with Lou, but only in the sense that she *had to* do so given the framing of the situation, that is, given that (a) Lou threatened to leave her if she refused to have sex with him, and yet (b) she wanted him to stay: she was thus forced in the sense of being subject to a hypothetical imperative or conditional norm (you have to do X if you want to achieve Y). Even so, it would still be difficult to qualify this as a case of Lou strictly "forcing" Chloe to have sex with him, because of background expectations about what is reasonable in a relationship (by and large, at least on what might be defined as the standard picture, it is more reasonable for two partners to a relationship to expect the relationship to have sexual intimacy than not). So, even though Lou is threatening to leave Chloe unless she delivers what he wants (namely, sex), and even though that is precisely what she does *not* want, he is still giving her a choice (however much a choice framed as an ultimatum), and the choice (or what he wants) is consistent with what people generally or standardly expect out of a relationship like the one between Lou and Chloe: the empirical or statistical criteria by which a relationship between a couple might be described seems to suggest that there may actually be some justification for Lou's ultimatum (the empirical criteria, in other words, seem to converge with moral criteria of what counts as a reasonable demand that can be made on others). What these considerations suggest, then, is that Lou's threat is not properly a threat—or, at least, it is less of a threat than might at first sight appear—even if it not an *offer* that he is making (it is more like an ultimatum), and what he is "offering" is something that, if he gets his way, will make Chloe worse off than she would otherwise be. For a slightly different reading, see Murphy (1994), p. 218.

to speak of coercion in the case of a person making an offer, not a threat, such as a substantial sum of money that improves the situation of the recipient, in exchange for something in return, as in the excerpt quoted from the movie *Heaven Can Wait*.

If the formal, subjective conception reveals itself to be inadequate, we will need to correct it with a substantive (evaluative) criterion that is objective. As we will see in Chap. 3, Sect. 3.6, what counts as "*sufficient* coercive pressure" depends on what fundamental rights we recognize for individuals (such as the right to housing, to unemployment benefits, to health care, to education, or to private property), that is, the judgment will depend on a conception of basic rights with which to flesh out a conception of liberal equality. In such a conception of equal rights lies our "objective" corrective. I am calling it quote-unquote "objective" because it is not to be understood as embracing moral realism or objectivism but is rather objective in the sense of a conception of equality that applies to individuals independently of what their (subjective) preferences or desires may be. On an expansive view of liberal equality, the right to health care can be regarded as a basic right that is morally as well as legally ascribed to individuals regardless of what some of them think (that is, even if some of them object to it)—though, as we will see in Chap. 5, this does not mean that they therefore *must* exercise this right, nor, consequently, does such an ascription of rights necessarily come into contradiction with an antipaternalistic theory.[20]

---

[20] In this sense, I am arguing that a minimal, night-watchman libertarian state is woefully inadequate, or, stated otherwise, that there are some basic rights whose recognition entails a need for resources to be redistributed from the socioeconomically well-off members of society to its less advantaged members. Examples of such rights (and the list is not exhaustive) include the right to old-age pension, to disability and unemployment benefits, to housing, to health (and so to healthy food), to education, and to life and physical integrity, as well as freedom of movement, freedom of speech, freedom of enterprise, and the right to property. Underpinning such a list of basic rights—a list of enumerated rights, like the lists we find in many Western constitutions—is the core idea of the capabilities approach advanced by Martha Nussbaum and Amartya Sen, even if this approach, I would argue, ought to be set aside because it easily lends itself to paternalistic readings. It also needs to be underscored that is it not enough nor just to redistribute resources equitably or to accept socioeconomic inequalities as morally legitimate only so long as they work to the advantage of the least advantaged members of society, as John Rawls's so-called difference principle would have it. That is because different people, with different abilities and disabilities, will make different uses of resources, and even more importantly because there is no capability that can be exercised by everyone using the same resources (which will accordingly vary widely from one person to the next). It is therefore not enough nor just to have a scheme of redistributive justice or to justify economic inequalities only if they benefit the worst-off members of society: it is also necessary to protect each right on its own terms (freedom of movement, for example, cannot be protected like freedom of speech, nor is there any single set of resources through which both can be equally protected). This way of protecting basic rights, this "basic-rights welfare," can be defended on at least three grounds. The first of these is the argument previously mentioned in connection with coercion in the labour market. As we saw, workers who are unskilled or underskilled are forced to act as the market dictates, that is, they are forced to (a) sell their labour at whatever price the market determines, which price is likely to be lower than what is necessary to sustain a decent living, and (b) buy essential goods and services for a price set by the market, which price is likely to be higher than what they can afford, and absent any government-supported basic-rights welfare, they will be forced to *choose* between such goods and services (perhaps skimping on health care in order to be

Let us, for example, suppose that Unskilled Worker Wesley decides to work twelve hours a day without any rest breaks so as to pay for his son's heart transplant, an operation that, given the local economy, cannot be paid for by anyone working a regular eight-hour job, and let us further suppose that in Wesley's community health care is set up as a service that is bought and sold on the open market, with high deductibles and out-of-pocket costs even for people who are covered by a private health-insurance plan (Wesley would thus be underinsured and still be unable to pay for his son's operation). In this case, too, I submit, Wesley's decision to work twelve hours a day can be described as the outcome of excessive coercive pressure, strong enough or sufficient to vitiate or invalidate his consent, that is, to support the conclusion that he is actually being *forced* to work the hours he is working. To see this, we only need to imagine a different scenario in which Wesley has access to public housing (enabling him to save on rent) and a public healthcare system that will cover his son's operation at no direct charge to him. And now we can ask, what would Wesley do in such a scenario with a wider menu of options open to him? It stands to reason that, *rebus sic stantibus*, he would no longer choose to work twelve

able to make rent or pay their utilities), since they cannot afford to buy both on the free market. And yet, on the hybrid (subjective/objective) conception of coercion, as we saw, in order to determine when a source of coercive pressure is legitimate, or when the action of those who are subject to this pressure can be said to be insufficiently voluntary, we need to take account of the substantive *rights* recognized for individuals. Which shows this argument in favor of the resource-redistributive conception to be incomplete. The second ground lies in the *Harm to others Principle*, because I do not agree with the veil of ignorance procedure. advanced by Rawls. Since it represents an objectively greater harm, a physical or psychophysical harm, that of suffering physical or psychophysical distress resulting from an illness that a person cannot afford to treat, or from a lack of housing or heating, compared to the psychological or economic harm of a very wealthy person who cannot furnish their large boat with luxury items due to high progressive taxation.

The third ground lies in a minimal theory of human well-being, which starts out by recognizing that different people have different desires and ascribe different utilities to different goods, activities, and pursuits (some would much rather have a smoke than go out skiing; some prefer the beach to the mountains; some have a much higher pain tolerance than others; some crave salty food, while others are sweet-toothed; some like stamp collecting, while others like to collect porn movies; and so on); and then, given that premise, the theory posits some basic or primary goods that any rational and uncoerced agent, or at least the vast majority of such agents, will see as necessary to their psychophysical well-being; these goods—such as food, water, heating, and health care—are thus conceived as universal, in that no one can do without them, for they satisfy some basic needs; or, stated otherwise, anyone will need these goods regardless of the particular conception of the good they happen to espouse or the life plan they want to pursue. As mentioned, what makes this conception of coercion and compulsion objective (or substantive) is not that it posits some entities existing out there in a moral reality, but that it is meant to apply to individuals independently of what other preferences or desires they may have, and it is against the benchmark of objectivity so construed that, on the conception of coercion being advanced here, we are to judge whether an individual is being subjected to coercion. As with all concepts that figure as core elements of a culture or research tradition, so the concept of coercion cannot be brought into a general theoretical framework without being given a definition that in explicating the concept also to some extent makes it normative or *evaluative*: its definition, in other words, proceeding from the linguistic usages that have gained currency within a given community of speakers, draws boundaries that include some uses of the term *coercion* as adequate, while excluding others as inadequate.

hours a day. Without evidence to the contrary, we have no reason to believe that Wesley would want to work twelve hours a day (in the previous scenario, in other words, he would not have made that decision but for the fact that he had to find a way to pay for his son's operation). On the contrary, if the national healthcare system were paying people to sell their organs, say, their kidney, and Wesley decided to sign up for the offer so as to buy a luxury car or a vacation home—rather than use the money to buy an essential good or service, one that, had he been in a welfare state, and so in a system based on a conception of liberal equality, he would have access to as a matter of right—we would *not* say that his decision was made under excessive coercive pressure, a degree of pressure sufficient to vitiate his consent (it does not not fall above the baseline below which an act can still be said to be properly voluntary).

And yet in certain respects even an unqualifiedly objective, evaluative, "moralized" conception proves to be problematic. On such an unqualifiedly, strictly substantive conception, we have "coercion" whenever one person threatens another to do something that is deeply unjust, such as infringing the latter person's rights. The problem we run into here is that, on such a morally laden or moralized conception, we can no longer distinguish acceptable from unacceptable acts of coercion, or insufficiently coercive from sufficiently coercive pressures (the latter crossing the threshold beyond which an act can no longer be accounted as consensual).[21] And yet

[21] On "moralized" conceptions of coercion, see Anderson (2021) sec. 2.3. In response to this objection, Wertheimer offers a reply that I cannot quite wrap my head around. Wertheimer argues that it makes perfect sense to say that the state can *legitimately coerce* its subjects. What explains this contention is that in most contexts in which we might ask whether someone has been coerced into doing something, that very question reframes the moral or legal status of their action. To claim that someone acted under coercion is to claim that they cannot be blamed for their action, or at least that they are less blameworthy than if the action had been uncoerced. As Wertheimer goes on to argue, the case in which the coercion at issue comes from the state is by and large unproblematic, for it is clear that, most of the time, when the state forces us to do or not do something (e.g., paying our taxes or not committing murder or theft), we are at the same time *morally* bound to so act (or at least the coercion stands on moral grounds). "The moral considerations that (help) determine whether someone is coerced (in the sorts of responsibility-affecting contexts on which I have focused) are importantly distinct from the sorts of moral considerations that figure in the justification of state coercion" (Wertheimer (1987), p. 256). This is tantamount to saying that, in most cases, the state's use of coercion paradigmatically exemplifies what counts as a morally justified use of coercion, such that we are not faced with the problem of determining whether or not someone has been "forced" to act as they did, and so whether that person can be legally or morally held to account for that course of action. For we already know that they can be so held to account (we know, for example, that Taxpayer Ted *is* liable for not having paid his taxes, even if he would have had to sell his home in order to do so). The problem here is that the reason why the use of coercion by and large seems morally unproblematic for the state is precisely that, on the basis of moral considerations about the state's responsibility, we have already come to the conclusion that the state is legitimized in making use of coercion. However, this holds good not only for the state but also for any individual who makes legitimate use of coercion, as when a judgment creditor has a writ of execution enforced against a judgment debtor, or when someone acts in self-defence, being able to then raise a necessity defence. And from the very fact that we can sensibly ask this question—namely, Can the state justifiably use coercion?—we know that the concept of coercion is in part not moralized. If we are assuming a fully moralized conception of coercion, it makes no sense

we do want to be able to distinguish a mafia boss who explicitly makes me "an offer I can't refuse" from an officer of a national revenue service who threatens to garnish my wages or place a levy on my company's assets (thereby effectively putting the company out of business) unless I pay the back taxes I owe to the government, which taxes have been assessed consistently with a body of tax laws that have been validly enacted and, in addition, are grounded in a foundation that imparts moral legitimacy to them as well. The difference between these two cases is not that the mafia boss is coercing me, having violated my rights, while the revenue officer is not. The difference, in other words, is not between coercion and noncoercion, but between unjust or illegitimate coercion in one case (with the mafia boss) and morally legitimate or warranted coercion on the other (with the revenue officer).[22] The objective conception seems equally inadequate in dealing with "fringe" desires. Suppose that Unsavoury Spencer wants to kill his wife, and just as he is pondering over how he might execute his plan, Burglar Bobby breaks into their home and threatens to kill her unless he turns over all the valuables stored in the safe. We should be able to agree that this situation, with Spencer's preexisting plan, cannot quite be described as coercive, because what Spencer is being threatened with is something he wanted to do anyway, and so it does not, for him, compute as a harm. But that is not what the situation would look like if observed through the lens of a substantive, unqualifiedly objective conception predicated on a set of "standard" desires (what people can *generally* be expected to want), independently of what any particular individual may desire: through that lens we would have to conclude that Spencer *is* being coerced (that what we are looking at is a straightforward case of coercion), for the thing that Spencer is being threatened with falls into a category

---

to say that A is using coercion on B in a morally justified way, because what it means for A to use coercion, on Wertheimer's definition, is for A to threaten B with something that is morally unjustifiable, that is, something that falls below B's reasonable expectations about what courses of action A is morally justified in taking in relation to B. So if A is morally entitled to do X (having a writ of execution served on B if B should fail to pay the debt he owes to A), and A threatens B with X, then, on a truly moralized conception of coercion, we cannot speak of coercion, or at least we can do so only on pain of contradicting ourselves. Indeed, if we were to replace the term *coercion* with Wertheimer's definition of the term, we would obtain a proposition as follows: "A is morally justified in threatening B with something that is morally unjust (levying execution on B's assets), that is, with something that falls below B's reasonable expectations" (cf. ibid., p. 256). That Wertheimer's moralized conception of coercion is highly problematic can also be seen from other argumentative passages. Wertheimer contends that the legal theory of coercion addresses two fundamental questions: (a) whether something amounts to coercion to begin with (*Was* there coercion? Was B actually *forced* to do X?) and (b) whether there is any *liability* that attaches to someone's actions (Should B be held legally to account for the consequences of X?). Now, there is no way to distinguish these two questions unless we can single out some factual, empirical criteria by which to answer the first of the two (that is, whether there is any degree of coercion involved in the course of action at issue), and yet, on a moralized theory of coercion, that is precisely what cannot be done, or at least it is not clear that, on such a conception, we can always find or rely on such empirical criteria (cf. ibid., p. 172ff.).

[22] This objection can be found in Anderson (2021), sec. 3.2.

(the loss of a spouse) that most people *would* regard as a harm (even if Spencer, in particular, sees it as beneficial to him).[23]

Is it possible to arrive at an alternative conception of coercion that will avoid the pitfalls of the subjective and objective conceptions while preserving the core truths of each? I believe so. In fact that is sense in which I have been suggesting the possibility of working with a *hybrid* conception of coercion and compulsion. Needless to say, this entails a redefinition of the term *coercion* or *compulsion*, or an explicative definition of the term. As noted, I will be looking at the problem only from the standpoint of those who are on the receiving end of coercion, rather than from that of those who are doing the coercing (what might be called the "passive" rather than the "active" side of coercion), and from this point of observation, the question whether a situation amounts to coercion (whether it can be said to involve some kind of coercive pressure) will turn on a *subjective* conception, and so on a conception that applies independently of where the coercion is coming from, be it an individual (or a group of specific individuals) or a system as a whole.[24] On a subjective conception, then, we can still identify the "degree of coercive pressure" that is brought to bear on an individual. On this conception, as noted, coercion or compulsion arises whenever the options available to an agent are not sufficient to satisfy the desires the agent wants to fulfil, and when these limiting options are determined by forces external to the agent. On a hybrid conception of this kind, then, there can be no coercion unless some third person or persons or some external circumstance beyond the agent's control threatens to deprive the agent of something the agent regards as a good, or as beneficial, and so unless there is someone or something that frustrates

[23] Even Wertheimer's "moralized" conception of coercion doesn't go so far as to analyze this as a case of coercion proper. Indeed, in *Coercion*, Wertheimer (1987), chap. 11, p. 192, n. 1, argues that whenever someone is faced with two alternatives, and they say they have no choice, it is always by reference to *that* person's preferences and desires that the two alternatives need to be evaluated in determining how far apart they are, which of the two is better than the other, or how desirable or acceptable they are (what their valence is), exactly as we would proceed on a hybrid (subjective/objective) conception of coercion. So, on Wertheimer's theory, it seems that, on the one hand, whether a threat counts as a threat of *harm* depends in part on the victim's (subjective) desires, but on the other hand, whether the threat is *coercive* depends on a moral (objective) conception of coercion.

[24] I should note that this hybrid conception should only be concerned with the passive side of coercion, with the question of who is *being* coerced into something, without specifying who or what is bringing coercive pressure to bear on this person. And the reason is that, as Robert Nozick's analysis shows, a formal conception of *active* coercion is inevitably going to present challenges. Most notably, in making the assertion that A forced B to do X, we seem to be already implicitly laying some kind of blame on A. The assertion thus often appears to be morally charged (or moralized), even if—as we saw at note 15, and as will shortly be discussed with the case of the person who is about to drown—even a moralized conception raises problems of its own. Subjective (or formal) conceptions of coercion can in turn be placed into two buckets: we have moderate conceptions, on which the range of desires that count as relevant are restricted to those that the person being coerced (the putative "coercee") considers to be so under conditions such as rationality and coherence, and extreme conceptions, on which *any* desire counts as relevant (even if it does not meet a test of rationality or coherence, and even if there is no such desire-independent criterion that the coercee takes into account).

the agent's desires or the agent's ability to obtain something that matters to the agent. This subjective criterion acts as a limit on the range of situations that can properly qualify as coercion exerted against a given individual, and, more to the point, it rules out as noncoercive those situations in which someone is threatened with being deprived of something they do not consider to be of value, or a "good" (for it wouldn't make much sense to say that someone in such a situation is being "threatened").

The other component of this hybrid conception lies in the *objective* criterion, which enables us to determine or make explicit, where necessary, whether the coercive pressure at issue is sufficient as a basis for saying that the coercee did not act voluntarily in the matter at hand or for downgrading the degree to which the act was voluntary, and so for determining whether the coercive pressure was (a) morally *unacceptable*, as with the case of unskilled and underpaid Worker Wesley, who felt he had to work twelve hours a day in order to pay for his son's heart surgery, or whether the pressure was (b) morally *acceptable*, and so below the baseline, or *insufficient* to vitiate the consent of someone who claims to have been forced to act as they did, as with the fellow who decided to take advantage of a healthcare programme that pays applicants to sell their organs, and who then proceeded to use the money to buy a vacation home. This objective, evaluative criterion can only be framed by reference to a conception of justice, and the conception I am going to rely on is one of liberal equality. The objective criterion acts or can act as an *exclusionary* and *restrictive* criterion, since (a) it restricts the range of cases in which coercive pressure qualifies as unacceptable—thereby ruling out the claim that the coercee acted voluntarily, or at least lessening the degree to which the act at issue can be said to have been voluntary—and since (b) that range of cases (the ones that meet the objective criterion) is likely to be narrower than the range of cases in which, on a strictly formal conception, there can be said to have been some form of coercion.

In reality, the conception I am advancing is primarily formal, for what it asks us to do in determining the degree of coercive pressure, or whether there even was any coercive pressure, is to look at the options available to the coercee in relation to what the coercee desires (the conception is formal in that it hinges on a relation, that between desires and options). And yet, in order to determine whether this coercive pressure is sufficient to bring about a certain outcome—and so to exclude the claim that the agent acted voluntarily and is therefore to blame, or at least to reduce the degree to which the act was voluntary and the agent was to blame—we have to rely on a moral conception of some kind. Wertheimer might object that I am profoundly misconceived as to the way the concept of coercion is used in moral language or in the language of the law. But the reason why the concept of coercion is sometimes used in a moralized way in moral and legal discourse is that the concept follows a binary, all-or-nothing logic: an act was either done under the pressure of coercion, violence, necessity, and so on, or it was not. *Tertium non datur*. It would seem, therefore, that in these cases we cannot neatly separate the question of whether or not any coercive pressure was brought to bear on someone (looking at things from that person's standpoint) from the question of whether or not such coercion or compulsion is acceptable, that is, whether or not we ought to exclude or diminish responsibility for the act that was putatively coerced, and so whether or not the coercee's will has been vitiated (cf. Wertheimer 1987, p. 185).

Unlike Wertheimer, I believe that moral and legal discourse is nuanced and sophisticated enough to avoid these kinds of "linguistic pigeonholes," that is, this language is malleable enough to enable us to not only see *degrees* of coercion (to see coercion as a graduated concept) but also, and especially, to identify two underlying questions that are in fact quite different. The first question is whether someone—from *their* standpoint, that is, in relation to their *desires*—has been subjected to some form of coercive pressure, or, stated otherwise, whether the range of options open to them has been significantly narrowed down. The second question is whether that coercive pressure is sufficiently grave or harmful, or to what degree it crosses the threshold of gravity or harm in depriving someone of important resources or opportunities, and so whether such pressure is sufficient to vitiate the coercee's will, that is, to exclude that the coercee acted voluntarily and is therefore to blame, or else to find that the act was less than fully voluntary, and so to attenuate the coercee's responsibility. And I cannot see what we can gain—from a moral standpoint as well as from the legal standpoint of legislation and adjudication—by using the concept of coercion in such a way as to conceal the questions that underlie its use.[25]

[25] There are different ways for any legal system to explicitly resolve the two questions underlying the use of the term *coercion*. One approach could be to work at the legislative level, with legal provisions drafted in such a way as to clearly signal gradation ("an excessive or unwarranted degree of coercive pressure," "coercive pressure sufficient to vitiate consent," "the weight of coercive pressure," and so on). But the courts may still have to deal with concepts that only admit of a binary logic, as in "a contract is null and void if any fraudulent design, material mistake, or duress was involved in its formation," thereby failing the "meeting of the minds" requirement (no *consensus ad idem*). In such cases the courts could get around the problem by crafting language specifically designed to address it. Thus *violence* might be defined in the case law as any undue and unwarranted coercive pressure significant and ominous enough to cause someone to act in virtue of that pressure alone. Something to that effect can be found in the Italian Civil Code, the source of the aforementioned unenforceability cause (Art. 1427) stating that a contract can be voided for mistake, fraud, or duress, where *duress* is understood to include violence, since *violence* is in turn farsightedly framed as an evaluative concept: it must be "of such a nature as to impress itself onto the mind of a reasonable person, causing this person to fear for themselves or for their property, anticipating a harm both unjust and significant" (Art. 1435, my translation). It is clear from the foregoing examples that the term *coercion* can often be used in a moralized (or morally charged) way. An example is the previously discussed case of Committed Chloe, the woman who is put under coercive pressure by her partner, Lustful Lou, who demands sex from her or else he will break up with her, where the argument was made that she is not truly being *forced* to do anything (because she has other options), and if she *is* being forced, the language of coercion only applies in virtue of the moral baseness of Lou's threat. In the language of law the matter gets much more complicated, and I will not be dealing with it here except by pointing to the example of malfeasance, or misconduct in public office, as defined in the Italian Criminal Code, which describes it as the conduct of government officials or civil servants who in that capacity abuse the powers of the office to *force* or *press* someone to give or unduly promise to give anything of value to them or to any third party. There are moral grounds on which, in such circumstances, responsibility can be attributed to a malfeasor and diminished for those who yield to the pressure of malfeasance: this can be done on grounds of (a) coercion, (b) abuse of public office, or (3) what is "undue." Thus, for example, in the statutory language and case law of some common law jurisdictions, violent sex

What ought to emerge from the foregoing remarks is that the hybrid conception here defended comes with two main advantages as follows. For one thing, it enables us to distinguish the two previously identified questions, namely, whether the conditions of coercive pressure are met—where the criteria are primarily factual or empirical, and where the situation is assessed from the standpoint of the coercee—and whether such coercive pressure is strong enough to justify excluding or diminishing the coercee's responsibility and/or holding the coercer civilly or criminally responsible. For another thing, the hybrid conception accounts for the fact that in ordinary and legal language the term *coercion* is sometimes used in a moralized (or morally laden) way.[26] What the hybrid conception gives us, then, is a conceptual toolbox that can be put to good analytical use across a full spectrum of scenarios involving the use of the term *coercion* in the language. Three such scenarios can be identified, and I should note, too, that they can be analyzed without loss of clarity even when it comes to the problem of interpretation. Thus, if in ordinary, philosophical, or legal language the term *coercion* or *compulsion* is used in a vague or moralized way—as in "A is coerced into doing X or forced to do X" (Example 1)—the hybrid conception makes it possible to explicitly distinguish the two underlying questions by construing coercion as any coercive pressure sufficient to vitiate the coercee's consent. If, by contrast, the term *coercion* is used in ordinary or legal language in such a way as to make the moralized element only partly explicit—as in "A physically forced B to do X through the use of violence" (Example 2) or "B was unjustly coerced" (Example 3)—the hybrid conception enables us to make the evaluative element and the gradual nature of coercion even more explicit (by framing Example 3 as saying "B did not act in a way that was sufficiently free of unjust coercive pressures"), and it likewise enables us to interpret different requisites (such as "physical violence" or the act of "forcing" someone to do something, as in

crimes are referred to as cases of *forcible compulsion*, involving a use of coercive pressure strong enough to exclude the victim's consent, whether because the victim acted under a real threat of harm or was physically forced into the act. The question here is whether embedded in the concept of compulsion or that of what counts as forcible are moral and evaluative considerations, and whether such considerations *should* be integral to one or both of these concepts.

[26] Some commentators also make the claim that a person's will needs to be free of manipulation, but this is a requisite that within the frame of the theory of coercion put forward here seems superfluous. Unlike coercion, manipulation does not work by forcing someone to not fulfil a desire. Rather, in some cases it eliminates the desire altogether from the start by partly or momentarily depriving the individual in question of cognitive or mental capacity (this can be achieved by brainwashing or psychological conditioning or by way of a brain implant). In other cases, manipulation works through techniques of deception that cause the individual to form false beliefs—something a theory of the value of individual autonomy can account for by introducing the requisite that an individual's decisions need to be duly informed, through a knowledge, awareness, or understanding of the relevant facts (once this requirement is satisfied, there can no longer be any deceptive manipulation). In still other cases, manipulation works by exploiting an individual's lack of knowledge, education, or cognitive skills (illiteracy in any of its various forms) or an education or upbringing that is dogmatic or fundamentalist. This kind of manipulation gives rise to what is known as epistemic violence, a matter we will be taking up in Chap. 3, Sect. 3.6 and Chap. 5, Sect. 5.6.

Example 2) on the basis of different evaluative considerations suited to each requisite. If, finally, in what is the least likely scenario, the use of the evaluative requisite in ordinary or legal language is fully explicit and exhaustive—as in "B acted in a way that was sufficiently free of any kind of unjust coercive pressure" (Example 4)—the hybrid conception enables us to see that there is no longer any need to make that requisite explicit (it would be redundant to qualify the scenario as "sufficiently" free of coercive pressure in interpreting that pressure and what it entails).

In short, in the paradigmatic cases in which the antipaternalistic doctrine applies, a person's will to carry out an act that is deemed dangerous or harmful to them needs to be *sufficiently free of coercive pressures*. While the meaning of the term *coercive pressure* needs to be determined on the basis of a formal conception, the qualifier *sufficient* enables us to make explicit all the evaluative considerations that, where necessary, need to be in made in assessing whether the coercion at hand is acceptable, that is, whether it crosses the threshold beyond which the coercee's action can justifiably be said to have been nonvoluntary.

From the framework just outlined there follows an implication that can be illustrated by going back to the case of Unskilled Worker Wesley. Which is to say that if a libertarian should claim that Wesley is not actually *forced* to work twelve hours a day in order to pay for his son's heart transplant, even if he has no other way to pay for that expense, we shouldn't assume that the libertarian is thereby endorsing a formal conception of coercion. It is more likely that the libertarian is instead reasoning from a hybrid conception or from an objective, substantive conception informed by a theory of justice, like Nozick's (see Nozick (1974), chaps. 3ff.), that leaves little room for liberal equality. Indeed, a libertarian proceeding from a strictly formal conception would have to qualify as coercive not only the case of a specific individual making a specific threat against a specific victim, but also the case of a blue collar worker trying to make ends meet by working the assembly line eight hours a day while hoping to find an opportunity to work under a contract that pays the same salary for half the hours. But I doubt that the libertarian would concede that the factory grind, too, counts as coercion. In order to exclude this case from the realm of the coercive, thereby avoiding self-contradiction, the libertarian would have to rely on substantive or moralized criteria under which some coercive pressures can be deemed acceptable (where the pressures are qualified as coercive on the basis of subjective criteria and as acceptable on the basis of evaluative ones).

With that as background, we should ask: are there contracts containing clauses agreed to under "sufficient coercive pressures" in the sense just mentioned, as when the parties start out from unequal bargaining positions? It seems clear to me that the answer to that question is yes. In a typical free market system—where competition is imperfect, with oligopolies forming in key sectors (such as banking or insurance), and sometimes even outright cartels in others—it is quite common for jobseekers and consumers to be confronted with boilerplate clauses in take-it-or-leave-it contracts of adhesion, which some can decline to sign but whose terms and conditions for the most part cannot be negotiated (Feinberg (1986), pp. 250–251; Murphy (1981), p. 88ff.). If employees wanted contract clauses that worked more in their favour, they would have to go on long strikes that would often not achieve anything, because the negotiating powers of employees and their the labour unions would be far inferior to those of the corporate groups and business combines on the other side of the negotiating table, considering the wide range of tools available to the latter, who can threaten workers with layoffs and offshoring and with moving plants, manufacturing, and investment abroad. If a large employer, corporate group, or business combine, through such threats, succeeded in getting its employees to accept contract clauses that strip away rights the employees regard as fundamental—rights which the employees want to be able to enjoy (the subjective requisite of coercion), and which on a conception of liberal equality are understood to be fundamental (the objective requisite of coercion)[27]—in what sense might a state be called paternalistic for introducing legal restrictions on the content of collective bargaining agreements? Is this a label we could apply to a government that (a), on the basis of accurate and extensive surveys and field investigations, found that the vast majority of employees, if given a choice, would rather work under a good contract than under a bad contract—one that curtails their basic rights—and that (b), on that basis, proceeded to introduce legislation making such bad contracts illegal, thereby prohibiting workers from accepting such terms and conditions in their employment contracts? Or shouldn't a government protect workers from specific kinds of harms, from unfair and unjust coercive pressures, ones that bend their will—with the caveat, of course, that the large companies and business conglomerates that employ these workers may well in fact offshore those jobs?

These questions point to the much more complex and difficult problem of the validity of contracts and legal transactions that legal or natural persons may enter into. But this is not a problem that will be dealt with here, for it would take us on a long detour, requiring us to work out what basic rights workers and consumers are to be recognized as having on the basis of a conception of liberal equality, while at the same time balancing these rights against the legitimate interests of businesses, thereby determining the extent to which the free market can be regulated, and in what ways. With that said, I do believe, as mentioned, that we shouldn't necessarily

[27] The mechanics of the two requisites become apparent in cases where they come into conflict. Thus, for example, if workers wanted stronger rights and protections than what is warranted under the prevailing conception of justice (say, a four-hour work day), this would mean that if a collective bargaining agreement is struck requiring employees to work six hours a day rather than the four hours they are hoping to get, the coercive pressure that through such negotiations is brought to bear on them by employers and capital cannot be qualified as unacceptable (even if these are the terms that employees now *have to* take). In a much more unlikely scenario, the prevailing conception of justice may recognize workers as having rights and opportunities they are not claiming at all (such as the right to have sleeping accommodations set up on site, at the business owner's plant), and in this case, too, there would be no coercion if the business owners were to threaten their employees with consequences in case they should in fact use the plant as sleeping quarters (even if this is contrary to what the applicable conception of justice calls for). A bizarre case in which a system of rules is in place that attaches penalties for engaging in conduct that those subject to the rules do not want to engage in at all is depicted in Lasse Hallström's film *The Cider House Rules*, where seasonal apple pickers who sleep in their employer's cider house are subject to a rule that bars them from sleeping on the rooftop, even if none of them want to do so or even think it a good idea to do so.

take it as a mark of paternalism if legal provisions are enacted to protect consumers and employees by limiting their ability to determine the content of the contracts they enter into, especially when these contracts contain clauses that significantly cut against their interests: in fact I believe that these legal restrictions (like many that are in force in Europe today) are very often *not* paternalistic at all. For it may well be that in certain historical periods, in an imperfectly competitive market system like the one previously described, some of the decisions that people make as consumers, jobseekers, or prospective employees are not "sufficiently free of coercive pressure." What is more, the legal restrictions the government places on the content of certain contracts, thereby limiting the ability of individuals to determine the content of these contracts, may well prove to be indispensable, because unlike what happens in other contexts in which real threats are made that force someone to act contrary to their will or to believe that it would be risky for them to negotiate, the capitalist market system does not offer the possibility of properly *neutralizing* the coercive pressure that major market players can bring to bear on consumers and people in the workforce: the best that can be done in this regard is to limit the effects of that pressure.

Let us consider an example that may clarify that last point. If I were seriously ill and authorized a doctor to euthanize me because my nephew is threatening to kill my partner unless I request that procedure, an effective law-enforcement apparatus would step in and prevent my nephew from acting on his threat, making it empty. With that threat gone, it would be possible to actually establish what my wishes are (to be euthanized or not). But no such alternative scenario seems available to us when considering whether to enter into a contract or go through with any other legal transaction: in this case, we do not have the option of working within an alternative system that operates on a large scale and does not entail as much harm as the capitalist market system. And that is the sense in which I contend that we cannot completely neutralize the coercive pressure that consumers and the individuals making up the workforce face in their relations and interactions with large employers and distributors. What could perhaps be done, as hinted at, is carry out widescale surveys or do other fieldwork to find out what consumers and workers actually think about some fundamental questions relating to their contractual rights and obligations, and on that basis legislation could be introduced that would prevent them from entering into contracts that work against their interests so ascertained and defined, with legal limitations that can strike a proper balance between (a) what consumers and workers (including employees) consider to be reasonable terms and conditions and (b) what a free market system requires to maintain healthy competition and a thriving economy consistent with a conception of liberal equality.[28]

[28] On the antipaternalistic conception here defended, the state may not interfere in the decisions that individuals make under a set of standard conditions that come down to (a) rationality (and so also a lack of mental incapacity), (b) desires that are stable over time, (c) an awareness of the relevant facts, and (c) sufficient freedom from coercive pressures. As mentioned, I will not be concerned with government interference in decisions where these conditions are *not* met. Even so, it is worth commenting on the last of these conditions, requiring sufficient freedom from coercive

As we can see, these problems do not go to the core of the conflict between paternalism and antipaternalism, and so we need not dwell on them any further.

2.4 Binding Our Future Selves

I was saying in the previous section that we will not be going into the general problem of the limits that can be placed on the validity of agreements and contracts. But there are three exceptions I should mention: that of voluntary slavery contracts, that of what might be called "mortal combat contracts" (think gladiators), and that of buying and selling drugs. These will be discussed in Chaps. 5 and 7, and the reason why they will be taken up is that in some of the literature we find the attempt (however vain it may be) to work these cases in such a way as to extract from them arguments that can be deployed against antipaternalism. Then, too, the same cases bring into play the even broader and crucial problem of the limits within which an agent can assent to another exercising coercion over him or her. Coercion, in other words, can come in the form of two agents agreeing that one of them will use force to limit

pressures. For, as has also been mentioned, a problem arises where the coercive pressure at issue stems from the market forces that bear down on an individual: in determining whether these forces, or the coercive pressure they exert, are sufficient to exclude that the individual concerned acted willingly, or at least are sufficient for a finding of diminished voluntariness, we have to look at the basic rights and protections that individuals are recognized as having (such as freedom of expression, the right to property, and the right to pension and unemployment benefits). Thus, for example, the coercive pressure would be morally *unacceptable* if Metalworker Mike, working for low wages, felt compelled to work twelve hours a day in order to pay for his son's heart transplant if the state protected none of his basic rights or those of his children (the right to universal health care, for example, and to unemployment benefits). It would also be possible for a given legal and social community in the West to form a majority consensus, either in the legislature or in the highest court of the land, in virtue of which individuals are recognized as having a set of rights grounded in an antipaternalistic conception, such as the right to euthanasia and assisted suicide, the right not to wear a helmet while riding a motorcycle, or the right to use hard or recreational drugs, which rights can be exercised so long as the individuals concerned are rational and fully informed and their desires are stable over time. But it would also be possible that *no* such consensus forms in the community at issue, such that individuals lack certain basic rights (certain basic freedoms and social rights). In other words, it would be possible for *tragic cases* to happen that I would find it quite difficult to solve. For example, someone who decides to commit suicide or sell a kidney because they are unemployed and unable to find a job would have no constitutionally protected or judicially recognized right to unemployment benefits or to universal health care (and equally tragic would be the predicament of those who see no option but to migrate illegally and are in extreme poverty). Clearly, we cannot properly assess the merits or adequacy of an ethico-political conception just on the basis of a few rare tragic cases. Indeed, if it is true, as Justice Holmes commented, that "hard cases make bad law" (*Northern Securities Co. v. United States*, 193 US 197, 365 (1904)), then we can equally say, with Wertheimer, that "hard moral cases may make for bad philosophy" (Wertheimer (1987), p. 13). Thus we could set out to develop a moral conception concerned with the rights and duties of parents in relation to their children, and this conception may hold up reasonably well in the majority of cases, but it can easily fall apart if we apply it to a situation such as a Nazi concentration camp.

the action of the other, or, otherwise stated, A agrees to be forcefully restrained by B. An analysis of this problem will make it possible to briefly state the *second* of the two main arguments for the view that legal restrictions on freedom of contract are not necessarily paternalistic.

It seems to me that there are two situations in which agents have good reason to choose now, in the present, to limit their own future freedom of action by availing themselves of the force of others. The first situation is one in which we envisage our future selves as no longer being able to make decisions that are actually beneficial to us or in our best interest, having become irrational or incompetent or subject to coercion or compulsion.[29] For example, Trippy Tim and Spacehead Sonny agree to take LSD together under the supervision of a physician, whom they authorize to use whatever force may be necessary to prevent either of the two from harming the other while tripping. These arrangements are also known as Ulysses contracts, and it's easy to see why. In the *Odyssey*, the Homeric hero has himself bound to the mast of his ship so as to be able to listen the sirens' captivating but deceptive and mortal song. And on hearing the song, he desperately pleads with his crew (who in turn have been instructed to wax their ears so that they themselves do not fall captive to the song), exhorting them to tie him loose, which they refuse to do. As Donald H. Regan underscores, the reason why it seems to us that the crew acted appropriately as they did is not out of a sense that the "first Ulysses," having expressed his wishes beforehand, ought to prevail on the later, "second Ulysses." Rather, the reason is that, unlike the first Ulysses—rational and pondered in ordering his crew to tie him to the mast and not free him for any reason whatsoever—the second Ulysses was presumably "beside himself," having expressed his wishes in conditions of irrationality or lack of mental capacity (the spell into which he had been cast by the sirens' song) (cf. Regan (1983); Feinberg (1986), pp. 82–83).

This why the Ulysses pact is often resorted to in explaining the rationale behind the use of advance healthcare directives, or living wills. But while the two bear some significant similarities, they differ in other respects. Like the Ulysses pact, a living will is an arrangement under which we (as testators) make decisions that apply to our future selves in case we should become incapacitated and no longer able to decide for ourselves, and they apply across the entire arc of any such period. Our antecedent wishes are binding on others and even on ourselves. But living wills, where they are legally recognized, are envisaged for circumstances like reversible coma, a persistent vegetative state, serious forms of senile dementia, and late-stage Alzheimer's disease, and the majority of these circumstances differ from those under which Ulysses pacts are typically made. And this where the differences between the two come in. I should mention two in particular. For one thing, a living will—which, not incidentally, is referred to as a "will"—is primarily a *unilateral* act, a statement of desires that, at a specified time in the future, binds an

[29] An example in a democratic polity would be that of a constitution designed to prevent a political majority from setting up an autocratic government. This example can be compared to that of a law under which employees are barred from waiving their right to paid holiday leave. Cf. Regan (1983), p. 127ff., and Chap. 5 in this work.

indeterminate number of persons (relatives, loved ones, friends, doctors) who cannot be individually named *ex ante* at the time the will is drawn up (we cannot say who the doctor is that will be authorized to withdraw life support ten or twenty years from now, or in what hospital): contrast that with a Ulysses pact, where the agreement usually binds the very parties who have clinched it, an no one else besides. And, for another thing, the situations that fall within the scope of a living will, and in which the will can be carried into effect, are typically ones in which the testator has essentially lost all capacity, mental as well as physical, and whose freedom of action is therefore severely limited, if not inexistent, and not likely to come back (as when someone has fallen into a permanent vegetative state or reversible coma). And in this respect, too, a living will is different from a Ulysses pact, which does cover situations in which someone expects to lose their mental capacity, but the condition is temporary and reversible (as when someone is under the influence of alcohol or of a mind-altering drug or is in a state of shock, hypnosis, or temporary depression), and the person in that condition normally still retains some cognitive and physical abilities.

We can turn now to the second of the two previously mentioned situations in which there may be a good reason to enter into an agreement by which to limit one's own freedom through the force of others. In this second case, we want to rid ourselves of a clinically diagnosed compulsive desire or addiction (to alcohol or other substance) that is currently gripping us and is proving to be extremely difficult to break free of. So, for example, Addicted Adriel might enter into an agreement with Trusted Tyler to prevent his future self from doing certain things like smoking a cigarette or doing cocaine, to this end temporarily authorizing Tyler to do what she thinks is necessary to prevent those things from happening (cf. Feinberg 1986, p. 82). I do not know that this kind of case exactly coincides with a Ulysses pact. I will therefore treat it as a subclass, highlighting the following difference, which essentially comes down to the extent of the powers entrusted to Tyler, particularly as concerns her discretion to take appropriate measures or do "what she thinks is necessary" to prevent the outcome she has been empowered to prevent. The scope of Tyler's powers, in other words, needs to be commensurate with the task assigned to her: there is a limit on *what* she is empowered to do, as well as on *how long* she can keep exercising those powers. So, for example, there are no good antipaternalistic reasons why Tyler should be able to *kidnap* Adriel in order to prevent him from smoking despite his intense desire to do so, nor should she be able to hold him hostage *for an indefinite amount of time*, even if that would achieve the goal for which Adriel previously empowered Tyler to act. That is not the case with a Ulysses pact, where the protection is for a person who may become irrational or mentally incompetent for a time, and the agent entrusted with the protection may accordingly have much greater discretion. If, for example, Adriel is addicted to heroin and lapses into a state of intoxication no or begins to hallucinate, and as a result attempts to jump from the window of his fifth-floor apartment, Tyler is thereby empowered to tie him to his bed, and to keep him that way for as long as he continues to hallucinate. Tyler's powers therefore need to be gauged to the occasion, and it is one thing for Tyler to do what is necessary to protect Adriel from a tobacco addiction and another to protect him from a drug-induced hallucinatory or psychotic state. Only in the latter case is Tyler's agreement with Adriel Ulysses-like, because with a greater potential for harm come greater powers to protect from that harm. And it stands to reason that this should be so, considering how serious the withdrawal stage may be when trying to overcome an addiction (cf. Husak 2000, p. 70ff).

I doubt that there can be a third case in which we may have a good reason to hold our future selves bound by a decision of our present selves. But one case that does suggest itself is that of an individual in a free market system who enters into a contract in order to obtain something of value that would not otherwise be available. Suppose, for example, that Homeowner Hunter wants to renovate his home and thus enters into a binding contract with Home Renovator Ross: under the terms of this contract, Hunter binds himself to pay Ross for a service (the home renovation) that Ross would probably not perform outside the framework of the same contract, not being sure that he can trust Hunter just on his word alone. This agreement might conceivably be constructed as a case of Hunter binding his future self to a decision of his present self. But is that the best way to frame the situation? Perhaps not. In fact, as Regan comments, there are different reasons that justify the enforceability of contracts as legally binding instruments, chief among which is the need to protect the interests of others. In the example just introduced, this is the financial interest of the home renovator, Ross, who risks renovating Hunter's home without being paid by Hunter, and the contract is there as a guarantee, without which Ross would not be able to trust that, once his work is done—once he has delivered a thing of value—Hunter will live up to his end of the bargain and pay for that thing. And this point about trust can be generalized. If no one could rely on the ability to enforce contracts, or if contracts could be unilaterally cancelled at will, no one would enter into a contract or agree to do anything for anyone else in exchange for anything else of value (consideration), and the economy, and indeed society, would grind to a halt for lack of trust: normative chaos would ensue, a general state of lawlessness. Hence the need for enforceable binding contracts, restoring at least part of the trust that is necessary for a well-functioning society and a well-oiled market system.[30]

It would seem, therefore, that with service contracts we have a third case in which one person, Hunter, has an interest in binding his future self through the force

[30] Cf. Regan (1983), p. 130. See also Shiffrin (2000), p. 221ff.: "I want to begin by taking it for granted that the institution of contract is an institution in which the community assists people who make agreements by providing a measure of security in those agreements. We may provide this assistance to one another for many reasons. Primary among them is that the institution facilitates agreements and transactions between strangers as well as people who lack a sufficient basis for an independently generated mutual trust. This allows us to cooperate more easily and to secure our common welfare in a number of respects. It also permits individuals to pursue more-complex projects and plans and to act more independently. These opportunities enhance the value of their capacity for autonomy. Of course, the existence of such an institution may well affect what agreements are made, so one should not necessarily regard all agreements regulated by a system of contract as conceptually prior to or independent of the existence of the institution. Some will be made only because there is a background institution providing such security. Others would be made regardless."

exercised by another person, Ross, so that Hunter will not, at time T_1, go back on the promise he previously made to Ross at time T_0. But what does this reconstruction have to do with the idea that the justification for placing any limitation on the legal enforcement of contracts must necessarily be paternalistic? It would be so because, on this reconstruction, to enforce a legally binding contract against a nonperforming party is also to protect the autonomy of that party a time T_0, that is, before they decided to go back on the commitment made in signing the contract. To do otherwise—that is, to prevent some contracts on some occasions from being enforced—would therefore be paternalistic, for it would violate or limit the autonomy of the nonperforming party at time T_0 or that of both contracting parties, and it is paternalistic to violate anybody's autonomy at any time.[31] But it is doubtful that this reconstruction can hold up.

The question of the legal enforceability of contracts, or else of the limits that can be placed on such enforceability, clearly brings into play the question of the interests of others and whether these interests ought to be taken into account as worthy of protection by the state. But let us set this question aside for the moment and ask: if Hunter does not pay what Ross is owed under the home renovation contract, and Ross therefore sues for damages, on what basis is the state's use of coercion to enforce the contract justified? Is it Hunter's antecedent decision to protect an interest of his, as in a Ulysses pact? Is it the sacredness of the promise made? Is it that Hunter, from the past, binds himself in the present? And why should he do so? Is it because Hunter at time T_0 feared that at time T_1 he would not do the right thing and

[31] It is curious that this antecedent-versus-future-self reconstruction seems to find support in Feinberg, as if a promise were rendered binding in virtue of the stronger force of the commitment made by the promisor's antecedent self, which prevails over any of the promisor's present wishes (thereby preventing the promisor from going back on the promise made), suggesting that this antecedent commitment necessarily or essentially protects the promisor's autonomy. But in reality the reasons Feinberg brings into his argument clearly show that what the binding force of promises protects is not so much the promisor's autonomy as an idea of virtue, or the interests of others (the promisees or any beneficiaries of the promise), or the promisor's current interests that are not in conflict with his or her previous commitments. Indeed, Feinberg argues that when promises are recognized to be binding, a general climate of trust develops in the community as individuals hold themselves and others responsible for the commitments they have made in the past, or indeed for any previous course of action that may have reasonably caused others to rely on them in the present (a principle that in the law goes by the name of promissory estoppel). Otherwise no one could be held accountable for anything they may have said or done in the past. See Feinberg (1986), p. 83ff. But Feinberg's argument seems to hold up well only in the context of a tight-knit community, where everyone will know who the individuals are that do not honour their promises, and no one will trust these individuals, who therefore can no longer expect to benefit from the community's system of trust. But in any other context—or any context involving millions of people, outside the boundaries of an interconnected community, be it traditional, online, or in some trade or profession where everyone knows everyone else—the untrustworthy promisor can simply relocate or set up shop at some other place across the nation or even across the world and make a fresh start. An illustration of this possibility afforded by a loosely connected community can be found in Steven Spielberg's movie *Catch Me, If You Can*, based on a real story, which shows how difficult it proves for federal agents in the United States to catch the lead character, who has perfected the art of passing forged checks.

pay what he owes? Is it to protect Hunter's interest so that other home renovators and builders will trust Hunter to pay if he should seek their services? I don't think so. The main basis on which the state is justified in using coercion to enforce the contract in case Hunter, at time T_1, should fail to pay the amount he owes under the contract is the need to protect Ross's interests, and so the interests of the counterparty, and generally the need to safeguard the practice that makes it possible to trust that others will do what they agree to do, thereby enabling the practice of contract-making to take hold and thrive.[32]

The agreement between Hunter and Ross can be construed as one of two basic facts that, once established, count as necessary conditions justifying the use of coercion to enforce the relative contract, the other basic fact being that of noncompliance, which (once established) would prove harm to the counterparty. If Hunter hadn't promised to pay Ross for the renovation, or if Ross didn't trust Hunter to begin with and thus hadn't agreed to do the job, there would be no contract, thus no basis for contract damages. In other words, even if we could obligate people to always keep their promises and uphold their commitments, what we would be protecting is perhaps a virtue, such as personal integrity, or we would be protecting the interests of those who stand to gain from the arrangements they make under certain

[32]A similar argument has been made by Seana Valentine Shiffrin. "This posture of selective involvement or selective non-enforcement need not be motivated by *distrust* of either parties' ability to judge what is in their good (or the good of those under their control) or to act to secure their good. The refusal to enforce need not represent an effort to supplant the judgment or action of the contracting parties or an intention to stop them from engaging in (solely) mutually regarding immoral action. (Such efforts *would* be paternalist, on my account). Instead, the motive may reasonably be a self-regarding concern not to facilitate or assist harmful, exploitative, or immoral action. Put metaphorically, on moral grounds, the state refuses, for its own sake, to be a codependent. Consider a parallel case: it would be paternalist for me to hide your cigarettes to protect your health. Nonetheless, it would not be paternalist (and may be morally required) for me to refuse to buy you cigarettes or to refuse to retrieve them from a pilfering acquaintance if my motive for refusal is that I think that *I* should not perform substantial actions that contribute to your addiction or illness. An analogous claim may be made with contract: there are some agreements you have a right to form but no right to assistance in carrying them out and about which others may reasonably feel that they may or even must not assist." Shiffrin (2000), p. 224, italics in the original. But this argument is ambiguous. It is not the case that if we refuse to help someone because we think their behaviour is immoral, then our refusal is necessarily antipaternalistic. On the contrary, it may well be the case that we *are* engaging in paternalism, but of a *soft* or mild variety, where we selectively do good to certain individuals on the basis of what *we* think is good for them. That is different from strong or coercive paternalism, which deliberately and specifically limits the freedom of others. The point has to do with the meaning that in Shiffrin's argument needs to be ascribed to the expression "harmful, exploitative, or immoral action." Suppose, for example, that A enters into a "contract of prostitution" and the community views this as morally harmful to A: if on that basis the community refuses to enforce this contract in the event of noncompliance, thereby refusing to protect A's interest in such enforcement, then we would be looking at a case of paternalism (however much noncoercive). But there is no paternalism if, on the contrary, the reason why the community refuses to protect a contractual practice is that this practice is regarded as harmful to the community itself (that is, to people other than the parties to a contract) or that the practice unfairly harms those who no longer want to keep faith with the agreement (it might threaten, for example, the sex worker's freedom to say no until the last minute).

contracts. And if what is at stake is the virtue of integrity, we would be looking at a perfectionist theory (discussed in Chap. 3, Sect. 3.11), and so a theory that leans toward paternalism, but that would work against the current wishes of the noncomplying party: it would instead protect what (according to the theory itself) is understood to be *good* for Hunter—namely, his interest in keeping promises, and in particular the promise he made at the time he entered into the contract—but it would not protect his autonomy. A perfectionist theory defending the legal enforceability of contracts is a theory that protects the moral value of promises, the virtue of honesty, the individual's good in the sense of the intrinsic interest that anyone should have in being morally virtuous. But that is not the only possible justification for enforceability, and at any rate it debunks the thesis that enforcement against the noncomplying party is necessarily justified on the basis of the need to protect this party's autonomy. If, on the other hand, the justification rests on the need to protect the interests of the compliant counterparty (in the example at hand, Ross, who stands to be harmed by Hunter's nonperformance), then we *would* be reasoning on antipaternalistic grounds, but the reasoning would have little to do with the rational interests of the party who no longer wants to keep the promise made with the contract. For if the state wanted to only protect the rational and sufficiently uncoerced wishes the noncompliant party forms *after* signing the contract, it would have to forgo enforcement.[33]

Indeed, it may be that Hunter decides to enter into a contract with Ross because this is the only way to get Ross the home renovator to renovate Hunter's home (Hunter would not otherwise be able to count on Ross, who understandably does not place much trust in humankind). It is in this sense that Hunter can be said to enter into a contract in order to get something of value that would not otherwise be available to him. Hunter may well be a self-interested, self-serving agent intent on exploiting the free market system in order to extract a benefit from it at others' expense, but in normal conditions this option wouldn't be available to him. It would therefore be reasonable for him to enter into a binding contract. As he sees it, he has no other choice: he would *have to* do so. Once the benefit is gained (once the renovation is done), Hunter could choose not to pay, in which case it wouldn't be plausibly or normally justified to resort to coercion to exact compliance in order to protect an interest of noncompliant Hunter, since he has already benefited from the contract, and he might prefer to risk losing the trust of others (who will no longer be willing to work for him or transact any business with him) rather than pay what he owes to Ross. The justification for recourse to coercion seems to essentially rest on the need to protect the interest of parties other than Hunter (either that of the

[33] The point is aptly stated by David Archard in relation to slavery contracts: "Were society to enforce the contract and coerce the slave into continued obedience, it would clearly be limiting the freedom of that person. When society refuses to recognize the contract it respects the currently expressed wishes of the discontented slave. It permits people to act as they choose, namely as free individuals. I fail to see how prohibition of slavery is correctly described as paternalism." Archard (1990), p. 462.

counterparty, Ross, or that of the broader community of free agents who stand to benefit from a reliable contract-making practice).

It therefore seems bizarre to argue that enforcement is justified on the basis that Hunter's wishes at time T_0 should *preempt* any current wishes he may form at time T_1 (or, more accurately stated, on the basis that the decision he made when he signed the contract, committing himself to fulfilling all the obligations set forth in the contract, including his obligation to pay damages for any nonperformance, should prevail on his current wishes not to perform and not have to pay restitution). Hunter's intention may well have been to see if he could gain some benefit without having to give anything back in exchange, even knowing that he would incur some kind of penalty in case he should choose not to perform. In just the same way, we wouldn't say that a burglar who breaks into a house does so wishing to be sentenced to serve time in prison, even if that is what may in fact happen as a legal consequence of such breaking and entering. What we are looking at could also be described as a transactional scenario that Hunter can step into with any of three frames of mind, for it could be that he enters into the contract (1) fully committed to complying with its every term and condition, in which case the matter is moot; (2) intent on complying only so long circumstances do not turn against him, which is in fact the case we are considering; or (3) knowing from the start that he has no intention to comply, calculating that the value he can extract from the contract (i.e., having his home renovated) outweighs the risk of the legal consequences (including payment of damages) that might ensue as a result of his noncompliance. So, while the effect of the contract is that, by signing it, Hunter legally binds his future self, giving rise to obligations that will limit the future scope of his own freedom of action, that legally binding effect may not be something that Hunter genuinely wants to bring about but may be something he merely *expects* to happen and takes into account, his purpose being, not to hold himself bound by the contract, but to extract from it the benefit of the counterperformance without having to pay the agreed upon price, either knowing from the start that he was never going to pay and would try to see if he could somehow escape the consequences of his actions (as in case (3) above) or taking into account the possibility that he may at some point in the future be either unable or unwilling to pay (as in case (2) above).

In conclusion, if the community is unwilling to enforce a contractual practice because the practice is viewed as harmful to the community at large (to people other than the contracting parties) or as unfairly harmful to a party who is unwilling or no longer willing to perform—as in the case of a slave in a "contract of slavery" or a sex worker in a "contract of prostitution" who wants to be able to refuse to perform up until the last minute—then not only is there no paternalism, but we are protecting the noncompliant party's autonomy, the *currently* expressed wishes of rational and sufficiently uncoerced parties to the contract, *like a slave or a sex worker*. These are people who want to withdraw from the contract without being liable to payment of damages, and we are protecting the noncompliant party's autonomy on the ground that, in cases involving important decisions about one's own body, their current wishes may or should prevail over the counterparty's autonomy, or, in the case at hand, over the preferences of the slaveowner or the sex client, and so of those who use such contractual practices to get something they want. For the same reasons, it should generally be the case that all contracts under which someone's life and limb is at stake can be voided and hence be made unenforceable. Thus, for example, if a gladiator under contract loses a gladiator fight and the decision comes down that he should therefore be slain, he should be able to reject that call even if that is in violation of the contract and contrary to the wishes of the organizers of the games as counterparties. And the same goes for an abortion or a surrogacy contract or for a contract to undergo euthanasia or medically assisted suicide in a private clinic, or for a performance agreement to act in a pornographic movie or an agreement to engage in a session of sadomasochistic sex or obtain any other such personal services.

In these cases, when the noncompliant party withdraws from the contract, the counterparty should be able to recoup the money paid for the services the noncompliant party was contractually bound to provide. On the other hand, contracts of purchase and sale should normally be enforceable.

This means that a contract's enforceability depends on how we balance the autonomous preferences of a party to a contract who is noncompliant against the autonomous preferences of the counterparty: we have to balance the harm of noncompliance (the harm of making a contract unenforceable) against the harm the noncompliant party would suffer through enforced compliance or contractual damage compensation. This balancing of harms does not rest on a paternalistic basis but is instead worked out by reasoning and arguing within the framework of the harm principle. This is why we cannot solve all cases of enforceability of contract. For example, the Italian Court of Cassation has held that marriage contracts are in most of the cases unenforceable, arguing that if one of the spouses files for divorce and there is an economic imbalance between the parties, the economically weaker party would be disadvantaged in the ensuing divorce suit and could not mount a good defence. But that reasoning is flawed, for it is protective in the wrong way. What we need to protect, where divorce is concerned, are the autonomous preferences of the contracting parties: if one of the two parties has a higher income and is wealthier and wants to make sure that that income and wealth are protected in the event of a divorce, he or she should be able to do that in the marriage contract or prenuptial agreement, regardless of the financial situation the other spouse might face after the divorce is made final, having been negligent in failing to foresee that scenario at the time the marriage was contracted (He or she always has the option of making a living, without a degree, by working as waiter or waitress or caregiver or babysitter or nurse or cook). If one of the parties is economically disadvantaged and risks financial distress outside the marriage, the divorce proceedings are not the tool we should be using to prevent that from happening. For that amounts to redistribution of wealth, something that should instead be entrusted to the redistributive and welfare policies enacted by the government. The enforcement of prenuptial agreements against the will of one party to the contract does not imply any form of homicide, torture, rape, or excessive work shifts, as could occur in cases of slavery contracts, or any kind of rape, as seen in prostitution contracts.

For this reason, we cannot solve all cases of attribution of Hohfeldian positions, such as immunity and its correlative, by positing the inability to modify the legal and contractual situation of someone who has an immunity.

Just as, on a liberal conception, we protect the rational and sufficiently uncoerced wishes of terminally ill patients or of women who want to keep their options open and be able to decide at the last minute that they do not want to go through with euthanasia or carry a pregnancy to term, even if they previously expressed a wish to do so, so we need to protect the autonomy of a slave who has entered into a slavery contract but subsequently decides to withdraw from the contract, where the ability to withdraw makes such contracts nonbinding, and thus legally voidable. A more complex question is whether, apart from the cases considered, there are principled reasons why an agent's future self ought to be bound by an antecedently expressed commitment. I am leaning toward the view that the reasons we do have for that claim are not compelling enough to unqualifiedly support it. But, as just mentioned, the question is a difficult one, and it should furthermore be irrelevant in the debate between paternalism and antipaternalism. Indeed, it is difficult to imagine why someone should rationally (or self-interestedly) decide to frustrate (not fulfil) their future wishes by binding themselves to the wishes expressed by their antecedent self, any more than it would be rational for them to frustrate (not fulfil) their current wishes when these are rational and when doing so would cause harm to themselves. But that is not to say that there are no good reasons why someone should bind their future self to the wishes of their present self, to that end assenting to another's use of force. In fact such reasons do exist, and the ones that pertain to our discussion essentially come down to the prospect of an agent's future irrationality, addiction, compulsive behaviour, or lack of capacity—all scenarios which the agent in question wants to avoid. These reasons are perfectly consistent with the antipaternalistic theory here defended, central to which is the thesis that the state does not have the right to limit the freedom of adult individuals so long as they are rational and sufficiently free from coercion (or compulsion) and so long as they do not cause harm to others. And as we saw, the case involving someone who is irrational, lacks mental capacity, or has a diminished decision-making capacity is different from the case of contracts whose binding force and enforceability rests on the need to protect the interests of the parties to the contract (the financial interests of the counterparty or of an assignee to the contract or of a beneficiary) or the need generally to protect the interests of all those who rely on the contract-making practice and stand to gain from it.

The same conclusion is reached by Regan, arguing that, with the exception of the cases previously discussed, it makes no sense that the wishes expressed by someone's antecedent self should trump those of their current self. What must prevail is the more recent decision made or wish expressed, so long as this decision or wish is rational and uncoerced (cf. Regan (1983), pp. 128–29). Or at least that is so if what needs to be protected is the individual's autonomy. To clarify the argument, Regan employs the idea that there are different "temporal selves" which at different times operate and govern in any one person. Let us imagine that Idealistic Ian, in his youth, espouses the ideals of socialist solidarity, equality, and fraternity and enters into a legally binding contract with his dear friend Trusted Tiffany, agreeing that if Ian should at some future date win the lottery or should inherit wealth, as he expects to, Tiffany will prevent him from wastefully, extravagantly, or frivolously spending that money on himself (as by purchasing unnecessary luxury items, throwing lavish parties, or using the money to feed a cocaine or gambling habit) and will place two-thirds of his acquired wealth into a people's trust fund, because the money belongs to the people, and to the people it should therefore be returned as restitution. Let us further imagine that Ian subsequently does inherit, but that he is now a changed person, no longer idealistic, and does want to spend his wealth recklessly on cocaine, gambling, and prostitution. Should Tiffany allow him to do so? This is a case in which young Ian, on the basis of a wish expressed at time T_0, resolves to limit older Ian's freedom of action at time T_1, thereby overriding any contrary wishes he himself may form at time T_1. If older Ian, having tasted the pleasure of spending money on himself, changes his outlook on life and becomes a self-interested capitalist, why should his antecedent, and now vanished, self be allowed to control his current self?[34]

And, even more crucially, if we argue that Ian's antecedently expressed wishes should in fact prevail, in what sense would that be consistent with antipaternalism? I believe it is not. In fact, for one thing, as I have stressed, an antipaternalistic conception protects the current wishes of an adult rational agent who is free from coercion (compulsion), and though these current wishes may need to be so qualified, they are nonetheless the agent's *current*, and thus standing, wishes. And, for another thing, when Ian, at time T_0, believes in socialism, the later Ian does not yet exist: the Ian who at time T_1 will have morphed into a self-interested free-market capitalist is, for the time being, only a projection, a future possibility. When this Ian_1 does come into being, Ian_0 will be far away and not to be seen, or at least the part that accounts for his youthful idealism will be gone. There is, to be sure, enough of a psychological and biological line of continuity between the two Ians that we can always refer to them as "Ian," but the later of the two is a much-changed person, different from his earlier self.

And yet, in an apparent contradiction, Regan uses a similar argument to justify a paternalistic limitation on individual autonomy. As he argues, a requirement to wear a helmet while riding a motorcycle can be justified on the basis that in this way we are protecting the motorcyclist's "real self," which is a future self, the self of motorcyclists who, at a future time, having suffered a serious physical injury as a result of riding without a helmet, will wish that they could go back and wear the helmet, regretting the choice made by their antecedent self, who was underplaying the risk of riding unprotected without a helmet. If, in other words, having had a bad accident, one that caused a serious injury and thus a significant loss of autonomy, a motorcyclist wishes that he or she had never made that choice—if this motorcyclist were therefore a changed person, more prudent, one for whom a person's well-being over the long run outweighs what marginal increments in utility can be had in the present moment (as with the greater pleasure you would feel with the wind

[34]A similar example can be found in Regan (1983), p. 132ff.

running through your hair)—we would be faced with the dilemma of which of the two selves ought to be protected: should it be the antecedent self—the one who did not think to wear a helmet—or the later self, the one who regrets not having worn one? Regan suggests that we should favour the second (cf. Regan (1983), p. 125ff.). And yet the dilemma persists, for if we protect this future self, will be protecting a self who will never come into existence—one who will never come to regret riding a motorcycle without a helmet, precisely because we have made the helmet mandatory, getting this future motorcyclist to wear a helmet and not suffer any serious injury as a result of a road accident—but if we do *not* protect this future self, then we may be looking at the possibility of a motorcyclist who will deeply regret having chosen not to wear a helmet.

What Regan offers in this case is not the simplest solution to the dilemma. When someone chooses not to wear a helmet, their future self doesn't yet exist, nor do we know if it ever will. If their future self does come into existence, and will at that point regret the choice made by their antecedent self, the latter will have faded into the background: the part responsible for that choice will have gone. So why doesn't Regan apply the same solution here that he applied to the case of the youthful Ian who comes into a sizable inheritance? Why is it that in the case of the carefree motorcyclist he instead grants authority to a future self who doesn't yet exist and may never exist? Regan seems not to appreciate how unreasonably counterfactual and sweeping it would be to make a universal rule out of this case. Should we protect future selves whenever we detect one that may be in danger, or the future self of anyone we think is liable to make reckless choices in the moment that may preclude them from realizing the sum total of the utility that would derive from the (presumably wiser) choices they would otherwise be able to make over the course of a lifetime? And how to calculate this greater "utility"? On the basis of what preferences? Ours? Should we protect the future selves of anyone who takes on any degree of risk—the athlete in a combat sport or an extreme sport, the outdoorsperson on a hiking or boating trip, the businessperson venturing into a commercial enterprise—where it is our job to prevent these individuals from taking such risks, since they may later come to regret having done so?[35] Why should we protect someone from causing a loss or injury to their future self if, reasoning from an antipaternalistic stance, we do not want to protect an adult, rational, and uncoerced person from doing harm to their *present* self?

It seems to me that there is an implicit (not expressly recognized) assumption at work in Regan's argument, and it is that the motorcyclist's future self is more rational, reasonable, and mature than their antecedent self. In other words, there is a *true* self, with which the agent identifies, and that is the agent's future self, the one who regrets having made what subsequently looks like a reckless decision and who, in hindsight, would therefore have acted differently. In that sense, we are caught in a

[35] To be sure, Regan does *not* argue that we should protect anyone who takes a risk, that is, anyone who risks harming their future self. But then we have to ask why we *shouldn't* universalize his argument, that is, we should want to know what the *general* principle is that justifies Regan's solution to the motorcyclist's case. See Regan (1983), p. 126.

double bind. For we have to show that someone who takes a risk and later comes to regret having done so was not sufficiently rational at the time the risk was taken. Which is to say that—on a limited and formal conception of rationality, the only one we can work from (as will be argued in Chaps. 3, Sects. 3.2 and 3.4.2, note 63)—the agent in question has wishes that are clearly incompatible or beliefs that are patently false, or there is no cognitive framework the agent is explicitly or implicitly relying on to estimate (even if only loosely) the time and intellectual and material resources that need to be devoted to making decisions depending on how important or consequential they are, especially so where these decisions *are* in fact consequential, in which case more time and resources will be needed to (a) identify what options are feasible, (b) make sure that these are being assessed on the basis of true (empirically grounded) beliefs, and (c) identify and rank one's own preferences. But if that attempt fails, then we have to think that concealed in Regan's argument is a perfectionist element, and one on which the paternalistic thesis he is defending ultimately rests: embedded in his argument, in other words, is the underlying view or assumption that there is a virtue, such as prudence, which the agent in question ought to embody.[36]

In the final analysis, it seems to me that the argument with which Regan seeks to justify a helmet mandate for motorcyclists falls short—this for two main reasons. The first one, as mentioned, is that we don't really know what will happen to motorcyclists who don't wear a helmet, or which of any number of their potential selves will come into existence in the future. A motorcyclist may never have a motorcycling accident. Or they may get into a *deadly* accident (in which case, needless to say, they won't be able to regret the choices they made leading up to the accident). Or they may may survive an accident with serious injuries that they would have sustained even *with* a helmet on. Or they could get badly injured without any sense of regret. Or they could fall into a brief coma and quickly recover with no permanent damage. Or they could suffer permanent damage (paralyzed from the neck down, for example), feeling regret for the rest of their life for having chosen not to wear a helmet, and resenting everyone who allowed them to do so. It doesn't seem to make much sense, then, to protect someone from a risk they are willing to assume, and to do so by limiting their freedom to take that risk, if the reason for doing so is speculative, in that they *may or may not* come to regret the choice they have made that put them at risk.[37]

But there is still an important point to be discussed, which is the second reason why I think Regan's argument falls short. Let us suppose that we have data showing that of all motorcyclists who have an accident with serious injuries that they could have avoided had they only been wearing a helmet, 90 percent of them come to regret their choice not to do so. Is what we have here a case of insufficient rationality? Let us suppose that this is in fact Regan's contention. On that basis, if someone

[36] On moral perfectionism see Chap. 3, Sect. 3.11.

[37] And it is worth noting, too, that this is entirely consistent with the legal doctrine of assumption of risk.

at time T_0 chooses not to wear a helmet while riding their motorcycle, but then subsequently, at time T_1, comes to have deep regrets about that choice and decides to be more careful and prudent going forward, then we would have a clear indication that the decision made by their antecedent self (their earlier choice not to wear a helmet) was made in a state of diminished capacity or weakness of will, a state of insufficient rationality comparable to that of the "second Ulysses," the one who is tied to the mast of his ship listening to the song of the sirens and demanding that his crew tie him loose so that he can join the sirens (only to drown at sea). If that is what Regan is arguing and the reasoning is correct, then we would have an antipaternalistic reason for limiting the freedom of motorcyclists, the freedom of their current selves. But it seems to me that there is a problem with this argument, and that there is a different way of construing the meaning and implications of regret.

It is quite likely that some of those who come to have deep regrets about a past decision they made that put them at risk were indeed not sufficiently rational in making that decision (they may have been acting incoherently, for example, or they may have been affected by a serious personality disorder, or they may have been deluded about the likely outcome of their action). Although it may not be easy to determine whether someone was insufficiently rational at the time they took a risk, nor can we know whether they will come to regret the foolhardy decision they made, we do in this case have standard methods that we can rely on in making such a determination (we can simply talk to the person, for example, or do a psychiatric evaluation). But many other people who come to regret some heedless decision they have made *cannot* be said to have been insufficiently rational at that time. Let us suppose that Brodie Bather is swimming leisurely off the beach knowing that there have been shark attacks at that particular location, but they were very few and far between and the last one happened a very long time ago; furthermore, there is no shark-warning sign anywhere along the beach, and Brodie also happens to have done some research, finding out that the likelihood of another shark attack is extremely low, say, one in ten million, which is in fact statistically correct. And yet Brodie is attacked by a shark: he comes out badly injured and traumatized. Brodie deeply regrets having made that choice, and even more so considering that he has had an argument with his wife, as a result of which he goes out swimming off the beach on that day at that time, and would not have been doing but for that argument. Is Brodie's sense of regret rational? Such feelings of regret and remorse are, I think, quite common, especially when the loss is devastating and particularly difficult to process emotionally (as with the loss of a child or a loved one). In cases like these, people will often go back over what they did, scrutinizing the chain of causation that led to the loss, and it is often the little things they focus on—trivial, almost meaningless actions (like asking somebody to get something from the grocery store) that nonetheless turn out to have been a *condicio sine qua non* in relation to the loss (certainly, they would pass a but-for test in a court of law), as in the case of a father who postpones an evening jog with his son, who then gets into a deadly accident when the two would otherwise have been jogging, so the father is rent by guilt and remorse (since the son would now be alive but for the fact that the father called off their regular jog).[38] What are we to make of the father's deep regret in this and other similar situations: should it be taken as evidence that the father's previous decision was insufficiently rational, or is it the subsequent emotional response (the regret itself) that falls short of a rational standard?

Unless there are some patently false beliefs at work (ones that would have been easy to test), or some beliefs that weren't tested even if the (subsequently) distraught agent thought it important to test them at the time they were acted on—and there are no such beliefs in Brody's shark-attack case—then it is doubtful that the choice at issue can be labelled as insufficiently rational. Is it irrational to desire or want to achieve something when the prospect of getting or achieving that thing is slim or next to zero? Is it irrational to discount the possibility of an unfortunate turn of events (an unlikely one such as a shark attack in the circumstances previously described)? Or to be unwilling to accept that we cannot fully control our destiny, that we cannot fully protect ourselves from misfortune despite out best efforts to do so? Or to insist on not scaling back our aims and ambitions in light of what a "reality check" would suggest, and to instead persevere in working toward those goals, however seemingly unattainable they may be? I do not know that it is irrational to be unwilling to relinquish desires that we are unlikely to be able to satisfy (including the desire to always be shielded from terrible misfortunes). Perhaps any such rationality depends on the intensity of the desire, but it is not necessarily a symptom of insufficient rationality to refuse to lower our expectations to what is "within our reach," to settle for something less than what we envisage through our dreams and ambitions: if anything, such stubbornness evinces a lack of practicality or "street smarts"—a realism or practical mindedness into which it would be paternalistic to force others. At any rate, if someone deeply regrets not having acted differently in some particular circumstance in the past, if there is a choice they wish they hadn't made or a risk they hadn't taken, it may well be that they *were* acting rationally at the time they made that decision: what is irrational, in other words, may be the regret, and not the earlier decision to take a certain risk (as by riding a motorcycle without a helmet on or going for a swim where sharks have been known to attack).

References

Alemany M (2005) El concepto y la justificación del paternalismo. Doxa 28:265–303. https://doi.org/10.14198/DOXA2005.28.17

Alemany M (2006) El paternalismo jurídico. Iustel, Madrid

Anderson S (2021). Coercion In *Stanford Encyclopedia of Philosophy* (Summer 2021 edition), ed. Edward N. Zalta. https://plato.stanford.edu/archives/sum2021/entries/coercion/

Archard D (1990) Freedom not to be free: the case of the slavery contract in J. S. Mill's *on liberty*. Philos Quart 40 161: 453–465 https://doi.org/10.2307/2220110

[38] This is the father's deep regret in the 2001 film *La Stanza del figlio* (*The Son's Room*), directed by Nanni Moretti.

Atienza M (1988) Discutamos sobre paternalismo. Doxa 5:203–214. https://doi.org/10.14198/DOXA1988.5.11
Burrows P (1995) Analyzing legal paternalism. Int Rev Law Econ 15(4):489–508. https://doi.org/10.1016/0144-8188(95)00041-0
Del Bò C (2007) Laicismo, neutralismo e 'legal enforcement of morals'. Ragion pratica 1:17–36. https://doi.org/10.1415/24455
Diciotti E (1986) Paternalismo. Materiali per una storia della cultura giuridica XVI 2: 557–586
Diciotti E (2005) Preferenze, autonomia e paternalismo. Ragion pratica 1:99–118. https://doi.org/10.1415/19841
Dworkin G (1983a) Paternalism. In: Sartorius R (ed) Paternalism, Minneapolis, University of Minnesota Press, Chap. 2, 19–34
Dworkin G (1983b) Paternalism: some second thoughts. In: Sartorius R (ed) Paternalism Minneapolis, University of Minnesota Press, Chap. 7, 105–12
Dworkin R (2000) Sovereign virtue: the theory and practice of equality. Harvard University Press, Cambridge
Feinberg J (1983) Legal paternalism. In: Sartorius R (ed) Paternalism. University of Minnesota Press, Minneapolis. Chap 1
Feinberg J (1984) Harm to others. Vol. 1 of the moral limits of the criminal law. Oxford University Press, Oxford
Feinberg J (1986) Harm to self. Vol. 3 of the moral limits of the criminal law. Oxford University Press, Oxford
Ferrajoli L (1989) Diritto e ragione: Teoria del garantismo penale. Rome and Bari, Laterza
Ferrajoli L (1991) Proibizionismo e diritto. In: Manconi F (ed) Legalizzare la droga: Una ragionevole proposta di sperimentazione. Milan, Feltrinelli, pp 133–157
Fiandaca G (2010) Punire la semplice immoralità? Un vecchio interrogativo che tende a riproporsi. In: Cadoppi A (ed) Laicità, valori e diritto penale: "The Moral Limits of the Criminal Law"; In ricordo di Joel Feinberg, Milan, Giuffrè
Frankfurt HG (1988) Coercion and moral responsibility. In: Frankfurt HG (ed) The importance of what we care about. Cambridge University Press, Cambridge, pp 26–46
Gardner J (2007) Offences and defences: selected essays in the philosophy of criminal law. Oxford University Press, Oxford
Garzón Valdés E (1988) ¿Es éticamente justificable el paternalismo jurídico? Doxa 5:155–173. https://doi.org/10.14198/DOXA1988.5.08
Gert B, Culver CM (1976) Paternalistic behavior. Philosophy Public Aff 6(1):45–57
Husak DN (2000) Liberal neutrality, autonomy, and drug prohibitions. Philosophy Public Aff 29(1):43–80
Kant I (1891) The principles of political right: considered in connection with the relation of theory to practice in the right of the state (1791). In: Hastie W (ed. and trans.) Kant's principles of politics, including his essay on perpetual peace: a contribution to political science. T.&T. Clark, Edinburgh, Chap. II
Kennedy D (1982) Distributive and paternalist motives in contract and tort law, with special reference to compulsory terms and unequal bargaining power. Maryl Law Rev 41(4):563–658. https://digitalcommons.law.umaryland.edu/mlr/vol41/iss4/4
Kennedy D (1998) Law-and-economics from the perspective of critical legal studies. In: Newman P (ed) The New Palgrave dictionary of economics and the law, vol 2. Palgrave Macmillan, Basingstoke, UK, pp 465–473
Kronman AC (1983) Paternalism and the law of contracts. Yale Law J 92(5):763–798
Lamond G (1996) Coercion, threats, and the puzzle of blackmail. In: Simester AP, Smith ATH (eds) Harm and culpability. Clarendon Press, Oxford, pp 215–238
Mill JS (1971) On Liberty (1859). In: Robson JM (ed) Vol. 18 of collected works. Routledge & Kegan Paul, London, pp 213–310
Murphy JG (1981) Consent, coercion, and hard choices. Virginia Law Rev 67(1):79–95. https://doi.org/10.2307/1072833

Murphy JG (1994) Some ruminations on women, violence, and the criminal law. In: Coleman J, Buchanan A (eds) In Harm's Way: Essays in Honor of Joel Feinberg. Cambridge University Press. Chap. 10, Cambridge, pp 209–230

Nozick R (1974) Anarchy, State, and Utopia. Blackwell, Oxford

Nozick R (1999) Coercion. In: Socratic Puzzles. Harvard University Press, Cambridge, Chap. 1, 15–44

Pope TM (2004) Counting the Dragon's teeth and claws: the definition of hard paternalism. Georgia State Univ Law Rev 20(3):659–722. https://open.mitchellhamline.edu/facsch/280

Regan DH (1983) Paternalism, freedom, identity, and commitment. In: Sartorius R (ed) Paternalism. University of Minnesota Press, Minneapolis. Chap 8

Sartorius R (1983) Introduction. In: Sartorius R (ed) Paternalism. University of Minnesota Press, Minneapolis

Shapiro DL (1988) Courts, legislatures, and paternalism. Virginia Law Rev 74(3):519–575. https://doi.org/10.2307/1073259

Shiffrin SV (2000) Paternalism, unconscionability doctrine, and accommodation. Philosophy Public Aff 29(3):205–250

Spena A (2010) Harmless rapes? A False problem for the harm principle. Diritto e questioni Pubbliche 10:497–524

Sunstein CR, Thaler RH (2003) Libertarian paternalism is not an oxymoron. Univ Chicago Law Rev 70(4):1159–1202. https://doi.org/10.2307/1600573

Thaler RH, Sunstein CR (2003) Libertarian paternalism. Am Econ Rev 93(2):175–179. https://doi.org/10.1257/000282803321947001

Trebilcock MJ (1993) The limits of freedom of contract. Harvard University Press, Cambridge

VanDeVeer D (1986) Paternalistic intervention: the moral bounds on benevolence. Princeton, Princeton University Press

Waldron J (1993) Mill and the value of moral distress. In: Liberal rights: collected papers 1981–1991. Cambridge University Press, Cambridge, pp 115–133

Wertheimer A (1977) Victimless crimes. Ethics 87(4):302–318. https://doi.org/10.1086/292044

Wertheimer A (1987) Coercion. Princeton, Princeton University Press

West RL (1990) Taking preferences seriously. Tulane Law Rev 64(4):659–703. https://www.tulanelawreview.org/pub/volume64/issue4/taking-preferences-seriously

Zamir E (1998) The efficiency of paternalism. Virginia Law Rev 84(2):229–286. https://doi.org/10.2307/1073801

Zimmerman D (1981) Coercive wage offers. Philosophy Public Aff 10(2):121–145

Chapter 3
Arguments for and Against Paternalism

3.1 A Metatheory of Arguments for and Against Paternalism

In Chap. 2 a moral-political conception was outlined that I am calling *legal paternalism*, on which (a) the state, or someone acting under the state's authority, has the right to use coercion against the will of adult individuals even when the their choices are informed, uncoerced, and sufficiently coherent, and (b) such coercive power is legitimate only so long as it is exercised primarily to protect what are understood to be these persons' interests, or what is understood as being good for them, and in particular to make sure that the actions they take or fail to take (or otherwise attempt to take or to avoid) do not harm them or put them at risk of harm (or what is understood to be such), be it physical, psychophysical, economic, or of any other nature. For simplicity's sake, this conception will henceforth simply be referred to as paternalism (short for *legal paternalism*).

On the other end of the spectrum is the moral-political conception I am calling *moderate legal antipaternalism*, on which the state or an official acting under the state's authority may *not* use coercion in that way, that is, may *not* use coercion against the will of adult individuals if (a) the sole or primary purpose for doing so is to make sure that the actions they take or fail to take (or otherwise attempt to take or to avoid) do not cause harm to themselves (or what is understood to be such) or put them at significant risk of harm, be it physical, psychophysical, economic, or of any other nature, and so do not undermine their own good, and if (b) it is clear or is reasonable to assume that these persons' intentions—to engage in a course of conduct that is considered harmful or dangerous to themselves—have been formed in a sufficient rational way,[1] with sufficient mental capacity and taking the relevant facts into account, and as long as the choices so made are stable over time and are

[1] As will be argued in Sects. 3.2 and 3.4.2, the conception of rationality needed to define and defend antipaternalism so understood is a essentially a *formal* conception.

G. Maniaci, *The Unbearable Lightness of Legal Antipaternalism*, Law and Philosophy Library 151, https://doi.org/10.1007/978-3-031-96844-0_3

sufficiently free of coercive pressures. All the more so, on this conception, the state clearly may not limit the freedom of individuals if the actions they intend to take are not considered to be harmful or dangerous to themselves or to others. Indeed, on the moderate antipaternalism here defended, if someone's decision-making is not vitiated in the sense just outlined, their freedom of action can be limited by recourse to coercion only if it does harm to others. From here on out, for convenience's sake, this moderate legal antipaternalism will simply be referred to as *antipaternalism*.

Having so defined paternalism and antipaternalism, we can consider the arguments that can be made for and against these two conceptions. But before we get to these arguments, it will be useful to make a few clarifications, and four in particular. For one thing, as curious as it may seem, there is not much in the literature in the way of arguments for or against the two conceptions. There are, more to the point, two main arguments in favour or antipaternalism: the first one (here favoured) is what I would call the argument from individual autonomy;[2] the second one is a version of the utilitarian argument. Paternalism, for its part, can count on six main arguments: we have (*i*) the substantive rationality argument, (*ii*) the slippery slope argument,[3] (*iii*) the "regret and contagion" argument, (*iv*) an organicistic version of the utilitarian argument, (*v*) the argument from moral perfectionism, and (*vi*) the theological argument. In Sections 9ff., we will be looking at a range of arguments based on the sanctity of human life, human dignity, and the common good, which will be shown to be flawed: in one way or another they lapse into the fallacy of *petitio principii* ("begging the question") or they prove to be rationally inadequate, by which I mean that they are parasitic on one of the other arguments, on which they depend for their own validity, but which at the same time they conceal (thereby concealing the relation of dependence) by using language that is extremely vague (lacking semantic determinacy).[4] Also examined in Section 12 will be the theologi-

---

[2] Worth noting in this regard is that the concept of autonomy is understood as requiring different conditions to be met: we cannot be considered autonomous unless we act on the basis of desires that are (a) rational and (b) stable over time, a dual condition entailing that (c) we must be of sound mind—possessed of the mental capacity needed to make decisions for ourselves—and unless we make these decisions (d) taking all relevant facts into account and (e) without being coerced (or with a sufficient degree of freedom from coercive pressures).

[3] This argument comes in two varieties—one of which I am calling the culture-of-death argument (discussed at footnote 24)—and with that distinction the number of arguments comes to nine. Clearly, it is a matter of judgment whether two versions of a broader argument count as two arguments, and if we consider that there are further arguments still which I am not taking into account—viewing them as fallacious or as parasitic on other arguments (examples being the argument from human dignity, from the sacredness of human life, and from the common good)—we can see that this numbering exercise can even get arbitrary. So the point here is not so much to tally all the arguments in favour of paternalism and antipaternalism as to map them out, so that we can more easily locate each argument and find our bearings in the broader landscape it is part of.

[4] We should distinguish here between logical errors properly so called (i.e., formal and informal fallacies) from other defects of rationality in argumentation. So, for example, an argument can be rationally unsound if it is based on factually patently false premises or if it involves psychological distortions (such as wishful thinking), See Copi and Cohen (2002), p. 137ff. Similarly, if the justification or the reasons we are given in support of a conclusion are indeterminate, the argument can

cal argument, not because it is rationally untenable but because it turns out to be a very weak argument. And, as I will be arguing, it is one of the arguments held in concealment by the argument from the sanctity or dignity of human life.

The second clarification I'd like to make is that the arguments we will be looking at operate at a general level of abstraction: the guidance they offer is accordingly broad-gauged, which means that they apply to a full range of cases (such as euthanasia, riding a motorcycle without a helmet, and doing drugs) even if these cases each have their own peculiarities, each calling for special considerations. This is to say that I will not be getting into the detail of each of the moral and political issues that will be discussed, except the right to engage in violent sadomasochistic sex, not to wear a helmet or seat belts, to sell and consume drugs, the case of voluntary slavery contracts or of combats between gladiators, or the right to request and obtain euthanasia or assisted suicide. What this means, for example, is that the antipaternalistic conception here defended, if coherently applied, will support legalizing the sale and consumption of addictive or psychoactive drugs *in general*—assuming, of course, that such legalization does not cause harm to others or that, taking the balance of interests into account, it is likely to cause less harm than prohibiting the same substances. But though I do think these are safe assumptions to make, they can only be made on an empirical basis, and the empirical questions that need to be worked out to that end can be complex.[5] For example, given scientific discoveries could, on the basis of moral principles, lead to a partly different conclusion. If the bulk of scientific research on the matter should reveal that cocaine in the majority of cases leads people to engage in aggressive and violent behaviour that consumers cannot control, a *belief that science denies*, we would have to conclude that the use of cocaine is harmful to third parties.[6] And that would be a good reason, here an

be said to be insufficiently rational, all the more so when the person making the argument (say, a philosopher, jurist, or judge) seems dismissive about the possibility of making the argument more specific, either by failing to explain why they are not making that effort or leaving it be understood that one shouldn't bother to seek out those more specific reasons even if they presumably exist. Cf. Alexy (1989) and Maniaci (2008), chap. 1.

[5] The cost of prohibiting the sale and consumption of drugs, as we will see in the last chapter, is abundantly addressed in the literature, a survey of which suggests that this cost can reasonably be placed into four buckets. We have (1) the economic costs of the "war on drugs" (law enforcement, the legal process, detention), as well as the unrealized revenue from the uncollected indirect taxes that could be levied on the sale of drugs once they are legalized (See Miron (2004, 2010); Miron and Waldock (2010)). Next we have (2) the demand side (the crimes committed by those who have to turn to this market for the drugs they seek) and (3) the supply side (the cost of organized crime, inclusive of violence and homicide, along with the cost of the government corruption that may develop with organized crime, in the form of graft and bloated procurement contracts). And, finally, we have (4) the harm done to the integrity, life, and property of drug users, who in the illegal market find a higher-priced, lower-quality product than would be available in a legalized market (with lower quality and hygiene standards, or cocaine "cut" with various substances, and the like), while also facing a range of risks, such as overdosing, violence, exploitation, and blackmailing of users suffering from drug withdrawal syndrome. See Husak (2002), p. 82ff., p. 133ff.; MacCoun and Reuter (2004), p. 326.; UNODC (2007, 2008, 2009).

[6] See, for example, Beltramini (2010). As for the costs of antiprohibitionism, it has been argued that a legalized market would significantly increase the consumption of psychoactive drugs, leading to (1) greater harm to health as a result of such consumption and (2) greater harm to life and limb

antipaternalistic one, for prohibiting the sale of cocaine. Actually, science causes us that only the *abuse* of cocaine can lead to a paranoid reaction, which in some cases could lead to aggressive behaviour. All this will be discussed in Chap. 7.

Third, as noted, the arguments for and against paternalism we are concerned with will be analyzed specifically with an eye on the problem of how the state might be justified in its use of force. The paradigmatic case here is that of criminal punishment, but that is by no means the only case. For the state's coercive interference can also come in the form of administrative fines or in the form of taxes levied on the sale of given goods, and the costs to those fined or taxed can be significant. And here a point needs to be stressed that shouldn't even have to be made if it weren't for some misconceptions that so often seem to come up in the press or in other types of media. It was previously argued that if the antipaternalistic conception I am here defending is coherently applied, it can as a general proposition justify the sale and consumption of psychoactive drugs (such as heroin) so long as it can reasonably be assumed, as I think it can, that antiprohibitionism overall causes, on balance, less harm than prohibitionism. And the point here is that a conception of this kind is merely concerned with the limits that should be placed on the state's coercive power. What is being put forward here, in other words, is not a general conception of the good, nor is the point of the discussion to determine what plan of life, if any, it would be right for anyone to pursue. So, for example, while I firmly believe that doing cocaine or heroin is bad all around and is to be avoided at all costs—I would be devastated if my children were to take up the habit, just as I would if a friend or my partner were to take their own lives—this view which I hold with such moral and personal conviction has no bearing at all on the problem at hand of the limits of the state's coercive power, and the same goes for *any* such personal conviction about what is good or bad choice-making (when it does not harm others), whether it is my view or anyone else's: no such view should factor into an account of what the state through its officials is justified in coercively imposing on the members of the collectivity.

Finally, there is a complex dialectic at work between the *rhetorical* force of the arguments deployed and their *validity*. Some of the most common rhetoric seen in the political, moral, and legal debate offers arguments that are considered to be highly persuasive. However, as I will argue, many of these *rhetorically* persuasive arguments lack rational *validity*. And that is particularly concerning in *legal* argumentation, where judges and jurists in the West frequently resort to paternalistic arguments in interpreting the constitution and generally in balancing basic rights, such as the right to autonomy, the right to life, and the right to health.[7] If we look closely when the argument from human dignity, from the sanctity of human life, and from the common good are introduced in support of a paternalistic position, we can see that these arguments are fallacious or parasitic. More to the point, they are para-

owed to road accidents and workplace injuries and generally to violent crime (including beatings of minors and family members). See Husak (1992), p. 150ff.; Husak (2002), p. 151ff.; MacCoun and Reuter (2004), p. 333ff. As we will see in the Chap. 7, this argument is flawed.

[7] Most of the cases where paternalistic arguments are used to rhetorical effect in legal discourse are ones I have gleaned from French and Italian legal commentary and case law. See Maniaci (2012).

sitic on other arguments, which means that they suffer from a fallacy of *petitio principii* or from incoherence or excessive indeterminacy. As for the theological argument, it is not much used in the public debate, to be sure. But the suspicion, and not without good reason, is that this argument is actually felt to be appealing, or that paternalism is widely believed to be correct precisely in virtue of the theological argument even if those who hold this view are unwilling to cast it explicitly in those terms in public forums such as a parliamentary debate or a talk show or other broadcast programme. If people do in fact dissimulate in this way, this would at least explain something that would otherwise be incomprehensible, namely, the fact that, at least in Catholic-majority countries like Italy, bioethical issues ideologically divide secularists and Catholics across party lines and affiliations.

In any case, as we shall see, the theological argument proves to be very weak. Equally weak are the arguments from regret and contagion. As far as paternalism is concerned, the strongest arguments are the utilitarian/organicist argument and the perfectionist argument, and they are so because they do not seem to be affected by serious or obvious logical flaws, even if they too have rationality problems.The strongest argument in favour of antipaternalism is, instead, that of individual autonomy.

How to explain this disconnect between an argument's rhetorical force, driving its uptake, and its rational validity? And, specifically, how to explain the fact that rhetorical arguments against antipaternalism gain wide currency despite being logically fallacious? What explains this dynamic, I would submit, is that many of the authors who position themselves against antipaternalism have something to hide, so they fall back on arguments, such as the argument from human dignity, from the sanctity of human life, or from the common good, that are fallacious or are parasitic on paternalistic arguments—and in particular the utilitarian/organicist argument and the perfectionist argument—that do not suffer from the same fallacies.

What is being concealed may differ from author to author, and often it may be more than one thing. Thus, for example, some authors, as we saw, may want to conceal the fact that the argument they are truly making, and on which basis they would like to limit the freedom of individuals, is a theological argument, namely, the view that only God gives life and death, and no one can dispose of anything that is not theirs. Those who take this view know that they have to engage with people of different persuasions—atheists, agnostics, Epicureans, theists, neopagans, Hindus, Muslims, Jews, Buddhists, Confucians—and that it would be very difficult for them to deploy the theological argument in the space of public reason, a space in which that full range of views necessarily comes into the picture. And yet, revealed truth is too important for the theologically minded, so they cannot easily part ways with it.

Other authors, as I was commenting in the introduction, may not have come fully to terms with their own paternalism, meaning that they may not be willing to admit, even to themselves, that they are none too liberal, so they choose to run with argumentative strategies that do not attack the argument from individual autonomy head on. Many other authors are consciously and self-assuredly paternalistic, but they also recognize that the idea of individual autonomy carries a great deal of weight, at least in the West, and cannot easily be dismissed. To openly question the idea of individual autonomy would mean to have the presumption to look an adult, informed, uncoerced, and rational person in the eye and tell them, in public, that others know better than they do what is best for them and what achieves their good.

For all these reasons, as Feinberg underscores, paternalists will often refrain from mounting full-blown arguments taking explicit aim at the idea of individual autonomy and the values it embodies, since any such frontal attack would be bound to fail. So they take a different tack, attempting to undermine the antipaternalist conception from *within*, trying to poke holes in it, looking for incoherences, fallacies, and false statements—all flaws that are *internal* to the conception. To this end, some paternalists concoct all manner of fantastic made-up examples of awful and repugnant activities that an antipaternalistic conception would licence, such as public spectacles with gladiators engaging in mortal combat for a fistful of dollars, gruesome theatrical performances with sadists flogging masochists for audiences with lurid interest in blood and gore, slavery contracts voluntarily entered into, or public auctions for the sale of organs. These objections, introducing the prospect of appalling human pursuits, will be addressed in the fifth chapter.

3.2 The Argument from Substantive Rationality

No one in their right mind would want to commit suicide or engage in behaviour that would imperil their life or do serious harm to their health, as by fighting a duel, attempting a dangerous acrobatic stunt without a safety harness, riding a motorcycle without a helmet, practicing extreme sports, or playing sadomasochistic games. To be sure, it is only on rare occasions, as far as I can tell, that a contemporary philosopher will still resort to this argument so explicitly, that is, by carrying it to such extremes, but in ordinary conversation it does have considerable traction. As Ernesto Garzón Valdés[8] reminds us, arguments so explicitly framed can be found in Blackstone, for example, while Jonathan Dancy (in Moral Reasons) and John McDowell (1998) identify them in Kant. Dancy and McDowell seem right about Kant and Kantian authors because a Kant-inspired variant on this latter position has been advanced by Velleman (1999). He considers that a person's well-being can only matter if she is of intrinsic value and so that it is impermissible to violate a person's *rational nature* (the source of her intrinsic value) for the sake of her well-being.[9]

There may, after all, be a good reason why such arguments no longer seem to crop up so often in the professional literature, at least when it comes to suicide. Which is that contemporary psychiatry is quite explicit in denying that a desire to commit suicide is in itself a sure sign or folly or irrationality, this even as psychiatrists tend to agree that, statistically, a considerable number of suicides take place under psychopathologically altered conditions, such as deep depression or paranoid

[8] Garzón Valdés (1988), p. 169.

[9] For an argument against Velleman's objections, see also Young (2007); Sumner (2011).

schizophrenia.[10] Precisely because there is no longer any credence to the notion of a conceptual link between suicide and folly, much less between folly and activities that put one at high risk for life, this argument is nowadays presented much more subtly, making reference to the fact that someone intent on carrying out certain acts, such as committing suicide or duelling to the death, is inevitably afflicted by some temporary or permanent "incapacity," or has no reason to carry them out,[11] or is acting under a "distorted" judgment,[12] or fails to accord the proper weight to relevant considerations,[13] or lacks willpower, or is making not an irrational judgment but an unreasonable one[14]

Now, we can't have it both ways with these *explicantia*: we can speak of distortion, unreasonableness, weakness of will, or lack of reasons for action in keeping with a formal (internalist) conception or a substantive (externalist) one, but we cannot skip back and forth between these two conceptions depending on what suits the thesis we are advancing.

Thus we can point to distortion, unreasonableness, and the like as objective factors—such as relevant beliefs that are patently false, relevant permanent or temporary psychopathologies, serious intellectual disabilities, serious incoherences, easy-to-detect cognitive biases (such as wishful thinking and the formation of adaptive preferences)—objective factors which alter the formation of beliefs and preferences by making them insufficiently rational according to a conception of formal practical rationality, in which case we are not going to run into any significant problem. Problems do come up when the concepts of distortion, unreasonableness, and the like are used loosely and without rigour. But any such nonmethodical use of concepts is generally suspicious and dangerous, and therefore absolutely to be avoided. Indeed, if we embrace a formal conception of rationality, we are better off leaving usage of the term *unreasonableness* as we find it, that is, in the highly indeterminate, "morally compromised" way in which it presents itself in ordinary language.

On the other hand, we can use the notions of distortion, unreasonableness, lack of reasons for action, and the like, in a substantive sense, that is, in a way that clearly presupposes or explicitly invokes a substantive conception of practical rationality. It is difficult to make a compelling case for such a conception, especially in its monist

---

[10] See DSM-IV-TR 2000; VanDeVeer (1986), p. 267ff. For a penetrating critique of the idea that a desire to commit suicide is necessarily the result of a mental illness, and on suicide as the ultimate expression of human freedom, see Marra (1990), p. 227ff. In support of this stance, it might also be added that the ontology and aetiology of clinical depression are uncertain. It is not the case, then, that every depressive condition is irrational or that every such condition makes irrational any desire to commit suicide. Rather, depression is best understood as a *normal* response for coping with a state of severe or deep suffering resulting from a serious incurable illness or severe, chronic, physical disability. Cf. Feinberg (1986), chap. 27 ("The Choice of Death").

[11] Cf McDowell (1998), chap. 5; Scanlon (1998), chap. 1.

[12] Cf. Sunstein (1997), p. 1141ff.

[13] Cf Dworkin (1983a), p. 31.

[14] Cf Amarasekara and Bagaric (2004), p. 411.

or mildly pluralist version, the one that can coherently be used in favour of paternalism.[15] Indeed, on a (robustly) pluralistic version, we can accommodate an indefinite multiplicity of desires and plans of life, all rationally valid, and so an indefinite plurality of objective values—even if these values are in conflict, and even if they are incommensurable—from which different solutions can be arrived at, all equally acceptable, in dealing with any (or almost any) moral question we are confronted with.[16]

In conclusion, the metaethical conceptions in favor of antipaternalism are two. One is an internalist or formal conception of rationality or of reasons for action. The other is a radically or robustly pluralistic externalist or substantive conception of rationality or of reasons for action, where different objective values are incommensurable or in conflict each other and it is morally and rationally acceptable to balance them against one another, as we see with the conceptions espoused by Celano, Nagel, and Berlin.

In fact, some authors, among whom Bruno Celano, argue that from the point of view of the distinction and conflict between paternalism and antipaternalism there are no big differences between a (moderately) formal conception of reasons for action and a robustly pluralist substantive conception.[17]

In short, on an externalist or substantive conception of practical rationality, our reasons for action, or the reasons on which basis we should act in one way or another, are independent (totally or partially) of our preferences and desires. By contrast, on a moderate internalist or formal conception *à la* Bernard Williams,

---

[15] The same point is made in Feinberg (1986), p. 110ff., and Rawls (1971), para 64. So vast is the literature on formal vs. substantive practical rationality, or on internalism vs. externalism in regard to reasons for action, that even a summary overview wouldn't be able to convey a proper sense of it here. But on the formal or internalist theory of reasons for action, see Williams (1981), while on externalism in regard to reasons for action, see McDowell (1998), chaps. 6 and 7; Nagel (1986), p. 138ff.; Putnam (1981), esp. chap. 6; and Scanlon (1998), chaps. 1 and 2. For an overview of the arguments for and against these conceptions, and of the literature in which they are laid out, see Maniaci (2008), esp. chap. 2.

[16] Some authors, among whom Bruno Celano, argue that from the point of view of the distinction and conflict between paternalism and antipaternalism there are no big differences between a (moderately) formal conception of reasons for action and a sufficiently pluralist substantive conception. On the different senses in which we can understand ethical pluralism, (metaethical) subjectivism, moral realism and antirealism, and moral cognitivism and noncognitivism, see Barberis (2006, 2010); Celano (2006); and Villa (2007).

[17] The same point is made in Feinberg (1986), p. 110ff., and Rawls (1971), para 64. So vast is the literature on formal vs. substantive practical rationality, or on internalism vs. externalism in regard to reasons for action, that even a summary overview wouldn't be able to convey a proper sense of it here. But on the formal or internalist theory of reasons for action, see Williams (1981), while on externalism in regard to reasons for action, see McDowell (1998), chaps. 6 and 7; Nagel (1986), p. 138ff.; Putnam (1981), esp. chap. 6; and Scanlon (1998), chaps. 1 and 2. On the different senses in which we can understand ethical pluralism, (metaethical) subjectivism, moral realism and antirealism, and moral cognitivism and noncognitivism, see Barberis (2006, 2010); Celano (2006); and Villa (2007).

For an overview of the arguments for and against these conceptions, and of the literature in which they are laid out, see Maniaci (2008), esp. chap. 2.

these practical reasons depend on the desires we form and settle on once we have reasoned through the practical problem at hand and have made certain that our solution to that problem is grounded in rational argument, that is, once we have gone through a formal procedure of rational argumentation, one that clears our reasoning of flaws such as explicit contradictions between preferences, patently false beliefs, or easily identifiable biases such as wishful thinking or adaptive preferences. A (robustly monist or weakly pluralistic) substantive or externalist conception, by contrast, makes rationality conceptually a function of morality, for its starts out by identifying certain desires regarded as unqualifiedly *immoral*—examples being a desire to commit suicide or kill our neighbour because he or she is "not nice" to us—and on that basis says that these desires are thereby devoid of any valid or rational reason for fulfilling them. The most important objections against the substantive conception of rationality are two: (1) there are no objective values in the world or external reasons, namely, reasons wholly or (as in the case of colours) partly independent by our beliefs, preferences, and desires; (2) according to a substantive conception, an evil person, such as a dictator, murderer, serial rapist or kidnapper, can be considered an insufficiently rational person, or this person's actions can be considered nonrational or insufficiently rational, this on the ground that there are no reasons in that might justify these actions, which accordingly qualify as immoral, with the result that such individuals could not be held accountable for their actions in the criminal process: they could not be criminally punished, but confined in a psychiatric hospital for a brief period of time.

In general, an externalist or substantive conception of rationality is normally linked to a form of (robustly monist) moral realism.

There are various metaethical realist conceptions involved here. Now, the (robustly monist or weakly pluralistic) moral realism/externalism of reasons for action can be strong or weak. In the first case, the strong version, it is hardly tenable, ontologically or epistemologically, and indeed there are hardly any present-day authors who defend it. In a weak version, the moral realism/externalism of reasons is either useless, i.e., unfit to fulfil the purpose for which it is defended, or it is incoherent. In a strong version, some authors, especially noncontemporary ones, assert that there are "facts" (and "reasons") that are totally independent of people's beliefs and preferences, on the basis of which it can be established whether a value judgment is true or false, objectively right or wrong. Furthermore, they assert that such "moral facts" are supernatural (they exist and become knowable in the same exact way as supernatural facts), an example being a law revealed by God (Finnis 1980), or they are "natural" facts (Brink 1989), such as the existence of mountains, rivers, atoms, and so on. In both versions, these moral facts would be totally independent of human beliefs and preferences, which is why such moral realism faces insurmountable ontological and epistemological objections and has been abandoned by most contemporary authors (see e.g., Celano, Dancy, Martí, McDowell, Moreso,

Nagel, Putnam, Scanlon).[18] If there are moral facts that are independent of people's beliefs and preferences, then there will exist reasons for action ("Dictators must not be killed") that are external to or totally independent of subjective desires and preferences.

In a weak version, the moral realism/externalism of reasons essentially postulates that objective values—so-called moral facts (and thus reasons for action)—are or can also be "social facts" (Stavropoulos), "secondary qualities," such as colours (McDowell), objective facts or entities such as numbers (Scanlon), or "preferences expressed under ideal epistemic conditions" (Alexy, Habermas, Moreso, Nino). But none of these answers are satisfactory from the standpoint of moral realism itself.[19]

If values such as colours are secondary qualities, then the thesis is incoherent, and it falls back on strong realism. For a certain object to appear red, three conditions need to be satisfied: a certain neuro-perceptual structure of the subject, favourable environmental conditions (light), and the presence of a *primary* property (that is, a property totally independent of the percipient subject) in the object seen as red. If there were no primary property present in the objects (irrespective of the difficulty of empirically identifying what it is), a property on which their being red depends, this would imply that all living beings with the same perceptual characteristics, or who are assumed to have the same perceptual characteristics (like all humans who are not colour-blind), would each have to see every object as having the same colour under the same light conditions. And if there is a primary property of a *moral* type—that is, a property totally independent of the subject and of the subject's beliefs and preferences—this presupposes moral realism in a strong sense.[20]

---

[18] Cf. Celano (2006); Dancy (1993), chaps. 1 and 2; Moreso (2003), p. 20ff.; McDowell (1998), chaps. 6 and 7; Nagel (1986), p. 138ff.; Martí (2006), p. 84; Putnam (1981), chap. 6; Scanlon (1998), pp. 62–63 (and, generally, chaps. 1 and 2. On the debate between moral realism and anti-realism, see also Celano (1994), and Comanducci (1992).

[19] Cf. Stavropoulos (1996), chap. 4, esp. p. 111ff. (who seems to share the thesis that objective values also depend in part on social practices); McDowell (1998), chap. 7; Scanlon (1998), p. 63ff.; Moreso (2003), p. 37ff.; Nino (1989). Some of these authors, such as Putnam and McDowell, are also "constructivists" in epistemology, in what concerns the reasons for believing in something. But they also reject the realist epistemological conception, namely, the idea that cognitive subjects tend to be able, perhaps only by successive approximations, to neutrally and objectively describe what the characteristics of the world are, through theories and concepts that "reflect" reality as it is. You cannot have it both ways. A constructivist epistemology is sufficiently moderate to state that cognitive activity, in particular the activity of justifying beliefs, is subject to *empirical constraints*, which in some sense depend on empirical data from the outside world, from the "court of experience." Therefore, if such (empirical) constraints exist, one would then have to show that the activity of justifying moral judgments also has the same constraints, which does not seem possible. Or, if we accept a sufficiently strong or radical version of a constructivist epistemology, where cognitive activity is not subject to empirical constraints, we fall into scepticism or relativism in the strict sense, and in this case, there is no longer any problem, because there is no form of any kind of *objective* knowledge, whether scientific or moral. Thus, moral cognitivism and the externalism of reasons would be equally rejected (and ethical noncognitivism would triumph). Cf. Maniaci (2008), p. 144ff.; Iglesias Vila (1999), p. 187ff.; Davidson (1986), p. 307ff.; Villa (1999), pp. 128–130.

[20] For this objection, see Blackburn (1993), chaps. 8 and 9; Maniaci (2008), p. 178ff.

It is evident that moral values are not objective like natural numbers, because algebraic operations, such as 5 times 5 equals 25, have a degree of certainty and indisputability that is lacking in evaluative reasoning. I am no expert on the subject, but if mathematics is "the model of science that is based on deductions"[21]—on the basis of a given set of *primitive* concepts, and of axioms that are not demonstrable within the theory itself (axioms which some authors consider to be known or true "by convention," given the primitive terms, and which others consider to be necessarily true)—then it would appear to proceed by analytical rather than ampliative reasoning, given the definitions and the underlying primary terms.[22] And even if human beings were to agree on some very general and generic core values (knowledge, life, pleasure, play, rationality, friendship and love, honesty), our interpretation and application of these values to concrete cases would depend on complex balances (not on analytical reasoning), on which there is deep disagreement, whereas there is broad agreement among mathematicians on the correctness of many algebraic operations. Once a theorem is proved, be it Cantor's or Pascal's, no mathematician will doubt the theorem any longer, but there is no equally certain way to prove that euthanasia, abortion, progressive income taxation, or slavery are unjust (it is no coincidence that slavery has been held to be just for two thousand years). Indeed, according to some influential mathematicians and philosophers, "if the explanatory autonomy of the mathematical *eidos* was interpreted in a Platonic sense, one would need to specify what kind of Platonism it involves. It could be, for instance, an ontological Platonism, that is to say, a vision of mathematical entities as mind-independent objects, or a transcendental Platonism in Petitot's sense (henceforth, PTP), or still a dynamical Platonism in Lautman's sense (henceforth, LDP)."

> If we exclude the first variant, against which Longo seems to have directed his main polemics, the last two ones could in fact offer an optimal framework for investigating the main scope of such an autonomy. From PTP we learned in particular that "les idéalités mathématiques", although dependent on particular cognitive gestures (or "synthèses noétiques corrélatives"), retain a significant margin of formal autonomy, namely they aren't "cognitivement réducibles." Thanks to LDP, moreover, we understood that such idealities

[21] Tuzet (2006), p. 141.

[22] A similar thesis has been argued by Blackburn (1993), chap. 3. Some authors claim that this representation of mathematics does not explain "how it is possible for mathematics to be analytic and yet constantly give rise to new discoveries". Tuzet (2006), p. 142. The answer to that question could be that "just as in scientific research, so in logic and mathematics, observations are made, experiments are carried out, and hypotheses are confirmed. The only difference is that the observations relate not to external objects but to models or diagrams constructed by the imagination." Mathematics, then, would also proceed by means of "theorematic deductions," as Tuzet calls them following Peirce, in which the content of the initial premises, as well as the content of the initial icons or diagrams, is enriched in such a way as to lead to conclusions not implied by the initial premises. In this case, however, I agree with Tuzet that mathematics would be "informative," that is, it would yield new information only with respect to a new token of a certain, already known type (a token that can itself be general)—we would learn, for example, that so-and-so, an individual, tangible human being, is mortal)—but it would not be ampliative, i.e., productive of new knowledge in general. Cf. Tuzet (2006), pp. 149–150.

> or "êtres mathématiques" aren't "êtres statiques," but rather generators of other mathematical beings, of all mathematical theories. As you can guess, then, the explanatory autonomy of mathematical eidos, even if inscribed within a Platonic framework, shouldn't necessarily fall into a form of ontological Platonism. But there is more, if we really want to get into the study of such topics. On the one hand, PTP seems to be consistent with a naturalized approach to mathematics; on the other hand, PDL is carnal in a sense of the word that comes close to Châtelet's perspective. In fact, insofar as PTP excludes that mathematical idealities are "entités séparées et indépendantes" from the "actes, [les] états et [les] processus mentaux" which establish them as such, it roots a fundamental aspect of mathematical practice—the so-called "transcendental constitution of mathematical objectivity"—in the brain's neuro-cognitive activity. As for LDP, instead, after having remarked that "les schémas logiques [les idées ...] ne sont pas antérieures à leur réalisation dans une théorie," it presents some mathematical properties, such as "la non-commutativité de certaines operations abstraites de l'algèbre", in terms of formal features which are susceptible to be symbolized "sur le plan de l'expérience" by key aspects of mobile corporeality of Dasein (e.g. "la distinction de la gauche et de la droite"). Hence, research programs such as PTP or LDP could allow the explanatory autonomy of mathematical eidos to perfectly fit into an embodied framework without, however, consenting to any form of neural reductionism.[23]

On the other hand, it is obvious that there are human and institutional realities—such as currency or a state's territory, a novel or a concert—and these are different from natural realities. These are facts that, as is commonly said, have a dual level of existence—an empirical one (the piece of paper on which the image of Lincoln is printed), and a symbolic one, i.e., the meaning a certain community attaches to that empirical fact (currency as a medium for exchanging goods and services)—and so the occurrence of a human reality can make a certain judgment true or false ("So-and-so has five dollars"). But the human and social realities that make true or false the judgments we make about the moral values shared by a social group are conventional social practices (conventional in the broad sense, as opposed to being natural): they are complex sets of beliefs and behaviours, facts on which basis a descriptive judgment (as opposed to an evaluative one)—such as "According to community X, euthanasia should be allowed"—can be said to be true or false. There are no human, institutional realities that can make an "objective" value judgment correct: there can only be a belief relative to values shared by a community of people, that is, relative to a "shared intersubjective" value judgment.

So, while it is true that there exist not only atoms and rivers but also corrupt public officials and human sacrifices, the statements that make a judgment about them true or false ("So-and-so has performed a human sacrifice" or "So-and-so is a corrupt public official") depend on a set of beliefs and behaviours relating to what in a certain community is considered to be human sacrifice or a corrupt public official (and the way in which such statements depend on such beliefs is certainly complex and often difficult to determine). This does not imply that there are such things as "moral facts" that can make a judgment about the "objective" wickedness of human sacrifice true or false, where "objective" is understood to mean that something is independent of someone's preferences and beliefs (beliefs that are rational, autonomous, etc.). The idea that a thesis is ultimately rationally and morally correct

[23] La Mantia (2023), pp. 38–40.

when expressed under ideal or hypothetical epistemic conditions (consistency, knowledge of relevant facts, absence of nonrational biases, etc.) represents a form of moderate noncognitivism (or internalism of reasons) *à la* Williams if the hypothetical conditions are formal, while it represents a disguised form of externalism of reasons (or moral realism in the strongest sense) in the other case.

At any rate, in the most widespread weak variant, and irrespective of the argument I am making about moral realism, the previously mentioned contemporary moral realists are faced with a formidable challenge when it comes to identifying an objective and sure way to gain a knowledge of moral facts under ordinary epistemic conditions, nor do they believe that there is an objective and sure way to identify so-called moral authorities or sages, regardless of the correct reasons. To be sure, ideal or optimal epistemic conditions, if they are formal, may enable us to form better, more rational judgments, but they cannot point us to any objective value. Generally, such ideal or optimal epistemic conditions need to satisfy desiderata such as impartiality (on one interpretation) in order to yield some result, but the procedure itself cannot justify such impartiality. In this sense, few (or perhaps none) of the contemporary moral realists would advise parting ways with constitutional democracy to embrace forms of dictatorship based on the rule of a wise few. For there is no certain or objective way, under normal epistemic conditions, to come to an understanding of the tree of the knowledge of good and evil. Nor is there a way to identify the sages (regardless of the correct reasons).

3.3 The Slippery Slope (or Massacre of the Innocents) Argument

The so-called slippery slope argument comes in at least two variants. Here we will only be dissecting the more salient one,[24] which might also be referred to as the Massacre of the Innocents argument. This well-known argument is used in particu-

[24] On the other variant of the argument, sometimes referred to as the "death culture" argument, if euthanasia were to be legalized—and the same applies to other activities that put one's life at serious risk, such as engaging in extreme sports or doing hard drugs—then a culture of death and dying would take hold, gradually displacing the idea that life is sacred, while shifting public opinion toward the idea that life can, under certain conditions, be sacrificed. People, in other words, would be desensitized to violence, and that, in turn, would put us on a course toward rising rates of homicide, rape, and other kinds of violent crime– all activities which are harmful to others and which an antipaternalistic policy would not justify. This argument needs to be assessed from a conceptual as well as from an empirical standpoint. On the empirical side, we can look at the legalization of euthanasia or assisted-suicide in countries such as the Netherlands—on the Netherlands see Griffiths et al. (1998)—Belgium, Luxembourg, Switzerland—for a very helpful comparative study of relevant legislation see Lewis (2007); see also Griffiths et al. (2008), Germany, Spain, Oregon, Washington state, Vermont, California, Colorado, Hawaii, Maine, New Jersey, New Mexico, the District of Columbia, Canada, [for a brief account of events leading up to the enactment of the various pieces of legislation in the United States and in Canada see Sumner (2017)], New Zealand, and some of the states in Australia. Has this predicted course of events unfolded when euthanasia or

lar in relation to the problem of euthanasia, but it could easily be applied to similar other problems, such as physician-assisted suicide for patients who have been diagnosed with a terminal illness or someone with tetraplegia who is unbearably unhappy, as well as in relation to dangerous or harmful activities. The argument, in short, is that legalizing euthanasia or assisted suicide[25] would have consequences

---

assisted suicide was legalized in these countries or when abortion was legalized in any other country? Of all the people who would be involved in carrying out acts of euthanasia or assisted suicide, how many of them would begin to feel that human life is less than sacred? Very few indeed, I would submit: essentially only a few physicians, some of whom are now already carrying out these acts illegally. Is there any evidence to suggest that abortion providers or physicians who do not object to and practice euthanasia or assisted suicide have become serial killers or have killed their patients without consent? None at all. And the argument looks unconvincing from a logical and conceptual standpoint as well, for if we believe that euthanasia ought to be permissible, it does not logically follow that we should thereby commit to the idea that there are certain conditions under which murder or torture must likewise be permissible. And in point of fact, those who subscribe to the former idea do not generally subscribe to the latter. The moral and political principle under which euthanasia, assisted suicide, or violent sadomasochism might be legalized is entirely different from the principle that would justify violent acts that do harm to their unconsenting victims (as in the case of murder, rape, robbery, or assault and battery), and it would be a serious logical error to run the two principles together. Needless to say, the empirical standpoint is not disconnected from the logico-conceptual standpoint. If we take adult individuals with a capacity to make decisions for themselves—and who are also generally educated, better yet if they are part of a scientifically and technologically advanced society, like those of the West—and if we can safely assume that people so described are sufficiently rational not to make serious logical errors in reasoning out the most debated moral and political questions, then we must also assume that their reasons for action are not affected by serious incoherences. So, as a matter of logic, if someone holds to the view that euthanasia ought to be permitted, it does not follow that they must also believe murder or torture to be legitimate. In other words, if euthanasia and assisted suicide are justified on the basis of the antipaternalistic principle—which protects the individual's self-determination—and if, in so doing, this principle does not in any way justify doing actions that cause harm to others, then it is reasonable to assume adult individuals who are passably rational will not so act on that basis: they will not take the principle of individual autonomy to mean that they should justify to themselves or to others a course of action that might be harmful to others. Cf. Cornacchia (2003), p. 208; Amato (2011), p. 138ff. On the different versions of the slippery slope argument, see Canale (2023).

[25] There is no unanimity in the literature on the use of the term *euthanasia*. Some authors, e.g. Singer (2000), pp. 220, 222, speak of voluntary euthansia and involuntary euthanasia. As Biggs and Young [Cf. Biggs (2001), pp. 12, 60 ff.; Young (2022), section 4] point out, especially with reference to the current literature and the problem of legalizing euthanasia, the use of the term *euthanasia* in the case of involuntary euthanasia, makes no sense, this for two reasons. If the victim clearly expresses a wish against euthanasia, if death is contrary to the victim's own wishes and interests, as perceived by the victim, it is not clear why we should not speak of murder. If euthanasia was also a death caused to alleviate the suffering of the victim against his or her wishes, even killing an unhappy and unrequited lover, a husband suffering from erectile dysfunction, a person with severe heart disease, or nephropathy could be considered eithanasia. Second, it was typical of Nazi propaganda and language manipulation to use words that disguise the truth, such as special treatment (*Sonderbehandlung*); final solution (*Endlösung*); merciful death (*Gnadentod*, literally a death received by grace) to denote omicides, by means of gas or lethal injection; or mass slaughter of people deemed "inferior or worthless" (homosexuals, the disabled, the sick, gypsies, communists, Jews, etc.). After all, it was precisely *Gnadentod* that was the term used by Hitler in the famous Order, officially dated September 1, 1939, given to Reich Chancellery chief Bouhler and Dr. Brandt to authorize certain doctors to kill patients considered incurable. The largely secret Nazi

that even those in favour of the policy would not find palatable—consequences that are as tragic and morally unacceptable as they are unavoidable, namely, that a number of people—often the poorest and most vulnerable—would be "induced" to die

program of systematic extermination of adults and children with physical or mental disabilities was later named T4. T4 was an abbreviation for *Tiergartenstrasse 4*, the address in Berlin's Tiergarten district where the headquarters of the Gemeinnützige Stiftung für Heil-und Anstaltspflege, the public body for health and social welfare, was located. Apparently, the Nazis also used the code name EU-AKtion or E-Aktion (where *E* and *EU* meant "euthanasia"). And it does not seem reasonable to continue along the path of such mystification. See Biggs (2001), p. 12; http://it.wikipedia.org/wiki/Olocausto; http://it.wikipedia.org/wiki/Karl_Brandt#cite_note-12; http://it.wikipedia.org/wiki/Aktion_T4; http://www.ushmm.org/wlc/en/article.php?ModuleId=10005200; Young (2022). Broadly speaking, three basic concepts (which obviously have margins of indeterminacy or doubtful cases) are distinguished in most of the literature. The first is active euthanasia, the second is passive euthanasia, and the third is assisted (or medically assisted) suicide. Normally, when we speak of active (voluntary) euthanasia, we refer to a situation in which a seriously ill or terminally ill patient, in order to avoid profound suffering, asks his or her physician to cause his or her death by lethal injection. Euthanasia is defined as active euthanasia because if the physician had not performed the relevant action (lethal injection), the patient would not have died in the same manner or would have died at a later time.

The concept of passive (voluntary) euthanasia, on the other hand, normally refers to a situation in which, at the explicit request of a patient or on the basis of advance directives by the patient himself, the physician suspends a treatment, (e.g. hydration, nutrition, artificial ventilation) or omits to administer or perform a treatment (e.g., tracheal intubation, cardiopulmonary resuscitation, blood transfusion) necessary for the survival of a patient, who is generally no longer capable of expressing valid consent, following previous statements by the patient to that effect.

Euthanasia would be passive because, by failing to perform a relevant action or by performing a relevant action (withdrawal of artificial nutrition), the physician lets the patient die, i.e., lets the disease follow its natural course, which, in the absence of medical treatment, will cause the patient do die in a short time. The same distinction (between active and passive euthanasia) is often referred to in the Anglo-Saxon literature by distinguishing between intentionally causing death (of the consenting patient) and letting die (the consenting patient).

Finally, when we speak of assisted suicide, we normally refer to a situation in which the physician helps a seriously ill or severely disabled person to die, i.e., prescribes the necessary medication for him or her to carry out the wish to commit suicide painlessly or helps him or her materially (in the cases such as quadriplegic or severely disabled persons) to commit suicide (by preparing the medication and setting up the machinery necessary to administer it, leaving him or her to perform the last act). Cf. Biggs (2001), p. 60ff.; Bok (1998b), p. 162ff. On the distinction in Anglo-Saxon literature between voluntary euthanasia, non-voluntary euthanasia , and involuntary euthansia, and on the principle of Double Effect, which I cannot examine here cf. Biggs (2001), pp. 12ff., 54ff.; Amato (2011), p. 111ff., Biggs (2001), p. 44ff., Bok (1998a), p. 136ff., Brock (1992); D'Agostino (1998), p. 229ff.; D'Agostino (2011), pp. 226–227; Young (2022), sect. 4. For a fuller discussion of issues concerning the definition of *euthanasia* see, e.g., Beauchamp and Davidson (1979). On the fact that passive and active euthanasia are morally equivalent, Young comments as follows: "By contrast, active (voluntary) euthanasia is said to be morally impermissible because it is claimed to require an unjustifiable intentional act of killing to satisfy the patient's request (cf., for example, Finnis 1995; Keown in Jackson and Keown 2012). Despite its popularity and widespread use, the distinction between passive and active euthanasia is neither particularly clear nor morally helpful. (For a fuller discussion, see McMahan 2002). Whether behavior is described in terms of acts or omissions (a distinction which underpins the alleged difference between active and passive voluntary euthanasia and that between killing a person and letting her die) is often a matter of pragmatics rather than anything of deeper moral importance." (Young 2022, sect. 4). In other words, we cannot distinguish between actions and omissions when the person making an omission, as many paternalists think. has a duty to prevent the event, i.d. the patient's voluntary death.

against their will or would otherwise be harmed. These people are "innocent" not only in the sense that they would not have died had it not been for the legalization of euthanasia or assisted suicide, but also in the sense that they wouldn't really have given their consent to euthanasia or assisted suicide, or at least they wouldn't have done so in normal circumstances.

As the argument goes, once euthanasia or assisted suicide is brought under a standard medical or hospital protocol aimed at ascertaining whether the agent or patient has consented to the procedure and/or whether the consent meets certain requirements—i.e., the decision to undergo the procedure must be rational, informed, uncoerced, and stable over time—it is statistically inevitable that there should be errors, which may be owed to negligence or incompetence, or to outright abuse if the physician or family members are acting in devious or malicious ways, and in these cases some people would in fact be put to a "gentle death" treatment against their will. This is what would happen, for example, if an error were made in filling out a patient's medical chart; or if the patient is fragile, emotionally challenged, or uneducated and is thus misunderstood in an evaluation interview with a physician or psychiatrist; of if the patient's family puts undue pressure on the patient; or if the doctor acts in haste; or if the family and doctor are actually complicit in conspiring against the patient[26]

The Massacre of the Innocents argument is quite significant and cannot be underestimated. It is significant because it is based on the idea, one shared by antipaternalists, that it is absolutely imperative not to cause harm to unconsenting third parties. But it is also significant on account of how it resonates in the literature and of the powerful emotions it elicits, which come down to the fear that we or our loved ones might be made to suffer a terrible and unwanted fate. Which means that this argument is not necessarily in favour of paternalism, or at least we can call that proposition into doubt. In fact, at least in the way the argument is set up, it appears to be antipaternalistic, for it is designed to justify limiting the liberty of individuals, against their will, in order to protect the well-being of third parties (and thus avert a Massacre of the Innocents). If this argument were correct—rather than rationally invalid, as I think it is—it would probably be genuinely antipaternalistic, that is, it would justify certain restrictions on liberty (and so a prohibition on euthanasia) on antipaternalistic grounds. But the argument is instead typically advanced by paternalists, who use it as a way not to call the value of individual autonomy directly into question, and so to avoid addressing the many objections that can be raised against the theological and perfectionist arguments.[27]

[26] Cf. R. Dworkin (1993), p. 262ff.; Singer (2000), p. 215; Sunstein (1997), p. 1141ff.; Amato (2011), p. 134ff.; D'Agostino (2011), p. 225.

[27] This is precisely the use of the argument made in Sunstein (1997), p. 1141ff., and Bok (1998a). The way the slippery slope argument is standardly used against the legalization of euthanasia, it contains two inductive fallacies (improper analogy and generalization) and some incoherences when judged against the moral premises that most people most likely start out from, including the authors who make this argument. I haven't included this argument among the fallacious or parasitic arguments discussed in Sect. 3.9 through the end of this chapter, because these fallacies are

3.3.1 The Analogy with Capital Punishment

More to the point, the argument draws an analogy to an argument used to make the case against capital punishment: just as it is better that ten people guilty of murder should go unpunished than that a single innocent person be sentenced to death, so it is better that ten patients should be unable to get the lethal injection they want, because they cannot validly authorize their doctor to carry out the procedure, than that a single patient be put to a "soft death" when they are in fact "innocent," dying by euthanasia when in fact they do not want to undergo the procedure[28]

In challenging the Massacre of the Innocents argument, I will begin by pointing out what I think is wrong with the analogy it draws to the argument made against capital punishment. Which is to say that the force of the Massacre of the Innocents argument in the fact-finding context of a criminal trial is different from the force it carries in the context of euthanasia. (And I should note, as a preliminary matter, that while the Massacre of the Innocents argument will be dissected here with specific reference to euthanasia and assisted suicide, the analysis, suitably adapted, also applies to other dangerous or harmful activities that we might want to prohibit people from freely engaging in.)

To begin with—and without even considering the different theories that exist on the meaning and function of propositions like "It is proven that p"—there is undoubtedly a first degree of complexity to judicial fact-finding in the criminal trial, for the facts to be ascertained belong to the past (Did X kill Y? Was X having an affair with Y?), so we have no direct access to these facts, nor is the factual picture they amount to easy to reconstruct. Sometimes these facts are events that cannot even roughly be "replicated," as can be done with a scientific experiment in a lab.[29] So, even if we concede that there is such a thing an objective truth independent of our beliefs, and that we can develop concepts and frameworks suited to representing this reality in an objective, mind-independent manner, which some contemporary epistemologists of constructivist or sceptical persuasion deny,[30] still we do not have direct epistemic access, whether by observation or experimentation, to the facts at issue in a criminal trial, the reason being that the alleged facts are all about something that may or may not have happened *in the past*.

In the second place, even if we grant the possibility of developing scientific theories capable of describing reality in a genuinely objective way, it is a standard view in epistemology, at least since Karl Popper, that objectivity so construed, and so the truth of its description, is merely an ideal, considering that empirical observation is often, if not always, theory-laden, and human knowledge is always fallible, defeasible, subject to change and revision. There is therefore a critical gap between the

---

not evident or explicit, as they are in the case of the argument from human dignity or from the sacredness of human life.

[28] Cf. Alemany (2006), p. 274ff.; Feinberg (1992), p. 268.

[29] Cf. MacCormick (1978), p. 87ff., esp. 91.

[30] I am thinking in particular of Vittorio Villa (1999), p. 59ff.

scientific understanding we have of the world today, *hic et nunc*, and the factual reality of that world. If knowledge as a matter of general principle is fallible, all the more so is the knowledge we can attain of the facts at issue in a criminal trial.[31]

In the third place, we need to bear in mind that the ascertainment of facts in a criminal trial is subject to a third set of epistemic constraints: these are not general, like the first two, but specific to the context in which facts are ascertained in a trial: they are economic and temporal, preventing the judge or jury from arriving at something like the "truth of the matter" on the basis of our current scientific understanding of the world.

Finally, we have a set of specifically legal constraints on the ascertainment of facts in a criminal trial. These are limits on the kinds of evidence that can be introduced, making it even more likely that a fact cannot be proved at trial or that a supposedly proven fact is not actually a fact.[32] So we know that there is some likelihood that a defendant in a criminal trial will be found guilty of something they did not do, which is especially serious if they have been tried on a murder charge and the specific jurisdiction where the case is tried has the death sentence on the books, especially considering that once the punishment is meted out, there is no going back (no amount of subsequently discovered exculpatory evidence will restore a life taken by judicial error). We can certainly envision various kinds of procedures by which to reduce the likelihood that an innocent defendant will be sentenced to death. For one thing, as much as scientific theory may be falsifiable, defeasible, and always subject to revision, it also true that physics, chemistry, and biology, which could ground certain expert opinions at the trial, are now reliably predictive sciences. In the second place, a policy could be enacted requiring a particularly demanding burden of proof—such as DNA testing—in cases where the crime one is charged with carries the death penalty. Likewise, if more economic resources were made available for judicial fact-finding, and more time were made available for the fact-finding process, the likelihood of finding an innocent defendant guilty would go down, considering as well that a guilty verdict would be subject to appeal. But even with such measures, the likelihood of an erroneous finding of a material fact cannot be reduced to zero, in part because there is no such thing as irrefutable and definitive evidence for any fact. DNA evidence may have a very slim margin of error, but even that technology is not foolproof.[33]

In light of the foregoing remarks, we can easily understand why the analogy between euthanasia and capital punishment doesn't hold up. The background assumption we have to start from, and this is the assumption made in any

[31] Cf. Maniaci (2008), chap. 2.8; Putnam (1981); Quine (1990), pp. 6ff., 17ff.; Quine and Ullian (1970), p. 12ff.; Villa (1999), chaps. 2–4.

[32] Cf. Ferrer Beltrán (2004), pp. 46ff., 65ff.

[33] Apart from the possibility of technical or human error in collecting biological samples, and apart from the fact that the DNA data extracted from them needs to be interpreted, the point is not just that DNA testing always carries a margin of error (the Federal Bureau of Investigation in the United States estimates this number at one in a billion chances of error) but that DNA evidence can never in itself prove a defendant's guilt. See Poggi (2010).

antipaternalistic theory like Feinberg's, any decision made in regard to euthanasia and assisted suicide needs to go through an authorizing procedure—a complex one, involving several stages, designed to assess whether and to what extent the conditions obtain for a physician to perform euthanasia on a patient. It needs to be established, in other words, whether euthanasia is what the patient actually wants, which in turn means that the patient's wishes in that regard need to satisfy at least four basic criteria: it must be the case that patients are (a) rational (they have the mental capacity to make decisions for themselves) and (b) informed (aware of the relevant facts); that (c) their consent is stable over time; and that (d) they are uncoerced (or sufficiently free of coercive pressures).[34] Now, I will be expanding on these four criteria shortly, but from the start we can observe that the task of verifying whether they are met is nowhere as involved or epistemically challenging and constrained as the task of ascertaining the allegation of facts in a criminal trial. Indeed, for one thing, what needs to be ascertained in cases of euthanasia is not a complex set of facts that may or may not have happened at some time in the past, but a circumscribed set of facts revolving around a single person in the present: we want to know whether someone wants to die, to which end we want to make sure that they have mental capacity and understand what their medical prognosis is, whose accuracy can in turn be ascertained on multiple occasions over time. And none of these supporting facts need to be ascertained in the minority of cases in which a patient no longer has mental capacity but has drawn up an advance healthcare directive.

In the second place, by comparison with the criminal trial, the ascertainment of facts in euthanasia is much less dependent on complex scientific theories like those developed in physics or chemistry. To be sure, this ascertainment is amenable to the same falsifiability and defeasibility that any other form of knowledge is also subject to. So, for example, psychiatry could at some point in the future identify a previously unknown personality disorder. And, clearly, it could also be objected that some of the criteria are difficult to assess, particularly as concerns mental capacity, for an assessment of someone's capacity to consent likewise depends on highly involved and contentious debates in psychology and psychiatry (Under what circumstances can X be said to have full mental capacity?), in which arguments have to be made that in turn make it necessary to address no-less-controversial philosophical and ontological questions. So, for example, we have to ask, What empirical facts need to come about so that X can be said to want A? But in reality, despite the philosophical tangle in which the analysis of the concept of will is enmeshed, once we settle on a theory of formal rationality,[35] any ascertainment of a patient's informed consent, like the consent of a spouse or of a contracting party, rests on procedures which are well established in the law and in the legal and medical com-

[34] Similar procedures are envisioned by virtually all authors in favour of euthanasia. See, for example, Cadoppi (2008), p. 96; Diciotti (2005), pp. 108ff., 113ff.; Dworkin (1993), p. 32; Feinberg (1986), pp. 113ff., 344ff.; Garzón Valdés (1988), p. 165ff.; VanDeVeer (1986), chap. 4, esp. pp. 175ff., 225ff. These kinds of procedures are also a standard part of the laws legalizing euthanasia and of the draft laws introducing such legalization. See Pérez (2007), pp. 11–12.

[35] See Anscombe (1963); Frankfurt (1982); Amarasekara and Bagaric (2004), p. 411; Dworkin (1983a), p. 31; McDowell (1998), chap. 5; Scanlon (1998), chap. 1; Sunstein (1997), p. 1141ff.

munity, and through which the problem is simplified. Thus, for example, in reply to the question, "Do you take X to be your lawfully wedded wife?" you repeatedly answer "I do," and in a previous interview you did not show any sign of psychopathology or incoherent thinking. If these simplifying procedures are suitable for any type of medical activity, as well as for other sorts of activities, there is no reason why they shouldn't also be suitable for euthanasia.

In the third place, unlike in a criminal trial, the procedure through which it can be ascertained whether the criteria for consent have been met is not subject to particular economic, intellectual, or time constraints except as is dictated by the nature of the decision itself. Thus, if a patient has been given six months to live, it won't make much sense to mandate a four-month inactive period in which to weigh and think through the options before a decision to undergo euthanasia can be made and authorized. Clearly, there is a minority of cases (as when an urgent blood transfusion is needed) in which, by contrast, time *is* of the essence, but this problem can easily be solved by way of advance healthcare directives. At any rate, it doesn't take a great expenditure of time or financial resources to ascertain whether the criteria for a physician to be authorized to perform euthanasia have been met: what is needed, rather, is an interview videorecorded by a physician who will ascertain the patient's wishes and explain, for example, the diagnosis and prognosis, as well as an interview by a psychiatrist who will ascertain that the patient's decision is rational and sufficiently uncoerced.

In the fourth place, unlike what is the case with the admissibility of evidence in a criminal trial, which is subject to a complex set of rules and constraints, there are no particular legal constraints on ascertaining that the criteria for consent have been met.

The foregoing remarks explain why the analogy between euthanasia and capital punishment doesn't hold up: the likelihood that an innocent defendant should be sentenced to death is much greater than that an nonconsenting "innocent" patient should be euthanized.

3.3.2 The Massacre of the Innocents as a Paranoid Scenario

In fact, a scenario in which a physically and psychologically uncoerced patient is treated to a "soft death" despite not wanting to is highly unlikely,[36] almost paranoid, dare I say, for in order for that to happen, four jointly necessary and sufficient conditions would have to be satisfied in relation to a patient, who we will call Patient X:

(a) While an initial clinical exam finds that X is rational or has a baseline level of capacity—X, for example, is not affected by any serious mental disorder (such as schizophrenia) or by any serious form of senile dementia—X is nonetheless

[36] The same thesis, with analogous arguments, is advanced in Singer (2000), pp. 215–216. Fornero quotes and agrees with my argument. Cf. Fornero (2020).

psychologically very weak and pliant, easy to manipulate or influence, so much so as not to resist in the face of pressure from others to be euthanized.

(b) The physician (an oncologist, for example) steers X toward euthanasia, either negligently (through malpractice) or intentionally—in the latter case conniving with X's scheming family—by placing undue emphasis on the negative aspects of the prognosis or by underscoring the physical pain X is likely to suffer or the difficulty in managing and relieving the pain.

(c) Despite the fact that X does not want to be euthanized, this is the choice toward which X is steered by everyone with whom X has an emotional connection (a spouse or partner, for example, as well as family and friends): all these people intentionally push euthanasia on X, disregarding X's wishes, or they unwittingly cause X to lean toward that choice.

(d) The psychiatrist likewise steers X toward euthanasia, either negligently, failing to understand what X really wants, or with wrongful intent, by *pretending* not to understand.

Now, everyone in (a) through (d) has to be working toward the same goal, either through culpable negligence or with wrongful intent. In other words, it must be the case that X's physician, family and friends, and psychiatrist all have to misunderstand what X wants, and X must be psychologically too weak to push back and correct the misunderstanding, or it must be the case that all or at least many of them deliberately take part in a design to relieve themselves of the personal, economic, or emotional burden of having to care for X. And the likelihood of a collective mistake on such a grand scale or of such a coordinated scheme frankly strikes me as negligible, or it is a scenario than can be seriously entertained only under a paranoid mindset. As Hart says while we may not be angels—kind-hearted and always ready to make sacrifices for the sake of others—we are not devils, either, inherently self-interested and ready to take advantage of others or leave them to fend for themselves when they are in need. There is no logical or empirical reason, or even a statistical reason, at the limit, to think that everyone involved in the matter (family, doctors, and so on) are more devil-like or less angel-like or more obtuse or less intelligent than the average person, so that they will want to deceive X or will misunderstand what X wants. We might ask if it isn't enough for even only one of the conditions just listed to be satisfied. The answer, I submit, is no. For if scheming family members conspire to "unload the problem" by attempting to influence X's decision-making, this does not mean that the psychiatrist or the physician cannot see what is happening (it may well be that, when visiting X without any family members around, either one or both will sense that something is off and will accordingly pursue the matter until they uncover the pressure campaign and deception), nor does this mean that the psychiatrist or the physician will themselves try to talk X into making a decision that X may otherwise not want to make.

Indeed, if we want to be sure that X's decision is rational and sufficiently uncoerced, we will want X to be interviewed by a psychiatrist in private (without any friends or relatives in attendance): this psychiatrist will ideally be working independently of the physician, making an impartial assessment in which the psychiatrist cannot know what the physician or X's relatives and loved ones think is best for X, and we will want the interview to be videorecorded for extra measure. Otherwise, if we want to protect X from malpractice or any medical error, and X's close family, partner, spouse, or children have reason to believe that X has mistakenly been understood as wanting to die or that the diagnosis is wrong, they can be given the option of requesting an interview with another physician with X's consent. Or again, even if some family members are pressuring X into a decision that serves their own self-interest, this doesn't mean that they will *all* be doing so, and in fact this is quite unlikely, nor is it necessarily the case that X isn't thinking clearly and isn't perfectly capable of understanding what is happening and making an independent decision, particularly if the diagnosis is clear in what is still an early-onset disease whose worst effects have yet to manifest. By the same token, if X can have a thoughtful, accommodating, and unrushed interview with the physician (with the help of an interpreter if X cannot speak the language), it will be entirely unlikely that a misunderstanding should arise as to the duration of the disease, the lack of any cure or effective treatment, or X's intentions. In fact, with a cooling-off period in which X has an opportunity to mull over what to do, it becomes unlikely that X should make any rash decision or one dictated by sudden and uncontrollable emotions. Nor is it an objection that, in view of the constant advances in medical science, euthanasia might kill someone who in the near future might otherwise be treated and kept alive, for it is always up to the patient to decide whether it is worth waiting for such a treatment, having first been correctly informed about the medical advances that can reasonably be expected or hoped for.[37]

Some large-scale studies conducted in the United States[38] have found that communication between patients and physicians is often insufficient or inadequate, which would seem to call into question the optimistic outlook of those who envision a future scenario in which euthanasia can be carried out responsibly with all of the necessary safeguards.[39] What these studies have found, more to the point, is a significant percentage of cases in which there is no communication between patients and physicians, or patients are misunderstood as to their preferences for

[37] We could finally envision a set of procedural rules aimed further minimizing the possibility of error. These rules would be set up under the principle *in dubio pro vita*. Suppose, for example, that X has gone through the standard procedure (providing for an assessment by the physician and an independent interview with the psychiatrist), but subsequently comes to have second thoughts, and just before the injection is set to take place, X decides *not* to go ahead with the medical procedure: in this case, it is X's last-minute reversal that would govern, trumping any previous decision. Likewise, under the enhanced procedural framework, the procedure itself could not be said to have been properly carried to completion until all of the professionals involved (physicians, psychiatrists, and specialists) are unanimously agreed that X's express consent is rational, sufficiently free of coercive pressures, informed of the relevant facts, and stable over time.

[38] See Bok (1998a).

[39] See Bok (1998a), commenting that "intellectuals are more prone than practitioners in most lines of work to fall into the trap of believing that they can devise a set of rules to guide participants in an inherently dangerous practice" (ibid., 135).

cardiopulmonary resuscitation, or physicians refuse to carry out their patients' directives, or patients do not receive painkillers.

But when we look at these studies more closely, we will discover a more nuanced picture. It is not that in the majority of cases the physicians simply *misunderstand* what their patients are saying (a patient says that he or she wouldn't want to be given cardiopulmonary resuscitation should it prove necessary, and the physician takes those words to instead mean "Yes, I do want to be resuscitated"). Rather, what in many cases happens is that physicians altogether disregard their patients' preferences and directives relating to cardiopulmonary resuscitation and the administration of painkillers. So these cases have little to do with misunderstanding or miscommunication and a lot to do with an unwillingness or reluctance to carry out a patient's directives (and they can also be attributed to a certain degree of negligence in carrying out the required procedures). Why such reluctance? The answer lies in a certain way of conceiving medical practice that is widespread in the United States as well as elsewhere. In an article that is widely cited in the literature on medicine and bioethics, Leo R. Kass[40] argues that medicine ought to be regarded "an inherently ethical activity, in which technique and conduct are both ordered in relation to an overarching good, the naturally given end of health."[41] From this end, "we can infer the importance of certain negative duties," such as "Doctors must not kill".[42] And "as the Hippocratic oath indicates, there are specific restrictions to counter these temptations—no breach of confidentiality, no sexual relations with patients, no dispensing of deadly drugs".[43] If we consider that many painkillers, being essentially opioids, are therefore felt to be immoral, we can appreciate that the root problem is not one of misunderstanding but rather lies in a widespread secular and inherently paternalistic practice that confers a great deal of power on physicians, who are simply to be trusted to do good by their frail and defenceless patients—a practice that accordingly fails utterly to recognize the value of individual autonomy, and in particular the autonomy of those patients who are suffering the most. As Sissela Bok underscores, "When people die after prolonged suffering, the doctors say, 'We did everything we could.' They don't say, 'We put this person

[40] Cf Kass (1989), p. 29.

[41] Similarly, Hans Jonas argues that it would completely alter the core sense of the medical profession to attribute to the physician the role of "giver of death." "The role of killing should *never* fall within the physician's remit: in no case should the law ascribe such a role, since that would put in danger, or perhaps even destroy, the role of the physician in society" (Jonas 2000, p. 63, my translation; cf. Jonas 1997, p. 196). It is not clear, however, what the danger or slippery slope is that Jonas is referring to, though I would surmise that this is the danger that physicians might turn into serial killers or might stop treating their patients. As I discuss below (as well as at footnote 24), there is little, if any, basis for supposing this to be a danger. And at any rate, even if what Jonas articulates is only a hypothesis, and so no more than a worry, there is a solution for these kinds of concerns: the task of "giving death"—carrying out the procedure of preparing and injecting the lethal cocktail into a patient—could be entrusted to a cadre of specialized nurses rather than to physicians.

[42] Cf Kass (1989), p. 30.

[43] Cf. Dworkin (1998), pp. 13–14.

through hell before he died'".[44] It is clear that any code of professional ethics or any Hippocratic oath—oral or written, recent or centuries-old—ought to subscribe to any law authorizing patients to request euthanasia, and ought to do so in order to protect individual autonomy, and that physicians ought to be trained accordingly in medical school.

From this point of view, as noted, the reluctance and negligence of some physicians in taking account of their patient's directives may be overcome by way of adequate procedures, ones that are more difficult to get around (such as written consent forms and videorecorded interviews), and by adequate professional training, as well as by making changes to codes of professional ethics (as would be desirable), by recognizing physicians themselves as having a right to conscientious objection (albeit within limits), and by introducing meaningful penalties.[45]

3.3.3 Adults Do Not Have a Right to Be Loved

It could be objected here that the risk is not that patients are *misunderstood* as to their will: a patient expresses a wish to be kept alive but is taken to mean that he wants to die—a fantastical scenario, to say the least. Rather, the risk that this patient does want to die, and can frame this as a rational decision, but the decision is made under emotional pressure from family members or doctors or both: our patient no longer wants to live, and there can be no mistake about that, nor was his decision formed on an irrational (misinformed or paranoid) basis—it was, on the contrary, a rational decision—but it was rational precisely on basis that he doesn't want to be a burden on people who convey to him that they are unwilling to take care of him or on whom he doesn't want to be entirely dependent, for he doesn't feel that they have his best interest at heart.

As I was saying, even if pressure is exerted on someone so that they will choose to be euthanized, it would be quite extraordinary if this pressure were to be uniformly exerted by *everyone* around this person (by all doctors, family members, and

[44] Bok (1998a), p. 119, quoting a physician named William A. Knaus, in turn quoted in Colburn (1995).

[45] An interesting proposal has been put forward by Paolo Becchi, making the case that if we do not want euthanasia to be reduced to a hospital routine—a bureaucratized and impersonal medical practice, a medical service like any other—we would be better off with a system under which the procedure is be carried out "by the person who is closest to the dying person": "this would be the last and ultimate gesture of love and affection for a beloved one whose fate is irremediably sealed [...], for there are times when even death can be a gift." This would make it possible to do away with all the penalties the law imposes "on those who carry out euthanasia in the manner just described." This proposal does have its merits, to be sure, but in one respect it seems to fall short: it would make sense for the right to request assisted suicide or euthanasia to also be recognized for persons who do not have family members or a partner or spouse they can turn to, and even for persons whose partner, spouse, family, and friends refuse to "gift death". Becchi (2009), pp. 151–152.

friends), and even more extraordinary if they were to act in concert toward that end. And even if this were a likely scenario, any risk of its coming about can be minimized by "neutralizing" any economic incentive that doctors might have to pressure patients into choosing to die (more on this later). To be sure, just a single individual in whom the patient places a great deal of trust could conceivably exert on him an influence that an entire entourage couldn't match, even if they acted in concert, but I don't think that the law could, much less should, guarantee for anyone *a right not to be influenced by others or a claim-right to be emotionally cared for or a claim-right to be loved.* On the contrary, everyone has a right to influence everyone else, to exercise "emotional pressure" (though of a kind that, needless to say, should not translate into harassing or offending others, violating the privacy of the home, committing a breach of confidentiality, or doing bodily harm to someone). If a woman wants to have an abortion, we can, and indeed must, help her toward that goal by providing her with economic or psychological support, but if abortion is legal under the circumstances of the case at hand, then we cannot prevent her from aborting if her reason for doing so is that she's been abandoned by the man with whom she conceived the child, the man she loves, and she is unwilling to raise the child without him. Nor can we compel someone to be emotionally caring and loving toward someone else. We can compel parents to raise and support their children and give them an education and, all the more so, we can prohibit them from mistreating or abandoning their children, but we certainly cannot compel them to be caring and loving towards them. Nor can we obligate someone to be affectionate toward a relative who is gravely ill, providing this person with all the emotional support they may need. If we consider any decision one may have to make about their job or their children's education or about whether they want to carry a pregnancy to term or stay in a relationship or continue living: these and other similar decisions may be more or less important, tragic, or definitive, to be sure, but what they all have in common is that they may depend on or be influenced by the behaviour and attitudes of individuals with whom we have an affective or existential connection, which behaviour and attitudes may well not be supportive—they may in fact be indifferent, unaffectionate, and even hostile. But that is not to say that any of the decisions at issue are thereby somehow coerced or unfree.[46] If such lack of understanding or support one

[46] In Cornacchia (2003, p. 205), we instead find the thesis, offered without evidence, that "vulnerable individuals, particularly the elderly and the mentally ill, are pressured to make unfree choices under the external conditioning of society and the family" (my translation). Also offered without evidence or justification is the claim in D'Agostino (1998, p. 219) that, in cases of euthanasia, the patient-doctor relationship is an inherently asymmetric, and even violent, one in which the doctor's will "prevails over," or is thrust onto, that of the patient. Viafora (2009, pp. 116, 128), for his part, claims that "a certain number of the elderly and the chronically ill are induced into self-sacrifice by a sense of guilt, perceiving themselves to be a useless burden" (my translation), which, as the author further claims, carries the risk of transforming the right to die into a *duty* to die. From this premise he arrives at the conclusion that the right to make one's own decisions about one's own death should come second to the right to be treated and cared for until the end without having to feel like a burden or feel any shame for it. As I will discuss in Sect. 3.8, there is a way of understanding these two rights—the right to self-determination and the right to be cared for—that makes

may face in making a decision, even a decision concerning a life event, could be grounds for making it illegal to so behave, then we would be facing a situation in which broad swaths of human conduct in the ordinary interchange of life would have to be deemed illegal.

It goes without saying that the likelihood of abuse or error essentially depends on the strength of the guarantees of the procedure in place to establish whether and to what extent a patient has given consent—a procedure whose guarantees, as we have seen, seem to be very strong. Obviously, there always remains a marginal chance that an adult, rational, and competent individual may be "subjected" to euthanasia owing to the wilful wrongdoing or negligence of doctors and relatives, since there is no humanly imaginable procedure, however complex, that can provide an absolute guarantee against abuse or error. Likewise, there is always a marginal chance that human error or medical malpractice may cause a patient to die as a result of a surgical operation the patient himself sought or may precipitate the patient's death during a procedure aimed at ascertaining that the patient is brain-dead (a necessary precondition for organ removal) or during a procedure aimed at ascertaining that the patient has refused life-saving treatments or life-support delivered to keep him alive once he has been diagnosed with an incurable disease. This, in part, is because these procedures are normally deemed legal even if they lack strong guarantees, that is, the procedures for ascertaining a patient's consent are deemed legal even if they are much simpler than those that would have to be followed the case of euthanasia. By the same token, there is always some likelihood that someone may be killed intentionally as a result of a plot carried out by friends or relatives.

Now suppose we applied the same principle to a case in which A consents to have B carry out an activity, X, and there is a very small, and indeed negligible, chance that in carrying out this activity, B should commit an error leading to A's death—something that A doesn't want. In this case, according to this principle, X would have to be prohibited. But then we would have to make it illegal to give consent for a whole range of activities, such as carrying out surgical operations (both life-saving and non-life-saving), removing organs from subjects whose brain-death has been ascertained, or refusing life-saving therapies or life-support treatment to keep an incurable patient alive, or even driving a car with passengers. In short, we would have to prohibit people from consenting to any activity which they want to have carried out but in the course of which they may lose their life or bodily

---

them compatible: we have *both* a right to be left alone *and* a right *not* to be left alone, and the two are not in contradiction. But if what the author means is that we have a right to be *loved*, or a right not to feel guilty, or, better stated, a right to be cared for without having to feel any sense of guilt for the burden we are putting on our caretakers, then we should be able to appreciate, and this is the argument made in the text, that such a right can neither be achieved nor reasonably be claimed (unless, of course, it is meant as a right not to be subjected to humiliating and degrading treatment). As much as it may be morally questionable, it would not be illegal for family members to signal to patients that they are a "useless burden" and that it would help if they decided to put an end to their life by exercising their right to refuse costly medical care and to request voluntary discharge from hospital.

integrity against their will as a result of some slight negligence, unforeseeable circumstance, or force majeure, no matter how slight the risk that such loss may happen.

Cutting to the chase, there is no denying that a doctor should always inform a patient of the risks involved in any treatment plan—even where those risks are not particularly high—and obtain the patient's informed consent on that basis. This goes for any medical procedure (ranging from breast augmentation to abortion, appendectomy, liposuction, removal of cancerous tissue, or euthanasia), and the information provided should include the full spectrum of risks, especially when these are statistically significant, and even more so when at stake is the patient's bodily integrity or life, since this is always a possibility and we must always assume that no patient wants to risk his or her bodily integrity or life. Thus, from the outset, in walking the patient through the process of explaining the patient's condition and laying out the options, which may include euthanasia, the doctor needs to inform the patient of any risk of medical error that may occur, as in diagnosis or prognosis, no matter how low that risk may be, and also needs to inform the patient of any likelihood that at some point in the future a cure may be found for the condition, and even of the risk that relatives may pressure the patient to authorize the doctor to perform euthanasia.

Catastrophists, or disguised paternalists, often hiding their disregard for individual autonomy behind the slippery slope argument, keep churning out disturbing and worrisome statistical data on the spread of alcoholism and drug use among physicians, on the prevalence of stress syndromes, and on cases of malpractice and negligence among physicians.[47] What they do not seem to explain is why such data should have a deterrent effect only where euthanasia is at issue, and not in all the many cases in which patients undergo appendectomy, liposuction, a buttock-augmentation procedure, rhinoplasty (a "nose job"), or breast reduction or augmentation and suffer serious injury or even death as a result of malpractice or error on the part of the surgeon—an outcome they did not want going into the surgery (they are injured or killed against their wishes). Is the life of a terminal patient worth more than that of another patient undergoing plastic surgery? If a patient suffers serious bodily harm (such as brain or spinal-cord injury) as a result of negligence, is that less serious than the death of a terminal patient? If we can assume, as seems to be the case, that the underlying risk criterion for any medical procedure is that the more pressing or existential the need for the medical procedure (e.g., surgery or euthanasia), the more we are justified in taking the risk of a serious or fatal injury as a result of undergoing that procedure, then we have to ask: is the need for breast augmentation—a procedure in which a certain risk of serious or fatal injury cannot be avoided, but which nonetheless does not raise so many moral concerns—on balance more pressing or existential than a cancer patient's need to put an end to the mental distress and physical suffering caused by cancer? I do not understand the catastrophists' value judgments, nor do I understand what strikes me as the irrational reluctance to recognize that a homicide carried out, in the manner previously described, under

[47] Cf. Bok (1998a).

the guise of a nonexistent request for euthanasia is a much less likely scenario than the unfortunate series of injuries caused each year through medical malpractice.

The slippery slope argument, so structured, contains a couple of fallacies. The procedure for ascertaining consent to authorize a physician to carry out euthanasia is much simpler than that for complex surgical operations, in which negligence and malpractice are much, much more frequent. So, too, there is no basis for (inductively) generalizing from the experience of Nazi Germany to what the current medical establishment would do in the Western world.[48] There is no statistical or probabilistically grounded reason to think that once euthanasia is legalized, doctors would turn into so many serial killers, out of fatigue, a habit of killing, or "just for the sake of it"—killers ready to kill patients suffering from severe dementia or other severe mental impairments and mental disorders (see also n. 11)—not least because, as noted, any standard procedure for authorizing a physician to carry out euthanasia would normally apply to rational adults with full mental capacity and able to give valid consent. In countries where euthanasia or physician-assisted suicide has been legalized—the Benelux countries (Belgium, the Netherlands, and Luxembourg), as well as Spain, Germany, and Switzerland—no massacre of the innocents has taken place, nor have doctors turned into bloodthirsty Nazis.

If we are to authorize assisted suicide for patients with severe psychological illnesses or severe mental or neurological disabilities, the procedure for doing so will have to be in keeping with the current legal framework applying to such individuals: it will have to be even more complex than the procedure for mentally competent individuals, (but that should in any case be very speedy) meaning that it will have to provide for greater safeguards. For example, it will have to require a court speedy authorization based on impartial expert advice and the appointment of a qualified guardian, while taking other relevant factors into account, such the possibility of using alternative drug therapies intended to quell the desire to commit assisted suicide. In any event, while the need to protect a patient's autonomy should in itself be a sufficient basis for justifying the legalization of voluntary euthanasia for adult, rational, and mentally competent patients, it cannot be used as a basis for legalizing euthanasia for persons with severe mental disabilities, much less for persons in a persistent, not irreversible, vegetative state.[49]

---

[48] This inductive fallacy can be seen in Bok (1998a).

[49] In the view of Amarasekara and Bagaric (2004, p. 411), if voluntary euthanasia is legalized for adult, rational, and mentally competent patients, we would soon see that, on equality or nondiscrimination grounds, euthanasia would be legalized for patients who cannot express valid consent (because they have severe mental impairments), which in turn would inevitably lead to widespread negligence and abuse practiced on the *innocent*. As Young comments (2022, section 4), "it is sometimes said that if society allows voluntary euthanasia to be legalized, we will then have set foot on a slippery slope that will lead us eventually to support other forms of euthanasia, including, in particular, non-voluntary euthanasia. Whereas it was once the common refrain that that was precisely what happened in Hitler's Germany, in recent decades the tendency has been to claim that experience with legalized euthanasia in The Netherlands and Belgium, in particular, has confirmed the reality of the slippery slope. Slippery slope arguments come in various versions. One (but not the only) way of classifying them has been to refer to logical, psychological and arbitrary line ver-

3.3.4 The United States Scenario

In the final analysis, it is worth making a side note about the Massacre of the Innocents argument, which could just as easily fall under the rubric of "protecting the poor and the weak." What a survey of the literature will clearly reveal is that this argument, however one might call it, resonates in particular with authors in the United States.[50] What seems to concern these authors is that poor or underresourced relatives of patients who are themselves poor or underresourced would be reluctant, and very often unable, to bear the cost of the full-time caregiving and treatment (e.g., palliative care) needed to tend to gravely or terminally ill patients until they die, a treatment that is technically nontherapeutic, i.e., unfit for the purpose of recovery. In this sense, taking advantage of the indifference, superficiality, or malice of complacent insurance companies and hospitals—themselves reluctant, or not required, to bear the same costs—relatives would leave the patient to the fate of death, which feels psychologically and financially easier to bear. Or they would insistently pressure the patient/relative to opt for euthanasia. The same thing could happen with marginalized individuals, such as the homeless, who have no family to turn to or any community support to rely on.

This is a very important problem, affecting in particular those countries in which right to health still lacks a solid legal basis or otherwise cannot be genuinely exercised, a case in point being the United States, where millions of people, especially the poor and the marginalized, struggle to access to health care (and that is despite the Affordable Care Act signed into law by President Barack Obama in 2010). This concern seems hypocritical to me when expressed by those who hold to the view that the government has no obligation to protect the health of the less well-off, for in that case we have to ask: How can one (a) worry over the possibility that someone who is poor and gravely ill should mistakenly be euthanized while in hospital care,

---

sions. The common feature of the different forms is the contention that once the first step is taken on a slippery slope the subsequent steps follow inexorably, whether for logical reasons, psychological reasons, or to avoid arbitrariness in 'drawing a line' between a person's actions." For further discussion see, e.g., Rachels (1986); Brock (1992); Walton (2015).

But in fact the differential treatment is entirely justified here: the standard we use to weigh euthanasia for rational and mentally competent adults cannot be the standard we use for patients affected by serious mental impairments or disorders, for it is two different interests that are being protected here, namely, personal autonomy in the former case, freedom from pain in the latter. Freedom from pain is itself an unalienable right, and it belongs to all human beings, but the human beings it concerns is much smaller—certainly it is not a right that can be claimed by patients in a persistent vegetative state for five years. In this sense, as I remark in the text, the right to freedom from pain may justify recourse to euthanasia under procedures which are more complex than the procedures for authorizing other medical interventions (but that means to be very speedy), and which partly differ from one another, and in any event, save for cases involving patients who lack any mental capacity at all, the procedures need to always respect a patient's wishes. Similar objections and arguments can be found in Frey (1998), p. 73ff. The same procedure would be provided for minors of 12 to 15 years. Older adolescents, aged 16 and above, are old enough to make rational and competent decisions.

[50] See, e.g., Sunstein (1997), p. 1143ff.; Bok (1998a).

and yet (b) not have any qualms about that same person being denied life-saving treatment at the same hospital, or indeed at any hospital, because they are uninsured or otherwise unable to pay for that treatment? In the first case we are dealing with an unintentional and remote possibility of death, in the second with a very real and intentional refusal to save someone's life. How can the first case be qualified as homicide and the second not? There would be no hypocrisy, of course, for those who feel that government does have a role to play in providing health care.

It seems to me that the solution to the problem remains the same. An antipaternalistic moral-political conception needs to be an egalitarian conception and must always be geared toward protecting each individual's basic rights. To this this end, there are two conditions that need to be met by any procedure aimed at ascertaining whether a patient has consented to euthanasia:

(a) The procedure must preserve the right of every gravely or terminally ill patient to receive medical care, regardless of income or wealth, as well as the right to receive palliative care, for pain management and psychological support, if the illness has no cure.[51]
(b) There must be a government programme in place that covers the medical expenses of a gravely or terminally ill patient, so that family members will not be prompted to pressure the patient into choosing euthanasia out of fear that they should have to go into debt in order to pay for the patient's medical care. And because this social security coverage would be paid for by the government, the programme would potentially give rise to a conflict of interests between family members and the hospital; the former might be conspiring against the patient to have him or her euthanized, because they only want to receive the inheritance and do not care about or love the patient, while the latter would have an economic interest in *not* authorizing euthanasia, thus making money by providing medical care.

Of course, patients going through prolonged physical and psychophysical pain have a right to palliative care whose justification also rests on the (antipaternalistic) case for protecting the psychophysical well-being of patients themselves, which protection in part means that patients should not be left to suffer any unbearable pain, or indeed any unwanted pain, if it can be avoided. There are cases in which this antipaternalistic right to freedom from pain should be sufficient grounds for justifying euthanasia. In the case in which the patient is in deep sedation or is confused by morphine doses we can use an antecedent "living will" or an "advance directives." "'Living wills' or 'advance directives' are legal instruments for giving voice to people's wishes while they are capable of giving competent, enduring and voluntary consent, including to their wanting help to die".[52]

[51] Correctly underscoring this point—speaking of a proper "right not to become a burden on relatives"—is Lalatta Costerbosa (2003, p. 192). In the same vein, see Viafora (2009), p. 121ff.; Cass. civ. n° 21748 of 16 Oct. 2007 (better known as the "Englaro" ruling).

[52] Cf Young (2022) section 4.

But what if, as discussed, patients face pressure from doctors and family members hoping to have them consent to euthanasia? This is a danger that can reasonably be supposed to exist in any Western country, including those where the government generally recognizes a right to health independently of any private health-insurance policies anyone may take out. Indeed, on account of the growing cost of medical and health care, causing many hospitals in Europe to carry debts on their balance sheets, and the growing public debt that European countries are running up relative to the size of their economies, many of these countries have had to cut public spending—and that includes limiting the budgets provided to public hospitals, despite the fact that they are legally required to deliver health care to anyone who needs it. So the argument has been made that these financial pressures act as an incentive pushing doctors and psychiatrists at public hospitals to pressure gravely or terminally ill patients to refuse medical care that would sink the hospital further into debt.

I am not confident in saying that such pressures pose a serious risk in public or hospitals or independent-sector healthcare providers, where the right to health care is guaranteed for everyone. In fact, I'd like to be clear on the kind of risk we are talking about. We are talking about the risk that doctors working for a public hospital (and who have accordingly been recruited through an open, public competition) should deliberately mislead patients about their diagnosis or prognosis or should otherwise falsify documents or alter audio or video recordings so as to trick patients into requesting euthanasia. Is it statistically the case that doctors are a cohort with a higher proportion of criminals, serial killers, or dishonest individuals than in other social groups or professions? I would doubt that. And even if we did face a risk of undue pressure being put on terminally ill patients in the event that euthanasia should be legalized, we would be facing the same problem regardless of whether or not the procedure is legalized. As things stand, unscrupulous doctors can already persuade patients to exercise their right to reject medical care: they can mislead chronically or gravely ill patients about how serious their condition is or how effective the treatment for it is, or what the prognosis is, and can accordingly get these patients to sign a refusal-of-treatment form, especially if they are vulnerable and cannot fend for themselves (as may be the case with the elderly and the homeless).

Even today doctors can cut down on costs by using inadequate tools and treatments or by withholding critical information or treatments at times when either could be life-saving. At any rate, there are simple solutions that can be adopted for public hospitals and independent-sector treatment centres. For example, when a gravely or terminally ill patient receives cancer treatment, palliative care, or other kind of support, the hospital or treatment centre should be able to seek reimbursement from the state *unconditionally*, that is, regardless of whether the funds available to the treatment facility enable it to pay for those expenses, and even if the patient has a right to request euthanasia or physician-assisted suicide. Under such a scheme, the doctors and psychiatrists at the treatment facility would have no economic incentive to pressure the patient into requesting euthanasia, and in fact they may have exactly the opposite incentive.[53]

It could be objected that the danger, in this case, is that doctors and psychiatrists at the hospital where the patient is admitted might unduly deny authorization for euthanasia in order to "pocket" state reimbursements. No law is perfect. Even so, safeguards could be put in place to protect the patient against potential medical misconduct or futile medical care. These safeguards might include granting patients the right to be heard by a medical team from another hospital that may then authorize the procedure, as well as the right to be transferred to other hospitals; requiring doctors and psychiatrists to videotape their interview with the patient; and requiring

[53] If funds or medical resources are limited, palliative care could be delivered that is only focused on pain management, as through continuous sedation, and on providing material (or nonpsychological) support. It is worth pointing out in this regard that when euthanasia was legalized in the Netherlands in 2001, official studies were conducted finding that when terminally ill patients were offered palliative care or sedation (such as deep sedation), requests for euthanasia decreased significantly (from 2.5% of all such cases in the Netherlands in 2001 to 1.7% in 2005), but this also means that requests for euthanasia continued to me made among these patients, even as they were being offered the option of receiving palliative care. This leaves us with only two explanations: either (a) palliative care cannot entirely eliminate psychophysical pain or the fear of such pain or (b) there must be some reasons other than pain or the fear of pain that lead a terminally ill patient to choose euthanasia despite the option to receive palliative care; these persons, for example, might decide that they don't want to lose their autonomy or self-control or they might not want to be a burden on their family or caretaker. Cf. Onwuteaka et al. (2007), p. 7; Pérez (2007), pp. 11–12. The same argument is made by Young (2022): "It is sometimes said (e.g., Emanuel 1999; Keown in Jackson and Keown 2012) that it is not necessary nowadays for people to die while suffering from intolerable or overwhelming pain because the provision of effective palliative care has improved steadily, and hospice care is more widely available. Some have urged, in consequence, that voluntary euthanasia is unnecessary." Young (2022, section 4) says that "high quality palliative care commonly exacts a price in the form of side-effects such as nausea, incontinence, loss of awareness because of semi-permanent drowsiness, and so on. A rosy picture is often painted as to how palliative care can transform the plight of the dying. Such a picture is misleading according to those who have closely observed the effect of extended courses of treatment with drugs like morphine. For these reasons many skilled palliative care specialists acknowledge that palliative care does not enable an easeful death for every patient. Second, even though the sort of care provided through hospices is to be applauded, it is care that is available to only a small proportion of the terminally ill and then usually only in the very last stages of the illness (typically a matter of a few weeks). Notwithstanding that only relatively few of the dying have access to hospice care it is worth drawing attention to the fact that in, Oregon, to cite one example, a high proportion of those who have sought physician-assisted suicide were in hospice care. Third, and of greatest significance for present purposes, not everyone wishes to avail themselves of palliative or hospice care. For those who prefer to die on their own terms and in their own time, neither option may be attractive. As previously mentioned, a major source of distress for many dying patients is the frustration that comes with being unable to satisfy their autonomous wishes. Fourth, as also indicated earlier, the suffering that occasions a desire to end life is not always traceable to pain caused by illness. For some, what is intolerable is their forced dependence on others or on life-supporting machinery; for these patients, the availability of effective pain control is not the primary concern". (In relation to the preceding matters see Rietjens, et al. 2009; see Onwuteaka et al. 2012 for findings for the Netherlands; and, Ganzini 2009 for Oregon).

psychiatrists to give analytical reasons when they deny authorization, and to support these reasons by pointing to reliable sources in the scientific literature.

In the final analysis, I understand the tragic dilemma of many US authors and commentators who believe in a liberal-egalitarian conception, that is, in the need to protect certain social rights, particularly the right to health of less affluent, economically disadvantaged people who do not have sufficient income or assets to take out health insurance to cover expensive cancer treatments or surgery or pay for palliative care and treatment. What I take exception to is their ultimately paternalistic solution to the dilemma. Forced to choose, given a legal framework under which millions of US citizens can be left without access to critical health care, these authors would rather have a state that lets gravely ill patients suffer a slow, painful, and terrible death if they cannot cover the costs of cancer care, surgery, and pain medications, than a state which grants them access to assisted suicide. Both alternatives are tragic and deeply unjust. But I do not understand how the former can be considered preferable. In general, this means that when the state does not see it as its role to guarantee social rights—such as the right to housing, health care, unemployment benefits, or education—we have a *weak* form of coercion: a patient without health care can feel *compelled* to request euthanasia. This is a tragic dilemma, one whose different solutions are all quite unacceptable. But in this tragic case, or dilemma, I would always want the state to recognize all antipaternalistic rights, such as the right to participate in violent sadomasochistic sex or to act in a pornographic movie, or the right to euthanasia and assisted suicide, or the right to selling and buying drugs.

3.4 The Value of Individual Autonomy

Autonomy is clearly the central value protected under the antipaternalistic conception, which puts front and center the right to carry out the plan of life that corresponds to one's ideals, preferences, and values, or at least to pursue such a plan of life consistently with one's abilities and with the humanly possible.[54] It is this individual autonomy that one needs to be in possession of before one can be justified in engaging in activities that may be dangerous or harmful to oneself, or at least before one's intention to do so can be validly expressed. But this is a justification that individuals owe only to themselves. Which is to say that they are sovereign over their mind and body: their life and integrity do not belong to God, or to his representatives on Earth, or to nature or the community.[55]

[54] See Young (2022).

[55] Cf. Ferrajoli (2009); Scarpelli (1998), pp. 5ff., 37ff., 123ff.

But the concept of autonomy is clearly very complex.[56] Indeed, this is a composite concept, combining individual freedom, and opportunities, and the argument can be made that these ought to be respectively protected, nurtured, and created. For as Feinberg underscores, "if adults are treated as children they will come in time to be like children."[57] What we will do in this section, then, is key in on four conditions that all have to be satisfied at the same time in order that someone may be considered sufficiently autonomous, thereby crossing the threshold above which the state cannot be justified in coercing them into making choices against their will. These are the four conditions (or rather, the four *sets* of conditions) that we have already discussed: individuals are autonomous so long as they can be shown to be (a) rational, (b) sufficiently free from coercive pressures (sufficiently uncoerced), and (c) aware of the relevant facts (informed), and so long as (d) their wishes (or the choices they make) are stable over time. Let us therefore develop these conditions, where the idea, to repeat, is that they all need to be satisfied for any individual to be considered autonomous, such that the state is not justified in forcing these same individuals to make personal choices they do not want to make.

3.4.1 Formal and Bounded Rationality and Lack of Mental Capacity

At the Sect. 3.2, and in this section, especially at the footnote 63 below, a formal and limited or bounded conception of rationality is briefly sketched on which our reasons for action are anchored not to any independently established criteria or external reasons or objective values of what counts as a bad decision we should want to avoid (something that is "beyond the pale"), but to a formal argumentative process we go through to make sure that the reasoning on which basis we make any specific decision is free of error. A formal conception of rationality must also be bounded, as opposed to a theory of ideal rationality or rational choice theory, on which "people do not seek the best alternative in the feasible set, but limit themselves to what seems to be 'good enough' or satisfactory" (Elster 1986, p. 25).[58] In this section, this

[56] Although we won't be able to enter into this complexity, it is worth noting that the self-determination that is so central to autonomy is not as straightforward as one might make it out to be. Thus Celano (2007), Diciotti (1986), p. 581ff., Feinberg (1986), p. 27ff., and Raz (1986), p. 369ff. all underscore the limits of self-determination, pointing out that it is simply a caricature of the concept to take it to mean that people can *freely choose* their ideals and desires. "The notion of choosing, from ground zero, makes no sense. Sooner or later we find ourselves, as in Neurath's metaphor of the ship in mid-ocean, being reconstructed while sailing, in mid-history" (Feinberg 1986, p. 35). "We are social animals. No individual person selects 'autonomously' his own genetic inheritance [...], his country, his language, his social community and traditions [...]. We come into awareness of ourselves as part of ongoing social processes" (ibid., 46).

[57] Feinberg (1983), p. 3. A similar argument based on the idea of personal integrity can be found in Kleinig (1983), p. 68.

[58] See Elster (2016), p. 1.

formal and bounded conception will serve as a basis on which t0 identify some conditions under which a decision or action can be said to be insufficiently rational. We will then turn to some further conditions that are standardly taken to mean that someone lacks mental capacity, either in the moment (as with temporary insanity) or permanently (permanent mental incapacitation). Let us then look at these conditions.

We might place them into five broad buckets as follows: (i) psychological immaturity (especially among those who are underage); (ii) permanent or temporary psychopathologies, such as psychosis, bipolar or serious obsessive-compulsive disorders (with symptoms such as delusion, hallucination, disorganized speech, or catatonic, severe manic, or phobic behaviour), severe mental handicaps, and severe dementia; (iii) temporary intoxication induced by alcohol or drugs, including psychotropic drugs; (iv) states of shock; and (v) beliefs which are material to an issue but are demonstrably false or can easily be shown to be so by looking at the relevant literature, as well as explicit or easily explicable logical contradictions, to which we can add wishful thinking ("the shaping of beliefs by wants"[59] adaptive preferences (the irrational adjustment of wants to possibilities, like the fox who cannot reach the grapes and then forms false beliefs, saying the grapes is sour), and conformism ("the adaptation of one's preferences to those of other people"[60]): as when someone believes that something is advisable or morally right because an authority figure (e.g., their father, Kant, or the Pope) believes it to be so.[61]

From the standpoint of a formal and limited or bounded conception of rationality,[62] we would say that when these errors are at play and they are significant, the deci-

---

[59] Elster (2016), p. 25.

[60] ibid., 22.

[61] When someone so appeals to the argument from authority (whether religious, traditional, or otherwise), they can be said to suffer from insufficient rationality or autonomy, finding themselves in what Kant—in his essay "An Answer to the Question: What Is Enlightenment?"—referred to as "minority" (Kant 1996, p. 17), or *Unmündigkeit* (AK 8:35), an "inability to make use of one's own understanding without direction from another" (ibid.). For a full overview of the factors that may cause an agent to think and act nonrationally or to lack mental capacity, see Alemany (2006), pp. 227ff., 403ff.; Beauchamp and Childress (2013), p. 277; Feinberg (1986), p. 115ff.; Pope (2004), p. 667ff.

[62] As noted, it is essential that the conception of rationality we work from be formal. This is also the conception that psychiatrists should be working from in conducting interviews to determine whether someone is rational, regardless of the orientation they may espouse in psychology (be it that of Carl Jung, Jacques Lacan, Sigmund Freud, or Melanie Klein). A formal conception of rationality must also be a "satisficing" or bounded or limited conception, as opposed to a theory of ideal rationality or rational choice theory, on which "people do not seek the best alternative in the feasible set, but limit themselves to what seems to be 'good enough' or satisfactory" (Elster 1986, p. 25). On the idea of bounded rationality see Elster (2016), chap. I; Maniaci (2008), chap. I; Simon (1955, 1957), Rawls (1971), para 64. According to a theory of ideal rationality, rational choice theory, individuals must maximize their utility. For example, in the case of buying a house, we must identify all possible options, all the houses for sale in and around Palermo, Italy; we must identify all the empirically possible consequences of each option, that is, all the empirical characteristics of each option (whether there is an elevator, the floor of the house, whether there is heating, how big it is, the view, whether it is a new or an old house, the colour of the floor, whether the

bedroom faces west, etc.); then we have to assign a numerical value to each characteristic, and discuss all the reasons for and against a certain value attribution; and finally, we had add up the various scores and we will get the house that maximizes our preferences. Simon points out that people normally do not have all these material, intellectual, and temporal resources at their disposal and cannot employ them to make this decision, much less every decision. Simon argues that people begin the procedure laid out in the rational choice theory scheme but at some point they freeze up, say "good enough," stop identifying other options and characteristics and do not assign a numerical value to each characteristic. These assumptions of rational choice theories model the reasoning of a computer or a robot. People, says Simon, say "good enough" when the cost of additional information, another option, another house to see, another feature to locate, is greater than the gain people expect from that additional information. In this sense on Simon's theory, according to the theory of bounded rationality, there are two decision-making levels. The first concerns the search for options, the characteristics of each option, and another level consists in deciding how many resources to dedicate to each decision.

According to bounded rationality, a "rational discourse conducted under limited conditions" is a discourse in which a normative thesis is rationally justified, in the presence of limited material, intellectual, and temporal resources, if, and only if, the thesis is justified on the basis of explicitly logically correct reasons, free from biases (as denial, wishful thinking, adaptive preferences and conformism), and if it is justified (in the reasoned judgement, of the one advancing the normative thesis) on the basis of a sufficient set of theoretical reasons warranted, on the basis of empirical data, by the relevant scientific community, and when the normative reasons advanced in favor of that thesis are general and (in the reasoned judgment, , of the one advancing the thesis) offer a sufficient response to the objections raised, or that might be raised, within the discourse itself.

The reasoned judgment of a rational agent refers to the approximate scheme, devised (and/or used) by the person advancing the thesis, that determines how many and/or what theoretical and normative reasons one must considers in relation to standard types of decisions, and why. The requirement of the subjectivity of judgment is necessary because, based on a skeletal concept of rationality, each person must determine for himself, within certain limits, and provided he is consistent therein, what a sufficient degree of justification for his beliefs and preferences is. What "limits"? It is important to reiterate that the "sufficiency" requirement has a different meaning depending on whether we are dealing with theoretical reasons or normative reasons. In practical discourse, it is not rationally possible for all the theoretical reasons given to be false, given the "standards" of the relevant scientific community. It can be said that, surely, some of the theoretical reasons adduced must be sufficiently vouched for by the scientific community, or, more precisely, that it is not rational to adduce theoretical reasons that are considered patently false, unfounded, by the scientific community, reasons whose unfoundedness is not difficult to ascertain. On the other hand, in the case of normative reasons, it is largely left to the agent's discretion how many and/or which objections to respond to, as long as the decision is substantiated.

To the definition thus elaborated, it is possible to add a (non-exhaustive) set of maxims that complement the notion of rational discourse and that must be followed to determine the notion of "sufficiency," i.e., when an answer to objections is sufficient, etc.:

(a) the more *important* the decision to be made, or the end to be achieved, the greater should be the number of normative criticisms and objections considered, just as the greater should be the number of theoretically warranted reasons based on the empirical data adduced (maxim related to the importance of the decision);
(b) the more strongly a normative thesis is *contested* or controversial within the target audience, the more it must be argued (maxim relating to the degree of acceptance of the normative thesis advanced);
(c) one must respond first to objections that are considered reasonable, and then to objections that are considered unreasonable or absurd (maxim of the reasonableness of objections);

sion-making and action of the person concerned will be nonrational or insufficiently rational, according to a formal and bounded conception of rationality, meaning that the person who is making these decisions and acting accordingly lacks mental capacity in the moment (nonrational) or suffers from a permanent condition of mental incapacitation or from a serious mental or personality disorder that makes some or most of his or her actions nonrational or insufficiently rational.[63] In addition to these conditions, others could be listed that give rise to a cognitive impairment so severe as to prevent someone from doing almost anything (examples being a persistent vegetative state or an reversible coma). Of course these conditions of insufficient rationality or lack of mental capacity need to be *relevant*, that is, they need to be such that one cannot be said to have intended the harmful or dangerous act they did. Thus if Simon is affected by a phobic disorder and decides to kill himself because his partner has died, the phobic disorder cannot be the reason that causally explains his decision. As Feinberg notes in *Harm to Self*, however, an important exception needs to be made for persons diagnosed with a serious form of cancer whose chances of survival do not stretch beyond, say, six months, or persons with tetraplegia or ones at an advanced stage of a serious disease such as multiple sclerosis. For persons in these conditions it would be normal to go through a phase of anger or aggression, and especially to have a mood disorder, such as a state of anxiety or a reactive depressive state. If persons in these conditions request euthanasia or assisted suicide, neither their anxiety nor a depressive state is relevant to invalidating their consent to the procedure. As we can see, then, it is a high bar that a formal and limited conception of rationality sets for an action to be considered insufficiently rational, reducing this test to a minimal, bare-bones set of conditions that need to be met for someone to be considered rational. This makes ineffective

(d) one must respond first to new objections or to objections advanced against a new normative thesis, where the adjective "new" refers, in both cases, to the fact that the thesis or objection has never been discussed by the agent or in the relevant discourse community. Then, it is necessary to respond to objections already discussed, or objections related to a thesis already justified, in previous discourses (maxim of novelty of the normative thesis or objections advanced).

On the conflict between formal and substantive rationality, see Amarasekara and Bagaric (2004), p. 411; Dworkin (1983a), p. 31; McDowell (1998), chap. 5; Scanlon (1998), chap. 1; Sunstein (1997), p. 1141ff., and the sources at nn. 8 and 9. On the (very complex) relation between rationality, autonomy, and the use of (psychologically or physically) addictive drugs see Husak (1992), p. 81ff.; Husak (2000).

[63] It goes without saying that the list of conditions we are going through is deliberately nonexhaustive. It is very difficult to pin down the conceptual relations that hold between rationality and mental capacity, which concepts are not coextensive. Thus, for example, it may be that someone lacks mental capacity (either in the moment or as a permanent condition) and yet it would feel wrong to judge them to be irrational, as would be the case with people affected by senile dementia, and the same goes for children, who cannot be said to meet the threshold for the capacity needed to determine whether an action they have done is reasonable or reckless, rational or irrational, for in several circumstances they lack the capacity needed to make rational decisions or to judge whether a decision would be rational. In the law, this translates to a "threshold conception of natural competence," on which see Feinberg (1986), pp. 29–30.

the objection that from some standpoint, e.g., psychoanalytically, no one is perfectly rational (or, conversely, that everyone to some extent or in some way neurotic).

In particular, a psychologist cannot qualify a desire as irrational or psychopathological on the basis of its content, even if we are talking about a desire to practice boxing, wrestling, or extreme sports; or a desire to go through with medically assisted suicide; or a desire to use drugs, including hard drugs; or a desire to be mutilated or be cannibalized, or both; or a desire to be whipped to a bloody pulp or be choked, or both, but not killed, in a ritual of sadomasochistic sex, all desires whose fulfillment causes pleasure, not emotional distress, to the agent.

A psychologist can prevent people from engaging in such fringe conduct only they show pertinent symptoms that vitiate consent and are accordingly diagnosed with conditions such as a major depression, hallucination, paranoid delirium, or a serious obsessive-compulsive disorder. If someone is in fact diagnosed with a compulsive disorder—meaning that they engage in a behaviour they cannot control or avoid: they do so against their will and regardless of what gives them pleasure—they should be permitted to continue engaging in such behaviour only on condition that they agree to first undergo a month, two months in the case of voluntary grave mutilation, of psychotherapy with the use of psychotropic drugs (if the collateral effects are acceptable).

In that sense, rationality and mental capacity are *completing* conditions: they figure as *necessary* conditions in the four sets of conditions of autonomy that, if satisfied, are sufficient as a basis on which to say that the state is certainly not justified in using coercion against an individual—the other three such sets being the conditions testing to see whether individuals are informed of the relevant facts, stable over time in expressing their wishes, and sufficiently uncoerced. That framework does not prejudice or resolve the question of whether, and if so to what extent, it may be necessary to place limits on the freedom of action of individuals who are found to be insufficiently rational as a permanent condition or to lack the mental capacity to make decisions for themselves (as would be the case with individuals suffering from schizophrenia or a serious form of senile dementia). This, to be sure, is a question I will not be addressing, but the point is that the reason why it does not bear on the framework in question is that an antipaternalistic theory can be compatible with the view that some nonrational choices, as well as some "involuntary" choices, should fall *outside* the sphere of what the state can interfere in. And that view seems reasonable enough: it ought to be the case that some choices which people make are respected even if these choices are not rational or autonomous or if the people who make them are not entirely rational or do not have full mental capacity. And as Enrico Diciotti rightly observes, this means that we need to protect their psychophysical well-being: some of the wishes of someone who suffers from schizophrenia, for example, will need to be protected because that is integral to their psychophysical well-being[64] But this argument does not count against an antipaternalistic conception properly understood, simply because such a conception does not

[64] Cf. Diciotti (2005), p. 117.

or should not concern itself, if not marginally, with the actions carried out by persons with a temporary lack of mental capacity, persons with a permanent mental disorder or disability, or children. At its core, the antipaternalistic theory being defended here is only concerned with protecting the sphere of freedom that rational and mentally competent consenting adults enjoy from the encroachment of an organized polity.

The foregoing framework, then, is best understood as a set of conditions to be used, not in the positive to determine when government interference might be justified, but in the negative to determine when it is undeniably *not* justified.[65] In order to deal with the matter of persons who are not sufficiently rational or mentally competent—those for whom this is a permanent condition or who have yet to attain this condition—we will need a partly different argument, one that is not entirely predicated on the idea of autonomy or valid consent, precisely because in these cases (that is, with children or with people affected by schizophrenia or a serious mental disorder) there may not be a *rational will* that needs to be protected, but there is sure to be a *psychophysical well-being* to be protected (essential to which are these persons' desires).[66]

If practical rationality is understood, as it should, in the formal sense outlined at Sect. 3.2, it needs to be clearly distinguished from reasonableness. As such, rationality surely forms part of an individual's autonomy[67] but it does not give us a full picture of what autonomy is, for even if an insufficiently rational person probably cannot be said to be fully autonomous, there is much more to autonomy than just rationality. Clearly, when our wishes are formed in a nonrational way, they can be very different from our *real* wishes.[68] If someone finds out that they have a nonrational wish that is dangerous or harmful to themselves, it means that (unless they are affected by a serious neurosis or psychosis) they themselves will come to believe that they should have conclusive reasons for setting that wish aside and not acting on it. Suppose, for example, that someone simultaneously wanted to (a) smoke

---

[65] A relevantly similar (but not identical) thesis is defended in Garzón Valdés (1988), pp. 168–169. On the relation between rationality and voluntariness as conditions of valid consent, see the discussion in the next section.

[66] The same point is stressed in Diciotti (1988), p. 755. It is clear that in a minority of these cases, such as serious senile dementia, there is a rational will to be protected, namely, the wishes that someone so affected expressed, expressly or otherwise, when they were still mentally competent. Then too, in general, an antipaternalistic conception will indirectly be concerned with people who only *temporarily* lack mental capacity (they may not be aware of the relevant facts, for example, or they may be drunk), a condition that (however long it lasts, and throughout that time) will take away their ability to make decisions that are harmful to themselves, including *irreversibly* harmful ones. This raises the very complex matter of how antipaternalism relates to liberalism and the rights of children. This is an issue I will not be taking up here, but see Fanlo Cortés (2008), p. 141ff.

[67] See Feinberg (1986), pp. 61ff., 106ff., 126ff., 132ff.

[68] On the various types of consent taken into account in antipaternalistic conceptions centred around the idea of individual autonomy (and around the thesis that hypothetical-rational consent takes precedence over tacit or presently expressed consent), see Diciotti (1986), p. 574; Diciotti (2005), p. 110ff.; and Feinberg (1986), p. 172ff.

thirty cigarettes a day and (b) increase as much as possible their chances of being healthy for as long as possible, but they subsequently learn that their beliefs in that regard are, unfortunately for them, patently mistaken: they find out, for example, that it is false that smoking isn't bad for their health. This realization will force them to decide which of the two wishes, (a) or (b), they want to fulfil (since they come to understand that they won't be able to fulfil both at the same time). In this case, we can unhesitatingly say that in view of the fact that an individual's wishes are insufficiently rational—they might, for example, be incompatible or based on a patently false belief—it becomes inherently uncertain whether that person *really* has those wishes or *really* wants to act on them (as would be the case with the wish to smoke thirty cigarettes a day). And the same goes for other states of serious emotional or sensory disconnection (owing to drugs or alcohol, for example) under whose influence we cannot tell whether someone who wants to do some act Φ that is harmful or dangerous to themselves really wants to Φ once they come back to their senses.

This kind of ontological uncertainty, as it were, needs to be integrated with a statistical-probability study. There are actions which do serious harm or pose a serious risk to life and bodily integrity (such as attempted suicide), and which, statistically, are often carried out by persons with a psychopathological condition, (such as schizophrenia, bipolar disorder, or grave obsessive-compulsive disorder) or by persons under the influence of drugs. After all, there is often a correlation where the more an act is harmful or risky as described, the smaller will be the statistical percentage of people who would want to carry out that act. We can see that correlation at play if we consider, for example, that there are more consumers of marijuana than of heroin.

In conclusion, the central question is this: If the state interferes in people's lives to make sure that when someone decides to carry out a seriously harmful and irreversible action or one that puts them at a significant risk of causing harm to themselves, they are not insufficiently rational and do not lack mental capacity, how is it that such interference can be said not to undermine their autonomy?[69] There are two fundamental reasons why that can be said to be so. The first of these has to do with the procedure that needs to be in place to make sure that when someone is intent on doing something that carries the risk of serious or irreversible harm (as with acts of self-mutilation or suicide), they are not suffering from any serious mental disorder (of the kind that might cause hallucination, delirium, paranoia, or the like). This is an important procedure, typically involving an evaluation interview with a psychiatrist or other medical professional, and the point here is that, as discussed, this is not an assessment made "on a hunch." Rather, if any such procedure is to be used to authorize a schizophrenic person to engage in an act which causes or risks causing harm to themselves, it will have to be much more complex than an authorizing procedure for someone who cannot be so diagnosed or for an act that is not so harmful, taking a wide range of factors into account. These include the weight that altered states of mind may play in preventing someone from fulfilling their real wishes (if

[69] On this question, see Diciotti (1986), p. 574, and Feinberg (1986), p. 13.

Hal is hallucinating and as a result believes he is diving into a pool where dolphins are swimming, when in fact he is diving into a pool filled with tiger sharks, we can conclude that his wish is not to commit suicide), the ability to correctly understand a patient's wishes (something that may be difficult to do when the patient is speaking incoherently or behaving erratically), whether alternative therapies are practical and effective, and the psychological pain the patient may be undergoing. In short, when we are dealing with patients affected by serious mental disorders, the assessment of the patient's condition will be much more thorough than one for a "regular" patient, for it will have to look at their psychophysical well-being.

In the second place, if we were to carry out a comprehensive scientific survey asking people whether they would want the state to prevent them from doing or risking serious and irreversible harm to themselves (such as committing suicide, doing acts of self-mutilation, or doing something that carries a high risk of death) if they should find themselves in a state of temporary mental incapacity or should be behaving in a way that is clearly irrational (they may be under the influence of alcohol or of hard or pharmaceutical drugs, for example, or they may be in a state of shock), I would venture to say that the findings we would get from such a statistical-probability study would tell us that most people would indeed want the state to so intervene to prevent them from doing these things. And that would mean that we first have to ascertain these states of irrationality or any such inability to be intentional about what one is doing. In these cases the state would be protecting an individual's true wishes: these are intentions someone may have expressed at some earlier time (when they had full mental capacity), perhaps in an advance directive.[70] For these reasons, then—in combination with others, such as the interest in protecting everyone's psychophysical well-being—it may be justified for the state to interfere in the private sphere in order to *prevent* individuals from doing or risking

[70] It may be objected here that a genuinely antipaternalistic solution would consist in making it possible for anyone to draw up a "nonmedical advance directive" laying out instructions that anyone working in a capacity such as firefighter or police officer is bound to follow faithfully if the author of the same directive should decide to carry out an irreversibly harmful act, such as jumping off a building, in a state of temporary mental incapacity or irrationality. Such a solution, however, would be legally impracticable. Imagine a team of firefighters or police officers arriving at the scene and scrambling to find these instructions previously written by a drunken individual who is now preparing to jump off a building. The laws on the books need to be such that they can reasonably be applied. At the same time, there are antipaternalistic reasons for protecting the majority, and it seems safe to say that the majority of people who should find themselves in such circumstances would probably want to be brought to safety if they were in their right mind. There are antipaternalistic reasons for momentarily going against the wishes of some in the minority who does not want to be rescued. Indeed, if the rescue team should have to waste precious minutes looking for directives that a guy named Drew may have written instructing the team to rescue him if he should be found trying to jump off a building in a state of drunkenness, Drew may have already jumped to his death by the time those instructions are found, and that would clearly be irreversibly harmful to him, and contrary to his true wishes. In such cases, therefore, it would be reasonable for the balance of interests to come out in such a way that drunken Drew is momentarily rescued even if it subsequently turns out that this is not what he wanted as per his advance wishes. It is sufficiently liberal, as I see it, to enable someone to commit assisted suicide, if this is what they truly want, once they have been rescued and are no longer drunk or otherwise "out of their wits."

serious harm to themselves in a state of insufficient rationality or of momentary lack of mental capacity. As noted, however, I will not be making an argument stating what the conditions should be under which the state may be justified in interfering in the decisions of individuals affected by serious mental disorders or dementia or of individuals with a permanent lack of mental capacity. The last thing I'd like to say that I do not believe in *libertarian free will*. There could be a liberal-egalitarian conception without strong free will, because conscious desires are formed by unconscious desires, which in turn depend, deterministically or probabilistically, on our DNA, family upbringing, culture background, and later experiences that may aggravate some childhood traumas. According to a compatibilist conception, an action is freely performed, it is voluntarily performed, essentially when there are neither internal compulsions, such as serious relevant psychopathologies or incapacities, neither external compulsions, such as threats of harm from a third party.

3.4.2 Sufficient Freedom from Coercive Pressures

An agent can have mental capacity, with a reasonably coherent set of wishes and intentions, and not have relevant beliefs that are patently false, and yet may still carry out actions under coercion, or at least may *intend* to do so under coercion (though it is not clear that in such cases we can speak of "intention"), which coercion could be physical (an agent might be physically forced to commit suicide, for example), or it could be psychological (as when someone *threatens* to use force in a way the agent will perceive to be harmful: "If you do not kill yourself, we will kill your family").[71] Or the wishes one comes to have may be attributable in part to *epistemic violence*: an agent may have been subject to serious and constant social and economic discrimination since childhood and may consequently have interiorized a diminished self-image, a deep sense of inferiority to others in other social groups, coming to believe that these others have a right to intimidate, humiliate, or bully them, or the agent may have developed as sense of self-loathing, particularly if they belong to a social group subject to deep discrimination.[72]

In light of this picture, we would have to conclude that an intention someone may form to carry out actions that do harm to them or pose a danger to their life and limb needs to be not just a rational intention but one that is sufficiently free of coercive pressures (uncoerced, for short). The action in question, in other words, needs to be one the agent carries out in a sufficiently *voluntary* manner. This argument would

---

[71] The absence of psychological coercion is a condition that needs to be ascertained through an evaluation interview with the person concerned: except in exceptional circumstances in which there is solid evidence of such coercion, there may be other exceptional circumstances in which it may be justified for government officials or law enforcement to carry out an investigation (no matter how complex).

[72] See Bartoli (2008), pp. 32ff., 54ff. We will come back to the concept of epistemic violence in Chap. 5, Sects. 5.5 and 5.6.

suggest that the concept of what is rational can be distinguished, at least in part, from that of what is voluntary. A person may be psychologically forced to do something that is harmful to them, and in so doing may still be said to be acting rationally in the sense previously specified.

Three observations, however, are in order. First, as noted in Chap. 2, it seems reasonable to me to rely on a *hybrid* conception of coercion, or compulsion, in defining antipaternalism.[73] If we only look at the "passive" side of coercion—on the receiving end of it rather than from the standpoint of whoever or whatever is *doing* the coercing—whether a given situation counts as coercion is something that can be determined only on the basis of a *subjective* conception of coercion, regardless of who is exercising the coercive pressure (be it one or more specific individuals or the system as a whole).[74] On a subjective conception of coercion, we can also determine the *degree* of coercive pressure that someone is made to bear.

On a subjective conception of coercion, we have coercion only when a certain relation of salience obtains between one's wishes and the choices or options one has at one's disposal, where the set of available options is determined by external circumstances beyond one's own control. Thus, on a hybrid conception of this kind, no one can be said to be coerced if others are threatening to deprive them of something that doesn't matter to them—something they do not regard as valuable or as a "good"—and so if there is no wish proper that is being frustrated. As for the

[73] The hybrid conception of coercion can be understood in relation to Feinberg's manifold conception: see Feinberg (1986), p. 189ff. A problem that comes up in this connection is that of the conceptual relation between rationality and voluntariness. This is a very complex problem that will not be dealt with here. But to appreciate the difficulty involved consider, for example, that according to Diciotti (2005), p. 116, the only interference that, on an antipaternalistic theory, is justified is interference "in choices at once *not voluntary* (not autonomous) and *not rational*" (my translation). Yet it seems to me that each of these two requisites (voluntariness and rationality) is a necessary condition of valid consent independently of the other. What this means—if we think of a hostage situation, for example—is that when someone chooses to do something that does harm or poses a risk to themselves, that choice may be rational but not voluntary, and that would be sufficient to vitiate that choice (it can no longer be accounted as a choice proper). And, to add another layer of difficulty, consider the converse situation, in which a choice someone makes could be voluntary but not rational. Here it is tricky to determine when that is the case, or even *if* that is possible. For if the choice in question is not rational—the agent making the choice may be incoherent or may be making the choice on the basis of patently false beliefs—then we cannot exactly say what that person wants.

[74] It is worth underscoring here the point that this hybrid conception of coercion is only concerned with the passive side of coercion (with the fact of someone being coerced to do something, without considering by whom or what). For, as we can appreciate from Nozick's (1999) analysis, it is much more difficult to work out a formal conception of the "active" side of coercion (the side of the doer). In saying that A forced B to Φ, it seems that we are already taking it for granted that A bears some kind of responsibility for whatever Φ is. Our use of the concept of coercion would therefore seem to often be morally charged, and even a moralized conception is problematic (as we saw in Chap. 2, §2, n. 15, with the case of the person who is about to drown). In turn, we can distinguish two subjective (formal) conceptions of coercion—moderate ones and extreme ones—where a conception is moderate if we only consider to be relevant the wishes the agent considers that way (as ones that matter), and that agent satisfies certain requisites of agency (such as being rational and coherent).

objective requisite, we can use it to determine or make explicit, where necessary, whether the coercive pressure is *sufficient* to vitiate or invalidate any consent given to the action in question, and so whether (a) the coercive pressure is *unacceptable*—as in the case of Steve Steelworker, who resorts to working back-to-back twelve-hour shifts, without overtime, so as to pay for his son's heart transplant—or whether (b) the coercive pressure is instead *acceptable*, and so does *not* invalidate the consent, as in the case of Don Donor, who of his own accord decides to sell an organ to the national health service, under a purposely designed incentive programme, so as to save money for a future purchase, of a holiday cottage in Tuscany. This objective test for assessing the acceptability of coercive pressure depends on a conception of basic rights, and specifically, as I see it, on an egalitarian conception of rights.

The second observation is that from the foregoing remarks it follows as a corollary that the concept of sufficient coercive pressure depends on the concept of autonomy: once we define the former, we have also in part defined the latter. And in view of that fact it seems important to start out from a conception of autonomy at once liberal and egalitarian, one that (as we will see in Chap. 5) will help us work through some of the cases typically regarded as "hard" for an antipaternalistic theory to solve, as would be the case with someone who—rationally, stably over time, and with an informed understanding of all relevant facts—should give their consent to entering into a voluntary slavery contract or into a contract to waive their right to health.

Indeed, on an egalitarian antipaternalistic conception, if Rick Rightsholder should waive some of his basic rights (such as his right to life, liberty, or health) or agree to a significantly reduced enjoyment of them, or if he should "sell" those rights, to a third party, that would amount to unjust coercive pressure just in case the state, contrary to what it is bound to do, failed to guarantee for him an effective protection of all his other basic rights, such as his right to housing, to unemployment benefits or to benefits for people with disabilities, or to healthcare services for which he is eligible.[75]

As we will see in Chap. 5, once these basic rights are genuinely protected—that is, once we can rule out the prospect of Hapless Harry selling himself into slavery

[75] On liberal egalitarian conceptions, see Rawls (1971), chaps. 2ff., and Dworkin (2000), chaps. 1–3. Although I do not believe in the veil of ignorance procedure, which leads to unresolvable ethical dilemmas and is hypothetical in nature, nor in the Rawlsian principle of difference, because the latter may imply a significant increase in progressive income taxation, confiscatory taxation, as well as an increase in tax evasion and avoidance. Nor do I share Dworkin's belief that people are partially free to decide what to do, to choose the options they prefer, and therefore responsible, in this sense, for the economic risks taken., as in the case of libertarian free will; thus, I do not believe in compensatory justice solely for those events that, according to Dworkin, go beyond human control, such as disability and illness.

More complex would be the case in which Rick Rightsholder should waive some of his basic rights (such as his right to life, liberty, or bodily integrity) or agree to a significantly reduced enjoyment of them, or should "sell" those rights, in a context where neither the constitution nor any established case law offers protection of other basic rights (such as the right to health, to a pension, or to unemployment benefits). Should Rick, in this case, be permitted to make such a choice to cause or risk causing harm to himself? On this question, see Chap. 2, §3, n. 33.

so as to spare his family from a fate of misery or violence, once we can say that no other forms of psychological or epistemic violence are at play, and that consent is given rationally—voluntary slavery will come out looking like a theoretical proposition, a purely theoretical case,[76] in effect an inexistent practice,[77] so much so that, as Feinberg[78] argues, antipaternalism is perfectly consistent with a legal prohibition on voluntary slavery contracts. For if basic rights are protected, and there is no irrationality or any mental disorder at play, the likelihood that someone should sell themselves into slavery is so low (there may even be none) that the administrative procedure needed to validate the consent of the eccentric agent willing to go into slavery (making sure the agent is rational and sufficiently uncoerced) would carry costs for the community that far outweigh the potential advantage sought, namely, guaranteeing for the exceedingly rare and eccentric agent the ability to go into slavery in exchange for payment—and even then it wouldn't be possible for the procedure to fully eliminate the risk of abuse or error.

It was noted earlier, in putting forward a notion of uncoerced consent (or consent sufficiently free of coercive pressure), that behind this notion is a moral-political conception at once liberal and egalitarian, and as I am suggesting, it is on the basis of such a conception that we should determine exactly how many resources need to be allocated across the community to make its members free and equal, or to determine *how* free they need to be from the constraints of the natural and social lottery and the way the capitalist market distributes resources. In view of that rationale, we can see that the need for a corrective reallocation of resources in fact rests on *antipaternalistic* grounds, not only because its aim is to get to a point where individuals, as free and equal members of a community, can fully enjoy their autonomy, but also because we take it as a presupposition that certain circumstances that individuals find themselves in are the *harmful effects* of a free-market system that distributes resources inequitably (as would be the case with a mother who is poor and uneducated and resorts to prostitution or to selling a kidney in order to feed the family or to pay for a heart transplant which her child badly needs). It is clear, however, that according to a reasonable liberal-egalitarian conception people cannot be totally free and equal, that is, have the same resources and opportunities in a capitalist market or the socio-economic resources that give maximum benefit to the most disadvantaged, that is, an income at T1 higher than they would have had if national wealth had been divided equally at T0, as in Rawls's conception.

---

[76] The idea of a "purely theoretical case" (in connection with slavery contracts), as well as other hard cases (such as selling one's rights), will be discussed in greater detail in Chap. 5.

[77] Contrary to what I am arguing, Gerald Dworkin claims that there is no convincing reason why someone who should want to "legally" sell themselves into slavery should do so in a way that is irrational or less than voluntary. In reality, what Dworkin lists as factors that would make some0ne's actions nonvoluntary are psychological or cognitive factors such as the agent being distracted, misinformed, impulsive, weak-willed, or self-destructive (Dworkin 1983b, pp. 108–109), showing that he is not contemplating a scenario in which coercion, in some forms, is enabled by a lack of protection of basic rights such as the right to health, to education, or to unemployment insurance. Nothing in Dworkin's argument, therefore, does anything to undermine the thesis here defended.

[78] Feinberg (1986), p. 71ff.

The third observation is that in discussing the concepts of physical coercion, psychological coercion, and epistemic violence, I found it was sufficient to only look at some of the clear-cut, *paradigmatic* cases illustrating how those concepts are to be understood here. As noted earlier, it won't be necessary to analyse all the borderline cases that may or may not fit the description of psychological coercion, for example. It is important to emphasize, however, what surely should not constitute a "coercive pressure", liable to vitiate the individual's consent.

3.4.3 The "Affective" Pressures and the European Court of Human Rights

As was also noted in discussing the slippery slope argument, the decisions we make in our lives, and our lives themselves, often depend on the decisions, behaviour, attitudes, and feelings of others. If I love Laura and the feeling is not mutual, this unrequited love may very well cause me to be unhappy, insecure, and even irreparably distraught. There are countless sources of influence that we can be subject to in virtue of the way others behave toward us, ranging from the aggressive and hostile to the kind and loving, and these are things we cannot control, except on some occasions and then only in part. This consideration ties in with the liberal conception, essential to which is the idea that, while we have a right not to have our lives controlled by others (so long as we do not cause harm to them), we do not have a right not to fall under their influence and not to feel psychological or "affective" pressures from them (so long as these pressures are not sufficiently coercive), just as we do not have a right to be loved. In fact that would be absurd: if I am in love with Laura and Laura doesn't love me back, her lack of interest in me, even if she snubs me, doesn't rise to the level of coercive pressure, much less a coercive pressure that could legally invalidate a decision I might make to commit assisted suicide as a result of her rebuff. I cannot obligate her to love me, nor (again) do I have a right to be loved by her. At the same time, while she has the right to reject me, that doesn't give her a right to prevent me from committing assisted suicide as a result of that rejection, nor could any such putative right be grounded in any sense she might have that she shouldn't be made to feel guilty if I should commit suicide as a result of that same rejection.

Everyone has a right to influence others, to exercise emotional or "affective pressure" of the kind just described, whether the pressure is exercised wittingly or otherwise, and, needless to say, so long as the pressure is not abusive, translating into harassment, stalking, intimidation, invasion of privacy, breach of confidentiality, assault and battery, and the like. Likewise, if someone is gay and wants to commit assisted suicide because he is rejected by his parents on account of that fact—and if he meets other conditions, such as being a sufficiently rational adult, without any disease, and being at least twenty-three years old—his parents do not have a right to prevent him from acting on his suicidal intentions, nor do they have a right to prevent him from being gay. At the same time, however, he does not have a right not to be emotionally rejected by his parents (or by any siblings he may have). This is the fate that befalls the protagonist, a character with Down syndrome, in the 1996 movie *Le Huitième Jour*, directed by Jaco Van Dormael.

As we will see, if we are to protect individual autonomy, we also have to recognize the right of individuals not to be left to fend for themselves when in need. As resources allow, for example, individuals have a right to medical care, including any psychological and pharmacological therapy needed to deal with emotional distress, and to get support from organizations that fight discrimination (if they are facing discrimination on account of their sexual orientation) or from organizations that help victims of domestic abuse (if they are women in that situation), and the like. But that does not mean that we have a right to be happy or a right not to be subject to "affective pressure" (so long as it is not abusive in the sense specified a moment ago), nor does it mean that this pressure invalidates any consent given to its being exercised.

Let us run through some examples of putative coercion that, on this conception, do not actually qualify as coercion (bearing in mind that all of the examples are best viewed against the background of a liberal legal system in the West). One of them was discussed in Chap. 2, Sect. 2.3: if Lustful Lou, who is engaged to Committed Chloe, and they live with their parents, tells her that he will leave her if she refuses to have sex with him, and in response she agrees to have sex, there is no sexual violence or forcible sex involved. Or, consider: A and B are best friends and A says to B that he will no longer speak to B unless B lends him 10,000 euros. B agrees to do so but there is no extorsion, because B does not have a right to A's friendship (indeed nobody has a right to anybody's friendship), and A's pressure is therefore not coercive. The same goes for a woman who should decide to have an abortion because the father of the child has abandoned her: here, too, there is no invalidation of her decision on that ground alone. So, too, if a woman tells her husband that unless he buys her a house on Lake Como that she very much likes, she will sue for divorce and leave the conjugal home, considering that he makes enough money to support himself, and he agrees to buy the house, the property deed will be deemed valid (not vitiated by the circumstances under which it was obtained). The last, and most important example, I'd like to turn to is that of euthanasia. Consider a cancer patient with a prognosis of six months to live. If he is *affectively* abandoned by his family, who tell him that they don't care about him and are only waiting for him to die, and he consents to being euthanized, his consent will not be invalidated, for that would lead to some paradoxical circumstances, and he would suffer a double harm: not only has he been deprived of his family's emotional support, but he would also be denied the ability to carry out his decision, not to mention that he may even have changed his will in view of that decision. His right to receive euthanasia would be made contingent on whatever feelings his family may harbour toward him—which would be arbitrary and absurd. A similar argument, similarly arbitrary, was made by the European Court of Human Rights in *Pretty v. the United Kingdom*, holding that we cannot afford a situation in which anyone may request euthanasia just because they feel guilty, a "burden to others,"[79] and in particular to their family for the time and effort the family would have to devote to their care. But feeling like a burden is something that happens to us precisely when we do not get the material and emotional support we need from family and friends, and there is nothing we can do about that except turn elsewhere for financial and psychological support. We cannot obligate anyone to be loving and caring toward us: that would be an unreasonable and unenforceable claim, no matter how heartless the individuals who are asked to be that way. So, to underscore: if we deny someone the ability to request euthanasia just because they are making that decision in order not to feel guilty or a burden toward their caregivers, that would amount to harming them twice (which is unacceptable), while making it so that a basic right they enjoy is contingent on whatever others might decide who have no interest in their well-being.

3.4.4 Stably Held Wishes

It is not just the flesh that is weak. The spirit is, too. Some authors hold to the view that human nature is frail and pliant: even if our wishes are not strictly irrational or incoherent, we will quickly change them depending on what others are saying and on whatever the circumstances are at any given moment. What we wish for today, with all of our heart and mind, we may very well not wish for tomorrow. And even if there are things we cherish and value over others—love, life, and health over wine, tobacco, and the earthly pleasures—there are times when we cannot muster the willpower needed to tame the passions and live up to the values we hold dear. According to the same authors, even if we are not irrational in forming our wishes, we form them under the conditioning of a whole range of psychological and environmental factors, and that conditioning makes them ever unstable, changeful, uncertain, and makes our decisions difficult, if not tragic, owing to our inability to choose among alternatives we judge to be equally valid. As H. L. A. Hart was early to critically point out, when John Stuart Mill set out his harm principle, defending the thesis that we ought to "limit legal coercion to the class of actions which harm others",[80] he was thinking of "a normal human being" endowed "with too much of the psychology of a middle-aged man whose desires are relatively fixed, not liable to be artificially stimulated by external influences; who knows what he wants and what gives him satisfaction or happiness; and who pursues these things when he can".[81] He was thinking, in other words, of a stylized human being far removed from the people we meet in real life, from real people in flesh and blood.

Now, I would submit that, in normal conditions, rational human beings are much less frail and unstable than what some authors would have us believe. Even so, I

[79] *Pretty v. the United Kingdom*, no. 2346/02, § 29, ECHR 2002-III.

[80] Hart (1963), p. 5.

[81] ibid., p. 33.

would ask: Should the (relative) suggestibility and frailty of human beings be factored into a decision-making procedure that we want to justify on an antipaternalistic basis? And *can* we even do that? Here, too, I would suggest that the answer to both of those questions is yes. What I am positing, in other words, is that if someone intends to carry out actions that are irreversibly harmful or dangerous to themselves, and they want to do so without hindrance, that intention should be expressed in a way that is not only rational and uncoerced—in a condition of rationality and full mental capacity, and in circumstances of sufficient freedom from coercive pressure—but also stable: the wishes being expressed need to be "durable," rather than being liable to change on a moment's notice. And this is a condition that needs to be in place in order to make sure that when someone makes a decision with irreversible consequences, they are not doing so on a whim or under conditions of uncertainty, weakness of will, or emotional instability. It is only because there is no going back on such decisions that some checks need to be in place—and, importantly as well, these are not restrictions on what can be done but safety checks to ensure that what is decided on is not something one may come to regret. On this reasoning, it may even be justified to require "time out for reflection," or "cooling off periods," before taking actions that are irreversibly harmful or dangerous to life and limb, as when requesting euthanasia or deciding to do heroin.[82] For example, in conducting an evaluation interview with a patient who is gravely (but not terminally) ill, with an incurable disease or a chronic, serious, and disabling disease, or is severely disabled, and who is suffering physically or psychologically, and is requesting euthanasia, a doctor could request that the patient take two weeks to think through that decision just in case it may have been made hastily, as established by the law on euthanasia as in Spain in 2021. Young[83] insists that the suffering can also be only psychological, for example because the patient, "as a direct result of the illness, [...], only has available a life that is unacceptably burdensome (e.g., because the illness has to be treated in ways that lead to her being unacceptably dependent on others or on technological means of life support. [...]. In The Netherlands, for example, pain has been found to be a less significant reason for requesting assistance with dying than other forms of suffering like frustration over loss of independence".[84]

---

[82]Arguments to that effect can be found in Cadoppi (2008), p. 114ff.; Dworkin (1983a), p. 32; Young, section 2., (2022) (who speaks of an enduring, voluntary and competent wish to die), Feinberg (1986), p. 113ff.; and Von Hirsch and Neumann (2010), quoted and discussed in Cadoppi (2008), p. 3ff. As Cadoppi underscores, "when a choice is that dramatic (when it is a choice to die), the person contemplating it ought to be given enough time to reconsider it; no such opportunity would be available if the choice were to be made effective immediately, and such immediate killing would therefore have to qualify as criminal" (ibid., my translation).

[83]Cf. Young (2022), para 2.

[84]See e.g. Marquet et al. (2003); Onwuteaka et al. (2012); Emanuel et al. (2016).

A solution consistent with an antipaternalistic outlook is available as well for the problem of weakness of will. In cases where weakness of will is not so damaging as to make idle our capacity for rational and voluntary action (as so often happens in real life) but is still consistent with that capacity—it is simply the case, in other words, that our wishes are not sufficiently structured, and we don't feel we have the fortitude we need in order not to give in to certain temptations—there are legal solutions that can be relied on to protect us (up to a point) from the risk of doing some acts that we would not do if we were sufficiently rational or were acting in a way that we judge to be wise. There is an analogy here to the Ulysses pact discussed in Chap. 2, Sect. 2.4: cognizant of the magical power of the sirens' song, Ulysses (voluntarily) decided to have himself tied to the mast of his ship so that he could listen to the song without being raptured by it. In the same way, some people can voluntarily choose a driver's license that requires motorcyclists to wear a helmet while riding and drivers to wear seatbelts while driving, or we could (voluntarily) choose to take out a private health-insurance policy that restricts the activities we can do (such as using hard drugs).[85] In the same way, a law could be passed allowing people to buy heroin or cocaine in designated places (such as a pharmacy) and to use them in certain places, such as private clubs and homes, or public bathrooms, if they have applied for a special health card which they can obtain on condition that they sit through an interview in which a healthcare professional makes sure they understand the risks of using these hard drugs. This card could be valid for ten years.

[85] The literature on the question of weakness of will is too vast to be captured in any single snapshot. But see Maniaci (2008), p. 121ff.; Schiavello (2010), p. 35ff.; and Searle (2001). Similarly, as I am arguing, the law could by default (a) obligate motorists to wear a helmet or seatbelts while driving a motorcycle or driving a car, or (b) prohibit the consumption of hard drugs, unless the individuals concerned—having gone through a procedure designed to ensure that his will is rational, uncoerced, etc.—choose to opt out., In other words we could envision an (equally antipaternalistic) opt-out program enabling motorcyclists and drivers to choose a motorcycle or driver's licence that does not require them to wear a helmet or a seatbelt while riding or driving. To stick with the Ulysses-pact metaphor, this would be like allowing people to "untie" or unbind themselves from that requirement, so long as (a) the consent they give in choosing that scheme satisfies all the requisites of rationality; (b) they keep a health-insurance policy covering at least some of the costs of the medical care they would have to receive to treat any injuries they might sustain in the event of an accident, so that those costs (including disability compensation) are not externalized to the public at large; and (c) they qualify as "safe" motorcyclists and drivers. This last condition could be met by requiring them to have a clean driver's record (e.g., no tickets for serious moving violations for at least five years prior to applying for the special licence, as well as no significant accidents throughout that time, and high scores on the driving test), thus minimizing the risk of their causing harm to others (e.g., psychological trauma or post-traumatic stress disorder that motorcyclists or drivers may suffer when involved in an accident in which a motorcyclist or driver who was riding without a helmet or driving without seatbelt is seriously injured or even killed; that kind of psychological harm can be avoided with a law under which a driver or motorcyclist can be punished for homicide only if the harm caused to a motorcyclist without a helmet is inflicted with gross negligence or with the intent to harm). On this point see Dworkin (1983b), pp. 109–110, and Alemany (2006), p. 268ff.

3.4.5 *The Right to Be Let Alone and Not Be Left to Fend for Oneself*

We have so far been concerned to highlight the way that central to an antipaternalistic conception are criteria of consent requiring basic rationality or mental capacity, stably held wishes, and sufficient freedom from coercive pressure. But this is really a minimum baseline, and we also saw that agents need to be informed of the facts that are relevant to the courses of action they are contemplating: they need to be specifically "knowledgeable" about such action.[86] What does that mean? A great many of the cases that Garzón Valdés and Feinberg discuss involve insufficient rationality or voluntariness understood in light of a theory of formal and bounded rationality, as when individuals act compulsively, or on the basis of patently false beliefs, or under the influence of drugs or alcohol, or when they suffer from serious mental disorders.[87]

However, it may happen that we are sufficiently rational in our action and yet are unaware of some of the relevant facts. Our knowledgeableness, in other words, is limited, perhaps because our upbringing was constrained or our schooling and education inadequate, or we may have little or no access to the information needed to make a thoughtful decision, or we may have the information at hand but are unwilling to make use of the resources needed to obtain the information, choosing instead to use the same resources in pursuit of another aim, while also devoting other resources to that aim (including time, money, and the powers of the intellect). The question, then, is: How is it that in these cases it may be justified for the state to interfere in our decision-making by ascertaining that when someone wants to carry out an act harmful to themselves (such as assisted suicide) or an act that risks causing such harm, they are doing so on the basis of an adequate understanding of the relevant facts? Is it really the case that the beliefs we act on need to always have a basis in science—that they need to be consistent with scientific consensus, or what the majority of the scientific community holds to be true—even if our circumstances are such that we *cannot* devote the resources needed to acquaint ourselves with that body of knowledge, and even if we are *unwilling* to do so? If Misconceived Matt believes, falsely, that getting into a car accident at 50 kilometres an hour without a

[86] It is important to underscore that these four criteria—basic rationality or mental capacity, knowledge of the relevant facts, stability of intent, and freedom from coercion—need to be assessed contextually, and what they require as standards of consent may therefore vary accordingly. Feinberg (1986, p. 115ff.) quite reasonably argues that such standards need to be assessed on the basis of two sliding scales: (1) the more is at stake—that is, the greater the value of the good in question (be it life, bodily integrity, or what have you), or the greater the risk of damaging that good, and the greater the gravity of the relative decision or action—the higher the standard needs to be for valid consent; and (2) the more the decision or action is irreversible—that is, the likelier it is that the damage done cannot be undone—the higher that same standard needs to be. In short, the more the harm is serious or the decision irreversible, the more must the consent be informed, uncoerced, and so on.

[87] See Garzón Valdés (1988), p. 166.

wearing seatbelt will not cause significant injury to him, or that the withdrawal symptoms from heroin last no more than a couple of days, why should we be concerned about such matters from an antipaternalistic standpoint.

The reason why that is the case, it could be argued, is that if Matt knew that heroin withdrawal symptoms can cause severe pain in its acute phase and can last several days thereafter[88] he might rethink his heroin consumption and come to view it as contrary to *his own* best interest—contrary, that is, not to what *others* (and in particular the state and its officials) think is in his best interest, but to what he *himself*, if knowledgeable about the science, would think is in his best interest. But even then, we might ask: Why should we take account of what Matt would *counterfactually* consider to be in his best interest if he were informed of all the relevant facts, rather than simply going by what he wants to do before being so informed, or regardless of the information or notions he is operating on? Would this in fact amount to interfering in people's freedom of choice? Or is this about protecting individuals from making choices that, being based on false beliefs and the like, are not truly their *own* choices or are not sufficiently voluntary, as some would argue? This is what I am arguing, too, but the argument amounts to endorsing a form of "antipaternalistic interference," so we need to distinguish this kind of interference from the standard, *paternalistic* kind. And the distinctions are essentially three.

(1) Antipaternalistic interference in the freedom of others is *limited*, and that for three reasons. First, in technologically advanced and culturally open societies like those in the West, it is more likely than not that the information that can be obtained relating to matters of public interest is scientifically grounded and readily available. For example, it won't be difficult for the regular guy in the street, even someone who might be illiterate, to find out and understand that smoking is bad for your health (though it would concededly be more difficult, even for someone with an education, to find out what the likelihood is of getting cancer given a certain amount of cigarettes smoked).

Second, and relatedly, it won't take much time to inform somebody of relevant facts they might previously been unaware of, such as the fact that heroin is addictive.

And third, as discussed in Sects. 3.4.2 and 3.4.3, there are reasons why, strictly within antipaternalistic bounds, a procedure needs to be in place to make sure that when someone is contemplating actions that will do severe harm to them (putting their life and limb at risk, or even ending their life), the consent they give to such courses of action is not owed to their being irrational or lacking mental capacity (as would be the case if they suffered from serious mental disorders, whether permanent or temporary, or if they were under the influence of drugs or alcohol or had advanced dementia or a serious mental disability), nor is it owed to their being under some form of coercion. And, as discussed, there are two arguments for such a procedure, something like an evaluation interview with a psychiatrist or other medical professional to make sure that when someone intends to do an act that causes serious or even irreparable harm to them (as in the case of suicide), they are not affected

[88] See Husak (2000), p. 70ff.

by any serious mental disorder (e.g., schizophrenia or something that may cause hallucination, delirium, or other dysfunction). The first argument is that such a procedure would have to be much more thorough than one needed to establish consent with individuals who are not so affected or where the stakes are not so high, e.g. the procedure would have to be more complex for individuals affected by schizophrenia. The second argument is that if we were to conduct a survey across the population, coupled with a statistical probability analysis, asking people whether they would want society as a whole to prevent them from carrying out serious and irreversibly harmful actions (such as committing suicide, engaging in self-mutilation, or putting their life at risk), either under serious threat from somebody else or while in a state of temporary mental incapacity (they might be having a serious bout of depression or acting under the influence of drugs or alcohol, or they might be in a state of shock or hypnosis), my guess is that a good percentage of them *would* in fact say they want to be relieved of the threat or be prevented from so acting. And that means that a procedure needs to be in place to ascertain that individuals in situations of that sort are not acting irrationally or involuntarily. If that is correct, then it is clear, even inevitable, I daresay, that the same evaluation interview with a medical professional will lead whoever is being interviewed to be clearer about their intention—deciding to carry it out with even greater resolve or otherwise deciding to desist from it—in light of a correct and scientifically grounded understanding of the relevant facts, and will be able to achieve such greater clarity without much expenditure of time.

(2) An antipaternalistic restriction on an individual's freedom of action would be *procedural*, rather than substantive: it would not restrict the range of anyone's basic desires and ultimate goals—the plan of life they have chosen for themselves—but would only constrain the *way* these goals and desires are formed, or rather, the way in which the agent should *assess* them, in a proper setting and without rushing to any decision to act on those desires and pursue those goals. The point, in other words, is not to make it impossible for someone to pursue their plan of life—even if reckless, hedonistic, masochistic, or what have you—but rather to have them wait before they *act on* it: this would in effect be a *cooling-off period*, a "waiting period," but it would crucially make it possible to assess whether the plan or the intention expressed to carry it out is rational, based on a correct understanding of the relevant facts, and stable, over time, and uncoerced. And once the "safety" procedure is completed, the individuals concerned will be free to choose what to do, whether it be to carry on with their plan of life or consider another such plan, or even to carry into execution a plan to *end* their life. Paternalism, by contrast, comes in with its own plan or conception of life, a model which it imposes on everyone, and which some may espouse but which others wouldn't choose for themselves even if they had all the time and knowledge in the world.

Now, crucially, if that reasoning correct, and we want stay true to an antipaternalistic conception, a safety procedure of the kind discussed cannot be overly drawn out or unreasonably burdensome or demanding on the person being evaluated. For while we do want to make sure that when someone intends to carry out an act which does significant harm to them or puts them at great risk, their intention to do so is (*i*) rational, (*ii*) based on a knowledge of the relevant facts, (*iii*) stable over time, and (*iv*) formed in a way that is sufficiently free of coercive pressure, we also, and more importantly, want to ultimately protect their individual autonomy: this means protecting their right to follow their own plan of life, which in turn means protecting their *right to be let alone*. This is a negative right to liberty and is one of two pillars of the antipaternalistic and egalitarian conception here defended, the other being the right not to be left to fend for oneself or not be left to one's own devices: this means protecting individuals from any self-harming acts they may carry out when insufficiently rational or significantly unknowledgeable or ill-informed (unaware of some key facts through no fault of their own), but it also means protecting some basic rights, such as the right to life and health.

(3) This takes us to a very important justification for the safety procedure being discussed, and it relates to the right not to be left to fend for oneself or not be left to one's own devices, with its corollary, namely, the need to protect some basic rights of the individual. One circumstance in which this idea applies is that of individuals who are ignorant of the relevant facts but cannot reasonably be held responsible for that lack of knowledge, in which case there is an argument to be made for limiting their freedom, but only within antipaternalistic bounds, that is, only to enable them to gain the knowledge needed to make an informed decision. This is the kind of circumstance that someone could find themselves in if, for example, they were poorly educated or even functionally illiterate, such that they may not even be aware of the science pertaining to the question at hand (such as the science highlighting the relation between cocaine abuse and bouts of paranoia), or if they were set in a pervasive social environment that exposes them to systematic misinformation or even disinformation, or again if they were so burdened with various sorts of problems (having do to with their finances, their health, or their family and relationships) that they couldn't reasonably be expected to take the time to study up on the issue in question. It is thus possible for someone to be "unwilfully unknowledgeable" or "uninformed by virtue of circumstance": they lack the relevant knowledge, but not because they have in any way "chosen" to be uninformed. For this reason they cannot be held blameworthy for their unawareness—in fact, if they only could, they *would* want to have an adequate understanding of the relevant facts and science—in which case there are good reasons to doubt that they are in fact limited in their capacity to form rational intentions. It is in other words possible, or even likely, that if people could know what the consequences are of their "second-order unknowledge"—that is, their not knowing that they do not know some relevant facts the scientific community considers to be true, on the basis of experimental findings the average person is unaware of—they would want to be shielded from that second-order lack of knowledge. These remarks are very much in line with the idea that, as we saw in Sects. 3.4.2, human rationality is properly understood as a bounded rationality rather than an optimal or ideal one. No one reasons like a computer or behaves or makes decisions in keeping with the dictates of the classic theories of rational choice aimed at maximizing utility or preferences. An antipaternalistic theory needs to take people as they are, as they actually reason, rather than as they should *ideally* reason as per the rational choice theory traditionally espoused in economics.

As I will expand on in Chap. 4, there is ample empirical evidence from cognitive psychology showing that even when people, in their bounded rationality, adopt rational and simplified strategies for lowering the costs of making complex decisions, they will fall prey to cognitive biases that lead them to underestimate or altogether discount important facts and make significant errors of judgment. In numerous experiments (Kahneman 2011), for example, it has been shown that people with no background in probability theory tend to misjudge the likelihood of a certain event taking place. This is referred to as statistical illiteracy. In particular, it has been observed in psychology that many errors can be avoided simply by reframing the problem. Thus, depending on how a problem is numerically set up or framed, it can either hinder or facilitate people in making probability judgments. One way to help people in this task and reduce error rates, according to some studies (Kahneman 2011) is to frame statistical problems as natural frequencies, e.g. ratios using natural numbers (e.g., "a one-in-a-thousand chance") rather than stating the equivalent percentage expressed in probabilities, like numerals and decimal points (0.1%).

From the foregoing it emerges even more clearly how important it is to have a *supporting procedure* for making decisions, whether the decision is about having euthanasia, removing a brain tumour, using cocaine, having nasal reconstruction, or what have you. Such a procedure assumes that we all have some kind of statistical illiteracy or are subject to any range of cognitive biases, and so, before we make a decision of the sort just described (particularly as patients), we would have a doctor and a psychiatrist guide us through it by framing the data in such a way as to make it easier (rather than harder) for us to form a proper understanding of the likelihood of a certain event or side effect happening as a result of going through with the decision.

But the right not to be left to fend for oneself entails much more than that: it also entails a need to help people who are economically or socially disadvantaged by ensuring that they have a greater range of opportunities than their currently unfavourable circumstances allow. Suppose, for example, that a factory worker has been laid off and, having failed to find new employment and having seemingly exhausted all other options, is now contemplating suicide. In such a case, the right not to be left to fend for oneself would mean that this laid-off worker would be made aware that there is an unemployment insurance programme he or she may qualify for. Or suppose that we have two parents with joint custody over their child, but one of them is successfully manipulating the law to prevent the other one from seeing the child, causing great distress to the parent so outmanoeuvred: here, under this right, the distraught parent would be informed that there *is* help out there, perhaps in the form of a legal aid society with a dedicated unit that will represent him or her pro bono. Similarly, the same right would mean that when someone is diagnosed with a terminal illness, they would be informed of any palliative care they are entitled to receive, or it would mean informing a heartbroken widower that he has access to a new psychotropic drug that may safely replace the heroin he is currently using to cope with the loss of his loved one. In all of these cases we are empowering people in need by making them more knowledgeable about their options, thereby expanding the range of opportunities available to them, while making it clear to them that they have the final say in making a decision about the problem they are facing: if they ultimately decide that they are going to commit assisted suicide or keep using heroin, so be it. To be sure, a scheme of this kind would indeed restrict some people's freedom of action—by taking time away from them and requiring them to sit down for counselling or guidance even if they know from the start that they aren't interested in the options that will be presented to them (they are not interested in any new drug that may safely and effectively replace the heroin they are currently consuming, nor are they interested in any pro bono legal services, and so on)—but the burden placed on them would be limited: it would be limited to the time needed to gain a full picture of all the risks involved in choosing a certain course of action, while being informed of all of the other options that are available. And the net effect would on balance be positive, since for every individual who doesn't want to know about any of the potential downsides of choosing Φ or about what other options there may be or what rights can be exercised, or who is already aware of these rights and options but doesn't want to make use of them, there will be at least another individual who *will* be interested in being so informed. This may expand the good that is available to all those in this latter group, while enabling them to avoid any harm they stand to suffer—and if harm avoidance coupled with choice is the point, that is at bottom what antipaternalism is about.

And yet, with all of that said, we still haven't definitively solved the problem at hand. For even if the process here defended is merely procedural, and even if it may in part be aimed at expanding the opportunities available to individuals and empowering them to exercise some basic rights they may otherwise be unable to exercise, there is no way to get around the fact that this is in fact an interference—requiring individuals to undergo an assessment to make sure they understand the consequences of the course of action they intend to pursue and the attendant risks, and requiring them as well to take some time out if it is determined that they are rushing into a decision—and it may well be that some do not want any of that help and guidance. So the question arises: isn't this interference, limiting an individual's freedom of choice, however much only procedurally so, ultimately a form of paternalism masquerading as "benevolent antipaternalism"? Or is this about protecting individuals from choices that, being based on false beliefs or faulty reasoning, are not truly their own or are not sufficiently voluntary, as some would argue? The problem, more to the point, is whether the wishes one expresses hastily, or without considering some key pieces of information that ought to be taken into account, are to be regarded as *ipso facto* nonvoluntarily expressed or as different from one's "real" preferences (from what one "genuinely" desires), as Feinberg argues along with other authors who can be placed in the antipaternalistic camp (such as Rosemary Carter and John Hodson) or again whether Feinberg's model, as Diciotti argues,[89] uses autonomy and voluntariness as a cover for what is actually a significant limitation on the freedom of others, a limitation based on an objective concept of

[89] Cf Diciotti (1986), p. 584ff.

well-being hiding beneath the surface or on an equally concealed or undeclared utilitarian and consequentialist conception.[90]

The answer to this question, as I see it, probably falls somewhere between Feinberg's conception and the one defended by Diciotti. Which is to say that both Feinberg and Diciotti have captured some of the truth, but not all of it, and so are both partly wrong. The part that I think Feinberg gets right is that a wish, desire, or preference that is not formed rationally can be very different from what the agent authentically or genuinely wants. As we saw, if someone has a patently false belief and then realizes that this belief is indeed false, that realization may lead them to change their behaviour in a significant way. For example, they might have had a habit of smoking which they quit upon realizing that, contrary to what they previously believed to the case, smoking tobacco is actually *unhealthy*. But the only way in which we can say that someone with an unhealthy habit didn't really want to have that habit is if we assume that they fundamentally wanted to live the longest and healthiest life possible, even *before* quitting the bad habit. And we do have to make that assumption. This takes us to the least convincing aspect of Feinberg's conception, for it suggests that a wish, preference, or intention formed over a couple of weeks of thinking about it can be less real or authentic than a wish, preference, or intention formed over the course of two months of thinking about it.

If the foregoing is correct, then there are genuinely antipaternalistic reasons for limiting the freedom of individuals through a brief procedure aimed at making sure that when someone is intent on doing something that will cause significant harm to them (putting their life or bodily integrity at risk), they have not formed that intention irrationally or while lacking mental capacity (owing, for example, to dementia or a mental disorder), or under the influence of drugs, or on the basis of patently false beliefs, or under coercion. So, if on the one hand a procedure so conceived takes some degree of freedom away from people, albeit temporarily and unintrusively, on the other hand it does so to achieve precisely the opposite effect, namely, to protect their basic rights and widen the spectrum of the opportunities available to them, and in particular the opportunity to exercise basic rights which they may not be aware of and yet do enjoy, which in turn strengthens their autonomy, getting them to potentially rethink some of the reasons and beliefs that may be responsible for a wish they may have formed to carry out acts that are harmful or dangerous to themselves. As noted, this procedure would consist of a session in conversation with a psychiatrist or other medical professional who, without taking too much time away from them, would lay out before them all the relevant facts they need to have in making a decision, so that they have a proper scientific understanding of those facts and why they matter. In this way, with that knowledge in hand, they will be in a position to either solidify their own resolve to go through with that decision (including a decision to carry out an act that is harmful or dangerous to themselves or change their minds about it, and they would be able to do so in a way that is sufficiently free of cognitive biases and of any deception or misconception to which

[90] Cf. Feinberg (1986), pp. 12–13, 98ff.

their social context would expose them, free from ignorance of relevant facts when the agent is not fully responsible for such ignorance. So far we have a genuinely antipaternalistic justification for a procedure through which to determine whether the individuals in question have met the standards requiring them to be rational, sufficiently free of coercive pressure, and correctly informed of the relevant facts. The next question is whether, consistently with an antipaternalistic conception, we can also require individuals to take a cooling-off period (however brief it may be), in addition to having them sit for an interview to see whether they meet the three basic criteria just mentioned (rationality or mental capacity, sufficient lack of coercion, and knowledgeableness) and thus put them in a position where they can enjoy their basic rights.

Indeed, it could be objected that hidden beneath Feinberg's notion of "substantially nonvoluntary" conduct is a perfectionist ideal, under which individuals are to live up to a standard requiring them not to be rash or irresolute in their decision-making. This is a complex question. For one thing, according to our working definition of rationality, it is certainly the case that we cannot describe someone as sufficiently rational if they act impulsively, even if only to some degree, that is, if they have a tendency to act without considering the consequences of their action, or if their decisions are insufficiently certain or their desires insufficiently stable, or if they are too weak-willed. Secondly, these traits are typically associated with a variety of mental and personality disorders, such as anxiety disorders, intermittent explosive disorder (characterized by explosive outbursts of anger and/or violence) and borderline personality disorder. And, for another thing, even if we concede that impulsiveness, uncertainty, irresoluteness, and weakness of will are rational, so long as they are contained within bounds, I would venture to say that many people would want to be protected from themselves if they were to exhibit these traits, because that behaviour would be harmful or dangerous to them. If I am right in making this supposition, then we can also suppose that at least some of the people who so act (impulsively or with incertitude or weakness of will) don't *really* want to do so (they would rather not do so) or that they are deeply conflicted—hence the need to determine whether their desires are stable.

If that is the case, the justification being offered here for the evaluation procedure in question would be antipaternalistic, because in the end it strikes a balance between (1) a more or less significant minority of people who do not accept their own impulsiveness and instability and who, without an evaluation procedure or interview with a medical professional, are prevented from carrying out an irreversibly harmful or dangerous act which (a) puts them at risk of life and limb, and which (b) they may not truly want to carry out, and (2) a small minority of other individuals who do accept their own impulsiveness and instability and are sufficiently rational and unconflicted. The balance is struck through a procedure that imposes a burden on both the former and the latter, but the burden does not unreasonably intrude on anyone's life, and so it is a burden that is justified in an anti-paternalistic way for the former and the latter group, even if people in the latter group do not really want the procedure. For those who are impulsive, irresolute, and weak-willed but wouldn't want to be that way and yet cannot act otherwise, this internal conflict can presumably be taken to mean that they are not sufficiently rational in their action. So, in conclusion, if it is indeed only a small minority of people who would describe themselves as impulsive and weak-willed and yet can rationally accept that fact about them, then we have all the more reason to protect a more or less significant minority of people from potential harm or from irreversibly consequential or dangerous actions that they may not *rationally want* for themselves.

Perhaps another angle from which to view this argument is to take the cooling-off period or the informedness requirement as justified on the basis of a minimal, probabilistic idea of psychophysical well-being. In other words, while being informed of the relevant facts and thinking about the consequences of what we do before we do it may be essential to rational action, neither of these two conditions seems logically necessary, much less sufficient, in securing our psychophysical well-being or happiness, any yet they do seem to make such well-being and happiness more likely than if they are not satisfied: we can at least empirically observe about humans that people who do think before they act, with an understanding of the relevant facts, are more likely (than people who do not) to have the self-knowledge needed to avoid feelings of regret or angst or at least to keep these feelings from overwhelming them. If that is correct, then we are not going to be able to paint antipaternalistic theories as ultimately resting on an objective idea of psychophysical well-being that is smuggled in and hidden from view, an unspoken value (family, prudence, wisdom, or some higher calling) that is nonetheless taken as key to one's happiness or satisfaction. What emerges is rather an antipaternalistic conception predicated on the idea that (a) everyone decides for themselves what gives them happiness, well-being, or fulfilment, but (b) it is much easier to find out what that thing is through a procedure of discovery like the one I am suggesting—which really means taking some time out to understand oneself and the relevant facts—rather than through a procedure of chance like tossing a coin to see how it lands (heads or tails).

3.4.5.1 Four Classes of Individuals

On pain of being overly analytical, we can look at that whole idea in relation to the kinds of individuals it can be said to apply to, and there are at least four such classes of individuals it presumes to exist:

(A) We have individuals we might describe as "adrift and unthoughtful yet happy." They are (*i*) impulsive, irresolute, self-doubting, weak-willed, and superficial, with unstructured desires—such that they will not be inclined to seek out all the relevant facts or that they will easily come to regret their own actions—and yet (*ii*) they are all told rationally contented with that state of affairs.

(B) We have individuals who are "*unhappily* adrift and unthoughtful." They are (*i*) impulsive, irresolute, self-doubting, weak-willed, and superficial, with unstructured desires—such that they will not be inclined to seek out all the relevant facts or that they will easily come to regret their own actions—and (*ii*) this state of affairs makes them rationally *discontented*: they would rather not be the kinds of persons they are.

(C) We then have individuals we might describe as "unawaredly" unknowledgeable and biased." They may be undereducated, and even be unable to read or write, as well as statistically illiterate and cognitively biased. As a result, they are unaware of relevant facts and are unaware of that unawareness, but none of this is through any fault of their own: they cannot reasonably be held responsible for their lack of knowledge or for their cognitive biases.

(D) We finally have individuals who cannot be described as adrift and unthoughtful but are rather resolute and driven. They are not impulsive, irresolute, self-doubting, weak-willed, or superficial, with unstructured desires, but are on the contrary thoughtful, deliberate, self-assured, strong-willed, and disciplined: they know what they want and have a plan to get what they want, and they will carry out that plan.

With that breakdown in hand, we can go back to our "cooling-off," information-giving procedure and see that it could not be described as paternalistic for people in groups B and C: the rash and discontented, and the unknowledgeable and statistically illiterate. Those in these groups who seek authorization for assisted suicide or the consumption of hard drugs, and the like, would be presented with information that may help them overcome their statistical illiteracy and cognitive biases, and they could then revisit their decision in light of that newfound knowledge. The point, in other words, is to protect these individuals as intentional agents, or at least to help them work out any conflicting intentions or desires they may have and protect the one they come to recognise as their true and authentic intention or desire. By contrast, the cooling-off procedure *would* effectively amount to a real interference in personal freedom for people in groups A and D: the rash yet contented, and the resolute and driven. Even so, as I am arguing, it would still be antipaternalistically justified to have these individuals take some supplementary time out to think about their action, in addition to having them "tested" to see whether they meet the three basic criteria of rationality or mental capacity, sufficient lack of coercion, and knowledgeableness. Indeed, not only would this supplementary period be brief, but its point is to make sure that no harm is done to *others* in group B (the rash and discontented) or in group C (the unknowledgeable and statistically illiterate)—the kind of harm they wouldn't want for themselves or which they cannot with any certainty be said to want for themselves.[91]

[91] It might be objected at this point that I have so far been advancing two theses that stand in contradiction to each other. In this Sect. 3.4.5.2, I am claiming that there is a significant minority of people who tend to be "rash and adrift" in their decision-making, at once impulsive and irresolute, as well as superficial, weak-willed and discontented, even if they are competent adults (so we are excluding children, people with mental disorders or dementia, and the like). But in Sect. 3.3, the assumption was made that mentally competent adults with an education are sufficiently rational to engage in practical reasoning without making serious logical errors, including when thinking in the abstract about major moral and political issues (and all the more so if these competent adults are members of a scientifically and technologically advanced society), and it was argued that if we

Then, too, as just noted, the cooling-off safety procedure needs to be brief. Indeed, if the point is to make sure that the decision at issue is not taken rashly, superficially, or incoherently, or ignoring relevant facts, or for lack of fortitude or resolve, it will only take a short period of reflection to achieve that result, or at least to give the individuals concerned an *opportunity* to avoid making any rash or inconsiderate decision. So, for example, if someone has decided that they want to take hard drugs, it would be unreasonably intrusive to require them to spend a month mulling over that decision or to mandate that they submit to a periodic (annual or biannual) review to make sure that their decision is still valid (meeting, for example, the requirements of rationality). For example, for people who want to take hard drugs, it would be fair to require them to take a two-week cooling-off period after the interview with the doctor, during which they are informed of the more serious risks of heroin use and all explained in a leaflet with which they leave the interview. At the same time, there is clearly very little discretion that lawmakers would have to exercise in establishing how long the cooling-off period ought to be or how complex the procedure should be under which to determine whether the individuals

---

make this assumption, then we need to also assume that these individuals' own reasons for action will likewise be logical (not glaringly incoherent) and grounded in fact (there will not be any gaping hole in the facts that ought to be taken into account). Take euthanasia, for example. If we agree that this practice is permissible, there is no logical reason why we should thereby commit to the idea that there are conditions under which killing and torture are likewise permissible: in justifying euthanasia and assisted suicide, the antipaternalistic principle (a principle of individual self-determination) does not in any way logically justify doing serious harm to others or doing anything to them that they have not explicitly requested and consented to. And if we take that as a valid argument, then, we can reasonably assume that mentally competent adults with a capacity for practical reasoning will accept that argument and act accordingly. So the question is, Why is not contradictory to place this stylized, generally rational adult in the same conceptual space as the rash and weak-willed discontented adult whose decision-making *cannot* be assumed to be rational and informed? There are three main reasons we can point to showing why there is no contradiction here. First, it is much more likely for people to be sufficiently rational and coherent when thinking *in the abstract* about moral and political issues they see as fundamental than when thinking in concrete terms about questions which affect their own life and which matter to them personally, inevitably bringing their own experience and sensitivities into play, as happens in areas of life such as work, and with relationships generally. In this personal realm, we need to be self-aware and make sense of our own past (with all of its personal losses, separations, traumas, and narcissistic wounds, along with the errors made by our loved ones), which is a much more difficult enterprise than an exercise in abstract practical thinking. It is much more difficult to accept certain behaviour from family members, for example, or to decide whether to have an abortion or to change gender, than it is to reason about big-picture issues that we can look at from a distance, where we are asked to take a stance on whether it ought to be permissible for an unspecified individual to act thus and so. Second, going back to euthanasia as an example, it is a serious logical error to think that the (antipaternalistic) principle on which basis this practice is justified also entails that, by the same reasoning, we should legalize homicide, rape, and assault and battery, nor can any of these acts (or others that are harmful to others) be justified by saying that the aggressor was rash, superficial, frail, weak-willed, or discontented. That would be utter nonsense, and completely unrelated to the antipaternalistic principle, which is about protecting a person's autonomy—precisely the opposite of what all those violent acts do. And third, there is no reason to think that the people I am describing as rash, irresolute and discontented are a majority of the population: it may well be that they are instead a significant minority.

concerned are rational, aware of the relevant facts, and uncoerced in their decision-making. As I have said, for a patient who is gravely (but not terminally) ill, with an incurable disease or a chronic, serious, and disabling disease, or is severely disabled, and is suffering physically or psychologically, and is requesting euthanasia, a doctor could request that the patient take two weeks to think through that decision just in case it may have been made hastily. This is the requirement as established by the 2021 Spanish law on euthanasia.[92] He is against the idea that a severely disabled patient such as a quadriplegic can request euthanasia. But this condition is too restrictive: see e.g., Varelius (2014). For a patient who is terminally ill, but is not dying, a cooling-off peroiod of one day would be fair. The most difficult case is that of a person who is not physically ill or disabled and who suffers from major depression. Most often this is a reactive depression, a response to a mournful event, the death of a loved one, a dvorce, a layoff. The ontology of depression is uncertain from the perspective of psychiatry. Symptoms of depression are suicidal thoughts, insomnia, poor appetite, severe fatigue, weight loss, irrational negative thoughts about the future. Now, is the agent depressed with suicidal thoughts because he is depressed, or is he depressed with suicidal thoughts because he does not want to live without his wife or children who have died? Normally, reactive depression passes after a few monthsk, especially if treated with psychotherapy and psychotropic drugs. In that case we cannot authorize euthanasia right away: human life and the likelihood of recovery must be protected. A six-month cooling-off period, a period of clinical observation, could be required. If after six months the patient is still depressed, and the drugs are not working, then euthanasia should be authorized because that condition brings a severe form of suffering to the patient.

It would all the more be a violation of individual autonomy if the state were to systematically intervene in people's lives so as to put to a test of sufficient rationality and adequate knowledgeableness every single decision that anyone might make, whatever it might be, such as entering into an employment contract, moving in with a partner, having children, or buying a house, or indeed making any major purpose. This should be fairly intuitive, to be sure, but there are specifically two reasons why any such systematic interference would be in violation of individual autonomy. The first one is that the massive bureaucracy that would have to be set up to systematically assess every decision that anyone might make would require them to devote to the effort to answer the questions directed at them by government officials an amount of time and resources so taxing as to make it impossible for anyone to carry out the plan of life they have chosen for themselves. On the other hand , the cost of these interviews will be enormous. The second reason is empirical-statistical, in the sense that most of the practical problems we face, involving any aspect of life, are ones that different people—all rational, none of them coerced—will typically choose to solve in different ways depending on the kinds of values they cherish and how they understand those values, as well as on their history and experience and how they make sense of that experience. The Values in question are ones like love,

---

[92] See Young (2022), section 2.

play, friendship, family, solidarity and knowledge And since those ways of solving those problems can be described statistically as more rational or less irrational than actions that are harmful and dangerous to themselves, it would amount to a blanket violation of autonomy for the state to pass all these decisions through a filter or rational decision-making.

Not so with other kinds of decisions. As we have seen, there are actions which are dangerous or do serious harm to those who carry them out or which put them at great risk of life and limb, and (a) in some or even many cases, such as suicide (and serious self-mutilation) these actions are statistically carried out by individuals in an altered state of mind, whether because they have taken some substance or because they have a mental disorder (schizophrenia, clinical depression, bipolar disorder, obsessive-compulsive disorder); (b) in some cases in which someone is diagnosed as falling below a certain mental-capacity threshold and the condition is permanent, as might be the case with dementia, they wouldn't be permitted to carry out the harmful or dangerous acts in question; and, finally, (c) many people (and this, too, is a statistical consideration) would want to be prevented from carrying out such harmful and dangerous acts if they should be doing so irrationally or in a state of temporary lack of mental capacity, or if there is some fundamental piece of information they are unwittingly ignoring. So if, as I am arguing, the state is justified in setting up the safety procedure described—a procedure merely designed to make sure that when someone is intent on carrying out actions that place them at great risk of harm, their intention to do so is sound (not "vitiated" in the sense explained)—that justification is based not on metaphysical or ideological considerations in disguise but on a set of empirical premises about the way people statistically are and what they statistically say about themselves. To be sure, the statistical language I have been using is in part approximate and intuitionistic (referring to what "most" people would want for themselves, for example), but only because it awaits a serious statistical study to back up the intuitions. On the contrary, there are statistical and empirical data in psychiatry about people who commit suicide or self-mutilation. And the point of the statistical basis is precisely that we do not want to smuggle any ideology into the argument.[93]

[93] Cf. Garzón Valdés (1988), p. 167. For a discussion of the fictions or illusory problems sometimes sneaked into deontological conceptions that style themselves as antipaternalistic, see Diciotti (1986), p. 583ff., and Pope (2005), p. 137ff. The safety procedure aimed at determining whether one is actually or validly consenting to an action is thus exclusively concerned with actions that will kill them or do serious harm to their bodily integrity or actions involving a significant risk of serious and irreversible harm. And the reasons for so limiting the scope of the procedure are not, as mentioned, ideological but have to do with statistical probability. So, for example, it would be possible to look at two surveys in comparison, both of them scientifically conducted on representative samples. The first sample would capture a set we might describe as comprising all adults who are *prima facie* rational and mentally competent (it would therefore exclude anyone under psychiatric care). Here we would ask: What percentage of people in this representative sample reports that they want to commit suicide, do acts of self-mutilation, take hard drugs, or practice extreme sports or bondage, discipline, dominance, and submission, sadomasochism? And what percentage, by contrast, would want to practice "safe" sports, have children, be in a fulfilling and mutually rewarding relationship, have a gratifying job, or own a beautiful home? My guess is that from such

3.4.5.2 Four Final Considerations on Individual Autonomy

I would now like to make four final considerations. The first of these is that we can recognize two Hohfeldian positions. The procedure guarantees that someone satisfies the conditions of individual autonomy—where individuals are considered autonomous if they are rational, sufficiently uncoerced, and informed, and if their desires are stable over time—and through this procedure we can determine whether a harmful or dangerous decision, such as a request for euthanasia or medically assisted suicide is valid (rational, sufficiently uncoerced, et). For this reason, on the one hand, autonomous agents are entitled to Hohfeldian *claim* that each public hospital should have an obligation to make euthanasia or medically assisted suicide available to patients who meet the standard of autonomy assessed through the procedure. There is the problem of the many doctors who raise a conscientious objection, and in this case the rule ought to be that if more than half of the doctors in a public hospital raise that objection, the hospital will be required by law to hire only

---

a survey we would get the statistical finding that the greater the danger or harm an act or pursuit poses to someone, the less likely it is that this someone would want to do that act or engage in that pursuit. This would explain, for example, why marijuana is consumed on a much larger scale than heroin. The second sample would represent the population of adults who, by contrast, could *not* be described as rational or mentally competent. The statistical study conducted on this sample, drawing on empirical data provided by mental health institutions, would try to answer probability of questions such as these: Of all the people who have been "flagged" or taken in for psychiatric care, or who seek help after an attempted suicide or an act of self-mutilation, what percentage suffer from a mental or personality disorder? Of all the people who have actually taken their own lives or have committed self-mutilation, what percentage were suffering from such disorders at the time? And then, by comparison: Of all smokers or of all people who are engaged to their partner, what percentage suffers from a personality disorder? Suppose, for example, that the study finds that the incidence of psychosis among smokers is about the same as its incidence among the general population (such that if 5% of the general population suffers from some kind of psychosis, then we are likely to find that 5% of smokers does, too), suggesting that there is no significant correlation between smoking and psychosis. Let us now suppose that the incidence of psychosis or clinical depression among people who have committed suicide is 50%. And let us further consider an imaginary scenario in which—God forbid!—anyone considering a major decision such as buying a house or getting married, or even taking out an insurance policy, is required to take a test of rational consent before they are authorized to do so. If we look at these requests in comparison with requests that (under the same system) are made seeking authorization to commit suicide or carry out acts of self-mutilation, we can ask: Is it more or less likely that individuals in the former group will be making rational and competent decisions than individuals in the latter group? What the previous statistical data suggests (if we look at the two sets of data in comparison) is that the former group is *more* likely than the latter to be rational in its decision-making, and indeed *much* more so. And what that simple statistical thought experiment shows is that, on an antipaternalistic conception, we would not have good reasons to mandate that when people decide to get married or enter into a contract, they need to first undergo an assessment to determine whether their decision-making is rational and takes all the relevant facts into account. This is also because it would destroy people's autonomy to force them to submit to an interview with a psychiatrist to determine whether they are rational, whether they know the relevant facts, and whether they are uncoerced in relation to any decision, such as buying a dress, a house, or a car, or getting married, or having children.

doctors who do *not* raise the objection (and the hiring is to be done through merit-based recruitment, or open competitions).

On the other hand, we can recognize a Hohfeldian *no-claim* and *no-liberty* as concerns suicide, meaning that an agent has no the liberty to commit suicide and has not the claim to assisted suicide, outside the medically assisted procedure, the correlative of this no-claim is the no-duty of other agents to making assisted suicide or aiding in assisted suicide outside the procedure, and the correlative of this no-liberty is the claim, of other agents, not making assisted suicide, outside the procedure, and not aiding the agent to commit suicide and the claim preventing an agent from committing suicide (The others people have the claim that the agent does not commit suicide). In this sense, we can call on police officers or firefighters to forcibly prevent others from committing suicide, outside the medically assisted suicide. Committing suicide is simply not sanctioned.

The second consideration is that my model of the requirements of individual autonomy is equivalent to—yet more sophisticated, precise, and justified than—the informed consent model that Beauchamp and Childress introduced in biomedical ethics in *Principles of Biomedical Ethics*. On my model, someone is considered autonomous if they pass a test of rationality, mental capacity, informedness (or being aware of the relevant facts), stability of wishes over time, and sufficient freedom from coercive pressure. On Beauchamp and Childress's informed consent model, this usually means that the patient is informed of the diagnosis and the prognosis, even if it is inauspicious, as with an advanced-stage cancer that leaves the patient with only a short time to live. Beauchamp and Childress report statistical research showing that some people in certain cultural or ethnic groups would rather not know about any such terminal illness:

> In one study, UCLA researchers examined the differences in the attitudes of elderly subjects, sixty-five years old or older, from different ethnic backgrounds toward (1) disclosure of the diagnosis and prognosis of a terminal illness, and (2) decision making at the end of life. The researchers summarize their main findings, based on 800 subjects (200 from each ethnic group):
>
> Korean Americans (47%) and Mexican Americans (65%) were significantly less likely than European Americans (87%) and African Americans (88%) to believe that a patient should be told the diagnosis of metastatic cancer. Korean Americans (35%) and Mexican Americans (48%) were less likely than African Americans (63%) and European Americans (69%) to believe that a patient should be told of a terminal prognosis and less likely to believe that the patient should make decisions about the use of life-supporting technology (28% and 41% vs. 60% and 65%). Korean Americans and Mexican Americans tended to believe that the family should make decisions about the use of life support.
>
> Investigators in this study stress that "belief in the *ideal* of patient autonomy is far from universal" (italics added), and they contrast this ideal with a "family-centered model" focused on an individual's web of relationships and "the harmonious functioning of the family." Nevertheless, the investigators conclude that "physicians should ask their patients if they wish to receive information and make decisions or if they prefer that their families handle such matters." Far from abandoning or supplanting the moral demand that we respect individual autonomy, their recommendation accepts the normative position that the choice is rightly the patient's or a designated surrogate's. Even if the patient delegates the right to someone else, his or her choice to delegate can be autonomous.

Beauchamp and Childress conclude that patients can elect not be informed of fundamental information about their own health, information such as an inauspicious diagnosis and prognosis. This right not to know, or to remain uninformed about one's own medical condition, is very problematic because it prevents patients from exercising other fundamental rights independently. Nor do I think that this would be a frequent event. In this sense, it seems to me that only under certain conditions can patients exercise the right not to know. One of these, as just hinted at, is that patients need to be informed by their physicians that in exercising this right, they are thereby preventing themselves from exercising other fundamental rights. These are the right to draw up or change a will and the right to go to confession and seek absolution for one's sins; and for those who are in pain, the right to say goodbye to family, relatives, and friends; the right to receive palliative care; the right to be emotionally supported by friends and relatives at this difficult time; and above all the right to euthanasia and assisted suicide. This accompanying decision-making procedure satisfies the four requirements for a sufficient degree of autonomy and is based on the patient's informed, written, and videorecorded consent, under which there must be express authorization before proceeding to pharmacological or nonpharmacological therapy, such as radiotherapy, or any surgery, as well as before someone can take part in an experimental research protocol. Beauchamp and Childress distinguish four senses of informed consent, three of which are problematic. Sometimes some authors talk about informed consent in the sense of a "joint or shared decision" or a "fair transaction model." "Shared decision-making may appear to be a worthy ideal in medicine, but the proposed process of decisions being shared is vague"[94] and potentially misleading.

> It cannot be understood as a division of labor, with the clinician deciding A and the patient deciding B. If, alternatively, it is understood as an effort to reach a "joint decision," this position downplays the patient's fundamental ethical and legal right to know and decide. Approving and authorizing are not shared in an appropriate model of informed consent, however much a patient or subject may be influenced by a physician or other health care professionals. In short, this model neither defines nor displaces informed consent; nor does it appropriately implement the principle of respect for autonomy. If shared decision making is presented only as a plea for patients to be *allowed* to participate in decision making about diagnostic and treatment procedures, it continues the legacy of medical paternalism by ignoring patients' *rights* to consent to and authorize or decline those procedures.

This informed consent, understood as a "joint decision" is unacceptable. Beauchamp and Childress thus distinguish two main senses of informed consent:

> Two different senses of "informed consent" appear in current literature, policies, and practices. In the first sense, informed consent is analyzable through the account of autonomous choice presented earlier in this chapter: An informed consent is an individual's autonomous authorization of a medical intervention or of participation in research. In this first sense, a person must do more than express agreement or comply with a proposal. He or she must *authorize* something through an act of informed and voluntary consent. In an early and classic case, *Mohr v. Williams* (1905), a physician obtained Anna Mohr's consent to an operation on her right ear. While operating, the surgeon determined that the left ear actually

[94] See Beauchamp and Childress (2013), p. 122.

needed surgery. A court found that the physician should have obtained the patient's consent to the surgery on the left ear: "If a physician advises a patient to submit to a particular operation, and the patient weighs the dangers and risks incident to its performance, and finally consents, the patient thereby, in effect, enters into a contract authorizing the physician to operate to the extent of the consent given, but no further." An informed consent in this first sense occurs if and only if a patient or subject, with substantial understanding and in absence of substantial control by others, intentionally authorizes a professional to do something quite specific.

In the second sense, informed consent refers to *conformity to the social rules of consent* that require professionals to obtain legally or institutionally valid consent from patients or subjects before proceeding with diagnostic, therapeutic, or research procedures. Informed consents are not necessarily autonomous acts under these rules and sometimes are not even meaningful authorizations. *Informed consent* refers here only to an institutionally or legally effective authorization, as determined by prevailing social rules. For example, a mature minor may autonomously authorize an intervention, but the minor's authorization may not be an effective consent under existing legal or institutional rules. Thus, a patient or subject can *autonomously* authorize an intervention, and so give an informed consent in the first sense, without *effectively* authorizing the intervention (because of some set of rules), and thus without giving an informed consent in the second sense.

Institutional rules of informed consent have typically not been assessed by the demanding standard of autonomous authorization. As a result, institutions, as well as laws and courts, sometimes impose on physicians and hospitals nothing more than an obligation to warn of risks of proposed interventions. "Consent" under these circumstances is not bona fide informed consent. The problem arises from the gap between the two senses of informed consent: Physicians who obtain consent under institutional criteria can and often do fail to meet the rigorous standards of the autonomy-based model.[95]

In the same sense, it is unacceptable to read informed consent as a "fair transaction model." Franklin Miller and Alan Wertheimer challenge our view that "the first sense of 'informed consent' [the one I am arguing for here] ought to serve as the benchmark for the moral adequacy of institutional rules"[96] relating to informed consent. They propose a "fair transaction model" of informed consent. On this model, investigators and their subjects are all treated fairly by giving due consideration to (1) the reasonable limits of an investigator's responsibilities to ensure an adequate understanding on the part of subjects who consent to the research, (2) what is reasonable to expect these subjects to understand; and (3) the overall interests of subjects in participating in the research being conducted.

Sometimes, in biomedical contexts, some doctors have accepted a form of presumed consent. Beauchamp and Childress, for example, note the following:

Often medical students have learned and practiced on anesthetized patients, some of whom have not given an explicit informed consent. For instance, many teaching hospitals have allowed one or two medical students to participate in the examination of women who are under anesthesia in preparation for surgery. Anesthetized patients have been considered ideal for teaching medical students how to perform a pelvic examination because these

[95] Beauchamp and Childress (2013), pp. 122–123.

[96] See Miller and Wertheimer (2010), p. 58.

> patients are relaxed and would not feel any mistakes. When questioned about this practice, some directors of obstetrics and gynecology programs have appealed to the patient's general consent upon entering a teaching hospital. Such consent typically authorizes medical students and residents to participate in patients' care for teaching and learning purposes. However, it is not specific as to which procedures might involve participation by medical students.[97]

There are good moral reasons to find presumed consent insufficient and to instead require specific informed consent for such intimate examinations performed for educational or training purposes. As Beauchamp and Childress argue, presumed consent is not sufficient. In other situations—even if these are exceptions to express consent, when we need to prevent harm to nonconsenting third parties—a form of presumed consent can be accepted. Two cases are worth mentioning. We can have an opt-out decision-making model for organ donation from deceased donors and for tests to screen for AIDS infection and transmission. As Beauchamp e Childress note:

> In late 2006, the US Centers for Disease Control and Prevention (CDC) changed its recommendations about HIV testing and screening for patients in health care settings in which various other diagnostic and screening tests are routinely performed. (Here "diagnostic testing" refers to testing people with clinical signs or symptoms that could indicate HIV infection, while "screening" refers to testing everyone in a certain population.) The policies then in effect, and often embodied in state laws, require specific informed consent, usually in written form, for HIV testing, frequently accompanied by pre-test and post-test counseling. These policies reflected public concerns that had surrounded HIV testing from its beginning in 1985, particularly concerns about the psychosocial risks of stigmatization and discrimination as a result of a positive test. Because of these concerns, testing for HIV was treated differently than testing for other medical conditions, especially those with public health ramifications. Hence, policies at the time required specific disclosure of information and a decision, expressed on a written form, to accept or refuse testing.
>
> The 2006 CDC recommendations moved away from specific written informed consent, accompanied by counseling. In the health care context, the diagnostic testing of patients, in light of clinical signs or symptoms, was justified under implicit consent to medical care, while the screening of all persons ages thirteen to sixty- four, without clinical signs or symptoms of HIV infection, was justified if they were notified that the test would be performed and then given the opportunity to decline. This shift indicated that HIV and AIDS would no longer be treated as exceptions to conventional medical care and to conventional public health measures. The CDC justified its new recommendations primarily on two grounds. First, because HIV and AIDS are chronic conditions that can be effectively treated through anti-retroviral therapies (ARTs), although not cured in the sense of totally and permanently eradicating the virus, the new screening approach would enable more people who are infected to take advantage of available ARTs that could significantly extend their lives at a higher quality. Second, the information gained from screening could enable persons who are infected with HIV to take steps to protect their sex partners or drug-use partners from infection. The CDC estimated that in 2015 over 1.1 million people in the United States were HIV-infected and that one in seven, or approximately 157,000 individuals, were not aware of their infection. Studies after the 2006 recommendations established that treating individuals to reduce their viral load (the concentration of HIV in blood) to undetectable levels can dramatically reduce the risk of spreading HIV infection to sexual or drug-sharing partners. Hence, a slogan arose: "HIV treatment as prevention."

---

[97] Beauchamp and Childress (2013), p. 111.

> The CDC's changed recommendations did not eliminate patient autonomy in health care settings—individuals could still refuse testing—but, by shifting the default from "opt in" to "opt out," the CDC anticipated that more people previously unaware of their HIV infection would be tested and would gain knowledge that could benefit them and others. Despite these potential benefits, critics warned that in the absence of a requirement for explicit, written informed consent, compromises of autonomy were inevitable in the "opt-out" policy. According to one AIDS activist, "This is not informed consent, and it is not even consent, [but rather an attempt] to ram HIV testing down people's throats without their permission."
>
> In our judgment, this "opt-out" approach, undertaken within CDC guidelines, was and remains justifiable as a way to increase HIV testing without infringing personal autonomy. A strong consensus developed around this approach: By early 2018, all states in the United States had changed their laws regarding HIV testing in medical contexts from "opt-in," through specific, written informed consent, to "opt out."
>
> Another context in which an opt-out approach, sometimes called presumed or tacit consent, could be justified is organ donation from deceased individuals.

Under the "opt-out" decision-making model, someone is considered an organ donor by default unless they choose otherwise. This presumed consent rule is absolutely necessary if we are to increase the number of organ transplants from deceased donors, and the urgency couldn't be stressed enough, considering how many people die each year waiting for a transplant. That number came to 4500 deaths in 2012 in the United States and 7000 in 2020 in Europe. To avoid violating people's autonomy, it is necessary that the ministry or department of health send out an information leaflet explaining what the presumed consent rule is, making it clear that anyone wishing to opt out can do so by logging into a dedicated ministry website or by mailing a prefilled form to the ministry. On the autonomous-choice requirement under the "informed consent model"—a model similar to my own individual-autonomy model, but less sophisticated than my model and more redundant, and one whose justification is weaker—see Beauchamp and Childress 2013.[98]

The third consideration is about the principle of beneficence, which in the version espoused by many authors in biomedical ethics posits the need to avoid harming patients and to provide them with health care. My point here is that this principle is to be interpreted not in a paternalistic way but in an antipaternalistic one, and that on the latter interpretation it is redundant: to satisfy the beneficence the principle is meant to ensure, it suffices to rely on the principle of individual autonomy coupled with the harm principle.

As various authors have noted, there is normally a kernel of meaning common to the various senses of autonomy: individual, territorial, accounting, negotiating, and administrative autonomy. In all or most cases, the individual or collective subject has the power to identify or create the norms, rules, principles, and values that govern a given sphere of activity, as well as the power to act in accordance with these

---

[98] Earlier quotations are from Beauchamp and Childress (2013), chap. 4, "Respect for Autonomy," and especially the section titled "The Meaning and Justification of Informed Consent", p. 123ff.

norms, free from interference or coercive pressures. These pressures may consist of violence engaged in by third parties or in circumstances of serious need (such as poverty) owed to a lack of protection of basic rights[99] Alberto Romano, in particular, observes that, in the first place, this power still has to be defined as the possibility of performing legal acts, or at least legally relevant ones.[100] In the case of individual autonomy, the sphere of activity is life and the use of the body; in the case of collective bargaining, autonomy resides in the power to validly enact rules governing property relations. Massimo Severo Giannini describes private autonomy as "a subject's 'necessary position' of freedom and self-determination".[101]

My liberal-egalitarian theory is compatible with the feminist conception put forward by Laura Ronchetti and others who embrace a moderate form of relational autonomy. As Ronchetti comments, echoing the words of Simone de Beauvoir, "if relationality is constitutive of the subject, that means that subjects are not *born* autonomous but *become* so: 'each human being must develop and maintain the capacity to find his or her own law, and the task is to understand what social forms, relationships, and personal practices strengthen that capacity. Nedelsky highlights [...] that this is not so much a matter of 'choosing' one's law but of *finding* it, because one's law is forged by the social and relational context in which the subject is embedded"[102] The conception of individual autonomy defended here is thus compatible with the absence of strong free will, so-called libertarian free will, in which I do not believe, because our conscious desires depend on unconscious motivations that depend on how parental upbringing and sociocultural references have imprinted themselves into our brains on the basis of our DNA. Such a liberal-egalitarian conception is therefore compatible with feminist relational autonomy if and only if the individual has the right to break such affective, social, and economic relationships, especially those that originated from, and were not subsequently created on the basis of, a voluntary act of the individual (where *voluntary* is to be understood in the sense of sufficient freedom from coercive pressures, whether external, such as threats, or internal, such as serious phobias), an example being that of relationships with minor children or contracts freely entered into, such as a mortgage contract.

3.5 The Arguments from Regret and Contagion

We have already seen that, according to some authors, human nature is frail, and that people sometimes show themselves to be impulsive, uncertain about what they want or what to do, emotionally unstable, and weak-willed. Within certain limits—and I should stress that proviso—that idea is correct, even if it is probable only for

---

[99] See Ronchetti (2018), pp. 104ff., 120 ff., 191ff.

[100] See Romano (1987), p. 31. In the same vein, see Benvenuti (2006), p. 223, n. 190.

[101] See Giannini (1951), p. 851

[102] Ronchetti (2018), p. 120.

a minority of people and only for some decisions. And indeed, if we are going to set up a consent procedure consistent with an antipaternalistic conception, we will need to make sure that the requisites for consent take account of the relative suggestibility and frailty of human beings, meaning that when someone wants to carry out actions that are irreversibly harmful or dangerous to themselves, their intention to do so needs to be expressed not only in conditions of rationality, mental capacity, and sufficient freedom from coercive pressure, but also in conditions of stability, ensuring that their stated wishes are durable.

If there are limits within which it is correct to say that human nature is frail, it is incorrect to assert that human nature is frail even *beyond* those limits, and yet this idea of limitless human frailty can still be used in advancing a paternalistic conception. It can do so in two different ways. The first of these ways I will call the argument from regret, the second the argument from contagion. With both arguments, the problem addressed is what to do about people who want to undertake serious risks by doing something that is likely to do serious and irreversible (or significantly irreversible) harm to them, whether the harm is self-inflicted (e.g., doing heroin, speeding without wearing a helmet or a seatbelt, engaging in extreme sports, or even committing suicide) or whether it is inflicted by others enabled to do so (e.g., sadomasochism), On the argument from regret, the claim is not that everyone intent on carrying out these activities is inherently irrational or mentally incompetent, nor is it that these individuals are misconceived or have bad judgment, operating under a cognitive fallacy or other error in judgement. Rather, the claim is that, given the frailty of human nature, *no one* should be permitted to engage in any such activity, so that they will not come to regret their decision to engage in it, a decision which, on reflection, they may regret for their rest of their lives, or which they won't even be able to reconsider and regret (when it ends in death, as with a decision to commit suicide). The problem with this argument is that it *proves or assumes too much*, erring on the side of safety: it overcorrects, entailing a greater institutional commitment than is reasonable. For it would mean that the state, if it were to act coherently on this argument, would have to prevent human beings from making any practical decision of any important consequence, such as whether to practise extreme sports, boxing, or wrestling; whether to swim in shark infested waters; whether to have unprotected sex, contract AIDS; whether to drink two bottles of whiskey a day, or smoke two packs of cigarettes a day, whether to have children, and with whom; whether to get married, and with whom; whether to have an abortion or have gender-affirming surgery; or whether to have sterilization or plastic surgery or other medical surgery; or even a decision about what line of work to get into—all major decisions in one's life, all of them to some extent or in some respect irreversible. A policy of this kind would be quite invasive, intruding on most aspects of people's private lives. It would be so except where certain conditions are met, such as the insufficient rationality or mental incapacity outlined in Sect. 3.4.2, or in the absence of a cooling-off period for actions which are harmful and dangerous: under these conditions the state *would*, by contrast, be justified in intervening, whereas, outside of these conditions, we can explain how an agent might come to regret a decision, because, as we have seen in Chap. 2, it is the regret that is irrational (and we can explain why the state shouldn't intervene even if that decision is one the agent later comes to regret).[103]

The second argument from human frailty is what I am calling the argument from contagion, and what it does is shift the focus from the frailty of those who *themselves* engage in high-risk, or irreversibly harmful behaviour to the frailty of those *around* these heedless or "extreme" individuals—to the community they are part of. The idea here is that even the virtuous among us—those who are endowed with moral integrity—will be subjected to constant and systematic temptation: no matter how virtuous they may be, their human frailty is such that widespread exposure to vice and evildoing by others will cause them to themselves yield to such corruption, and the (paternalistic) metaphor that may well be used in making this argument is that of a young virgin who for the first time ventures out into the world without the safety and security afforded at home by her father. The contagion metaphor aptly conveys the idea of a society in which just *seeing* an example of vice or corruption is cause for alarm, being *in itself* harmful to the whole of society: the harm may not be tangible in a strictly physical or economic sense, but it is no less damaging, for it is a moral harm that eats away at the very fabric of society, hollowing it out from within by dint of constant exposure to temptation, the temptation offered simply in virtue of the fact that an unseemly individual may be passing by. For "if by his vices or follies a person does no direct harm to others, he is nevertheless (it may be said) injurious by his example; and ought to be compelled to control himself, for the sake of those whom the sight or knowledge of his conduct might corrupt or mislead".[104]

The argument from contagion presupposes the very impossibility of distinguishing between rational, competent human beings from human beings who are not, as is often the case with children or people with a psychotic disorder. This is not just morally unacceptable: it is in the first place based on an implausible, if not demonstrably false, conception of human nature. At any event, even if it *were* possible for someone to fit the description of an adult individual who is (a) rational (not suffering from a serious personality disorder), informed of the relevant facts, and sufficiently uncoerced, and yet at the same time (b) so frail as to be unable to resist the temptation from the example of others—which strikes me as unlikely, if not impossible—I do not think there is good reason to protect individuals so described from such contagion. As Mill put it (for all the respect owed to our primate forebears), "[t]he human faculties of perception, judgment, discriminative feeling, mental activity, and even moral preference, are exercised only in making a choice. […] The

[103] In this connection Dworkin (1983a, p. 31) comments that "part of what is involved in claiming that the man who doesn't fasten his seatbelts is attaching an incorrect weight to the inconvenience of fastening them is that if he were to be involved in an accident and severely injured he would look back and admit that the inconvenience wasn't as bad as all that." In speaking of an "incorrect weight" here, Dworkin is framing the argument in terms of substantive rationality as previously outlined in Sect. 3.2, but in so doing he conflates the argument from substantive rationality with the argument from regret. On the complex relation between the rationality of a choice (e.g., a choice to ride a bicycle without wearing a helmet) and the rationality of any subsequent regret an agent may come to have about making that choice, see Sect. 3.4.

[104] Mill (1971), p. 280.

faculties are called into no exercise by doing a thing merely because others do it, no more than by believing a thing only because others believe it. [...] He who lets the world, or his own portion of it, choose his plan of life for him, has no need of any other faculty than the ape-like one of imitation".[105]

On top of that, the argument from contagion cuts against some constitutional principles and moral intuitions that I think are strongly rooted in Western, classically liberal societies, since it may justify ethnic, sexual, or social discrimination. For example, it could conceivably be put to use to prohibit certain behaviours as public displays of sloth, cowardice, greed, or selfishness. It could even make it possible to build ghettos for racists who refuse to sit next to black people or ethnic minorities on public transport, for people who do not want to live in the same neighbourhood as members of the LGBTQ+ community, or for communists who do not want to share the homeland with anarcho-capitalists. It goes without saying that the argument from contagion can be understood as a variant of the utilitarian/organicist argument, which we will turn to in the next section. To that extent, it is open to the same objections that can be raised against the utilitarian/organicist argument, including the objection that questions whether it is at all or exclusively an argument in favour of paternalism, but is rather an antipaternalistic argument in favour of unacceptable restrictions on individual freedom.

3.6 The Utilitarian Argument

The utilitarian argument can be used to support a *paternalistic* doctrine, particularly to justify the prohibition on assisted suicide or on the consumption of certain drugs, or it can be used in favour of *antipaternalism*. In its paternalistic use, its turns into a holist or organicist argument, holding that it is wrong for individuals to put their own life or limb in danger, or indeed to cause any kind of serious harm to themselves, because they are by nature relational: as realational beings, they are embedded in a community, forming with it ties of mutual dependence that cannot be legitimately severed, for these are ties of sustenance, on which hinges their own economic, psychological, and psychophysical well-being as well as that of others in the community (which includes family, friends, partners, and colleagues). As the argument goes:

> No person is an entirely isolated being; it is impossible for a person to do anything seriously or permanently hurtful to himself, without mischief reaching at least to his near connexions, and often far beyond them. If he injures his property, he does harm to those who directly or indirectly derived support from it, and usually diminishes [...] the general resources of the community. If he deteriorates his bodily or mental faculties, he [...] disqualifies himself for rendering the services which he owes to his fellow-creatures generally; [...] and if such conduct were very frequent, hardly any offence that is committed would detract more from the general sum of good. Finally, if by his vices or follies a person does no direct harm to

[105] ibid., p. 262.

> others, he is nevertheless [...] injurious by his example; and ought to be compelled to control himself, for the sake of those whom the sight or knowledge of his conduct might corrupt or mislead. [...] If gambling, or drunkenness, or incontinence, or idleness, or uncleanliness, are as injurious to happiness [...] as many or most of the acts prohibited by law, why (it may be asked) should not law, so far as is consistent with practicability and social convenience, endeavour to repress these also?[106]

And yet the idea of qualifying as "legally binding" most of the affective, social, and economic ties an individual establishes with the community, or with some of its members—and especially the "native ties" that individuals do not freely form themselves by marriage or contract—is not only morally aberrant—for it turns the individual into an instrument in service of the state or of an organized community, with the aim of achieving the greatest utility for the greatest number—but also seems to conflict (or be incoherent) with many of the rights protected by the constitutions of countries in the West (examples being Articles 13, 16, and 32 of the Italian Constitution),[107] as well as with many laws informed by those principles. I am thinking of criminal and civil laws, and of the constitutional principles on which basis they are justified, that make it permissible, within limits, for a citizen or resident with nondependent children not to work, to permanently expatriate, or to panhandle without nuisance to others, or laws that do not criminally or civilly punish suicide, attempted suicide, refusal of life-saving medical treatment, divorce, or life-threatening activities carried out within the privacy of one's own home (such as binge drinking that may lead to alcohol intoxication and death), or even the decision that a misanthropic old man may make to sever all ties with society by retreating to his country mansion.

The ties we choose to form within the community may well give rise to duties, as when we enter into a marriage or a contract, but these are duties owed to specific *individuals*, e.g., to a spouse or a party to a contract, or to our forebears or offspring (if someone has a minor child and is not gravely ill or seriously disabled, or does not suffer from any debilitating condition of the kind that would lead one to request euthanasia or assisted suicide, they are jointly and severally obligated with the other parent to support that child). It may be that anyone is free to do anything at will regardless of the community or society that sustains the individual and makes that action possible, so long as no harm is done to others—but still, the idea is that once we choose to do something like enter into a contract and no one is coercing us into that contract, we make a commitment out of which a duty arises that will typically be recognized by a contemporary liberal constitution, and rightly so: these duties, consistently with Mill's conception,[108] are not duties owed to the community; also,

[106] Mill (1971), pp. 280–281.

[107] Article 13 establishes the inviolability of personal liberty, Art. 16 freedom of movement and residence, and Article 32 universal health care.

[108] See Mill (1971), pp. 281–282. The only exception here might be that of an imminent danger on a wide scale, something that Feinberg (1986, p. 22) himself considers in the example he offers of the "a beleaguered garrison of settlers under attack from warlike Indians. [...] At the peak of the excitement, John Wayne becomes so bored and depressed that he withdraws with the announced

they are binding and are more mandatory, inescapable, less subject to exception, and less defeasible than duties owed to the original community, like the obligation to pay taxes, which can be avoided with a decision not to work, or permanently expatriate, or to panhandle without nuisance to others.

3.6.1 The Right to Beg and the European Court of Human Rights

In regard to the right to panhandle without nuisance to others, the European Court of Human Rights has established that the "fine imposed on a destitute and vulnerable Rom person for harmless begging," followed by a five-day prison sentence for nonpayment, violates the right to privacy guaranteed by Article 8 of the Convention for the Protection of Human Rights and Fundamental Freedoms (hereinafter the "European Convention on Human Rights"). This was the judgment the European Court of Human Rights issued on January 19, 2021 (Cour eur. dr. h., arrêt *Lăcătus c. Suisse*, 19 janvier 2021), and it was immediately welcomed by associations campaigning for the rights of people living in precarious conditions, as well as by attentive observers of Strasbourg jurisprudence. The case concerns an applicant from the Rom community who on several occasions was charged with begging on the public highway in Geneva, Switzerland. Geneva's criminal law provides for a fine for begging in the street, and if the fine is not paid, it provides for pretrial detention. The applicant, who had been ordered to pay CHF 500 but was unable to pay, was kept in custody for five days. Having challenged the measure and exhausted domestic remedies, she appealed to the European Court of Human Rights (ECtHR) in Strasbourg.

The ECtHR provided an interesting overview of European laws on begging, before concluding that the complaint based on Article 8 of the Convention was admissible. Following a classic line of reasoning admitting the infringement of the rights protected by Article 8, and seeking to justify this infringement, the Court held

intention of killing himself. 'After all,' he says, 'my life is my own and what I do with it is my own business.'" But if in this example John Wayne "could not be more wrong" (ibid.), the justification for that conclusion would nonetheless be antipaternalistic, since the lives of many others—hundreds, if not thousands—are at stake. As Feinberg puts it, this is a situation in which "anyone who does not help inflicts serious harm on all the others" (ibis., p. 23), and so a restriction on any one person, being necessarily other-regarding, would be justified on the basis of the (antipaternalistic) harm principle. Nor can it be objected—turning to what we might term "rights to harmful conduct to themselves" such as the right to assisted suicide or the right to consume hard drugs—that if these rights were to be exercised *en masse* by the bulk of the adult population, all at once or within a short span of time, we would witness an implosion of society, but this scenario is false for two reasons. First, because these rights, to assisted suicide or to consume hard drugs would be exercised by a small minority. Second, because for the same objection, invoking the same hypothetical scenario, could equally be raised against a whole range of constitutionally protected rights, which would be exercised by the majority, such as the right to health care, the right to an abortion, the right not to procreate, or the right to permanently expatriate.

that the interference was not justified. The Court gave an interesting overview of the various laws and regulations in force in the member states of the Council of Europe (points 19ff.):

- Of the thirty-eight member states studied, nine do not prohibit begging as such.
- In eighteen of them, begging is prohibited at the regional level, and of these, six prohibit only intrusive or aggressive forms of begging.
- Eleven of the states studied ban begging at local level. Penalties vary from state to state. They can be classified as contraventions or délits, or as entailing an administrative sanction at local level.

Hybrid systems also exist, as in France, where the ban can be national (present in the penal code for aggressive begging, article 312.12.1) and local (through the mayor's administrative police powers). For example, in France, in a ruling dated July 9, 2003, the Conseil d'État more specifically proposes a grid for analyzing the legality of *anti-mendicité* bylaws. Such an order is legal if it is:

- of such a nature as to "preventively ensure the safety, convenience and tranquillity necessary for users of public thoroughfares during periods of tourist influx";
- limited in time and space, so that the people concerned are not subjected to "excessive constraints other than those required to meet the objectives pursued."

In the case in point, this criterion has been met, since "the order issued by the mayor of Prades prohibits acts of begging only during the summer period, from Tuesday to Sunday, from 9 a.m. to 8 p.m., and in an area limited to the town center and the vicinity of two supermarkets."

The High Assembly subsequently clarified the contours of its control by sequencing it as follows: the administrative police measure must, in order to be deemed lawful, be appropriate, necessary and proportionate. A measure is appropriate if it makes it possible to achieve the general interest objective in question, in this case ensuring public order. That is necessary when it is the least intrusive way of achieving the objective in question, and it is proportionate when it does not create excessive burdens in view of the desired result. The order handed down by the interim relief judge of the Besançon administrative court is unprecedented in that it establishes a new fundamental freedom within the meaning of article L521.2 of the Code of Administrative Justice, but also in that it is the first time that an anti-mendicity order has been challenged via an interim relief procedure. However, the judge applied a classic review of the legality of the administrative police measure.

He concluded that "the infringement of the freedom to help others for humanitarian purposes caused by the disputed order is neither sufficiently serious, nor manifestly illegal".

In the case of the Bisontin anti-begging ordinance, the interim relief judge accepted the fundamental freedom to help others for humanitarian purposes, based on the principle of fraternity. He added, however, that "the applicant cannot usefully claim, on the basis of the principle of fraternity, any fundamental freedom to beg" (recital 5).

This is the French judgement. Returning to the ECtHR judgement, the applicant invokes article 8 of the European Convention on Human Rights, which in its first paragraph states:

> Everyone has the right to respect for his private and family life, his home and his correspondence.

The Court points out that this is a new question of law, namely, whether "a person who is punished for begging can rely on Article 8 of the Convention" (paragraph 53). The Court then accepted that the concept of private life protected by Article 8 is broad and may encompass the notion of human dignity, which is "seriously compromised if the person concerned does not have adequate means of subsistence" (paragraph 56). The Court departs from the approach of the French administrative court in that it accepts that "the right to turn to others for help is part of the very essence of the rights protected by Article 8 of the Convention". The Court accepts that the applicant's right to respect for her private and family life has not been respected. However, interference with the exercise of this right may be justified if it was provided for by law, inspired by one or more legitimate aims and necessary in a democratic society. The legitimate aims invoked by the government are the defence of public order and safety, economic well-being, and the protection of the rights and freedoms of others. The Court then examines the necessity of the measure in a democratic society. It points out that any interference "must be based on a pressing social need and be proportionate to the aim pursued" (paragraph 99), and that a "general prohibition of certain conduct, such as that in the present case, is a radical measure requiring solid justification and particularly serious review by the courts, which are authorized to weigh up the relevant interests at stake" (paragraph 101). The Court notes that, in the present case, the law imposing general penalties for begging does not allow for such a balancing of the interests at stake, without taking into account, in particular, the vulnerability of the individual and whether or not the begging is aggressive.

As regards the margin of appreciation left to the state, the Court points out that this is necessarily limited by the fact that a particularly important aspect of an individual's existence is at stake. Weighing up the interests at stake, the Court found that the applicant had the right "inherent in human dignity, to be able to express her distress" and "to try to remedy her needs by begging", given her situation of manifest vulnerability.

The Court concluded that the penalty imposed was not proportionate to the legitimate aims invoked by the government. Because of the applicant's vulnerability, the measure imposed when she had no other means of supporting herself "undermined her human dignity and the very essence of the rights protected by Article 8" (paragraph 115). The interference was therefore not necessary in a democratic society, and the measure therefore violated Article 8 of the Convention. In short, the French administrative courts recognize a fundamental freedom to help others for humanitarian purposes, based on the constitutional principle of fraternity, but refuse to recognize a fundamental freedom to beg. The European Court of Human Rights, on the other hand, recognizes as inherent in human dignity a right to be able to express one's distress and try to remedy one's needs by begging, on the basis of Article 8 of the Convention. (Louise Montesuit, Le Cadre Juridique de la Mendicité en France, 31/07/2021, https://blog.landot-avocats.net/2021/07/31/le-cadre-juridique-de-la-mendicite-en-france-article-de-l-montesuit/.) The right to beg implies the right not to work, even if some constitutions—such as the Spanish Constitution of 1978, at Article 35, and the 1946 French Constitution, at Article 5 of the preamble, establish a duty to work but do not esbalish a correspoding penalty. Similarly to the previously cited French judgment, this judgment of the ECtHR is compatible with the provision that, without providing for criminal penalties, prohibits begging in historical centers at certain times of day.

3.6.2 *Duties to the Community: Defence, Economic Solidarity, and Contributing to "the Material or Spiritual Progress of Society"*

The same even goes for the duty to defend the motherland: even in those countries where this translates into conscription (and many countries no longer have that requirement), that duty can be defeated by conscientious objection. As is stated in the German Constitution at the article 12a, paragraph two, "Any person who, on grounds of conscience, refuses to render military service involving the use of arms may be required to perform alternative service. The duration of alternative service shall not exceed that of military service. Details shall be regulated by law" (https://www.constituteproject.org/constitution/German_Federal_Republic_2014).

The Spanish Constitution at the Article 30, § 2 says that "The law shall establish the military obligations of Spaniards and shall regulate, with due guarantees, conscientious objection, as well as other causes for exemption from compulsory military service, and may impose, where appropriate, a substitute social service" (https://www.senado.es/web/conocersenado/normas/constitucion/detalleconstitucioncompleta/index.html#preamb).

Similarly, the duty to pay taxes arises only when someone has some kind of taxable income or asset. And likewise, the "duties of political, economic, and social solidarity" set forth in Article 2 of the Italian Constitution are standardly taken to be conditional duties: they are conditional on someone having a taxable income or asset, and they do not translate into any kind of specific performance required of any individual, such as working or not expatriating permanently.

So it cannot be compellingly argued that to fulfil the duties of economic and social solidarity is to preclude the right to euthanasia and assisted suicide. In fact, as we will see later, Italian law generally grants citizens the right not to work, to panhandle without nuisance to others, and to expatriate permanently (so long as they don't have any outstanding tax liabilities or any unfulfilled contractual obligations). The fulfilment of any duties of economic and social solidarity normally presupposes no more than that the duty-holder should be able-bodied and have an income—the only two conditions absent which one cannot be held bound by these duties. These duties of economic and social solidarity do not typically presuppose a duty to live and work; on the contrary, since no one is bound to the impossible (*ad impossibilia nemo tenetur*), no one can assert any corresponding rights against someone who is not alive and able-bodied and has no income. If the state can require individuals to do work or render a service that does not involve any payment, that has to do with the individual at issue having committed a crime or receiving unemployment benefits. As is stated in the German Constitution, at the Article 12, paragraph 3, "Forced labour may be imposed only on persons deprived of their liberty by the judgment of a court". In Spain even this kind of forced labour is not legally possible. According to Article 25, § 2, "Punishments involving deprivation of liberty and security measures shall be aimed at rehabilitation and social reintegration and may not consist of forced labor".

There is no law under which a state can force individuals to render such services merely on the basis of a duty of economic and social solidarity: no one, for example, can be compelled to care for someone under a "caregiving order" (the only exception being when that someone is a child or a parent who lacks mental capacity). Although caregiving duties owed to family members can be entrusted to third parties who are paid for their caregiving work, the Italian Supreme Court has found that there *is* a duty of "moral support" owed to minor children or to a spouse.[109] The only exception concerns the means of subsistence owed to a spouse, to economically dependent children, or to forebears (which the state provides for in any case through social security, old-age pensions, caregiving allowances, or basic universal income): these are obligations that cannot be gotten out of simply by deciding that one will not do the work in question.[110]

It should be noted, however, that even in the case of caregiving duties, duty-holders can evade these duties if they are unable to provide such means through no fault of their own, which is usually the case with people who request euthanasia or assisted suicide, since these are usually people who are gravely ill or are suffering from severe disabilities, or simply from severe depression. In this sense, it would be inhumane and cruel to ask people who are unable to fulfil their duty of solidarity to do so. In conclusion, given how important it is to care for children and give them an education, and given that having a child is most often and substantially a choice, a balance could be struck between a parent's right to self-determination and the obligation to care for children, a balance that could be achieved by excluding assisted suicide for parents who have minor or otherwise dependent children and are not suffering from serious illness or severe disability. I will not tackle the very

[109] According to an interpretation of Articles 570 and 591 of the Italian Criminal Code (on family abandonment and road injury, respectively), there is no abandonment of an incapacitated elderly parent if the latter is put in the care of a government aid agency, and as for the obligation to provide means of subsistence under Article 570, i.e. for elderly parents, it is unclear whether this obligation also applies to offspring who themselves lack such means blameless.

[110] cf. Crespi et al. (2001), p. 1806ff.

complicated problem of recognising a right to assisted suicide for young adults who have minor children and are suffering from severe depression.

Recognising citizens as having a constitutionally protected right not to work or to panhandle without nuisance to others may seem to be at odds with Article 4, second clause, of the Italian Constitution, under which every citizen has a duty "to perform an activity or function that contributes to the material or spiritual progress of society" consistently with "personal potential and individual choice." There are two possible ways to interpret this clause in keeping with a liberal ethics. On a liberal interpretation, it is up to individuals themselves to determine which activities or pursuits best contribute to the "material or spiritual progress of society," and if that pursuit, as it turns out, consists in not working, growing orchids, and being supported by a mother-in-law, who could raise a constitutionally based objection to that? Such an interpretation is certainly plausible and consistent with standing case law and legislation, under which there can be no civil or criminal liability for choosing to permanently expatriate or not work (without unemployment benefits): unlike with the public security authority the state can exercise in the matter of suicide, no public authority has a right or an obligation to prevent individuals from following such pursuits unless a crime is committed, as when someone fails to comply with a caregiving duty owed to a family member, like a sons or a parent. If someone is in a bitter conflict with their family or with their superiors at work, it may make perfect sense to them that the best contribution they can make to the nation consists in expatriating permanently—breaking all emotional, social, and economic ties, and not creating new ties in the place to which they expatriate—or retiring for life to their country estate and reap the fruits of the land.

Doesn't a charming elderly misanthrope with adult and independent children have a right to retire to his country estate for life, break off all family, emotional, social, and economic ties (except those necessary for cultivating the land), seclude himself indefinitely, order seeds and any other goods over the internet, and live only in his beloved greenhouse, with his books, films, and wines, enjoying the fruits of his land? That strikes me as an inevitable constitutional interpretation. In this case, contrary to what Francesco D'Agostino (1998) claims, it would not be true that life is necessarily about sharing experiences, because the old misanthrope would not be sharing his aesthetic (visual, gustatory, auditory) experiences with anyone, with any living creature that can share such experiences, as they are not the plants in his orchard. The same goes for euthanasia and assisted suicide: there are circumstances in which some gravely ill people believe that the greatest contribution they can make to the nation is to disappear for good. In the final analysis, we cannot argue both ways with what I would call the ultimate freedom, the freedom from suffering, where someone who is gravely ill chooses euthanasia or assisted suicide, severing all emotional and social ties: either we make the case that this act is a contribution to the nation (and this is how the agent making that choice would see it), or we deny that proposition, by denying that this someone can contribute to the nation by dying in that manner. In this latter case, we need to be able to explain to such individuals how it is that (a) they can possibly make a contribution to the spiritual progress of the nation by being forced to live a life of suffering—one in which they would be feeling deep resentment toward a community and a state that are forcing them to live in conditions they do not want to live in—while at the same time (b) the state is according the same right—the right to cut off all emotional and social ties—to individuals who choose to indefinitely expatriate (to a place where they may not even disclose where they are coming from) or to an old misanthrope who chooses to retreat to his country estate. The only way this argument can be made is by claiming that an individual can be seen as making an actual contribution to the spiritual growth of the nation simply in virtue of being alive, having in the meantime severed all emotional and social ties with the homeland, as by indefinitely expatriating abroad, and not doing anything of artistic value or doing any work that might advance our understanding of anything in the world or might contribute to the economy. That would strike me as an absurd argument, not least because it is hard to see how someone can be forced to make a contribution to the "spiritual progress of society,".

Finally, and this, too, is a similarly plausible interpretation and consistent with standing case law and legislation, it is taken for granted that people who are unemployed and destitute or people who beg for a living find themselves in situations of serious mental or social hardship: it can therefore be reasonably supposed that they have not *chosen* to do what they are doing, which means that, under Article 4 of the Italian Constitution, are not even in a position to contribute to "the material or spiritual progress of society." This interpretation also applies to people who want to resort to euthanasia and assisted suicide, typically on account of a serious illness (including depression) or a severe disability. Indeed, if their condition is so severe as to cause them to want to end their life, they, too, cannot be said to have "chosen" not to contribute to the "material or spiritual progress of society." Or, stated otherwise, they themselves believe that they can no longer contribute to that progress, but they have come to that belief on the basis of a disabling condition that is beyond their control. This is not to say, of course, that no one with a serious illness or disability can contribute to material or spiritual progress: that will depend on their values or philosophical or religious views, among other things.

In conclusion, it is worth recalling that the Charter of fundamental Rights of European Union, Treaty of Nice 2001, itself, at Article 5, states that no one can be forced into labour.[111] It follows that, "Article 4, second clause, of the Italian Constitution, with its sweeping language about 'personal potential and individual choice,' ends up acting more as a limitation on state action than as an obligation of private citizens" (ibid.). In other words, there do not seem to be the legal prerequisites—in the Italian legal system or generally in the European system—for public security authorities to compel citizens to work, to subject individuals to anything like a "compulsory labour treatment" akin to the compulsory *medical* treatment that, by contrast, authorities do have the power to impose on individuals affected by serious mental disorders whose life and body integrity are in danger or there is an important risk to harm others. In other words, the right not to work is also a right in

[111] cf. Bifulco et al. (2008), p. 128.

the sense of a claim that can be asserted against the system, the state, and its organs so that they do not interfere in the sphere of the individual nonworker as it the case with the exceptions for caregiving duties for sons, spouses and parents or the case of individuals who have committed a crime or have received unemployment benefits or are doing alternative civilian service).

Equally aberrant would be the ethical-political notion, paternalistic or otherwise, that an individual's freedom (outside of any contractual liability) can be restricted not only to avoid causing loss of income to third parties, but also to avoid causing psychological suffering to a majority of relatives, friends, partners, colleagues, or neighbors. This would amount to prohibiting any number of acts or activities on the ground of the hurt they may cause to others, for example, interfaith marriage (for the fear this would strike in those committed to the traditional family), working overseas (so as not to upset family members who want their family to be close-knit and close by), or even divorce (owing to the emotional distress this would cause to the spouse). A similar argument is advanced by D'Agostino in stating that "no one is master of their own life [...], because human life is not a *solipsistic experience* but a *sharing of experiences*," making euthanasia detrimental to "the coexistence that is constitutive of human experience"[112] As Mill notes, it is unacceptable and very dangerous to give the majority the power to prohibit anything it deems socially disadvantageous. Indeed, logically and conceptually, "there is no violation of liberty which it would not justify"[113]

One might doubt—as I do—that this is a genuinely paternalistic argument. Indeed, the point of paternalism isn't just to prevent individuals from harming themselves, whether physically or psychologically, or to forbid socially harmful behaviour, but to safeguard what is believed to be their own good, or what is in their own best interest. The utilitarian/organicist argument supports paternalism by claiming that individuals are part of, and organic to, a single social body, from which it follows that it is in *their* best interest to fulfil their assigned roles in the community, such as the role of taxpayer, soldier, spouse, parent, or worker.[114] That would be like saying that not only does the good of the community, in general, lie in maximizing the utility of the majority of the people—in maximizing their pleasure or rational preferences or desires—but also that the good of an individual coincides to a great extent with the utility of the greatest number even when that individual is part of a small minority whose desires are frustrated in order to increase the utility of the majority, as might happen with someone's desire to use drugs or engage in sadomasochism. Of course, this is not an exclusively paternalistic argument. Indeed, I could argue that someone should be prevented from consuming narcotics or freely living out their homosexuality not because this is not part of their good, but merely because it would cause some kind of psychological distress to the majority of the community

[112] D'Agostino (1998), pp. 214, 218, my translation.

[113] Mill (1971), p. 288ff.

[114] On the conflict between liberalism and organicism, see Bobbio (2006), chap. 9.

(as by provoking anger or disgust within the community) or, in the case of drugs, it would cause financial loss, particularly lost income.

Finally, some might take a "moderate," or less radical, utilitarian/organicist view that in the name of a reasonable pluralism accepts a compromise solution that brings the principle of utility into balance with that of autonomy. For example, a moderate utilitarian/organicist might consider it unacceptable for the state to restrict the freedom of some so that they may increase the psychological well-being or happiness of others, their fellow citizens—in short, to be slaves to the happiness of others—but might at the same time consider it reasonable for an individual not to cause significant loss of income to the community. And yet any compromise struck for the sake of reasonable pluralism needs to be consistent. If we prevent individuals from taking drugs because that would cause medium- or long-term economic and social loss to the community— assuming that that is in fact the case—then we should coherently also make it illegal to not work or to work fewer hours, as well as to refuse life-saving treatment, permanently expatriate (cutting off all ties with one's community of origin), or seclude oneself permanently so as to work the land. For all of these activities would lead to the same result.[115]

Equally problematic is the idea that every human being forms nurtures emotional relationships they may not rightfully break up altogether. Indeed, on a moderate version of this argument, individuals may be recognized as having a right to engage in conduct that may cause displeasure, anger, ill-will, resentment, or regret to parents, siblings, and friends, as by working abroad, engaging in questionable professions (pimping or prostitution), or marrying someone against the wishes of their own family. No one should be a slave to their family. But what one does not have a right to do, on this moderate argument, is cause intense and prolonged suffering to others in the family, like that of a parent who discovers that his or her son or daughter has become a cocaine or heroin addict and as a result no longer has a working, emotional, social, economic or sexual life. For it is one thing to do drugs and another to work abroad or expatriate. The analogy, then, does not stand. Doing drugs, the argument goes, completely alters the social and emotional lives of those who use them, destroying them and dragging anyone close to them, including their family, into the abyss.

Paternalistic and prohibitionist rhetoric, especially on the subject of drug use, is widespread. There are certainly some people whose lives have been destroyed by the use of cocaine or heroin—people whose physical and mental health has greatly deteriorated with the use of these substances. But the statistics are clear. Users who reach such a level of moral and material despair, of physical and mental suffering, are a small minority. The majority, 75–80%, are recreational or occasional users, even of hard drugs. People whose lives are destroyed by drugs are normally a minority of the minority of compulsive users, who are 20–25%. And in most cases there are many factors, not just one, that lead to such consequences (unemployment,

[115] On the incoherence of the classic argument according to which it is prohibited to use drugs because that would reduce social welfare or economic productivity, see von Hirsch (1996), p. 262.

social marginalization, bereavement, depression), including prohibition itself (which greatly increases the likelihood that users will share infected needles, and so that a user will contract HIV or hepatitis, as well as the likelihood that poor-quality or poorly cut cocaine or highly concentrated forms of cocaine will be sold).[116]

[116]As we will see in the last chapter, according to some estimates from the 2000s, for example, only a fourth of cocaine users have health issues: "Estimates for Italy show that 1,300,000 individuals out of 32,230,000 in the age bracket from 15 to 54 made use of cocaine in 2003. It can be estimated that within this population of users, about 300,000 individuals are 'problem users,' meaning that they have conditions related to their use of cocaine that pose a serious health problem (Molinaro et al. 2006, p. 78, my translation). On the psychological and physical disorders brought on by chronic use or abuse of cocaine, see Serpelloni et al. (2006), pp. 201ff., 259ff. Husak (1992, p. 97; 2002, p. 105) reports medical data suggesting that, unlike with the use of tobacco and alcohol, there is a range of serious diseases (such as vascular disease and cancers of various kinds) for which cocaine and heroin use is not a significant risk factor. As stated in the 2009 *Annual Report on the State of the Drugs Problem in Europe* (EMCDDA 2009), the use of crack and cocaine is associated with serious health conditions, including cardiovascular disease and mental health issues, particularly with intensive and regular users, whose patterns of consumption "may lead to chronic health and social problems and to the need for treatment" (ibid., 60). These problems are particularly acute for a small group of users that includes those who inject cocaine intravenously (less than 7% in Europe: ibid., p. 67), polyaddicts, and regular crack users. This "set of users includes members of socially excluded groups, including current and former opioid users. Most of them have intensive patterns of cocaine use, possibly using crack or injecting the drug, which may perpetuate or exacerbate existing health and social problems, and may complicate their treatment for opioid use" (ibid., p. 60). The 2009 EMCDDA report also notes: "A survey carried out in the United States estimated that frequent cocaine users had a seven-fold higher risk of nonfatal myocardial infarction than nonusers" (ibid., 65, citing Qureshi et al. 2001). And: "In a study among patients attending a hospital emergency department in Barcelona for problems directly related to cocaine use, the main complaints were anxiety or agitation (48%) and thoracic pain or palpitations (25%)" (ibid., p. 66). As far as addiction is concerned, there is research suggesting that "one-third of all people who smoke become chronic smokers, 23% of those who try heroin become heroin addicts, and 17% of those who try cocaine become cocaine addicts" (Bricolo et al. 2006, p. 138 [my translation], citing Bierut et al. 1998; Cadoret et al. 1995; Pickens et al. 1995; and Tsuang et al. 1996). Also pointing in the same direction is the 1995 Cocaine Project Briefing Kit, outlining the results of an international study on cocaine conducted by the WHO and funded by UNICRI (WHO/UNICRI 1995, p. 28), as well as the aforementioned EMCDDA report, according to which "those who only experiment with the substance [cocaine] on one or a few occasions make up the largest group" (EMCDDA 2009, p. 60; cf. 62–64; EMCDDA 2022). It is a far smaller group that makes a dependent or intensive use of cocaine. Similar data is reported in Husak (1992), p. 124. Similarly as well, the 2009 EMCDDA report says: "A study conducted in the United States showed that about 5% of cocaine users can become dependent in the first year of use, though not more than around 20% of users developed dependence in the long term" (EMCDDA 2009, p. 66, citing Wagner and Anthony 2002). The same report also says: "Clients entering outpatient centres because of cannabis use often also report the use of other drugs. Based on a data collection in 14 countries, 85% of them take another drug, mostly alcohol (65%) or cocaine (13%), and some report use of both alcohol and cocaine (12%)" (EMCDDA 2009, p. 45, citing EMCDDA Selected Issue 2009). According to the National Survey on Drug Use and Health (NSDUH) in the Unites States 2021 (https://www.samhsa.gov/data/report/2021-nsduh-detailed-tables) the total consumers of illicit drugs among persons aged 12 and older, in the past year, in 2019 were 57,200,000, about 20.8%. Consumers of cocaine in past year among persons aged 12 or older in 2019 were 5,468,000, about 2.0%, 2.1% among people aged 18 and older. Consumers of marijuana in past year among persons aged 12 or older in 2019 were 48,242,000, about 17.5%, about 18% among persons aged

18 and older and about 35.4% among persons aged 18–25. Consumers of crack in past year among persons aged 12 or older in 2019 were 778,000, about 0.3%. Consumers of heroin in past year among persons aged 12 or older in 2019 were 745,000, about 0.3%. Consumers of methamphetamine in past year among persons aged 12 or older in 2019 were 1,999,000, about 0.7%. Consumers of Hallucinogen—ketamine, methoxetamine (MXE), phencyclidine (PCP), dextromethorphan (DXM), and nitrous oxide, LSD, MDMA or ecstasy—in past year among persons aged 13 or older in 2019 are 6,010,000, about 2.2%. Consumers of illicit drugs in past year among people aged 12 and older who have a substance use disorder are 8,313,000 and cocaine consumers in past year among people aged 12 and older who have a substance use disorder are 1,011,000, about one-fifth, 18%, and the percentage of the population among aged 12 and older who consumed cocaine in the past year with a substance use disorder was 0.4% in 2019, one-fifth of the total of consumers of cocaine. Consumers of marijuana among people aged 12 and older in the past year with a substance use disorder were 4,836,000, about 10% of total consumers. Consumers of heroin among people aged 12 and older in the past year with a substance use disorder were 438,000 in 2019, 0.2% of the population from 12 to 64, about 58% of the consumers of heroin. Consumers of Hallucinogen among people aged 12 and older in the past year with a substance use disorder were 274,000 in 2019, about 4.5% of the consumers of hallucinogen Consumers of methamphetamine among people aged 12 and older in the past year with a substance use disorder were 1,048,000 in 2019 about 50% of the consumers of methamphetamine Consumers of alcohol in the past year among persons aged 12 and older with a substance use disorder are 14,500,000 in 2019, about 8.10% of total consumers. The total consumers of alcohol in the past year among persons aged 12 and older in 2019 were 179,144,000. The percentage of consumers of alcohol in the past year among persons aged twelve and older with a substance use disorder was about 5.3%, 5.6% among people aged 18 and older in 2019. The population in the United States in 2020 among people aged 15 and older was about 271,464.,00 The percentage of consumers of illicit drugs in the past year among persons aged 12 and older with a substance use disorder was about 3% in 2019 and it is statistically proven that only a minority of users of marijuana, cocaine, MDMA and Hallucinogens—only 20–25%,— normally develop a significant form of addiction. Heroin and methamphetamine, in the afore mentioned survey in the United States, reveals a substance use disorder in about 50% of consumers. But only *severe substance use disorder* is defined as addiction in the literature. Substance use disorder (SUD) is the persistent use of drugs (including alcohol) despite substantial harm and adverse consequences as a result of their use. The National Institute of Mental Health (NIMH) states that "Substance use disorder (SUD) is a treatable mental disorder that affects a person's brain and behavior, leading to their inability to control their use of substances like legal or illegal drugs, alcohol, or medications. Symptoms can be moderate to severe, with addiction being the most severe form of SUD". Substance use disorders (SUD) are considered to be a serious mental illness that fluctuates with the age that symptoms first start appearing in an individual, the time during which it exists, and the type of substance that is used. It is not uncommon for those who have SUD to also have other mental health disorders. Substance use disorders are characterized by an array of mental/emotional, physical, and behavioral problems such as chronic guilt; an inability to reduce or stop consuming the substance(s) despite repeated attempts; operating vehicles while intoxicated; and physiological withdrawal symptoms. Drug classes that are commonly involved in SUD include: alcohol (alcoholism); cannabis; opioids; stimulants such as nicotine (including tobacco), cocaine and amphetamines; benzodiazepines; barbiturates; and other or unknown substances. In the Diagnostic and Statistical Manual of Mental Disorders 5th edition (2013), also known as DSM-5, the DSM-IV diagnoses of substance abuse and substance dependence were merged into the category of substance use disorders. The severity of substance use disorders can vary widely; in the DSM-5 diagnosis of an SUD, the severity of an individual's SUD is qualified as *mild*, *moderate*, or *severe* on the basis of how many of the 11 diagnostic criteria are met. The International Classification of Diseases 11th revision (ICD-11) divides substance use disorders

3.6.3 *The Right to Cause Great Suffering Implies the Right to Cause Less Suffering*

In any case, apart from any prohibitionist rhetoric, even the moderate version of this argument proves untenable. This for two reasons. The first is that if drug users have a right to cause *great* suffering to friends and family members, then so much the more do they have a right to cause *less* suffering.

What is it that, in principle, would cause parents or siblings to suffer more than anything else vis-à-vis their loved ones (other than their dying or falling seriously ill, of course)? I don't think it is any occasional drug use these loved ones may make, at least so long as that doesn't lead to dire consequences. What *would* make people who love us suffer more than anything else is our shutting them out completely, permanently, without any going back. The words that would make them suffer the most are not, I submit, "I do cocaine every now and then" but "I hate you. I never want to see you again, hear your voice, hear your footsteps, or even hear *about* you." It is this total and deliberate severing of all bonds that I think would

---

into two categories: (1) harmful pattern of substance use; and (2) substance dependence. The diagnostic criteria are as follows:

addiction—a biopsychosocial disorder characterized by persistent use of drugs (including alcohol) despite substantial harm and adverse consequences;

addictive drug—psychoactive substances that with repeated use are associated with significantly higher rates of substance use disorders, due in large part to the drug's effect on brain reward systems;

dependence—an adaptive state associated with a withdrawal syndrome upon cessation of repeated exposure to a stimulus (e.g., drug intake);

drug sensitization or reverse tolerance—the escalating effect of a drug resulting from repeated administration at a given dose;

drug withdrawal—symptoms that occur upon cessation of repeated drug use;

physical dependence—dependence that involves persistent physical-somatic withdrawal symptoms (e.g., fatigue and delirium tremens);

psychological dependence—dependence socially seen as being extremely mild compared to physical dependence (e.g., with enough willpower it could be overcome);

reinforcing stimuli—stimuli that increase the probability of repeating behaviors paired with them;

rewarding stimuli—stimuli that the brain interprets as intrinsically positive and desirable or as something to approach;

sensitization—an amplified response to a stimulus resulting from repeated exposure to it;

tolerance—the diminishing effect of a drug resulting from repeated administration at a given dose. Symptoms of a substance use disorder include behavioral, physical, and social changes. Changes in behavior include being absent from school or work; changes in appetite or sleep patterns; personality and attitude changes; mood swings; and anxiety. Signs include physical changes such as weight gain or loss, tremors, and bloodshot eyes. Different substances used can give different signs and symptoms. Substance use disorders can range widely in severity, and there are numerous methods to monitor and qualify the severity of an individual's SUD. The DSM-5 includes specifiers for severity of an SUD. Individuals who meet only two or three criteria are often deemed to have *mild* SUD. Substance users who meet four or five criteria may have their SUD described as *moderate,* and persons meeting six or more criteria as *severe.* In the DSM-5, the term *drug addiction* is synonymous with *severe substance use disorder.*

make our loved ones experience the most suffering, not least because with a definitive rejection, they would no longer be able to know anything about us—whether or not we are in good health, whether we are out on the streets dealing drugs. And, as noted, such cutting off of all emotional ties and show of utter contempt for the person we break away from is precisely what in most liberal countries governed by the rule of law we normally have a right to do, no matter how close the person we are estranging or how harmful the act may be to them. The right to affectively abandon, to hate. And if we have this right, and if such estrangement or rejection is felt by my many as the ultimate hurt or suffering (apart from our loved one dying or falling gravely ill), then we have a right to cause a *lesser* form of suffering, like the kind that would be experienced by someone whose child or sibling ends up doing drugs. As evidence for that claim, we need only consider that in the rationale for laws prohibiting murder, rape, kidnap, and the like, we do *not* find the need to protect people from the emotional distress they would experience if their sons or daughters committed such crimes. In fact, if that *were* the case, the punishments for such crimes would have to be less severe if the offender's parents and loved one were themselves criminals, completely satisfied that their son or daughter has followed in their footsteps, pursuing a criminal career; conversely, the punishments would have to be *more* severe the looser the emotional ties are that bind offenders to their loved ones.

At any rate, this argument is incoherent even if the kinds of behaviour in question cause our parents or friends to suffer in the extreme, whether the harm associated with such behaviours consists in death or the risk of death or bodily injury in the medium to long term, as happens with people who consume cocaine or heroin. Indeed, we have the same result—namely, a sufficient risk of death or bodily injury in the medium to long term, causing friends or parents to reach that degree of suffering—in the case of people who practice extreme sports or boxing or wrestling, or who swim in dangerous waters where sharks have been spotted, or people who frequently have unprotected sex and may contract AIDS, or who refuse life-saving treatments, or eat only junk food and become obese as a result, or drink two bottles of whiskey a day, or smoke two packs of cigarettes a day.

In the second place, the argument of the necessary relationality of human beings fails to take into account that love, in its various forms—that of spouses, lovers, friends, parents—cannot be the object of an obligation or a promise, because it is something that largely escapes our rational control, our will. One cannot purposely "decide" to love or fall in love. In many European civil codes, there is rightly no obligation requiring parents to love their children: there is an obligation to raise, educate, support, and care for them, but not to love them. A legal obligation to love someone would be just as absurd as a legal obligation to forget and overcome an unhappy love or to go hungry. Similarly, some civil codes in Europe obligate children to help their parents materially or economically in certain situations of hardship (such as illness or poverty). But there can be no obligation to love or not to hate one's parents. And if there can be no such obligation, there is no way that an emotional bond can reasonably be turned into a legal bond ("You are prohibited from consuming narcotics because your parents would stop loving you or because any mutual affection would be lost"). If, fearing the punishment meted out by the state, we felt compelled not to make use of cocaine, would it follow that our (affective) relationship with our sibling becomes closer and more authentic just because our sibling would plunge into desperation if we did make use of cocaine? A personal relationship is either (affectively) authentic, sincere, or it is not a genuine relationship at all. The state could conceivably compel someone's offspring to visit them if they have fallen ill or to abstain from conduct that would cause them to feel emotional pain, as by making use of cocaine, but this would have nothing to do with building a close and genuine affective bond between parents and their children—which is the only reason that, on the paternalistic argument considered here, could reasonably justify prohibiting someone's offspring from making use of hard drugs or engaging in any other self-harming conduct. But no one can be *forced* to love someone else or feel affection for them. So the only consequence of this argument is that it would justify forcing someone's offspring or siblings to be deceitful, that is, to pretend as if they genuinely felt something (love or affection) that may not exist. And I do not believe that such a cynical interpretation, the only one that makes any rationally sense, could even remotely be accepted by the same authors who advance that line of argument.

3.6.4 Mill's Utilitarian Arguments in Favor of Antipaternalism

There is, however, a variant of the utilitarian argument which be used in support of antipaternalism, and which in fact has been so used, notably by Mill, whose argument in this respect can be distilled down to two statements:

(a) First, allowing people to live as they wish, rather than forcing them to live as others believe they should, increases overall utility, that is, people's own well-being and happiness, and so also their economic productivity, because satisfied people can be expected to work harder and better, making a greater contribution to social progress and to economic growth (I would call this argument "free choice as a conduit to development").
(b) Second, we are each our own best judge when it comes to our own good, or that which advances (or at least does not harm) our own interest (I would call this argument "hands-off paternalism").[117]

The first statement seems plausible enough to me, for if the state were indeed to systematically and intrusively interfere in the freedom of individuals—deciding, for example, what entertainment is allowed, what books can be read, what clothes can be worn, or where to go on vacation, or even what line of work we should pursue or who we should marry, and *that* we should marry in the first place—the outcome would inevitably be a generalized malaise, a situation of widespread psychophysical frustration and suffering, an unbearable state of affairs that, as is easy to

[117] cf. Mill (1971), pp. 260ff., 267ff., 277; Diciotti (1986), p. 566ff.; Kleinig (1983), pp. 28–32.

imagine, would at the very least crush the creativity of individuals, their economic productivity, and their entrepreneurial and social initiative, very likely to devastating effects, with an endemic spread of anxiety disorders, depression, even suicide, and people fleeing abroad en masse.[118] That said, the "development through free choice" argument does appear to be consistent with a certain brand of paternalism, for in Western constitutional democracies where laws are enacted whose rationale is paternalistic, the restrictions placed on individual freedom normally do not go to the core of the life projects that people may want to pursue but instead stop at the margins, generally not choosing any activity for individuals to carry out but requiring them to carry it out in a certain way (as by wearing a helmet while riding a motorcycle), and when activities *are* prohibited, they tend not be ones that are core to one's identity (e.g., doing drugs), or they tend to be "fringe" pursuits (e.g., hardcore sadomasochism). As objectionable as any interference in individual freedom may be, I would submit that no one of a liberal cast would consider that kind of paternalistic legislation to be so oppressive as to snuff out individual creativity, nor would they compare such restrictions to the interference practiced by a totalitarian state.

The second statement, however, seems less convincing, for it cannot be taken to be essentially true once appropriately qualified. As Garzón Valdés points out, it is certainly true, barring very serious mental disorders, that we are each in a better position than anyone else to know what we desire or what our state mind is at any given moment, or what we are now feeling. But knowing what what's in our own best interest is something else entirely: we cannot leap from what we desire *in the moment* to what we *genuinely* or *essentially* desire simply on the basis of how we are feeling right now. It takes a rational understanding of our own desires to get to that point, where we can not only identify what we desire beyond the fleeting moment of our feelings, but also find and select rationally suitable means for fulfilling that desire consistently with a theory of formal rationality. We therefore need to process our desires accordingly, which in turn means that we need cognitive and emotional capacity, something we may lack if we have an entrenched set of false beliefs about the world or if we have some kind of relevant mental or mood disorder or a neurosis.[119]

In fact, various studies in cognitive and experimental psychology reveal that people tend to make certain cognitive biases, as when estimating probabilities, a classic example being the gambler's fallacy,[120] or that, in some specific situations,

[118] The truth of this statement does not depend on any objective metric of utility—on an "objective" concept of well-being established *a priori*—but is rather tied to what are arguably the preferences of most people in the Western world when it comes to their mental and physical well-being.

[119] After all, Mill himself seems to have been on board with this idea, for he did accept that the state can interfere in the freedom of children, as well as of individuals with a temporary or permanent mental incapacity, so as to prevent them from doing harm to themselves. See Mill (1971), p. 294; cf. Garzón Valdés (1988), p. 158ff.

[120] This fallacy consists in believing that when a random event has taken place a disproportionate amount of times in the past, it is less that 50 percent likely to happen again in the future. For example, if we flip a coin and it comes out heads 19 out of 20 times, the fallacy consists in believ-

people tend to get trapped into a conformist logic, showing a "blind obedience to authority".[121] Even so, making allowance for these widespread cognitive errors and the others previously identified, and making allowance as well for mental disorders that some people may suffer from, it is certainly the case that adult, functionally rational, and reflective people know better than anyone else what their own basic desires are, what gives them psychophysical well-being and what does not. As evidence for this claim—not quite in keeping with scientific protocol in the subject matter but psychologically very interesting nonetheless—I would submit that many scholarly articles devoted to the topic of paternalism also reveal in an exemplary way their authors' personality and outlook, their likes and dislikes. Garzón Valdés, for example, takes issue with people who think that mountaineering, though it involves some degree of danger, is an activity objectively more uplifting and enjoyable than smoking.[122]

Similarly, neither Garzón Valdés nor Gerald Dworkin[123] can understand why someone would rationally prefer not to wear seatbelts or a helmet when driving a car or riding a motorcycle, since this kind of "pleasure" is evidently far removed from either author's character.[124] And so it is that Garzón Valdés considers it irrational to choose not to wear a seatbelt or a helmet. If these drivers believe, as one assumes they would, that it is important to safeguard their physical integrity, and then choose not to act accordingly, with little sacrifice to their own convenience, it follows that they are not sufficiently rational. Ergo, the state's coercive intervention would be justified. Unlike these authors, and like many other motorcyclists in a county like Italy, I fully understand why it might be regarded as an inconvenience to wear a helmet while riding a motorcycle: it could even be felt to be unbearably annoying, especially in the summer and in the city.[125] But I do have to say that seatbelts while driving are a different matter. Indeed, speaking for myself, I cannot

ing that the next time we flip the same coin, it is more than 50 percent likely to come out tails, when in fact either outcome is equally likely.

[121] See Zimbardo (2007), p. 266ff.

[122] I point this out noting that, as a smoker himself, or at least as a former smoker, Garzón Valdés can certainly appreciate the pleasure of smoking. See Garzón Valdés (1988), p. 170. One who contends that mountaineering is *intrinsically* more valuable than smoking is Donald Regan (1983, p. 120).

[123] See Garzón Valdés (1988), p. 166; Dworkin (1983a), p. 31.

[124] On this unresolved bind in Garzón Valdés's theory, see Atienza (1988), p. 211.

[125] At the risk of making light of a serious point, I am going to sort the kinds of inconvenience at issue into four buckets: functional (a helmet restricts your field of vision), sense-perceptive (it gives discomfort, particularly by making your head feel hot in the summer), mood-suppressive (it deprives you of the carefree state of mind you might experience with the breeze brushing up against your face, also in the summer), and aesthetic (it messes up your hair, assuming you are a carefully groomed person who doesn't want to look dishevelled). I should also want to offer an impression I have about safety: it seems to me that the risk of fatal or serious accidents in the city is much overblown, at least if we only count automobile drivers and motorcycle riders who are reasonable—those who drive safely and have the skill needed not to get into an accident. Although I do say this anecdotally, drawing on my own experience, it is not difficult meeting people who I think would meet that description of the reasonably safe motorist, like me, for example, and have

understand how the simple act of buckling up may be felt to be a significant inconvenience—as Garzón Valdés points out,[126] a seatbelt is not a straitjacket—even if I do know people who do see this as just such an inconvenience, and indeed one that is intolerable. At any rate, the question comes up: if it is rational for smokers to give up years, or even decades, of their life for the pleasure of smoking tobacco, why shouldn't it be rational for motorcyclists to increase the risk of a head injury, or even death, for the pleasure that comes from feeling wind-blown or in order not to feel discomfort?

In this sense, it seems to me that this part of Mill's argument, properly construed, is still valid. In other words, it does seem to be the case that, so long as we meet the criteria of autonomy—we are rational, mentally competent, relevantly informed, and sufficiently uncoerced—we are each in a position to our own best judge as to what our basic desires and preferences are, what our emotional responses will be, and above all what can make us feel good or amuse us. And these desires can often be difficult for others to understand. Indeed, as Mill points out:

> The same things which are helps to one person towards the cultivation of his higher nature, are hindrances to another. The same mode of life is a healthy excitement to one, keeping all his faculties of action and enjoyment in their best order, while to another it is a distracting burthen, which suspends or crushes all internal life. Such are the differences among human beings in their sources of pleasure, their susceptibilities of pain, and the operation on them of different physical and moral agencies, that unless there is a corresponding diversity in their modes of life, they neither obtain their fair share of happiness, nor grow up to the mental, moral, and aesthetic stature of which their nature is capable.[127]

As evidence for that contention, I should point out how difficult it is for some people (including some prominent philosophers) to put themselves in the shoes of others. But even more important is the fact that Mill's second statement (capturing the second part of his argument) can be used against paternalistic moral-political conceptions even by those who do not endorse a utilitarian conception but still justify antipaternalism on the basis of the principle of individual autonomy and liberal equality.

Last but not least, there remains an important point to be discussed. Enrico Diciotti argues that in the debate between paternalism and antipaternalism, utilitarianism offers a better moral-political conception than conceptions focused on upholding the principle of individual autonomy. Diciotti argues that even a utilitarian doctrine can reach the same conclusion as a doctrine based on the principle of autonomy: on either basis, we can argue that individuals ought to be allowed to do anything that is harmful or dangerous to themselves, so long as they are rational, relevantly informed, and sufficiently uncoerced, and so long as they do not cause harm to others[128] That much is true. However, that outcome is only contingent: there

never been in or caused an accident, not even a minor one, despite the fact that they have regularly driven for twenty or thirty years.

[126] See Garzón Valdés (1988), p. 160.

[127] Mill (1971), p. 270.

[128] See Diciotti (2005), p. 112ff.

is nothing conceptually necessary about it. In other words, utilitarianism considers it important or necessary to maximize utility, that is, the pleasure, advantage, or preferences of the majority of people. To be sure, it *is* possible for the majority of people in a historically given community to desire that each person be free to do anything that does not cause harm to others or to be free to put others at risk of harm so long as they have proper consent (i.e., consent not vitiated by an agent being irrational or coerced). But it is just that—a possibility: there is nothing conceptually necessary about it. It is equally possible that the majority of people in another community would want everyone in that community to be obligated to do what maximizes the wealth of the community (as with migrants, who are a minority, working thirteen hours a day in order to increase GDP) or what maximizes overall pleasure across the population. A utilitarian doctrine, in other words, may be put to paternalistic ends or it may otherwise impose significant restrictions on individual freedoms. Not so with a doctrine that consistently protects the principle of individual autonomy: even the most cautious of these doctrines would always rule out the ability of an organized community to coercively interfere in the freedom of individuals, where the basic idea is that so long as individuals are rational (uncoerced, informed, and mentally competent), and so long as the only harm they may do to others is done with proper consent (satisfying those same conditions), they are free to do what they want in the privacy of their own home, such as engaging in violent sadomasochism. On the other hand, utilitarianism, even rule-utilitarianism, which takes account of Harsanyi's expectation effects[129] is dangerous, because it could justify banning same-sex marriage, or enslaving illegal migrants who are supposed to work from dawn to dusk on tomato and other vegetable plantations, if that satisfies the majority's utility.

3.7 Seven Objections to the Moral Perfectionism Argument

On the perfectionist argument, it is imperative that each individual be directed—by persuasion or, if necessary, by force—toward an ideal of moral excellence or spiritual growth, an ideal of virtue or human flourishing. In this sense, an organized community would have a right or even a duty to paternalistically educate, or even forcibly compel, citizens to embody a series of virtues while avoiding the correlative sin: bravery, not cowardice; industriousness, not laziness; thoughtfulness, not recklessness; mutual support, not self-dealing; generosity, not greediness; temperateness, not lustfulness; a striving for greater knowledge and cultural literacy, not ignorance. And citizens can even be compelled to maintain the psychophysical integrity needed to cultivate these and other virtues.[130] Apart from the fact that

[129] See Harsanyi (1975); Ferraro (2013).

[130] On the concept of perfectionism and its various conceptions, see Wall (2021); cf. Mill (1971), p. 278ff.

perfectionism may translate into outright legal moralism—on which the state may prohibit individuals from engaging in practices deemed morally unacceptable (such as sadomasochism), and may do so even if the practice at issue is not harmful to themselves or to others (such as practicing oral or anal sex)—the perfectionist argument can be used to justify paternalistic limitations on individual freedom on the ground that virtue requires that we abstain from certain actions or practices that will or may harm our mental and physical integrity.[131] It could be argued on this basis, for example, that if someone has been diagnosed with a terminal illness, such as an incurable cancer that is bound to give them mental as well as physical agony, they are to stoically endure that condition, bravely accepting their painful fate.

There are at least four objections that can be raised against the perfectionist argument. Let us take them up in turn.

The first of these is that the perfectionist argument cuts against some well-established principles of limited government embodied in Western constitutions and against a core of liberal principles that people are broadly committed to in the West in societies marked by moral and cultural pluralism. On this objection, moral perfectionism would make it possible for the state to interfere in the freedom of individuals in a whole range of areas, prohibiting them from, say, squandering away their money on sex or gambling, from eating junk or ultra-processed food, or from lazing about, even dictating how much they should work. In other words, what holds for the utilitarian/organicist argument previously discussed also holds for the perfectionist argument: from a logical-conceptual point of view "there is no violation of liberty which it would not justify".[132]

The second objection, related to the first, is that the moral perfectionist argument finds few, if any, footholds in contemporary Western constitutions, particularly the Italian one. Indeed, the Italian constitution does not contain language about the pursuit of models of virtue or human flourishing, about duties owed to oneself, about ideals of moral excellence. And the same goes for many Western constitutions, such as the German Constitution of 1949, (https://www.constituteproject.org/constitution/German_Federal_Republic_2014) the French Constitution, as La Declaration des Droits de l'Homme et du Citoyen de 1789 (article 4, "La liberté consiste à pouvoir faire tout ce qui ne nuit pas à autrui", article 5 "La loi n'a le droit de défendre que les actions nuisibles à la société. Tout ce qui n'est pas défendu par la loi ne peut être empêché, et nul ne peut être contraint à faire ce qu'elle n'ordonne pas"; https://www.conseil-constitutionnel.fr/le-bloc-de-constitutionnalite/declaration-des-droits-de-l-homme-et-du-citoyen-de-1789), Le Préambule de la Constitution du 1946; (https://www.conseil-constitutionnel.fr/

[131] On the other hand, Amarasekara and Bagaric (2004, p. 411) make the point that "autonomy appears to be an instrumental good, not one which is of intrinsic value. Certainly it is not the case that all expressions of autonomy are conducive to human flourishing." And yet, like many other authors, they do not clarify what perfectionist value is to be held up against autonomy, that is, what virtue is at stake, nor do they take up the objections that may be raised against the argument they make about autonomy as an instrumental good.

[132] Mill (1971), p. 288ff.

le-bloc-de-constitutionnalite/preambule-de-la-constitution-du-27-octobre-1946) and the Spanish Constitution of 1978. None of the perfectionist vocabulary has any foothold in the Italian, German, Spanish or French Constitution. The text sets forth duties of economic and social solidarity, duties owed to third parties, where at stake is not what one owes to oneself but the interests of *others*.

Third, as Elio Sgreccia himself recognizes in his handbook on bioethics (Sgreccia 1997), Western culture is at the farthest remove from an ethic based on the virtue of putting up with pain and illness—assuming, of course, that this is indeed a virtue and not a form of masochism. Western culture, hedonistic and materialistic, is permeated with the idea of rejecting illness, old age, and death. Western medicine is entirely focussed on pain *relief*, indeed on getting rid of pain altogether. A society so described is inherently unreceptive to a perfectionist argument, or an argument against euthanasia or assisted suicide, prohibiting people from making that choice if they are terminally or gravely ill, especially if the argument is made on the basis of the virtue of courage, understood here as the virtue of withstanding pain.

Fourth, it might be doubted whether an ethical state, that is, a state that imposes an ideal of moral excellence, a model of virtue, can consistently exist without raising questions of rationality. It is certainly possible for the state to *enforce* a model of morality through the threat of punishment as a way to discourage people from engaging in behaviours inconsistent with that model, such as working less than eight hours a day or squandering money on paid sex. But does this amount to making people more virtuous? In other words, isn't it paradoxical to impose virtue by force, mandating something that in fact may be impossible? Isn't acting intentionally, based on one's own convictions or sense of regret, an integral part of being virtuous? Can you really *compel,* with the force, someone to embody any of the virtues, such as kindness or courage? Most likely not.[133] This is an empirical false belief.

This last objection to the perfectionist argument in turn faces two counterobjections that could be raised against it. The first is that a perfectionist ideal need not be made to rest on a *teleological* ethics but can be cast within the framework of a *deontological* ethics. The idea is that there are moral duties which everyone has and which we cannot fail to recognize—and should we fail in that sense, there is nothing left for the community but to forcibly herd the wayward flock, putting the sheep back on the right path. As D'Agostino says, "If I rationally, clear-headedly choose to forge a life in which I act not for the good of others—out of love for them, as by saving someone's life when they are in mortal danger—but for my own good, within the enclosure of my own self-interested subjectivity, I demonstrate my human and existential poverty" (D'Agostino 2009, my translation).[134]

---

[133] Cf. Dworkin (2000), p. 268; Schiavello (1998), p. 63ff.

[134] On the deontological version of moral perfectionism, see Wall (2021), sect. 1.1, where the idea is referred to as "objective goods perfectionism."

On this counterargument, then, the state cannot allow me to behave so self-interestedly, with such spiritual poverty, as to request, for example, euthanasia or assisted suicide.

Even the deontological version of the perfectionist argument is open to several objections. I will list three. First, just as is the case with the teleological version, even if the state can force me not to engage in certain behaviour (e.g., not to request assisted suicide), it cannot force me to genuinely fulfil a moral duty to be less self-interested or spiritually poor in my action, for in complying with a *legal* obligation not to request assisted suicide, I am not *genuinely* fulfilling a moral duty to be less self-interested or spiritually poor: I am being *forced* to live up to that (purportedly) higher moral standard, and so am not actually fulfilling a moral duty, for I am not doing so out of spontaneity. And if I am not acting spontaneously, if I am "unwillingly fulfilling a moral duty"—a rather bizarre, if not nonsensical, conceit—I am not genuinely fulfilling that duty. Second, it is very problematic to identify a reason or purpose behind these moral duties. Generally, moral duties are based on, and justified by, the rationale that we shouldn't cause harm to others: we should therefore not kill, steal, bear false witness, betray friends or partners, and the like. Not so with the purported duty not to request assisted suicide or euthanasia: there are no third-party interests to be protected here. And third, if moral duties (on the deontological conception) are entirely decoupled from any teleological ideal, it follows that fulfilling such duties doesn't necessarily advance the aim of realizing one's true well-being, flourishing, nature, or interests, if these interests or this well-being are understood in a psychological sense, where psychophysical well-being is achieved by fulfilling a set of basic desires, those which agents form when they are sufficiently rational, aware of the relevant facts, and sufficiently free of coercive pressure, and which they maintain stably over time.

A deontological perfectionist could (a) concede that the point of fulfilling a moral duty not to request euthanasia or assisted suicide is not to avoid harming third parties, nor is it to achieve the psychophysical well-being or fulfil the basic desires of the duty-bearers themselves, and yet could still (b) contend that fulfilling such a duty serves their interests. If so, what kinds of interests might these be? Presumably they would be metaphysico-transcendent interests, and quite likely religious ones. Three points are worth making here. The first is that a justification of this kind, where a moral or legal duty is made to rest on metaphysico-transcendent assumptions, would in this case be open to the same challenges as the theological argument considered in Sect. 3.1: the argument that only God gives life and death, and so no one can dispose of anything that is not theirs. The challenge, in short, is that there is no way to know with any degree of certainty whether such interests exist: no hard evidence for them have been forthcoming for as long as there has been empirical observation, so it seems no more likely that they do exist than that anyone today should be able to perform a miracle. The second point is that if such duties are to be justified in institutional, legal, public discourse—that of legislators, judges, and jurists—any such justification would have to proceed on a secularist basis, a secularist conception, which is contrary to the use of religious beliefs. And third, talk of specific metaphysico-transcendent interests does not seem to sit squarely with cultural pluralism, in a context where being different faiths and religions exist, with divergent interpretations of moral and religious duty.

Let us turn to the second counterobjection mentioned three paragraphs earlier, one that could be raised even if a perfectionist conception were to be based on a teleological ethics. The basic idea is that there are "specifically human needs, desires, inclinations, and capacities, and that to fulfil them, to exercise these capacities, is to fulfil human nature (to realize the human good)," or human virtue (Celano 1994, p. 566, my translation). This means that we cannot at the same time not exercise these capacities, and so not embody the corresponding virtues, and still account ourselves to be human. For "a virtue, such as courage, is to be understood as a character trait, and more precisely as a disposition to make a choice to exercise the underlying capacity [...], a capacity whose exercise and acquisition is a necessary condition" (ibid.) or a sufficient condition for the fulfilment of human nature. And what this also means is that virtue is not something that one either has or does not have. It is possible to educate individuals to flourish in the right way, to discover which goals they need to achieve as a necessary condition for realizing their true well-being or which desires they need to fulfil if they are to be truly happy. And like any education worthy of its name, an education in virtue, in *true* happiness, *true* well-being—as opposed to an incomplete or spurious well-being, the kind obtained by satisfying false needs—can legitimately *also* make use of the threat of a future harm, of a punishment. In this way, while people may initially act out of fear of this threat—the threat of the punishment meted out by the state—complying on that basis with the mandated model of virtuous behaviour, they will gradually come to appreciate how important these virtues are for their happiness and well-being (and will do so thanks in part to their participating in programmes designed to give them an education in virtue), not unlike an unruly child who needs to be "grounded," or otherwise punished, in order to be able to understand why it is important not to hurt or otherwise harm others.[135]

[135] For a further counterobjection see Dworkin. Teleological moral perfectionism, based on a certain conception of human nature, corresponds to what Steven Wall calls "human nature perfectionism," as distinct from the deontological "objective goods perfectionism." It is worth pointing out here that a teleological ethics is underpinned by a "functionalist" theory of human nature on which it is in the nature of humans to have certain desires or needs, such as a desire to marry and have friends and children. But this theory, I would contend, very often reveals itself to be an ideology in the pejorative sense of the term—a false theory, one that behind a facade of purportedly objective notions, such as well-being or happiness, conceals a design to impose models of behaviour or an ideal of character. The idea that human beings, by virtue of their nature, have certain ends whose attainment is necessary to realize their well-being and happiness makes sense only if we proceed from a theory of what, within the limits of possibility, can be empirically ascertained, a theory about the subjective well-being of some group of people in a given historical context or, universally, of *all* historically situated people. So if a flesh-and-blood person is serene, happy, and satisfied even without embodying values such as prudence, temperance, or industriousness or the values associated with the family, this does not mean that this or other persons have thereby corrupted their nature: it simply means that it is not necessary to nurture these values in oneself to achieve well-being or happiness. In fact, "the teleological project of assigning a human nature to us is vitiated by the fallacy of composition" (Celano 1994, p. 577, my translation); "in the vast

This last argument is open to at least two objections. I should begin by noting that adults are not unruly children. If they were forced to behave in a way they consider unfair (e.g., a ban on the consumption of tobacco), they would probably react with hatred and resentment directed at the institution that forces them to do so. At any rate, we have seen that the use of force to compel virtuous behaviour does nothing, in itself, to make people virtuous or set them on a path toward virtue: what is also needed is a dialogical, persuasive education in virtue. But even here, if the idea is that people can be educated to flourish in the right way, to discover which goals they need to achieve as a necessary condition for realizing their true well-being, this education in virtue comes up, in the first place, against an objection we can call "coercion". Once a prohibition is placed on a certain behaviour (such as smoking tobacco), and on top of enforcing penalties for breaking that rule, the state also requires smokers to go through a tobacco education and prevention programme, what good would that do if people are *forced* to sign up and hear the arguments in favor of the virtues? The element of compulsion makes it very unlikely that any enrolee will persuade themselves that smoking tobacco is a bad choice. For decades, modern psychotherapeutic and psychoanalytic theories have understood that participation in education and prevention or rehabilitation programmes needs to be voluntary, for otherwise the programmes would fail in their mission. In fact, even if someone can be compelled to participate in an education and prevention programme or a "virtue-building" programme, they cannot be compelled to *commit* to it, in the sense that they could go through the motions of attending, all the while drifting away with the mind, and legitimately so, in a reverie about what they really want to do (e.g., smoke). And I suspect that the likelihood of that happening would indeed be quite high. In the second place, current paternalistic states in the West prohibit certain behaviours, but they do not roll out compulsory educational "virtue-building"

majority of cases, the definition of human nature in functional terms—the notion of a 'well-functioning' human being—has served, and continues serve, the purpose of affixing a stamp of factual objectivity or 'natural necessity' on normative and evaluative assumptions expressive of particular moral conceptions" (ibid.); "in the vast majority of cases, terms such as *abnormal* and *pathological* have been, and continue to be, conveyors of prejudices [...] whose purveyors, wittingly or otherwise, have an interest in presenting as *free* of prejudice" (ibid., italics added). Even where we have needs, desires, and inclinations that are typical of human beings, such as breathing or the instinct for survival, this doesn't mean that we cannot detach ourselves from them, or from some of them, nor does it mean that we must necessarily satisfy them. "From the fact that something is part of human nature it does not follow that we must conform to that nature" (ibid). The same idea has been expressed by Uberto Scarpelli: "Another meaning of *nature* is 'that in virtue which every entity tends toward an end,' and precisely in this tendency lies its nature. Nature so understood is inherently normative, such that something proves to be good and just inasmuch as it promotes this tendency, and bad and unjust inasmuch as it gets in its way. Behind this idea lies a very long and complex history going back to Aristotle; the idea of a tendency toward an end was then extended to include not only this-worldly ends but also otherworldly ones [...]. Then came the Scientific Revolution and modern thought, under which finalism was discarded [...]. Teleological thinking now retains a role only in the human sciences, where behaviour is explained in relation to *the aims that individual set for themselves or otherwise accept*" (Scarpelli 1998, p. 43, my translation, italics added).

programs for adults (e.g., programmes that would train people to withstand pain). And that is perfectly understandable, since compulsory participation in such programs would be experienced in the West as an intolerable violation of autonomy. As a result, if current prohibitions on euthanasia and assisted suicide were to be implemented on a perfectionist and compulsory basis, they would prove to be ineffective. Indeed, as we have seen, people cannot be "compelled" to be virtuous or threatened with penalties for "breach of virtue," for that would defeat the very logic of virtue, which is a logic of internal and voluntary change.

Even with the perfectionist argument, as with the utilitarian/organicist argument, it may be objected that there exist moderate perfectionists who, in the name of a reasonable pluralism, are willing to endorse a compromise solution where perfectionism is brought into a balance of acceptability with the principle of autonomy. In other words, while moderate perfectionists, expressing a sentiment that is widely shared in the Western world today, would consider it unacceptable for the state to coercively restrict individual freedom so as to get us to be more virtuous in the use we make of our own assets or body (forcing us to make generous or unselfish or temperate or not greedy choices in that regard), they might instead accept that the state should compel us to exercise the virtue of courage, requiring us to withstand physical or psychological pain, resist the temptation of assisted suicide in coping with a serious or terminal illness, or reject the escapist choice of taking refuge in drug-induced artificial worlds.[136] The problem with this "reasonable" perfectionism is precisely that it requires a coherent balancing between the principle of individual autonomy and the need for individuals to embody the virtues of an ethical state. The problem, more to the point, is that in order for this coherence to obtain, we need a sufficiently definite criterion by which to govern this balancing, for otherwise we would be looking at the prospect of unfettered interference in individual freedom. It doesn't seem to me that such a criterion exists, and even if we assume that it does exist, its use would lead to paradoxical or unacceptable outcomes. This for at least four reasons.

For one thing, concepts such as "brave," "virtuous," "hard-working," and "selfish" are ethically thick, meaning that they inevitably involve value judgments, and

---

[136] A similar argument against euthanasia has been advanced by Francesco D'Agostino, commenting that "if we are endowed with such serene lucidity as to be able to plan our own death by the hand of others, we should also have it in us to execute that plan by our own hand [...]. And if, as patients, we reject the idea of suicide because we lack the courage for it, doesn't this mean that our strong and serene will, a will of true fortitude, is thereby diminished [...]?" (D'Agostino 1998, p. 238, my translation). Here D'Agostino commits an empirical error. A patient's will is normally not simply to die but to die in a certain way (one that is painless, dignified, safe, assisted, comfortable), and not to attempt a solitary and probably painful or ineffective suicide by improvised means. He does not understand this important truth when he argues that in order for euthanasia to be legal, a patient requesting the procedure needs to be "unable without assistance to end her life" (Young 2022, para 2). Looking at the contemporary world, D'Agostino also laments the disappearance of "the *ars moriendi*—the art of dying well, with a human acceptance of the terrible event" (ibid, 240). It is worth noting, in this connection, that even drug addicts, despite their addiction, could be perfectly capable of taking on certain family and work responsibilities.

controversially so. Some authors even argue that these value judgments are akin to facts and cannot be separated from the factual, meaning that they determine the *truth conditions* of a statement such as "So-and-so is brave." I doubt, for example, that it is cowardly to request euthanasia if we have fallen gravely ill in a way that causes physical or psychological agony. In fact a choice to endure the agony could easily be viewed as masochistic. A prohibition on assisted suicide on perfectionistic or "virtuous" grounds would therefore raise serious problems of indeterminacy, with no limits on the kinds of criminal laws that could be introduced by an ethical state using language that contained such thick concepts.

For another thing, we have a coherence problem. If we assume that courage consists in withstanding physical or psychological pain and facing up to difficult situations and to our responsibilities—as when grappling with the loss of a loved one or a strained marriage or with loss of employment—and that it is, by contrast, cowardly to run away from these and other hardships, as by seeking peace of mind in heroin or LSD, and that this activity should accordingly, on that basis, be prohibited, then why shouldn't it also be prohibited to systematically seek peace of mind by recourse to hypnosis or ritual fasting or to other drugs, such as alcohol, antidepressants, or sleeping pills? Assuming that it is cowardly to avoid physical and psychological pain by requesting euthanasia, and that the procedure is therefore, on that basis, prohibited, why shouldn't it also be prohibited to request anaesthesia or pain killers for any painful surgery, such as an appendectomy? Assuming that it is cowardly to request assisted suicide if we have been diagnosed with a serious or terminal illness, and the procedure should therefore be prohibited, wouldn't it also be cowardly to flee to a foreign country to escape the consequences of the hurt of a romantic disappointment?

3.7.1 The Hamlet's Objection and Other Objections

Assuming it is cowardly to request assisted suicide if we have been diagnosed with a serious or terminal illness, since we are doing so out of fear of pain, wouldn't it be equally cowardly to desist from suicidal intentions out of fear of death or the afterlife? This is a point about human character that Shakespeare was early to express:

> For who would bear the whips and scorns of time, / Th' oppressor's wrong, the proud man's contumely, / The pangs of despised love, the law's delay, / The insolence of office, and the spurns / That patient merit of th' unworthy takes, / When he himself might his quietus make / With a bare bodkin? / Who would fardels bear, / To grunt and sweat under a weary life, / But that the dread of something after death, / The undiscovered country from whose bourn / No traveler returns, puzzles the will / And makes us rather bear those ills we have / Than fly to others that we know not of? / Thus conscience does make cowards of us all [...].[137]

[137] Shakespeare, *Hamlet*, act 3, sc. 1, ll. 78–91.

Assuming that it is cowardly to shirk our family, social, and financial responsibilities by taking refuge in heroin, perhaps because we are mourning the loss of a loved one, wouldn't it also be cowardly to permanently cut ties with our social and family environment and take refuge in the Alaskan backcountry or a Buddhist hermitage built in a pristine forest, or to wander about homeless in Mexico City or take up painting in Tahiti?.[138] The only coherent conclusion for a moral perfectionist would seem to be that if we want to punish drug addicts because they lack courage or because, in the medium to long period, they put their life or physical integrity at risk, in sucha away as to prevent the cultivation of certain virtues, we should also punish the hermit who systematically fasts, the couch potato who loves to binge on junk food and becomes obese, anyone addicted to psychotropic drugs or who systematically overdrinks, or who engages in extreme sports, who has unprotected sex and contracts AIDS, who swims in dangerous waters where dangerous sharks have been spotted, or who practices boxing or wrestling. It might be objected that the law does not deal with marginal, niche phenomena: *De minimis non curat lex*, as the Latin phrase goes. How many hermits are there? How many "total couch potatoes" are addicted to junk food and become obese? And yet, on the principle of rationality and reasonableness, requiring coherence in the law, the law should also punish the hermit, the alcoholic, and the couch potato who loves to binge on junk food and becomes obese. At any rate, even the law currently on the books deals with marginal cases, having to do with LSD, for example, or with the sacramental use of peyote (in this last regard, in the US context, see *Employment Division v. Smith*, 494 U.S. 872 [1990]). It might still be objected that while it is comparatively easy to arrest drug dealers and users, a policy of punishing couch potatoes or alcoholics would require a police state, one that uses surveillance technology to systematically spy on people in their private lives. But that is not necessarily the case. For one thing, it may be equally difficult punish drug dealers and users, since drugs are very often sold and consumed in the home. And, for another thing, there are two intuitively simple measures that could easily be adopted without significant investment. The first is a card, like a national medical card, that records any transaction involving the sale of alcohol or junk food: if you exceed a threshold number of transactions, this will automatically trigger an alert sent to authorities who will review your case or issue a fine. A similar system could be set up requiring psychologists to report clients who book appointments for a hypnosis session. The second is a scheme under which the Department of Labour or a similar government agency would be required to report people who quit their jobs or remain unemployed for a set amount of time, and this could be supplemented with a reporting system for people who go missing or retreat to a convent. Of course, the effects of drug use vary depending on the type of drug at issue. Not all of drugs have the effect of taking users to a place of oblivion where they can escape reality, but I would suggest that there does seem to be a common

[138] This is, respectively, the real story of Christopher McCandless, recounted in the film *Into the Wild* (2007), directed by Sean Penn; the fictional story of two Buddhist monks in the film *Spring, Summer, Fall, Winter ... and Spring* (2003), by Kim Ki-duk; and, finally, the fate of the homeless protagonist in *Amores Perros* (2000), by Alejandro González Iñarritu.

use case. It could be argued, in other words, that people who make use of nonmedical drugs have a common psychological profile, in that they lack the strength needed to accept reality, that is, their own mental or physical limitations, and they accordingly turn to drugs to cope with these limitations or enhance their mental or physical performance. Finally, some might argue that some choices that people make to escape reality (such as permanent expatriation or hermitism) or choices that can do harm to the mind and body (such as ritual fasting carried out systematically over time) can be justified on the basis of the need for individuals to strike a balance between different virtues, values, and principles. For example, permanent expatriation could be justified on the basis of the need to balance perfectionist values with the principle of the free movement of people and things in a globalized world. Such balancing would doubtless be constitutionally legitimate. Or someone may feel they need to balance certain familiar virtues (such as industriousness) with ascetic or religious values that would justify their retreating to a hermitage or systematically carrying out ritual fasting. But here, too, we would face a coherence problem. Consider a scenario in which, on the one hand, people are allowed to stop working (thereby ceasing to contribute to the nation's economic growth), or take refuge in a convent (shirking family responsibilities), or do harm to their own body by continuous and systematic ritual fasting), all for the purpose of enabling them to nurture their spirituality, but on the other hand a prohibition is placed on practices that similarly do harm to the mind and body or enable individuals to shirk their responsibilities or to not work, and these latter actions are put in place on "secular" grounds, such as the need to enable individuals to seek pleasure, push the limits of their intellectual capacities and physical strength, complete sporting feats that no one has ever accomplished, contribute to the historical and cultural progress of the nation, or put an end to their own suffering or pain. It is difficult to see how those two regimes could justifiably coexist within the same system, not least because that would stand in contradiction with the secularist disestablishment principle of the separation of church and state.

Third, it is possible to determine whether an agent's choice to carry out a certain action is rational and sufficiently uncoerced, and the procedure for making such an assessment would be complex but transparent. And through such a procedure, while also making some assumptions, it is also possible, albeit more difficult, to determine whether a certain behaviour that causes harm to others was wilful, a case of wrongful intent. But here we should ask, isn't it possible for someone who performs an action to have different conscious motivations behind for that action? It may be possible, in other words, that they had different motivations for a certain act. So, for example, isn't it possible that is someone who takes LSD or makes a nonsacramental use of peyote, "cravenly" avoiding a challenging situation or shirking their responsibilities, is also on a spirit quest, striving for a greater awareness of the universe by unlocking the doors of sensory perception or the boundless potential of the unconscious? isn't it possible that free-solo climbers or waterfalls kayakers seeking to push the limits of their mental and physical strength, are also simply adrenaline junkies? Isn't it possible that extreme paragliders interested in contributing to the progress of humanity, accomplishing feats that no one has ever accomplished before, are also seeking a glorious death? And what about someone who retreats to a bunker to immerse themselves in reading (perhaps attempting their own translation of Proust's *In Search of Lost Time*), or someone who goes into seclusion to meditate and fast, or someone who decides to binge-watch an entire season of an animated sitcom while binging on junk food: or isn't it possible that they trying to avoid facing up to difficult personal situations, trying to shirk financial, social, or family responsibilities, all the while doing harm to their mind and body, are also nurturing their spirituality?[139]

Fourth, the usual unresolved problem remains; you cannot impose virtue by force or impose *effective* virtue education programs.

A final consideration. It is important to point out that antipaternalism could justify the use of public resources to finance films and associations and set up public debates and educational programs in schools for the purpose of guiding citizens toward activities that are believed to promote greater intellectual, emotional, and spiritual enrichment, like not doing hard drugs.

3.8 Fallacious or Rationally Inadequate Strategies

As we saw in Sect. 3.1, several argumentative strategies in support of paternalism are fallacious or rationally inadequate because parasitic. These arguments suffer from circularity, inconsistency, or serious vagueness. They form a cluster that lacks rational support, and they can further be broken down into two subgroups: (1) arguments that rely on circular concepts of mental incompetence or nonvoluntary action and (2) arguments that appeal to the sanctity of human life, human dignity, and the common good (often used in combination).

These arguments unfortunately enjoy widespread rhetorical use. So how can we explain their appeal, considering that they are, after all, fallacious? The answer, as previously suggested, is that the authors who use them seem to have something they want to conceal, which leads them to deploy arguments that are either fallacious or parasitic on more robust paternalistic arguments, that is, on the utilitarian/organicist argument and the perfectionist argument. As we have seen, for example, there are authors whose work conceals that their true commitment is to a theological argument—namely, God gives life and death, and no one should dispose of what does not belong to them—in light of which they seek to restrict individual freedom.

It would be just as difficult to use strong versions of either the utilitarian/organicist argument or the perfectionist argument, the former turning the individual into an instrument of the collectivity to advance the aim of maximizing overall happiness across the population, the latter coherently lending support to policies designed

[139] A vivid illustration of the way that junk and ultraprocessed food can damage one's physical and psychological health is offered in the 2004 documentary film *Super Size Me*, directed by and starring Morgan Spurlock, who in the film puts himself through a month-long diet consisting exclusively of food selected from the McDonald's menu. Cf. Kechagias et al. (2008), p. 57.

to clamp down on any number of recreational activities or activities expressive of one's sexuality, in a way that would now be considered unconstitutional, as well as morally unacceptable by many citizens, in many, albeit not all, Western states. And I should also note an irony here, which is that utilitarian/organicist and perfectionist arguments are often premised with the caveat that, clearly, we cannot use religious arguments in public debate. Hence the need to press forward with nonreligious arguments. But there is a Latin phrase for such use of disclaimers: *Excusatio non petita, accusatio manifesta*. The irony, then, is that the more one prefaces an argument by saying that it is nontheological, the likelier it is that they are disguising a theological argument, that is, precisely the kind of argument they just said they were not going to use.[140]

Why is the theological argument difficult to use, and indeed little used, in contemporary Western democracies? Like any other metaphysico-transcendent argument of that kind, the argument is subject to at least three objections that are difficult to overcome. For one thing, not only is it a metaphysico-transcendent argument of a religious nature—concerning entities that are supersensible or supernatural, whether in whole or in part—but it is an argument based on an intricate set of metaphysico-transcendent beliefs, having as their object some very complex facts that would have to pass a twofold test: they would first have to be shown to hold, and then (granted that they *can* be shown to hold), they would have to be shown to be "active," that is, capable of having an effect on sensible, empirical reality, and constantly so on countless occasions. And it is difficult to see how they could pass even the first one of those two tests, considering that, by definition, they lack empirical evidence (even if this doesn't *ipso facto* disqualify an argument as irrational). From an ontological and epistemological point of view, the metaphysico-transcendent assumptions, therefore, are unverifiable and unfalsifiable in the sense that they are neither rational nor irrational, there is no sufficiently certain logical or empirical evidence in favour of or against these assumptions. They are totally arbitrary. Then, as we know with sufficient certainty, on the basis of an inductive argument, that water boils at a hundred degrees Celsius at sea level, just as we know, on the basis of a Peirce abductive argument, that it is probable that the white beans above the kitchen table came from the sack of white beans under the table, or that the woman killed with a backstab in her flat knew her murderer, because there are no signs of forced entry to doors and windows, and people do not normally open to strangers, therefore we do not know with sufficient certainty whether God exists—much less whether God actually "wills" anything, or deals with human affairs, or establishes when we are born and when we die, or has laid down some code morality that we must all follow, or considers it legitimate (or not immoral) for someone to renounce life (once given), including by requesting the help of third parties, or thinks it right that

[140] One author who employs this strategy is Mario Romano, who comments as follows: "I view it as excessive to assert a genuine right to choose the time and manner for ending one's life. Although we cannot argue on religious grounds in a secular system, it seems to me that even a conception completely devoid of any religious underpinnings cannot be stripped of communitarian elements" (Romano 2010, p. 165, my translation).

human beings should to be free to sin (they are not predestined to do so), as by committing assisted suicide (as long as they do not harm others), so that those who have *not* sinned (the virtuous among us) can be rewarded in the afterlife.

We cannot say with any sufficient certainty whether God considers it right for the state to allow individuals the freedom to act in morally wrong ways—as by committing assisted suicide (so long as they do not cause harm to others)—or whether God wants the community to forbid what God considers sinful, or whether God would consider it morally right to legalize euthanasia. Couldn't it be that case that God cannot countenance suffering and believes in the principle of individual autonomy? Couldn't it be the case that God sees the world through a *liberal* lens? Assuming, and not conceding, that according to the head of the Catholic religious confession, who considers himself the authoritative interpreter of God's will, God is against euthanasia and wants the community to prohibit it, there are so many metaphysico-transcendent premises that would have to hold true here that we cannot verify the theological argument against autonomy in question with the certainty needed to for it to be acceptable (or with the "relative certainty" with which we can verify the second law of thermodynamics). We have considered almost seven metaphysico-transcendent premises–God exists (1); God actually "wills" anything (2); God deals with human affairs (3); God has laid down some code morality that we must all follow (4); God does not consider it right for the state to allow individuals the freedom to act in morally wrong ways—as by committing assisted suicide or God wants the community to forbid criminally what God considers sinful (5); the head of the Catholic religious confession is the authoritative interpreter of God's will (6); according to the head of Catholic Church God is against euthanasia and wants the community to prohibit it (7). The fact that all these seven metaphysico-transcendent premises are true is, from the point of view of the logic of calculating probability, radically improbable.[141] This objection of course applies to any such complex, multifaceted metaphysico-transcendent argument, and so not only to religious arguments of this sort but to also to "secular" ones, assuming that such arguments exist.

Second, the theological argument would seem to violate the secularist disestablishment principle of the separation of church and state, under which the state is to not impose the dogmas of any single religion. And third, the argument seems to conflict with the principle of cultural pluralism. Atheists, agnostics, theists, Epicureans, neopagans, Christians, Jews, Buddhists, Confucians, Muslims, Hindus, Taoists, and indeed people of any creed, should be able to peaceably coexist under a single polity and not impose their beliefs on others.[142]

[141] The probability that two events are simultaneously true is given by the product of the probability that the first will occur and the probability that the second will occur. Therefore, if the probability that "God exists" is 50%, the probability that "God exists" and "God has a will" is 25%. The probability that all these seven metaphysico-transcendent premises are true is one in one hundred and twenty-eight, that means a probability of 0.0078125.

[142] Apparently subscribing to the second and third objection are Dworkin (1993), and D'Agostino (1998, p. 214).

Other authors do not seem to be fully aware that they are paternalists, that is, they appear not to accept, even to themselves, that they are not liberal under the pluralist standard of the third objection above. So they turn to argumentative strategies that do not frontally attack the principle of individual autonomy. Many others recognize that they are paternalists, but they also appreciate that in the twenty-first century, at least in the West, the principle of individual autonomy is deeply entrenched and sits like a boulder blocking the path along which the paternalist is marching. To openly question individual autonomy is to have the presumption to look someone in the eye—someone who is an adult, rational person, who knows the relevant facts, is sufficiently free from coercive pressures, and whose desires are stable over time—and tell them, publicly, that others know better than they do what is good for them.

3.8.1 *Never Failing to Invoke Mental Incapacity and Nonvoluntariness*

One argumentative strategy that doesn't stand up to rational scrutiny and yet is widespread is as follows. It is first argued that a liberal state has the right to coercively restrict individual freedom in two cases: when someone may cause harm to a third party, and when they do something that is harmful or dangerous to themselves, and in some relevant respect they lack rationality, sufficient freedom from coercive pressures, knowledge of relevant facts, and mental capacity, perhaps because they are wildly incoherent or uninformed, or they suffer from a serious mental disorder or they are in a state of momentary insanity. At this point a circular notion of incapacity or nonvoluntariness smuggled in so as to prevent individuals from carrying out activities that are dangerous or harmful to their integrity (cf. Garzón Valdés 1988, p. 164). In short, a notion of incapacity is constructed that stealthily brings in utilitarian/organicist or perfectionist values or a substantive conception of rationality on which it is based.[143]

[143] There is a different kind of mistake that Macario Alemany seems to be making. He first develops a conception of "basic capacity" resting on a conception of (predominantly) formal rationality and on the principle of autonomy. We thus have the familiar list of vices of consent or voluntary action: uninformedness, inconsistent preferences, mental disorders, cognitive bias, duress, etc. But then, when this broad framework is applied to concrete cases—as with the question of whether the state should make it legal to sell and consume heroin or ride a motorbike without wearing a helmet—we see that not everything hangs together coherently. Indeed, Alemany speaks of "trivial interference," and does so on the assumption that "not wearing a seatbelt or a helmet on a motorbike cannot be significant component of any plan of life" (Alemany 2006, p. 408ff.; my translation) or that the consumption of drugs should be permitted only when "the reason for consumption is purely recreational" (ibid., p. 418 ff.). In reality, the notion of "trivial interference," as well as the distinction between recreational and nonrecreational uses of drugs like heroin, is incompatible with antipaternalism as outlined not only here and in Feinberg's theory but also in Alemany's own theory. If we have a drug user who is now addicted to heroin and wants to keep making use of that drug, and we want to say that desire is unvitiated, we have to go back to the decision made at a previous moment,

Let three examples illustrate.

For our first example we can turn to the familiar principle that a physician may legitimately carry out euthanasia on a seriously ill adult patient if, and only if, that patient is rational and mature and the choice is thought-through and informed.[144] All well and good—were it not that the next move invariably consists in specifically denying that terminally ill patients who want to be killed by lethal injection are rational, mature, and adequately informed, for if they did meet that description, they would *not* give so much weight to the fact that they are experiencing psychophysical suffering considered to be unbearable.[145] As Young (2022) comments: "Perhaps, though, what is really at issue in this objection is whether anyone can ever form a competent, enduring and voluntary judgement about being better off dead, rather than continuing to suffer from an illness, prior to suffering such an illness". Keown (cf., Keown in Jackson and Keown 2012) talks about the use of advancet directives in cases in which the patient cannot give a *current*, rational, and competent satement, owing for example of deep sedation, and in these cases the authors seem to use a circular concept of rational and competent wishes.

Turning now to our second example, consider the argument that since seriously ill, or elderly patients or people with childhood trauma are frail, vulnerable, and suggestible, they cannot, by definition, have the mental capacity or autonomy needed to make decisions form themselves when the stakes are so high.[146] If that were the case, and if we were to act on that argument, we would fall into the paradox whereby the people sick, elderly or with childhood trauma are barred from making important personal decisions (some of them in a sense wholly or partially irrevers-

when this person started taking drugs, knowing that there was a risk of becoming addicted to the drug.

[144] In Belgium, for example, the law on euthanasia reads: "Doctors who carry out euthanasia do not commit an offence if they have ascertained that: the patient is of full age or an emancipated minor who at the time the request is made is mentally competent and conscious; the request is made voluntarily, carefully, and on multiple occasions and is not coerced." Loi relative à l'euthanasie (28 May 2022), chap. II (Des conditions et de la procédure), Art. 3(1): "Le médecin qui pratique une euthanasie ne commet pas d'infraction s'il s'est assuré que: le patient est majeur ou mineur émancipé, capable et conscient au moment de sa demande; la demande est formulée de manière volontaire, réfléchie et répétée, et qu'elle ne résulte pas d'une pression extérieure [...]." *Moniteur Belge*, 22 June 2022, p. 28515, https://www.ejustice.just.fgov.be/eli/loi/2002/05/28/2002009590/moniteur.

[145] Indeed, on some conceptions that style themselves as deontological or as based on the principle of autonomy, "the fact that someone's behaviour is irrational [or else nonvoluntary] is inferred from the fact that they are doing harm to themselves, such that the overriding criterion comes to be, once again, harm avoidance" (Diciotti 1986, p. 585; my translation). As Diciotti points out, as much as theories of this kind may purport or aspire to be deontological, they are in effect consequentialist (or otherwise nondeontological) theories in disguise.

[146] Cf. Sunstein (1997), p. 1142ff.; Amarasekara and Bagaric (2004), p. 410. Luigi Cornacchia even speaks of an "unsolvable paradox of vulnerability" in virtue of which weaker individuals, such as aging or sick people, would be unable to exercise the "right to make their own decisions" or would even be prevented from exercising that right (Cornacchia 2003, p. 207; my translation), though he doesn't specify in any detail how that would happen. In the same vein, see D'Agostino (1998), pp. 218–219.

ible), such as getting married; having an abortion; having gender-affirming surgery; giving consent to life-threatening operations; refusing life-saving treatment; determining whether, with whom, and how to raise children; or drawing up a will. There are many circumstances and events that can make someone fragile, vulnerable, or unhappy: betrayal, divorce, separation, a failing romantic relationship, bereavement, a family quarrel, being unable to reunite with one's own family, having possessive or unloving parents, getting uprooted from one's native land, not being able to have children, getting fired from one's job, a serious neurosis, a childhood trauma. And yet it would be absurd to legally qualify the vulnerability or anguish attendant on such circumstances as a condition barring someone from carrying out certain "acts in the law," particularly acts through which patients may consent to medical treatment of any kind. If vulnerability or emotional distress were in fact a disabling condition preventing someone from properly consenting to medical treatment, then in at least half of the cases in which a patient consents to such treatment, the authorization would have to be deemed invalid. In part, that is because deciding whether to authorize a certain medical treatment or surgical operation is a very complex decision, one that involves weighing numerous pros and cons, such as the risk of significant side effects and the different probabilities of such effects occurring. These kinds of decisions are often much more difficult and complex than someone's decision to request euthanasia once they have been diagnosed with a terminal or grave illness with a gloomy prognosis.

Our third, and final, example concerns cases in which a patient is supposed to show signs of depression. Here the argument is made that patients in this condition cannot authorize a doctor to euthanize them, the understanding being that depression is a mental disorder—and a serious one at that—and is therefore a mentally incapacitating condition. As evidence for that claim, and this is where the whole line of reasoning turns circular, it is pointed out that patients in that condition no longer value as they should a whole range of activities and pursuits (such as forming friendships, playing with children, or contemplating the beauty of nature) that should otherwise be regarded as meaningful.[147]

In conclusion, the fallacious or rationally inadequate argumentative strategies we have passed in review make it possible to claim that someone is rational or competent—or makes rational, competent, or voluntary decisions—only if these decisions, or those who make them, possess a certain qualifying property, but the scope or meaning of this property is vague or morally controversial: different people will understand it in different ways, for which reason it is deliberately left unspecified. Examples of such a property are psychological maturity (regardless of age), thoughtful judgment at peace with oneself, reasonableness, normality, and emotional balance. And the catch here is that if someone is diagnosed with an illness that causes great suffering, with a gloomy prognosis, and they no longer see the good in life—they may no longer be responsive to loving relationships, for example, or embrace

[147] For a close analysis of these fallacious argumentative strategies, see Alemany (2006), pp. 273–274; Feinberg (1986), p. 359.

the virtue of courage—they are at once demoted to a status of unreasonableness or immaturity, which on this line of argument disqualifies them from making rational or competent decisions for themselves.[148]

3.9 The Argumentative Triad: The Sanctity of Human Life, Human Dignity, and the Common Good

Another rationally inadequate argumentative strategy consists in using widely disputed or extremely vague concepts, on a level of generality close to that of R. M. Hare's "primarily evaluative" concepts.[149] The three main here are those of human dignity, the sanctity of human life, and the common good. These arguments, such as they are used in the debate between paternalism and antipaternalism, can be said to beg the question (*petitio principii*) or to be parasitic, for they all seem to depend on any of the six arguments in favour of paternalism previously listed in Sect. 3.1. The idea of the sanctity of human life, for example, can be understood to mean any of the following three things, at least: (1) human life is a value to be cherished in itself, rather than being instrumental to the realization of other values; (2) human life is a supreme, absolute value that cannot be sacrificed to other values, such as privacy, public order, or freedom of enterprise; or (3) human life is an unwaivable, inalienable value.[150] From the standpoint of the debate between pater-

[148] On the legalization of euthanasia, for example Cornacchia comments that "the making of decisions for oneself through the agency of others must still be 'reasonable': there must be a valid justification for it. The taboo of the sanctity of human life can be challenged, but only where the community has a sense of boundary situations" (Cornacchia 2003, pp. 205–206; my translation).

[149] Primarily evaluative concepts, according to Hare, are ones in which the evaluative meaning is primary to the descriptive meaning, as happens when a word's "evaluative meaning is constant for every class of object for which the word is used" (Hare 1952, pt. II, sect. 7.4, p. 118). The chief example here is the word "good": a good knife and a good story are different things, to be sure, but when I call them "good" I am equally commenting on both the knife and the story. The same kind of reasoning also applies to the word "right."

[150] An in-depth discussion can be found in Dworkin (1993), p. 97ff. Even the idea that life is *inherently* valuable is open to question. Thus, according to Peter Singer, "we usually value life because it is the basis for everything *else* that we value, whether it be happiness, appreciation of beauty, creativity, love, or the exercise of our rational faculties" (Singer 2000, p. 203; italics added), or even the very idea that life is a gift from God. Equally controversial is the idea that life is truly, and not just figuratively, an absolute value, one that, without exception, prevails over any other value. Just think of the economic and social costs the community would have to bear if it had to (a) protect every person who has been threatened and has a certain statistical probability of being killed by loan sharks, kidnappers, terrorists, or abusive partners or disgruntled former partners; (b) guarantee that all members of the community have access to the most advanced medical treatments; (c) forbid road, rail, and air traffic that inevitably causes accidents, even if it is regulated to minimize the risk of accidents, and even this scenario is unlikely because it is extremely expensive, by requiring all drivers and pilots to take blood-alcohol tests or by monitoring the speed of all vehicles on the road. It shouldn't be hard to imagine similar implications for the three understandings of the sacredness of life just mentioned in the run of text.

nalism and antipaternalism, the first two understandings are not relevant, since the question that specifically comes up in that connection is whether an individual's life can be sacrificed to protect the mental or economic well-being of others. The question here is not whether and to what extent individuals can be allowed to take their own life or harm their own physical integrity—which is the central issue in the debate—but whether and to what extent they can be allowed to harm others or their interests (including by taking their life).

The third understanding is the only one whose implications are relevant to the debate between paternalism and antipaternalism. And yet the argument from the sanctity of human life, though relevant as an argument in favour of paternalism, is clearly circular (vitiated by *petitio principii*), or it is rationally inadequate (parasitic), in the sense that it likely presupposes one of the other six arguments previously identified in Sect. 3.1, such as the utilitarian/organicist argument or the perfectionist one. Indeed, if we are to argue that life and physical integrity are inalienable and unwaivable goods, and so that the state can interfere in individual freedom to prevent people from harming themselves or putting an end to their own life, we need to assert that these goods are "sacred"—which means that they are unalienable or unwaivable (the implication following from the third understanding of the sanctity of human life). So, for example, if at issue is the prohibition on euthanasia or on assisted suicide, and I simply state, without further comment, that the principle of the sanctity of human life needs to be balanced with the principle of autonomy, my argument will be totally indeterminate.[151] Even more dangerous and rationally untenable—though equally prevalent in political, moral, and legal dis-

[151] If we look at the case law of the Italian Constitutional Court, it won't take long to find out that, while the court doesn't generally use the expression "sanctity of human life," it does appeal to the same principle by speaking of the "supreme good of life," the "inviolability of human life," or "human life as an absolute good." A dogmatic use of the principle of the sanctity of human life is made by the criminal lawyer Mario Romano, who states that the fundamental reason for prohibiting euthanasia is that "one's life is a good not solely dependent on one's own will" (Romano 2010, p. 166; my translation)—without in any way elaborating on that statement. Further on, he argues that the need to prohibit euthanasia rests as well on "a fundamental public ethic that must naturally also translate into a generous, tangible, moral, and material solidarity toward those who are coping with the tragedy and toward their family and loved ones" (ibid.). The "solidarity" Romano is referring to probably includes the completely understandable need to provide palliative care for those whose life has been struck by tragedy (the seriously or terminally ill), as well as psychological and economic support for them and their family. And yet we have to ask, how can the moral and material solidarity invoked by Romano be reconciled with his insistence on not allowing someone to end their own life when they are in great psychological and physical pain? In other words, how is it supportive of patients in that state, and how is it respectful of their fundamental wishes, to force them to choose between constant, severe pain and some form of more or less continuous sedation? In what sense of "solidarity" does that even make sense? Even more doctrinally assertive than Romano is Elio Sgreccia, who invokes the doctrine of the Catholic Church, and in particular the 1980 "Declaration on Euthanasia," which qualifies euthanasia as a "violation of the divine law, an offense against the dignity of the human person, a crime against life, and an attack on humanity." In the same vein, Sgreccia states that "suicide is to be condemned because it is contrary to the inviolability of life, to the dignity of the human person, and to the respect owed to the Goodness of the Creator" (Sgreccia 1997, pp. 362, 379; my translation).

course (both in legal scholarship and in the case law)—is the claim that we need to balance the principle of individual self-determination with the right to life, a right conceived as unwaivable, asserting this right against individuals who, by rational, autonomous, and uncoerced deliberation, have decided that they no longer want to live. What seems to be happening here is that, through fanciful rhetorical acrobatics, the right to life or health, a right that in most liberal democracies is constitutionally protected, transmogrifies into what in effect is a duty to live or a duty to safeguard one's own health, even against the wishes of rights-holders who may autonomously and rationally choose otherwise.[152]

It is worth asking, at this point, what might be the *core meaning* of the sanctity of life, or the meaning that ties together all three of the previously listed understandings of the concept, namely, life as a value in itself, life as an inalienable or supreme value, and life as an unwaivable and inalienable good. Here we might follow Ronald Dworkin, who suggests that we look at life in the same way as we do other things we consider worthy of protection, like the Amazon rainforest, the Mayan culture, a Rembrandt painting, or an endangered species of butterfly. One way in which they become sacred is through their "history": we protect them "because they embody processes of human creation we consider important and admirable".[153] The common thread that runs through our three understandings of the sanctity of human life, or the core they all share, can in this sense be described as being at once "creative" and "genetic" or "evolutionary":[154] there is a "creative investment" that nature, humankind, or God has put into the genesis of life, art, or anything we account to be inviolable—and the older the genesis and the more exalted the author, the greater the hallowedness. Hence the widespread sense that none of those creations ought to be in any way damaged, or the effort to create them frustrated.

So that's one explanation for the inviolability of that which is created through an investment of effort, and whose genesis dates back centuries, even millennia. But we should still want to ask, what makes such an investment important? Or, on the flip side, what accounts for the gravity of frustrating the creative effort? Leaving aside metaphysico-transcendent explanations—relating to the creation of the world or the gift of life by God, or positing "a mysterious inexorable force unifying all Life in itself", "the procreant urge of the world"[155]—there is certainly something unique and unrepeatable about the processes of cultural and natural creation, for these are things that we humans cannot create or recreate in a laboratory, and whose "laws" we cannot entirely modify; and even if our outlook is secular, this uniqueness and unrepeatability in part explains the awe and wonder we feel at life and its creation, as well as the pain we feel when life is destroyed or when someone (vol-

[152] Cf. Milan Court of Appeal, order of 17 Oct. 2003, with comment in Ferrando (2004); Milan Court of Appeal, order of 15–16 Nov. 2006, in Guida al diritto: Settimanale di documentazione giuridica, 1 (2007), p. 39; Bonaccorsi (2008), pp. 433–435; Guerra (2008), p. 439ff., and the literature cited therein.

[153] Cf Dworkin (1993), p. 75.

[154] ibid., pp. 74, 76.

[155] ibid. p. 79, quoting Walt Whitman's 1855 poem "Song of Myself".

untarily) renounces it.[156] As Dworkin himself points out, however, that account isn't quite satisfactory. We think that the disappearance of Mayan culture is lamentable or inherently bad not only because it is unique and unrepeatable but also because we ascribe value to it: we do so independently of its uniqueness and unrepeatability, on the basis of other values, considerations, and conceptions, and ones that are not only moral. Consider the tradition of crucifixion as punishment in pagan times, the tradition of hunting witches and burning them at the stake in the sixteenth and seventeenth centuries, or the sati tradition in India (requiring a widow to sacrifice herself on her husband's funeral pyre). Historically, these too are unique and unrepeatable cultural practices, and yet we do not lament their disappearance, any more than we lament the disappearance of AIDS or of Tyrannosaurus Rex.[157] Which brings us back to the question above. If life is considered sacred, in the sense of being unwaivable and inalienable, that is because someone ascribes a particular value to it. And even if there may be individuals who are not ascribing that value to life—they may want to commit suicide, for example—there is a community that is doing so (a community inclusive of friends and family), and the ascription of values in that community can only be based on values in the two previously identified classes of values: perfectionist or utilitarian/organicist.

3.9.1 The Argument from Dignity, Torture and Cruel, Inhumane, or Degrading Treatment

The same argument applies to statements such as "Legalizing euthanasia is contrary to human dignity." The moment we specify what human dignity consists of, we get an argument that is either circular (vitiated by *petitio principii*) or parasitic, because it is so vague and capacious as to be able to take any argument in its premises, including the theological argument, the utilitarian/organicist argument, and the perfectionist argument.[158] In fact, this is most likely to be the case. There are two characteristics of human dignity that can explain why.

---

[156] As Celano comments, "is this one of the most profound and well-established ways in which it is possible to understand the claim that something is as it is "by nature" or that it happens that way. So understood, the term *nature* designates "anything that is not human-made and [...] does not depend on human activity, including all entities and events that [...] come into being, develop, and die in accordance with laws that are not human-posited and cannot be modified by humans. We use *natural*, in short, for the totality of things which are not contingent on humans, and 'over which [humans] have no power'" (Celano 2021, my translation).

[157] cf. Dworkin (1993), p. 76.

[158] Much more scathing is the assessment we have from Winfried Hassemer. "It is disheartening to study discussions of human dignity [...]. One cannot escape the impression that the concept is bent to the strategic interests of the arguer, that its persuasive force is turns monolithic, being put to use and consumed within argumentative chains that would be quite weak but for their recourse to human dignity [...]. The widespread strategy of enhancing weak arguments with the vital breath of a principle such as that of human dignity might explain the equally widespread tendency not to

First, human dignity is indeed a highly indeterminate concept, one that accordingly lends itself to being used in the most disparate ways, often without analytical rigor. And essentially all authors agree on this point. In just a snapshot of the literature, we find that dignity is described as (a) a vague, controversial, deeply ambiguous, and inherently uncertain concept;[159] (b) a moral and legal concept whose boundaries are exceptionally fluid, more changeful than those of any other such concept, and so an intangible concept, owing precisely to its ability to take in innumerable and indefinite contents (Pirozzoli 2007); (c) a solemn, transcendent concept, prone to hegemonic expansion;[160] (d) a concept indefinite enough to be applicable to the most diverse cases and be made to support the widest variety of rights, and so a concept that cannot meaningfully be put to use in the law without specifying it;[161] and (e) a concept almost impossible to define in the abstract, so much so that the best we can do is enumerate the different rights it supports.[162]

Second, "dignity is a notion that can have a strong emancipatory force, especially when it comes to strengthening the social rights of individuals,[163] but at the same time it can be used with apodictic arguments to significantly curtail the rights of others. [...] Dignity [...] is a tool that can be used to expand the sphere of individual autonomy,[164] as well as to establish some baseline conditions that need to be met in order for individuals to freely construct their identity, but at the same time it is also liable to be used to impose a set of mainstream values, to the detriment of pluralism and diversity".[165] In this sense, the principle—with its tendency to establish itself as hegemonic—has been characterized by Benoît Jorion[166] as potentially

work argumentatively with that principle in a proper sequence, one step at a time, but rather to put it on the battlefield and leave it there to do its thing. [...] Those who diligently enunciate the principle of human dignity, and then derive from it what they are looking to get out of it, have not done their argumentative duty" (Hassemer 2007, p. 62, my translation). In the same vein, see Jorion (1999), p. 220. A dogmatic use of the argument from human dignity can be found in Sgreccia (1997), pp. 362, 379.

[159] See Champeil-Desplats (2007), p. 14ff.; Hassemer (2007); Jorion (1999); Maestri (2009), p. 516; Pirozzoli (2007); Resta (2002), p. 825ff.; Ruggeri and Spadaro (1991), p. 347.

[160] Cf. Jorion (1999), p. 215ff.; Pirozzoli (2007), p. 324.

[161] Cf Moutouh (1999), p. 160.

[162] Cf. Jorion (1999), p. 215ff.; Pirozzoli (2007), p. 324. On the question of human dignity, see also Becchi et al. (2012).

[163] As Benoît Jorion (1999, pp. 218ff., 222ff.) observes, especially with respect to French legislation and case law, the principle of human dignity has been used as a basis for a range of human and basic rights that include the right not to be subjected to torture or to degrading and humiliating treatment or punishment, the right to develop one's own personality, the right to decent housing, the right to a living wage, and the right to decent working conditions.

[164] In this connection, and with the same emphasis on French legislation and case law, Hugues Moutouh (1999, p. 174ff.) lists several groups of people who have benefited from the legal recognition of rights based on the principle of human dignity. Among the groups he lists are sick people (especially people with AIDS), employees, children, and foreign nationals, and generally all socially and economically disadvantaged people. In the same sense, see Resta (2002), p. 825ff.

[165] Cf. Resta (2002), pp. 825–828, my translation.

[166] Cf. Jorion (1999), p. 224.

"liberticidal." Where does the threat to the freedom of others lie? Let us consider three sources.

First, this is an argument that easily lends itself to being used to justify paternalistic or, worse still, authoritarian policies, especially in the bioethical debate. To this end it suffices to point to certain acts or activities as against dignity (examples might be practicing oral sex, having abortions, consuming pornography, or using contraceptives), and that is in itself an argument for prohibiting them. As Jorion comments, "we can ask to what extent Picasso, Schiele, or Bacon could have been reproved for assaulting human dignity in virtue of their representation of the human being": "Every era has its own people who criticize and despise degenerate art".[167]

Second, apart from being elevated to the rank of a constitutional principle in several countries in the West—enshrined in the very first article of the German Basic Law—human dignity is part and parcel of the contemporary argumentative discourse, not only in constitutional debates but also in political speech and jurisprudential writing, as well as in statutory and case law. The principle, in other words—its advance seemingly unchecked and unbound—is cropping up in the most diverse legal contexts across the West, not only in legislation and in judicial opinions but also in an array of international conventions.[168]

And third, and this is no small matter, dignity often serves as "a knock-down argument capable of closing the discussion at the outset, barring the way to any further argumentative effort [...]. In other words, in ordinary moral conversations, in international documents, in the argumentative practices of courts (national as well as international), in legal scholarship, in parliamentary discussions, and in current legislative practice, dignity is frequently appealed to as a conversation stopper, as an 'exclusionary reason,' settling every issue and signalling that no further discussion will be tolerated".[169] In that same vein, Umberto Vincenti describes the argument from human dignity as "mythical, an argument capable of putting an end to a discussion, while also stemming the progress of research into a fact, an event, or a context".[170] In fact, the principle of human dignity is often considered intangible, absolute, inviolable, not subject to any balancing—a principle that always trumps any other conflicting principles that may come into the picture, including principles of constitutional rank.[171]

Given how widespread the argument from human dignity has become, and how ideologically salient it is among judges and jurists in the West, many commentators recognize that this principle can no longer be done away with in moral or legal argumentation, nor should it, but at the same time they agree that it needs to be

---

[167] Ibid., p. 228, my translation.

[168] Cf. Jorion (1999), p. 208ff.; Moutouh (1999), p. 168ff.; Resta (2002), p. 819ff.

[169] Tesauro (2011), my translation; similarly, see Simon (2002).

[170] Cf. Vincenti (2009), pp. 107–108, my translation.

[171] Cf. Champeil-Desplats (2007), p. 17ff. The literature on balancing is quite vast. See Aleinikoff (1987); Alexy (2002); Atienza and Ruiz Manero (1996); Barberis (2003); Champeil-Desplats (2002); Dworkin (1977); Gianformaggio (1985); Guastini (1998), p. 230; Guastini (2004); Maniaci (2005); Pino (2007); Troper (2007).

corrected in some important ways. As Winfried Hassemer puts it, "the current argumentative approach to the principle of human dignity [...] is very dangerous, not least for the good health of the principle itself. Still, this does not mean that this approach should be given up: it means that it needs to be put to work more judiciously".[172] The most important way in which the principle needs to be corrected is by stripping it of its absolutist and transcendent sense, so as to enable it to work as an antipaternalistic principle.[173] But what does it mean to interpret human dignity as an antipaternalistic principle, as happened with the *Englaro* opinion rendered in 2007 by the Italian Court of Cassation (a case that in Italy drew much media attention?[174]

To begin with, we need to distinguish between two kinds of applications for the principle of human dignity: the first concerns cases where the state or the community interferes in the freedom of individuals to carry out actions that are harmful to *others*; the second concerns cases where at issue are actions that can only be harmful to *oneself*. As concerns the first application, the principle can be understood to mean that all human beings have the same dignity and are entitled to equal consideration and respect. For example, they have a right not to be subjected to torture or to cruel, inhumane, or degrading treatment or punishment, even when they have committed the worst crimes, such as rape or murder, and are serving sentences for such crimes under serious restrictions of personal liberty. By the same token, under the same principle, human beings have a right not to be subjected to sexual harassment, discrimination (based on suspect classes such as race, gender, or sexual orientation), just as they have an equal right to privacy, safe working conditions, and a minimum wage. Indeed, common to all these cases is that they all involve harm caused by and to third parties without consent: the harm may be physical, psychophysical, economic, or any other kind of third-party harm, but the point is to afford equal protection from it, in full agreement with Mill's harm principle and with an antipaternalist conception. And one of the implications of the principle of human dignity so understood—as consistent with Mill's harm principle—is that it is

---

172 Hassemer (2007), p. 58, my translation.

173 Cf. Jorion (1999), p. 232. Even if Jorion doesn't expressly mention paternalism or antipaternalism, he is quite attuned to the distinction between an antipaternalistic, individualistic conception of human dignity and a paternalistic one, the latter of which he characterizes as absolutist, transcendent, substantial: "If dignity is conceived as one of the attributes of freedom, humans can demand that their dignity be protected against any encroachment, and their dignity cannot be turned against them to restrict their freedom. For individuals are free to define what is good for them. [...] If freedom is one of the attributes of dignity, an appeal to human dignity can be used to *limit* individual freedom" (Jorion 1999, p. 218). [...] Here dignity is no longer a right recognized *for* the individual: it may become a right asserted *against* the individual" (ibid., pp. 218, 231, my translation).

174 "It would certainly be inadmissible to draw any kind of distinction between lives worthy of being lived and ones unworthy of being lived, particularly when the lives in question are those of individuals who are in some way incapacitated. [...] The individual's right to health [...] encompasses the right to lose one's health, to become ill, to go untreated, to live the final stages of one's existence according to one's own canons of *human dignity*, and even to allow oneself to die" (Cassazione Civile, no. 21748 of 16 Oct. 2007, italics mine).

inadmissible for the state to draw (much less enforce) a distinction between lives worth living and lives unworthy of being lived (as might be thought to be the case when someone is in a reversible persistent vegetative state or is suffering from a serious mental disorder),[175] where the third-party harm is that of the state, or indeed anyone, acting on such a distinction to end their "unworthy" life regardless of their wishes.

The argument from human dignity, then, can prove useful where individuals, especially the weaker and more disadvantaged ones, need to be protected from third-party aggression or interference in cases where (1) someone's free and rational will can be ascertained and is contrary to the interference or where (2) it is impossible to ascertain this will, even on the basis of previous statements they may have made or on the basis of their past conduct. But two background conditions need to be met in order for the argument to be legitimately used in such cases. First, there must be a legislative or regulatory gap that the argument fills within a given legal system. And second, it must in any event be specified how someone's human dignity is harmed in the case at issue, or what concrete harm is caused by a certain act, practice, or conduct. In cases involving torture, for example, the harm obviously consists in a severe interference in the corporeal-perceptual sphere, causing the infliction of serious physical and psychological pain and suffering, which may even be permanent. Importantly, however, the argument from human dignity so understood—as an argument used to protect individuals from third-party harm—applies, with its two conditions, regardless of how bad or despicable an individual may be: even a dictator or a murderer is owed a minimum degree of human dignity, that is, a minimum degree of protection from harm that others may do acting contrary to his or her will (whether that will is real or presumed to be such). Or at least that seems to be the universal core that the principle of human dignity contains, and what it entails, as applied to cases involving third-party harm or interference in someone's free and rational will.

This brings us to the second kind of application for the principle of human dignity, where at issue are cases in which the state or the community interferes in the freedom of individuals to carry out actions that are harmful not to others to *themselves*. Here, contrary to what was just argued with respect to the first application, there can be no minimum core of protection that human dignity, on an antipaternalistic understanding of the principle, should be able to afford to individuals, for the only criterion that counts here, as far as their human dignity is concerned, is what *they*, and not others, decide for themselves, particularly when it comes to determining whether and to what extent their own life is worth living. In short, human dignity, on this understanding of the principle as applied to harm done to oneself, is a principle entirely predicated on the idea of individual freedom—the freedom to decide for oneself what counts as harm done to oneself. To take the contrary view is

[175] For a concurring view, see D'Agostino (1998), p. 213.

to fashion human dignity into a liberticidal principle, as is typical of the ethical state.[176]

For example, a person could legitimately say that if he or she has been in a permanent vegetative state for five years, or if he or she is gravely ill with a prognosis of six months, his or her life would no longer be worth living, but this is only based on his or her values or ideals. In other words, a person can be better off dead, because the life that remains for that person has no positive value for her,[177] whereas some of those who hold that a person's life is inviolable, using an objective, trascendent, or paternalistic sense of dignity, or an ideal theory of interests as elaborated in the Chap. 1 deny that a person can ever be better off dead.[178]

What we can take away from the foregoing is that in the debate between paternalism and antipaternalism—specifically when it comes to the question of whether uncoerced rational adults ought to be able to do or to significantly risk doing physical or psychophysical harm to themselves, and to only themselves—the argument from human dignity turns out to be rationally inadequate, as well as dangerous. In fact, as discussed, human dignity is an exceedingly vague concept, one that, as a result, lends itself to a wide variety of uses and is therefore apt to become controversial. We can therefore take it that when this argument is deployed, it is likely to presuppose (a) a theological argument, (b) a utilitarian/organicist argument, or (c) a perfectionist argument, and in such a way that not one of those arguments is explicitly acknowledged or discussed, even if it is the real argument—in effect a theological, utilitarian/organicist, or perfectionist argument cast in the guise of an argument from human dignity. So, for example, I might argue that the state can forcibly prevent individuals from consuming heroin because that would undermine their human dignity as a particular form of respect that individuals owe to themselves. And I would be able to make this claim because what matters in the debate between paternalism and antipaternalism is only the respect that individuals owe to *themselves*, rather than to others, and the assumption here is that heroin users only do harm to themselves, or at least that any harm they do to others (be it physical, psychological, or economic) is irrelevant from the standpoint of a paternalistic argument. The argument I would be making, then, is that individuals who use heroin have no self-respect and undermine their own welfare. But why would that be the case? If we dig deeper, we would find that this respect that everyone owes to themselves, requiring them to do what is good for them, is likely to be ultimately grounded in (a) the respect everyone owes to God and the divine will (and this is the theological argument), or (b) the need to spare their own family the pain they would suffer knowing

---

[176] For example, if someone has been in a permanent vegetative state for five years, they could legitimately claim that their life is no longer worth living, and what would justify the claim is that this is a decision made about their *own* life on the basis of their *own* values, ideals, or worldview. This is a conception that some judges and jurists call personalist, both in connection with the right to health and with human dignity. See Bonaccorsi (2008); Champeil-Desplats (2007), p. 20; Guerra (2008), p. 439ff.

[177] A possibility which is discussed by, e.g., Foot (1977); McMahan (2002); Bradley (2009).

[178] e.g., Keown in Jackson and Keown (2012).

that there is a heroin user in their midst or the need not to break emotional, social, economic ties with children, parents, siblings, relatives, and friends who do not tolerate the agent consuming heroin (this is the utilitarian/organicist argument), or (c) the ideal of the virtuous life that everyone is to pursue (the perfectionist argument). If I confine myself to claiming, apodictically, that consuming heroin undermines the respect that everyone owes to themselves, without in any way elaborating on that claim, my argument will not support my claim. In fact, it will not be an argument at all, for it would remain totally indeterminate.

Similarly, if I say that we as individuals are to determine on our own and for ourselves whether an action we might do that does no harm to others violates our own dignity as human beings or violates the respect we owe to ourselves, I am saying that we are each sovereign over our own mind and body. In other words, I am using the argument from individual autonomy as the basis of the argument from human dignity. That is an antipaternalistic understanding of equal dignity among humans, and one that, importantly, makes it possible to forever dispel "Hitler's shadow," a trope still occasionally resorted to in discussions of euthanasia and other related topics.[179]

3.9.2 The Argument from the Common Good and Its Organicist Metaphor: If the Individual in Some Way Fails, so Does the Community

The same fate, finally, befalls some typically communitarian arguments on which the identity, well-being, good, strength, life, health, wealth, and success of the community as a whole necessarily depend on the identity, well-being, good, strength, life, health, wealth, and success of the individual. If the individual in some way fails, so does the community—the two being inextricably bound up. Now, if we rule out metaphysical conceptions that posit an "ontological primacy of the community"[180]—where the idea is that the community exists above all individuals as an entity with a mind, body, and life its own, and so an entity that can be described as "living," and more or less healthy and strong (mentally or physically)—this argument shows itself to be flawed in the same way as the previous ones. Indeed, a closer look at the need to protect the "life," "health," or "strength" of the community will

[179] "For fifty years, Adolf Hitler has cast a long and dark shadow over discussions of euthanasia. His shadow still persists, to the extent that every time euthanasia is debated, the slippery slope appears beneath our feet, and the Holocaust lies at the bottom of it" (Singer 2000, p. 201). It "may be simply that the attitude that made the Holocaust possible was the attitude that some lives are not 'worthy' of being lived because they fall below some ideal standard of racial and genetic purity. Whether this view is correct is a huge and complex historical question [...]. It may well be right. If it is, then the attitude that lies at the root of the Holocaust is, fortunately, an attitude that very few people hold today" (ibid., pp. 202–203).

[180] Dworkin (2000), pp. 226–227.

disclose either of two scenarios, each with its own underlying purpose. In the first scenario, that purpose is to prevent harm from being done to third parties (e.g., to prevent A from killing or mugging B or to prevent B's parents from psychologically abusing or mistreating the son, B, thereby depriving B of emotional moorings and a safe space in which to have a healthy emotional development),[181] and that kind of protection (of individuals from external harm) is entirely compatible with an antipaternalistic conception. In the second scenario, the need to protect the life, health, identity, strength, of the community is instead invoked to justify placing paternalistic restrictions on individual freedom, either on the basis of the utilitarian/organicist argument or on the basis of the argument from contagion. To return to the previous example: we want to prevent individuals from using heroin, and we justify that restriction by pointing to the fact that this would be bad for the community, whether this is the close community of friends and family (who stand to suffer from seeing a friend or family member with an addiction or who might feel like they have failed their friend or loved one) or the majority of the community or society as a whole, which takes an economic loss with every new heroin addict, especially if, on the argument from contagion, others should imitate that behaviour. On the contrary, the life, health, strength, good, and well-being, of the community does not depend significantly or extensively on the behaviour of a small minority of individuals. As we shall see in the last chapter, there is a small minority of people who use cocaine, MDMA, and heroin, as in fact happens according to the European Drug Report 2022. According to this report, it is estimated that in the past year 3.5 million adults consumed cocaine, 2.6 million MDMA, and 2 million amphetamines. About 1 million Europeans are heavy consumers of heroin or another illicit opiate in the past year; 3.5 million or 1 million out of a population of about 450 million in the European Union means 0.7% of consumers of cocaine or 0.22% of consumers of opiates. As we will see in the last chapter, the majority of consumers, including of hard drugs, 75–80%, are occasional; only a minority, normally 20–25%, is compulsive, and develops a significant addiction (marijuana, cocaine, MDMA, Hallucinogens). About 50% of consumers of heroin and metamphatemine, in United States, develop a substance use disorder (see the cited survey at the footnote 117). But only *severe substance use disorder* is defined as addiction in the literature. (See the footnote 117). According to different studies, as we will see in the last chapter, it is estimate that in case of legalization, this number of users would not grow or would grow no more than 15–20%, especially among consumers of cannabis.

People who are gravely ill or terminal ill who want euthanasia are also a small minority.

None of the foregoing should be understood to diminish the salience of some communitarian arguments. It is obvious that people depend on community in various ways. As Feinberg puts it, "we are social animals. No individual person selects

[181] It is no accident that Martha Nussbaum lists among the "central human functional capabilities" our "being able to have attachments to things and people outside ourselves; to love those who love and care for us," all the while "not having one's emotional development blighted by overwhelming fear and anxiety, or by traumatic events of abuse or neglect" (Nussbaum 2000, p. 79).

'autonomously' his own genetic inheritance or early upbringing. No individual person selects his country, his language, his social community and traditions. [...] We come into awareness of ourselves as part of ongoing social processes."[182] This appreciation for the salience of the community is echoed by Ronald Dworkin:

> People need security and the economic benefits of division of labor. No one could lead an adequate human life without the mechanisms of community that rationalize production and consumption [and] provide public goods like police and armed forces [...]. But people depend on community in ways that go beyond these evident economic and security benefits. They need a common culture and particularly a common language even to have personalities, and culture and language are social phenomena. [...] people need community not only for culture and language but for identity and self-reference, because people can only identify themselves, to themselves, as members of some community to which they belong.[183]

Dworkin is quick to caution, however, that such "evident dependence [on community] does not [...] suggest that a community must be morally or in any other way homogeneous in order to benefit its members in the right way",[184] so he contends with the view that "people need a morally homogeneous community as a necessary conceptual background to a moral and ethical life".[185] But regardless of where we land with respect to this last claim, we have here an opportunity to look at the flip side of the nexus between individuals and the community. And here there can be no denying that just as individuals are dependent on the community they belong to, so the community depends for its spiritual and material well-being on the well-being of the majority of individuals who belong to it. To the extent that these individuals in some way struggle in life, so will the community struggle as a whole.

And yet everyone's life would be derailed or reduced to naught if the state were to be entrusted with the task of coercively preventing people from behaving in such a way as to cause unhappiness in the community, or a loss of wealth, ranging from the intimate community of family and friends to the extended community of society as a whole, and where the unhappiness spans the gamut of negative emotions, ranging from boredom and disappointment to shame, anger, and disgust. And even if the aggregate happiness the community would gain by having someone in their number act or not act in some way far outweighed the unhappiness this person would feel by acting or not acting in that way (e.g., pursuing a career in journalism instead of consuming LSD or writing obscene books), would that justify compelling that behaviour, or forcing it on anyone?[186] Clearly not.

In conclusion, as Ronald Dworkin (2000, p. 230) underscores, "people belong to a variety of communities, and most people can belong to many more if they choose. They belong—or may belong—to families, neighborhoods, alumni groups, fraternal associations, factories, colleges, teams, orchestras, ethnic groups, expatriate

---

[182] Feinberg (1986), p. 46.

[183] Dworkin (2000), pp. 219–220.

[184] Ibid., p. 219.

[185] Ibid., p. 221.

[186] The point is aptly underscored in VanDeVeer (1979), p. 183.

communities," and religious communities.[187] These smaller, more cohesive communities can nurture individuals by giving them a sense of identity, belonging, and emotional attachment that they can develop through a shared set of values or experiences, fulfilling a need that I would even count as a right, especially in a liberal society—pluralist, multiethnic, and multicultural. For even if such a society (the national community) provides a setting in which people can form bonds of affection, it is *through* that society that they can form those bonds and not necessarily *with* it: although it is certainly possible for the members of a national pluralist polity to identify with the polity itself as a source of affection and meaning, that is not likely to be the case. And that brings us to a point that Feinberg makes about the ideal of a liberal polity and community (and what the typical embodiment of that ideal is). On the one hand, as just mentioned, a liberal community is not a close-knit community of like-minded people who find connection through a shared set of values and ideals around which they coalesce: it is more like a community of individuals, where everyone is free to find meaning however they choose and through whatever pursuit or form of experience the choose, and in this sense it is a society in which everyone has a right to be left alone. But on the other hand, we should not take this to mean that a liberal community (the overall polity) is a collection of lone, self-sufficient individuals, each doing what they think is best for them, isolated monads or "free-floating molecules"[188] strategically acting to advance their own good regardless of what bonds of affection there may be that give people a sense of togetherness and attachment. Rather, a liberal polity is "a complex network of subcommunities"[189] or intermediate groups situated between the national polity (with its form of government) and the family of origin or the individuals who belong to it: the communities it harbours are essential to everyone's life, and this is the communitarian element, but in it everyone is free to pursue their own happiness, and this is the liberal element. Needless to say, they are free to do so as long as they do no harm to anyone else, consistently with Mill's harm principle, developing their own nature and inclinations, whether these are formed by genetic endowment, upbringing, cultural heritage, later experiences (what is more probable) choice, destiny, astral influence, or divine will.[190] In this way, anyone who has grown into a rational adult, and indeed anyone who is figuring out what that means, can choose the (intermediate) community or communities that best suit their nature and inclinations. And, subject to the harm principle, it makes no difference in that regard what these communities are: they may be a club of sadomasochists, or a swingers' club, a prayer group, an association of railway workers or philosophers, a house of opium, a chess club, a group of escorts with political ambitions, an environmentalist organization or one that is devoted to advancing LGBTQ+ issues, a Nazi rock band, or a Woody Allen or Britney Spears fan club.

[187] On the looser but equally useful bond an individual can form with a liberal national community (one that is pluralist and tolerant), see Dworkin (2000).

[188] Feinberg (1990), p. 108.

[189] Ibid., p. 92.

[190] See, generally, Feinberg (1990), chap. 29.

References

Aleinikoff TA (1987) Constitutional law in the age of balancing. Yale Law J 96(5):943–1005

Alemany M (2006) El paternalismo jurídico. Iustel, Madrid

Alexy R (1989) A theory of legal argumentation: the theory of rational discourse as theory of legal justification (trans: Adler R, MacCormick N). Oxford University Press, Oxford

Alexy R (2002) A theory of constitutional rights. Oxford University Press, Oxford. Orig. pub. as *Theorie der Grundrechte* (Frankfurt: Suhrkamp, 1986)

Amarasekara K, Bagaric M (2004) Moving from voluntary euthanasia to non-voluntary euthanasia: equality and compassion. Ratio Juris 17(3):398–423. https://doi.org/10.1111/j.1467-9337.2004.00275.x

Amato S (2011) Eutanasie: Il diritto di fronte alla fine della vita. Giappichelli, Turin

Anscombe GEM (1963) Intention, 2nd edn. Harvard University Press, Cambridge (Orig. pub. Basil Blackwell, 1957)

Atienza M (1988) Discutamos sobre paternalismo. Doxa 5:203–214. https://doi.org/10.14198/DOXA1988.5.11

Atienza M, Ruiz Manero J (1996) Las piezas del derecho: Teoría de los enunciados jurídicos. Ariel, Barcelona

Barberis M (2003) Filosofia del diritto: Un'introduzione teorica. Giappichelli, Turin

Barberis M (2006) Il lessico del dissenso. Ragion pratica 1:47–64. https://doi.org/10.1415/22177

Barberis M (2010) La strana coppia: Relativismo etico e pluralismo dei valori. In: Villa V, Maniaci G, Pino G, Schiavello A (eds) Il relativismo: Temi e prospettive. Aracne Editrice, Rome

Bartoli C (2008) La teoria della subalternità e il caso dei dalit in India. Rubbettino, Soveria Mannelli (Catanzaro)

Beauchamp TL, Childress JF (2013) Principles of biomedical ethics. Oxford University Press, Oxford

Beauchamp TL, Davidson AI (1979) The definition of euthanasia. J Med Philos 4:294–312. https://doi.org/10.1093/jmp/4.3.294

Becchi P (2009) Diritto di morire e diritto di lasciar(si) morire: Dialogando con Hans Jonas, oltre Jonas. In: Argiroffi A et al (eds) I diversi volti dell'eutanasia: Prospettive teologiche, etiche e giuridiche. Aracne Editore, Rome, pp 141–156

Becchi P, Belvisi F, Pacillo V (eds) (2012) La dignità umana: Testo e contesto. Themed section, Ragion pratica 1:5–182. https://www.rivisteweb.it/issn/1720-2396/issue/101

Beltramini A (2010) La droga della violenza. Focus, May 2010

Benvenuti F (2006) L'istruzione nel processo amministrativo. In vol. 1 of *Scritti giuridici*. Milan: N.p. (1st ed. Padua: CEDAM, 1950)

Bierut L et al (1998) Familial transmission of substance dependence: alcohol, marijuana, cocaine, and habitual smoking: a report from the collaborative study on the genetics of alcoholism. Arch Gen Psychiatry 55(11):982–988. https://doi.org/10.1001/archpsyc.55.11.982

Bifulco R et al (eds) (2008) Commentario alla Costituzione. UTET, Turin

Biggs H (2001) Euthanasia: death with dignity and the law. Hart Publishing, Oxford

Blackburn S (1993) Essays in quasi-realism. Oxford University Press, Oxford

Bobbio N (2006) Liberalism and democracy (trans: Martin, Soper K). Verso, London

Bok S (1998a) Euthanasia. In: Dworkin G, Frey RG, Bok S (eds) Euthanasia and physician-assisted suicide: for and against. Cambridge University Press, Cambridge

Bok S (1998b) Physician-assisted suicide. In: Dworkin G, Frey RG, Bok S (eds) Euthanasia and physician-assisted suicide: for and against. Cambridge University Press, Cambridge

Bonaccorsi F (2008) Rifiuto delle cure mediche e incapacità del paziente: La Cassazione e il caso Englaro. Danno e responsabilità 4:432ff. (Comment on Cassazione Civile, sez. I, judgment no. 21748 of 16 Oct. 2007.)

Bradley B (2009) Well-being and death. Clarendon Press, Oxford

Bricolo F et al (2006) Meccanismi di azione della cocaina e implicazioni per i trattamenti farmacologici. In: Serpelloni G et al (eds) Cocaina: Manuale di aggiornamento tecnico sci-

entifico. Editrice La Grafica, Mori (TN), pp 137–144. https://www.politicheantidroga.gov.it/media/1981/23pluscocaina.pdf
Brink D (1989) Moral realism and the foundations of ethics. Cambridge University Press, Cambridge
Brock DW (1992) Voluntary active euthanasia. Hastings Center Rep 22(2):10–22. https://doi.org/10.2307/3562560
Cadoppi A (2008) Liberalismo, paternalismo e diritto penale. In: Fiandaca G, Francolini G (eds) Sulla legittimazione del diritto penale: Culture europeo-continentale e anglo-americana a confronto. Giappichelli, Turin, pp 83–124
Cadoret RJ et al (1995) Adoption study demonstrating two genetic pathways to drug abuse. Arch Gen Psychiatry 52(1):42–52. https://doi.org/10.1001/archpsyc.1995.03950130042005
Canale D (2023) Conflitti pratici: Quando il diritto diventa immorale. Laterza, Rome and Bari
Celano B (1994) Dialettica della giustificazione pratica: Saggio sulla legge di Hume. Giappichelli, Turin
Celano B (2006) Pluralismo etico, particolarismo e caratterizzazioni di desiderabilità: Il modello triadico. Ragion pratica 1:133–150. https://doi.org/10.1415/22182
Celano B (2007) L'eguaglianza nella cultura giuridico-politica occidentale moderna: Una mappa concettuale. In: Squarcini F (ed) Mai praticamente uguali: Studi e ricerche sulla disuguaglianza e sull'inferiorità nelle tradizioni religiose. Società Editrice Fiorentina, Florence, pp 11–43
Celano B (2021) Lezioni di filosofia del diritto. Costituzionalismo, Stato di diritto, codificazione, diritto naturale, positivismo giuridico. Giappichelli, Turin
Champeil-Desplats V (2002) Raisonnement juridique et pluralité des valeurs: Les conflits axio-téléologiques de normes. In: Comanducci P, Guastini R (eds) Analisi e diritto 2001: Ricerche di giurisprudenza analitica. Giappichelli, Turin, pp 59–70
Champeil-Desplats V (2007) Dignité de la personne. JurisClasseur Libertés, 540 ff
Colburn D (1995) US Patients' Dying Wishes Often Ignored. Washington Post, 22, https://wapo.st/4eyLxoI
Comanducci P (1992) Assaggi di metaetica. Giappichelli, Turin
Copi IM, Cohen C (2002) Introduction to logic, 11th edn. Prentice-Hall, Upper Saddle River, NJ (15th ed., New York and London: Routledge, 2019)
Cornacchia L (2003) Il dibattito giuridico-penale e l'eutanasia. In: Zanetti G (ed) Elementi di etica pratica: Argomenti normativi e spazi del diritto. Carocci, Rome, pp 195–208
Crespi A et al (2001) Commentario breve al Codice Penale: Complemento giurisprudenziale. CEDAM, Padua
D'Agostino F (1998) Bioetica: Nella prospettiva della filosofia del diritto. Giappichelli, Turin
D'Agostino F (2009) Il grande sofisma sulla fine della vita: Ogni libertà anche nella morte non può svendere la mia libertà. Avvenire, March 6, 2009. https://bit.ly/dagostino-2009-fine-vita-avvenire
D'Agostino F (2011) Testamento biologico. In: Bioetica e biopolitica: Ventuno voci fondamentali. Giappichelli, Turin
Dancy J (1993) Moral reasons. Basil Blackwell, Oxford
Davidson D (1986) A coherence theory of truth and knowledge. In: LePore E (ed) Truth and interpretation: perspectives on the philosophy of Donald Davidson. Basil Blackwell, Oxford
Diciotti E (1986) Paternalismo. Materiali per una storia della cultura giuridica XVI 2:557–586
Diciotti E (1988) Interferenze paternalistiche. Rivista internazionale di filosofia del diritto LXV 4:748–756
Diciotti E (2005) Preferenze, autonomia e paternalismo. Ragion pratica 1:99–118. https://doi.org/10.1415/19841
DSM-IV-TR (2000) Diagnostic and statistical manual of mental disorders, 4th edn. Text revision. American Psychiatric Association, Washington, DC
Dworkin R (1977) Taking rights seriously. Harvard University Press, Cambridge
Dworkin G (1983a) Paternalism. In: Sartorius R (ed) Paternalism. University of Minnesota Press, Chap. 2, Minneapolis, pp 19–34

Dworkin G (1983b) Paternalism: some second thoughts. In: Sartorius R (ed) Paternalism. University of Minnesota, Chap. 7, Minneapolis, pp 105–112
Dworkin R (1993) Life's Dominion: an argument about abortion, euthanasia, and individual freedom. Alfred A. Knopf, New York
Dworkin G (1998) The nature of medicine. In: Dworkin G, Frey RG, Bok S (eds) Euthanasia and physician-assisted suicide: for and against. Cambridge University Press, Cambridge, Chap. 1
Dworkin R (2000) Sovereign virtue: the theory and practice of equality. Harvard University Press, Cambridge
Elster J (ed) (1986) Rational choice. Readings in social and political theory. New York University Press, New York
Elster J (2016) Sour grapes: studies in the subversion of rationality. Cambridge University Press, Cambridge
Emanuel E (1999) What is the great benefit of legalizing euthanasia or physician-assisted suicide? Ethics 109:629–642. https://doi.org/10.1086/233925
Emanuel EJ et al (2016) Attitudes and practices of euthanasia and physician-assisted suicide in the United States, Canada and Europe. J Am Med Assoc 316:79–90. https://doi.org/10.1001/jama.2016.8499
EMCDDA (2022) Trends and Developments (European Monitoring Centre for Drugs and Drug Addiction). Publications Office of the European Union, Luxembourg. https://www.emcdda.europa.eu/publications/edr/trends-developments/2022_en
EMCDDA (European Monitoring Centre for Drugs and Drug Addiction) (2009) Annual report on the state of the drugs problem in Europe. Publications Office of the European Union, Luxembourg. https://www.emcdda.europa.eu/publications/annual-report/2009_en
EMCDDA Selected Issue (2009) Polydrug use: patterns and responses. European Monitoring Centre for Drugs and Drug Addiction (EMCDDA). Publications Office of the European Union, Luxembourg. https://www.emcdda.europa.eu/publications/selected-issues/polydrug-use-patterns-and-responses_en
Fanlo Cortés I (2008) Bambini e diritti: Una relazione problematica. Giappichelli, Turin
Feinberg J (1983) Legal paternalism. In: Sartorius R (ed) Paternalism. University of Minnesota Press, Minneapolis, Chap. 1
Feinberg J (1986) Harm to self, vol. 3 of the moral limits of the criminal law. Oxford University Press, Oxford
Feinberg J (1990) Harmless wrongdoing, vol. 4 of the moral limits of the criminal law. Oxford University Press, Oxford
Feinberg J (1992) An unpromising approach to the 'right to die'. In: Freedom and fulfillment: philosophical essays. Princeton University Press, Chap. 11, Princeton, pp 260–282
Ferrajoli L (2009) Trattamenti sanitari forzati. Ragion pratica 1:357–363. https://www.rivisteweb.it/doi/10.1415/29425
Ferrando G (2004) Stato vegetativo permanente e trattamenti medici: Un problema irrisolto. Familia: Rivista di diritto della famiglia e delle successioni in Europa (Nov.–Dec.). 1167ff. (Comment on Milan Court of Appeals, order of 17 Oct. 2003.)
Ferraro F (2013) L'utilità dei diritti. ETS Pisa
Ferrer Beltrán J (2004) Prova e verità nel diritto. Bologna: il Mulino. Orig. pub. *As Prueba y verdad en el derecho* (Madrid: Marcial Pons, 2002, 2nd ed. 2005)
Finnis J (1980) Natural law and natural rights. Clarendon Press, Oxford
Finnis J (1995) A philosophical case against euthanasia. In: Keown J (ed) Euthanasia examined: ethical, clinical and legal perspectives. Cambridge University Press, Chap. 2, Cambridge, pp 23–35. https://doi.org/10.1017/CBO9780511663444.004
Foot P (1977) Euthanasia. Philos Public Aff 6(2):85–112. https://www.jstor.org/stable/2264937
Fornero G (2020) Indisponibilità e disponibilità della vita. Una difesa filosofico giuridica del suicidio assistito e dell'eutanasia volontaria. Utet, Torino

Frankfurt HG (1982) Freedom of the will and the concept of a person. In: Watson G (ed) Free will. Oxford University Press, Oxford, pp 81–95. Orig. pub. in The Journal of Philosophy 68, 1 (1971): 5–20. https://doi.org/10.2307/2024717

Frey RG (1998) The fear of a slippery slope. In: Dworkin G, Frey RG, Bok S (eds) Euthanasia and physician-assisted suicide: for and against. Cambridge University Press, Cambridge, Chap. 3

Ganzini L (2009) Oregonians' reasons for requesting physician aid in dying. Arch Internal Med 169(5):489–492. https://doi.org/10.1001/archinternmed.2008.579

Garzón Valdés E (1988) ¿Es éticamente justificable el paternalismo jurídico? Doxa 5:155–173. https://doi.org/10.14198/DOXA1988.5.08

Gianformaggio L (1985) L'interpretazione della costituzione tra applicazione di regole e argomentazione basata su principi. Rivista internazionale di filosofia del diritto, 4th series 62(1):65–103

Giannini MS (1951) Autonomia (saggio sui concetti di autonomia). Rivista trimestrale di diritto pubblico 2:851–883. Republished under the title Autonomia. In: Studi in onore di Luigi Rossi (Milan: N.p. 1952). Now in vol. 3 of *Scritti*, 1949–1954 (Milan: N.p., 2003)

Griffiths J et al (1998) Euthanasia and law in the Netherlands. Amsterdam University Press, Amsterdam

Griffiths J et al (2008) Euthanasia and law in Europe. Hart Publishing, Oxford

Guastini R (1998) Teoria e dogmatica delle fonti. Giuffrè, Milan

Guastini R (2004) L'interpretazione dei documenti normativi. Giuffrè, Milan

Guerra G (2008) Rifiuto dell'alimentazione artificiale e volontà del paziente in stato vegetativo permanente. Danno e responsabilità 4:438ff. (Comment on Cassazione Civile, sez. I, judgment no. 21748 of 16 Oct. 2007.)

Hare RM (1952) The language of morals. Clarendon Press, Oxford

Harsanyi JC (1975) Rule utilitarianism and decision theory. Erkenntnis 11 1, also In: Social Ethics, Part 1, May, 1977, 25–53

Hart HLA (1963) Law, liberty, and morality. Stanford University Press, Stanford

Hassemer W (2007) Argomentazione con concetti fondamentali: L'esempio della dignità umana. Ars Interpretandi: Rivista di ermeneutica giuridica 1:57–70. https://www.rivisteweb.it/doi/10.7382/71837

Husak DN (1992) Drugs and rights. Cambridge University Press, Cambridge

Husak DN (2000) Liberal neutrality, autonomy, and drug prohibitions. Philos Public Aff 29(1):43–80. http://www.jstor.org/stable/2672864

Husak DN (2002) Legalize This! The case for decriminalizing drugs. Verso, London

Iglesias Vila M (1999) El problema del discreción judicial. Centro de Estudios Constitucionales, Madrid

Jackson E, Keown J (2012) Debating euthanasia. Hart Publishing, Oxford

Jonas H (1997) Tecnica, medicina ed etica: Prassi del principio responsabilità (trans: Becchi P, Benussi A). Einaudi, Turin. Orig. pub. as Technik, Medizin und Ethik: Zur Praxis des Prinzips Verantwortung. Frankfurt, Insel Verlag, 1985

Jonas H (2000) Sull'orlo dell'abisso: Conversazioni sul rapporto tra uomo e natura (trans: Becchi AP). Einaudi, Turin

Jorion B (1999) La dignité de la personne humaine ou la difficile insertion d'une règle morale dans le droit positif. Revue du Droit Public et de la Science Politique en France et à l'Étranger 1:197–233

Kant I (1996) An answer to the question: what is enlightenment? (1784). In: Gregor MJ (trans and ed) Practical philosophy. Cambridge University Press, Cambridge, pp 11–22

Kass LR (1989) Neither for love nor money: why doctors must not kill. Public Interest 94:25–46

Kechagias S et al (2008) Fast-food-based hyper-alimentation can induce rapid and profound elevation of serum alanine aminotransferase in healthy subjects. Gut: Int J Gastroenterol Hepatol 57(5):649–654. https://doi.org/10.1136/gut.2007.131797

Kleinig J (1983) Paternalism. Manchester University Press, Manchester

La Mantia F (2023) Almost an introduction: from the basilar notions to the legacy of Gilles Châtelet. In: La Mantia F, Alumni C, Zalamea F (eds) Diagrams and gestures. Springer

Lalatta Costerbosa M (2003) Eutanasia e filosofia morale: L'autonomia e le sue insidie. In: Zanetti G (ed) Elementi di etica pratica: Argomenti normativi e spazi del diritto. Carocci, Rome, pp 179–194
Lewis P (2007) Assisted dying and legal change. Oxford University Press, Oxford. https://doi.org/10.1093/acprof:oso/9780199212873.001.0001
MacCormick N (1978) Legal reasoning and legal theory. Clarendon Press, Oxford
MacCoun RJ, Reuter P (2004) Drug war heresies: learning from other vices, times, and places. Cambridge University Press, Cambridge
Maestri E (2009) Genealogie della dignità umana. Diritto & questioni pubbliche 9:509–520
Maniaci G (2005) Razionalità e bilanciamento tra principi del diritto: Un inventario, un'intuizione, una proposta. Ragion pratica 2:335–364. https://doi.org/10.1415/20841
Maniaci G (2008) Razionalità ed equilibrio riflessivo nell'argomentazione giudiziale. Giappichelli, Turin
Maniaci G (2012) La force du pire argument: La rhétorique paternaliste dans l'argumentation morale et juridique. La Revue des Droits de l'Homme (June). http://wp.me/P1Xrup-dK
Marquet RLA et al (2003) Twenty five years of requests for euthanasia and physician assisted suicide in Dutch general practice: trend analysis. Br Med J 327:201–202. https://www.jstor.org/stable/25455084
Marra R (1990) Suicidio e diritti: Un'alternativa a costruzioni eziologiche e programmi terapeutici. Materiali per una storia della cultura giuridica XX 1:211–236
Martí JL (2006) La República Deliberativa. Marcial Pons, Barcelona
McDowell J (1998) Mind, value, and reality. Harvard University Press, Cambridge
McMahan J (2002) The ethics of killing: problems at the margins of life. Oxford University Press, Oxford. https://doi.org/10.1093/0195079981.001.0001
Mill JS (1971) On Liberty (1859). In: Robson JM (ed) Vol. 18 of collected works, 213–310. Routledge & Kegan Paul, London
Miller FG, Wertheimer A (eds) (2010) The ethics of consent: theory and practice. Oxford University Press, New York
Miron JA (2004) Drug war crimes: the consequences of prohibition. The Independent Institute, Oakland
Miron JA (2010) The Budgetary Implications of Marijuana Prohibition. https://scholar.harvard.edu/files/miron/files/budget_2010_final_0.pdf
Miron JA, Waldock K (2010) The budgetary impact of ending drug prohibition. Cato Institute, Washington, DC. https://www.cato.org/white-paper/budgetary-impact-ending-drug-prohibition#
Molinaro S et al (2006) Epidemiologia dell'uso e del consumo problematico di cocaina in Italia. In: Serpelloni G, Macchia T, Gerra G (eds) Cocaina: Manuale di aggiornamento tecnico scientifico. Editrice La Grafica, Mori (TN), pp 77–86. https://www.politicheantidroga.gov.it/media/1976/14pluscocaina.pdf
Moreso JJ (2003) El reino de los derechos y la objetividad de la moral. In: Diciotti E (ed) Diritti umani e oggettività della morale. Publications of the Siena University Department of Historical, Legal, Political, and Social Sciences, Siena
Moutouh H (1999) La dignité de l'homme en droit. Revue du Droit Public et de la Science Politique en France et à l'Étranger 1:159–196
Nagel T (1986) The view from nowhere. Oxford University Press, New York
Nino C (1989) El constructivismo ético. Centro de Estudios Constitucionales, Madrid
Nozick R (1999) Coercion. In: Socratic puzzles. Harvard University Press, Chap. 1, Cambridge, pp s15–s44
Nussbaum MC (2000) Women and human development: the capabilities approach. Cambridge University Press, Cambridge
Onwuteaka P et al (2007) Summary evaluation of termination of life on request and assisted suicide (review procedures) act. In: Programme on evaluation of legislation (in Dutch), part 23. ZonMw, The Hague

Onwuteaka P et al (2012) Trends in end-of-life practices before and after the enactment of the euthanasia law in the Netherlands from 1990–2010: a repeated cross-sectional survey. Lancet 380:908–915

Pérez CB (2007) Memoria y anteproyecto de ley orgánica de modificación del código penal y de regulación de la eutanasia y la asistencia al suicidio. Master en Derecho, Barcelona, Universitat Pompeu Fabra

Pickens RW et al (1995) Common genetic mechanisms in alcohol, drug, and mental disorder comorbidity. Drug Alcohol Depend 39(2):129–138. https://doi.org/10.1016/0376-8716(95)01151-n

Pino G (2007) Conflitto e bilanciamento tra diritti fondamentali: Una mappa dei problemi. Ragion Pratica 1:219–276. https://doi.org/10.1415/24465

Pirozzoli A (2007) Il valore costituzionale della dignità: Un profilo giurisprudenziale. Rassegna parlamentare 49(2):323–353

Poggi F (2010) Tra il certo e l'impossibile: La probabilità nel processo. Diritto & questioni pubbliche 10:457–477

Pope TM (2004) Counting the Dragon's Teeth and Claws: the definition of hard paternalism. Ga State Univ Law Rev 20(3):659–722. https://open.mitchellhamline.edu/facsch/280

Pope TM (2005) Is public health paternalism really never justified? A response to Joel Feinberg. Oklahoma City Univ Law Rev 30:121–207. https://open.mitchellhamline.edu/facsch/285

Putnam H (1981) Reason, truth and history. Cambridge University Press, Cambridge

Quine WVO (1990) Pursuit of truth. Harvard University Press, Cambridge

Quine WVO, Ullian JS (1970) The web of belief. McGraw-Hill, New York

Qureshi AI et al (2001) Cocaine use and the likelihood of nonfatal myocardial infarction and stroke: data from the third national health and nutrition examination survey. Circulation 103(4):502–506. https://doi.org/10.1161/01.cir.103.4.502

Rachels J (1986) The end of life: euthanasia and morality. Oxford University Press, Oxford

Rawls J (1971) A theory of justice. Belknap Press of Harvard University Press, Cambridge

Raz J (1986) The morality of freedom. Clarendon Press, Oxford

Regan DH (1983) Paternalism, freedom, identity, and commitment. In: Sartorius R (ed) Paternalism. University of Minnesota Press, Chap. 8, Minneapolis, pp 113–138

Resta G (2002) La disponibilità dei diritti fondamentali e i limiti della dignità: Note a margine della Carta dei diritti. Rivista di diritto civile, XLVIII 6(2):801–848

Rietjens JAC et al (2009) Two decades of research on euthanasia from the Netherlands: what have we learnt and what questions remain? J Bioeth Inq 6:271–283. https://doi.org/10.1007/s11673-009-9172-3

Romano A (1987) Autonomia nel diritto pubblico. In: Vol. 2 of Digesto delle discipline pubblicistiche. UTET, Turin

Romano M (2010) Danno a sé stessi, paternalismo legale e limiti del diritto penale. In: Cadoppi A (ed) Laicità, valori e diritto penale: "The Moral Limits of the Criminal Law"; In ricordo di Joel Feinberg. Giuffrè, Milan

Ronchetti L (2018) L'autonomia e le sue esigenze. Giuffrè, Milan

Ruggeri A, Spadaro A (1991) Dignità dell'uomo e giurisprudenza costituzionale: Prime notazioni. Politica del diritto 3:343–377

Scanlon TM (1998) What we owe to each other. Harvard University Press, Cambridge

Scarpelli U (1998) Bioetica laica. Ed. Maurizio Mori. Baldini & Castoldi, Milan

Schiavello A (1998) Diritto come integrità: Incubo o nobile sogno? Saggio su Ronald Dworkin. Giappichelli, Turin

Schiavello A (2010) Perché obbedire al diritto? La risposta convenzionalista ed i suoi limiti. ETS, Pisa

Searle JR (2001) Weakness of will. In: Rationality in action. MIT Press, Chap. 7, Cambridge, pp 219–237

Serpelloni G, Macchia T, Guerra G (eds) (2006) Cocaina: Manuale di aggiornamento tecnico scientifico. Editrice La Grafica, Mori (TN). https://www.politicheantidroga.gov.it/it/attivita/attivita-e-progetti/le-pubblicazioni/cocaina-manuale-di-aggiornamento-tecnico-scientifico/

Sgreccia E (1997) Bioetica: Manuale per medici e biologi. Vita e Pensiero, Milan
Simon HA (1955) A behavioral model of rational choice. Q J Econ 69(1):99–118. https://doi.org/10.2307/1884852
Simon HA (1957) Models of man: social and rational. John Wiley & Sons, New York
Simon J (2002) Human dignity as a regulative instrument for human genome research. In: Mazzoni CM (ed) Ethics and law in biological research. Brill/Nijhoff, Leiden, pp 35–45. https://doi.org/10.1163/9789047403067_006
Singer P (2000) Writings on an ethical life. Ecco Press, New York
Stavropoulos N (1996) Objectivity in law. Clarendon Press, Oxford
Sumner L (2011) Assisted death: a study in ethics and law. Oxford University Press, Oxford
Sumner (2017) Physician-assisted death: what everyone needs to know. Oxford University Press, New York
Sunstein CR (1997) The right to die. Yale Law J 106(4):1123–1163. https://doi.org/10.2307/797150
Tesauro A (2011) Spunti problematici in tema di dignità umana come bene penalmente rilevante. Diritto & questioni pubbliche 11:885–952
Troper M (2007) Le réalisme et le juge constitutionnel. In: Le réalisme en droit constitutionnel. special issue. Cahier du Conseil constitutionnel 22 (June):125–131. https://www.conseil-constitutionnel.fr/nouveaux-cahiers-du-conseil-constitutionnel/le-realisme-et-le-juge-constitutionnel
Tsuang MT et al (1996) Genetic influences on DSM-III-R drug abuse and dependence: a study of 3,372 twin pairs. Am J Med Genet 67(5):473–477. https://doi.org/10.1002/(SICI)1096-8628(19960920)67:5<473::AID-AJMG6>3.0.CO;2-L
Tuzet G (2006) La prima inferenza: L'abduzione di C. S. Pierce fra scienza e diritto. Giappichelli, Turin
UNODC (United Nations Office on Drugs and Crime) (2007) World Drug Report 2007. http://www.unodc.org/unodc/data-and-analysis/WDR.html
UNODC (United Nations Office on Drugs and Crime) (2008) World Drug Report 2008. http://www.unodc.org/unodc/data-and-analysis/WDR.html
UNODC (United Nations Office on Drugs and Crime) (2009) World Drug Report 2009. http://www.unodc.org/unodc/data-and-analysis/WDR.html
VanDeVeer D (1979) Coercive restraint of offensive actions. Philos Public Aff 8(2):175–193. https://www.jstor.org/stable/2264933
VanDeVeer D (1986) Paternalistic intervention: the moral bounds on benevolence. Princeton University Press, Princeton
Varelius J (2014) Medical expertise, existential suffering and ending life. J Med Ethics 40:104–107
Velleman J (1999) A right of self-termination? Ethics 109:606–628
Viafora C (2009) Il diritto a morire con dignità: Quattro tesi sull'etica dell'accompagnamento. In: Argiroffi A et al (eds) I diversi volti dell'eutanasia: prospettive teologiche, etiche e giuridiche. Aracne Editore, Rome, pp 99–128
Villa V (1999) Costruttivismo e teorie del diritto. Giappichelli, Turin
Villa V (2007) Relativismo: Un'analisi concettuale. Ragion pratica 1. https://doi.org/10.1415/24457
Vincenti U (2009) Diritti e dignità umana. Laterza, Bari and Rome
Von Hirsch A (1996) Extending the harm principle: 'remote' harms and fair imputation. In: Simester AP, Smith ATH (eds) Harm and culpability. Clarendon Press, Oxford, pp 259–276
Von Hirsch A, Neumann U (2010) 'Indirekter' Paternalismus im Strafrecht—am Beispiel der Tötung auf Verlangen (§ 216 StGB). In: von Hirsch A, Neumann U (eds) Paternalismus im Strafrecht: Die Kriminalisierung von selbstschädigendem Verhalten. Nomos, Chap. 5, Baden-Baden, pp 71–98. https://doi.org/10.5771/9783845224374-71
Wagner FA, Anthony JC (2002) From first drug use to drug dependence: developmental periods of risk for dependence upon Marijuana, Cocaine, and Alcohol. Neuropsychopharmacology 26(4):479–488. https://doi.org/10.1016/S0893-133X(01)00367-0
Wall S (2021) Perfectionism in moral and political philosophy. In: Zalta EN The Stanford Encyclopedia of Philosophy. https://plato.stanford.edu/archives/fall2021/entries/perfectionism-moral/

Walton D (2015) Slippery slope. In: Ht Have (ed) Encyclopedia of global bioethics. Springer, Berlin, pp 2623–2632
WHO/UNICRI (1995) Cocaine Project Briefing Kit. Unpublished. World Health Organization (WHO) and United Nations Interregional Crime and Justice Research Institute (UNICRI)
Williams B (1981) Internal and external reasons. In: Moral Luck: Philosophical Papers 1973–1980. Cambridge University Press, Chap. 8, Cambridge, pp 101–113
Young R (2007) Medically assisted death. Cambridge University Press, Cambridge
Young R (2022) Voluntary Euthanasia. In: Zalta E The Stanford Encyclopedia of Philosophy. https://plato.stanford.edu/archives/sum2022/entries/euthanasia-voluntary/
Zimbardo P (2007) The Lucifer Effect: understanding how good people turn evil. Random House, New York

Chapter 4
Liberal Theories and Behavioural Economics or Heuristics and Biases Psychology

4.1 Introduction

In Chap. 3 we looked at the basic arguments that nonliberal authors have put forward in favour of paternalism: the perfectionist argument, the utilitarian-organicist argument, and the very popular slippery slope argument. In recent years, however, a paternalistic argument has been advanced by authors claiming to be liberal, an argument based on the findings of cognitive science, that is, on the idea that human beings are prone to make numerous cognitive errors in their everyday reasoning.

Behavioural economics or heuristics and biases psychology studies the numerous cognitive errors that people fall into when making choices or decisions. Both Daniel Kahneman, in *Thinking Fast and Slow* (Kahneman 2011), and Richard Thaler and Cass Sunstein, in *Nudge* (Thaler and Sunstein 2008), cite numerous examples of cognitive errors studied in cognitive psychology.[1]

A problem arises for a moderate liberal theory, a Millian theory such as the one defended here. According to such a theory, the state has a *prima facie* right to exercise coercion to limit individual freedom only when individuals cause unjust harm to third parties or, in some cases, when adult individuals carry out acts that are harmful or dangerous to themselves and these acts are nonrational or are carried out by someone who lacks mental capacity (either temporarily or permanently) or is insufficiently free of coercive pressure, or again when an act does not proceed on sufficiently stable desires or on an adequate knowledge of the relevant facts. As mentioned in Chap. 2, I will not specify exactly in which cases the state does or does not have this right. There are some cases in which the state would seem to certainly have this right. If we suffer from a mental disorder that is significant enough to lead us to do something that is harmful or dangerous to us—we may be suffering from hallucinations and, seeing a Caribbean beach in front of us, may decide to take a dive, when in fact we are about to dive into the Tiber in January — doctors and nurses (acting on the authority of the state) would have a right to prevent us from taking our own lives. Likewise, if we temporarily lack mental capacity—we might be in a state of shock or may be drunk—

[1] See also Kahneman et al. (1982), Gilovich et al. (2002), Greene (2008), Ariely (2009), Dovidio et al. (2013) and Viale (2020).

G. Maniaci, *The Unbearable Lightness of Legal Antipaternalism*, Law and Philosophy Library 151, https://doi.org/10.1007/978-3-031-96844-0_4

> the state would have a right to prevent us from carrying out a harmful act. On the contrary, it seems clear that if we are suffering from schizophrenia, constantly having hallucinations of huge aliens coming after us and torturing us, and there are no drugs that can cure such hallucinations, and we express a desire to die, then that desire needs to be protected. And the same goes for a child with an incurable disease that causes terrible suffering: if the child expresses a desire to die, that desire needs to be protected.

Let us see why cognitive errors may pose a problem for a liberal theory. In reasoning vitiated by widespread cognitive errors or biases or by common framing errors, our judgments would seem to have the same effect as false beliefs, widely regarded as symptoms that we are insufficiently rational or, at any rate, that our decisions are not based on a knowledge of the relevant facts. If a decision is in fact based on a false belief, the means we identify to achieve the goal pursued through that decision could be unsuitable. Similarly, if we commit a relevant cognitive error—especially one that is very difficult for us to detect and hence avoid, unless we are cognitive psychologists—then our decision could be unsuitable for achieving our desires.

In this case, a decision based on widespread cognitive errors could even be considered not fully voluntary, because my guess is that most people, if they knew how frequently cognitive errors are made in decision-making, would probably want to be protected, that is, they would want the state to temporarily prevent them from carrying out harmful or dangerous acts on the basis of cognitive errors, just as they would want to be protected from such acts if they are carried out in states of temporary severe depression or illicit substance intoxication, or again in a state of shock or hypnosis. In other words, if we realized that we are smoking tobacco due to a cognitive error, we might, with good reason, decide to stop smoking, and we might also come to see our previous smoking habit as not truly voluntary, since we were operating under a cognitive error that was preventing us from achieving the goal we really wanted to pursue, namely, to live a full life not cut short by lung cancer. In short, in a moderate liberal theory—one that protects individual autonomy, such that all adult persons who are sufficiently rational and uncoerced and have mental capacity enjoy a right to live their life according to their desires, values, principles, and philosophical and religious conceptions—that individual autonomy seems threatened by the incidence of cognitive errors, if we agree, as the science suggests, that people sometimes make decisions, even important ones, on the basis of flawed reasoning.

So, in what follows, I will analyze some of the most common cognitive errors identified in heuristics psychology, as well as some of the flaws contained in the most popular psychological theories on heuristics and cognitive error, and then, in light of that analysis, I will argue that moderate liberal theories could consistently solve the problems posed by the prevalence of such errors.

4.2 A Sampling of Cognitive Errors

Let us take, for example, the substitution error that Kahneman calls "answering an easier question".[2] As the name suggests, this is where we unwittingly replace a difficult question with an easier one: we are asked, "How much would you like to contribute to save an endangered species?" and we replace that with "How much emotion do I feel when I think of dying dolphins?"[3] Another phenomenon is the affect heuristic, "in which people let their likes and dislikes determine their beliefs about the world" (ibid). Kahneman points to a study by Paul Slovic in which a group of people were interviewed about the benefits and harms of certain technologies, such as cars, water fluoridation, and food preservatives. The same subjects were then made to read texts that stressed either the benefits of those technologies or their low risk, with some people learning about the benefits and others about the low risks: it was found that those who learned about the benefits changed their minds about the risks and, conversely, those who learned about the low risks changed their minds about the benefits (ibid., Chap. 9, "The Affect Heuristic").

Another phenomenon that is widely studied in psychology is known as the anchoring effect, "when people consider a particular value for an unknown quantity before estimating that quantity" (ibid., Chap. 11). So, for example, if the unknown quantity is the age at which Gandhi died and "you are asked whether Gandhi was more than 114 years old when he died you will end up with a much higher estimate of his age at death than you would if the anchoring question referred to death at 35" (ibid.).

Another phenomenon still is the representativeness heuristic, in which the probability that A belongs to class B is "evaluated by the degree to which A is representative of B, that is, by the degree to which A resembles B" (ibid., Appendix A). In one experiment, subjects were asked to estimate the probability that someone is an engineer on the basis of a personality description chosen at random from a pool of such descriptions, knowing that 30 of those were descriptions of engineers and 70 of lawyers. It was found that "subjects evaluated the likelihood that a particular description belonged to an engineer rather than to a lawyer by the degree to which this description was representative of the two stereotypes, with little or no regard for the prior probabilities of the categories" (ibid.; cf. Chap. 14, "Predicting by Representativeness").

Equally common are availability biases—errors made when, in order to identify the amount of a category or the frequency of an event, one relies on the ease with which a paradigmatic case of that event is recalled from memory, examples being divorce rates among Hollywood stars, sex scandals among politicians, the frequency of airplane crashes, or maritime pollution hazards. As Kahneman comments, "the world in our heads is not an accurate replica of reality; our expectations about the frequency of events are distorted by the prevalence and emotional intensity of the messages to which we are exposed" (ibid., Chap. 13, "Availability and Affect").

Also numerous are framing errors, in which people respond differently to the same question depending on how it is framed. For example, the statement that a vaccine has a death rate of 0.001% tends to be perceived very differently than the equivalent statement that the vaccine causes the death of one person for every 100,000 vaccinated people: the latter statement feels much more frightening. When asked, "Would

---

[2] Kahneman (2011), Chap. 9.

[3] Ibid., chap. 9, "Substituting Questions".

you buy a 100-euro ticket to a concert a second time if at the gate of entry to the concert you realized that you lost the ticket?" people tended to say no, but they tended to say yes when asked, "Would you have bought a concert ticket if instead of losing the ticket you had lost 100 euros from your wallet?" The statement that a certain type of surgery has a 90% survival rate tends to be perceived much differently than the equivalent statement that the same surgery has a 10% mortality rate: the first one feels positive, the second one negative (ibid., Chap. 34, "Emotional Framing"). Another cognitive error, mentioned by Sunstein, is conformity. In some lab experiments it was found that when the majority of people in an experiment make false statements, the remaining participants also tend to make false statements, thereby making blunders, or errors they would be expected to avoid if they were acting on their own.[4]

The findings of behavioural economics are largely correct. But before we can understand why moderate liberal theories can rely on this body of research to solve the problems associated with the most common cognitive errors, we need to make a brief premise—a general premise about heuristics and biases research as a field of inquiry, and some more specific remarks about Kahneman's argument.

On the basis of many experiments that have been carried out, Kahneman and Tversky conclude that our minds seem ill-equipped to correctly estimate probabilities (Samuels et al. 2002). And yet, as Samuels, Stich, and Bishop argue, these challenges do not mean that it is altogether impossible to make such estimates (ibid.). Other experiments in which participants are asked to answer questions about relative frequencies suggest that the mind seems to perform better, with more accurate answers, when the question is framed not in percentages (e.g., 5%) but in natural numbers, natural frequencies (5 in 100).

For example, here is an experiment conducted by Cosmides and Tooby (1996). One in 1000 Americans has disease X. A test has been developed to detect when a person has disease, but the test can yield false positives. In particular, out of 1000 people who are perfectly healthy, 50 test positive. The subjects in the experiment were asked, out of 1000 Americans chosen at random, how many of those who test positive actually have the disease? In the experiment, 76% participants answered this question correctly, this in contrast to only 15% of participants in experiments where probability problems were framed as percentage questions. The hypothesis of some authors is that "our hominid ancestors were immersed in a rich flow of observable frequencies that could be used to improve decision-making [...]. So if we have adaptations for inductive reasoning, they should take frequency information as input." (ibid., 16). There are cases, then, in which human reasoning can be said to be fallacious, in that it does not apply the rules of probability calculation. But this does not mean that our reasoning is therefore always, or even normally, inconsistent with those rules. These findings are consistent with those reported by Kahneman, whose discussion of framing errors likewise shows that human reasoning involving relative frequencies tends to be more accurate when the problem is framed in natural

[4] Further cognitive errors are listed and discussed in Trout (2005), p. 393ff.

numbers, natural frequencies (1 out of 1000), than when it is framed in percentages.

In the second place, it is wrong to think, as one might take away from Kahneman's experiments, that human beings are normally irrational, incapable of reasoning based on deduction, induction, and abduction. In contrast, many evolutionary psychologists recognize that "our cognitive architecture resembles a confederation of hundreds or thousands of functionally dedicated computers (often called modules) designed to solve adaptive problems endemic to our hunter-gatherer ancestors. Each of the devices has its own agenda, and imposes its own exotic organization on different fragments of the world. There are specialized systems for grammatical induction, for face recognition, for dead reckoning, for construing objects and recognizing emotions from the face".[5] I would add that if we think of instrumental rationality—with its boundless technical applications: the technique for carrying a heart transplant, an air-traffic-control system, and so on—it is difficult to espouse the idea that human beings are normally irrational. How can we reconcile our vast know-how—everything that human beings know how to do—with the numerous cognitive errors identified by Kahneman? The answer, according to Samuels, Stich, and Bishop, is that heuristics and biases research do not show that deductive and inductive judgments made by human beings are usually incorrect: what they instead show is that human beings can often be deceived if we exploit the cognitive processes through which they make the decisions they end up making.

In the third place, one may question the underlying conception behind Kahneman's research on heuristics and cognitive biases. This is not a conception of bounded rationality but one of rationality as optimization, on which human beings are considered rational to the extent that they reason correctly, using all the rules of logic and probability, and make decisions accordingly, and they are, by contrast, irrational to the extent that they violate these rules. This, of course, is an outdated conception, the one that Samuels et al. (2002) operate on in *Ending the Rationality Wars*. To appreciate the problem with this kind of conception, we need only observe how the authors are themselves very well acquainted with probability calculus and yet—or perhaps precisely for that reason, as if possessed by a curse of knowledge—take it for granted that everyone should be equally familiar with that discipline and should make decisions accordingly. But that seems quite unrealistic. Apart from some probabilities we can "ballpark" or intuitively grasp as rules of thumb (e.g., a one-in-a-million chance that we will be hit by an asteroid if we decide to go out to dinner tonight), the rules and principles of probability calculus—the ones in light of which, on this conception, rationality can be ascribed to an agent—form a specialized body of knowledge whose use requires formal training, a skill that needs to be acquired in much the same way that we need to acquire the ability of a mathematician or a logician. Can someone really be considered irrational because they struggle with the kinds of calculations involved in probability calculus or mathematical calculus? Probably not. Which why it is important to appropriately frame cognitive errors: on the one hand are the kinds of errors that amount to faulty reasoning judged

[5] Cf. Samuels et al. (2002), p. 242, quoting Cosmides and Tooby (1995, p. xiii).

against the benchmark of perfect rationality, with an optimal argumentative procedure carried out in optimal conditions, where agents are assumed to have the time, resources, and intellectual powers needed to solve hypothetical problems; on the other hand are the cognitive biases that most people, most of the time tend to have in real life, where conditions are not ideal for making the best (most rational) decision, and where no one can be assumed to have unlimited powers of reasoning and computational capacity, that is, where we have to assume a bounded rationality.

We can now turn to the more specific observations I think are worth making about Kahneman's (2011) *Thinking, Fast and Slow*. For all the insights this book has to give, it does contain some errors: an interpretive error (at least one that stands out), a *non sequitur*, and an inconsistency. An example of an interpretive error can be found in Kahneman's analysis of different regulatory frameworks on organ donation, where a claim is made about the psychology at work when people are prompted to make decisions about post mortem organ donation. Kahneman claims that the majority of potential donors commit a framing error: when the default option is an opt-out box that says "I do not want be an organ donor," (an opt-out policy presumes that every person in a country is willing to be an organ donor after they die) people tend not to tick the box, and when the default option is an opt-in box that says "I want to be an organ donor,", (an opt-in policy presumes that every person in a country is not willing to be an organ donor after they die), people likewise tend not to tick the box (Kahneman 2011, Chap. 34, "Good Frames"), the implication being that an opt-out form will deliver more organ donors than an opt-in form. From an examination of European legislation on post mortem organ donations, it emerges that there are essentially two models of legislation: one with an opt-out default (in which the presumption is for consent, unless that is expressly denied), and one with an opt-in default (in which the presumption is for denial, save for an express statement of consent). The default position is the status quo, and the framing error that Kahneman points to is not in fact a framing error: it consists precisely in taking that position for granted, thereby going for the status quo, presumably out of laziness or selfishness or to avoid the costs of deliberation, namely, the time needed to think through the choice at hand, the theory being that unless we have already gone through that deliberation, and have formed an opinion accordingly, we will not be making the extra effort to do so on the spot, when filling out a form, choosing instead to go with whatever default has been chosen for us (because that is the easier choice).

Kahneman also reports an experiment in which real-estate agents were asked to assess the market value of a house, and it was found that in making that assessment they were significantly influenced by the asking price (apparently more so than by other information they had that was relevant to the house's market value): this is the anchoring effect. The effect seems to be real, but from it we cannot logically draw, in the case at hand, any definitive conclusions about the behaviour of real estate agents or of potential buyers. This is a *non sequitur*, for it overextends the premise. The real-estate agents had an opportunity to see the house and review a "comprehensive booklet of information" about the house and the local real-estate market, but had no reason to suspect that the asking price had been manufactured (having been skewed away from the actual list price), nor did they have any reason to ignore that information, since it is good practice to take the asking or list price into account in appraising a house and see how it compares to that of other properties in the same area and to the prices listed in the assessment roll pertaining to the house: the greater the gap, the likelier it is that the house is under- or overvalued, as the case may be.

There are numerous framing errors that Kahneman illustrates, and from them he concludes that in many cases there is no such thing as an agent's true or authentic preference: there are only preferences expressed within a frame, or context, and from the agent's point of view, rather than from the point of view of the community that wants to influence or manipulate the agent; and indeed, from the agent's standpoint, one frame, or context, is as good as any other (ibid., Chap. 34, "Empty Intuitions"). This conclusion seems to contradict what Kahneman himself states elsewhere, claiming that there are frames that determine an agent's rationality: these are broad frames or a joint evaluation, where multiple scenarios are evaluated at the same time. And if that is the case, that is, if there are frames through which agents are enabled to achieve greater rationality, it follows that through these frames they can express their true and authentic preferences. If we are to identify these preferences (an agent's real preferences), it is crucial that we work from a weak notion of rationality. If someone has two contradictory desires, they cannot fulfil both of these desires at the same time. A desire to enjoy tobacco, for example, is inconsistent with a desire to live a healthy life and as long as possible, even if we believe that smoking tobacco is good for our health and we accordingly smoke a pack of cigarettes a day. That belief is false: that is what makes the two desires inconsistent, and what lies behind the framing error. If we are to avoid the error, it suffices that we reframe the problem, looking at it through a broader frame that will enable us to evaluate it from two different points of view, or from the standpoint of two framings that each shed their own light on the problem. We saw that with the vaccine example: if we should want to scare people away from a vaccine, it is not enough to point out that the vaccine has a mortality rate of 0.001%; we need to reframe that statistic by saying that one person for every 100,000 people who get the vaccine die. In just the same way, we can reframe the riskiness of a surgical operation by pointing out its 90% survival rate or its 10% mortality rate (even if the two are equivalent), or we can reframe the riskiness of a therapy for a serious disease by highlighting that the therapy saves the lives of 200 out of 600 people who go through the therapy or by highlighting that it will not be effective for 400 out of 600 people who go through it, and who will therefore die of the disease as a result (ibid.)

Kahneman would reply that there is no contradiction in his argument, but that in some cases in which a decision involves a broad frame or joint evaluation, the framing affords greater rationality, while in other cases the same kind of framing does not afford that rationality. Or, stated otherwise, the same problem may be jointly evaluated in light of two sets of frames, both broad, but only one of those two sets affords greater rationality. It is not the broad framing in itself that affords that rationality, but the way the framing is specifically constructed. But Kahneman in no way justifies that distinction, which seems to detract from his argument.[6]

[6]About adjudication, judicial heuristcs and biases cf. Efran (1974); Guthrie et al. (2001); Bibas (2004), pp. 1–12; Gigerenzer and Engel (2004); Englich et al. (2005); Harley (2007): Guthrie et al. (2007); Klein et al. (2010); Danziger et al. (2011); Abrams et al. (2012); Ellsworth (2012); Jones (2013); Skorinko et al. (2014); Girvan (2016), p. 215; Leibovitch (2016); Levinson et al. (2017); Wistrich and Rachlinski (2017); Brewer and Bradfield (2019); Griffin (2016).

4.3 How Moderate Liberal Conceptions Respond to the Problem of Cognitive Biases

As noted at the outset, moderate (or moderately antipaternalistic) liberal conceptions need not fear the most common cognitive biases and framing errors. As much as these biases and errors may be widespread, it doesn't follow from that factual premise that we should thereby do away with individual autonomy as a principle that is core to any liberal conception, and which needs to accordingly be protected.

If consistently interpreted, the moderate liberal conceptions here defended, such as Joel Feinberg's theory or John Stuart Mill's, distinguish between two kinds of activities: (a) ones that do not normally cause serious harm to the agent's own health or life or do not pose any serious risk of causing such harm (examples being buying a car or a house, getting married, choosing a particular diet, or choosing to be an organ donor)[7] and (b) activities that, by contrast, do normally cause or risk causing (what is understood to be) that kind of harm (examples being euthanasia, assisted suicide, taking hard drugs, or riding a motorcycle without wearing a helmet).

The point is that with activities of type (a) above—those that are not inherently harmful to the agents who carry them out, meaning that the risk they pose is not the standard course which any agent should expect—it is wrong for the state to interfere and compel agents not to engage in such activities, even where these agents are not fully informed about the risks and consequences of these activities or are not sufficiently rational in choosing to engage in them. For that would be tantamount to embracing a very strong type of coercive paternalism inconsistent with the broadly liberal outlook espoused throughout the Western world (apart from any specific politics one may commit to: progressive or conservative). The justification for a system in which the state cannot coercively interfere in such activities is that, even if human beings are fallible, making cognitive errors and misjudging themselves as well as others, they are in an incomparably better position than anyone else, including loved ones and government psychologists, to understand their own desires and moral principles. Nor does it seem reasonable or economically feasible to subject people to interviews with bureaucrats or government psychologists entrusted with evaluating their rationality and mental capacity or with ascertaining that they are informed of the relevant facts and sufficiently uncoerced in making decisions about activities of this type (a), such as buying a house or choosing what to wear. The bureaucratic machine needed to run such a system would not only be financially unsustainable: it would also be perceived as an excessive encroachment on individual freedom, a form of control that would stretch across the vast majority of

[7] Clearly, a marriage can end in a separation or divorce, with a bitter legal fight; a house can prove to be a bad investment; and a diet may well cause great harm to the body if misconceived or not based on any good science. But that is not the normal or expected course for such activities: it is simply part of the contingency of life that comes with any kind of activity, even crossing the street on a crosswalk, which on this conception cannot be prohibited, or otherwise viewed though a paternalistic lens, simply because it involves some risk to the agent's own health or life.

activities that one may choose to engage in. When it comes to activities of type (b)—those that do qualify as inherently harmful or dangerous, such as assisted suicide or the consumption of hard drugs—it would, by contrast, be reasonable for the state to require individuals to submit to such interviews, but only to determine whether the individuals concerned are sufficiently rational and mentally competent, as well as sufficiently informed and uncoerced, and whether their desires are stable over time. But that would not amount to prohibiting such activities: it would only be a process that individuals would have to go through before acting on their decision.

In Chap. 3, the need to evaluate individuals under these criteria (sufficient rationality and mental capacity, coupled with sufficient informedness and freedom from coercion and stability of wishes) was justified on the basis of a liberal antipaternalistic conception. The argument, in short, was that it does not undermine individual autonomy to require people to submit to such evaluations if they are intent on carrying out inherently harmful activities of type (b), where the harm is serious and irreversible, as in the case of assisted suicide[8] and there are two reasons why that is so.

The first reason is that the procedure needed to evaluate individuals in these cases—who may be suffering from a mental disorder such as schizophrenia—are much more complex than those needed to evaluate individuals who do not suffer from such conditions (which may involve hallucinations, paranoid delusions, and the like). Indeed, there are numerous factors that a doctor or psychiatrist needs to take into account in making an assessment of mental fitness consistent with the criteria in question. These professionals have to consider, for example, the extent to which someone's psychopathological symptoms is to account for the desires they form (thus, if we are hallucinating that we are about to take a dive into a dolphin pool, when in fact we are standing before a tiger-shark pool, it is probably not our desire to commit suicide: it is our hallucination, and not a grasp of the reality around us, that explains our desire to dive into the pool). The evaluation also needs to take into account whether someone's desires are coherent and ascertainable (it may be difficult to even understand what someone wants if their speech or behaviour is disorganized), as well as the need for drug treatment (to deal with the hallucinations, for example) and the mental suffering one may be going through. It is there fore a complex picture that that needs to be constructed in evaluating someone's psychophysical well being.

There is then the second reason why, as I contend, it would not undermine individual autonomy for the state to require people to submit to a mental-fitness evaluation before deciding to do what I am here calling type (b) acts, ones that are inherently and irreversibly harmful to the agent, such as committing assisted suicide or engaging in self-mutilation. And this is a speculative reason, to be sure, in the sense that it is based on a personal conviction, but the claim it makes is nonetheless empirical and seems reasonable enough: this is the claim that a scientific statistical-probabilistic survey would show that a great many people would like the

[8] See Diciotti (1986), p. 574; Feinberg (1986), p. 13.

community to prevent them from carrying out seriously or irreversibly harmful actions or actions with a high risk of harm if they should find themselves in a condition of temporary incapacity or clear irrationality: they may be having a bout of depression, for example, or they may be high on drugs, or in a state of shock or hypnosis. In such special scenarios, we would want a procedure by which to ascertain the temporary incapacity. If someone in a temporary state of mental incapacity wanted to commit suicide, the state would step in and prevent them from doing so, and in that way would protect their real will, a will often expressed at an earlier time, perhaps in an advance healthcare directive if they have drawn one up.[9] Through the same procedure for ascertaining adequate mental capacity, rationality, and freedom from coercion, and without further expenditure of time, individuals could learn about the relevant facts and come to appreciate the full spectrum of their options: they might, for example, learn about a new drug against anxiety and depression. European law requires individuals to take a cooling-off period of reflection before making irreversible decisions, as when contemplating gender-affirming surgery, abortion, sterilization, or assisted suicide, and that requirement can be justified by the need to protect individuals from any impulsiveness or weakness of will they might want to be protected from or to protect individuals who have no other way to get the facts they need to make an informed decision, perhaps because they are illiterate and not responsible for their ignorance.

A moderate liberal theory might, however, allow for some interference that is neither coercive nor detrimental to individual autonomy, as with the nudging advocated by Thaler and Sunstein (2008). Some interferences in the market have no paternalistic thrust, because they would simply serve to prevent the corporate world from exploiting the weaknesses, ignorance, and common biases of consumers. There are various ways of structuring people's choices (choice architecture), as by

[9] Some might argue that a genuinely antipaternalistic solution would be to let everyone write their own advance healthcare directive, laying out instructions that civil servants such as police officers, firefighters, or ambulance medics would have to follow just in case, at some future time, we should find ourselves in a condition of temporary incapacity or irrationality in which we might decide to carry out a harmful and irreversible act, such as jumping from the eighth floor of a building. But such a solution would not be not practical. Imagine firefighters or the police frantically searching for an advance healthcare directive previously drawn up by someone who is drunk and intent on jumping from the eighth floor of a building. Laws must also be reasonably enforceable, and there are antipaternalistic reasons to protect the majority—a majority that in such cases would probably want to be saved—even if on the basis of these reasons the state should temporarily constrain a minority of people who would not want to be saved in those same cases. In fact, if firefighters waste precious time searching for the advance healthcare directive drawn up by Drunken Drew, who is intent on committing suicide and succeeds in doing do before the directive is found, at which point it is discovered that Drew would have wanted to be prevented from committing suicide, that would be irreversibly harmful to drew in the worst way possible, since he is no longer alive. True, it could instead have turned out that Drunken Drew did in fact want to die (as specified in his advance directive), in which case it would have been a "disservice" to him to prevent him from jumping to his death, but that is not an irreversible course of action (Drew can find other ways of committing assisted suicide once he has sobered up), and so, in the balance of interests, and given the unknowns, it seems much preferable, or compatibly antipaternalistic, to go with the chosen course and prevent Drew from jumping.

requiring firms to provide disclosures about their products and services. Thaler and Sunstein give the example of extending warranties, for a fee, on common products ranging from cell phones to washing machines. Manufacturers would be required to inform customers of the probability of their products failing within the extended warranty period, a probability that in reality is usually very low. This might induce consumers to be more rational and consistent in the choices they make. In fact, corporations and multinationals are in a position of advantage relative to consumers, and are especially aware of various tricks by which to manipulate them: if the choices presented to consumers were structured in such a way as to avoid such pitfalls, consumers would stand to benefit, and that would be a reason for introducing legal requirements to that effect.

Similarly, in many countries warning labels inform potential consumers of the risks of using a given product (the typical example being the warning messages placed on cigarette packs). Even so, many people make serious mistakes when making important choices, such as buying a house or deciding whether or who to marry. In these cases, it is difficult to imagine even noncoercive interference. It might be conceivable to require city clerks tasked with keeping marriage records to prompt engaged couples to consider the statistical probability that their marriage will end in divorce (that figure currently stands at 50% in Italy) or to consider that during the period when they are falling in love—some 12–36 months from the first intimate contact—the brain produces endorphins, such as dopamine or phenylethylamine, which alter the mood and increase euphoria, while also predisposing the couple to accept each other's flaws. What this data suggests is that it would be inadvisable to get married in that period of new relationship energy (the honeymoon phase). But that is as far as a liberal theory can go: the kind of state it supports can do no more than make available the kind of information that people ought to take into account before committing to any course of action. But the more central point here is that, as much as we all make mistakes when making all sorts of decisions, big and small alike, there is no one who knows what we want better than we do—not a government psychologist or any other expert or civil servant, and not even the people who are closest to us and know us best. As Mill was early to argue, "with respect to his own feelings and circumstances, the most ordinary man or woman has means of knowledge immeasurably surpassing those that can be possessed by any one else. The interference of society to overrule his judgment and purposes in what he only regards himself, must be grounded on general presumptions".[10]

Whatever cognitive errors an individual makes, we cannot know what they would do once they discover a cognitive error, nor could a psychologist know. The mistakes we make have a lot to do with the difficulty of knowing ourselves, and understanding others, and no one can replace our judgment when it comes to certain choices, especially deeply personal ones such as choosing a partner or getting married. It is true that with other kinds of decisions, such as buying a house or a car, some find it quite helpful to turn to others with expertise in the area. As was argued

[10] Mill (1971), p. 277.

earlier, however, this does not make it reasonable, or even economically viable, to restrict people's freedom in such decision-making scenarios by requiring them to submit to interviews with civil servants or psychologists at public hospitals for the purpose of ascertaining that they are mentally competent and sufficiently rational and informed. This, moreover, is a position that finds support even among paternalists, and I am thinking in particular of Sarah Conly (2013), who argues in favour of coercive paternalism in health care advocacy, among other areas.

Again, looking to Thaler and Sunstein's theory, a moderate liberal theory can justify nudging as a kind of interference that is neither paternalistic nor coercive, so long as this kind of soft influence is aimed at promoting behaviour that advances the public interest or helps avoid the harm that others may suffer (where that is considered uncontroversial, e.g., saving lives or enabling people to live well in old age), and so long as the scheme under which to promote this kind of behaviour does not violate any constitutional principles. An example of such a scheme is the use of a default option in a choice architecture. This is the "easy" option, the one that individuals tend to lapse into of "fall for," whether unthinkingly, out of laziness (so as not to go through the effort of actually deliberating about a specific choice), or out of selfishness or, according to Kahneman (2011), on the basis of cognitive error. An example would be a retirement savings plan of the kind that employers might offer to their employees, where the default option—the one promoted as the wise financial decision—defines an elective-deferral contribution (an amount withheld from the salary and paid into the retirement plan) that is large enough to secure adequate savings for employees once they retire, so that they do not have to then rely almost exclusively on old-age insurance payments issued by the government.

In the same vein, Thaler and Sunstein cite numerous studies, relative to Western countries, where the percentage of people who, in a given country, respond to a survey saying that they are willing to be organ donors is much higher than the percentage of people who, in the same country, actually make that choice when filling out mandatory forms. This is understood to happen on account of laziness or selfishness, which leads many to choose the default option. In Austria, for example, the default on such forms is an opt-out box (where you are assumed to be an organ donor unless you expressly choose not to be one), whereas in Germany the default is an opt-in box (where, conversely, you are assumed not to be an organ donor unless you expressly choose to be one), and as it turns out, the percentage of organ donors in Austria (under its opt-out scheme) is much higher than the percentage in Germany (under its opt-in scheme). So, on a liberal conception, we would have an opt-out scheme (donor by default), since that would ensure a larger supply of life-saving organs (a public interest to be promoted), while still giving people the freedom to choose not to be donors.

Given what we know about human beings and their tendency to stick with the default (the "easy" or least-effortful choice), its use as part of an opt-out architecture should be the exception rather than the rule: it should be limited to cases in which we want to avoid causing harm to third parties and where the default option (the presumption of consent) is uncontroversial (something that most people can be assumed to agree to), and, needless to say, it should always be consistent with constitutional principles. An offending example is that of income tax returns in Italy, filed on tax forms where taxpayers are assumed to want to donate part of their income to the Catholic Church or to other religious institutions, such as the Italian Buddhist Union: filers have to expressly opt out of that choice; otherwise they will be making a religious donation amounting to 0.8% of their income, under a scheme where the total revenue so collected is allotted to each religious denomination according to the overall share of donations it has received from filers who have not opted out (and a share of those revenues will also be set aside for the state).

In this way, the Catholic Church gets the largest share of the revenues so collected, about 80%, or 1 billion euros. Even more troubling is that the scheme is outlined on the tax forms in fine print, in such a way that most people won't even notice the choice they are making. This default, termed *favor religionis*, is not intended to help save lives (as is the case with organ donations), nor is it morally uncontroversial (it is not a choice that most people would make), and it sits poorly as well with the constitutional principle of the separation of church and state. There is a good argument to be made that this also amounts to a violation of individual autonomy, considering that the fine print makes the scheme nontransparent, exploiting the fact that most people won't make the extra effort of entering into the arcane minutiae of their tax forms, or are other otherwise unaware of the scheme, which seems clearly designed to raise funds for the largest religious establishment in the country—namely, the Catholic Church—without making it apparent that this is what is happening.

Conly (2013) makes a case against framing people's choices through nudge tactics like the ones envisaged by Thaler and Sunstein, arguing that they are manipulative, in that they take place behind people's backs, exploiting their cognitive biases, and are therefore unacceptable. But Conly's argument misses the mark. As we will see shortly, it is very often possible to structure people's choices by framing the options available to them without manipulating the outcome (meaning the choice that people end up making), to this end using broad frames or a joint evaluation, in such a way that people will avoid the most common cognitive errors. Moreover, there is no alternative to a choice architecture: the information must be given or the choice must be made within some kind of frame, however broad it may be, nor is there any alternative to the use of defaults. In this sense, Conly's argument, however correct it may be in principle as a defence of individual autonomy, cannot be translated into practice. As the legal maxim says, *ad impossibilia nemo tenetur* (no one is bound to do the impossible, or "ought" implies "can"). If the issue is post mortem organ donation, for example, there is no way to avoid a default on any consent form: it will have to be either *for* donation (unless people explicitly opt out of it) or *against* donation (unless people explicitly opt in). There is no third option (*tertium non datur*) apart from making organ donation either mandatory or prohibited, either way severely restricting individual freedom.[11]

[11] In the same vein, Cominelli (2018, pp. 300, 302) argues that defaults, while inevitable, can be framed consistently with individual autonomy.

And even if we concede that Thaler and Sunstein's nudging is manipulative, that argument—to the extent that it holds up—loses much of its force, and becomes moot and almost pointless, once we consider that the alternative is coercive paternalism, under which people have no freedom at all, and so do not have *any* autonomy to begin with.

Finally, in order to avoid any manipulative effects that could indeed exist, Thaler and Sunstein's theory would have the state from inform citizens of the reasons why a choice is offered or why it is framed in one way rather than another. For example, in the case of the elective 0.8% donation on Italian tax forms, the most liberal solution would certainly be not only to identify the state as the default recipient (the entity that gets the amount unless taxpayers explicitly opt out of the scheme) but also to prominently print on the tax form itself a notice stating that this is in fact the default option (the choice they make by doing nothing, or not checking any boxes) and that this is precisely the option that, statistically, most people tend to choose as the "easy" option requiring the least amount of effort. And if it is manipulative, and hence inconsistent with individual autonomy, to nudge people toward a specific default, it is all the more inconsistent with individual autonomy to *force* that choice on them, as coercive paternalism would do, even if the rationale for that coercion (namely, preventing people from making cognitive errors) is clearly explained in a way that no one can ignore.

There is then the matter of acts or practices that are likely to do serious or irreversible harm to the agent, causing death or compromising the agent's health, as with euthanasia, assisted suicide, doing hard drugs (cocaine or heroin), or riding a motorcycle without wearing a helmet. Here, on a liberal conception, we would be permitted to carry out these acts or engage in these practices once we pass a simple mental fitness test, this being the procedure previously discussed where someone sits down with a doctor (and also a psychologist for euthanasia and assisted suicide) for an evaluation aimed at assessing whether they have mental capacity and are sufficiently rational, aware of the relevant facts (about the possible diagnosis and likely prognosis), and sufficiently uncoerced, and that the desires they express are sufficiently stable over time. Procedures of this kind are already required by law in several Western states for people contemplating euthanasia and assisted suicide (Belgium, the Netherlands, Luxembourg, and Switzerland), gender-affirming surgery, or abortion. Such an evaluation would prevent people who want to take such actions from falling into the most common cognitive biases and framing errors.

Take, for example, the errors that Kahneman attributes to substitution. As discussed, this is where we unwittingly replace a difficult question with a simpler one. Thus, for example, the question "How much would you contribute to save an endangered species?" is replaced with the heuristic question "How much emotion do I feel when I think about dying dolphins?" (Kahneman 2011, Chap. 9, "Substituting Questions"). The idea is that we will be much less likely to make this kind of error if we discuss the pros and cons of any intended course of action with a doctor or other expert, for in the course of such a conversation we would have to explain the *reasons* why we want to do what we say we want to do; at the same, this would also make it easier for us to assess whether the wish we are expressing is consistent with other preferences we have, and it would also alert us to any false beliefs we may be operating on. It is also worth pointing out that what Kahneman describes as the substitution heuristic is not inherently or necessarily a cognitive error. It is not necessarily a cognitive error, for example, to factor our emotions about dying dolphins into our reasoning about the need to save them as an endangered species and about the means by which to do so. This becomes a cognitive error only if the emotional pain we feel when thinking about a dying dolphin becomes a reason for saving *all* endangered species. What Kahneman, drawing on the work of the psychologist Paul Slovic, calls the affect heuristic, "in which people let their likes and dislikes determine their beliefs about the world" (ibid., "The Affect Heuristic"), is easily avoided by providing patients with the correct beliefs. Similarly, as we have seen, framing errors are easily avoided: to this end it suffices to ask the same question through a broad frame or a joint evaluation, a frame specifically created to avoid common cognitive errors.

In support of the proposal I am making about requiring individuals to submit to an evaluation interview before deciding to do anything irreversibly harmful to themselves, I should add that Kahneman himself claims that if we are made to know the real benefits and harms of a certain activity, our preferences will change accordingly and rationally. Indeed, that is precisely the point of such a procedure if it were to be implemented, as I am arguing it should consistently with a moderate liberal theory. At the same time, there is no reason to think that the procedure would trigger any anchoring effects, where (as mentioned) "people consider a particular value for an unknown quantity before estimating that quantity" (ibid., Chap. 11). For the information laid out during the interview would consist simply of factual or statistical data (the science), without including any information that is irrelevant to the decision at hand or that would otherwise be intended to skew the decision-making process in favour of one outcome or another.

Equally unlikely is that the procedure envisaged under the liberal theory would trigger an availability bias, when (as mentioned) we identify the amount of a something or the frequency of an event relying on the ease with which a paradigmatic case of that event is recalled from memory. For example, in assessing the frequency of heart attacks among cocaine users or the percentage of recreational users of any such substance who become addicted to that substance, we might think of acquaintances or celebrities who fit that description, using these cases to fill the statistical space for the phenomenon in question. But in an evaluation interview with a physician, none of that anecdotal evidence would count toward an assessment of probability or relative frequency, for it would not be the interviewees who supply their own evidence for their conclusions: the evidence would instead be supplied by the physician presenting hard facts and statistics, and would also do so expressing this data not in the form of difficult-to-grasp percentages (e.g., 0.1%) but in the form or ratios using natural numbers (1 in 1000), that is, using broad frames.

4.4 The Problem of Tobacco Smoking

More difficult to solve are cases where the activity in question is harmful to our health over the long run and yet is socially accepted or at least tolerated by the bulk of the population. Examples are smoking tobacco or consuming red meat or junk food, such as fast food that is high in fat or LDL cholesterol, or indeed any ultraprocessed food. Here, some authors propose, for example, a ban on the importation and sale of cigarettes. One such author is Sarah Conly, who argues that coercive paternalism is justified when we know that (a) consumers make choices that are likely to cause serious harm to their health in the long run, and (b) they make cognitive errors in estimating such harm (such as lung cancer for smoking and obesity and all its comorbidities for a diet mainly based on junk food). But what are the cognitive errors that Conly points to? She points to wishful thinking ("when we believe something is safe only because we are in fact already engaged in doing it"), anchoring ("falsely assuming that since smoking has not perceptibly hurt us in this one instance, it never will"), and time-discounting ("disproportionately discounting future pains when trading them off against present pleasures").[12]

Conly does not advocate the strong brand of coercive paternalism know as perfectionist paternalism, in which the state forces the virtues on individuals, requiring them to be industrious, chaste, generous, and the like, nor does she believe in the idea of ultimate ends that are objectively good (to be imposed by force) or inherently irrational (to be made illegal). Nor does she believe in a coercive paternalism based on a utilitarian-organicist conception, on which the state can coercively interfere in the freedom of individuals by prohibiting them from carrying out acts (such as suicide) that would result in putting an end to the many emotional, social, economic relationships they have created, in that they can no longer carry out the basic roles they carry out in society (as husband, son, grandson, friend, worker, taxpayer, and so on). Conly instead defends a weak type of coercive paternalism, where paternalism is justified only on the basis of the findings of social psychology and behavioural economics pointing to the fact that, when it comes to certain decisions, people tend to make numerous cognitive errors that prevent them from achieving the very ends they want to achieve, rather than the ends that the state or those in their family or their social world would want them to pursue (ibid., p. 150).

Conly does, however, run into trouble when she turns to the question of tobacco, where the argument is at once inconsistent and based on questionable factual premises. The inconsistency concerns the claims she makes about the black market that would be created once a substance such as tobacco is banned. She first notes that people know that smoking tobacco is harmful, and claims that marijuana and alcohol are perceived as less harmful, as if to suggest that no black market in harmful substances exists. She then concedes that there does exist a black market in harmful substances such as heroin, noting that heroin can be initially enjoyable. This is unlike what she claims about tobacco. But if tobacco in not enjoyable, why would

[12] Conly (2013), p. 169.

people start smoking? Conly claims that if people continue to smoke even if they do not enjoy the experience of smoking, that is entirely attributable to addiction. But then why do they even start smoking? Then, after claiming that it is completely unnecessary, and unnecessarily costly, to prohibit the consumption of alcohol—because experience shows that a black market would immediately form, and policies would have to be implemented to clamp down on the illegal dealing in alcohol—Conly claims, without evidence, that no such thing would happen with a ban on tobacco: the benefits of enforcing the ban would outweigh the costs, reducing the harms caused by the black market in tobacco that would inevitably form as a result, and so a ban would not in this case be unnecessary. But that is inconsistent with the argument made against a ban on alcohol.[13]

Conly's argument also rests, as mentioned, on some questionable empirical claims. Conly essentially relies on Robert Goodin's "The Ethics of Smoking" (Goodin 1989) to show that many smokers make several cognitive errors. But the empirical studies on which Goodin's argument is based do not support Conly's argument, not even in part. The fundamental cognitive error that Conly attributes to smokers—namely, believing that something is safe only because they are in fact already doing it, rather than doing it because they believe it is safe—can only be attributed to about 20% of smokers. In fact, the remaining 80% of smokers are not even misconceived about the harms of smoking: they know that smoking is harmful. And we are talking about statistics from the 1980s. In today's information environment, with its public service announcements and easier access to reliable sources, the percentage of people aware of the harms of tobacco smoking is certainly much higher.

In fact, Goodin's argument against smoking tobacco is mainly based on other science, most crucially the science showing that nicotine is addictive, and it has since been listed as such in the *Diagnostic and Statistical Manual of Mental Disorders* (DSM-IV-TR 2000, pp. 265–266). Thus, after a short time, a smokers' choice to smoke would no longer be truly voluntary. But Goodin's argument is actually quite weak, because while it is true that nicotine is addictive, the withdrawal symptoms are not even close to those of cocaine or heroin. We are talking about irritability, a melancholy mood, difficulty concentrating, a decreased heart rate, headaches, constipation, increased hunger, anxiety, insomnia, impatience, and other minor psychological complaints lasting for a few weeks. As with other addictive substances, the acute phase, with peak symptoms, occurs in the first week from the time the last cigarette was smoked; then, in most cases, the symptoms diminish significantly.

What other cognitive errors does Goodin attribute to smokers on the basis of empirical studies? According to many studies, a good portion of smokers, some 40–50%, know the statistics about the probability of getting lung cancer, and some even pessimistically overrate smokers' overall risk of getting lung cancer, and yet they believe that the statistics do not apply to them. They believe that they are less

[13] Conly (2013), pp. 150ff., 170ff.

susceptible than the average smoker; they believe that their own probability of getting lung cancer is lower than the average smoker's.[14] This *optimism bias* has also been noted with regard to car drivers, most of whom "consider themselves to be safer, more skillful, and less likely to be involved in an accident than the average driver".[15] What Goodin describes is certainly a cognitive error, and it is so for many of those who claim to be less susceptible to lung cancer than the average smoker, but it may not be so for everyone. That depends on empirical data that I am not aware of. From an epidemiological standpoint, tobacco consumption is neither a necessary nor a sufficient condition for lung cancer. It simply greatly increases the risk of lung cancer, by about 23% for men and 13% for women compared to nonsmokers. But there are other contributing factors, especially environmental ones. Studies on the impact that genetic factors have on the development of lung cancer are controversial, but some studies confirm their existence. According to Kanwal et al. (2017, p. 539), "the risk of lung cancer in individuals with a family history of cancer among first-degree relatives is increased by 50% compared with those without a family history, and this association is not affected by gender, ethnicity, histological types and other known lung cancer risk factors." If, as would seem to be the case, genetic predisposition, or family history, is among the factors affecting the probability of getting lung cancer, in the sense that genetic family history is triggered when another risk factor is present, then some percentage of smokers, say 10%, could have a basis for claiming that if their parents or grandparents or uncles did not get lung cancer despite smoking, they too are less likely to get lung cancer by comparison with others who have a relative who got cancer, and who accordingly falls in the average. We would need a specific empirical study that looks at (a) smokers with a smoking relative who has had lung cancer in comparison with (b) smokers with a smoking relative who has not had lung cancer, and on that basis we could assess how much more likely smokers in group (a) are to get lung cancer relative to smokers in group (b).

Setting aside the question of the degree to which family history affects the likelihood of a smoker getting lung cancer from smoking, let us assume, with Goodin, that about 40% of smokers make the cognitive error of believing that they are less susceptible to cancer than the average smoker. How might we explain these smokers' optimism bias?

Weinstein (1982, 1987) has noted the same optimism bias in relation to some health hazards. The subjects in Weinstein's study claimed to have a lower

[14] See Leventhal et al. (1987); Park et al. (2009); Khwaja et al. (2009); Shiloh et al. (2009); Weinstein (1998); Weinstein et al. (2005). In reality, studies on tobacco smokers' risk perception give mixed results that are difficult to interpret. Some show a certain pessimism among smokers, while others show excessive optimism about the likelihood of getting lung cancer. Some authors' complex explanation for this contrast is that smokers are ashamed of their cognitive errors, denying them when interviewed (either in person or over the phone), and expressing them freely only when they are own their own with a written questionnaire to fill out. Second, some studies do not accurately report the percentage of smokers surveyed who think their risk of getting sick is lower than that of the average smoker.

[15] DeJoy (1989), p. 333.

probability than other people that something should happen to them that is either harmful to their health or fatal, including drug addiction, alcoholism, attempted suicide, sunstroke, skin cancer, lung cancer, asthma, biliary colic, deafness, and death by murder. A first explanation is that the optimism bias is a strategy for reducing stress and anxiety in the face of significant threats to one's own health and life. But there is no documented evidence for the validity of this explanation, because the research so far conducted does not find any correlation between the seriousness or severity of the threat to one's health and the seriousness or severity of the cognitive error. And the reason we would look for such a correlation is that, as some authors suggest, if the cognitive error is a strategy for reducing the stress connected to possible threats, we should see the idea of one's own invulnerability establishing a stronger and stronger foothold as the health threat becomes increasingly severe. We might think, for example, that we are more invulnerable than the average person to lung cancer and yet less invulnerable than average to a flu. It may well be that this is a defence mechanism for coping with the stress and anxiety of a truth we do not want to face, and in that sense it may be rational to hold such a belief—for it is rational to want to protect oneself, however flawed the means we choose by which to do that—but nothing about the logic of that belief seems rational. It seems absurd, in short, to think that the greater the threat to our health, the greater our invulnerability to that threat.

A second explanation is that the optimism bias protects our self-esteem: many of us feel reassured thinking that we have a better-than-average ability to protect ourselves from negative events whose occurrence depends crucially on our own conduct. There are other explanations, too, not incompatible with the previous ones, and they include overconfidence—erroneously believing that we are more prudent than average—and plain ignorance, where we are simply unaware of the causes, risk factors, and incidence of many diseases, erroneously believing that we not especially at risk for them.

In offering to finally explain how people fall victim to optimism bias, specifically where they believe that they have a lower-than-average probability of something very harmful happening to them in the future, Weinstein points to four kinds of incorrect inferences and assumptions that people tend to make: (1) if the event has not yet happened to us, this will be taken to mean that it will *never* happen to us; (2) if the event is infrequent, it will be taken to mean that it is even less frequent than it actually is; (3) if the occurrence of the event depends on individual conduct, it will be perceived as something that we can easily avoid; and (4) if we have no experience with the event or problem, it will be perceived as something we shouldn't have to worry about. The curious aspect of Weinstein's study is that he complains that people do not engage in what I would call "statistical hyperrationality." According to Weinstein, people who are more at risk than others should remind themselves every day that they have a serious or high probability of attempting suicide or becoming heroin addicts in the next decade. But who could make a point of regularly reminding themselves of such a gloomy prospect and not fall into a general state of depression?

Some of the explanations that Weinstein offers for the optimism bias obviously do not apply to tobacco smokers, even if most of them are in general terms aware of the risks of smoking and the frequency of lung cancer, just as they know that the disease can develop even after decades of smoking, and, obviously, they know that they can avoid lung cancer or reduce their risk for it if they quit smoking. Some tobacco smokers, however, believe that the general statistics about the probability of getting cancer do not apply to them. Is there a way to interpret this cognitive error of tobacco smokers as one that is not a determining factor in a smoker's decision to start smoking? Yes, there is. It is possible—and I am stressing possible, rather than certain—that some smokers (say, 30% of them) who actually make the cognitive error of optimism bias, should rationally decide that it is on balance preferable to smoke, and risk giving up a few years of their life, than live a longer life without smoking. This is not to say that it would be rational for people to want to die of lung cancer, but that it may well be rational for them to accept the *risk* that this could happen. And that would explain why some people immediately stop smoking as soon as they get the first symptoms of a smoking-related disease, such as emphysema or a curable cancer. However, after carrying out such balancing, in a rational way, smokers may forget and deceive themselves, because they do not want to constantly remind themselves that they are engaging in deeply harmful behaviour, so they deceive themselves about the probability of getting sick, about their own invulnerability.

This defence mechanism, self-deception, is much more widespread than one would think. There are unresolved issues and internal conflicts that people are always dealing with in their personal lives, especially when it comes to the more important decisions, and in fact some people just believe what they want to believe: on a deep level they sense some hard truths that they consciously reject—truths about themselves, their partners, their children, their parents—and they deceive themselves because they are unable to accept the bitter truth. They deceive themselves about the ambivalent, love/hate relationships they have with their parents, siblings, or partners, or about a neurosis they may have, or about some serious mistakes their parents may have made and which they cannot bring themselves to forgive or are unconsciously reluctant to forgive. It seems to me that the choices people make, or the things they choose to do, can easily be ranked on a "self-deception scale": at one end of the scale are the hard choices, like those that people confront in their relationships with their loved ones, and this is where the self-deception tends to be strongest, where we are unconsciously dealing with conflicts that we might choose to resolve by wishful thinking or other erroneous ways of thinking; at the other end of the scale are the easy choices that we can actually make on a rational basis, because we are less likely to be dealing with unconscious conflicts, and even if we are always dealing with our own unresolved issues in making these choices, the choice problem is one we can nonetheless approach on a rational basis, as might be the case when at issue is whether to pass a law that would legalize euthanasia, assisted suicide, gay marriage, and the like; at midrange we would find ourselves making choices that can be rational, less subject or not subject to unconscious conflicts, and hence to self-deception, even if our decision-making behaviour can be rash, superficial, or uncertain, or it may be affected by weakness of will, as when making a personal choice to consume tobacco or narcotic substances, or to request euthanasia or assisted suicide, or to engage in sadomasochism or perform bloody religious rituals.

Another cognitive error that, according to Goodin, some smokers make is to forget about the harm of smoking once smoking has become a habit. As we have seen, this, too, may not be a decisive cognitive error. As just discussed, it may happen that some smokers balance the positive effects of smoking (the pleasure it gives) against its negative effects on the lungs, and that after a while, through self-deception, they forget the negative effects. It would in fact be an annoying nudge to have to continually remind oneself on a daily basis that tobacco consumption increases the risk of serious harm to one's health. As a result, smokers forget about the harm of smoking, or even remove the belief they had about that harm, and yet the risk balance behind that self-deception could be perfectly rational, that is, even if someone vividly reminded them of the increased risk of cancer, they would still want to smoke (without any change in their desire to smoke). And even without the personal reminder, they would get the reminder from the warning labels on cigarette packs, so it is almost impossible to forget; then, too, as we have seen, many smokers are aware of the the statistics relating to the probability of getting lung cancer from smoking.

Finally, Goodin (1989, p. 582) points to time-discounting errors, in which young smokers irrationally "attach relatively little importance to future pains relative to present pleasures in their utility functions," thus discounting the harm they will suffer in the future as a result of their present actions. This, too, is not necessarily a cognitive error. Is it possible for there to be a "rational squanderer" of one's own physical, intellectual, and economic resources? Here too, I would suggest that it is. From Jim Morrison to Freddy Mercury, from Kurt Cobain to Amy Winehouse, to the character of Count Mascetti in Mario Monicelli's film *Amici Miei*, there are people who rationally squander their own resources. The rationale for this behaviour—like that of spendthrifts who use up all of their wealth in a short time, only to live from hand to mouth for the rest of their life—rests on two assumptions. The first one is that there is no sure tomorrow: we can never know what the next day will bring. The second one is that it is better to live in lavish extravagance, with hotels, escorts, and luxury cars, for a few years now than to slog through life with ordinary means, having to budget for everything. The idea, in other words, is that if we plan our financial future in such a way as to distribute our income evenly across all the years we expect to live, we would never be able to experience the unbridled luxury we desire, not even for a short period.

The same goes for those who put their body and their psychophysical energy to use for risky or unhealthy activities, such as unprotected sex or drinking alcohol and doing drugs. It can be completely rational to be wasteful with one's own resources, whether they are physical, psychological, or financial. And, contrary to what Goodin suggests, if Spendthrift Steve is squandering his resources, or is not maximizing his average utility in such a way as to have enough of a cushion for retirement, this does not in itself mean that he is being irrational or is committing a cognitive error. The only basis for saying that he has in fact done so is to look at any sense of regret he may come to have at the end of the run: if he does come to regret his actions, that may suggest that he was indeed acting irrationally. But that is not a definitive litmus test of irrationality: Steve may have changed his mind about his approach to life, or it may be that what is irrational is not his previous course of action but his present regret. This notion that people who squander their resources are necessarily irrational can hold up only on the basis of a cryptopaternalistic theory, on an objective theory of interests positing that life is always inherently valuable and that no one moment in one's life is any more or less valuable than any other moment. What this assumes is that none of the things we choose to do in life can have an opportunity cost, despite the fact that our resources are limited and that there is no way to avoid making choices in life, as if a person cannot, rationally, squander all his resources and then, rationally, die young.

We have seen that Conly's claim that smokers often make several cognitive errors is empirically questionable, but that is not her only error. For one thing, she assumes that smokers would stop smoking once they discover a cognitive error in their decision to smoke. This is not known. We don't know what smokers will do once they discover a cognitive error in their decision to smoke, just as we don't know how people would balance their values and interests once they discover a false belief, such as that it is false that smoking is good for your health.

For another thing, the tenor of Conly's argument suggests that it is not so essential to respect people's capacity for autonomy, and consequently that it is okay to cause them to suffer by preventing them from making their own decisions, through their own independent powers of judgment, even if they prove to be sufficiently rational in making such decisions, and even if the decision is not irreversibly self-destructive, such as a decision to commit suicide within the next 24 h. What seems to matter most, on her conception, is that the decision should be right from some objective point of view: for example it should be perfectly balanced from a psychological point of view. According to this way of thinking, when a decision is wrong, we should be prevented from acting on it. But how many people in the world could pass that test of objective correctness or be perfectly balanced from a psychological point of view in their decision-making? I would suggest that there are very few such people, and that even when we are far from level-headed and judicious by any objective standard—if we engage in harmful conduct, for example—we have a right to be left alone so long as we are not harming others. People who engage in harmful conduct—and in that category I would count tobacco smoking and drugs—may be doing so because they have suffered physical, sexual, or psychological abuse or some kind of abandonment that they cannot process on their own, and they can regain their emotional balance through a relationship, or they can seek help, or help may be made available to them in the form of psychotherapy. But from the fact that they have underlying issues that can be addressed through psychotherapy it does not follow that they should thereby be compelled to go through such therapy so that they can be set on the right course, the one that leads them to make the right decisions.

Everyone should be free to live their life and pursue their own goals according to what drives them, even if their drives are self-harming, and so long as the individuals concerned are sufficiently rational and autonomous, implying that their drives cannot be *irreversibly* self-destructive and that the same individuals can lead a functional life (they do not suffer from any severe depression or any psychotic disorder or borderline personality disorder). This does not mean that these "nonfunctional" individuals can be compelled to go into therapy, but it does mean that if their behaviour causes harm to others, apart from the harm it causes to themselves, it would be justified to prevent them from causing that outside harm. Anything beyond that would cross over into the camp of the illiberal. And to advocate for any more restrictive policy when it comes to issues such as tobacco smoking, as by prohibiting the use of tobacco products, would be to fail to understand the consequences of such a prohibition: smokers might seek tobacco on the black market or, if behind their desire to smoke lies a self-harming impulse, they might switch to drugs or alcohol, or again they might seek comfort in junk food, which would be harmful to their health in other ways. The logic of prohibition is always at root wrong, not only because, as just commented, we can't prohibit people from exercising their autonomy just because they have impulses that cause them to do some degree of harm to themselves, but also because prohibition is always prohibitively costly to the community, its enforcement inevitably requiring some kind of "war" on whatever substance is being prohibited (and history suggests that these kinds of wars are never-ending and largely ineffective, no matter how many resources are poured into them).

But even assuming that this is all wrong—that is, even assuming that smokers commit several cognitive errors, do not make decisions rationally, and deceive themselves, and that sufficiently autonomous people do not have the right to live as they choose if they are even only slightly subject to self-harming drives—there remains a possible liberal solution to the problem, and that is the solution already discussed. In other words, even if we assume that people commit several cognitive errors in choosing to start smoking or to not quit smoking, why can we not adopt the scheme that moderately liberal antipaternalistic theories adopt for activities widely considered to be risky or harmful? Under this scheme, as discussed, persons intent on carrying out these activities would be required to have a conversation with a doctor or other medical professional or counsellor entrusted with laying out the key facts and statistics about smoking and with pointing out the most common cognitive errors that people make in choosing to smoke. This would mean that, as with the consumption of hard drugs and psychotropic drugs, so with the consumption of tobacco people would have to obtain medical authorization before they take up smoking. The scheme might be set up as follows: (1) would-be smokers submit to an interview with a doctor or other health professional or counsellor (an interview where they get the facts about the risks of tobacco smoking and learn about the cognitive errors involved in any decision to smoke); (2) having gone through the interview, they can decide whether they want to take up smoking anyway; (3) if they do make that decision, they obtain an authorization to do so, perhaps through their health insurance card; and (4) they are required to periodically renew their authorization by submitting to a new interview, perhaps every 10 years, where the doctor, health professional, or counsellor looks for any self-deception interviewees may be trapped into in regard to their own invulnerability to the harms of smoking and in regard to their risk of exposure relative to nonsmokers. I think that Conly would respond by arguing that cognitive errors are incorrigible and intractable, so any interview or sit-down session with any professional would be pointless.

In the literature we find two senses in which the *incorrigibility* and *intractability* of cognitive errors is understood, only one of which, I would argue, is correct. One place where we can find the sense that strikes me as incorrect is in an article by Trout (2005), who suggests that all or most cognitive errors are incorrigible in the sense that, once a given problem or piece of information is framed in a certain way, in a certain context, it is inevitable for respondents or recipients of that information to make the error in question, no matter how careful they are about not making any error. Thus, to return to the Gandhi example in Sect. 4.2, if we are asked to guess the age at which Gandhi died, and in the framing of the question we are given an incorrect anchor (114), we are very unlikely to guess correctly. The same goes for other cognitive errors. What I think makes this sense of *incorrigibility* incorrect, or at least unhelpful, is that even if we are indeed very likely to make the wrong guess under one framing, that does not necessarily hold for all possible framings: it may well be that under a different framing (such as one in which the anchor is 35), we will be more likely to guess correctly. The sense of *incorrigibility* and *intractability* that, by contrast, strikes me as correct, is the one in which I think Conly uses the term. According to this sense, most or all cognitive errors are understood to be incorrigible or intractable in that there is going to be bias no matter the framing or context through which a given problem or piece of information is presented, such that, whatever bias we are dealing with, there is no way in which it can subsequently be corrected. But I think that Conly is wrong to claim that most cognitive errors are incorrigible and intractable in this second sense.[16]

Contrary to what Conly claims about intractable irrationality in relation to cognitive errors like the optimism bias (as when a smoker believes that he or she is less exposed to the risk of lung cancer than the average smoker) or the affect heuristic, the representativeness heuristic, the anchoring effect, the framing effect, the availability bias, confirmation bias, and the choice-supportive bias,[17] there is nothing in

---

[16] A similar claim is made by Trout, who argues "that these biases are, in general, extremely difficult for individuals to correct, and so are, for practical purposes, psychologically incorrigible" Trout (2005, p. 408). But Trout also discusses "debiasing strategies," drawing a distinction between outside strategies and inside strategies: "Outside strategies place a priority on welfare, inside strategies on liberty" (ibid., p. 420). Trout's outside strategies can be understood to include the strategies previously discussed where information about probabilities is conveyed in terms of relative frequency using natural numbers or natural frequencies, rather than percentages, or where a default value is used as a way to indicate the better of two options, or at least the one that is favoured.

[17] Choice-supportive bias is the tendency to retroactively play up the positive attributes of an option we have previously selected or to play down the negative attributes of the ones we have not selected, or both, thereby representing the choice we made as better than it actually was. Confirmation bias is where we look for evidence that supports something we already believe, all

Kahneman and Tversky's studies to suggest that these cognitive errors cannot be avoided or corrected through a rational and relaxed interview with a doctor or other medical professional, as happens today with regular drug prescriptions; rather, as we have seen, these studies offer good reasons why we should want to make the effort to avert or eliminate cognitive errors.

A similar scheme could be introduced for driving a car without wearing seatbelts or riding a motorcycle without wearing a helmet. As Thaler and Sunstein propose, a special license could be issued for these cases, making such activities legal. Under the scheme, anyone who wants to obtain the license would be required to undergo training that brings to their attention the statistical frequency of accidents and head traumas, the mortality rate, and the damage resulting from the impact of a human body against a windshield at low speeds, such as 50 km/h—to be clear, that would be like falling from the third floor of a building, and the like. (Under this proposal, however, it would be forbidden to show photos of people who have been seriously injured in a traffic accident as a result of which they might have sustained a head injury or been severely disabled.) For example, some studies have shown that the mandatory use of a helmet leads to a reduction in the rate of mortality for motorists (the reduction in mortality rate changes according to different statistical research or survey from 40% to 17.8%) and a reduction in the head-trauma rate (the reduction in head-trauma rate changes according to different statistical research or survey from 44% to 16.8%). "Relative risk is the ratio between (1) the probability that those exposed to a certain risk factor (e.g., not wearing a helmet) will undergo a certain event (e.g., head injury) and (2) the probability that those not exposed to that risk factor (e.g., wearing a helmet) will undergo the same event (e.g., head injury). So when we say that the risk of incurring a serious or fatal head injury is 2.0 for someone who doesn't wear a helmet relative to someone who does, we mean that

---

the while ignoring any contrary evidence. It seems unlikely that individuals should make either of these two cognitive errors when they sit down for an interview with a medical professional entrusted with laying out the key facts pertaining to the choice at hand (as when thinking about requesting assisted suicide or taking hard drugs) and assessing whether the interviewees are mentally fit (whether they have mental capacity and are sufficiently rational and uncoerced), so as to assess whether they really want to make those choices. It is unlikely because, in this scenario, there is no previous choice that one might embellish, nor is there any cherry-picked evidence that one selects for oneself: there is only the evidence and information that the medical professional offers as relevant and reliable. To be sure, other cognitive errors may be much more difficult to avoid, as is the case with the tendency to accept the default as one's chosen option, or the halo effect, or again the "eye level is buy level" effect in retail merchandising, but these errors are unlikely to arise in the context of a structured conversation with a health professional. What seems clear, in conclusion, is that the experiments that cognitive psychologists set up are not the simple and obvious ones that are sure to yield predictable results, in such a way as to suggest that cognitive errors can be corrected. Consider, for example, the anchoring effect with the Gandhi example we should by now recognize. Two groups of people are asked to guess the age at which Gandhi died, but the framing of the question is anchored at 140 for one group and 35 for the other: the first group tends to answer that Gandhi died at 67, the second group at 50, suggesting that the majority of people are susceptible to anchoring. But what if people in both groups are subsequently told that Gandhi actually died at the age of 78, and the experiment is then repeated with the incorrect anchors: how many people would still get the date wrong?

the first person is twice as likely as the second to sustain such an injury" (Taggi 1999, my translation).

At the same time, applicants would have to score high on their drivers tests and would also have to show that they are prudent, or that they are unlikely to, and should not, commit serious violations of the highway code. In addition, considering that in the event of a fatal accident involving another motorist, the latter could be held liable for vehicular manslaughter, the scheme would provide that the motorist is exempted from criminal and civil liability if the motorcyclist or the motorist was not wearing a helmet or seatbelts at the time of the accident (unless, of course, the motorist is found to have acted with malice or gross negligence).

Conly also makes other proposals, such as banning trans fats and the use of food stamps to purchase soft drinks (considering that a correlation has been established between the consumption of soft drinks and obesity). These kinds of restrictions would be consistent with a moderate liberal theory as previously outlined, and the same goes for proposals to mandate smaller portions at fast-food restaurants (Conly would put such a ban on *any* restaurant, not just fast-food establishments, but that would be too restrictive for a moderate liberal theory of the kind here envisioned). Conly justifies these proposals on various grounds, and three in particular. First, she argues that since trans fats have no taste or smell, nothing would change for consumers except that they would avoid doing harm to their own health. Second, these proposals do not force people to necessarily eat a healthy diet based on fruits and vegetables, nor would the proposals ban fast or junk food itself. They simply make it more difficult to buy and eat unhealthy foods: if the portions at fast-food restaurants are smaller, there is nothing to prevent customers from ordering a second or third portion. And third, obesity is associated with a range of comorbidities, such as diabetes and some types of cancer: these entail considerable healthcare costs for the wider community, justifying policies under which the state would intervene to curb these costs. Under this slate of proposals, not only would fast-food menus carry smaller portions, but the items on the menu, including soft drinks, and indeed junk food generally, would be specifically taxed by levying an indirect tax such as VAT, just as tobacco is currently taxed (an average tax of 75% in Europe today). Putting an indirect tax on the consumption of a harmful substance would make it possible to legalize that substance without the state incurring significant costs. This would also apply to a range of risky or harmful activities, such as smoking tobacco, consuming fast food or carbonated drinks; drinking alcohol; or taking hard drugs (such as cocaine, heroin) or smart drugs (MDMA, cognitive enhancers), or cannabis, since the revenues from taxation normally outbalance the healthcare costs sustained to treat the conditions associated with these activities, not to mention that legalizing the sale and consumption of these substances would mean that the state no longer has to devote resources to the effort to fight drug trafficking on the black market.[18]

[18] Two economists, Miron and Waldock, have calculated that anti-prohibitionist policies on drug sales and consumption, such as those under the "tax and control" system, with or without a state monopoly, could imply, by a very conservative estimate, "that drug legalization would reduce government expenditure by about $41.3 billion annually. Roughly $25.7 billion of these savings

In the same vein, there needs to be affordable private insurance to cover all the medical and disability expenses for individuals who suffer an injury in a car or motorcycle accident and were not wearing a helmet or a seatbelt at the time of the accident. The premiums for liability car insurance in Italy in 2024 typically fall into three brackets as follows (covering both third-party bodily injury and property damage): 494–685 euros in a low-risk class; 924–1190 euros in a high-risk class for drivers aged 60 or older; and 1949 euros in a high-risk class for drivers aged aged 20 or less. This insurance covers up to 15 million euros per accident for third-party death or bodily injury. Premiums will increase by 50 to 190 euros per year for third-party bodily injury and property damage if the insurance company pays out an amount in excess of five million euros. The premium for bodily injury suffered by the driver (the policies cover medical and disability expenses) and for damage

---

would accrue to state and local governments, and roughly $15.6 billion would accrue to the federal government. Approximately $8.7 billion of the savings would result from legalization of marijuana, $20.0 billion from legalization of cocaine and heroin, and $12.6 billion from legalization of all other drugs. Legalization would also generate tax revenue of roughly $46.7 billion annually if drugs were taxed at rates comparable to those on alcohol and tobacco. Approximately $8.7 billion of this revenue would result from legalization of marijuana, $32.6 billion from legalization of cocaine and heroin, and $5.5 billion from legalization of all other drugs". Similar estimates are made by Husak.

The legalization, in other words, could bring in, by a very conservative estimate, about $88 billion in increased revenue per year, counting lower expenditures and higher revenues, in the United States of America alone: lower expenses due to the fact that it would no longer be necessary to wage a fight against drug trafficking, and higher revenues due to indirect taxes on drug use, once legalized. It would be sufficient for cocaine, hashish, or marijuana to be sold at a price that incorporates indirect taxes, i.e., VAT or excise taxes, equivalent to those in place today for tobacco sales (in Europe, this is an average of 75% percent of the price). It is not possible, nor is it important here, to make precise calculations regarding Italy. If we stipulate a per capita consumption of narcotics, and per capita costs, for to the use of police forces, criminal trials, and the detention of drug dealers somewhat lower than in the United States, where the level of consumption and the intensity of the war on drugs is very high, we should expect an increased revenue of about 10 billion euros per year in Italy alone, where the population is about one-sixth that of the United States. It would, however, be a huge amount, about half of the Meloni government's 2024 budget of 24 billion euros. Other studies show far more optimistic prospects of lower expenditures and higher revenues in the event of legalization, and they also seem empirically well-founded. A study in which David and Ofria consider the cannabis market alone, has calculated lower expenses and higher revenues amounting to increased tax revenues ranging from 6 to 8.7 billion euros, depending on the price at which a dose of cannabis would be sold. Based on official data, David and Ofria calculated about 540 million euros in costs that the state would have had to bear to fight cannabis traffiking, calculating prison expenses, and 228 million euros for public order and security in 2011. They then calculated how much the tax revenue could be from the sale of as many doses of cannabis as are assumed to have been consumed in 2011, making different estimates depending on whether the dose is sold for 12, 10 or 8 euros, with an indirect tax of 75% percent. The amount of drugs consumed was estimated based on AquaDrugs' surveys of drug residues in wastewater purifiers. That would be an average of 36 doses per thousand inhabitants in Italy in 2011, which means a tax-revenue increase, of approximately between 5.3 billion and 8 billion euros, depending on whether the single dose is sold for eight, ten, or twelve euros. See David and Ofria (2017). The retail price of cannabis per gram is about the equivalent of 12 dollars in Italy and thhe equivalent of between 10 and 12 dollars in other European contries.

caused to the driver's own property ranges from 30 to 45 euros per year, and it typically does not cover injuries suffered without wearing a helmet or a seatbelt. Consider, then, a scheme under which motorcycle and car drivers aged eighteen or older who choose not to wear a helmet or a seatbelt can do so on condition that they take out a personal-injury-protection policy which caps benefits at two million euros and which they need to renew every year in order keep their drivers' licences: on a conservative estimate, such a policy would cost from 190 to 270 euros per year, almost six times more than regular mandatory car insurance for personal injury protection.

The premium for liability car insurance for a twenty-year old driver in a high risk class with a policy limit of 15 million euros is 1949 euros. It follows that an insurance premium with a policy limit of two million euros is priced at 12% of that amount, at less than 235 euros. The probability of an accident causing personal injury is the same as the probability of an accident causing third-party bodily injury or property damage, given that the risk of injury without wearing a helmet or a seatbelt is higher (about 16.8% higher), but there is no risk of making payments for third-party bodily injury or property damage, or for the death's driver, because if the driver dies, there can be no compensation (even if the driver was wearing a seatbelt or a helmet). In Italy, only 10% of head traumas need intensive care, and from 1985 to 1987, with the 1986 law that was passed making helmets mandatory for minors of age driving mopeds and for all drivers of motorbikes, the number of people injured in motorcycle accidents fell: the figures went from 29,700 to 24,500 injuries with probable head trauma over a six-month period (5200 fewer injuries over that period). That means that, over the course of a year, in Italy, a total of nearly 1000 people were injured who were not wearing a helmet and needed intensive care, in a healthcare landscape with an overall capacity of 7500 ICU beds, which translates to 45,000 intensive care hospitalizations for an average period of 2 months. Traumas and head injuries are classified into three groups as follows. (1) Mild head trauma: This is the majority of head-trauma cases, in which there is no loss of consciousness, or the period of unconsciousness does not exceed 20–30 min. (2) Moderate traumas: These are often difficult to diagnose, with those affected generally noticing mental changes only when they return to common daily activities. The most common post-traumatic symptoms of mild head trauma are as follows: physical problems (headache, dizziness, nausea, excessive fatigue), cognitive impairments (memory loss, attention and concentration deficits), mood and/or behavioural changes (anxiety, depression, agitation, irritability). (3) Severe head trauma: These head injuries are accompanied by loss of consciousness during or immediately after an accident. Although the duration and severity of symptoms vary greatly, many patients continue to have significant issues in the months following the event, particularly in the form of headaches, memory lapses, and difficulties in daily life. In the vast majority of cases, neuropsychological, cognitive, speech, and physical rehabilitation is very effective if the treatment—usually lasting for several months—is begun within the first months after the head trauma. (If the trauma results in serious disability requiring a full-time caregiver, that will cost 1670 euros a month, plus 200 euros for rent in a caregiving facility out in the province and 400 euros for food and utilities: that adds up to 2200 euros per month, 26,400 euros per year, and 1,848,000 over the course of 70 years. Intensive care cannot cost more than 152,000 euros.)

Even if I am arguing in favour of legalizing psychoactive drugs (such as heroin and cocaine), while regulating their use, as we will see in the Chap. 7, and levying an indirect tax on them, with tax-inclusive pricing that would also apply to unhealthy foods, it is well worth remembering that in all Western countries where the right to health care is protected under some kind of universal healthcare programme, it is by and large the healthcare system that bears the economic cost of the medical care needed to treat the conditions of individuals who engage in risky activities such as smoking, doing drugs, eating too much junk food (whether by choice or by circumstance), or having unprotected sex, or in forms of reckless behaviour such as speeding or practicing boxing, wrestling, or extreme sports.

But the range of decisions that people may make to do anything that is irreversible or highly risky or harmful is not limited to the cases we have surveyed (such as requesting euthanasia, taking hard drugs, or practicing extreme sports): it can be made to also include risky decisions where a lot is at stake for the decision-maker, and I am thinking in particular of financial decisions, such as taking out a loan (including a mortgage) or making an investment through a bank or an investment company: it wouldn't be incompatible with a moderately liberal conception like the one here outlined to mandate an interview with a financial advisor entrusted with determining whether the person contemplating the financial decision in question is making a cognitive error (a form of consumer financial protection). The reason why such a requirement wouldn't be incompatible with such a moderately liberal conception is that the purpose of the interview—for financial decisions as well as for all the other risky or irreversible decisions previously discussed—is not to compel the interviewee to decide in one way or another but to offer guidance in the form of a diagnostic analysis of anything that may be wrong with his or her decision-making process. Any further requirement or restriction would instead be inconsistent with such a conception. So, contrary to what Conly argues for, I cannot see how it might be justified to cap the amount of debt that one can take on, not only because this would interfere with individual autonomy but also because the financial system already has risk management built into it as it stands. With consumer loans, this comes in the form of collateral (and a mortgage, or home loan, is essentially that: a lien on a house). The same goes for a business, which would typically be required to put up collateral before it can secure a loan, while also providing financial documentation showing that the business itself is creditworthy. At the same time, it would certainly be consistent with a moderately liberal conception to put a cap on the interest that banks can charge on the loans they issue to consumers (this, too, would be a form of financial consumer protection), since the rationale for such a cap would not be to limit a consumer's individual autonomy but to avoid the harm that consumers can suffer as a result of their financial transactions.

More complex, finally, is the issue of pension plans. As Conly (2013, p. 23) notes, "the pension plan a group of employees has depends not so much on what would most efficiently advance their retirement goals, but largely on the 'default option' they are offered." This means that they tend not to opt for a pension plan if that is not the default, even if they would be better off opting in. This problem could be solved by making the pension plan mandatory—again, not in order to restrict an employee's freedom of choice but to avoid the harm that a choice not to opt for such a plan may cause to the state, at least with employees who fail to save adequately for retirement and then become eligible for a social-insurance programme that would have to make disbursements to provide for these employees in old age, making up for the financial irresponsibility of their younger days. Their injudicious behaviour can in this sense be considered an externality, a cost that will eventually weigh on the community. Hence the justification, on the liberal grounds explained, for making opt-in pension plans mandatory.

References

Abrams DS, Bertrand M, Mullainathan S (2012) Do judges vary in their treatment of race? J Leg Stud 41(2):347–383. https://doi.org/10.1086/666006

Ariely D (2009) Predictably irrational: the hidden forces that shape our decisions. Harper, New York

Bibas S (2004) The psychology of hindsight and after-the-fact review of ineffective assistance of counsel. Utah Law Rev 55(1):1–12. https://scholarship.law.upenn.edu/faculty_scholarship/9

Brewer N, Bradfield AD (eds) (2019) Psychological science and the law. Guilford Press, New York

Cominelli L (2018) Cognition of the law: toward a cognitive sociology of law and behavior. Springer, Cham

Conly S (2013) Against autonomy: justifying coercive paternalism. Cambridge University Press, Cambridge

Cosmides L, Tooby J (1995) In: Baron-Cohen S (ed) Foreword to Mindblindness: an essay on autism and theory of mind. The MIT Press, Cambridge, MA, pp xi–xviii

Cosmides L, Tooby J (1996) Are humans good intuitive statisticians after all? Rethinking some conclusions from the literature on judgment under uncertainty. Cognition 58:1–173. https://doi.org/10.1016/0010-0277(95)00664-8

Danziger S, Levav J, Avnaim-Pesso L (2011) Extraneous factors in judicial decisions. Proc Natl Acad Sci USA 108(17):6889–6892. https://doi.org/10.1073/pnas.1018033108

David P, Ofria F (2017) Perché legalizzare la cannabis: Una analisi di costi e benefici. Economia e politica 9(14):1–6. http://www.economiaepolitica.it/politiche-economiche/perche-legalizzare-la-cannabis-una-analisi-di-costi-e-benefici/

DeJoy DM (1989) The optimism bias and traffic accident risk perception accident. Analysis & Prevention 21(4):333–340. https://doi.org/10.1016/0001-4575(89)90024-9

Diciotti E (1986) Paternalismo. Materiali per una storia della cultura giuridica XVI 2:557–586

Dovidio JF, Hewstone M, Glick P, Esses V (eds) (2013) The SAGE handbook of prejudice, stereotyping and discrimination. SAGE Publications, London

DSM-IV-TR. (2000) Diagnostic and statistical manual of mental disorders, 4th edn Text Revision. American Psychiatric Association, Washington, DC

Efran MG (1974) The effect of physical appearance on the judgment of guilt, interpersonal attraction, and severity of recommended punishment in a simulated jury task. J Res Pers 8(1):45–54. https://doi.org/10.1016/0092-6566(74)90044-0

Ellsworth PC (2012) Legal reasoning and scientific reasoning. Alabama Law Rev 63(1):895–918. https://repository.law.umich.edu/articles/1416/

Englich B, Mussweiler T, Strack F (2005) The last word in court—a hidden disadvantage for the Defense. Law Hum Behav 29:705–722. https://doi.org/10.1007/s10979-005-8380-7
Feinberg J (1986) Harm to self. Vol. 3 of the moral limits of the criminal law. Oxford University Press, Oxford
Gigerenzer G, Engel C (eds) (2004) Heuristics and the law. The MIT Press, Cambridge, MA
Gilovich T et al (eds) (2002) Heuristics and biases: the psychology of intuitive judgment. Cambridge University Press, Cambridge. https://doi.org/10.1017/CBO9780511808098
Girvan EJ (2016) Wise restraints? Learning legal rules, not standards, reduces the effects of stereotypes in legal decision-making. Psychol Public Policy Law 22(1):31–45. https://doi.org/10.1037/law0000068
Goodin RE (1989) The ethics of smoking. Ethics 99(3):574–624. https://doi.org/10.1086/293100
Greene JD (2008) The secret joke of Kant's soul. In: Sinnott-Armstrong W (ed) The neuroscience of morality: emotion, brain disorders, and development. Vol. 3 of moral psychology. The MIT Press., Chap. 2, Cambridge, pp 35–79
Griffin LK (2016) Criminal adjudication, error correction, and hindsight blind spots. Washington and Lee Law Review 73(1):165–215. https://scholarlycommons.law.wlu.edu/wlulr/vol73/iss1/5
Guthrie C et al (2001) Inside the judicial mind. Cornell Law Rev 86(4):777–830. https://scholarship.law.cornell.edu/facpub/814
Guthrie C et al (2007) Blinking on the bench: how judges decide cases. Cornell Law Rev 93(1):1–43. https://scholarship.law.cornell.edu/facpub/917
Harley EM (2007) Hindsight bias in legal decision making. Soc Cogn 25(1):48–63. https://doi.org/10.1521/soco.2007.25.1.48
Jones CE (2013) The troubling new science of legal persuasion: heuristics and biases in judicial decision-making. The Advocates' Quarterly 12:41–49
Kahneman D (2011) Thinking, fast and slow. Farrar, Straus and Giroux, New York
Kahneman D, Slovic P, Tversky A (eds) (1982) Judgment under Uncertainty. Cambridge University Press, Cambridge. https://doi.org/10.1017/CBO9780511809477
Kanwal M et al (2017) Familial risk for lung cancer. Oncol Lett 13(2):535–542. https://doi.org/10.3892/ol.2016.5518
Khwaja A et al (2009) Do smokers value their health and longevity less? J Law Econ 52(1):171–196. https://doi.org/10.1086/589655
Klein DE, Mitchell G (eds) (2010) The psychology of judicial decision making. Oxford University Press, Oxford. https://doi.org/10.1093/acprof:oso/9780195367584.001.0001
Leibovitch A (2016) Relative judgments. J Leg Stud 45(2):281–330. https://doi.org/10.1086/687376
Leventhal H et al (1987) Is the smoking decision an 'informed choice'? Effect of smoking risk factors on smoking beliefs. JAMA 257(24):3373–3376. https://pubmed.ncbi.nlm.nih.gov/3586266/
Levinson JD et al (2017) Judging implicit bias: a National Empirical Study of judicial stereotypes beyond black and white. Florida Law Rev 69(1):62–114. https://scholarship.law.ufl.edu/flr/vol69/iss1/2
Mill JS (1971) On liberty (1859). In: Robson JM (ed) Vol. 18 of *collected works*. Routledge & Kegan Paul, London, pp 213–310
Park ER et al (2009) Risk perceptions among participants undergoing lung cancer screening: baseline results from the National Lung Screening Trial. Ann Behav Med 37(3):268–279. https://doi.org/10.1007/s12160-009-9112-9
Samuels R, Stich S, Bishop M (2002) Ending the rationality wars: how to make disputes about human rationality disappear get access arrow. In: Renée E (ed) Common sense, reasoning, and rationality. Oxford University Press. Chap. 11, Oxford, pp 236–268. https://doi.org/10.1093/0195147669.003.0011
Shiloh S et al (2009) Being 'At-risk' for developing cancer: cognitive representations and psychological outcomes. J Behav Med 32(2):197–208. https://doi.org/10.1007/s10865-008-9178-z

Skorinko JL et al (2014) Effects of perspective taking on courtroom decisions. J Appl Soc Psychol 44(4):303–318. https://doi.org/10.1111/jasp.12222

Taggi F (1999) L'uso del casco per la riduzione dell'incidenza e gravità del trauma cranico secondario alla guida di veicoli a due ruote motorizzate. Conference report presenting early results from the PREVIS project (Prevenzione Incidenti Stradali), funded by the Italian Ministry of Public Works

Thaler RH, Sunstein CR (2008) Nudge: improving decisions about health, wealth, and happiness. Yale University Press, New Haven

Trout JD (2005) Paternalism and cognitive bias. Law Philos 24(4):393–434. https://doi.org/10.1007/s10982-004-8197-3

Viale R (ed) (2020) The Routledge handbook of bounded rationality. Routledge, London and New York

Weinstein ND (1982) Unrealistic optimism about susceptibility to health problems. J Behav Med 5:441–460. https://doi.org/10.1007/BF00845372

Weinstein ND (1987) Unrealistic optimism about susceptibility to health problems: conclusions from a community-wide sample. J Behav Med 10:481–500. https://doi.org/10.1007/BF00846146

Weinstein ND (1998) Accuracy of smokers' risk perceptions. Ann Behav Med 20(2):135–140. https://doi.org/10.1007/BF02884459

Weinstein ND et al (2005) Smokers' unrealistic optimism about their risk. Tob Control 14(1):55–59

Wistrich AJ, Rachlinski JJ (2017) Implicit bias in judicial decision making: how it affects judgment and what judges can do about it. In: Redfield SE (ed) Enhancing justice: reducing bias. American Bar Association, Chicago, pp 87–130

Chapter 5
The Dark Side of Antipaternalism

5.1 Four Challenging Cases for Antipaternalists

As discussed in Chap. 3, the value of individual autonomy presents a significant obstacle for paternalists. To question this value is to presume to look an adult and autonomous person in the eye and publicly declare that they do not truly understand their own good and what constitutes their well-being. Others, it is assumed, know better what is good for them. In many contexts, explicitly challenging the value of individual autonomy is neither politically nor socially realistic.

For these reasons, paternalists often refrain from directly opposing the concept of individual autonomy. Instead, they aim to weaken the antipaternalist stance from within, identifying what they pretend to be inconsistencies, fallacies, and false statements inherent in the concept. A favoured strategy is to imagine scenarios of "terrible and repugnant" activities that would be permissible under an antipaternalist framework, such as public gladiator fights ending in death for a handful of dollars, theatrical performances where sadists whip masochists, or voluntary slavery contracts. It is therefore crucial to analyse what would actually be permissible or prohibited under a consistently developed antipaternalist conception. The four cases I will examine are voluntary slavery contracts, the definitive transfer or alienation of fundamental rights, violence towards presumably "consenting" women, and extremely violent or deadly gladiator fights. We will discover that there are sound and coherent antipaternalist arguments for prohibiting each of these activities. For reasons discussed in the second chapter, I will not address the issue of the validity of consent in marriages or contracts with potentially unequal clauses that appear to or actually harm the interests of one of the parties involved (e.g., the employee versus the employer or multinational, the small business owner versus the large corporation, the small retailer versus the large distributor). Two exceptions are made: slavery contracts and gladiator fights, as these are particularly notorious, thorny, and

G. Maniaci, *The Unbearable Lightness of Legal Antipaternalism*, Law and Philosophy Library 151, https://doi.org/10.1007/978-3-031-96844-0_5

sensational cases, extensively discussed by Feinberg, often cited as examples of horrendous activities that would be allowed under an antipaternalist conception.

Before analysing these four cases, a general premise is necessary which addresses most of them and summarises the conclusions reached in the second chapter. There are certainly two fundamental reasons why an agent's purpose in binding their future self, authorising the use of coercion by others, is rational: a compulsion (gambling, drugs) from which one seeks liberation, or a justified fear of future incompetence, irrationality, or coercion that could lead to dangerous or harmful decisions. A third, very dubious case arises when a person, in a free-market system, acquires a benefit through a contract that they could not have otherwise obtained. However, as seen with contracts, if a person does not fulfil their contractual obligation, it would be quite peculiar to assert that their prior will to authorise coercion against themselves in case of nonfulfilment, expressed at the time the contract is entered into, should prevail over their current will not to fulfil and avoid payment of damages. In case of nonfulfilment, the main interest justifying the use of coercion is that of the nondefaulting party or third-party reliance; hence the need to protect a contractual practice as a whole. Outside the two certain scenarios mentioned earlier (compulsive addiction and future irrationality or incompetence), it seems irrational for a person to have an interest in their past self's will prevailing over their current self's will. The only exception is the case of advance directives, when there is, for instance, the event of future incompetence (a permanent vegetative state). Apart from this exception, antipaternalism thus protects the agent's current will, rational and free from coercion, but still current. Contrary to certain libertarian or perfectionist conceptions, the idea that an agent's prior will should always prevail over their current will is not an implication of antipaternalism, even if the prior will was enshrined in a contract or written agreement. Obliging people to always keep their commitments or promises perhaps protects a virtue, such as integrity, or the interests of those who profit from certain contracts. For example, it protects a contracting party from a counterparty's unjustified nonfulfillment or generally, as we have seen, third-party reliance and the very possibility that a certain contractual practice may develop and spread. If, in fact, a given contract were nonbinding, if everyone could freely withdraw from it, harming the expectations of others or of third parties, few would have an economic interest in entering into it. However, compelling people to always keep their commitments, including of a contractual nature, is not an implication of antipaternalism—although it is compatible with it in some cases—nor is it an implication of antipaternalism to always protect the interests of those who profit from certain contracts. Moreover, I do not believe that compelling people to always keep their commitments, including of a contractual nature, is always morally justified.[1] In summary, when a community withholds its protection from certain

[1] Mill held that an individual's sovereignty over their own mind and body does not extend to the freedom to enter into contracts of voluntary slavery (the right to be free not to be free). Some scholars perceive this exception as residual perfectionism in Mill's conception, possibly a form of liberal perfectionism, while others view it as a genuine contradiction (the only one, perhaps, in his theory). Efforts have been made to justify this exception within an antipaternalist framework. For further discussion of this matter, see Archard (1990); Arneson (1980), pp. 470–89; Feinberg

contractual practices, such as voluntary slavery or prostitution, on the grounds that these practices unjustly harm third parties (who are not the contracting parties) or unjustly harm a party who no longer wishes to honour the agreement (such as a slave seeking freedom from the contract, or a prostitute deciding at the last moment against performing the sexual act), this is not paternalism. Rather, we are safeguarding the autonomy, the current rational and uncoerced will, of the slave or prostitute. This current will, which may and should take precedence in cases of significant acts of disposition of one's own body, overrides the former will of the slave (which no longer exists due to the change of mind), as well as the autonomy of the other contracting party, countering the interests of the master or the prostitute's client, and of those who profit from these contractual practices.

(1986), p. 75ff.; Mill (1971), p. 118ff. I will not argue extensively in favour of one interpretation or another of Mill's assertion. However, I believe that Mill would fundamentally agree with my argument: that in cases of contractual nonfulfilment, the primary interest justifying the use of coercion is that of the third party, the nondefaulting contracting party, or third-party reliance, i.e., the need to protect a contractual practice in its entirety. In other words, outside the two certain scenarios mentioned earlier, compulsive addiction and future irrationality or incompetence, it seems irrational for a person to have an interest in their past self's will prevailing over their current self's will. This interpretation is informed by Mill's discussion of the problem of slavery contracts in the context of the value of commitments mutually made by individuals and the value of promises. Mill states that "it is fit, as a general rule, that those [mutual] engagements should be kept. Yet [...] this general rule has some exceptions. Not only persons are not held to engagements which violate the rights of third parties, but it is sometimes considered a sufficient reason for releasing them from an engagement, that it is injurious to themselves. The principle, however, which demands uncontrolled freedom of action in all that concerns only the agents themselves, requires that those who have become bound to one another, in things which concern no third party, should be able to release one another from the engagement: and even without such voluntary release, there are perhaps no contracts or engagements, except those that relate to money or money's worth, of which one can venture to say that there ought to be no liberty whatever of retractation." Mill argues that the given word, *enshrined* in an agreement, has no value in itself, but only if failure to fulfil a previously made commitment harms the other party, proof of which is that each can release the other from their commitment. Why does Mill assert that, as a general rule, one does not have the freedom to rescind agreements concerning money or the value of money? Because in these cases, the harm from nonfulfillment is evident and particularly significant, i.e., the harm is economic. In the absence of economic or other types of harm—as in the case of marriage, according to Mill—failing to keep a promise is not significant in itself. Nor does failing to keep one's word harm the autonomy of the person who does not fulfil their promise. Mill demonstrates that he does not formulate any exception to the harm principle or the principles of antipaternalism. What Mill states is merely an application of the principle of harm to others. If disregarding a contractual commitment harms the interests of third parties, then the state may intervene, for example, by offering the injured party the possibility of compensation or damages. Likewise, if fulfilling the contractual promise causes excessive harm to one of the two contracting parties, because contractual fulfilment has become too burdensome for or detrimental to one of the contracting parties (and is not wanted by the latter) or to third parties, then the state may intervene, making the contract no longer binding or unenforceable. As Mill states, "But by selling himself for a slave, he abdicates his liberty; he foregoes any future use of it, beyond that single act. He therefore defeats, in his own case, the very purpose which is the justification of allowing him to dispose of himself. [...] The principle of freedom cannot require that he should be free not to be free" (118). Put another way, as I will argue in the text, and as Feinberg says, if a slave has a change of mind and wants to withdraw from the contract, he or she must have the right to do so, because it is the last will that counts in cases of serious and irreversible acts of disposition of their body. See Feinberg (1986), p. 73.

5.2 Slavery Contracts

(a) Imagine Humbert, who lives in a shack with his three children, without water, sewage, or heating, and relying only on a small stove for warmth in the winter. Humbert, a widower without higher-education qualifications, faces serious health issues that prevent him from sustaining regular employment and survives by performing sporadic manual labour, such as construction work. At a certain point, he decides to enter into a contract of voluntary slavery in exchange for a substantial sum of money, enabling him to purchase a decent home, secure an income for his children, and take out a life insurance policy with his children as beneficiaries. Should the state prevent Humbert from entering into a slavery contract? According to some antipaternalists, if Humbert's consent is rational, informed, stable, and free from external threats, then he should be allowed to do so. From a paternalistic viewpoint, however, we might prevent Humbert from signing such a contract, as it would be contrary to his supposed "interests," encompassing his freedom, sexuality, health, and life, all of which his *master* would have the right to control as he pleases.

The response from a liberal-egalitarian antipaternalist doctrine, as explored in Chap. 3, Sect. 3.4, which protects liberty and social rights, differs. The point is that Humbert, *rebus sic stantibus* (things being as they stand), has only two choices: continue a life of extreme misery or "sell himself into slavery." If we allow Humbert to enter a voluntary slavery contract, are we protecting his will, or are we also endorsing a market system that, through contracts, allows some individuals in severe economic hardship to relinquish their freedom for monetary compensation, while enabling others to make significant profit from this situation? Are we safeguarding Humbert's will, or are we also protecting a free-market system that allocates goods and services based on supply and demand, where Humbert's skills and competencies are not deemed economically rewarding, a system where Humbert's capabilities are insufficient for him to acquire essential goods and services, a free-market system that allows for the signing of slavery contracts and protects those who profit from them? Both, evidently. We are safeguarding Humbert's tragic choice, but also the free-market system that, except through a slavery contract, does not "allow" Humbert to obtain essential goods and services through the work he knows or can perform.

The intervention that a liberal-egalitarian antipaternalistic doctrine would deem justifiable in this case involves, on the one hand, temporarily preventing Humbert from entering into a slavery contract and, on the other hand, ensuring the effective protection of his fundamental liberty and social rights. These rights include access to housing with essential services such as running water and electricity, entitlement to benefits in cases of involuntary unemployment or disability, the right to certain free healthcare services, and the right to dignified work. This state intervention does not necessarily have a paternalistic justification; it is not so much about protecting Humbert's well-being against his will to become someone else's slave, but rather about preventing others from acquiring economic benefits in ways considered morally unacceptable or unjust, thereby causing harm to Humbert.[2]

Once Humbert's fundamental rights are secured, would he still choose to "sell himself into slavery"? The answer is clearly no, at least not to satisfy his previous intention (to obtain a decent home and a guaranteed minimum income for his family). In this case, can we say that we have fulfilled some of Humbert's fundamental desires? Or have we limited his autonomy by preventing him from realising his fundamental desires? I would argue that we have protected his autonomy by providing him with goods that are likely necessary (though not necessarily sufficient) to pursue his plan of life, whatever it may be. The reason we have fulfilled some of Humbert's fundamental desires is that we have not restricted his freedom by telling him, "You cannot enter into a slavery contract because it is against your interests." Instead, we have expanded the range of real options available to Humbert. Once Humbert has three options, namely, (1) entering into a voluntary slavery contract in exchange for a substantial sum of money; (2) obtaining a house from public housing, receiving a subsidy in case of involuntary unemployment, and not entering into a slavery contract; or (3) continuing to live a life of extreme hardship and not entering into a slavery contract, he would presumably choose the second option.

The state's intervention in this scenario is not, ultimately, paternalistic because, rather than prohibiting Humbert from undertaking an action—entering into a slavery contract—it expands the range of available alternatives based on a liberal-egalitarian ethical and political conception. According to Mill's harm principle, the organised community can always use coercion or force to protect itself, that is, to prevent a single member or the majority of the community, through a free-market system, from causing economic or psychophysical harm to another person against their will. In this case, the organized community has prevented the free-market system from causing harm (economic or psychophysical) to a community member, Humbert, by expanding the sphere of his fundamental opportunities. This harm could stem from entering into a slavery contract or continuing to live a life of extreme hardship, which Humbert himself considers harmful. Thus, the state's intervention is not paternalistic, especially since the state does not compel Humbert to choose a particular plan of life, as it is Humbert—and not the state—that has decided that he should live in a more dignified house, rather than enter into a slavery contract. Indeed, Humbert has a right to a dignified house, not an obligation to live in one. If he does not want to, he can always renounce it.

One might argue that the state's intervention remains paternalistic because Humbert, rather than signing a slavery contract and exercising the right to a house and to unemployment subsidies, might ultimately prefer a cash equivalent to squander on prostitutes and gambling. If Humbert had no children to feed and raise, in which case prohibition might be envisaged to prevent harm to third parties, i.e., the children, one might even consider a "dual track" public welfare system. On one hand, the state could allow an individual to alienate a social right, such as the right

[2] In a similar vein, see Feinberg (1986), p. 80; Arneson (1980), p. 472.

to housing, health, or pension, to third parties or to the state itself. On the other, the state would ensure the enjoyment of a set of minimum rights, for survival—for example, the right to sleep in a public dormitory, to emergency medical care, to a hot meal at a charity association—granted for reasons of human solidarity, to those who have alienated their social rights, such as the right to housing, health, or pension (presumably to the state) and squandered the cash equivalent of some of those rights. While other people who have not alienated such rights, in exchange for "consideration," would be entitled to much more substantial protection of health, education, and housing rights.

Would a state that denies people with social rights the possibility of transferring their ownership through consideration to third parties or demanding the monetary equivalent from the state be paternalistic? I do not believe so at all. If the purpose of protecting social rights is to restore some minimum conditions of equality among people, or to establish conditions of equal or greater opportunities, in terms of primary goods necessary for the pursuit of any plan of life, if the purpose of protecting such rights is to modify the distribution of goods and services by the market jungle and natural lottery, why should we compensate those who refuse this fair compensation? If someone prefers to turn down the opportunity, offered by the community, to acquire goods and services, such as housing, less expensive healthcare services, and unemployment subsidies, that they would have much difficulty obtaining in the free market, why should we offer them consideration for the right they renounce?

Certainly, the state's intervention in this context would *not* constitute coercive paternalism. If an individual prefers to endure the psychological or physical suffering arising from living without any "help" in the market jungle, freely participating in its resource-distribution mechanisms and rejecting the opportunity to obtain certain goods from the state, there is no one to stop them from doing so. However, one might contend that this amounts to noncoercive paternalism, albeit paternalism, because the state is protecting the individual's good (greater opportunities or more equal access to certain resources) potentially against their will. The very justification for the distribution of resources or benefits could be paternalistic. The state does not use coercion to impose a certain behaviour on an individual but increases or decreases the range of options available to them based on what the state considers primarily to realize the individual's well-being (acquiring primary goods and services, such as housing, health, and education), even though the individual's will might be contrary to the value judgments underlying the state's distribution. Indeed, the state might deem superfluous some pursuits (such as gambling or having sexual relations with expensive escorts) that the individual might consider essential to their well-being. In this work, I am primarily concerned with the legitimisation of *coercive* paternalism.

In any case, it is easy to argue that denying holders of social rights the right to demand monetary equivalents of these rights could have an antipaternalist justification. As always, it suffices to identify harm to third parties. If resources that could be allocated to protecting the mental and physical health of suffering individuals—building public housing complexes, improving conditions in prisons or hospitals, increasing minimum social pensions, or raising involuntary unemployment allowances—are instead used by individuals originally entitled to certain social rights (the right to housing, health, or pension) for other purposes, i.e., to protect other rights (the right to have sexual relations with a luxury escort, the right to gamble a significant sum of money at a casino, the right to attend a peep show every week), we are harming the interests of third parties (less affluent people, jobless people, prisoners, pensioners), offering weaker protections to individuals in need, causing economic and psychophysical harm to other individuals. When resources are scarce, this is inevitable. In conclusion, there is an economic budget behind a social right, which budget depends on resources not of the individual but of the collectivity. If the individual could alienate certain social rights to people who are not entitled to them, it would mean that he or she could freely make use of the economic budget behind the social right, that is, could freely make use of resources that are not his or her own, causing harm to the community.

To summarise, if Humbert wishes to enter into a slavery contract because, in a free-market system, it is the only way to ensure a dignified life for his family through a decent sum of money, this should be temporarily prevented to protect the fundamental rights he holds or should hold. Some might argue that I have merely shifted the problem. It's true that if the state protected Humbert's fundamental rights and the right to housing and to an unemployment subsidy, Humbert would likely not want to enter into a slavery contract. But what if the state is too poor to protect people's fundamental rights? If the state, in an economically and technologically underdeveloped context, lacks sufficient resources to protect such fundamental rights? I am not sure that this is a realistic scenario, because in situations of great poverty, even identifying fundamental needs and rights can be contextualised, considering only minimum survival needs (adequate food, shelter, etc.).

5.2.1 Voluntary Slavery Contracts as Off-Market Contracts

However, imagine that the state cannot protect Humbert's fundamental rights. Should we allow him to enter into a slavery contract? Would it be realistic for an entrepreneur to offer a slavery contract to Humbert? I do not believe so, as we will see later, because such contracts would be either off-market or contrary to the interests of many workers. As Feinberg says, they are more a theoretical than a realistic case.

If a business owner needs labour and wants to cut down as much as possible on costs, they might consider drafting a contract where Humbert works as a slave for 14 h a day without breaks, instead of the 7 h, let's assume, stipulated by national collective bargaining agreements. However, in this scenario, the entrepreneur would not want to pay Humbert a substantial sum of money; it would not make sense for the entrepreneur to pay Humbert more than the cost of two workers each working a seven-hour shift. Moreover, a slavery contract incurs additional costs, such as board or lodging. The business owner would want to pay Humbert less than what two workers on two seven-hour shifts would cost, otherwise the contract under which

Humbert works as a slave for 14 h without a break would not be worthwhile. And yet, since Humbert is compelled by poverty to accept a 14-h workday, and since such an exhaustive shift is detrimental to Humbert, the state can intervene, at no extra cost, by requiring the entrepreneur to employ Humbert for a work shift not exceeding 7 h, thus forcing the business owner to reduce profits. At this point, if the entrepreneur genuinely needs the labour, they would be forced to employ Humbert for a seven-hour shift.

One might counter-argue: If two workers on two seven-hour shifts cost the business owner 50,000 euros a year—a stipulated amount based on national collective bargaining agreements, including taxes and social security contributions—couldn't Humbert and the business owner draft a contract for a fourteen-hour slavery shift, where Humbert earns 30,000 euros a year, more than he would if employed for a seven-hour shift? Both would benefit, with Humbert earning 30,000 euros a year instead of 25,000, and the entrepreneur incurring a cost of 30,000 euros instead of 50,000. Generally speaking, it can be argued that certain or many workers' rights, such as paid holidays, daily rest, minimum hourly wages, and safe working environments, are rights that protect the autonomous preferences of workers, i.e., the autonomous preference for no negotiating these terms with employers. If negotiation on these rights were possible, if there were no maximum set hours for work shifts and overtime, there could easily be a race to the bottom in the labour-supply market, where some, driven by extreme poverty and/or by slightly greater economic resources, might accept increasingly worse working conditions because of unjust threats to not hire workers or threats of layoffs, offshoring, or reduced production, such as 14-h shifts, contracts without paid holidays, or unsafe work environments, against the autonomous wishes of the great majority of workers who does not want to work under these conditions and who can withstand 2 or 3 months of strike. In a short time, the market might only offer contracts with exhausting shifts, without paid holidays, or with unsafe work environments, harming the autonomy of those desiring not to work under these conditions. On the labour-demand side, employers could exert unjust coercive pressures (threats to not hire workers or threats of layoffs, offshoring, or reduced production), which vitiate the consent, to induce workers to accept contracts with fewer protections and rights, such as 14-h shifts.

Imagine another scenario involving Lolita, a 40-year-old secretary in a law firm. She is a woman of average intelligence and attractiveness, living in a small but comfortable rented home. Her life, filled with numerous failed love affairs and the impossibility of having children, is viewed by Lolita as sad and lonely. Imagine a billionaire proposes a slavery contract to Lolita, with clauses prohibiting murder, serious injury, torture, or suicide, but requiring certain sexual, domestic, and social services in exchange for ten million euros. Lolita could spend this sum as she wishes in the year before the slavery contract begins. For instance, Lolita might have to pretend to be the proposer's wife on certain occasions. If Lolita's fundamental rights—free movement, health, education, housing, and unemployment benefits—were (or had been) protected before signing the contract, but Lolita despised her life and preferred to live a year of wealth and pleasure before becoming the billionaire's slave, why should we prevent her from doing so?

The difference from Humbert's case is that protecting Lolita's spendthrift preferences, such as shopping and travelling to Australia and the Caribbean, does not necessarily fall under the protection of her fundamental rights under a liberal-egalitarian conception. In this hypothesis, wouldn't allowing Lolita to enter into a slavery contract amount to protecting her rational will, informed by relevant facts and stable over time, to freely dispose of her own body, as well as the interests of the contract beneficiary, which interests in this case might not be considered inequitable or morally unacceptable?[3]

---

[3] I should offer only a few comments about the problem of selling one's own body parts. It is not problematic to sell blood or male and female gametes. Consider a free market in which someone sells an organ on the basis of a contract as envisaged by Becker and Elias (2014). The reason for prohibiting such contracts is that they undermine the principle of substantive equality, considering that such organs would come with a hefty price tag (in the range of 50,000 US dollars), which means that only wealthy people would be able to take advantage of an increased supply of organs. The idea, then, is to increase the supply of organs in order to avoid deaths (4500 in 2012 in the United States; 7000 in Europe in 2020) and to shorten waiting lists: "In 2012," Becker and Elias report, "95,000 American men, women and children were on the waiting list for new kidneys, the most commonly transplanted organ." And the solution to that supply problem should instead be as follows: where a national health service or a healthcare agency exists, it will buy organs from ordinary living people (say, 15,000 euros per organ)—to this end using public funds, the most probable source being the European Social Fund (for example, 7,500,000 euros for Spain)—and distributing the new organ supply, removed from living donors, among rich and poor people who are waiting for an organ donation (a kidney, lung, or half liver), on the basis of criteria of necessity and urgency. Clearly, before organ donors can give their consent, it will be necessary to make sure that they meet the criteria of autonomy, meaning that in an interview with a doctor it needs to be determined that donors making this choice are rational, capable of understanding the choice they are making, informed of the relevant facts, and sufficiently free from coercive pressures, and it also needs to be ascertained that the decision itself is stable over time. In particular, as concerns the need to ensure an informed and knowledgeable decision, organ donors need to be made aware of the possible side effects of removing an organ such as a kidney. Individuals below the poverty line—5,7 million people in Italy—may be prohibited from selling their organs, since their vulnerable position would put them at risk of being seriously exploited, in a scenario where they may become the organ reservoir for the entire country, and their life expectancy may shrink. A condition of poverty may be temporary; the removal of a kidney is permanent.

Every autonomous person has a right to commodify himself or herself on the basis of the principle of individual autonomy. Against the right to commodify oneself, one can make the classic perfectionist and utilitarian-organicist arguments, which meet the objections we looked at in Chap. 3, since according to these objections classic perfectionist and utilitarian-organicist arguments are based on false empirical premises or inconsistencies.

Another solution, not incompatible with the previous one, is to adopt an opt-out system for consent when it comes to organs from a deceased person. On this implicit consent model, consent is the default option, meaning that individuals are deemed to be organ donors unless they choose otherwise on the form they receive from the Ministry of Health. See Maniaci (2020). For the commodification argument, see Maniaci (2022).

Cannibalization is normally a practice that serial killers and psychopaths engage in, but there are exceptions. In 2001 in Germany, Armin Meiwes video-recorded himself mutilating, drugging, bleeding, killing and cannibalizing Mr. Brandes with the latter's consent (He said: "I always wanted it"). On the antipaternalistic model I am putting forward, this act of homicide would be considered legal so long as both parties consent and their consent is rational, sufficiently free from coercive pressures, and based on a knowledge of the relevant facts and is stable over time, and so long as the assessment is carried out by a psychologist at a public or private hospital relying on a formal conception of rationality, with all the guarantees provided for euthanasia and assisted suicide, such as a cooling-off period or a video recording (see the section on the slippery slope argument and the value of individual autonomy in Chap. 3). This behaviour of consensual mutilation, homicide and cannibalisation adopted by Brandes and Meiwes can be considered an extreme case of sadomasochism? Meiwes would be sadist and Brades masochistic. I don't know, it is possible. In any case, the DSM-5 (Sexual Masochism Disorder DSM-5302.83(F65.51), similarly to the DSM-IV, explains that sexual masochism disorder is diagnosed in individuals who experience sexual arousal in response to extreme pain, humiliation, bondage, or torture. The masochist will have unrelenting fantasies with urges to be beaten, bound or humiliated during sex. (…) diagnostic criteria requires that the patient experience (1) emotional distress, such as shame, guilt or anxiety related to sexual fantasy, urges or sexual experiences or (2) social, or working, or economic impairment. Milder forms of masochism between consenting adults, sometimes also referred to as "BDSM," or "Bondage, Discipline, Dominance, Submission," are not classified as disorders by the DSM-5. Diagnosis occurs when certain criteria are met. Let see the Diagnostic Criteria for Sexual Masochism Disorder:

- Recurrent intense fantasies, urges, or behaviors involving real acts of receiving extreme physical pain, torture, or humiliation for sexual arousal.
- Present for at least 6 months
- Results in significant (1) impairment in daily life (relationships, occupational or social functioning) to social, working, relational, economic life or (2) emotional distress related to sexual fantasy, urges or sexual experiences. In the case of Brandes and Meiwes there is not emotional distress, and nor exactly social, economic, impairment. Brandes simply dies. If the case of Brandes were an example of impairment then all cases of euthanasia and assisted suicide would be one. The concept of impairment, applied to sadomasochism, is probably ideological, based on the wrong substantive conception of rationality, and should be removed from DMS-V, like all so-called sexual perversions or paraphilias (fetishism, voyeurism, frotteurism, exhibitionism). This is the argument and the thesis of Khan (2015). He says that "quantitative and qualitative empirical studies of SM practitioners indicate that they fall within normal ranges in psychological and social functioning. (…) [After the author] examines research on one negative consequence of the inclusion of SM in the DSM: It may interfere with the therapeutic relationship with clients who practice SM or have SM desires by reinforcing broader societal stigma and encouraging diagnostic misuse. (…) [He] reviews an emerging body of research that reverses the "SM as pathology" discourse by showing the therapeutic and healing potential of bondage-discipline-dominance-submission-sadism-masochism (BDSM) practice and ethos. Based on this review, the conclusion argues that there is no valid reason to continue identifying SM as a potential mental disorder, and furthermore, there are detrimental effects of its association with pathology in the DSM-5."

As for incest between parents and their children, this ought to be considered illegal because there is a strong presumption of violence or irrationality and of psychic inferiority of the sexually abused child. As for incest between siblings—an example being the case of Patrick and Susan in Germany outlined below—the practice can be considered legal so long as the same safeguards and requirements are maintained as for cannibalism (there needs to be mutual consent and it needs to be rational, based on a knowledge of relevant facts, and sufficiently free from coercive pressures, and the consent needs to be stable over time). Patrick and Susan were raised in separate families throughout their childhood and into their teens; they began an incestuous relationship in 2001, when he was 23 and she was 16, and because of the incest Patrick was sentenced twice to prison. Over time they had four children, two of whom were disabled. The argument that the incestuous relationship should be prohibited because children who are born of incest have a greater likelihood

As we saw at the beginning of this chapter, there are sound antipaternalist reasons to prevent slavery contracts, even under Lolita's conditions, from being considered binding or enforceable. Good reasons exist because, in case of nonfulfilment, the defaulting slave should not be condemned either to the specific performance of the service (as a slave) or to payment of damages. In other words, if Lolita's current will were to withdraw from the previously signed slavery contract and the state forced her to abide by this contract, we would be protecting not her autonomy but the interests of her "master," or those who profit from the proliferation of such contractual practices (slavery contracts).[4] And not necessarily would such third-party interests be deemed worthy of protection under the harm principle.

But let us leave these reasons aside and imagine that, once formed, slavery contracts are enforceable,[5] like many others, and that Lolita's choice is indeed irreversible. Are there other antipaternalistic reasons to prevent Lolita from entering into such a contract? Gerald Dworkin suggests that it would be truly sad if we lived in a world where we, as "good" citizens, were forced to return an escaped slave to our neighbour or where slave hunters proliferated, going after for those who, after squandering the received sum, escape a cruel fate of slavery. In reality, I do not believe this is the case. A person who, in exchange for a large sum of money to squander, agrees to become the slave of a sadistic billionaire probably despises their life and has no concrete hope of changing it. In this sense, if someone had to choose between committing suicide to end a life they hate and becoming the slave of a sadistic billionaire after squandering some of their money, we should not complain if they chose the latter option.

The scenario we have considered so far is to allow slavery contracts to be formed under the above conditions, those of Lolita, i.e., upon payment of large sums of money. In this context, I genuinely believe that legalising slavery contracts would not lead to their widespread adoption, simply because they would be pushed "out of the market." Wealthy and powerful individuals, who have huge sums of money at their disposal, can and do obtain similar *services*—domestic, sexual, and even

of being disabled does not work and is inconsistent. On the basis of this argument, we should ban sexual relations between two young persons affected by Down syndrome or two parents who have a genetic sexually transmitted disease. As for zoophilia or bestiality, i.e., sexual relations between humans and nonhuman animals, the practice can be legalized if ways are found to ascertain the psychophysical wellbeing of the nonhuman animal. As Evan Rachel Wood says in Woody Allen's 2009 movie *Whatever Works*, "they think that according to them love is the answer for every case. But I told them of Jethro Page down in my country. He got caught doing it with a sheep. He was making love to a sheep. And everybody laughing, you imagine that. [...] Beautiful, as Boris would say, 'Whatever works.'"

[4] As we saw in Chap. 2, the point is perfectly captured by Archard (1990), p. 462: "Were society to enforce the contract and coerce the slave into continued obedience, it would clearly be limiting the freedom of that person. When society refuses to recognize the contract it respects the currently expressed wishes of the discontented slave. It permits people to act as they choose, namely as free individuals. I fail to see how prohibition of slavery is correctly described as paternalism."

[5] For insights on the tragic consequences resulting from the irrevocability of slavery contracts, see Feinberg (1986), p. 81.

"masochistic"—from multiple workers or employees, rather than from a single "slave," probably at a lower price and without any contractual obligations for sustenance, food, or accommodation. As Marlon Brando's character in Gillo Pontecorvo's film *Queimada* says, why would an entrepreneur want to *have* a slave or a spouse when they can secure the same services from hundreds of workers or paid "lovers," who can be freely dismissed and to whom they owe nothing beyond payment for the service rendered? Similarly, a slavery contract under Lolita's terms would not be appealing to groups of entrepreneurs who might be interested in employing workers at no cost.

However, if slavery contracts turned out to be profitable from a market perspective, under conditions much less favourable to the future slave than to Lolita—hypothetically, ten million euros—it would undoubtedly indicate that entrepreneurs anticipate deriving a significant profit margin from such contractual practices and that the consent of the "future slaves" is marred by coercion. Given the ongoing phenomenon of globalization, the unceasing migration of the poor and the desperate from all over the world to wealthier countries, and the phenomenon of enslavement, increasingly documented by sociologists and criminologists, there is a real, high, and empirically founded risk that unscrupulous multinational corporations and criminal associations could enslave groups of migrants against their will under the legal guise of slavery contracts.[6]

Therefore, it would not be sufficient to ensure that the fundamental rights of individuals like Lolita—the right to health, education, housing, and pension—be protected in order for such contracts to be freely entered into. It is crucial to prevent wealthy and powerful multinationals from corrupting officials to "enslave" individuals with psychological issues and/or serious economic problems. This type of corruption appears to be widespread in Italy, as indicated by numerous reports from the Italian Court of Auditors and other sources. In this regard, it should be prohibited for wealthy and powerful multinationals to bear the costs of procedures aimed at verifying the requirements of consent (rationality, sufficient freedom from coercive pressures, etc.) of potential "voluntary slaves," as this could jeopardise the impartiality and integrity of public officials tasked with such assessments. Furthermore, the work of these public officials should be very well remunerated.

Finally, one might question the sensibility of entering into gratuitous slavery contracts, that is, without any economic or other benefits resulting from the contract. In such cases, there would be substantial doubts about rationality. As we saw in Chap. 2, it is not rational for an agent to decide to bind their future self, authorising the use of coercion by others, in the absence of a compulsive addiction (such as gambling or drugs) from which to free oneself, a well-founded fear of future incompetence, irrationality, or coercion that might lead to harmful or dangerous decisions, or the prospect of obtaining some current or future benefit. Why would anyone enter into a gratuitous slavery contract? A permanent bond of slavery implies that the

[6] See issue 35 of (2010) of the journal *Ragion Pratica*, edited by Mauro Barberis and Costanza Margiotta and devoted to the topic of slavery.

agent can no longer satisfy their own preferences but must only satisfy the preferences of the "master," obeying their commands. Why should an individual frustrate their current and future preferences without fulfilling some other current preferences, such as a preference for expensive cars? Furthermore, even if an agent desired to live "as a slave" to someone, that is, to obey another person's wishes every day, why, assuming this is rational, would they need a binding contract? Could they not in fact choose to do so without legal constraints? If their future preferences changed rationally, why should they remain bound by the decisions of their previous self?

5.3 Conclusion on Slavery Contracts

As we have observed, allowing the voluntary formation of slavery contracts is compatible with antipaternalism, once it is ascertained that the requisites of consent, rationality, and knowledge of relevant facts are satisfied, and provided that the efficiency and impartiality of the public bodies tasked with these assessments and granting the necessary authorisations are protected. However, this is not the only solution congruent with antipaternalism, nor is it the best. To understand why, a fundamental distinction needs to be made between "purely theoretical"[7] "statistically nonexistent" cases, such as consensual incest between adult parents and children, voluntary slavery contracts, fights to the death between gladiators, and other statistically more prevalent cases, such as euthanasia, drug use, riding a motorcycle without a helmet, or sadomasochistic sex. Purely theoretical cases involve activities that very few adults, rational and free from coercion, would desire to engage in. There are *three* fundamental differences.

(1) First, a first difference is statistical. Once rationality, knowledge of the relevant facts, and freedom from coercion are ensured, including the protection of fundamental rights, it is highly likely that, at least in the Western world, a more or less significant minority of people would still want to consume narcotics, request euthanasia, engage in sadomasochistic sex, or participate in extreme sports. These would be examples of statistically more widespread activities. In contrast, serious and scientifically sound statistical investigations would likely determine that only 0.0001% of adult, rational, and uncoerced individuals would desire to participate in a gladiator fight to the death or enter into a slavery contract, even under the advantageous conditions offered to Lolita.[8] This

[7]As Feinberg (1986, p. 81) points out, "slavery contracts are theoretically interesting constructs with which to test theories, but otherwise are of very little practical interest."

[8]Doubts may arise concerning the actual effectiveness or credibility of statistical surveys on individuals' desires to enter into slavery contracts. Conducting such a survey would not be as straightforward as gathering data on known facts, such as birth, marriage, or divorce rates, but it would not be exceedingly complex either. It would involve presenting respondents with a simple questionnaire containing a few variables. For instance, given a certain definition of slavery, would you wish to enter into a slavery contract for ten million, 1 billion, or ten billion or more euros? Moreover,

implies a serious presumption of nonvoluntariness in engaging in such conduct (see Feinberg 1986, p. 79).

(2) Second, the cost of procedures aimed at verifying the fulfilment of consent requirements would be significantly lower in cases of euthanasia or extreme sports, whereas it would be much higher in the case of voluntary slavery contracts (see Feinberg 1986, p. 79). In the case of euthanasia, for instance, the same hospital doctors and psychiatrists where patients are admitted and request euthanasia would be "used." Consultations would be brief. In the case of extreme sports, the verification of consent would be carried out by the same agencies or associations that issue the relevant certificates or licenses, as already happens today with licenses for driving a car or practicing certain types of sea diving. Authorization for the use of narcotics could be issued by the same private and public facilities that deal with detoxification and treatment of drug addicts or by private or public doctors.

The procedure through which to verify consent requirements in cases of slavery contracts or gladiator fights to the death would be considerably more expensive for three reasons. First, a dedicated public office would likely have to be set up. Second, given the strong presumption of nonvoluntariness in entering into such contracts, investigations would need to be far more thorough. And third, it would be essential to ensure that corrupt officials, influenced by powerful multinationals, do not authorise the signing of a slavery contract or the holding of a fight to the death despite not meeting the valid consent criteria. As we have observed, private entities could have significant economic interests in having numerous workers enter (voluntarily or otherwise) into certain slavery contracts, especially under conditions far less favourable than those offered to Lolita. These private economic interests are typically absent in cases such as sadomasochistic sex, euthanasia, riding a motorcycle without a helmet, or drug use (if these drugs are sold by the state and not by private entities). In other words, as Mill (1971, p. 113ff.) understood, whenever an individual's disposition of their body implies profit, gain, or economic exploitation by third parties, the situation changes dramatically. The economic interest of third parties profiting from harmful or dangerous activities undertaken by agents might lead them to exert considerable coercive pressures on these agents, potentially "tainting" their will. More importantly, the protection of profit or economic exploitation by

---

surveys and polls on motivations and intentions are quite common and, despite some historically significant errors, generally have high pragmatic success and predictive capacity. Consider the opinion polls on voting intentions in politics conducted in the run-up to elections. Surveys based on hypothetical scenarios are deemed equally reliable, provided there are few variables to consider (e.g., "Would you vote for the Italian Democratic Party in Italy if it allied with *Sinistra e Libertà* [The Left and Freedom?]"). In essence, while there might be challenges in conducting these surveys, their utility and necessity in informing policy decisions, especially on matters as significant as slavery contracts, cannot be understated. In any case, objections to the effectiveness of such surveys are practically irrelevant. There are no viable alternatives. Would the alternative be to allow a group of philosophers to decide whether the majority of the population wants to enter into slavery contracts? Or should we resort to drawing lots?

third parties is not the primary objective of an antipaternalistic doctrine, which aims to protect individual autonomy and the rational, free will of those who wish to engage in activities dangerous or harmful to themselves.

(3) Another significant difference is that in some "purely theoretical" cases, the state can intervene, protecting certain social rights, to remove some of the causes leading many people to make certain decisions, causes such as poverty in the case of voluntary slavery contracts, whereas in other cases, such as drug use or euthanasia, there is nothing that the state can do to remove one of the fundamental causes leading some people to make such decisions, namely, their unhappiness. The state cannot guarantee the right to happiness, ensure that marriages do not fail, that friends do not fall into the traps of alcohol or religious fundamentalism, that parents do not make serious mistakes, or that love relationships do not end. We cannot shield people from all the consequences of such unhappiness or from the outcomes of their economic, social, or emotional failures. Similarly, we can and should guarantee a terminal patient's right to effective palliative care and physical assistance, but in many cases we cannot "avoid" the onset of the disease and its consequences. We cannot prevent the patient from suffering due to the fear of more suffering, from not wanting to be totally dependent on others (economically, physically, or psychologically), from transitioning between brief, painful states of wakefulness and long states of unconsciousness due to strong painkillers. We cannot prevent a terminally ill patient, despite medical care and the loving assistance of friends and family, from not accepting their loss of autonomy, such as the inability to make love, engage in sports, or work.

Excluding economic motivations, one might wonder who would wish to submit to the will of another person and suppress their own desires to fulfil only those of someone else. Beyond sadomasochistic practices, the fundamental motivation appears to be a spiritual journey of self-discipline and self-annihilation or the expiation of a serious sin.[9] However, anyone can embark on this spiritual path without any contract, submitting to the will of another as and when they wish, without legal bindings. They can achieve their goals without entering into a contract. There is no reason why a subsequent will, not to annul oneself or not to atone for a particular sin, should succumb to a previous one.

[9] See Feinberg (1986), p. 73. In cases where an individual displays a weakness of will when embarking on a spiritual journey within a convent, sect, or religious group, and in the absence of significant economic interests or exploitation of labour by the group itself, a more rigorous, stringent procedure could be envisaged to ascertain the individual's willingness to leave a particular convent or sect.

5.3.1 *Two Argumentative Strategies Against Voluntary Slavery Contracts*

In conclusion, it is overall preferable, a stance shared by Joel Feinberg, to establish a legal prohibition of "voluntary slavery" contracts, using two argumentative strategies. The first strategy allows for the slave to withdraw from the contract at will (*ad libitum*), while the second strategy involves criminal penalties for the slaveholder. The first strategy, which we are already familiar with, aims to protect the party who no longer wishes to honour the agreement (such as a slave seeking to break free), safeguarding their autonomy, their rational will, free of coercive pressures—their current will to renege on the contract without being liable for damages or other penalties. In cases of significant acts of disposition of one's own body, this will should, and must, prevail over the previous will of the slave (which no longer exists, having changed their mind), over the autonomy of the other contracting party, and against the interests of the master or of those profiting from these contractual practices. Such a power to withdraw at will, without any liability for damages or penalties upon withdrawal, would render these slavery contracts nonbinding and not legally valid as slavery contracts.

The second strategy is based on the presumption of nonvoluntariness in voluntary slavery contracts, a presumption grounded not in "a priori" concepts or metaphysical or ideological considerations, but on serious, scientifically conducted empirical investigations. It is presumed that any person, or 99.999% of them, in the Western world—once we have ascertained their rational consent, knowledge of the relevant facts, stability of consent over time, and sufficient freedom from coercive pressures—would not wish to enter into slavery contracts, even under the favourable conditions offered to Lolita. Hence, there are substantial "antipaternalistic" reasons to prohibit voluntarily entering into such contracts (Feinberg 1986, p. 79ff.). Firstly, the bureaucratic procedure by which to verify the aspiring slave's consent would be costly to the community, amounting to economic harm to the community itself, and so to a real harm to third parties on an antipaternalistic conception. It is not worth it just to protect a few eccentrics who want to become someone else's slave, especially since they can *in fact* do so without a contract. Secondly, there is a need to avert the medium-to-high—a real risk, empirically grounded on statistical-probabilistic bases—that masses of marginalised, exploited migrants, or individuals with severe mental disorders, may be "legally" enslaved against their will, which would represent a blatant harm to third parties. Thirdly, we must prevent the proliferation in the market of labour contracts with gruelling, slave-like shifts, which workers would be forced to accept under penalty of poverty and unjust threats of dismissal, offshoring, or reduction of production, undercutting the autonomy of many workers who wish to enjoy a daily rest, paid holidays, and other rights. The prohibition of slavery contracts, under which the slaveholder is penalized, is justified by the reasonable presumption that the slaveholder has coerced the slave into signing the contract or taken advantage of a mental disorder.

5.4 Transfer or Alienation of Fundamental Rights

To reiterate the point, the transfer of fundamental rights,[10] with or without payment or consideration, should be prohibited for antipaternalist reasons. Using the classic tripartite division of rights—rights to liberty, political rights, and social rights[11]—

[10] The literature on the subject of fundamental rights is vast. On the definition of fundamental rights, see Ferrajoli (2001), p. 5ff.; Alexy (2001), esp. p. 173ff.; Pino (2010), p. 12ff. It is very important to distinguish between the transfer of a fundamental right, with or without payment or consideration, the irrevocable waiver of our entitlement to them, and the waivability of its enjoyment or exercise. According to Ferrajoli, "the unwaivability of fundamental rights concerns not the exercise or the enjoyment of a right but the waivability of our entitlement to them." And the fundamental rights are, by definition, unwaivable, where "waivability is not a merely a de facto waiver or any nonexercise or nonenjoyment of a right, but a decision about a right with binding effects. More precisely, it designates any legal act of alienation or transfer of a patrimonial right. It therefore does not include suicide [...], nor does it include a waiving of the exercise, enjoyment, or enforcement of a fundamental right." The only disagreement between myself and Ferrajoli seems to be that Ferrajoli takes it for granted, or does not exclude the fact, that the unavailability or alienation of fundamental rights, as he understands it, can have a paternalistic justification and that this paternalistic justification is morally acceptable (see Ferrajoli 2001, p. 16). In this section, however, I argue that the unwaivability of fundamental rights or their nontransferability can perfectly have an antipaternalistic justification and that this is the only morally acceptable justification that protects the autonomy of individuals. And it is the same protection of individual autonomy that explains why it is important for fundamental rights to be waivable with regard to their exercise or enjoyment. And this explains why if we attribute to John the right to commit assisted suicide under certain conditions, we do not necessarily have to enforce (or oblige Titius to fulfil) the contract by which John obliged himself to commit suicide. Cf. Ferrajoli (2001), p. 140ff. On the importance of distinguishing between the alienability of fundamental rights, the waivability our entitlement to them, and the waivability of their exercise, as well as on why it is important that the exercise of certain fundamental rights (such as the right to health or life) be waivable by the holder, i.e., why it is important that an adult and rational person be able to validly waive the exercise of the fundamental rights he or she holds (unless there is harm to others or unless we should protect the autonomous preferences of all or some of the holders of these rights), see Jori (2001), p. 89ff. and below in the text. In many legal systems, for example, there is a rule that grants workers the right to paid holidays, and this right is interpreted as, or is established by the same rule to be, unwaivable with regard to their exercise or enjoyment, meaning that workers cannot validly waive temporalily, de iure, the entitlement or, de facto, the exercise of the right: they are "required" to take holidays. And this unwaivability protects them from stronger private entities, namely, employers, safeguarding their autonomy and their qualified consent, their freedom from coercive pressures. It protects the autonomous preference of workers to not negotiate the terms of their employment. Indeed, as mentioned, if workers were allowed to negotiate with their employers, they would likely face legal coercive pressures, with the employer threatening layoffs or offshoring or threatening to cut back on production—all to induce workers to waive, in whole or in part, de iure or de facto, their right to paid holidays, daily rest breaks, or a safe workplace environment (for the same salary). On unwaivable rights, see Zaller (2010, 2015); Sunstein (2001); *Pellegrino v. Robert Half International*, 181 Cal. App. 4th 713 (2010); *Barrentine v. Arkansas-Best Freight System*, 450 U.S. 728 (1981); Vaver (2006); Austin and Klimchuk (2014), p. 292; Perritt (2017); Bigliazzi Geri et al. (1986); Cian and Trabucchi (2001), arts. 10ff.; and Rescigno (1982), p. 47ff.; and more recently Del Giudice et al. (2015) and Del Giudice (2015).

[11] The literature on this subject is vast. See Marshall (1950); Celano (2007); Schiavello and Trujillo (2000); Ferrajoli (2001), p. 22ff.

and the traditional understanding of this categorisation,[12] we can assert that for some rights to liberty, it is even hard to conceive how such a transfer to third parties could take place. For instance, how could someone alienate their freedom of expression? Typically, this right is interpreted as a combination of Hohfeldian positions, such as the claim that the state and other entities not interfere using force, the permission to express one's opinion, and the permission not to express it. Even if interpreted as a right to positive actions (like the right to equal access to the media according to market rules), it remains a right attributed to all, thus making its sale nonsensical. The same applies to other rights to liberty, such as freedom of the press or of religion. By protecting these rights, the state normally restricts itself, creating a protected space where the individual can act freely. However, if the state does not limit one person's freedom to publicly criticise the government, how could that person transfer this freedom to another person, considering that this other person enjoys the same protection from the state, i.e., the right to publicly criticise the government's actions?

Regarding political rights, like the right to vote, they should be nontransferable and inalienable, not for paternalist reasons, but to protect democracy. If it were possible to transfer one's voting right to others, there would be some individuals whose votes count two, three, or four times. One could argue that preventing citizens from establishing a dictatorship through democratic procedures, i.e., protecting the value of democracy against the citizens' will, is paternalistic. I cannot delve deeply into this topic here, but it seems that dictatorships achieved through "sufficiently" free elections, as in part happened in Italy and Germany in the Fascist and Nazi periods, are either desired by citizens whose preferences have been formed in an insufficiently correct manner (due to inconsistencies or reliance on false beliefs), or are established in historical moments when the population is in a state of poverty and desperation akin to Humbert wanting to enter into a slavery contract to escape deep misery. In the case of a people "choosing" dictatorship, however, no one would propose an acceptable alternative, so the "constitutional" prohibition could be justified by the need to protect the interests of third parties who could likely suffer severe and irreversible economic, psychophysical, or physical harm from the dictatorship itself: this would happen to future generations or certain political, linguistic, ethnic, or sexual minorities, whose fundamental rights would likely be violated, since they would be "treated" as scapegoats of a likely severe economic situation, as happened in the Nazi-fascist and communist regimes in the former USSR.

As concerns the alienation of social rights, which are predominantly rights to positive actions or services, I already explained in Sect. 5.2 why I believe that prohibiting the alienation or gratuitous transfer of these social rights to third parties is not necessarily paternalistic, because the transfer of a right to unemployment benefits to someone who does not have this right is equivalent to transferring the economic resources of the welfare state.

[12] For a penetrating analysis and critique of the traditional way of understanding the distinction between social rights and rights to liberty (a distinction that cannot be explored in depth here), see Diciotti (2006), p. 73ff. Holmes and Sunstein (1999), p. 255.

It is very important to distinguish between the transfer of a fundamental right, with or without payment or consideration and the waivability of its enjoyment or exercise. Obviously, what has been argued concerns the transfer of fundamental rights, with or without payment, not the temporary waiver of our entitlement, or of exercise, of such rights, such as the right to health or housing. From an antipaternalistic perspective, waiving temporally, de iure, the entitlement, or, de facto, the exercise, of rights would always be allowed under the conditions we know,[13] unless there are autonomous preferences of the rights-holders—preferences that are essentially rational and sufficiently free from coercive pressures—to not negotiate a temporary waiver, de iure, of the entitlement, or, de facto, of the exercise, of the right in

[13] Having addressed the transfer of fundamental rights, with or without payment or consideration, and the temporary waiver, de iure, of the entitlement, or, de facto, of the exercise, of such rights, the only remaining aspect is the irrevocably *waiver of the entitlement* to fundamental rights without transfer to anyone else. About this argument cf. Fornero (2020). If there are good antipaternalistic reasons, as there are, to prevent people from transferring their fundamental rights to third parties, are there also reasons to prohibit them from irrevocably waiving the entitlement to these same rights? This would be a fairly rare case. Why would anyone want to not just waive the exercise of the right to health at a particular moment in their life but forever renounce the right to health? This would be akin to binding oneself for the future, preventing one's future self from enjoying the right to health, should they wish to. I see no reason why a person would adopt this behaviour. As I stated in Chap. 2, antipaternalism always protects, except in the case of advance directives, the agent's current will, rational and free from coercion, but nonetheless current. If the agent changes their mind in the future and wishes to exercise their right to health, a right which they had previously waived, I see no reason not to fulfil their "new" will. There are undoubtedly two fundamental reasons why an individual can rationally bind their future self, to this end using force by third parties. These are to rid oneself of a current substance addiction or to safeguard against potential future incompetence or irrationality. A third, a very doubtful case occurs when, in a free-market system through a contract, a person acquires a benefit that they otherwise could not have obtained. However, the case of irrevocable waiving entitlement to rights does not fall into any of these categories. What would be the benefit that an individual can gain by definitively waiving entitlement to the right to health? It makes no sense. An individual can always choose, at a given moment X, to not exercise their right to health, but if they change their mind, there is no (antipaternalistic) reason not to protect their new choice. Some eccentric might claim that they feel great annoyance at having to renew, each time, their request not to be treated and that avoiding this annoyance would be the benefit they acquire by waiving, forever, their entitlement to the right to health. But even if this were the case, the right to health is a right to positive performances. If an individual does not want to exercise it, there is no state "opposition" or "impediment" to overcome; it is enough not to go to the hospital, to a doctor, or to a pharmacy, except for the possible opposition of family or friends. Someone who embraces a bizarre religious ideal of total self-mortification of the body and mind might believe it is right to remain entirely at the mercy of providence, fate, or natural forces, so if "Someone in Heaven" has decided that they must suffer greatly due to an illness, then it is right that they suffer greatly. Even in this case, I do not understand why our "devotee" should forever renounce their right to health. They could simply choose not to exercise it, staying in their cave. If, however, our devotee preferred to not even have the option of the "satisfaction" of the right to health, preferring not to have to waive the exercise of the right to health, preferring never to have had it, or preferred for no one to offer them the possibility of satisfying it, this is not legally possible (that is so for antipaternalistic reasons, that is, to protect all others who want to be treated). If, finally, our devotee also suffered from a weakness of will, the solution would be the same as the one provided in Chap. 3, Sect. 3.4. The same argument holds for the case of an eccentric anarchist who does want to definitively waive his or her right to vote.

question or the availability of the right, as in the case of workers' rights to paid holiday and daily rest, or unless it is necessary to avoid harm to third parties. Indeed, under the concrete conditions of the capitalist market, once the right to paid holidays or daily rest becomes legally available, meaning its exercise can be validly waived, the right-holder (the worker) could not express autonomous consent to waive temporarily, de iure, the entitlement, or, de facto, the exercise, of that right, but would likely face unjust coercive pressures (threats of not hiring workers, threats of layoffs, offshoring, or production reduction), which vitiate the consent, to waive temporarily, de iure, the entitlement, or, de facto, the exercise, of the right, unacceptable pressures that cannot be eliminated (unless the right is declared legally unwaivable) and would turn the right into a mere *paper right*, which is effectively impossible to enjoy. According to a reasonable theory of rights, for rational and competent adults, a subjective right does not necessarily protect the agent's current will, the will they express in the here and now, *hic et nunc*, but rather the will they would express if they were rational, informed of relevant facts, and sufficiently free from coercive pressures. In many legal systems, for example, there is a rule that grants workers the right to paid holidays, and this right is interpreted as, or is established by the same rule to be, unwaivable, meaning workers cannot validly waive, with a contract, the entitlement, or the exercise, of the right: they are "required" to take holidays, and this unwaivability protects them from stronger private entities, namely, employers, safeguarding their autonomy and their qualified consent. It protects the autonomous preference of the great majority of workers to no negotiate the terms of their employment. Indeed, as already mentioned, if negotiation with employers were possible workers could face, and would likely face, unacceptable legal coercive pressures (threats of layoffs, offshoring, or production reduction) to induce them to waive temporarily, in whole or in part, de iure or de facto, their paid holidays, daily rest, or a safe working environment.

5.4.1 The Right to a Name and the Right to Counsel

One other case in which the unwaivability of a right, the impossibility of validly waiving the exercise of a right, could be envisaged is the case where we need to avoid harm to third parties, as with the right to a name, in which case it would be preferable to speak of a *right/duty* to a name (a duty imposed by expressly valid criminal or administrative laws, such as the regulations prohibiting the falsification of identity documents and giving false particulars to public officials).

As concerns the inalienability and the unwaivability of the right to counsel and to a fair trial, it is hard to imagine to whom this right could be sold, since everyone has a right to counsel. Could a public prosecutor make an agreement with the defendant who, in exchange for a large sum of money for their family, would waive their right to counsel? In any case, inalienability and unwaivability, meaning the impossibility of validly waiving the exercise of a right, is justifiable to protect the interests of third parties. Can an individual waive their right to present a legal defence, even if they are incapable of legally defending themselves? The answer is usually no. The role of the defendant's lawyer is to protect not only the interests of the defendant themself, interests that the defendant can clearly decide not to assert, but also public interests, relating to the purposes of the trial itself, essentially the search for truth, the introduction of evidence in court (fact-finding), through the adversarial process between prosecution and defense. Thus, the need for a lawyer is also justified to protect public interests, the interests of third parties, which a defendant cannot dispose of. Many third-party interests depend on the proper conduct of a trial, as is the case with the interest in punishing the true perpetrator of a crime. In this case, rather than speaking of the unwaivability of the right to counsel, it is better to speak of the right/duty to present a defense.

5.5 Violence Against Women: Limits of Consent in a Social Patriarchal Context

Let us consider the case of a woman, Samantha, married to a violent husband, who consents to her husband's abuse, whenever and however he wishes. The abuse typically results in either minor or permanent injuries. Both Samantha and her husband are part of a patriarchal "social group." This patriarchy extends to the family (in a broad sense), neighbourhood, friends, and the community they live in. Let us say that the woman's consent to being abused is clear, explicit, coherent, rational, and based on a knowledge of the relevant facts.[14] Under what conditions can we say that her consent is sufficiently free from coercive pressures? The solution to this case can also be applied to other similar cases of social and cultural discrimination, such as those against gay people or members of linguistic minorities.

Firstly, the law should prevent unreasonable inequality or discrimination in the allocation of rights under the laws governing marriage, child custody in the event of separation, and inheritance. For instance, if the social group to which Samantha belongs shares certain values and principles, typical of some patriarchal conceptions, under which Samantha would lose any right to the couple's common property, or to her original dowry, or would lose custody of the children or part of the inheritance if she separates from her husband, there would be enormous coercive pressures on Samantha not to leave the group and her husband. In this case, we should, on the one hand, deny the validity of Samantha's consent to be abused by her husband and, on the other, ensure that such a situation is not legally tolerated, i.e., Samantha should be given the right to legally separate, to obtain child custody on the same terms as her husband in case of separation, and to receive a share of the marital property, even against the will of her social group.

[14] Therefore, it is clear that if the victim's psychological attitude is that of someone who wants to escape from someone perceived as a tormentor, the fact that they can only fulfil that wish in an inconsistent and irrational manner is not a reason to consider their consent as validly given.

Secondly, the state should provide Samantha with a real, economic opportunity to *leave* the group—i.e., the state should grant and effectively protect certain fundamental rights, such as the right to life, health, housing, employment, or a subsidy in case of involuntary unemployment—allowing her not to be economically dependent on her husband and family. Especially in cases of brutal violence or repeated threats, Samantha should be granted the concrete right to protect her physical integrity, and possibly a new identity and residence in a different location, far from her violent husband.

However, this might not be enough. Imagine that, once Samatha is separated from her husband and group of origin, she is provided with a house in a public housing complex, or with a rent allowance while looking for a job, or with job training organised by regional agencies or volunteer associations, or with free medical care, or all of the above, and that she is given custody of the children in case of divorce. Even so, we have not given her a new "community." The emotional and social bond with her community of origin could be definitively broken. And it is likely that Samantha—because she is, for example, an immigrant from another country, speaks another language, or adheres to another religion—may not have another community of affection and relationships to join. The fear of losing the emotional and relational bond with the community of origin could be a strong deterrent for Samantha to leave her original social group. Other deterrents could be the fear or certainty of not finding an acceptable alternative, of not being accepted in a different context, that of a community of people who have a different culture and religion, who are members of a different ethnicity.

In this regard, I believe that a liberal-egalitarian state should establish, in all cases of "escape from an oppressive and discriminatory social group," a procedure for the social and emotional reintegration of the person fleeing. This procedure should, of course, be independent of the reasons for the discrimination by the group, or the group's ethnicity. The reasons can be religious, or social; the groups to which one belongs may be Christian, Muslim, Jewish, or atheist; the relevant discriminations may be towards gays, women, or other minorities. It is not only about ensuring the survival of the discriminated person or guaranteeing the satisfaction of their primary needs such as living in a house or protecting their health but also about giving them an opportunity to create a new, socially satisfying relational life. How? This could be achieved, for example, through the help of volunteer associations that help women flee patriarchal and oppressive groups, fostering acquaintances with other women who have had similar experiences, and/or with other groups that share the same language or religion, or other groups that have a different language and religion but are much more tolerant, open, and egalitarian.

Therefore, we grant Samantha the right to effective protection of her physical integrity, away from the violence and threats of her husband, the right to health, housing, and employment, the right to legally separate from her husband, to obtain custody of the children in case of separation, and to receive a share of the marital property, as well as the right to social and emotional reintegration into a different context, a true "right to exit" from the group of origin. We have given her a concrete opportunity, an economic and social opportunity, to leave the oppressive group.

However, once it is ascertained that, despite the concrete opportunity to escape from the patriarchal group, her consent to be abused by her husband persists and that such consent is rational, based on a knowledge of relevant facts, and stable over time, can we judge her consent to be sufficiently free from coercive pressures? Once we have neutralised physical and psychological coercion, once we have concretely protected this woman from her husband's threats, there remains the problem of *epistemic violence*. What happens if Samantha has internalised self-representation, a debilitating and mortifying identity model, if she is convinced that she "is worth less" than her husband, that her place is, regardless of any violence he commits, next to him, that the core family can never be "broken"?

Determining whether a person has really suffered some form of epistemic violence is challenging. The risk, as with all theories of this kind, from Freud to Marx, is that the diagnosis of epistemic violence is unfalsifiable, meaning there are no objective bases on which to determine whether someone has been subjected to this form of violence and when. The risk, as Bartoli points out, is twofold. On the one hand, there is a lapse into populism, assuming that people's preferences, even if rational, based on a knowledge of the relevant facts, and stable over time, are always considered expressions of their "true interests," of their good, and thus "freely" expressed. On the other hand, there is a lapse into paternalism, assuming that supposed victims of an oppressive social system, "desperate housewives," or members of oppressed linguistic or ethnic minorities, have no idea of what their good is and need someone to guide them so that they can "see the light" (see Bartoli 2008, p. 61ff.)

A possible solution could be as follows. We can identify a fundamental, conceptually necessary prerequisite for the presence of epistemic violence, and several "indicators," certain conditions whose (joint) occurrence makes it highly probable that an individual has suffered some form of epistemic violence, particularly *four* indicators.

5.6 Symptoms of Epistemic Violence

The fundamental premise is that epistemic violence likely originates from economic, social, cultural, or psychological discrimination exercised by the majority of a social group against a minority within the same group. This "minority" can be numerical, as in the case of a linguistic or religious minority, or a minority in terms of economic and social power, as with women in Western societies, at least from the Roman Empire until the latter half of the twentieth century, black people in South Africa under Apartheid and in the United States (from the era of slavery until at least the end of Jim Crow with the modern civil rights era of the 1960s), or the Dalits in India. For epistemic violence to occur, it is necessary, historically, for a *doxa* to form within a group, debilitating or mortifying for a subsocial group identified on the basis of characteristics generally present from birth, or from adolescence in the case of homosexuality, and independent of their will, characteristics such as sex, skin colour, or ethnicity, or even one's religious background. This *doxa* will generate some form of economic and social exploitation. These characteristics generally identify more what people are—women, black and brown, Jewish, homosexual—rather than what they do. It is also necessary that such a cultural model be imposed through education from an early age and be likely to be passed down within the same exploited, discriminated subgroup (see Bartoli 2008, pp. 32ff., 54ff.).

First Symptom A first symptom of epistemic violence is that the "subaltern," the epistemically violated subject, who "uses categories and representations that are externally produced and self-debilitating" (ibid., 58, my translation) engages in discourse that is incorrect due to its being inconsistent or founded on empirically false beliefs, for example, "Women or black and brown people are intellectually inferior to men or whites" or "The Aryan or white race is biologically superior." Alternatively, the epistemically violated individual might explicitly use conformism, based on tradition or authority, as an argument to justify a moral principle or a general value judgment, or they might base their plan of life, in its fundamental aspects, on complex, articulated metaphysical transcendent beliefs with a very low probability of being true, e.g., "The indissolubility of marriage and the right of the husband to command his wife are established by the will of God," paraphrasing what Saint Paul says in the Bible, though the same Saint Paul adds that the husband cannot mistreat his wife because he must treat her as his own flesh, just as Jesus treats the church).

Second Symptom Another important indicator, the second, is when someone is, even unconsciously, a habitual, uncritical conformist, adapting their preferences, opinions, and principles to those of the dominant social group or to the opinions of the dominated group, such as their family of origin. This implies that the epistemically violated subject often lacks the ability to develop second-order desires, preferences, and reflections, i.e., desires or preferences about other desires or preferences, or the ability to "view" the principles and values of their ancestors, familial or cultural, with sufficient detachment to identify fallacies, gaps, inconsistencies, new arguments, or different adaptations to previously unconsidered cases.

Third Symptom Another sign of epistemic violence is self-loathing, a form of "dependency very common among disadvantaged minorities. Self-loathing is contempt toward oneself or one's own group, generating a desire to disappear and a pleasure in being marginalized" (ibid.). Self-loathing clearly implies more than a mere belief ("I believe women are inferior to men"), but a feeling of contempt toward oneself, of a kind that is likely to give rise to unhappiness, guilt, or deep internal conflicts.

Fourth Symptom The last important symptom (the fourth) of (suspected) epistemic violence is linguistic and conceptual incompetence, which in turn depends on illiteracy or having received a dogmatic, rigid education not based on the values of moral, cultural, or religious "pluralism." This conceptual incompetence likely leads to an inability to rationally justify certain value judgments, like "Women should devote themselves to their husband and children" or an inability to analyse the reasons for or against a certain thesis or to come up with arguments in support of their preferences. Therefore, in assessing someone's cultural subalternity, and especially in avoiding such subalternity, it is fundamental to ensure that everyone has the right to a secular and "plural" education, inspired by some fundamental principles and values: the separation between reason and faith, between metaphysico-transcendent assumptions and empirically founded beliefs, between the scientific community and religious "authority"; the freedom and (epistemological) limits of scientific research; the pluralism of values, plans of life, and lives worthy of living; the development of each individual's critical and argumentative skills, their cognitive and emotional capacities. Equally important is that a certain degree of pluralism, if not democracy, be guaranteed, protecting the right to criticism within each religious or cultural group, so that each member has a concrete opportunity to develop ideas, opinions, and preferences in a sufficiently free and autonomous manner.

It is, of course, quite challenging to determine whether and to what extent these four indicators are necessary or sufficient conditions for epistemic violence. Are each of these indicators necessary for a form of epistemic violence to exist? Certainly not. The fundamental premise of epistemic violence is, by definition, necessary but not sufficient. Certainly, all four factors, in conjunction with the fundamental premise, are sufficient. In reality, I believe that all the "indicators" considered harmonise with each other, representing a coherent whole where "everything" is connected, in the sense that they usually cluster. If one is missing, it is likely that others will be, too. What I mean is that a person who is illiterate and uneducated, having suffered severe social, economic, and psychological discrimination by the dominant social group, will likely not have the capacity to develop ideas, concepts, or values alternative to those of the social group they belong to, and is therefore likely to be largely conformist with respect to the dominant *doxa*. It is also likely that such a person will engage in discourse that is not sufficiently rational, as by using arguments based on the "inevitability" of certain moral laws, justifying certain choices on the basis of the so-called "moral" authority of a person invested with sacred power ("As is stated by the head of our religious community, it is unbecoming of a woman to leave here home and husband"), qualifying certain behaviours as "against nature," or using magical/fideistic arguments, because an important, essential part of their plan of life is based on metaphysico-transcendent assumptions.

Consider, for example, the religious belief that "a widow who performed *sati* [i.e., the ceremony in which the widow throws herself onto the funeral pyre of her deceased husband] would absolve herself and her spouse of all sins," transforming herself into a martyr to be counted among her kin. "Indeed, the couple, purified by the woman's sacrifice, would immediately reach a celestial abode, sweetened by songs of praise sung by angelic maidens" (ibid., 63). Equally insufficiently rational would be the belief that women are, by nature, intellectually inferior to men, because it is based on premises that, today, are considered patently false from an empirical standpoint,[15] or the belief that divorce between parents is always the cause of moral and psychological damage to children, damage greater than what they would endure under a quarrelsome, violent, or deeply unhappy marriage, at least for one of the spouses.

Finally, as mentioned earlier, a victim of epistemic violence, someone who suffers from strong social and cultural discrimination, might easily engage in discourse that, if not outright insufficiently rational, lacks a broad and coherent justification. Such a person might find themself in a dilemma when asked to justify unequal treatments. "Why can a husband be unfaithful to his wife, but not vice versa?"; "Why is it that a husband can and should work while a wife cannot?"; "Assuming that children always need at least one parent at home with them—as opposed to a competent babysitter—why should it be the wife who takes on this role?"; "Assuming that one of the parents must prepare and cook food for the children—rather than buying it out or hiring a cook—why should this chore be for the wife?"; "On what clinical and experimental psychology studies is the idea based that men are incapable of adequately raising and educating a child?"

This does not exclude the possibility that a person's preferences can be rational—based on a knowledge of relevant facts, stable over time, formed in a manner sufficiently free from unwanted physical and psychological violence or epistemic violence—and yet at the same time be, for example, masochistic sexual preferences whose satisfaction increases the risk of injuries to one's integrity but brings pleasure and well-being to the "victim." However, in the case of masochistic sexual preferences, the psychological and social framework would likely be different from that of a person who is a victim of discrimination and psychological and epistemic violence from their social group. In the case of masochism, one is not typically dealing with a person—man or woman, often terrified, suffering—claiming to be unable to escape their tormentor—such as a husband, or even the patriarchal family or social group they belong to—and desperately wanting to do so, but failing in that effort, someone whose sexuality is normally not experienced in a masochistic way, since sexual pleasure does not mix with pain. In the case of masochism, we are more likely dealing with a person for whom physical suffering, especially in a sexual context, brings pleasure, but who might not accept mistreatment or discrimination in other contexts, in relation to professional fulfilment, leisure time, education, or the upbringing of children.

To summarise what has been discussed so far, we could say that a woman might validly consent to being mistreated by her partner when the following is ascertained, through a rigorous procedure, such as an interview with a psychiatrist, a doctor, or an experienced volunteer from an association against violence towards women:

(a) Consent must be rational, informed by all the relevant facts, and stable over time.
(b) Consent must be "sufficiently free from coercive pressures" when the right to escape from an oppressive and discriminatory social group is guaranteed. This involves the effective protection of fundamental rights such as the right to hous-

[15] From a biological/evolutionary point of view, by contrast, females traditionally have a less developed build and musculature than males.

ing, health, pension, and employment, with fair pay, adequate to ensure a dignified life. This includes the right to equal distribution of rights within the family of origin in case of separation (marital property, custody of children, etc.) and the right to social and emotional reintegration into a nonpatriarchal or nonoppressive context.

(c) Consent must be sufficiently free in the sense that, based on the indicators just discussed, it is certain or likely that the person in question is sufficiently autonomous and is not (still) a victim of any form of unwanted physical, psychological, or epistemic violence. This framework should allow a woman who truly wishes to, to remain with a man/husband who abuses her, even when she has a real economic, social, and emotional alternative.[16]

This situation is reminiscent of the fate chosen by Pilar, the female protagonist in the powerful and starkly realistic film *Te doy mis ojos*, by Icíar Bollaín. The film confronts the challenging and harrowing theme of psychological and physical violence against women, a plight that, regrettably, shows no signs of abating. Pilar, played by Laia Marull, after initially fleeing from the atmosphere of violence and fear established by her husband, returns to him, despite his continued abuse and his fits of rage. Even as Pilar secures a job that economically emancipates her from her husband, and despite the social and emotional support from her sister and friends, she deeply loves him. She continues to love him, in spite of everything, and strives to change him, to alter his violent nature, even through the group psychotherapy he goes to. The film thus narrates an impossible love, woven with passion and violence, disappointment and bitter reconciliations, telling the story of two fragile individuals who are changing, but in divergent directions. One moves towards freedom, self-fulfilment in her career, social and professional gratification, toward greater autonomy and self-mastery. The other sinks deeper into the quicksand of suffocating possessiveness, of impetuous and irrational jealousy, unable to overcome the profound sense of inferiority that burdens him. In the end, Pilar leaves her possessive and violent husband, a man unable to change. However, the crux of the matter is that her definitive decision to leave him, a second time and for good, does not seem, within the film's narrative, more rational or more "autonomous" than her decision to return to him the first time, to give him a second chance, despite his relapses, his intermittent crises, and the renewed psychological violence she endures. If her husband had been immediately arrested and convicted for the violence Pilar suffered, she probably would not have had the opportunity to give herself and him this second chance. But is this conclusion acceptable?

[16]For instance, it is conceivable that Samantha, the abused wife, might secretly contact, unbeknownst to her husband, a domestic abuse centre. This centre could inform her of her rights and the existence of a real opportunity to find refuge in another city. She could be temporarily accommodated in one of their shelters, find a job through a network of associations and public entities, initiate legal proceedings for divorce and sole custody of the children, receive counsel from a lawyer and a psychologist at the centre, obtain a restraining or protection order against her husband, prevent her abusive husband from discovering her new residence, and maintain contact only with friends or relatives who agree to keep this secret. Nevertheless, despite such a concrete opportunity, Samantha might decide not to leave her husband or to return to him.

5.7 Conclusion Regarding Violence Against Women

The phenomenon of violence against women, encompassing both physical and psychological abuse, is alarmingly severe and persistent.[17] It is a phenomenon that inflicts significant harm on others, not just the women who fall victim to it, but also their children, who are indirect victims. Children, even if they do not directly suffer violence from their fathers, and even if they are not the direct object of beatings, threats, or insults, suffer serious traumas, deriving from frequently feeling fear, terror, and anguish and from witnessing scenes of violence, often helplessly (Adolfi et al. 2011; p. 4; de Concini et al. 2005). There is a certain likelihood that children who endure violence may become violent themselves in adulthood. Furthermore, mothers cannot mortgage their children's future or decide on their psychological well-being in this manner (as they might, according to an antipaternalistic doctrine, decide on their own well-being). This largely hidden phenomenon, subject to few reports, necessitates stringent repression without any leniency. Additionally, as documented by domestic abuse centres, many women struggle (psychologically or economically) to break free from the cycle of violence and to report their violent partners. This difficulty is often linked to a lack of appropriate facilities to safeguard the fundamental rights of women, particularly the right to be effectively and defini-

[17] See ISTAT (2015). Here are some figures. "Over the past 12 months, 1.15 million women (5.4%) have been victims of violence, but the majority of these cases go unreported. An estimated 96% of nonpartner-violence and 93% of partner-violence cases remain in the shadows. A third of these victims endure both physical and sexual violence. Shockingly, 690,000 women have suffered repeated violence from partners when they already had children, with 62.4% saying that their children have witnessed one or more episodes. Partners are identified as the primary perpetrators in the majority of physical violence cases and are also significantly responsible for various forms of sexual violence, including rape and coerced sex. A notable 69.7% of rapes are committed by partners, 17.4% by someone they know. Only 6.2% were committed by strangers. The risk of experiencing actual rape, rather than an attempted rape, is higher in relationships with closer connections between perpetrator and victim. Strangers, followed by acquaintances and colleagues, are more likely to commit physical sexual harassment. Domestic violence cases are predominantly severe, with 34.5% of women categorising the violence as very serious and 29.7% as fairly serious. Women who have a current partner who is physically violent (35.6% compared to 6.5%) or verbally abusive (25.7% compared to 5.3%) experience higher rates of violence. Additionally, women whose partners show attitudes of devaluation or disregard in daily interactions face a violence rate of 35.9%, in contrast to 5.7% for those without such experiences. The prevalence of violence is also higher among women with partners who frequently get intoxicated, with 18.7% against 6.4% for those whose partners do not, and particularly those whose partners get drunk daily or nearly daily (38.6%) and once or more a week (38.3%). Furthermore, women who grew up in a household where their father was violent towards their mother have a 30% chance of experiencing violence, compared to 6% for those who did not have such a background. The percentage of those who are violent with their partner is 30% among those who witnessed violence in their family of origin, 34.8% among those who experienced it from their father, 42.4% among those who experienced it from their mother, and 6% among those who did not experience or witness violence in their family of origin." Although the concept of violence employed in the study is quite broad, encompassing "psychological forms such as denigration, behavioral control, isolation strategies, intimidation, and significant economic restrictions imposed by partners," the data remains deeply concerning.

tively protected from intimate partner violence, and the economic opportunity to leave their original social group (Gamberini 2007; del Frate et al. 2009). However, the issue of violence against women is too complex to be comprehensively addressed here. The specialised literature in legal, criminological, medical, and psychological fields is vast. Therefore, I will confine myself to a few brief observations, three in particular.

Firstly, what percentage of women in the Western world, once it has been ascertained that they satisfy the criteria of rational consent, awareness of the relevant facts, temporal stability of desires, and sufficient freedom from coercive pressures, would consent, like Pilar, to being abused or harmed for love or in an attempt to redeem a violent partner? Certainly, it would be a minority, perhaps a small one, but how small? This is very hard to determine. Various studies, reports, and surveys have been conducted by domestic abuse centres, antidiscrimination associations, and national bodies.[18] For instance, there are countless reasons why abused women not report abuse or withdraw existing complaints, retract statements at trial, or refrain from testifying despite having filed a complaint. Some authors have identified two main ones (see Hoyle and Sanders 2000, p. 23ff.). The first (involving a minority) is that the trial and conviction of a violent partner are not deemed necessary to achieve the victim's primary objectives, with the initial arrest often seen as sufficient to stop the violence, enable the woman to escape, or initiate divorce proceedings. Secondly, in the majority of cases, a cost-benefit analysis leads many to conclude that a criminal trial and conviction would have far worse consequences, particularly the fear of revenge or retaliation by the abusive partner, jeopardizing the safety of the woman or her children. This fear is compounded by the difficulty of ensuring protection from further violence, harassment, or stalking, especially if the woman is not willing to relocate, find a new job, or obtain a new identity.[19] Additionally, managing child custody with an abusive ex-partner adds further complexity.

Secondly, the utopian ideal of achieving rational, informed, and uncoerced consent in such cases is genuinely challenging to realize. I will illustrate this with two examples. Firstly, the abusive partner often creates an environment so intimidating and fear-inducing that only the implementation of an actual right to escape and reintegrate into society in a new location, facilitated by domestic abuse associations, social support structures, and protection programmes, can make a significant difference. However, these programmes require substantial public resources, which are

[18] Some authors cite the attempt to salvage an emotional relationship as one of the five primary reasons women do not leave their violent partners. See Creazzo et al. (1999), p. 27.

[19] Taking into account that separation or the desire for separation by a woman, and generally the choices that women make to assert their autonomy and not be submissive, are fundamental causes of femicide, so the fear of revenge exacted by an abusive partner is well founded. See Adolfi et al. (2011), p. 4. "Instead, we know from research that victim action, calls for help, and separation—whether in progress or planned—*in themselves* raise the degree violence carried out by the abuser" (Romanin 2011, p. 89, my translation).

not always available.[20] Secondly, various studies have identified patterns of insufficient rationality or epistemic violence in abused women, especially in cases of prolonged maltreatment. Symptoms of post-traumatic stress disorder, entrenched and unjustified guilt ("It's my fault I am being abused"), likely inconsistencies ("I deserve to be mistreated if I behave this way"),[21] denial ("Nothing serious has happened; there are no problems in our marriage"), and difficulties in attributing the violence to the partner ("He is a good man, it's the alcohol or drugs that are making him violent") indicate a sense of irrational powerlessness.[22]

Thirdly, let us assume, as this is the matter at hand, that the consent of a victim of physical and psychological violence could "justify," as a justificatory defence, the crime of causing injuries, even serious and permanent ones. This implies preventing the emergence of a criminal act, provided that their consent is rational, informed of the relevant facts, stable over time, and sufficiently free from coercive pressures as specified (unwanted physical and psychological violence, as well as epistemic violence), along with the guarantee of the right to escape from an oppressive social group. In this case, the legal framework for the crime of inflicting injuries, even serious and permanent ones, would be analogous to that currently in place for sexual abuse, where the absence of valid consent is a determining requirement for the emergence of a criminal act. The freedom to make choices about one's physical integrity would be akin to sexual freedom. Would this lead to greater difficulty for the legal system in punishing perpetrators of abuse against nonconsenting women? Would there be more evidential challenges? Could the abusive partner's lawyers successfully argue that the woman consented (even if in reality she did not), attempt to delegitimise her, or present arguments (such as the woman's reluctance to flee or

[20] "In Italy, protective measures are limited, and the few that exist are often still unknown to the general public. For instance, domestic abuse centres are not yet a widespread reality recognised by everyone: ISTAT has found that only 2.8% of women who have suffered violence from a partner or ex-partner, and 2.4% of others, have sought help from these centres. Shelter homes [...] have scarce security measures, which almost always only include the secrecy of the address (in any case, hospitality in these centres is not secure enough if the woman at high risk of being killed lives in the same city as her abuser). The transfer from one shelter home to another outside the original territory, even in Emilia-Romagna, where such facilities are more widespread than in the rest of Italy, is made difficult or impossible by administrative constraints [...]. The criminal complaint in itself does not provide effective protection for the very few victims who report. Women, forced to hide due to violence in intimate relationships, cannot conceal their personal data, as is possible for witnesses in the justice system, who can benefit from a witness protection programme" (Romanin 2011, pp. 98–99, my translation).

[21] According to a formal and limited conception of rationality, outlined in Chap. 3, Sect. 3.2, Sect. 3.4.1, profiles of insufficient rationality (such as inconsistency) exist to the extent that, through an interview with psychologists or social workers, the victim realises that it does not make much sense to feel guilty and think that she deserves to be denigrated, insulted, or mistreated due to aspects of her character or behaviour that she herself cannot change or that are very difficult to change (a consolidated trait of her character; a pattern of emotional reaction; a physiognomic trait; being desired by other men; a rooted cognitive, linguistic, or manual incapacity; or emotional weakness).

[22] See Creazzo et al. (1999), p. 27.

end the relationship) in favour of her consent? What would happen? Is there a risk that unscrupulous lawyers might "abuse" the justificatory defence—exploiting fragile women—to exonerate abusive husbands?

And yet, what would be the greatest, most well-founded risk? What poses the greater risk? The risk of abuse, the risk that violent husbands may go unpunished if we modified the legal framework to allow consent to exempt offenders from the crime of causing injuries, even severe and permanent ones? Or is there the risk that a small minority of women who truly and rationally, in full autonomy, and independently of masochistic sexual preferences, wish to temporarily live in a "violent" love relationship, in the hope that their partner will keep their promises, stop drinking, or find stable employment, are prevented from doing so under the current legal system, which does not recognise their consent as a defence to the charge of causing injury? I do not have the expertise or the tools to make such evaluations. Based on the reports and surveys cited, it seems to me that the risk of harm to third parties, the risk of impunity of abusive partners and of psychophysical harm to children, where, as is often the case, they are present, is significant, while the second risk, limiting women's autonomy while awaiting *redemption* of the violent partner, is on the contrary insignificant. If serious and scientifically based statistical analyses of the desires of women who are victims of violence, as well as criminal law analyses of the risks of impunity for violent partners, confirm this hypothesis regarding the magnitude of these risks, we would have a founded risk of harm to third parties, a genuinely antipaternalistic reason to prohibit such forms of abuse (regardless of the existence of an alleged consent of the victims).

Is it possible to reconcile the two needs? To protect the choice of a small minority who, like Pilar, want to give a second chance to an abusive husband, and the need to severely repress the phenomenon of violence against women? According to the solution just adopted, the legal system would prohibit (and criminalise) injuries and abuse regardless of the victim's dissent. This is based on a presumption of nonvoluntariness, not grounded in "a priori" concepts or metaphysical or ideological considerations, but, as we have seen, in empirical research, to the extent that serious and well-documented statistical and probabilistic investigations ascertain, as seems plausible, that the desire to temporarily live in a "violent" love relationship, awaiting the partner's redemption, is, as we have seen, not as rare as the desire to enter into a contract of slavery but is still quite rare. It is presumed that the vast majority of women in the Western world would not give their consent, once it has been ascertained that they meet the criteria of the rationality of consent, awareness of the relevant facts, stability of consent over time, and sufficient freedom from coercive pressures.

This solution, much like the one regarding slavery contracts, could also satisfy the second requirement, that of women like Pilar. If a woman wishes to submit to her husband's violence because she is deeply in love with him, or because she is attempting to redeem him, despite the protection of all the rights mentioned above, she could still do so without legal authorisation, because whether or not there is epistemic violence, her conception of happiness, however bizarre it may be, must ultimately prevail. Only in a police state, which systematically monitors citizens in their homes through ambient, phone, or satellite wiretapping, could many cases of abuse be discovered and punished. A woman who is abused and goes to the hospital can, if she wishes, tell any "story": that she fell down the stairs or that she was attacked by a masked robber. And even if social workers had well-founded suspicions, in many cases it would be difficult for the violent partner to be convicted without the wife's testimony.[23] A similar principle could justify the fact that the very crime of injury, if not serious, is punishable under the Italian Penal Code only if the offended person files a complaint, as is the case with many cases of sexual violence.[24]

In conclusion, the argument presented in this enquiry has been that an activity that is neither dangerous nor harmful to the agent himself or to others should not be limited or prohibited even when the person engaging in such an activity is not deemed to be perfectly rational or autonomous in light of a balancing of preferences, and the conclusion we can draw coherently with that argument is that it is important to punish physical violence as well as psychological violence (or threats). But a woman in a patriarchal society who is a victim of epistemic violence has a right not to work, to take care of and raise her children on her own, and to wear a veil in public. The burqa is problematic because it completely covers the face, making it impossible to see who is behind the veil, and yet in a variety of settings—a government office, a bank, an insurance agency—it is important to be able to see everyone's face. Nobody can walk into a bank wearing a motorcycle helmet.

5.8 The Spectacle of Death

Another particularly challenging case concerns seriously dangerous/harmful actions committed in the context of a performance, such as at theatre or a stadium or on TV. The scenario is that some individuals consent, often for pay, to participate in extremely violent shows or games where there is a very high risk of losing one's life or sustaining physical injury, or even a certainty of death or permanent injury in case of defeat. Imagine a TV show where contestants play Russian roulette, a stadium where "gladiators" engage in violent or lethal battles in front of screaming crowds, or a sport like *Rollerball* as envisioned by Norman Jewison in his film of the same name, a fast-paced and violent sport where players on roller skates or motorcycles

---

[23] In a similar vein Hoyle and Sanders (2000), p. 16ff., who propose a legal framework that balances public interest in prosecuting abusive partners and allowing victims in dire psychological, economic, and social straits to escape the cycle of violence, against the need to preserve some degree of autonomy for the victims of such violence. They suggest that crimes of abuse and serious injury are prosecutable by the state, and temporary restraining measures like immediate arrest could be implemented. The same applies to police investigations, including phone and ambient wiretapping. However, in cases where there are no child victims of the violence, and in the absence of testimony or a complaint from the woman who is the victim of violence, it would not be possible to bring the accused to trial and convict them of the alleged crime.

[24] Similar arguments can be found in Scarpelli (1998), p. 157.

clash on a circular track, using brutal moves and strikes to score points by throwing a ball into a metal basket.[25]

Principally, based on the discussions in the previous sections, these cases could be solved similarly to slavery contracts, namely, by prohibiting such activities for analogous reasons. This prohibition would be consistent even if such violent confrontations did not occur in front of an audience or for pay or other benefits (which is even more improbable). Firstly, these are statistically very unlikely cases. How many people, in conditions of rationality and sufficient freedom from coercion, would wish to enter into such contracts and, once defeated in battle, would choose to be killed rather than be spared? Very few, I believe.[26] Evidence of this is that gladiators in ancient Rome or as depicted in movies (*The Running Man*) were mostly compelled to do so, meaning they could not choose, once defeated, between death and exiting the scene. We protect the current wishes of the gladiator, not the wishes set forth in the contract, by inserting an *ad nutum* (at will) termination clause in the contract as in slavery contracts.

Secondly, we would have to ascertain through very costly bureaucratic procedures that a person's willingness to participate in a gladiator fight or Rollerball match is rational, informed of the relevant facts, stable over time, and sufficiently free from coercive pressures. Thirdly, some of this person's fundamental rights would have to be guaranteed: this applies, for example, to the right to free movement, health, education, and housing, and to unemployment benefits in case of involuntary job loss. Another important guarantee, as we saw in the case of slavery contracts, is related to the impartiality and correctness of officials in conducting procedures to verify that potential gladiators meet consent requirements (rationality, absence of coercion, knowledge of the relevant facts), to prevent wealthy and powerful multinationals from corrupting officials to coerce people with psychological difficulties and/or serious economic problems to compete in such games, should the profit from these shows be high.

If these reasons are not convincing enough to prohibit such spectacles, though I believe they are, in the case of the spectacle of death, there is an additional problem, namely, that of the "spectacle" itself. We saw in Chap. 3, Sect. 3.3, note 24, that the "death culture" argument does not hold, as the protection of individual autonomy is sufficient to morally justify the right to request euthanasia or assisted suicide from one's doctor, or the right to engage in sadomasochistic sex or extremely dangerous individual sports. These rights are not (necessarily or normally) justified by sadism, cruelty, contempt for others' lives, or a love for violence, as is the case with activities that cause harm to nonconsenting third parties (murder, rape, robbery, abuse). In other words, the "death culture" argument is unconvincing because agreeing with the idea that euthanasia should be permitted does not logically imply agreeing that

25 Examples can be found in Kristol (1994), p. 47ff.

26 Joel Feinberg speaks of a reasonable presumption of nonvoluntariness in Feinberg (1994), p. 52ff., 57ff.

there are conditions under which murder and torture should also be permitted; indeed, this is mostly not the case.

In other words, legalising euthanasia or other activities involving significant risk to life does not necessarily propagate a *culture of death*, where human life is perceived as a less significant value, one that can be sacrificed under certain conditions leading to more murder, abuse, or rape, i.e., harm to nonconsenting third parties, which an antipaternalistic doctrine would not justify. In discussions of euthanasia, assisted suicide, noncompetitive extreme sports, and sadomasochism, we are referring to activities that, on the one hand, involve relatively *few* individuals, a minority of the society, such as terminally ill patients, those who are suffering severely, extreme-sports enthusiasts, and sadomasochists. On the other hand, these are people who voluntarily relinquish their lives or personally risk their life and physical integrity during these activities. The settings and methods for these activities are often *private* and vary in location, time, and manner. These activities take place in remote mountains, hospital rooms, bedrooms, brothels, opium dens, turbulent rivers, private residences, or the open sea.

A different discussion is necessary for situations where violence and death become a public spectacle, enjoyed by thousands or millions of spectators. These spectators do not risk their lives or physical integrity, nor do they materially or emotionally assist, like a doctor in assisted suicide, in the harmful or dangerous act, which the individual alone could not perform, at least not in the same way as in cases of euthanasia, assisted suicide, sadomasochistic practices, or drug use. Spectators of extremely violent fights do not facilitate the harmful/dangerous action; they do not take part in its execution. Instead, they merely derive enjoyment from the violence or death of others, witnessing scenes of individuals inflicting harm or killing each other.

At this juncture, the issue becomes empirical. Can witnessing death and violence—not cinematic or theatrical violence, nor violence occurring in fiction, but a real spectacle of death and bloodshed—actually lead, not those who fight or risk their lives in dangerous actions, but rather the paying spectators, to perceive life and the physical integrity of others as a value of lesser importance? This would require relevant empirical studies, though it is unclear how these could be conducted. However, it seems plausible. Protecting minors and individuals with psychological difficulties would be a sufficient reason to prohibit the broadcast of such violent and deadly spectacles on unencrypted television channels or the web or in public venues. I doubt that the justification spectators might offer for watching a violent spectacle is respect for others' will or individual autonomy. I believe the most plausible reasons are twofold: sadism, the pleasure derived from torture, or the sublimation of one's own violent impulses and frustrations, and the sense of powerlessness that most human beings feel in the face of both minor and major injustices and abuses endured over the course of their lives. This view is explicitly taken in films like *Rollerball*, where such a violent and bloody sport is deemed necessary for an ideal of social order and peace. History also seems to support this direction. In Ancient Rome, many gladiators, whether professionals or novices, were criminals, slaves, convicts, prisoners of war, or Christians. Particularly sought after were hardy convicts and war prisoners, who had survived years of combat and suffering. This suggests that the tradition of gladiator fights fostered and presupposed the idea that the life and physical integrity of certain people (slaves, convicts, prisoners) were less important, thus more liable to be sacrificed, than the lives of free citizens of certain ranks. This was the culture underpinning the bloody gladiator fights to the death.

As is clear, the viewing of a spectacle of violence and death is justified by the spectators for entirely different reasons than those invoked to legalise the undertaking of other harmful/dangerous actions, i.e., respect for individual autonomy. *One* of the two likely reasons, sadism, poses a serious danger to the integrity and lives of others, i.e., it can reasonably increase the likelihood of actions that infringe on the rights of others, actions such as murder and rape, something that an antipaternalistic conception cannot allow.[27] Therefore, I do not in principle believe that organising and conducting spectacles like gladiator fights or Rollerball events should be allowed, not least because violent films can equally effectively sublimate the frustrations of spectators, assuming empirically that that is how things work, whereas it would undoubtedly be possible to play sports professionally, for pay and entertainment, even very dangerous ones, like car or motorcycle racing, circus acrobatics, boxing, and wrestling, that do not translate into actual bloodbaths or gratuitous violence, as far as that is actually the case.[28]

[27] This is a point on which Feinberg (1994, pp. 54–55) insists.

[28] I do not believe that forms of "violent" pornography would have the same effects as a spectacle of real violence. The reason is that in the case of fiction, a part of the viewer, a part of their self or ego, knows that what they are seeing is not "real," that no one is actually being raped or whipped. Indeed, its cathartic value could be precisely this. Even though the viewer, or their superego, knows that what they are seeing is not real, and so that no immoral or illegal action is actually being committed, another (unconscious?) part of their ego sublimates in what they see the weeks or years of abuse suffered at the hands of a boss or mother-in-law, fantasizing about doing something unedifying to their tormentors. In fact, there are four kinds of "violent" pornography. The first is videos in which a woman is raped and is seen in the video enjoying the rape: this is a small minority of the pornographic videos on the web (YouPorn or RedTube). This is the real *violent* pornography. A second kind of violent pornography *are fiction videos* of sadomasochistic sex, including violent ones, in which one is willingly bound and whipped to a bloody pulp or in which hot wax is thrown on the genitals, and this is a very tiny minority of pornographic video on the free web, almost nonexistent. In these cases, it is clear that the "victim" is consenting and the viewer knows that it is only fiction. A third kind of violent pornography is snuff movies, in which someone is tormented and killed and mutilated against their will: these "productions" are not available on the free web or on cable or satellite TV. Clearly, snuff movies should be prohibited. In any case, for those who, after watching sadomasochistic pornography, might want to experience certain "thrills," there is always the possibility of sadomasochistic clubs, escorts, accommodating girlfriends, or virtual sex. The fourth kind of violent pornography is *real shows* or video recordings of violent sadomasochistic sex sessions, and it could instead be argued that these are equally dangerous, because they could elicit violent impulses in the viewer. If this were the case, I do not think someone of a liberal cast would have particular problems in banning the sale of such recordings and limiting their use to the sadomasochistic club or circle that produced them. In any case, the above applies. One of two things will happen: either the viewer remains inactive, after watching a real sadomasochistic scene, i.e., remains a latent sadomasochist, or the viewer joins the sadomasochistic club located in their city (or the nearest such club). The real difference from gladiator fights is, in this sense, con-

One might object that if rational and competent adults wish to undertake violent and dangerous feats, and also wish to earn from showcasing their talent and courage, why should they not be able to enter into private contracts to receive/offer such performances? Why should spectators not *enjoy* the talent and courage of other human beings? A possible reason for this was discussed earlier. While it is true that spectators can legitimately enjoy a show of talent, as in a fight, or someone's courage, I see no reason why the fight should end with the killing or maiming of the loser, i.e., I do not see what the killing or mutilation of the defeated player has to do with the show of talent, courage, or strength, or with respect for individual autonomy (see Feinberg 1994, pp. 57–58). And the killing/mutilation of the defeated player would be reasonably justifiable, from the spectator's point of view, on the basis of the two reasons identified earlier: sadism/love of violence or sublimation of one's impotence, with the real risk of increasing the likelihood of harm to third parties.[29]

---

siderable. If someone, after watching a sadomasochistic sabbath, wanted to experience certain thrills, they would have a certain probability of finding consenting persons, while the probability of finding someone who, voluntarily, would allow themselves to be mutilated and killed violently is much reduced. There remains the problem of the very violent kind of pornography, in which a girl enjoys being raped. According to some studies of Malamuth, for 2–3 weeks the belief that a girl enjoys of a rape remains in the minds of Malamuth students who watched this kind of video. In these cases, there should be a further experiment in which at the beginning and the end of the video, a prominently displayed message appears saying "Real women do not enjoy rape." I believe that the belief about women enjoying rape would not in this case arise.

[29] With the analysis just offered of the last difficult case, that of gladiatorial combat, I can also respond to a potential objection: the claim that the thesis I support is inconsistent. Why, in Chap. 3, Sect. 3.3, did I think it irrelevant that a patient, once euthanasia is legalised, might be misunderstood by doctors, while I consider significant the risk of a battered, raped woman retracting her statement in court, exonerating her violent husband? Why did I find irrelevant the risk of unscrupulous doctors persuading lonely and fragile patients to request euthanasia? Why is the risk of unintended harm to others relevant in prohibiting voluntary contracts of slavery, violence on (presumed) consenting women, and gladiatorial fights but not in prohibiting euthanasia? This is a matter of consistency and scientific objectivity. The difference is as follows. If the risk of unintended harm to others is medium to high, rationally or scientifically grounded in statistical probabilistic research, consistent with other legally relevant analogous situations, and concerns statistically insignificant desires (as defined earlier in Sect. 5.3), then it makes sense to take the risk into account. If the risk of unintended harm to others is low, statistically or scientifically unfounded or very doubtful, and/or inconsistent with other legally relevant situations, and concerns statistically more frequent desires, this probably means that some authors consider it significant for specious reasons. For instance, it is known that a certain percentage of seriously ill or terminal patients (in conditions of rationality and freedom from coercion) desire to request euthanasia, whereas it is very likely that only very few people (rational and free from coercion) would want to enter into a contract of slavery, be continuously abused by their spouse, fight as gladiators, and be killed in case of defeat in a fight to the death. Equally insignificant, as we saw Chap. 3, Sect. 3.3, is the risk that a sufficiently rational patient is "misunderstood" when stating their wish (or lack thereof) to authorise their doctor to assist in their suicide. The risk of being "killed" by doctors seeking to save on hospital costs may be exaggerated in some of the literature, but is a real risk nonetheless, even if euthanasia is not legalised. However, it is a risk that can be neutralised within certain limits. The risk that a patient requests assisted suicide because they are fragile and not sufficiently loved by their relatives is indeed very concrete and realistic. For reasons of consistency, however, not being

5.8.1 *Duff, Violent Sadomasochism and the European Court of Human Rights*

In conclusion, Anthony Duff, like other authors, uses examples of this kind, such as fights to the death between gladiators, in an attempt to weaken an antipaternalistic conception and to question the importance of individual autonomy (cf. Duff 2001, p. 31ff.). According to Duff, outside the hypothesis where the gladiators' consent is vitiated by irrationality or coercion, or the hypothesis where the viewing of such spectacles significantly increases the risk of harm to third parties (homicide, battery, abuse), which hypotheses the author evidently does not consider founded, an antipaternalistic doctrine should, for reasons of consistency, allow such spectacles to be organised. Alternatively, if an antipaternalist wanted to prohibit them, he or she would have to grant their (theoretical) failure. The only way to prohibit such activities, says Duff, is to recognise that they offer an inhumane and degrading spectacle, one that humiliates and degrades those who participate in it, just like violent practices carried out in sadomasochistic clubs (but which do not involve the killing or mutilation of any participant) (see Duff 2001, p. 39ff.). The practices that unfold in such clubs, according to Duff, should also be prohibited. What has been said so far show not only how unconvincing Duff's argument is, but also how fallacious it is.

There are three aspects that Duff fails to consider. First, as I mentioned in Chap. 2, Duff does not take into account that there is a significant difference between cases like euthanasia, extreme sports, and riding a motorcycle without a helmet and cases where an agent binds themself, in return for payment, under a voluntarily signed contract, to participate in a violent fight or a fight to the death. The difference is that committing to an antipaternalistic doctrine, contrary to certain libertarian or perfectionist conceptions, does not logically imply preferring the agent's prior will over their current will. As I said in Sect. 5.1, forcing people to always keep their commitments or promises protects, perhaps, a virtue, such as integrity, or the interests of those who profit from such spectacles. Forcing people to always keep their promises is not an implication of antipaternalism (even if it is, in some cases, compatible with it), nor do I believe it is always morally justified. Antipaternalism protects the agent's current wishes (except for advance directives). Therefore, according to a strictly antipaternalistic and liberal egalitarian conception, the defeated gladiator should be allowed to choose between death and exiting the scene. If, in fact, the defeated gladiator, about to be killed, pleads for mercy, as would happen in 99% of cases (except for the few who would want to die with "honour"), this means that their current wish is not to be killed, and on the basis of the value of individual autonomy, this wish must prevail over the prior wish expressed at the time the contract is signed. If the other gladiator kills them anyway, this does not mean respecting the autonomy or wishes of the defeated gladiator. It means committing a murder. And I have no doubt that 99% of defeated gladiators would choose to exit the scene.

sufficiently loved is not a condition that can reasonably be considered to "vitiate" someone's will, for otherwise the execution of many human actions should be prevented.

Anyone with a minimal survival instinct, when forced to choose between death and the end of their career as a gladiator—considering that it is evident that no one would offer them contracts of this kind anymore, having failed to honour previous commitments—would choose the latter option.

Indeed, I would be concerned about the psychological state of a gladiator who ultimately chooses to be killed. Such a choice would amount to a veritable suicide, which, according to the antipaternalism defended here, should not be the result of a decision made under conditions of severe physical or psychological weakness (due to wounds and defeat), amid bloodthirsty and baying crowds, but should be a choice made in more serene, rational conditions, free from coercive pressures (unless the will to commit suicide had been explicitly ascertained beforehand). However, if defeated gladiators were allowed to choose between death and bowing out, I believe that would signify the end of such spectacles, as no one would pay to watch a show that almost *never ends* in the only way that would justify the ticket price. Alternatively, the producers of such shows would be required to refund part of the ticket. By prioritising the earlier wish of the defeated gladiator, a wish expressed when signing the contract, we would not be enabling a violent show with fully consenting participants. We would be protecting, in 99% of cases where the current wish of the defeated gladiator is contrary, the interests of those profiting from these shows (producers and victorious gladiators) and the morbidity of the spectators. We would be sacrificing the value of human life on the altar of profit, the most brutal capitalist exploitation, and sadism. History seems to offer clues that point in the same direction. Did gladiatorial fights in ancient Rome not thrive precisely because the defeated gladiator was not given another choice, precisely because the defeated gladiator could not retreat unharmed after being defeated? This is not surprising, considering many gladiators were slaves, prisoners of war, or, from a certain point onward, Christians sent to slaughter.

Secondly, Duff overlooks another important aspect of history, one highlighted in Chap. 2. If the gladiators' union, despite numerous battles, fails to modify certain contractual clauses imposed by the producers of such spectacles, despite the majority of gladiators demanding it, clauses which entail that the spectacle should end with the killing of the defeated, or clauses which impose severe economic penalties on defeated gladiators who decide to withdraw "dishonourably," the consent of the gladiators could be considered vitiated, as it was not formed in a manner that was sufficiently free from coercive pressures, where the pressures are those of the market not offering better options to the worker/gladiators—unless, of course, the market offers different options, e.g., compelling spectacles but not to the death, even if they bring in less money.[30] And historically, there were no gladiator unions in ancient Rome.

Thirdly, Duff fails to address an obvious objection to his argument. If we prohibit the staging of very violent or to-the-death fighting shows or violent sadomasochistic

[30] Even Feinberg (1994, p. 58) emphasises that, given the freedom to decide and negotiate, many gladiators and spectators would demand fair fighting rules, excluding killings and mutilations.

practices, because they are inhumane and degrading, why should we not also ban other activities that some people, even entire communities, find equally disgusting and degrading, such as orgies, prostitution, pornography, swinging, or anal or oral sex? "Disgusting," "degrading," and "inhuman" are terms that are almost primarily evaluative in Hare's sense, with widely indeterminate meanings, just like the concept of dignity analysed in Chap. 3. In this sense, Duff appears to be a typical, albeit moderate, paternalist. He mixes metaethical objectivist conceptions with typically paternalistic rhetorical strategies that are fallacious or insufficiently rational, maintaining that engaging in certain behaviours is not (necessarily) contrary to individuals' well-being, happiness, and serenity (as in a certain Aristotelian tradition), but is contrary to our very "nature as humans," our humanity. According to Duff, people who, like gladiators, voluntarily participate in very violent fights during which they can suffer/inflict even mortal injuries, or groups of sadomasochists who voluntarily inflict wounds and injuries on each other through "torture rituals," are treating themselves and other participants in the game like animals, "dehumanising" themselves, harming "the humanity within themselves."[31]

Just like Duff, I fail to grasp how one might find violent, bloodthirsty fighting (even "without the last blood") or sadomasochistic torture enjoyable, exhilarating, or pleasurable, whether as a spectator or as a participant. The question is why the state should prohibit these kinds of behaviour through the use of force. Is it sufficient that they be considered "inhuman" or "degrading" by the majority of the community? Underneath this fallacious or insufficiently rational rhetorical strategy ("the humanity in ourselves"), Duff conceals the utilitarian/organicist or perfectionist argument he truly espouses, the virtue he really wants people to practice, seeming to hide his prejudices and to not clarify whether he has truly reconciled with his demons.[32] Duff's biases appear evident.

[31] Further evidence supporting my argument is that some authors, such as Kristol, consider pornography "dehumanising." Indeed, the difference between pornography and eroticism, according to many, lies precisely in this: pornography, like any obscene activity, deprives people of their typically human dimension, treating them as sexual beings, not as fully human beings. See Kristol (1994), p. 48; Duff (2001), p. 41.

[32] It is unclear whether Duff has fully confronted his own biases, as it is difficult to discern his degree of "torment" from these prejudices, or how aware he is of them, or whether he is being deliberately opaque to protect his space for public reasoning. At note 81 of "Harms and Wrongs," Duff (2001) acknowledges that the current practice of boxing—with its degree of violence, the physical harm often inflicted, and profit as a fundamental driver, along with the degrading spectacle of shouting crowds wanting to see blood—makes it a borderline case, not so different from the scenario of gladiators killing each other in combat. By *borderline case* he means that it is a liminal case, at the threshold of what can legitimately be prohibited. So if Duff is almost willing to even prohibit violent, lucrative boxing, what would be the analogy with violent sadomasochistic practices that should also be banned? Is there a principle that can make Duff's arguments and examples coherent? I offer a conjecture. The way Duff describes the practice of duelling or jousting, where gentlemen or aristocrats of bygone eras fought to defend their honour or show their courage; the fervour with which he condemns male homosexual masochistic practices; and his criticisms of a sports world that only follows money and profit—all these things suggest a perfectionist, tentatively communitarian morality with Victorian echoes, male chauvinist, but not liberal. This moral-

Just like the House of Lords in a 1993 ruling, and the European Court of Human Rights in a famous 1997 decision,[33] Duff posits a significant difference, probably incoherent, between a club of sadomasochists who inflict serious but nonpermanent wounds on each other—injuries that are significant but not lasting, healable within weeks at most—and fighters in boxing and wrestling who under the rules governing these sports inflict medically comparable injuries, if not more serious ones, and quite easily at that: in the case of boxing fights there are cases of boxers losing an eye, or their hearing, or falling into a coma, or having their jaw and ribs broken, or even collapsing and dying. None of this happens normally with sadomasochistic rituals. Why fighters in boxing and wrestling, under the rules governing these sports, could inflict medically comparable injuries, if not more serious ones, and sadomasochists could not inflict serious but nonpermanent wounds on each other—injuries that are significant but not lasting, healable within weeks at most?

However, the nature of this distinction remains unexplained and therefore incoherent. Why are sadomasochists behaving like "animals" while boxers and wrestlers are not? Is there a prejudice concerning the homosexuality of the sadomasochists in question, a misogynistic prejudice under which the "virility" and (supposed) bravery of the fighters is extolled, all the while condemning the (supposed) weakness or "perverse" pleasure of others? Is it a prejudice about the taboo of libertine

ity centres on "manly values" such as physical strength, courage, and martial virtues in combat; the need to protect the family, country, and personal honour; and fighting or competition (without gratuitous or excessive violence) as realms where these virtues are tested, where anyone can prove their worth, strength, or bravery (see Duff 2001, pp. 39–40). However, an ironic sadomasochist might reply to Duff: Yes, it takes courage to participate in a wrestling or boxing match. But it also takes courage (and physical endurance) to whip and be whipped to blood with a cat-o'-nine-tails, or to pour hot wax on one's one genitals or have it poured by others. (On these disturbing practices see Green 2001). Nor can it be said—the ironic sadomasochist might continue—that sadomasochists are the only ones who enjoy their activity. Some wrestlers, boxers, and free-climbing enthusiasts also find great pleasure in what they do (despite the pain, physical effort, and fatigue).

[33] The case Duff refers to is the following. In 1987, in Britain, during a police search, video tapes were found showing sadomasochistic gatherings attended by 44 British citizens over time. These were (homo)sexual meetings during which various kinds of suffering were inflicted, either barehanded or with various instruments, often on the genitals, or through flagellation rituals that at most culminated in healable wounds. All these activities were freely conducted in private and with the consent of the victims, all of whom were adults, and apparently for no other purpose than sexual pleasure. There were various charges. The most significant was that of voluntary injury (*coups et blessures*, "assault occasioning actual bodily harm") under a British law of 1861. All three of the main defendants, M. Laskey, M. M. Jaggard, and Brown, were convicted at trial and then on appeal. Equally unsuccessful was their appeal to the House of Lords, which in 1993—the judgement cited by Duff—denied, in particular, that consent could be considered a justification in the case of injuries inflicted during sadomasochistic practices. Finally, when brought before the European Court of Human Rights, the case was decided by the Court on 19 February 1997, which dismissed the appeal brought by Laskey and the other defendants, upholding the previous rulings and conviction. See "Laskey, Jaggard, et Brown c. Royame-Uni," *Recueil des arrêts et décisions de la Cour Européenne des droits de l'homme*, 1997/I; *R v Brown* [1993] UKHL 19, [1994] 1 AC 212; and Green (2001).

sexual pleasure? It is unclear. Perhaps the answer lies in the puritanical tradition that may underpin such prejudices, but I will not delve deeper into the matter.

In conclusion, it is entirely consistent, from an antipaternalistic standpoint, to prohibit shows involving gladiators fighting, maiming, and killing each other, this for three reasons. Firstly, similarly to the case of slavery contracts, these are "statistically negligible cases", activities that very few rational and uncoerced individuals would desire to engage in. Therefore, according to a strictly antipaternalistic and liberal egalitarian conception, the defeated gladiator should be allowed to choose between death and exiting the scene. If, in fact, the defeated gladiator, about to be killed, pleads for mercy, as would happen in 99% of cases (except for the few who would want to die with "honour"), this means that their current wish is not to be killed, and on the basis of the value of individual autonomy, this wish must prevail over the prior wish expressed at the time the contract was signed. If the other gladiator kills them anyway, this does not mean respecting the autonomy or will of the defeated gladiator. It means committing murder. We protect the current wishes of the gladiator, not the wish set forth in the contract, by inserting an *ad nutum* (at will) termination clause in the contract, as we would with slavery contracts.

The bureaucratic procedure for ascertaining whether the gladiators' consent is rational, informed, and uncoerced is excessively costly for the state's administrative agencies. Also, as we have seen, the public officials tasked with these verification procedures would need to be highly paid, and the procedures themselves would have to be conducted correctly and impartially, and with various oversight mechanisms, to prevent wealthy and powerful multinationals from exploiting the situation.

Secondly, it is right to prohibit such shows if, and to the extent that, it is ascertained that watching these shows would significantly increase the risk of harm to third parties by promoting violence and sadism. Thirdly, these would generally be contracts between private parties, where we should always protect the current will of the defeated gladiator, making such shows likely unprofitable for their organizers.[34] That is, it would be unlikely that anyone would want to produce such shows.

[34] It must be said, in fairness, that most of these objections do not apply to a TV game where participants play Russian roulette. In this case, the agent's current wish would always be protected. If participants in the game have already pressed the trigger five times in a six-shot magazine, and there is one remaining lethal bullet, it is likely that the agent would decide to quit the game, that is, choose not to commit suicide (unless the purpose of participating in the game was to commit suicide on live TV). And it is likely that he or she would be forced to leave the game, while if there are two or more than two chances of pressing the trigger with only one lethal bullet, the agent can choose to risk and continue playing. If the participant in the game decides to continue playing and dies, there would be no murder, nor can it be said that those watching the show derive sadistic pleasure, because, strictly speaking, in this show no one kills or mutilates anyone else: there is no violence perpetrated by anyone on anyone else. Rather, this would be tantamount to witnessing a live suicide, both terrible and distressing, but certainly less violent than the gladiator spectacle. One could point out the viewers' terrible cynicism, their indifference, but that would not be much different from that which many people feel towards African tragedies, nor do I believe that such indifference would greatly increase the risk that viewers commit homicides or abuse after watching the game. Nor do I believe there would be the problem of the coercive pressures of the market as

There would therefore be a presumption of nonvoluntariness, not only with respect to potential gladiators but also with respect to potential producers of these shows.

References

Adolfi L et al (2011) Il costo di essere donna: Indagine sul femmicidio in Italia; i dati del 2010. Casa delle Donne per Non Subire Violenza, Bologna. http://www.ristretti.it/commenti/2011/luglio/pdf2/ricerca_femminicidi.pdf

Alexy R (2001) Teoría de los derechos fundamentales. Translated into Castilian by E. Garzón Valdés. Centro de Estudios Constitucionales, Madrid

Archard D (1990) Freedom not to be free: the case of the slavery contract in J. S. Mill's on liberty. Philos Q 40:161ff

Arneson RJ (1980) Mill versus paternalism. Ethics 90(4):470–489

Austin LM, Klimchuk D (eds) (2014) Private law and the rule of law. Oxford University Press, Oxford

Bartoli C (2008) La teoria della subalternità e il caso dei dalit in India. Catanzaro, Rubbettino

---

in the case of workers/gladiators, because most participants in Russian roulette would be "ordinary people" trying their luck to win millions on live TV. Unlike with fighting, no particular physical skills are needed to play Russian roulette. This would not be a "profession" like that of gladiators. The only reason to ban such shows would be the first. The procedure by which to ascertain the fulfillment of the wishes of the participants in the game would be, for the aforementioned reasons, very costly, and would therefore entail (economic) damage to the community. Nor, obviously, as we know, could the costs of the procedure be covered by the organizers of the show or by the aspiring game participants who end up winning (because this would mean that the salary of the officials who ascertain the fulfillment of the consent requirements would always depend on the same TV production system, and this would entail significant risks). And yet the case seems particularly difficult because I have the impression that, unlike with contracts of slavery, there would be many more people who (rationally and independently of constraints) would want to participate in the game and risk. It is historically a known fact that during phases of recession and economic depression, there is an increase in suicides, suicides by people who have lost their property or job, and so their only source of income. In any case, there would need to be an empirical, statistical investigation to ascertain how many people would normally want to participate in similar shows in exchange for the possibility of winning large sums of money. I think that many participants in these shows would be depressed, in which case this participation would be not allowed. Even if it were allowed to organize, participate, and watch such a TV show—something that I do not believe an antipaternalist (for reasons of consistency) should necessarily accept—based on what was said earlier, it would be a game visible only on encrypted, not generalist, channels, but with individual shows that can be purchased, with special codes, for a fee, to prevent minors from viewing the same shows (as happens, on cable or satellite TV, in the case of pornographic films). This, together with the absence of a large live audience, as is inevitable on TV shows, could perhaps make such shows less convenient than other shows for those who produce them, being shows that would not be watched by millions of viewers, like certain football matches in stadiums. But I would not bet my money on this. After witnessing on TV long lines of Sunday tourists who, in Italy, out of curiosity, voyeurism, and morbidity, went to visit the places where an "ogre uncle" confessed to having barbarously killed his fifteen-year-old niece (perhaps with the complicity of his daughter), I should think that it is possible that there are few things that some so-called "good" people would not be capable of doing (outside of killing, raping, or abusing anyone, of course), including enjoying the game of Russian roulette on TV.

Becker GS, Elias JJ (2014) Cash for kidneys: the case for a market for organs. Wall Street J 18:2014. http://online.wsj.com/article/SB10001424052702304149404579322560004817176.html?reflink=desktopwebshare_permalink
Bigliazzi GL et al (eds) (1986) Diritto civile. Vol. 1, Norme, soggetti e rapporto giuridico. Turin, UTET
Celano B (2007) L'eguaglianza nella cultura giuridico-politica occidentale moderna: Una mappa concettuale. In: Squarcini F (ed) Mai praticamente uguali: Studi e ricerche sulla disuguaglianza e sull'inferiorità nelle tradizioni religiose. Società Editrice Fiorentina, Florence, pp 11–43
Cian G, Trabucchi A (2001) Commentario breve al Codice civile: Complemento giurisprudenziale. Padua, CEDAM
Creazzo G et al (1999) Maltrattate in famiglia: Suggerimenti alle donne che si rivolgono ai servizi sociosanitari. Casa delle Donne per non Subire Violenza, Bologna. https://www.casadonne.it/wp-content/uploads/2014/04/manuale2medici992.pdf
De Concini E et al (2005) Violenza assistita, violenza vissuta: La violenza domestica assistita dai bambini. Seminar proceedings, Bologna, 21 January 2005. Casa delle Donne per Non Subire Violenza, Bologna. https://www.casadonne.it/wp-content/uploads/2008/01/minori_seminario_210105.pdf
Del Frate N et al (2009) Prevenzione e intervento sul maltrattamento e sulla violenza sessuale. Casa delle Donne per Non Subire Violenza, Bologna. https://www.casadonne.it/cosa-facciamo/progetti/prevenzione-e-intervento-sul-maltrattamento-e-sulla-violenza-sessuale/
Del Giudice F (2015) Manuale di diritto ecclesiastico: Chiese, culti e religioni nell'ordinamento italiano, 16th edn. Naples, Edizioni Giuridiche Simone
Del Giudice F et al (2015) Manuale di diritto del lavoro, 33rd edn. Edizioni Simone, Naples
Diciotti E (2006) Il mercato delle libertà. il Mulino, Bologna
Duff RA (2001) Harms and wrongs. Buffalo Criminal Law Rev 5(1):13–45. https://doi.org/10.1525/nclr.2001.5.1.13
Feinberg J (1986) Harm to self. Vol. 3 of the moral limits of the criminal law. Oxford University Press, Oxford
Feinberg J (1994) Harmless wrongdoing. In: Dworkin G (ed) Morality, harm, and the law. Westview Press, Boulder
Ferrajoli L (2001) Diritti fondamentali. In: Vitale E (ed) Diritti fondamentali: Un dibattito teorico. Laterza, Rome and Bari
Fornero G (2020) Indisponibilità e disponibilità della vita. Una difesa filosofico giuridica del suicidio assistito e dell'eutanasia volontaria. Utet, Torino
Gamberini A (2007) La rete con i servizi pubblici: Le forze dell'ordine. Proceedings of the seminar Lavorare in rete con le forze dell'ordine. Casa delle Donne per Non Subire Violenza, Bologna. https://www.casadonne.it/wp-content/uploads/2013/03/gamberini_lavorare_in_rete_12_settembre_2007.pdf
Green R (2001) (Serious) sadomasochism: a protected right of privacy? Arch Sex Behav 30(5):543–550
Holmes S, Sunstein CS (1999) The cost of rights: why liberty depends on taxes. Norton, New York
Hoyle C, Sanders A (2000) Police response to domestic violence: from victim choice to victim empowerment? Br J Criminol 40(1):14–36
ISTAT (2015) La violenza contro le donne dentro e fuori la famiglia. Press release, Italian Ministry for Rights and Equal Opportunity Survey, 5 June 2015. https://www.istat.it/it/archivio/161716
Jori M (2001) Aporie e problemi nella teoria dei diritti fondamentali. In: Vitale E (ed) Diritti fondamentali: Un dibattito teorico. Laterza, Rome
Khan U (2015) Sadomasochism in sickness and in health: competing claims from science, social science, and culture. Curr Sex Health Rep 7:49–58. https://doi.org/10.1007/s11930-014-0039-1
Kristol I (1994) Pornography, obscenity and the case for censorship. In: Dworkin G (ed) Morality, harm, and the law. Westview Press, Boulder
Maniaci G (2020) ¿Incentivos económicos a la cesión de órganos entre vivos? Doxa: Cuadernos de Filosofía del Derecho 43:341–368

Maniaci G (2022) Argomenti pro e contro: La legalizzazione della gestazione per altri. Diritto e Questioni Pubbliche 2:137–166
Marshall TH (1950) Citizenship and social class. In: Citizenship and social class and other essays. Cambridge University Press, Cambridge. Chap. 1
Mill JS (1971) On liberty (1859). In: Robson JM (ed) Vol. 18 of collected works. Routledge & Kegan Paul, London, pp 213–310
Perritt HH Jr (2017) Employee dismissal law and practice. Wolters Kluwer, New York
Pino G (2010) Diritti e interpretazione. il Mulino, Bologna
Rescigno P (ed) (1982) Trattato di diritto privato. Vol. 2, Persone e famiglia. Tome 1. UTET, Turin
Romanin A (2011) Vittime ad alto rischio: Due progetti europei per il triennio 2010–2012. In: Karadole C, Pramstrahler A (eds) Femicidio: Dati e riflessioni intorno ai delitti per violenza di genere. Casa delle Donne per Non Subire Violenza, Bologna. https://www.casadonne.it/wp-content/uploads/2014/04/femicidio_pdf1.pdf
Scarpelli U (1998) Bioetica laica. Baldini & Castoldi, Milan
Schiavello A, Trujillo I (eds) (2000) Ragion pratica 14, special issue on social rights and rights to liberty
Sunstein CR (2001) Human behavior and the law of work. Va Law Rev 87(2):205–276
Vaver D (ed) (2006) Intellectual property rights: critical concepts in law. Routledge, London
Zaller A (2010) What labor code requirements can employees waive? California Employment Law Report 19
Zaller A (2015) Five Legal Concepts Every California Employer Needs to Understand. California Employment Law Report, 17

Chapter 6
The Concept of Harm in John Stuart Mill's and Feinberg's Harm Principle

6.1 Harm Principle and the Concept of Protected Legal Interest as a Principle of Criminalization

The concept of harm is central to a liberal or antipaternalistic view, like the conception put forward by John Stuart Mill,[1] with respect to justifying the use of criminal coercion. One of the foundational theses of antipaternalism is the idea that the exclusive or principal reason why the state can use coercion is to prevent harm to others. The other thesis, in brief, is that antipaternalism protects the autonomy, or sovereignty over mind and body, of rational individuals who are sufficiently free from coercive pressures. In Chap. 2 we defined the concept of *moderate legal antipaternalism*. This is the ethical political conception according to which the state, or an agent authorized by the state, does not have the right to use coercion against the wishes of an adult individual solely or primarily to prevent that individual, through action or omission, from causing what is regarded as a significant harm to themselves or from risking such harm, such as physical, psychophysical, or economic harm (thus undercutting their own good), if it is certain or likely that the wishes of this adult individual to engage in dangerous and/or harmful activities has been formed rationally, in a state of mental capacity, on the basis of a knowledge of the relevant facts, stably over time, and in a manner sufficiently free from coercive pressures. Even more so, the state obviously cannot limit the freedom of the individual if the action they wish to perform causes no harm to themselves. As already mentioned, according to the moderate antipaternalism expounded here, if the individual's consent is not, in the specified sense, vitiated, their freedom of action can be limited, through coercion, only if it causes harm to others. This is the famous *Harm to Others Principle* developed by John Stuart Mill.

---

[1] On the concept of harm in Mill's *On Liberty*, see Tincani (2009), Ten (1980).

G. Maniaci, *The Unbearable Lightness of Legal Antipaternalism*, Law and Philosophy Library 151, https://doi.org/10.1007/978-3-031-96844-0_6

What is the importance, from a philosophical legal perspective, of the harm principle? The fundamental importance of the harm principle is that, in criminal law, it can give sense and content to the concept of *protected legal interest, as a principle of criminalization*,[2] according to which an act can be deemed criminal only if it violates a legally recognized interest (a constitutionally protected interest or at least one that is not incompatible with the Constitution), the idea being that there can be no criminally punishable harm where there is no legally protected interest. This reconstruction of the harm principle is a way to specify, within in a liberal ethic, the concept of criminally protected legal interest, as a principle of criminalization, which, as is known, has a wide margin of indeterminacy. The harm principle can thus serve as a hermeneutic interpretive criterion for arguing in favour of or against a strict or broad reading of criminal statutes, and even more importantly it can be used to constrain lawmakers drafting legislation establishing whether some act is to be deemed criminal as an act that harms an interest worthy of protection. According to many authors, the concept of criminally protected legal interest is fundamental under international criminal law (see footnote 2) and can be derived from various constitutional provisions, such as Articles 13 and 25 of the Italian Constitution, and it is deemed a fundamental constraint on lawmakers, such that the Constitutional Court should declare the unconstitutionality of criminal statutes that conflict with the harm principle.

But what does *harm* mean? What is the correct interpretation of this principle? After analyzing various types of harm, after evaluating which harms are or are not relevant from the standpoint of a fully liberal ethic, I will show why the criticisms that Arthur Ripstein, Ronald Dworkin, and others levy against the harm principle fail to hit the mark.

Actions that concern ourselves only (self-regarding actions), and so actions that can cause harm only to ourselves, must be distinguished from actions that cause harm to others, from actions that harm the interests of others (other-regarding

---

[2] Cf. Alexander and Kimberly Kessler (2008); Gómez Lanz (2023); Eser (1965); Atadjanov (2019); Altman (2012); Ambos (2013); Ambos (2014); Ambos (2015); Boot (2002); Cassese (2003); Fleck (2008); Bergsmo et al. (2022a); Bergsmo et al. (2022b); Tianying (2022); Nakhjavani and Mirzaagha (2022); Motilewa Quadri et al. (2022); Stella (1973), p. 3ff.; Gallo (1969), esp. p. 8ff.; Bricola (1973), p. 14ff., 82ff.; Musco (1974), p. 55ff. (chap. 2); Mantovani (1977), p. 445ff.; Mantovani (1996), p. 91ff., 99; Vassalli (1982), p. 629ff.; Zagrebelsky (1982), p. 417ff.; Pulitanò (1985), p. 134ff.; Fiorella (1987), p. 793ff.; Ferrajoli (1989); Insolera (1990), p. 726ff.; Patrono (1993); Fiandaca (1991) p. 61ff.; Fiandaca (2001), p. 5, 7–9; Fiandaca (2003), p. 203ff.; Fiore (1994), p. 278ff.; Fiore (1998), p. 274ff.; Dolcini and Marinucci (1994), p. 333ff.; Moccia (1995), p. 343ff.; Neppi Modona (1996), p. 259ff.; Donini (1996), p. 18ff., 25ff., 45–46, 117ff., 140ff.; Donini (1999), pp. 267–75; Donini (2002), p. 111ff.; Donini (2003), esp. pp. 90–100; Donini (2008), p. 1546ff., 1552ff.; Mazzacuva (1997), p. 75ff., 83ff.; Palazzo (1996), p. 74; Palazzo (1998), p. 350ff.; Cavaliere (1998), p. 133ff.; Grosso et al. (2000), p. 103ff.; Manes (2002), p. 720ff.; Manes (2005), p. 129ff., 209ff.; Manes (2012), p. 99ff.; Manna (2002), p. 35ff.; Valenti (2003), p. 953ff.; Valenti (2012), p. 359ff.; Neppi Modona (2004), p. 89ff.; Caterini (2004); Riondato (2005), p. 96ff., 117ff.; Catenacci (2006), p. 1415ff.; Vinciguerra (2006), p. 2:2077ff.; Zuccalà (2004), p. 1:791ff.; Zuccalà (1984); Fiore (2006), p. 91ff.; Merli (2006), p. 283ff.; Romano (2011), p. 33ff.

actions). Conversely, an antipaternalistic conception is inapplicable. The concept of harm is clearly descriptive and prescriptive in nature, or secondarily evaluative. As Fiandaca notes, "the notion of 'harm' [...] is neither purely conceptual nor purely empirical; it is instead a notion deeply imbued with value judgments" (Fiandaca (2010), p. 225, my translation). It is therefore a notion that has an inevitable normative evaluative dimension, as well as a factual one, insofar as it is not a semantically "empty" concept. There are clearly entities, facts, and events that cannot be qualified as "harm" (a house, a chair, lightning, a fish). Just as easily, one can imagine paradigmatic cases of actions that concern only the acting agent, without harming the interests of others. An example would be the sadomasochistic sex practiced by a John Doe, a wealthy person, at his home, unknown to relatives, friends, and neighbours. It is, in fact, a practice that satisfies an interest of John Doe; that causes him bodily injuries that will take at most two weeks heal; and that is highly unlikely to cause any economic, physical, or psychophysical harm, or any emotional stress, to other nonconsenting agents. The medical expenses for treating such injuries are, in fact, always borne personally by John Doe. A paradigmatic case of an action that harms the interests of others could, of course, be killing, robbing, or kidnapping another individual. However, there are some cases where the answer is not so straightforward.

What, then, is the preferable notion of "harm"? Obviously, there are different possible definitions of "harm," as well as different definitional strategies, some of which are wrong. First, does it make sense to develop a completely "subjective" concept of harm? An entirely subjective definition of *harm* rigorously applies the principle *Volenti non fit iniuria* ("To a willing person, it is not a injury"), according to which, if a person performs an action that permanently modifies their body in a way considered dysfunctional by the majority of people, and does so on the basis of a rational and uncoerced will, there is no actual harm. For example, it would make no sense to say, on the basis of a completely "subjective" definition of harm, that John Doe, by blinding himself, has caused "physical harm" to himself. It would make no sense because, in this scenario, it was his interest to blind himself: the act satisfied his rational preferences. If one argues that physical or economic harm is a subclass of harm in general, and that John Doe has caused no "harm" to himself, because the result, that is, his blindness, was consistent with his will, then one must logically conclude that there can be no physical harm in John Doe's case.

I do not believe that such a definition is appropriate, even if it is logically possible, because it is somewhat counterintuitive and too far removed from ordinary language. The meaning of concepts like "harm" and "need" historically depends on the most widespread desires and interests among human beings, namely, the interests in survival, maintaining bodily integrity, and health. In this sense, there is no reason to modify how these terms are most commonly used. It makes perfect sense to assert that John Doe, by blinding himself, has done *physical harm* to himself, even if he did so voluntarily and rationally, because the concept of physical harm is partly "objectified" (objective) and refers to a lesion, a permanent alteration of the body that prevents one from performing a function that for centuries has been considered as fundamental by the vast majority of humans.[3] This does not mean, of course, that John Doe should not have the right to blind himself, if he so wishes. It must be added that, in reality, severe self-mutilation is sometimes the result of a personality or mental disorder described by psychiatrists. Obviously, the change in values and customs also changes how words are used, so I would never claim that someone who has changed their sex, permanently altering their body, has caused "permanent harm" to themselves.

In other contexts, however, the concept of harm is inevitably subjective, meaning that it is dependent on the agent's preferences and interests. For example, someone who gambles a million euros at a casino and loses it all could be said to have suffered an economic loss, because (in a certain sense) that happened against their will. However, we would not say that a person who donates the same amount to a religious cult or creed, like Opus Dei or evangelicalism, has suffered an "economic loss," even though we might think the money gambled and lost at the casino (or thrown out the window for passersby) could have been used more wisely.

Given that the concept of harm has different layers, one of which is certainly "objective," a second problem arises. Joel Feinberg's strategy, and that of other authors, is to provide a very vague, indeterminate definition of "harm." On the other hand, in line with a liberal ethical and political conception, they argue that the state may use coercion not only to prevent harm to others but also to prevent certain offences against individuals. In particular, Feinberg distinguishes *hurts* (such as hyperactivity, fatigue, insomnia, weakness, tension, or feeling too hot or cold); *offences* (unpleasant mental states, such as irritation, frustration, disgust, embarrassment, anxiety, guilt, anger, shame, remorse, regret, or boredom, caused by someone's wrongful conduct); and true *harms* (such as physical, psychophysical, or economic harm). Both hurts and offences are unpleasant, painful mental states, but they are not true harms unless they are prolonged experiences that occur intensely and continuously. The "offences" to nonconsenting others that Feinberg believes could be prohibited by criminal law are those that are serious and are caused by someone's wrongful conduct, and they relate to the disgust, shame, embarrassment that we feel (or some feel) due to certain behaviors engaged in by others (intentionally urinating or vomiting in public, having sex in the street) (see Feinberg (1984a), p. 45ff.; 1985, 2ff.).

So, what how do Feinberg and others define *harm*?

Harm is defined as "the wrongful setback to a person's interest or rights deemed worth protecting" (see Feinberg (1984b), p. 36ff.; Spena (2010); Duff (2001), p. 17ff.). This definition of *harm* is not wrong, but it is too vague, leading to the risk of falling into paternalism, whether utilitarian in nature, considering a "harm" to be an injury to what the majority considers a socially relevant interest, or perfectionist, where what is relevant is the interest in a "proper flourishing" of the human being devoted a life of integrity, virtue, and courage. For example, one might consider it

[3] For this reason, it makes sense to assert that someone is a victim of harm even if they are not aware of it or do not see themselves as victims of harm (see Wertheimer (1979), p. 308).

relevant to assert an affective interest—the interest of parents, friends, or partners—in an agent behaving in a way they consider right or correct, a way that does not offend or displease them. Similarly, if an interest deemed worthy of protection were *any* interest an individual considers such, then the interest in not being psychologically harmed by a partner or the interest in living in a virtuous and courageous community could be relevant. But the only correct interpretation of the Mill's and Feinberg's Harm Principle, as we will see, is a principle based on a liberal ethic (cf. Lieberman (2012); Feinberg (1986); Stanton-Ife (2017); Mill (1971)). The harm principle is incompatible with moral perfectionism, the idea that an interest worth protecting is an individual's proper flourishing, in the pursuit of ideals of moral excellence.

Given that it is preferable not to include the "Offence Principle"[4] among the reasons that legitimise a state's use of coercion (though this is not an argument I can make here), the core of the liberal conception is to create a protected space within which an individual can move freely, free from illicit interference by others, be it interference from the state or from private entities. People can be prohibited from defecating, urinating, littering, dumping garbage, dismembering corpses, or intentionally vomiting in public or in public spaces, whether on the streets, on buses, or in the metro, because such actions cause cumulative, aggregative, or incremental harm. A single incident may not cause significant harm or create health hazards, but it can induce nausea, embarrassment, or disgust. However, if practices such as defecating, urinating, littering, dumping garbage, dismembering corpses, or intentionally vomiting in public space or in the streets become widespread—especially among homeless individuals, those who sleep in their cars, people washing car windows on the street, or others who refuse to participate in proper waste disposal—public health problems can arise. Such practices significantly increase the risk of spreading pathogens and bacteria, compounded by the presence of cockroaches and rats in the filth and garbage. This leads to an encroachment on the bodily autonomy of others, which causes psychological harms, who are compelled to come into contact with contaminated materials (vomit, feces, urine, corpses) and/or dirty and dangerous animals and insects (like cockroaches and rats, whose presence causes psychological harm to many people who hate and have fear of them). That is why we utilize sewers to dispose of feces, urine, or vomit, and why we quickly segregate waste in designated containers. Vomiting on a bus generally provokes a similar biological and psychological response, often causing those who witness the act to feel nauseous themselves. A comparable reaction—nausea and vomiting—can occur in response to a coprophagist eating feces from a box on the bus or to a homeless person whose odor is exacerbated by a lack of hygiene. Additionally, playing loud

[4] On the harm principle, the offence principle, and paternalism, see Simester (2005, 2006, 2010, 2011); Simester and von Hirsch (2002, 2006, 2009, 2011); Simester and Sullivan (2007); von Hirsch (1986, 1996, 2000, 2006, 2008a, 2008b); von Hirsch and Neumann (2010); von Hirsch (2010); Simester and Sullivan (2005); von Hirsch and Ashworth (2005); Raz (1987); Persak (2007); Diciotti (1986, 2005); Feinberg (1983, 1994); Dworkin (1983); VanDeVeer (1986); Maniaci (2012); von Hirsch and Simester (2006).

music on a bus or on an apartment overnight causes incremental harm, which may lead to hearing problems or insomnia problems. According to some psychologists, engaging in sexual activities in public can cause existential harm, which interferes with children's bodily and perceptual development. This may lead to recurrent psychological harm or emotional distress in young children, as well as unprotected imitative behavior in adolescents. Such behaviors can result in the transmission of diseases like AIDS or HPV, or in unwanted pregnancies. Specific studies indicate that the exposure of very young children (ages 6-9) to highly sexualized, though not pornographic, material for a very limited time elicits essentially two types of reactions.

On one hand, many children do not fully grasp the meaning of the scenes they observe; on the other hand, many experience discomfort and negative emotions when confronted with such material. It is easy to imagine that these negative emotions can become entrenched, with their intensity potentially increasing if exposure is prolonged or repeated over time.[5]

In male children, who are beginning to develop or have already developed an Oedipal complex, nudism can provoke emotional distress, because the sight of an adult male with a very large penis of their own can be distressing, embarrassing, anxiety-provoking, even castrating.[6] It is clear that sex or nudism in public should only be punished with a fine.

Therefore, it is preferable that this space be as rigorously defined as possible, clarifying what we mean when we talk about harm to others. It is a protected sphere that, more rigorously, and depending on the case, may consist in "protected liberty"—i.e., the conjunction of (a) the granting to the holder a permission to do or not do X (circulate freely or being cared for), with a correlative obligation on other agents, including the state, not to interfere in X (circulating freely or being cared for), and (b) the state's obligation to coercively interfere with those who want to prevent me from doing X or the obligation of the state to give all the public structures and resources necessary to make possible for the holder do X (circulate freely, as in the case of freedom of movement within the state's territory, or being cared for in the case of the right to health)—or it may simply consist in the imposition of an obligation on other individuals, including the state, to refrain from doing X (as in the case of the inviolability of one's home).

For this reason, I will list seven types of harm, sufficiently determined, to assess whether they can be considered grounds for using criminal coercion:

---

[5] Cf. Etzioni (2004), pp. 38–39; Oddone-Paolucci et al. (2000), p. 48ff; Jackson Harris and Barlett (2009). Another very serious risk, especially connected with internet pornography (chat porn sites), is so-called online sexual solicitation, which is when "one person attempts to persuade another person to talk about sex or engage in a sexual activity." Whitaker, Bushman (2009), p. 1055. Thus, the risk is that pre-adolescents will fall prey to dangerous people, such as paedophiles or blackmailers.

[6] Precisely because nudism can cause emotional distress, parents can decide to take their child to a nudist camp and explain to them that there is nothing wrong with nudism. It depends on the parents' upbringing.

(1) *Physical harm.* Injury to life or to physical integrity.
(2) *Psychophysical harm.* An injury to psychophysical health, where the injury is sufficiently continuous over time, examples being severe anxiety disorders, major depression, or bipolar disorder.
(3) *Economic harm.* Injury to a business asset or to the ownership of an asset.
(4) *Existential harm.* Significant interference, i.e., willful interference in the bodily sphere, where the interference is sufficiently continuous over time; significant interference, i.e., willful interference in a person's perceptual sphere, where the interference is sufficiently continuous over time; or interference in the integrity of the person, i.e., in the safety and security of the home or in the right to a name or to identity or in the right of publicity (including reputational damage) or in confidentiality.
(5) *Psychological or mental harm.* Intense mental pain, sufficiently prolonged over time, e.g., over many days or weeks, often accompanied by more or less severe symptoms, such as distress, insomnia, lack of appetite, melancholy, or weakness. This is normally intense pain that follows a bereavement, a serious emotional loss, a debilitating accident, or an illness.
(6) *Relational harm.* Not being esteemed or appreciated in a certain social group, in terms of the quality/quantity of social relations or friendships or of participation in various events, associations, or meetings, such as parties, dinners, trips, or excursions.
(7) Harms, in terms of lost temporal opportunities or resources, which result from violations of the rules of impartiality governing the administrative state or from violations of constitutionally protected residual fundamental rights, provided they are compatible with a liberal egalitarian conception (such as the right to education). For example, John Doe receives a bureaucratic service much later than due because of abuse of office or corruption, or he is unjustly forced to waste time to obtain the same service. If the service is not received or if an agent receives a bureaucratic service that is not due, there could be economic harm—loss of profit in the former case, fiscal harm in the latter.

In addition to the harms identified above, we can also identify mere psychological stress, i.e., the set of unpleasant mental states, normally of short duration (hours or a few days) that an agent experiences when in a situation such as hyperactivity, fatigue, insomnia, weakness, tension, feeling excessively hot or cold, irritation, frustration, disgust, embarrassment, anxiety, guilt, anger, shame, remorse, regret, boredom, displeasure, or envy (in turn, stress can, from a psychological point of view, coincide with some of these negative emotions, such as anxiety, tension, and anger).

Therefore, it is preferable that the space or the sphere in which the individual is sovereign, in which others cannot interfere harming him, be as rigorously defined as possible, clarifying what we mean when we talk about harm to others. It is a protected sphere that, more rigorously, and depending on the case, may consist in three spaces: (1) the mind and the body, the bodily and perceptual sphere; (2) the property, the home, the domicile, the car; (3) the identity, such as name, imagine, honor, reputation, privacy. The right to health, for example, concerns the integrity of life and body.

6.2 So-Called Moral Harm

I have intentionally not included so-called moral harm among the possible harms to others. Why? I will not discuss in depth whether it makes sense to talk about moral harm, meaning by *moral harm* the fact that by performing certain actions, individuals do not "flourish" in the right way or become worse, corrupt, or perverse, because they do not cultivate the virtues, the qualities that could make them better. I will limit myself to some brief observations.[7]

The first aspect to consider is that qualifying moral harm as a possible harm to others largely nullifies the very opposition between paternalism and antipaternalism. If antipaternalism asserts that the state cannot exert force against an individual to prevent them from causing harm to themselves, while it can limit their freedom if they cause harm to others, and if moral harm is also harm to others, practically any limitation of freedom could be allowed. For example, producers, actors, authors, directors, projectionists, distributors, and retail sellers of pornographic films or authors and producers of heavy metal or satanic-music-videos or CDs, could be deemed agents who "cause" the corruption of consumers or increase the likelihood that consumers may suffer *moral harm*, who will corrupt themselves by purchasing the aforementioned merchandise. Thus, if moral harm were a harm to others, according to Mill's theory, the state should be able to intervene through criminal punishment. Even if it were argued that it is consumers, based on their own will, who decide to let themselves be corrupted, this could still be said to be action carried out in concert to commit a crime, the crime of moral corruption or of incitement to corruption. Now, Mill's conception, the liberal conception, was born precisely to prevent the prohibition of such actions, so it makes little sense, as Waldron (1993), p. 126) says, to consider moral harm a harm to others (the same goes for causing moral disproval or disgust in others, which could be considered a type of psychological stress or harm).

However, there are good reasons to think that the concept of moral harm itself, so understood, should be abandoned, because it is in contrast with the results of contemporary psychology, criminology, and sociology. The ancient, but never completely extinct, idea underlying the concept of "moral harm" is that evil or immorality is a sort of "moral disease," an inner disharmony, an imbalance in the individual, like a fracture in the soul of the agent, as D'Agostino and Finnis say in regard to homosexuality; or, according to some even older conceptions, evil or immorality even results from a disharmony in the entire universe of which the individual is a part (as the wizard Merlin says in the movie *Excalibur*, to lie is to murder part of the world). The idea is that criminals cannot be happy, serene, "balanced," or satisfied with themselves (as one of the good fairies in *Sleeping Beauty* says about the evil Maleficent, who, as the good fairy says, will surely be unhappy): they cannot be at peace with themselves, for in committing bad actions, they thereby corrupt themselves, doing harm to themselves.

[7] For more exhaustive arguments, see Feinberg (1984b), p. 66ff; Waldron (1993).

Unfortunately, contemporary criminology shows how such an idea is completely unfounded scientifically. This description of the deranged criminal may apply to a serial killer suffering from severe personality or mental disorders, such as Ed Gein or Jeffrey Dahmer, or to a rapist strongly opposed by the community to which he belongs. But it certainly does not apply to associative forms of crime. From unscrupulous multinationals which pollute the environment and which, in the name of profit, harm the lives, physical integrity, and health of thousands of people in poorer countries, to the mob associations that control the drug-trafficking and prostitution market, the relevant literature speaks of a crime often devoid of remorse or guilt, where perpetrators are not at all "sick" but fully aware and satisfied with their actions. And if criminals are unhappy, anxious, or distressed, they are so not because of remorse or guilt, but because they live in constant fear of being killed or injured by rival gangs, betrayed by false friends, or arrested by law enforcement. Not only that, corrupt lawyers and board members, unscrupulous financial speculators, "godfathers" of various kinds, or mob killers—these people can often be, in private, excellent fathers, affectionate husbands, caring uncles, and kind neighbors. That such a conception no longer makes any sense is also demonstrated by the fact that even in contemporary ordinary language, where changes occur very slowly, the expression "moral disease" or "moral harm" is very rarely used in this sense (moral harm, for example, is used by Italian lawmakers and judges in the sense of psychological harm).

A proponent of the idea of moral harm might object that this idea makes sense even if criminals suffer no "perceptible" negative consequence, no "empirically" psychologically verifiable corruption as a result of their wickedness, even if the corruption does not translate into any (vaguely) observable data, such as unhappiness, sadness, pain, imbalance, lack of psychophysical well-being or anguish (except for the occurrence of the very behavior that is considered corrupt). This is because criminal or immoral persons cause a "harm" to themselves simply because, in any case, they harm an interest *of their own*, for example, the interest in not exploiting prostitutes or not engaging in oral sex. And it does not matter how much the person in question claims to have some rational interest or preference for oral sex, because a proponent of the idea of moral harm knows that immoral persons somewhere have an interest in not engaging in oral sex, because they cannot not have an interest in being morally better persons, and engaging in oral sex does not make them such. Here I will only comment on the radically "ideal" conception of individual interests according to which there are "objective" interests completely independent of the rational desires or preferences of the individuals themselves, and independent as well of any connection with an element of an individual's "motivational set": this, in my opinion, is a prescientific, premodern, and deeply misleading conception, bordering on absurdity. On the basis of this conception, one could in fact claim that John Doe has an interest in doing X (but where does this interest exist if not in relation to an element of his self?) even if in the manifestations of his self—including his unconscious self—or in his desires, rational preferences, or motivations, there is no tangible, observable sign that such an interest X exists.[8] (On this point, see Chap. 1.)

6.3 Why Psychological Harm Is Not, on Its Own, a Sufficient Ground to Use Criminal Coercion for Adults

Having outlined seven potential harms—namely, physical, psychophysical, economic, existential, relational, and psychological harms and harms resulting from violations of the rules of impartiality governing the administrative state, to which are added mere psychological stress and so-called moral harm—and noting that these definitions do not fully align with what Italian legal scholarship and case law call "moral harm" or "existential harm," I will put forward two fundamental theses.

The first of these theses is that, for various reasons, a liberal ethical and political conception aimed at justifying state coercion should not consider psychological harm, relational harm, mere psychological stress, or so-called moral harm as sufficient grounds for criminal coercion, regardless of their perceived injustice, except in cases where children suffer psychological harm or emotional distress repeated times. Children can indeed suffer psychological harm or emotional distress from material and/or emotional abandonment, which must be absolutely prevented, this in contrast to adults, who normally do not have a right against emotional abandonment. Specifically, mere psychological stress, even if it could be considered a form of harm, should not be viewed as a *significant* harm to others in the case of adults.[9] Psychological stress represents an interest whose violation not only fails to provide sufficient reason to limit individual freedom through force but also does not enter into the balancing of interests to determine the severity of other harms. Psychological harm is directly relevant and should be seen as an indicator of the severity of what I have termed existential harm, as in the case of stalking, while relational harm is only indirectly relevant, its significance being subordinate to the presence of psychological harm; however, neither relational nor psychological harm, on its own, should be considered a sufficient reason for criminal punishment.[10] Finally, as I have argued, I do not think it is in any sense conceptually appropriate to include "moral harm"

---

[8] On the concept of moral harm and its connection to an ideal conception of interests, see Mangini (2010).

[9] I will not discuss here the problem of the reasons that may warrant noncontractual forms of liability, i.e., tort liability.

[10] Whether and to what extent we should consider "mental distress" a *harm to others* is, of course, one of the most important problems that a liberal conception of criminal law needs to address (see Wertheimer (1979), p. 306). It is instead possible, and quite rightly so, to consider psychological harm as one of the fundamental indicators (or symptoms) of the *severity* of interference in the bodily or perceptual sphere (i.e., a fundamental indicator or symptom of existential harm). As the severity of the interference increases, it logically follows that the corresponding penalty should be greater, with additional aggravating factors and accessory sanctions. See Tobagi (2009).

among the *harms* done to others, much less to consider moral harm a *prima facie* or conclusive reason for exercising criminal coercion.

Why should these harms, despite being considered unjust, not be viewed as sufficient reasons to employ state coercion? The reason is that mere awareness of certain relevant facts could lead to psychological harm or stress. For instance, John Doe might feel anger, disgust, embarrassment, intense irritation, envy, anguish, shame, or other forms of mental suffering simply because he *knows* (without having to see or hear) that John Smith (his friend, relative, or neighbour) is engaging in oral or anal sex with other consenting men, using cocaine, or having sex with escorts at his home. Although this knowledge may cause psychological harm to some who are aware of the "disturbing" acts in question, it does not, in Western legal systems, constitute sufficient grounds for imposing a civil, administrative, or criminal penalty on the person committing these acts. The fact that conduct causes disgust, embarrassment, anger, resentment, hatred, or other negative emotions is not, on its own, sufficient reason to use criminal coercion. And this, as Ten points out, is the only plausible interpretation of Mill's thought. According to Ten, liking and disliking do not, in Mill's conception, represent harm to third parties. Conversely, anyone's private life could be destroyed. (Ten (1980), p. 14ff).

For the sake of consistency, therefore, the same should apply to other acts that in some legal systems are subject to civil or criminal penalty, such as active euthanasia, marriage between homosexuals or between multiple consenting individuals, and the use of narcotics.

Even if these acts are carried out in places partly or fully open to the public, such as a hospital room, a town hall, a brothel, or an opium den, they can be regarded as predominantly private events in terms of the participation or knowledge of third parties, despite the legal value of the act and the presence of a public official in the marriage, which can be attended only by invitation (unless the spouses wish otherwise) and which those who do not wish to attend do not have to. Evidence of this includes the fact that some celebrities marry in private, some even secretly, while other celebrities sell image rights to their marriage. Even a public will drawn up by a notary in the presence of witnesses is a public act and is drafted by a public official, but from the perspective of subjects other than the testator and witnesses, it is an entirely private event. It could be argued that if the celebration of a marriage between same-sex individuals is a predominantly private event, other events might not be, a case in point being when the homosexual parents of a child conceived through artificial insemination or through commercial surrogacy attend an open-house event where the child goes to school or a homeowners' meeting. However, these events, like many others, do not depend on the marriage but on having a child and on two homosexuals living together. Other rights connected to marriage would, in any case, be exercised privately or mostly privately, examples being the right to visit a spouse in hospital, the right to inherit from a spouse upon the spouse's death, or succession rights in connection with a rental contract, rights to practice sodomy. Even in relation to private sodomy, knowledge of which could lead some people to feel disgust, nausea, embarrassment, and which those people would like to ban, there is, unlike nudism or vomiting or defecating in public, no existential or incremental harm either for adults or children. In the case of two homosexuals kissing each other in public, there is no willful or intentional interference in the perceptual sphere of adults or children; therefore, there is no existential harm, as there would be in the case of a person pursuing me with the intent to touch me, urinate on me, vomit on me, or shout at me against my will. The disgust or shame felt by other people is a possible consequence of the kiss.

What about the case of a lesbian girl coming out? There is a significant difference between the interference of a telephone or sexual harasser in the sphere of the victim and that of the lesbian girl in relation to her father. The lesbian girl does not significantly interfere in her father's bodily sphere; she does not use her father's body and does not typically interfere intentionally with his perceptual sphere, nor does she normally alter the course of his life, except in the context of his wish for his children to be virtuous people (based on a certain idea of virtue).

Her interference is primarily affective. In contrast, the interference of a telephone or sexual harasser in the victim's bodily or perceptual sphere is significant because it is intentional. The psychological harm caused is not merely a possible consequence of their actions; it is inherent to those intentional actions. The homosexual girl could potentially interfere with her father's perceptual sphere, for example, by telling him she is lesbian or when he sees her with her girlfriend in public. However, such direct communication, the coming out, is usually concentrated in a very limited timeframe and space, and it may cause psychological harm as a possible consequence of the intentional act of coming out, rather than being an intrinsic or intentional part of her being homosexual or of engaging in sexual acts that involve her body.

Being homosexual does not affect the life plan her father has envisioned for her, except in the selfish conception he may have constructed. It also does not imply that he must encounter her, as she may live in a different neighborhood or city. One could argue that the daughter might have anticipated her father's reaction, given his past homophobic attitudes, suggesting potential intentional malice. There are two counterarguments to consider. First, no one can predict with certainty how a parent will react to *their* daughter's homosexuality. Therefore, while coming out is an intentional act, the psychological harm caused is merely a possible, not a certain, consequence of that action. Secondly, even if there were existential harm, which there isn't, it would not constitute unjust harm; as we will see, the mere fact that X causes harm is only prima facie grounds for punishment. Otherwise, we would have to punish all companies that, by competing with others, cause them economic harm, which is generally considered just.

It would not be an unjust harm because, in parent-child relationships, it is important for children to have the opportunity to declare their sexuality at least the first time. Such communication, therefore, such coming out, is necessary, as there is no other way for one to disclose their sexual identity to their family. However, if the daughter were to force her homophobic father to see her with or without her girlfriend during Thanksgiving or Christmas, after coming out and after he expressed a desire no longer to see her, or to listen to the erotic details of her relationship with her partner, that could potentially lead to existential harm or harassment.

Secondly, and this is the second thesis I am putting forward, I agree with Feinberg and other authors on the need to justify the use of force that causes *unjust* harm to others. It is evident that there are scenarios where causing harm to others is legitimate, such as economic harm in a free-market system that complies with competition rules and antitrust regulations, or physical harm without malice or negligence. This can be harm materially caused by an agent's action, even if the agent neither intended the harm nor could foresee it (as with force majeure or fortuitous events). Another way to express this is to assert, as Gardner ((1996), p. 127ff.) or Lamond ((1996), p. 237) do, that the purpose of the harm principle is to rule out the punishability of certain types of conduct, specifically those that do not cause harm to others. The fact that an act or type of conduct causes harm is a necessary but not sufficient condition to warrant the use of coercion under the criminal law. This latter thesis can be interpreted in two ways. The first interpretation is that the fact that an act or type of conduct causes "unjust" harm is both a necessary and a sufficient reason to punish that act or conduct, where the qualification of *unjust* depends on the application of the principle of culpability (conduct is punishable if it causes harm and is carried out with malice or negligence) and on the outcome of a balance struck between competing harms. This is in particular a balance that guides the attribution of meaning to "fundamentally similar normative evaluative criteria, in what concerns both their characteristics and functions, in assessing the constitutionally relevant parameters of criminal policy that have been handed down and developed in the context of constitutional case law such as that in Germany and Italy" (Fiandaca (2010), p. 226, my translation). These criteria, which Feinberg calls *mediating maxims*, include "the degree of the offense, the need to resort to punishment (a need evaluated in part by looking at available protection alternatives), their suitability to achieve the objective of protection, and the cost-benefit balance in terms of punishability and nonpunishability of the behaviour in question" (ibid.). This balance also serves to determine the severity of the penalty. According to this first interpretation, in line with Mill's thought, causing unjust harm is the only reason for using criminal coercion against an individual, the only criterion in virtue of which it is possible to discriminate between illicit acts of different gravity. According to the second interpretation, only conduct that causes "unjust" harm is criminally prosecutable, that is, conduct that, in addition to *harming* someone, *wrongs* them *morally*: as a moral wrong, the conduct is in this sense also immoral from a perfectionist or utilitarian point of view, interpretation that I would reject.

However, it is not important that we delve further into the concept of "unjust harm" at this point. In other words, I will not develop an exhaustive analysis of all the reasons, all things considered, that justify the use of the state's coercion. I have simply dealt with the concept of harm to others that represents the central core of the reasons that can justify the use of force by the state. This means establishing the paradigmatic cases in which the state has a good *prima facie*, not conclusive, reason to use force, rather than establishing when the state has a good conclusive reason to do so all things considered. For it is possible that, in some cases, as noted, the state ought not to intervene even if harm has been caused to others (the reason being that the harm is not unjust).

6.4 Ripstein's Sovereignty Principle

Various objections have been raised against the harm principle, and here I will examine some of them. The previously discussed concept of existential harm addresses a problem rightly posed by Ripstein (2006). Ripstein argues that the concept of harm does not always work, because there are activities whose prohibition we generally agree on even if they do not cause physical or material harm. Examples include invasion of privacy and property without causing any damage to the property, such as harmless trespass, or someone entering our home to nap without breaking in or stealing.[11] Ripstein suggests abandoning the concept of harm and replacing the harm principle with the sovereignty principle (see also Tadros (2011), p. 59ff.). Ripstein's goal aligns with mine: to construct a protected sphere—encompassing the corporeal and mental sphere, the privacy of one's home, and one's personal identity—within which the individual can move freely, short of causing harm to others or risking such harm. I am convinced that Ripstein's purpose can be achieved by developing the notion of existential harm, conceding that (a) the paradigmatic cases of harm, indeed the overwhelming majority of cases, are always represented by permanent (or long-lasting) modifications of the external world, of the body, of the mind, of the goods belonging to the individual; (b) these modifications are deemed unfavorable by the individual themself; and (c) they are the result of the performance of a human action but are logically and empirically independent of the action performed by the agent. In the case of injury to bodily integrity or property, we can distinguish the action of the agent (e.g., firing a gun) from the result of the action (death or injury to the victim's bodily integrity), which is the harm caused.

In existential harm, the harm consists precisely in interfering in ways the victim does not want (in a deliberate violation of the bodily sphere, invasion of privacy or property, a violation of someone's identity, and the like). This is not because, very often, there is no physical or material harm in cases of interference in the bodily sphere or a violation of the safety and security of person and property. For instance, those who suffer sexual harassment, defamation, stalking, anonymous calls, invasion of the privacy of the home, insults—all actions involving existential harm—usually endure more or less serious consequences, such as psychological harm, leading to anger, shame, a desire for revenge, guilt, or a sense that one is no longer protected in their privacy, and a loss of self. The reason for these stipulations is in part that trespass or interference in the bodily sphere should be prohibited anyway

[11] Another case of an activity that we cannot but prohibit even if it lacks the element of physical or material harm is that of so-called harmless rape. This refers to a rather rare case of rape occurring without the victim suffering any physical, psychophysical, or psychological injury: the victim, for example, might remain asleep throughout the rape, wake up without any trace of the violence on their body, and remember nothing of what happened. Shortly thereafter, the rapist dies in a car accident, without having told anyone about the incident and without anyone having seen the act. The case of "harmless rape" can also be easily resolved on the basis of the definition of existential harm, since, like kidnapping, it remains a significant and intentional interference in a person's bodily sphere. On this point, see Spena (2010); Gardner (1996, 2007); Lamond (1996).

if it is not wanted by the victim, regardless of the severity of the psychological consequences the violation produces, and because other similar kinds of suffering can occur as a result of someone performing legally permitted actions. In this sense, it must be conceded that the concept of "existential harm" is in part stipulative, proposing a use of the term *harm* marginally in contrast with ordinary language. However, for one thing, this is a very limited, marginal contrast with ordinary language, not affecting most cases of application of the concept of harm. These are marginal, peripheral cases of the use of the concept. The fundamental core, namely, physical, psychophysical, and economic harm, remains in place. The same applies to paradigmatic cases of existential harm, such as sexual harassment, insults, anonymous phone calls, stalking, or someone defecating or urinating on us: these are cases in which there is a psychological harm, a nonpermanent harm in a physical or material sense. And, for another thing, philosophical and legal language is full of partly stipulative definitions. That is normal.

One might conclude, with Ripstein, that it is better to abandon the harm principle and replace it with the sovereignty principle, but I am not sure that this is the best solution. It would undoubtedly be a possible, acceptable solution. Equally acceptable would be to couple the harm principle with the sovereignty principle for all violations of autonomy, of the individual's protected sphere, that do not cause harm understood in a physical or material sense. However, I believe there are two reasons against using the sovereignty principle. On the one hand, the harm principle still captures the fundamental core of the reasons justifying the state's use of force, meaning that, in the vast majority of cases, force is justified to prevent others from suffering physical, psychophysical, or economic harm or from being exposed to the risk of such harm. On the other hand, while the sovereignty principle effectively captures the idea of the individual's protected sphere—the body, mind, home, and territory where the individual reigns supreme—the harm principle captures another idea, likewise Millian and liberal, that the use of criminal coercion by the state amounts to *violence* and that such violence is justified only to prevent further violence to others. The harm principle, extended to existential harm, tells of a world where *violence* means not only physical violence, as a modification of the external world, violence done to people's goods or bodies, but also violence violating the will of other people in certain protected areas. It is this wrong, this harm, not understood in a physical or material sense, that the harm principle is concerned with. Interfering in individuals' protected sphere (in their body, mind, home, or identity), against their will, regardless of the (psychological) consequences the interference produces, is a form of violence, a harm. In fact, what matters if the state is to intervene is not just the harm, whether physical, economic, or otherwise material, or whether it consists in an invasion of the privacy of the home. It is necessary that the harm—whether physical, economic, or otherwise material, or whether it interferes in the bodily sphere—be something the victim *does not want*. After all, both criteria—the causing of "existential harm" as part of the harm principle and the sovereignty principle—have the same flaw. They are quite indeterminate until we fill them with content. Saying that the state's coercion under the criminal law is justified if and only if we violate the sphere in which the individual is sovereign tells us little about what this sphere is. In a sexist and patriarchal world, the space in which the individual is sovereign and supreme could also include his family, wife, and children. And the concept of existential harm itself can be expanded or narrowed in various ways. Yet, as I said earlier, much less indeterminate is the core of paradigmatic case, that of physical, psychophysical, economic, and existential harm, covered by the harm principle in ordinary language use.

6.5 Dworkin and the Fair Impact on an Ethical Environment

Finally, the need for all these distinctions—the need to differentiate between various types of harm (physical, psychophysical, economic) and the need to differentiate, from a liberal perspective, harm that is relevant to others and harm that is not, as well as the general semantic indeterminacy of the concept of harm—is considered by some authors as a clear symptom of the failure of the entire argumentative strategy initiated by John Stuart Mill and as the very *demise* of the harm principle. The strength of the harm principle, as defined by Mill, supposedly lies in offering a simple, clear, precise, and unequivocal criterion for justifying the use of state coercion: the existence of harm to others. The need to distinguish between different types of harm—some of which are irrelevant, unjust, or insufficient to warrant coercion under the criminal law, fatally weakens this argument (see Wertheimer (1979); Del Bò (2007); Donini (2010); Sartorius (1983)).

This objection, however, misses the mark for several reasons. Firstly, there are no concepts without some degree of (potential) indeterminacy, meaning dubious cases of application. Even the simplest concepts, like those used in physics to measure space, are affected by this—all the more so with, complex concepts, which are intersections of conflicting ontological and cultural views. Even so, most cases where the concept of harm is applied are paradigmatic. Who would doubt in the current Western community that physical, psychophysical, or economic harm is indeed *harm*? The same goes for certain clear cases of existential harm. If kidnapping or systematic interference in one's body or invasion of the privacy of the home is not violence against an individual, I do not know what is. Equally evident, as we have seen, would be the turmoil in Western society if we were to consider as relevant, that is, as harms to others justifying coercion under the criminal law, moral disgust or psychological stress or anger that neighbours or John Doe's parents might feel with regard to his behaviour (like divorcing his wife or having sex with escorts), not to mention the absurdity of the idea of "moral harm" as harm to others.

However, there is another reason not to abandon the harm principle: what is the alternative? The alternative is a return to the *enforcement of morals*, in either a liberal or an illiberal guise. Let us see what Dworkin says about this:

> Every community has an ethical environment and this environment makes a difference to the lives its members can lead. A community that tolerates homosexuality, where homosexuality has a strong presence, provides a different ethical environment than one where homosexuality is forbidden, and some people believe themselves harmed by this difference.

> They find it much harder, for example, to raise their children to absorb instincts and values of which they approve. (Dworkin (2000), pp. 213–14)

However, the majority does not have a right to eliminate anything it sees as harmful to the ethical environment. "Each member of the majority has only a right to a fair impact on his environment: the same impact as any other single individual. He has no right to an environment that would make it easiest for him to raise his children to hold his favored opinions" (ibid.). The solution according to the Harm Principle is better. With regard to two homosexuals kissing in the street, as I said, in a pub, on the metro, on the bus, at high school, or at university, the kiss is done intentionally, with intentional malice, and the psychological result due to interference in the perceptual sphere of adult homophobes is only possible, i.e., there is a possibility that the kiss will provoke disgust or anger or disapproval in some adult homophobes. From the point of view of the harm principle, this is not an existential harm, because the interference in the perceptual sphere of adult homophobes is not intentional and does not provoke recurrent psychological harm or emotional distress in children.

Is the harm principle to be replaced by the "principle of fair impact on one's own ethical environment"? What is a fair impact? Does the molester not have a right to a fair impact on the surrounding environment? One could argue that if the molester or harasser has a right to fondle store clerks, they have a right to publicly slap or beat him. Is that a fair impact? And doesn't a nudist have a right to a fair impact? The nudist has the right to show himself nude on the bus, just as others have the same right. Is that a fair impact? If a person has the right to watch pornographic movies on websites from the comfort of his home and to pay someone to protect his PC from viruses, do hackers paid by Fundamentalist Christian Associations have the right to infect his computer with viruses or malware linked to porn sites? Conversely, do producers of pornographic movies have the same right to infect websites belonging to Fundamentalist Christian Associations with viruses? Is that a fair impact? If professors at school or university have the right to speak out against government homophobia or racism, do students, who may be fundamentalist Catholics homophobes or supremacists and fascists racists, have the right to label them as, respectively, "faggot's friend" or "nigger's friend"'? Is that a fair impact? Neo-Fascist, racist and far-right movements or parties in Occident have the right to distort reality about migrants, claiming that many of them are criminals, that many of them steal jobs from Italians, that many of them are rapists, that many of them steal resources from the welfare state, especially in health and education, while associations and leftist movements have the right to criticize fascists and far-right movements on anti-immigration policies, telling the truth about migrants and distort reality about far-right movements (But, how could the reality and ideology of far-right parties and movements be worse)? Is that a fair impact?

One could claim that I have a right to look at my neighbour's photo albums by invading the privacy of his or her home, no less than he or she has a right to look at my photo albums, and that I have a right to a fair impact on the personal identity of each member of the community, e.g., my neighbor, and vice versa, or that (from an active as well as a passive point of view) I have a right to a moderate, fair dose of defamation, no less than my neighbour does. So, at homeowners' meetings, everyone has a right to an equal opportunity to defame everyone else, and everyone has a right to spread rumors about their neighbor, rumors that are in equal parts a fascinating mix of falsehood and truth, plausibility and implausibility, superficiality and accuracy. Future generations will judge. I do not know what a *fair impact* is, but above all, I do not see how replacing the harm principle with a principle that is indeterminate, and indeed much more indeterminate, can be of any use.

References

Alexander L, Kimberly Kessler F (2008) Culpable acts of risk creation. Ohio State J Crim Law 5:375ff

Altman A (2012) Genocide and crimes against humanity: dispelling the conceptual fog. Soc Philos Policy Found 29:280ff

Ambos K (2013) Treatise on international criminal law, vol I. Oxford University Press, Oxford

Ambos K (2014) Treatise on international criminal law, vol II. Oxford University Press, Oxford

Ambos K (2015) The overall function of international criminal law: Striking the right balance between the rechtsgut and the harm principles. A second contribution towards a consistent theory of ICL. Crim Law Philos 9:301–329

Atadjanov R (2019) The protected legal interests of crimes against humanity and other core crimes under international law: a comparative analysis. In: Atadjanov R (ed) Humanness as a protected legal interest of crimes against humanity, pp 277–307 First Online: 14 June 2019, https://link.springer.com/chapter/10.1007/978-94-6265-299-6_6#ref-CR22

Bergsmo M, Buis EJ, Tianying S (2022a) Protected interests in international criminal law. In: Bergsmo M, Buis EJ, Tianying S (eds) Philosophical foundations of international criminal law: legally-protected interests. Torkel Opsahl Academic EPublisher, Brussel

Bergsmo M, Buis EJ, Tianying S (eds) (2022b) Philosophical foundations of international criminal law: legally-protected interests. Torkel Opsahl Academic EPublisher, Brussel

Boot M (2002) Genocide, crimes against humanity, war crimes: Nullum crimen sine lege and the subject matter jurisdiction of the International Criminal Court. Intersentia, Antwerp, Oxford, New York

Bricola F (1973) Teoria generale del reato. Novissimo Digesto Italiano, vol. XIV

Cassese A (2003) International criminal law, 3rd edn. Oxford University Press, Oxford

Catenacci M (2006) I reati di pericolo presunto fra diritto e processo penale. Studi Marinucci v II 14: 15ff. Milan, Giuffrè

Caterini M (2004) Reato impossibile e offensività: Un'indagine critica. ESI, Naples

Cavaliere A (1998) Riflessioni sul ruolo dell'offensività nella teoria del reato costituzionalmente orientata. In: Giostra G,. Insolera G, Costituzione, diritto e processo penale, Milan, Giuffrè, p 133ff

Del Bò C (2007) Laicismo, neutralismo e 'legal enforcement of morals. Ragion pratica 28:17–36

Diciotti E (1986) Paternalismo. Materiali per una storia della cultura giuridica XVI.2: 557–586

Diciotti E (2005) Preferenze, autonomia e paternalismo. Ragion pratica 24:99–118

Dolcini E, Marinucci G (1994) Costituzione e politica dei beni giuridici. Rivista italiana di diritto e procedura penale:333–373

Donini M (1996) Teoria del reato: Una introduzione. CEDAM, Padua

Donini M (1999) Teoria del reato. Dig. Disc. Pen. XIV, 267–75. UTET,Turin

Donini M (2002) Prospettive europee del principio di offensività. Verso un codice penale modello per l'Europa. In: Cadoppi A (ed), Offensività e colpevolezza., CEDAM, Padua, p, 111ff

Donini M (2003) L'art. 129 del progetto di revisione costituzionale approvato il 4 novembre 1997: Per una progressione 'legale,' prima che 'giurisprudenziale,' dei principi di offensività e di sussidiarietà. Alla ricerca di un disegno: Scritti sulle riforme penali in Italia. Padua. Orig. pub. in Crit. dir., 1998, 95ff
Donini M (2008). 'Danno' e 'offesa' nella tutela penale dei sentimenti: Note su morale e sicurezza come beni giuridici, a margine della categoria dell''offense' di Joel Feinberg. Rivista italiana di diritto e procedura penale
Donini M (2010) 'Danno' e 'offesa' nella c.d. tutela penale dei sentimenti: Note su morale e sicurezza come beni giuridici, a margine della categoria dell''offense' di Joel Feinberg. In: Cadoppi A (ed), Laicità, valori e diritto penale: The Moral Limits of the Criminal Law; in ricordo di Joel Feinberg Milan, Giuffrè, pp 41–99
Duff A (2001) Harms and wrongs. Buffalo Crim Law Rev 5:13–44
Dworkin G (1983) Paternalism. In: Sartorius R (ed) Paternalism. University of Minnesota Press, Minneapolis, Chap. 2, pp 19–34
Dworkin R (2000) Sovereign virtue: the theory and practice of equality. Harvard University Press, Cambridge
Eser A (1965) The principle of "Harm" in the concept of crime: a comparative analysis of the criminally protected legal interests. Duquenne Law Rev 4:345ff. Available at: https://dsc.duq.edu/dlr/vol4/iss3/2
Etzioni A (2004) On protecting children from speech. Chicago-Kent Law Rev 79:3
Feinberg J (1983) Legal paternalism. In: Sartorius R (ed) Paternalism. University of Minnesota Press, Minneapolis, Chap. 1, pp 3–18
Feinberg J (1984a) Fairly imputing harms. Chap. 6 in harm to others. Vol. 1 of The moral limits of the criminal law. Oxford Academic, Oxford
Feinberg J (1984b) Harm to others. Vol. 1 of the moral limits of the criminal law. Oxford University Press, Oxford
Feinberg J (1985) Offense to others. Vol. 2 of The moral limits of the criminal law. Oxford University Press, Oxford
Feinberg J (1986) Harm to self. Vol. 3 of The moral limits of the criminal law. Oxford University Press, Oxford
Feinberg J (1994) Harmless wrongdoing. In: Dworkin G (ed) Morality, harm, and the law. Westview Press, Boulder, pp 111–135
Ferrajoli L (1989) Diritto e ragione: Teoria del garantismo penale. Rome and Bari, Laterza.
Fiandaca G (1991) Considerazioni sul principio di offensività e sul ruolo della teoria del bene giuridico tra elaborazione dottrinale e prassi giudiziaria. In: Stile AM (ed) Le discrasie tra dottrina e giurisprudenza in diritto penale, Naples, Jovene, 61ff
Fiandaca G (2001) L'offensività è un principio codificabile? Foro italiano V:7–9
Fiandaca G (2003) Nessun reato senza offesa. In: Fiandaca G, Di Chiara G (eds) Una introduzione al sistema penale per una lettura costituzionalmente orientata, Naples, Jovene, 203ff
Fiandaca G (2010) Punire la semplice immoralità? Un vecchio interrogativo che tende a riproporsi. In: Cadoppi A (ed) Laicità, valori e diritto penale: The Moral Limits of the Criminal Law; in ricordo di Joel Feinberg. Giuffrè, Milan, pp 207–232
Fiore C (1994) Il principio di offensività. IP: 278ff
Fiore C (1998) Osservazioni in tema di clausole di irrilevanza penale e trattamento della criminalità bagatellare: A proposito di una recente proposta legislativa. Critica dir: 274ff
Fiore C (2006) Il contributo della giurisprudenza costituzionale all'evoluzione del principio di offensività. In: Vassalli G (ed) Diritto penale e giurisprudenza costituzionale. ESI, Naples
Fiorella A (1987) Reato in generale. Enciclopedia del Diritto 38: 793ff
Fleck D (2008) The handbook of international humanitarian law, 2nd edn. Oxford University Press, Oxford
Gallo M (1969) I reati di pericolo. Foro penale
Gardner J (1996) Justifications and reasons. In: Simester AP, Smith ATH (eds) Harm and culpability. Oxford University Press, Oxford, pp 103–129

Gardner J (2007) Offences and defences: selected essays in the philosophy of criminal law. Oxford University Press, Oxford
Gómez Lanz K (2023) The attack on the protected legal interest: a criminalisation principle and an element of the criminal offence? Ius Novum 17(3):19–31
Grosso C et al. (2000) Documento n. 2 su Inoffensività e irrilevanza del fatto negli 'Allegati alla I Relazione della Commissione Grosso' In: Grosso CF, Per un nuovo codice penale, vol. 2, CEDAM, Padua, pp 103ff
Insolera G (1990) Reati artificiali e principio di offensività: A proposito di un'ordinanza della Corte Costituzionale sull'art. 1, VI comma, l. n. 516 del 1982. Rivista italiana di diritto e procedura penale: 726ff
Jackson Harris R, Barlett CP (2009) Effects of sex in the media. In: Bryant J et al (eds) Media effects: advances in theory and research. Erlbaum, Psychology Press.
Lamond G (1996) Coercion, Threats and the Puzzle of Blackmail. In: Simester AP, Smith ATH (eds), Harm and culpability. Oxford University Press, Oxford, pp 215–238
Lieberman JK (2012) Liberalism undressed. Oxford University Press, Oxford
Manes V (2002) Der Beitrag der italienischen Strafrechtswissenschaft zur Rechtsgutslehre. Zeitschrift für die gesamte Strafrechtswissenschaft 114:720–735
Manes V (2005) Il principio di offensività: Canone di politica criminale, criterio ermeneutico, parametro di ragionevolezza. Giappichelli, Turin
Manes V (2012) I recenti tracciati della giurisprudenza costituzionale in materia di offensività e ragionevolezza. Diritto penale contemporaneo 1:99–110
Mangini M (2010) Atti osceni e danno morale. Diritto e questioni pubbliche 10:383–414
Maniaci G (2012) Contro il paternalismo giuridico. Giappichelli, Turin
Manna A (2002) I reati di pericolo astratto e presunto e i modelli di diritto penale. In: Curi U, Palombarini G (eds) Diritto penale minimo, Donzelli, Rome, p 35ff
Mantovani F (1977) Il principio di offensività del reato nella Costituzione. Aspetti e tendenze del diritto costituzionale. In: Scritti in onore di Costantino Mortati, Milan, Giuffrè, 445ff
Mantovani F (1996) Il principio di offensività nello schema di delega legislativa per un nuovo codice penale. Prospettive di riforma del codice penale e valori costituzionali. Giuffrè, Milan, p 91ff
Mazzacuva N (1997) Diritto penale e Costituzione. In: Insolera G et al. (eds) Introduzione al sistema penale. UTET, Turin, pp 75ff., 83ff
Merli A (2006) Introduzione alla teoria generale del bene giuridico; Il problema, le fonti, le tecniche di tutela penale. ESI, Naples
Mill JS (1971) On liberty (1859). In vol. 18 of collected works, J. M. Robson (ed) Routledge & Kegan Paul, London, pp 213–310
Moccia S (1995) Dalla tutela dei beni alla tutela di funzioni: Tra illusioni postmoderne e riflussi illiberali. Rivista italiana di diritto e procedura penale: 343ff
Motilewa Quadri K et al (2022) Forging a modern African perspective on 'unity' as a collective legal interest in international criminal law. In: Bergsmo M, Buis EJ, Tianying S (eds) Philosophical foundations of international criminal law: legally-protected interests. Torkel Opsahl Academic EPublisher, Brussel
Musco E (1974) Bene giuridico e tutela dell'onore. Giuffrè, Milan
Nakhjavani SA, Mirzaagha M (2022) On 'Unity' as an emerging legal interest in international criminal law. In: Bergsmo M, Buis EJ, Tianying S (eds) Philosophical foundations of international criminal law: legally-protected interests. Torkel Opsahl Academic EPublisher, Brussel
Neppi Modona G (1996) Reato impossibile. Dig. Disc. pen., XI, UTET, Turin, 259ff
Neppi Modona G (2004) Il lungo cammino del principio di offensività. Studi in onore di M. Gallo: Scritti degli allievi, 89ff. Turin, Giappichelli
Oddone-Paolucci E, Genuis M, Violato C (2000) A meta-analysis on the published research on the effects of pornography. In: Violato C et alii (eds) The changing family and child development. Aldersgate UK, Ashgate Publishing
Palazzo F (1996) Meriti e limiti dell'offensività come principio di ricodificazione: Prospettive di riforma del codice penale e valori costituzionali. Giuffrè, Milan

Palazzo F (1998) Offensività e ragionevolezza nel controllo di costituzionalità sul contenuto delle leggi penali. Rivista italiana di diritto e procedura penale: 350ff

Patrono P (1993) Diritto penale economico e interessi umani fondamentali. CEDAM, Padua

Persak N (2007) Criminalising harmful conduct: the harm principle, its limits and continental counterparts. Springer, New York

Pulitanò D (1985) Bene giuridico e giustizia costituzionale. In: Stile AM (ed) Bene giuridico e riforma della parte speciale, Naples, Jovene, p 134ff

Raz J (1987) Autonomy, toleration, and the harm principle. In: Hart HLA, Gavison R (eds) Issues in contemporary legal philosophy. Oxford University Press, Oxford

Riondato S (2005) Un diritto penale detto "ragionevole": Raccontando Giuseppe Bettiol. CEDAM, Padua

Ripstein A (2006) Beyond the harm principle. Philosophy Public Affairs 34(3):215–245

Romano M (2011) La legittimazione delle norme penali: Ancora su limiti e validità della teoria del bene giuridico. Criminalia: 33ff

Sartorius R (1983) Introduction. In: Sartorius R (ed) Paternalism. University of Minnesota Press, Minneapolis, pp 1–3

Simester AP (2005) Is strict liability always wrong? In: Simester AP (ed) Appraising strict liability. Oxford University Press, Oxford. Chap. 2

Simester AP (2006) The mental element in complicity. Law Quart Rev 122(4):578–601

Simester AP (2010) Betrachtungen über Moral und Paternalismus. In: von Hirsch A, Neumann U, Seelmann K (eds) Paternalismus im Strafrecht: Die Kriminalisierung van selbstschädigendem Verhalten. Nomos Verlagsgesellschaft, Baden-Baden

Simester AP (2011) Enforcing morality. In: Marmor A (ed) The Routledge companion to philosophy of law. Routledge, New York. Chap. 31

Simester AP, Sullivan GR (2005) On the nature and rationale of property offences. In: Duff RA, Green SP (eds) Defining crimes: essays on the special part of the criminal law. Oxford University Press, Oxford, pp 168–195

Simester AP, Sullivan GR (2007) Criminal law: theory and doctrine, 3rd edn. Hart Publishing, Oxford

Simester AP, von Hirsch A (2002) Rethinking the offense principle. Legal Theory 8(3):269–295

Simester AP, von Hirsch A (2006) Regulating offensive conduct through two-step prohibitions. In: von Hirsch A, Simester AP (eds) Incivilities: regulating offensive behaviour. Hart Publishing, Oxford. Chap. 7

Simester AP, von Hirsch A (2009) Remote harms and non-constitutive crimes. Crim Justice Ethics 28(1):89–107

Simester AP, von Hirsch A (2011) Crimes, harms, and wrongs: on the principles of criminalisation. Hart Publishing, Oxford

Spena A (2010) Harmless rapes? A false problem for the harm principle. Diritto e questioni pubbliche 10:497–524

Stanton-Ife J (2017) Must we pay for the British Museum? Taxation and the harm principle. In: Bhandari M (ed) Philosophical foundations of tax law. Oxford Academic Books, Oxford. Chap 2

Stella F (1973) La teoria del bene giuridico e i c.d. fatti inoffensivi conformi al tipo. Rivista italiana di diritto e procedura penale: 3ff.

Tadros V (2011) Harm, sovereignty, and prohibition. Legal Theory 17(1):35–65

Ten CL (1980) Mill on liberty. Clarendon Press, Oxford

Tianying S (2022) The legal interests protected by war crimes. In: Bergsmo M, Buis EJ, Tianying S (eds) Philosophical foundations of international criminal law: legally-protected interests. Torkel Opsahl Academic EPublisher, Brussel

Tincani P (2009) Harm principle: Il Principio del danno. In: Sciacca F (ed) L'individuo nella crisi dei diritti. Il Melangolo, Genoa, pp 55–80

Tobagi B (2009) Come mi batte forte il tuo cuore: Storia di mio padre. Einaudi, Turin

Valenti A (2003). La 'musa negletta': quando la Costituzione non ispira più il legislatore nelle scelte di incriminazione. Indice pen: 953ff

Valenti A (2012) Principi di materialità e offensività. In: Insolera G et al (eds) Introduzione al sistema penale, vol 14. UTET, Turin, p 359ff

VanDeVeer D (1986) Paternalistic intervention. Princeton University Press, Princeton

Vassalli G (1982) Considerazioni sul principio di offensività. Studi Pioletti, Milan, p 629ff

Vinciguerra S (2006) Appunti sulla inoffensività, la tenuità dell'offesa e la tenuità del reato in Italia nel secondo Novecento. Vol. 2. Giuffrè, Milan, pp 2077–2121

von Hirsch A (1986) Injury and exasperation: an examination of harm to others and offense to others. Mich Law Rev 84(4/5):700–714

von Hirsch A (1996) Extending the harm principle: 'Remote' harms and fair imputation. In: Simester AP, Smith ATH (eds) Harm and culpability. Oxford University Press, Oxford, pp 259–276

von Hirsch A (2000) The offence principle in criminal law: affront to sensibility or wrongdoing? King's Law J 11(1):78–89

von Hirsch A (2006) Toleranz als Mediating Principle. In: von Hirsch A, Seelmann K, Wohlers W (eds) Mediating Principles: Begrenzungsprinzipien bei der Strafbegründung. Nomos, Baden-Baden

von Hirsch A (2008a) Harm and Offence: Schädigungsprinzip und Schädigungsprinzip als Kriterien für die Kriminalisierung von Verhalten. In: Dietrich Herzberg R, Putzke H (eds) Strafrecht zwischen System und Telos: Festschrift für Rolf Dietrich Herzberg zum siebzigsten Geburtstag am 14. Mohr Siebeck, Tubingen

von Hirsch A (2008b) Direct paternalism: criminalizing self-injurious conduct. Crim Just Ethics 27(1):25–33

von Hirsch A (2010) Nachwort: Indirekter Paternalismus und die normative Basis des Tòtungauf-Verlangen-Verbots. In: von Hirsch A, Neumann U, Seelmann K (eds) Paternalismus im Strafrecht: Die Kriminalisierung van selbstschädigendem Verhalten. Nomos Verlagsgesellschaft, Baden-Baden

von Hirsch A, Ashworth A (2005) Proportionate sentencing: exploring the principles. Oxford University Press, Oxford

von Hirsch A, Neumann U (2010) 'Indirekter' Paternalismus im Strafrecht am Beispiel der Tòtung auf Verlangen (§ 216 StGB). In: von Hirsch A et al (eds) Paternalismus im Strafrecht: Die Kriminalisierung van selbstschädigendem Verhalten. Nomos Verlagsgesellschaft, Baden-Baden

von Hirsch A, Simester AP (2006) Penalising offensive behaviour: constitutive and mediating principles. In: von Hirsch A, Simester AP (eds) Incivilities: regulating offensive behaviour. Hart Publishing, Oxford. Chap. 4

Waldron J (1993) Mill and the value of moral distress. In: Liberal rights: collected papers 1981–1991. Cambridge University Press, Cambridge, pp 5–42

Wertheimer A (1979) Victimless crimes. Ethics 87(4):302–318

Whitaker JL, Bushman BJ (2009) Online dangers: keeping children and adolescents safe. Wash Lee Law Rev 66

Zagrebelsky V (1982) Contenuti e linee evolutive della giurisprudenza in tema di rapporti fra tassatività del fatto tipico e lesività. In: Vassalli G (ed) Problemi generali di diritto penale, Giuffrè, Milan, p 417ff

Zuccalà G (1984) Sul preteso principio di necessaria offensività del reato. Studi Delitala 3, Milan, Giuffrè, 1700ff.

Zuccalà G (2004) Due questioni attuali sul bene giuridico: La pretesa dimensione 'critica' del bene giuridico e la pretesa necessaria offesa ad un bene. Rivista trimestrale di diritto penale dell'economia 3(4):1 791ff

Chapter 7
The Harm Principle, Vulnerability, and the Criminalization of Drugs

Politics and hysteria, not science and sound principles, continue to fuel our drug policy.
—Douglas Husak, *Legalize This!* (2002)

I can't believe you used to bring my daughter here, to this place. [Harlem]

[…] To this place. What's that shit. Right now, all over this country, a hundred thousand white people from the suburbs are driving around downtown, asking every black person they see, You got any drugs? What kind of effect you think this has on the psyche of a black person, on their possibilities? […] The product's marked up three hundred percent. You can go out on the street and make five hundred bucks in two hours and then do whatever you want for the rest of the day.

—Dialogue between Robert, the father of a teenage addict named Caroline, and Seth, her boyfriend, who introduced her to drugs, in Steven Soderbergh's 2000 film *Traffic*

Arrest me, but forget her.

Arrest you? Think I'm a fool?

Not at all. You located Olivier in two days. Nice going.

Olivier?

The dealer. Why not arrest him?

Want me to arrest everyone? […]

You never bust suppliers?

All the time. We work years, bust an Iranian gang. And then Iraqis took their place. Or the Lebanese, Turks, Italians. There's too much demand. It's an invasion.

—Dialogue between Sébastien, the father of a cancer patient who needs heroin to manage his pain, and Gilles, a police officer, in Denys Arcan's 2003 film *The Barbarian Invasions*

G. Maniaci, *The Unbearable Lightness of Legal Antipaternalism*, Law and Philosophy Library 151, https://doi.org/10.1007/978-3-031-96844-0_7

7.1 The Consequences of Criminalizing Drugs

There is a relationship between antiprohibitionism and antipaternalism. In a nutshell, according to antipaternalism (a complete definition can be found in Chap. 2), the state cannot use coercion to limit the rational and competent choices made by an adult individual who is sufficiently free from coercive pressures (e.g., threats), who knows the relevant facts, whose relevant desires are stable over time, even where these choices cause (what is considered) harm to the individual making the same choices, so long as the harm does not affect any third parties. This is John Stuart Mills' famous *Harm to Others Principle*, under which (to reiterate) an autonomous individual's freedom of action can be restricted, through the use of coercion, only if it harms others.[1] In short, antiprohibitionism advocates legalizing the consumption and sale of drugs (marijuana, cocaine, heroin, Ecstasy) whose sale (and sometimes consumption) is punished with criminal penalties or with severe administrative fines in many countries of the Western world. So there seem to be two kinds of prohibitionists: the paternalist and the antipaternalist. Paternalistic prohibitionists would like to restrict people's freedom to consume narcotics for their own good. Then there are the prohibitionists who explicitly use the harm principle, because they claim that legalizing the sale and consumption of drugs would cause certain economic and psychophysical harms to the community. For example, it is claimed that legalization of illicit drugs would result in a significant increase in their consumption, which would lead to an increase in the harm caused to the health of users, as well as to violent behaviour of users of certain drugs (e.g., cocaine), healthcare costs incurred by the community for the treatment and detoxification of users, or road or workplace accidents.

In this chapter, I will argue two theses. The first is an antiprohibitionist thesis. I will argue that it would be preferable to legalize the sale and consumption of drugs, that is, it is likely that prohibitionism results in more harm (be it economic, physical, psychophysical) and entails more costs than antiprohibitionism and antipaternalism. The second thesis I will argue, related to the first, is that prohibitionists use the harm principle in a false, specious, or grossly overblown way. This disingenuous use of the harm principle has longstanding origins; it can be found in Sir Devlin's (1959–1965) "The Enforcement of Morals" and also recently in Katharine A. MacKinnon's and Diana Russell's studies of pornography (Russell 1993; MacKinnon 1987, 1989). Devlin argues that the legalisation of sodomy would have resulted in harm to third parties, because homosexuals are, in Devlin's false belief, essentially, spineless, debauched, effeminate, incapable of defending the nation, of defending their community with arms or force (On this point see Hart 1963).

As I have shown elsewhere, MacKinnon's and Russell's argument identifying the harms and the violence against women that would result from the consumption of pornography is a road paved with fallacies of all kinds (see Maniaci 2016). The same thing happens with the harms feared by prohibitionists on the subject of the

[1] On the concept of relevant harm to others, see Chap. 6, Sect. 6.1.

legalization of drugs when they use an argument we will be discussing, that of the zombie epidemic.

Before assessing why antiprohibitionism and antipaternalism result in less harm and less cost than prohibition, let us consider the fundamental argument in favor of an antipaternalistic or liberal conception, the value of individual autonomy, and the right of individuals to live their own lives, as far as is humanly possible, in accordance with their own values, desires, plans, and philosophical and religious conceptions. Without dwelling on the notion of individual autonomy (outlined in Chap. 3), we can say that, in principle, the conditions an agent must possess or can reasonably be presumed to possess, in order to achieve a sufficient degree of autonomy are four: sufficient rationality and capacity, the need for the agent's preferences to be stable over time, sufficient freedom from coercive pressures in the formation of the agent's preferences, and a knowledge of relevant facts.[2] All adults, if they so desire and if they are sufficiently autonomous—i.e., they satisfy the four previously listed conditions—would in this sense have a right to make their own decisions about their own body, including a decision to take drugs.

A particular problem facing liberal, antipaternalistic conceptions is the problem of vulnerability, a problem that, as we saw in Chap. 3, paternalists often seize on to limit individual freedom. The problem is what is meant by vulnerability. If it is stated that a seriously ill, or elderly patient, or a person with childhood trauma, is frail, vulnerable, or suggestible, and so by definition not competent or insufficiently autonomous to make decisions, such as euthanasia or drug use, this paternalistically and deceptively restricts his or her freedom.[3] If this were the case, one would fall into the paradox of preventing sick and/or elderly people from making important decisions, some of them irreversible, such as getting married; having an abortion; giving consent for life-threatening surgeries; refusing life-saving treatment; determining whether, with whom, and how to raise their children; or drafting a will. There are many circumstances or events—betrayals, divorces, separations, bereavements, constant family quarrels, possessive or detached parents, an inability to

[2] On the meaning of these conditions for a sufficient degree of autonomy, see Chap. 3. For activities that do not normally cause or run the risk of causing serious harm to health and physical integrity, such as buying a dress, a house, or a car or going on a diet, the requirements of sufficient rationality, knowledge of the relevant facts, and freedom from coercive pressure are presumed to be present, unless there is evidence to the contrary in specific cases or unless particular decisions, such as that of workers forgoing their paid leave, warrant presumptions to the contrary, because it would be significantly costly for the administrative state and highly restrictive of the freedom of individuals to mandate public interviews to determine whether they are sufficiently rational or knowledgeable of the relevant facts in making these kinds of decisions. For harmful or dangerous activities, such as consuming cocaine or heroin, or requesting euthanasia, interviews with a private physician or at a public hospital can be set up to ascertain the requirements of autonomy. See Mill (1971).

[3] An author even speaks of an "insuperable paradox of vulnerability," one which is an unspecified as to its consequences, and which would seem to exclude the most vulnerable, such as the elderly and the sick from the "right to make their own choices," including about euthanasia: see Cornacchia. In the same vein, see D'Agostino (1998), pp. 218–219.

reunite with one's own family, getting uprooted from one's own homeland, unhappy romantic relationships, an inability to have children, or job failures—that can make a person fragile, vulnerable, or unhappy. And yet it would be absurd to qualify the fragility or distress that the occurrence of such events gives rise to as a legally obstructive condition for the performance of certain actions. When does vulnerability represent an obstacle from a liberal point of view and result in a form of incompetence? It does so when there is an issue of rationality (from the point of view of a formal conception) or of mental capacity, as when a person has a severe neurosis or borderline personality disorder.

Let us see why, as I said, the enactment and enforcement of a body of antipaternalistic and antiprohibitionist drug legislation would likely result in more benefits than costs to the community,[4] that is, why the costs—including but not limited to bureaucratic costs—would be far outweighed by the benefits. I will point out four reasons. Our analysis of these reasons will inevitably lead us toward the defense of an antiprohibitionist thesis. Let us look at them.

First, in order to carry out most of the authorization procedures for authorizing harmful/dangerous actions, such as consuming cocaine and heroin, one could use, and indeed rationalize, the work of existing institutions and medical personnel (in hospitals, for example), without having to create new institutions. For example, cocaine and heroin could be sold in pharmacies upon presentation of a health card issued upon authorization by a private or hospital physician.

Second, some people would be unwilling to bear the economic costs (the fees built into the price of narcotics), the temporal costs (the time needed for the procedure), or the psychological costs (incurred in connection with the interview with the doctor) involved in obtaining medical clearance for consumption. Other people would be unwilling to go through with the procedure itself once they find out that they have false or inconsistent beliefs. I think that many people will continue not to consume narcotics, even though they might be authorized to do so.

Third, the bureaucratic costs of the procedures could in part be covered through the payment of a fee, an indirect tax embedded in the price of the cocaine or marijuana.

There is, finally, another reason, the fourth, why antipaternalism and antiprohibition are much more convenient than paternalism and prohibition, in that any additional economic costs of adopting antipaternalist or antiprohibitionist laws would always be lower than the economic benefits of antipaternalism and antiprohibition itself. Indeed, there are areas where antipaternalistic and antiprohibitionist laws—sad to say but true—could bring in huge profits for the state, as would happen with

[4] In any case, after nearly a hundred years of failed prohibitionist policies, the time has come to try a different path, to empirically observe what the costs and benefits of antiprohibition and antipaternalism would be.

the legalization of the illegal drug market, of part of the prostitution market (when there is consent, not coercion, of the prostitute), or of gambling.[5]

First of all, legalization of certain activities, such as gambling and prostitution, always leads to higher tax revenues, if only because certain activities/professions would no longer be carried out "off the books," but in the light of day, with associated payment of direct taxes, income taxes, and any pension contributions. There are, secondly, many studies related to the costs of prohibition in the area of drug sales and consumption. These costs or harms can reasonably be broken down into four types (cf. Husak (1992), p. 51ff.; Tincani (2012)).

7.2 Four Types of Harms of Drugs Prohibitionism

(1) Economic costs related to the "war on drugs" (investigations, prosecutions, imprisonment of drug producers and distributors) and lost revenues, i.e., indirect taxes that could be imposed on the consumption of certain drugs, once their sale is legalized (similar costs are incurred in the prohibition of gambling or of prostitution).
(2) Harms resulting from crimes committed by consumers purchasing drugs, which on the illegal market normally have very high prices.[6] To avoid such harms within a legal framework, controlled administration of cocaine and heroin could be carried out for compulsive and underserved consumers.
(3) Harms arising from crimes committed by organized crime (murder, injury, kidnapping, extortion, and money laundering, as well as the bribery of politicians, police officers, judges, or government administrators).[7]

---

[5] I say "part of" the prostitution market because, clearly, it is not right to legalize the slavery of sex workers, some of whom, a minority, one in seven according to the European Commission, are in various ways forced into prostitution.

[6] That this is a classic argument validly made by antiprohibitionists is underscored by Alldridge (1996), pp. 243–244.

[7] Husak distinguishes three types of crimes dependent on the sale and use of drugs. Two of these, the most important, are related to prohibition, i.e., systemic crime (violence and harm committed by criminal organizations) and economic crime, i.e., theft and robbery committed by users to obtain the coveted dose (given the high price of the same dose in the illegal market). The third type of crime would be "pharmacological," where the crime is dependent on the cognitive and emotional alteration that narcotics cause in users. On the alleged pharmacological effects, widely overstated in the media, that would turn users into so many Mr. Hydes, see Sect. 7.2 below. See Husak (2002), p. 84. On police corruption induced or caused by drug trafficking, see Husak (2002), p. 149ff. Since the criminogenic source par excellence is prohibition itself, it makes little sense, as Alldridge points out, that the argument on the criminogenic effects of drug consumption should be put forward by prohibitionist judges and jurists. On the damage caused by prohibitionism, see also MacCoun and Reuter (2004), p. 326; Rolles (2009), p. 71ff. On the distorting effects of criminal organizations on the economy, see, generally, Lavezzi (2014). These effects are greater the more powerful the criminal organizations are (and the more prosperous the sources of profit). See Wikipedia (2023b); Miron and Earleywine (2010).

(4) Harms to users' physical integrity, life, and property as a result of their drug use under conditions of poor hygiene, poor quality control, violence, or exploitation ("cut" substances, overdosing, blackmailing of users in withdrawal.)[8]

Even the World Drug Report 2022 recognizes the advantages of legalization of cannabis.

> A combination of drivers, public policy concerns and ambitions have led to countries and state-level jurisdictions in Canada, the United States and Uruguay legalizing the entire cannabis supply chain and adopting measures allowing the production and sale of cannabis for non-medical use by commercial and for-profit entities.
>
> Reducing both law enforcement costs, especially the policing of possession for personal use of cannabis, thus freeing up resources to address more serious crimes.
>
> Those concerns or aspirations include:
>
> Permitting non-medical use of cannabis among adults while preventing its use among adolescents
>
> For governments and authorities themselves to generate revenue from the cultivation, production and sale of cannabis, depriving organized crime groups of income and investing part of the revenue in prevention of substance use and treatment of drug use disorders, thus protecting public health and safety.
>
> Addressing criminal justice responses because treating the possession of cannabis for personal use as a criminal offence had led to many people being arrested and acquiring a criminal record, with ethnic minorities being disproportionally affected by such policies in countries such as the United States
>
> Establishing a regulated market to ensure product quality (THC content) and prevent the use of hazardous contaminants in production
>
> Analyzing the impact of cannabis legalization
>
> Preventing organized crime groups from generating profits from the illicit trade in cannabis. (World Drug Report 2022, sect. 3)

There is no single antiprohibitionist strategy, particularly when it comes to the drug market. There are different proposals, e.g., Friedman's more "libertarian" proposals, i.e., (1) relying on the self-regulatory mechanisms of free-market competition, allowing drugs to be sold, with very few restrictions (e.g., for minors) like any other good in a free-market regime. There are more restrictive, statist proposals, such as (2) creating a market system with more restrictions, controls (e.g., where individuals can be cleared to buy certain drugs at pharmacies by showing a health card), and a level of taxation that would cover, in whole or in part, the costs of education highlighting the risks and harms of drug use and the social and health costs of drug abuse, or (3) entrusting to the state, under a monopoly regime, the production and/or refining and distribution of drugs. Taradash argues that any solution based on legalizing the market would likely have the same effect on the supply side, drastically reducing the price of drugs, while immediately putting criminal organizations

---

[8] On the various forms of exploitation and blackmail that consumers can suffer from drug dealers who control a monopolistic market at a local level, see Alldridge (1996), p. 247.

out of business and stifling induced crime, but here I will only take into account the assumptions made in relation to the second and third systems of drug-market regulation, those involving a system of taxes and oversight controls.[9]

Two economists, Jeffrey Miron and Katherine Waldock, have calculated that antiprohibitionist policies on the selling and consumption of drugs, such as those under the "taxation and control" (or oversight) model, with or without a state monopoly, could mean, by a very conservative estimate,

> that drug legalization would reduce government expenditure by about $41.3 billion annually. Roughly $25.7 billion of this savings would accrue to state and local governments, and roughly $15.6 billion would accrue to the federal government. Approximately $8.7 billion of the savings would result from legalization of marijuana, $20.0 billion from legalization of cocaine and heroin, and $12.6 from legalization of all other drugs. Legalization would also generate tax revenue of roughly $46.7 billion annually if drugs were taxed at rates comparable to those on alcohol and tobacco. Approximately $8.7 billion of this revenue would result from legalization of marijuana, $32.6 billion from legalization of cocaine and heroin, and $5.5 billion from legalization of all other drugs. Miron and Waldock (2010), p. 1

In the United States alone, in other words, and by a very conservative estimate, legalization could bring in about $88 billion in increased revenue per year, counting lower expenditures and higher revenues: lower expenditures attributable to the end of the fight against drug trafficking, coupled with higher revenues from indirect taxes on drug use once the drugs are legalized. It would be sufficient for cocaine, hashish, or marijuana to be sold at a price that incorporates indirect taxes, i.e., VAT or excise taxes, equivalent to those in place today for tobacco sales (in Europe, this is an average of 75% of the price). It is not possible, nor is it important here, to make precise calculations regarding Italy. Supposing that per capita consumption of narcotics and per capita costs for the use of police forces, criminal trials, and the detention of drug dealers are somewhat lower in Italy than in the United States, where the rates of drug use are very high and the war on drugs very aggressive, we would be looking at an increased revenue of about 10 billion euros per year in Italy alone, where the population is about one-sixth that of the United States. It would, however, be a huge amount, equal to about half of the Meloni government's 2024 budget bill of 24 billion. Other studies show far more optimistic prospects of lower expenditures and higher revenues in the event of legalization, and they also seem to be empirically well founded. A study by Piero David and Ferdinando Ofria calculated, for the cannabis market alone, that legalization would increase tax revenues by 6 to 8.7 billion euros, depending on the price of a dose of cannabis, and counting lower expenses and higher revenues. On the basis of official data, David and Ofria (2017) calculated about 540 million euros in costs that the government incurred in 2011 in its effort to fight the sale of cannabis, counting prison expenses and 228 million euros for public order and security. They then calculated how much the tax revenue could be from the sale of as many doses of cannabis as are assumed to have been consumed in 2011, making different estimates depending on whether the dose was

[9]A detailed analysis of these proposals is carried out in Taradash (1991), p. 170ff., and Rolles (2009), p. 20ff.

sold for 12, 10, or 8 euros, with an indirect tax of 75%. The amount of drugs consumed was estimated on the basis of AquaDrug surveys of drug residues in wastewater purifiers. That would be an average of 36 doses per 1,000 inhabitants in Italy in 2011, which means a tax-revenue increase ranging from 5.3 billion euros to 8 billion euros depending on whether a single dose was sold for 8, 10, or 12 euros. The retail price of cannabis per gram is the equivalent of about 12 dollars in Italy and between 10 and 12 dollars in other European countries.

In any case, engaging in harmful or dangerous activities, such as consuming tobacco or heroin, entails healthcare costs for the community. At the same time, however—tragic to say but true to fact—it also reduces costs, because some consumers, especially of tobacco, die prematurely, which means that the state no longer has to spend money on those old-age pensions and healthcare costs.

Add to that a reduction in the crimes that users commit to finance their "vice," in that free cocaine and heroin could be administered, for example, to compulsive or addicted heroin or cocaine users who are poor or not wealthy (see Husak 1992, p. 54).

Of course, it is not easy "to calculate the tax rate that needs to be levied on each substance in order to achieve the twofold result of reducing consumption without fostering the emergence of a black market and partially covering its social cost" (Taradash (1991), p. 177, my translation; cf. Rolles (2009), p. 41ff.). And yet, as Miron points out, not only is this possible, but there is clear evidence that such taxation can be imposed without engendering a significant illegal market. And the strongest evidence is the absence of a significant illegal market for tobacco or alcohol in Europe.

It is not important a detailed proposal here, nor would I have the tools to make such a proposal. Suffice it to recall, however, that according to the 2009 and 2012 United Nations Reports, one kilogram of cocaine could be purchased wholesale in 2007 for about $2000 in Colombia ($2400 in 2010), the producer country par excellence; $2000 per kilogram means $2 per gram. And the retail price for a kilogram of cocaine was about $110,000 in Italy in 2010 (in the US, that figure was $120,000 per kilogram in 2010), and so about 50 times the wholesale price. According to the World Drug Report 2019, the wholesale price of a kilogram of cocaine in Colombia was $1500 in 2017; in Western Europe, the retail price of a gram of cocaine ranged from $80 to $100, $92 on average in Italy.

Now there are many studies indicating that production and refining costs are only a small part of the retail price: 4%. According to a study by Jonathan Caulkins, even just transportation on ships is negligible, as are inventory costs. Then, too, there are no marketing or advertising costs or taxes. Excluding money-laundering costs (2–4%), the real problem for traffickers, Caulkins says, are importation costs (about 12%), the cost from police seizures (which cause significant losses: about 10%), and, finally, the high costs of illegal labor (13%), from individual couriers to retail dealers, from those who "pack" the stuff to those who act as "lookouts" (to warn if the police come).

In sum, in total, according to Caulkins, profit margins should hover around 55% of the final selling price, which would compensate organized crime for the high risks—the risk of being injured or killed by rival gangs or police in a firefight, as well as risk of being sentenced to many years in prison.[10] This means that after deducting costs, we get a huge profit margin, at least 2,500 to 3,000%, which in turn explains why no deterrent, not even life imprisonment or the death penalty, can prevent the illegal trade. As I argue in the epigraphs quotes from the movies *Traffic* and *The Barbarian Invasions*, the illegal drug market is an unstoppable force; the demand for drugs, a true invasion, is too high for the illegality of the market to halt the supply of drugs.

Taking into account that, once the sale and consumption of drugs is legalized, the costs of importing labor from economically developing countries—in 2020, these countries were Colombia, Peru, and Bolivia for cocaine; Morocco, Afghanistan, Pakistan, and Lebanon, for cannabis; Afghanistan, Myanmar, Mexico, and Laos for opium (World Drug Report 2022, sect. 3)—would be much lower (say, 20% of the current sale price for drugs), and that Western importing states could completely forgo profits (such as marketing and advertising, which are also inadvisable) by merely introducing an indirect tax that raises the price of drugs by 100% over the net cost of production and distribution, they would be able to sell narcotics at a retail price (say, $40 per gram of cocaine) that is 60% lower than the actual price in the illicit market, which averaged $112 per gram of cocaine in Italy, in 2007, and 92 dollars in 2019, making it unlikely that a thriving underground market could develop. Indeed, the state, as is the case with so-called "natural monopolies" (distribution of water or electricity), could buy and sell narcotics with very low profit margins.

Third, as for organized crime, it is clear that one of its most important sources of profit would disappear. Greatly diminished, in part due to the legalization of part of the prostitution and gambling market, would be the turnover of organized crime, its ability to bribe the political, financial, and banking systems, corruption that inevitably leads to an increase in the cost of public contracts (cf. Husak (1992), p. 53ff). So fewer crimes would be committed by users because it would take less money to purchase drugs. In addition, there could be less costly or free controlled administration for severely dependent and low-income consumers. Of course, Less crime means less damage to health, less injury to the physical integrity and lives of others, less medical expenses incurred by the community, fewer police investigations, and fewer criminal trials.

In 2009, A. M. Costa, executive director of the United Nations Office on Drugs and Crime (UNODOC), argued that in the event of legalization, organized crime would shift its business to other markets—such as trafficking in arms, human beings, or organs—making the legalization of narcotics completely futile. But this

[10] See Caulkins and Reuter (1998), p. 595ff. It must be said that Caulkin and Reuter's study dates back to (1998), when the retail price of cocaine was much higher than in 2006. According to Costa Storti, due to globalization, profit margins and the costs of distribution and of transport have further decreased, in absolute value, but we do not know, or the author does not say, how much in relative terms (percentage-wise). In any case, because import and labor costs had fallen to 35%, this would mean that, in relative terms, profit margins would have risen by 65%. See later in the text and note 30.

argument faces a very strong objection. In some fundamental respects, the illegal market is not very different from the legal market. It is governed by the law of supply and demand. Organized crime cannot create demand for illegal goods and services. It cannot increase the demand for weapons, slaves, or organs at will. It can certainly arrange to increase supply, to better meet existing demand, or to intercept new needs, more sophisticated needs (e.g., new weapons) or new market sectors, but it cannot significantly alter demand. Put explicitly, if consumers stop buying narcotics from the mafia, does that mean they will start acquiring semi-automatic guns or AK-47 assault rifles?

In this sense, the likelihood that organized crime can recover profits from drug trafficking by selling weapons or slaves is very low. Crime cannot decide to sell as many weapons or to market as many slaves to recover the profits lost from drug trafficking (cf. World Drug Report 2009, p. 3; Rolles 2009, p. 92).

Fourth, drug quality would be much better, and clean syringes could be administered for free; in short, there would be fewer infections. Hepatitis and AIDS infections, for example, are widespread among heroin addicts because of prohibition. There would also be fewer overdose deaths, and less damage to health and property.[11] In fact, several empirical studies show that producers and sellers in illegal drug markets, having profit as their sole purpose, tend to produce psychotropic substances that are much more risky (to health) because they are more potent and concentrated (Rolles 2009, p. 124), examples being crack and the synthetic cannabinoids (HHCs) identified in the 2022 European Drug Report, while legal markets for psychotropic substances, as in the case of alcohol, tend to (or can) produce less harmful and less concentrated variants (cf. Husak 1992, p. 54ff.; World Drug Report 2022, sect. 3). Even in a legal market some pharmaceutical companies could be induced to produce new drugs that have the same positive effects as existing ones (euphoria, relaxation, mood elevation) but not the same harmful effects. Finally, it should be considered that ending drug control would bring enormous international benefits, not only in terms of saving the many resources the United Nations spends on the fight against drugs, but with respect to the huge incidence of crime, murder, injury, robbery, political and judicial corruption, and money laundering committed in producing and distributing countries by the gangs that in Mexico, Colombia, and Bolivia seek to control the narcotics market. These are countries in which the level of corruption of officials, police, politics, the level of violence and of insecurity in the streets, and fear of citizens for their safety reaches levels unthinkable for an average European (cf. Rolles 2009, p. 84ff.). Drug-consuming countries in Europe, North America, and Australia could even decide which producing countries to buy from, excluding, for example, states that aid or finance terrorism, e.g., Afghanistan if it were ruled by the Taliban, which in UN World Drug Report 2008 was listed as

---

[11] Cf. Taradash (1991), p. 196. On the spread of hepatitis and AIDS among heroin addicts due to prohibition, see Husak (2002), p. 137ff.

the largest producer of opium in the world.[12] According to World Drug Report 2022, sect. 3:

> Of the 57 countries where illicit opium production was reported over the last decade, three alone collectively accounted for 97 per cent of estimated illicit opium production in the period 2017–2021. Afghanistan remained by far the world's largest source of opium, accounting for an estimated 86 per cent of global illicit production in 2021. Afghan opium supplies markets all over Eurasia and Africa, and a negligible proportion reaches North America and Oceania. Opium produced in South-East Asia, mostly in Myanmar (6 per cent of global production) and the Lao People's Democratic Republic (about 1 per cent), supplies markets in East and South-East Asia and Oceania, while opium produced in Latin America, mostly in Mexico (close to 6 per cent) and to a more marginal extent in Colombia and Guatemala (less than 1 per cent), accounts for most of the heroin supplied to the United States and the relatively limited heroin markets of South America.

7.3 The False Use of Harm Principle in the Arguments in Favour of the Criminalisation of Drugs

It could be counterargued, however, that an antiprohibitionist policy would entail some additional costs, and two in particular.

According to some authors, such as Robert J. MacCoun and Peter Reuter, as a result of the legalization of the narcotics market, there would be a significant increase in the consumption of narcotics, an estimated 1000 to 2000%. In fact there would be a kind of epidemic of narcotics consumption, and so there would be (1) greater damage to health (damage from the consumption of the substances, affecting, for example, the mucous membranes or respiratory tract, or a potential increase in heart attacks due to the consumption of cocaine),[13] and (2) increased damage to

[12] Other disadvantages of prohibitionism include the violation or erosion of civil rights; the deep distrust that many young people feel toward politicians and doctors who shamelessly lie about the effects of consumption and prohibitionism; the criminalization and marginalization of the poorer classes and of African Americans, often enlisted among drug dealers; the destruction of the work ethic due to the enormous ease of "making money" through drug dealing, the overcrowding of prisons through mass incarceration; and the restricted access to some drugs for medical purposes. These disadvantages are reported by Husak (1992, p. 55ff.), and some are obviously specific to the United States. "Politics and hysteria, not science and sound principles, continue to fuel our drug policy" Husak (2002), p. 145.

[13] It must be said that, according to some estimates, only a quarter of consumers have health problems. "The estimates relating to the use of cocaine applied to the Italian population aged between 15 and 54, amounting to 32,230,000 people, indicate that approximately 1,300,000 subjects used this substance in 2003. Within this population of users, approximately 300,000 subjects can be estimated who have characteristics of cocaine use that represent a serious problem for individual health (problem users)" (Molinaro et al. (2006), my translation). On mental and physical disorders caused by the abuse or chronic use of cocaine, see Serpelloni et al. (2006), p. 201ff., 259 ff. Husak reports medical opinions according to which the use of cocaine and heroin, unlike tobacco and alcohol, is not a significant risk factor for many serious diseases (such as vascular diseases and tumors of various kinds). See Husak (1992), p. 97; Husak (2002), p. 105. The 2009 Annual Report on the State of the Drugs Problem in Europe (EMCDDA 2009) reports that intravenous intake of

crack and cocaine is associated with the highest health risks (including cardiovascular and mental problems). Furthermore, chronic health problems and treatment needs concern intensive and long-term users, health conditions which are further aggravated for a marginal group of consumers, i.e., those who take cocaine parenterally (less than 7%), poly junkies, and chronic users, especially crack users—in other words "members of socially excluded groups, including former or current opioid users, most of whom follow intensive patterns of cocaine use, probably using crack or injecting the substance, with negative consequences on the duration or severity of existing health and social problems, which can also complicate treatment for opioid addiction" (EMCDDA (2009, p. 66, 74). In general, the EMCDDA report points out that "frequent cocaine users are seven times more likely to suffer a non-fatal myocardial infarction than those who do not use the substance" and that several studies show that many hospitalizations "urgency in hospital (for palpitation, chest pain, agitation) are due to taking cocaine" (EMCDDA (2009), p. 72). "In 2020, only Czechia, Spain, Luxembourg and Norway reported meeting the World Health Organization's 2020 targets of providing 200 syringes per person who injects drugs per year and having 40% of the population of high-risk opioid users on opioid agonist treatment. This points to a continuing need to scale up treatment and harm reduction provision for opioid users and those who inject drugs. The prevalence of high-risk opioid use among adults (15–64) is estimated at 0.34% for the EU adult population, equivalent to around 1 million high-risk opioid users in 2020. There were 514,000 clients in opioid agonist treatment in 2020 in the European Union, suggesting that overall treatment coverage is around 50%. However, this figure masks the fact that there are considerable differences between countries in the extent to which those with opioid problems are likely to be able to access opioid agonist treatment, and in some countries the provision is clearly insufficient" EMCDDA (2022). According to the European Drug Report, cocaine users entering treatment are 14,000 (first-time entrants) and 16,000 (previously treated entrants), about 1%. "Our overall assessment is that drug availability and use remain at high levels across the European Union, although considerable differences exist between countries. Approximately 83.4 million or 29% of adults (aged 15–64) in the European Union are estimated to have ever used an illicit drug, with more males (50.5 million) than females (33.0 million) reporting use. Cannabis remains the most widely consumed substance, with over 22 million European adults reporting its use in the last year. Stimulants are the second most commonly reported category. It is estimated that in the last year 3.5 million adults consumed cocaine, 2.6 million MDMA and 2 million amphetamines. Around 1 million Europeans were high-risk users of heroin or another illicit opioid in the last year. Although the prevalence of use is lower for opioid use than for other drugs, opioids still account for the greatest share of harms attributed to illicit drug use. This is illustrated by the presence of opioids, often in combination with other substances, which was found in around three quarters of fatal overdoses reported in the European Union for 2020. *It is important to note that most of those with drug problems will be using a range of substances*" EMCDDA (2022). "Problem drug users are people who engage in the high-risk consumption of drugs. For example, *people who inject drugs, people who use drugs on a daily basis* and/or people diagnosed with drug use disorders (harmful use or drug dependence), based on clinical criteria as contained in the Diagnostic and Statistical Manual of Mental Disorders (fifth edition) of the American Psychiatric Association, or the International Classification of Diseases and Related Health Problems (tenth revision) of WHO. People who suffer from drug use disorders/people with drug use disorders—a subset of people who use drugs. Harmful use of substances and dependence are features of drug use disorders. People with drug use disorders need treatment, health and social care and rehabilitation" (World Drug Report (2022), sect. 3).

"North America is the world's largest market for cocaine. The prevalence of past-year cocaine use in 2020 is estimated at 2 per cent among the population aged 15–64, translating to 6.4 million past-year users." According to the National Survey on Drug Use and Health in Unites States (NSDUH 2021), past-year consumers of illicit drugs among persons aged 12 or older in 2019 were in total 57,200,000, about 20,8%. Past-year consumers of cocaine among persons aged 12 or older physical integrity resulting from an increase in traffic accidents, workplace accidents, and violent crimes in general (injuries and child and domestic abuse).[14] There is a lack of studies giving a definitive answer to the question of increased consumption, because a program to legalize all drugs has not been attempted in any country recently. As Husak points out, no one in this field has the gift of clairvoyance; no one knows for sure what would happen once the sale and consumption of narcotics were to be legalized and regulated, not least because, as we will see later by analyzing the Dutch case, the trends in drug use in different Western countries (e.g., peak marijuana use in the United States in 1978–1979, peak cocaine use, also in the United States, in 1985) show that it is largely influenced by social and cultural factors that have little to do with the use of state coercion. Evidence of this would be the decline in alcohol and tobacco consumption in the 1980s, despite consumption and sale being legal, and the subsequent increase in the 1990s (Cf. Husak 2002: p. 160; Husak 1992: p. 11ff., 155). However, there are four arguments that work

in 2019 were 5,468,000, about 2.0%, 2.1% among people aged 18 or older. Past-year consumers of marijuana among persons aged 12 or older in 2019 were 48,242,000, about 17.5%, about 18% among persons aged 18 or older and about 35.4% among persons aged 18–25. Past-year consumers of crack among persons aged 12 or older in 2019 were 778,000, about 0.3%. Past-year consumers of heroin among persons aged 12 or older in 2019 were 745,000, about 0.3%. Past-year consumers of methamphetamine among persons aged 12 or older in 2019 were 1,999,000, about 0.7%. Past-year consumers of hallucinogens—ketamine, methoxetamine (MXE), phencyclidine (PCP), dextromethorphan (DXM), nitrous oxide, LSD, MDMA, or Ecstasy—among persons aged 12 or older in 2019 were 6,010,000, about 2.2%. Past-year consumers of illicit drugs among people aged 12 or older who have a substance use disorder are 8,313,000, and past-year cocaine consumers among people aged 12 or older who have a substance use disorder are 1,011,000, about one-fifth, 18%, and the percentage of the population among 12 or older who consumed cocaine in the past year with a substance use disorder was 0.4% in 2019, one-fifth of the total of consumers of cocaine. Past-year consumers of marijuana with a substance use disorder among people 12 or older are 4,836,000, about 10% of total consumers. Past-year consumers of heroin with a substance use disorder among people aged 12 or older were 438,000 in 2019, 0.2% of the population aged 12–64, about 58% of the consumers of heroin. Past-year consumers of hallucinogens with a substance use disorder among people aged 12 or older were 274,000 in 2019, about 4.5% of consumers of hallucinogens. Past-year consumers of methamphetamine with a substance use disorder among people aged 12 or older were 1,048,000 in 2019, about 50% of consumers of methamphetamine. Past-year consumers of alcohol with a substance use disorder among persons aged 12 or older were 14,500,000 in 2019, about 8.10% of total consumers. Past-year consumers of alcohol among persons aged 12 or older in 2019 were in total 179,144,000. The percentage of past-year consumers of alcohol with a substance use disorder among persons aged 12 or older in 2019 was about 5.3%, 5.6% among people aged 18 or older. The population in United States in 2020 among people aged 15 older was about 271,464,000. The percentage of past-year consumers of illicit drugs with a substance use disorder among persons aged twelve or older was about 3% in 2019. See Wikipedia (2023a); World Drug Report (2008).

[14] Cf. Donini (2008), p. 86; MacCoun and Reuter (2004), p. 333ff. Apocalyptic frescoes by prohibitionists (especially Americans and/or US government officials) are not uncommon. Daniel Lungren, for example, former attorney general of California, believes that the legalization of drugs would lead to an increase in homelessness, unemployment, the need for social assistance, loss of productivity, reimbursements for the disabled, the school dropout rate, lawsuits, medical costs, chronic mental illnesses, accidents, crime, child abuse, and abandonment. Cf. Husak (1992, p. 150ff.), Husak (2002, 151ff).

strongly against the "drug epidemic" or "zombie" argument, where *zombie*, in this context, refers to drug addicts, with blunted perceptions, hungry for money and drugs. Hence, it can be said that the harm principle is invoked by such prohibitionist authors in a false or specious way.

First, if legalizing of narcotics would lead to a significant increase in consumption, this means that prohibiting such substances should cause an equally significant reduction in their consumption.[15] And this is very doubtful. Several studies have analyzed the levels of alcohol consumption before and after the so-called "prohibitionism" of alcohol itself in the United States (1920–1933), the levels of opiate consumption in the United States before and after prohibition, and the impact on cocaine consumption owed to a massive use of resources in the fight against drugs from the mid-1980s onwards, in the United States. These studies show that there is no correlation between prohibiting the sale and consumption of drugs and any significant reduction in the consumption of alcohol, opiates, or cocaine, and therefore that prohibiting the sale and consumption of drugs or ramping up the effort to choke the market in drugs, where this effort is undertaken, at best results in a decrease in consumption never exceeding 20%.[16]

Other authors argue that it would exponentially increase consumption because legalizing the sale and consumption of drugs brings with it the disappearance of penalties and especially an important symbolic effect, namely, the idea that from a certain point onward, taking narcotics is acceptable or legitimate. The argument of deterrence—greater penalties, greater repression equals less consumption—is sadly put forward by some US authors in defiance of the available empirical data (cf.

[15] Furthermore, as Taradash commented as early as 1991, "antiprohibitionists can today attribute to the prohibitionist system a constant growth in the number of consumers of illicit drugs and in the number of countries and even continents involved in consumption and trafficking, as well as a resurgent market in drugs that have long disappeared (such as cocaine) and the introduction of new drugs that are more dangerous to health (such as crack)" (Taradash (1991), p. 160). The same thing could be said of the "resurgence" of heroin in the 1990s and in the subsequent decades.

[16] Cf. Miron (2004), p. 34ff., 37ff. With great acumen and precision, Miron dismantles the strongest empirical argument always put forward by North American prohibitionists, namely, that during Prohibition in the United States there was a significant reduction in alcohol consumption (see Husak (1992), p. 154). In reality, Miron shows that there are no reliable data relating to that period on the reduction in alcohol consumption, and that the official data mainly concern the decrease in deaths from cirrhosis, which is a typical disease associated with alcoholism. In reality, deaths from cirrhosis decreased significantly from 1910 onwards and then stabilized around 1920, i.e., at the time of the introduction of the federal prohibitionist law; therefore, the reduction in deaths from cirrhosis could hardly depend on this federal law. Furthermore, there was a decrease in deaths from cirrhosis (before 1919) both in the northern states of the United States which had already adopted prohibitionist laws and in those where such laws (before 1919) had not been adopted. Robert J. MacCoun and Peter Reuter agree on the fact that during Prohibition the consumption of alcohol decreased insignificantly; they instead underline that after the Harrison Act of 1914, making opiates illegal, their consumption fell, even though, and this is a decidedly ironic aspect, the per capita consumption of cocaine before 1914, when it could freely be purchased and marketed in many North American states, was much lower than it was in the 1990s. This would show, once again, the modest impact of the policies of criminalization and enforcement of prohibition by the state (both in one sense and in the other). See MacCoun and Reuter (2004), p. 307ff.

MacCoun and Reuter 2004, 96ff., 305ff.). If the criminalization of consumption, and aggressive enforcement of prohibitionist policies, led to a significant reduction in per capita consumption, some US states which prohibit the consumption and sale of cannabis, cocaine, and other drugs should have a very low number of per capita users, and states that have implemented policies decriminalizing the consumption of moderate amounts of marijuana, cocaine, and heroin starting in the 1990s or have recently legalized the sale and consumption of cannabis should have seen a significant surge in consumption. In contrast, some US states which prohibit the consumption and sale of cannabis, cocaine, and other drugs have high levels of cocaine and marijuana use, a higher rate than almost any European country,[17] in many of which (as in Italy) there is either no criminal penalty for consumption or only an administrative penalty, and decriminalization or legalization of cannabis in other countries,

---

[17] The 2009 World Drug Report calculates that in 2007 there was a percentage of cannabis users equal to 12.3% in the United States, surpassed only by Italy with 14%. In US states which prohibit the sale and consumption of cannabis, annual cannabis consumption reached 13.5% of the population in 2015, and 13.9% in 2016. See World Drug Report 2018. Here is the data according the World Drug Report 2022 for Europe: in 2020 in the Netherlands, 10%; Czechia 9.5%; England and Wales, 7%; Spain, 10.5%; Ireland, 7.5%; Croatia, 10.2%; Austria, 6%; Sweden and Norway, 4%; Germany, 7%.

Compare that with the fact that in 2007 the United States, with its 2.8% of cocaine users, was "beaten" only by Spain (3%) and Scotland (3.8%). The World Drug Report 2013 reports, for 2011, a percentage of cocaine users of 1.5% in North America and 1.2% in Central and Western Europe, confirming higher percentages in Italy, Spain, and Great Britain compared to other European countries. According to the 2022 World Drug Report, the percentage of crack and cocaine users in 2020 in United States was about 2.3% of people above the age of 12. Cf. SAMHSA (2020) and Johnston et al. (2022). "North America is the world's largest market for cocaine. The prevalence of past-year cocaine use in 2020 is estimated at 2 per cent among the population aged 15–64, translating to 6.4 million past-year users" (World Drug Report 2022, sect. 4). "The prevalence of the use of cocaine products among the adult population in Europe in 2020 was estimated at 1 per cent, more than double the global average. In the European Union, cocaine is the second most used drug after cannabis, and the third most frequently reported primary drug upon entry into drug treatment. The use of cocaine is concentrated mainly in Western and Central Europe, with an estimated prevalence of 1.4 per cent, or 4.6 million past-year users, making the subregion the second largest market for cocaine in the world" (World Drug Report (2022), sect. 4). In Western and Central Europe users of cocaine increased about 50% from 2014 to 2019. Very troubling is the trend of cocaine use among high school students aged 15–16 in Western and Central Europe in 2019, which was 4.2% in the UK, 2.6% in France, 2.2% in Italy, 2% in Spain, 1.8% in the Netherlands, and 1.2% in Germany. World Drug report 2022, sect. 4. According to the National Survey on Drug Use and Health (NSDUH (2021), past-year consumers of illicit drugs in United States among persons aged 12 or older in 2019 were in total 57.200.000, about 20.8%. Past-year consumers of cocaine among persons aged 12 or older in 2019 were 5,468,000, about 2.0%, 2.1% among people aged 18 or older. Past-year consumers of marijuana among persons aged 12 or older in 2019 were 48,242,000, about 17.5%, about 18% among persons aged 18 or older and about 35.4% among persons aged 18–25. Past-year consumers of crack among persons aged 12 or older in 2019 were 778,000, about 0.3%. Past-year consumers of heroin among persons aged 12 or older in 2019 were 745,000, about 0.3%. Past-year consumers of alcohol among persons aged 12 or older in 2019 were in total 179,144,000. The percentage of past-year consumers of alcohol with a substance use disorder among persons aged 12 or older was about 5.3%, 5.6% among people aged 18 or older, in 2019. The US population in 2020 among people aged 15 or older is about 271,464,000.

including some US states and Mexico, does not seem to have led to any significant increase in consumption.

On the contrary, several studies show that many people do not consume drugs simply for moral or prudential reasons, such as avoiding harm or risk to their health or avoiding disapproval from their target social group, and that the existence of forms of stigma or social exclusion has a much greater effect than an increase in expected legal penalties or the likelihood of being punished by the state (cf. MacCoun and Reuter 2004, p. 88ff., 90ff., 99ff.). This explains the conditions under which the deterrence argument can, in general, work. The deterrence argument—according to which criminalizing a behavior (such as consuming cocaine) decreases the expected utility from engaging in that behavior, because of the likelihood of being punished—does not work with narcotics not only because the argument, such as it is commonly presented in relation to drug use, presupposes the very thesis it sets out to prove (*petitio principii*), namely, that many people do not consume controlled substances precisely because that behavior is punished, but also because, as mentioned, the latter thesis is largely false.[18]

Second, the available empirical data tells us that despite more than 54 years (since 1970) of de facto legalization of marijuana consumption in coffee shops in the Netherlands, the level of per capita marijuana consumption in the Netherlands is not much higher than in the US states which prohibit the consumption and sale of cannabis, cocaine, and other drugs, Great Britain, Spain, Italy, and other European countries, where the sale of marijuana is prohibited, and that the number of coffee shops has declined over the past decade. In these US states, annual cannabis consumption reached 13.5% of the population in 2015, and 13.9% in 2016. According to the 2021 National Survey on Drug Use and Health (NSDUH 2021), past-year consumers of illicit drugs among persons aged 12 and older in 2019 in the United

[18]The deterrence argument, from Bentham and Beccaria onwards, only works within a group of people who have already decided to commit a crime, such as rape or murder. In this case, increasing the disutility expected from carrying out the act in question (for example, murder) will lead, if criminals are sufficiently coherent and informed of the relevant facts, to a decrease in murders. But this only applies within a group of potential murderers. Conversely, we should see a proportional growth in murders if the price of a murder carried out by a professional killer on the black market were to decrease significantly. The argument, therefore, applied to drugs, works if it is demonstrated that the fundamental reason why people do not consume drugs is that their sale is illegal. But this assumption is refuted by different studies, including, see below, the levels of consumption in the Netherlands—lower in 2015, a little higher in 2020—which changes which are independent of legalization. Secondly, the argument according to which legalizing a behavior undermines the symbolic effect of criminalization is very dubious. The argument presupposes that the majority of people avoid engaging in certain behavior not for moral reasons (killing is wrong) or for fear of a violent reaction from the potential victim, or out of cowardice, a sense of guilt, or for fear of retaliation from the victim's family, or fear of being despised, marginalized, and estranged from parents, partners, friends, relatives, colleagues, or fear of losing one's job, or for reasons of mere calculation of legal costs/benefits (the concrete risk of being condemned versus the possible gain), but out of a kind of legalistic conformism according to which if the state establishes "X is illegal," there will be a reason for not doing X; therefore, it is better to behave obediently. I won't comment further. For the use of the deterrence argument and the symbolic value of criminalization, see MacCoun and Reuter (2004), p. 87ff., 99ff.

States were 57,200,000 in total, about 20.8%. Past-year consumers of cocaine among persons aged 12 or older in 2019 were 5,468,000, about 2.0%, 2.1% among people aged 18 and older. Past-year consumers of marijuana among persons aged 12 or older in 2019 were 48,242,000, about 17.5%, about 18% among persons aged 18 or older and about 35.4% among persons aged 18–25. Annual consumption rates in Western and Central Europe are as follows: France (11.1% in 2015), Spain (9.5% in 2015), Czechia (9.4% in 2015), Italy (9.2% in 2013/14), Switzerland (9.1% in 2016), and the Netherlands (8.7% in 2015). The World Drug Report 2022 reports the following data relative to 2020: the Netherlands 10%, Czechia 9.5%, England and Wales 7%, Spain 10.5%, Ireland 7.5%, Croatia 10.2%, Austria 6%, Sweden and Norway 4%, Germany 7% in 2018.

According to the World Drug Report 2022:

> Around 29 million people are estimated to be past-year users of cannabis in Europe. Annual prevalence of cannabis use in Western and Central Europe has fluctuated between 6 and 8 per cent over the past decade (2010–2020). Among the countries in Europe that have reported recent survey data, many countries indicate a trend of an increase in cannabis use in recent years. Cannabis use in the European Union reflects the global trend for a higher prevalence among adolescents and young adults (15–24 years old), with past-year use among this age group estimated at 19.2 per cent.
>
> As of January 2022, legal provisions allowing the production and sale of cannabis for non-medical use have been approved in Canada and Uruguay, as well as in 21 jurisdictions of the United States (18 states, two territories and the District of Columbia). Canada and most of the 21 jurisdictions in the United States allow for production and sale by for-profit industry, while in Uruguay there is a partially controlled and state-regulated retail market. There are differences in the level of regulation and control from jurisdiction to jurisdiction, which is likely to have varying impacts on cannabis use and related harms and public health and safety outcomes.
>
> Cannabis use and frequency of cannabis use have increased in the countries and state level jurisdictions that have legalized non-medical use of cannabis. In the United States and Canada, the increase in cannabis use started long before legalization. In the United States, a clear expansion of the cannabis market started in 2007/08, long before the first state legalized cannabis, with the main increase being observed in the daily and near-daily use of cannabis and among those aged 18–25 years and those aged 26 years or older compared with men, but the gap between use of cannabis by men and by women is narrowing. The trend in the last two decades was more marked (with higher rates of increase) in the jurisdictions that legalized non-medical use of cannabis than in those jurisdictions that did not. As a long-term trend, past-month cannabis use declined after a peak in 1979 before resurging. Legalization by itself does not account for the larger increase in cannabis use in those states where cannabis was legalized. In states that have legalized non-medical use of cannabis, such as Colorado, cannabis use has traditionally been above the national average.
>
> Long-term trends in past-month cannabis use in the United States, by age group, 1971–2020 show an increase, from 2007 to 2020, of the use with a percentage very high of 20-23% in consumers aged 18-34. Trends in cannabis use from 2012 to 2020, in past-month and past-year use show a little increase, 5%–10%, in States that have legalized cannabis use compared to States that have not legalized it.
>
> Cannabis use in Canada and Uruguay has also increased post legalization, though not at the same rate of increase or to the same level of use as in the United States. In Uruguay, cannabis use began to increase from much lower levels than in the other two countries.

> Scientific literature indicates early initiation of substance use can be particularly harmful for the developing brain of adolescents. Cannabis use among adolescents in state-level jurisdictions and in countries that have legalized cannabis in general seems to have remained stable following legalization, although it remains much higher in these jurisdictions than in most countries that have not legalized non-medical cannabis. In Colorado, based on the Healthy Kids Colorado Survey and the Youth Risk Behavior Survey, past-month use of cannabis among high school students declined between 2005 and 2019. (World Drug Report 2022, sect. 3)

Data tracking the legalization of marijuana sales and consumption in Colorado show that there has been no increase in use among young people (EMCDDA 2018). Even in Colorado, where marijuana was legalized in 2012, there was no significant increase, just as there was no significant increase in California in 2018 or in Uruguay. (See the track record of legalization of cannabis sales and consumption in Colorado in Sana's 2019 article published in *il Fatto quotidiano*, an Italian daily newspaper.)

In summary, the author states that, as predicted by antiprohibitionists, tax revenues have increased enormously, a billion dollars in five years (since 2014), the price has come down by 35%, drug quality has improved, the illegal market has greatly declined, and consumption by young people over 21 has not increased, in fact it has decreased by about 20% in ten years, while in five years there has been a twofold increase in drivers involved in a fatal traffic accidents and testing positive for THC. And a 2017 study found that compared to the prelegalization period, there has been a fivefold increase in emergency room visits for mental illnesses (hallucinations and disorientation) and physical illnesses (nausea, vomiting) related to marijuana use, particularly food use. The doubling of marijuana-positive drivers does not necessarily imply a doubling of marijuana use or traffic accidents, because in the vast majority of cases the drivers had taken alcohol or other drugs, so they would still have died. A predicted by Miron, there has probably been a nonsignificant increase (20%–25%) in marijuana use among adults aged 40–50 and younger people, aged 16–21, and individuals previously addicted to alcohol and other psychoactive substances have added marijuana, as was the case in the fatal accidents. In other words, people who previously did not consume marijuana and after legalization added it to other drugs, testing positive for THC, were already used to driving under the influence of drugs. The World Drug Report 2022 shows similar data:

> Studies of the effects of the legalization of non-medical use of cannabis on traffic accidents have produced mixed findings, and there is little difference in cannabis- or alcohol-related traffic fatalities between the states that have and those that have not legalized non-medical use of cannabis in the United States. The number of fatalities in which the driver tested positive for cannabinoids as the only substance present increased in Colorado from 23 fatalities in 2013 to 42 in 2019. Colorado may show an increase in traffic fatalities involving cannabis use, it has been argued that this upward trend would have taken place whether or not non-medical use of cannabis had been legalized. In Colorado, citations for driving under the influence of cannabis use increased by 17 per cent between 2014 and 2017, but the number of citations that involved cannabis and other drugs doubled, and those that involved cannabis and alcohol increased fourfold. The overall rates of people charged with drug-impaired driving increased fivefold between 2009 and 2020. It is possible that at least part of this increase was due to better detection rather than an actual rise in drug-impaired driving. (World Drug Report 2022, sect. 3)

As I said, the growing number of people involved in fatal traffic accidents who tested positive for THC does not mean a significant increase in fatal traffic accidents:

> A simultaneous quadruple confluence of increasing prevalence of use, increasing intensity of use (in terms of both frequency and quantities), increasing THC content of cannabis products, and increasing hospitalization due to cannabis use and cannabis use disorders all likely interact multiplicatively in the context of studying the impact of legalization". In the United States, cannabis exposure cases from 2010 to 2017 increased following legalization of nonmedical use of cannabis in the state-level jurisdictions.
>
> In Colorado, cannabis-related emergency room visits and hospitalizations (including treatment of cannabis use disorders and dependence) increased considerably since 2013 but have shown a general stabilization since 2018. In emergency room visits, patients may present anxiety, panic attacks, public intoxication, vomiting and other, non-specific symptoms that could be precipitated by the use of cannabis products with varying THC content. This is especially the case with high-THC edible cannabis products, which take longer to reach peak psychoactive effects, which a person is unable to regulate. Following the same trend as in Colorado, in California, after the opening of the retail sales market, emergency room visits and admissions for primary cannabis increased by 56 per cent from 2016 to 2019. (World Drug report 2022, sect. 3)

There is a very simple reason why the increase in emergency-room visits does not indicate a significant increase, perhaps not even an increase in consumption. Unlike in the black and nonlegalized market, in the legalized market there is among adults widespread consumption of sweets, drinks, and candy prepared with marijuana, which did not exist or were not widespread in the illegal market, whose food consumption explains the hospitalizations for food-related illnesses. In other words, it is possible that those who were already consuming marijuana by smoking it switched to sweets and beverages with legalization, perhaps increasing the doses a bit, these products being particularly good, and it being probably more difficult to calculate how much marijuana one is taking in with a sweet than with a cigarette, unless the label states so (assuming, however, that they read and understand it).

7.4 Suicides and Suicide Attempts Related to Cannabis Use

> Research shows that depression is associated with cannabis use and frequency of cannabis use. Suicide rates in the United States increased between 2002 and 2018, particularly among people aged 18–34, and rates remains higher in states that have legalized cannabis than in states that have not.
>
> There was a significant increase in the use of cannabis (from 28 percent to 37 percent) among patients seeking consultations with a psychiatrist, especially among patients aged 18–24. In Colorado, the proportion of suicides in which cannabis was present, for which toxicology data were available, increased more than threefold between 2006 and 2018. Attention, this does not mean that the rates of suicide are threefold, but only the suicide positive to THC. In contrast, the proportion of suicides in which alcohol was present increased only slightly, from 35 per cent to 40.6 per cent over the same period.
>
> However, there was no statistically significant difference in terms of psychotic disorder diagnoses before or after legalization, but there was an increase in the proportion of those

diagnosed with a personality disorder in the post-legalization period (increase from 39.6 per cent to 44.9 per cent).

Overall, in the United States, past-year cannabis use disorder, daily cannabis and non-daily cannabis use were associated with a higher prevalence of past-year suicidal ideation, plans and attempts among young adults aged 18–23 of both sexes, with significantly higher prevalence among women than men. As cannabis use and harmful patterns have increased in United States. The association between cannabis use and depression also increased significantly between 2005 and 2016. A national survey shows that individuals with depression have higher odds of any past-month cannabis use and daily or near-daily use of cannabis compared with those without depression observed that in the post-legalization period (2018). (World Drug Report 2022, sect. 3)

This study used data from the National Youth Risk Behavior Survey to examine the association between adolescent marijuana, tobacco, and alcohol use and suicidal ideation and attempts over a period of six years (2011–2017), as attitudes and laws became more permissive of marijuana use. We used logistic regression to control for possible confounders, estimate marginal prevalence ratios (PR's), and assess changes over time. Marijuana was more strongly associated with suicide attempts than ideation, and more frequent use was associated with significantly greater risk. The effect has not changed substantively since 2011, despite changing attitudes toward marijuana. Marijuana is broadly comparable to other substances: results for tobacco were similar, though frequent alcohol use had a significantly stronger association than other substances.

Kahn et al. (2022)

The best explanation for these empirical data is that, once cannabis is legalized, people who are already seriously depressed or have another serious personality disorder—e.g., fragile and vulnerable patients seeking counselling with a psychiatrist—will use cannabis to relieve their suffering more frequently than before legalization, because of a small increase of consumption (25–30%), but that the cause of suicides, suicidal ideation, or plans and attempts to commit suicide among young adults aged 18–34 is often not cannabis but a major depression independent of the use of cannabis. That explains many surveys and studies. For example, "individuals with depression have higher odds of any past-month cannabis use and daily or near-daily use of cannabis compared with those without depression observed that in the post-legalization period (2018)." Here is another example. The increase in suicides among people who have tested positive for THC started in Colorado long before legalization, in 2006, and in Colorado suicide rates between 2006 and 2018 are not threefold: only the suicide rate among people who have tested positive for THC have increased threefold. Here is another example still. "There was a significant increase in the use of cannabis (from 28 per cent to 37 per cent) among patients seeking consultations with a psychiatrist, especially among patients aged 18–24." According to the research conducted by Kahn et al. (2022), marijuana, tobacco, and alcohol use is associated with suicide attempts or suicide ideation in adolescents. But it is clear that smoking tobacco cannot cause depression or other mood disorders.

The explanation according to which depression, and not the use of cannabis, is often the cause of suicide, suicide ideation, suicide plans, or suicide attempts does not in any way explain all the empirical data. It does not explain the higher suicide rates in states that have legalized recreational and medical marijuana use, nor does it explain the association between daily or regular cannabis use and a higher prevalence of past-year suicidal ideation, suicide plans, and suicide attempts among young adults.

Here it is worth quoting an important study:

"Objective:

Cannabis use is associated with suicide-related outcomes in both adolescents and adults, and may be increasing amid shifting cannabis policies. However, little is known about the impact of medical marijuana legalization (MML) and recreational marijuana legalization (RML) policies on youth suicide. Using 20 years of national data, we examined associations between MML, RML, and suicide-related mortality among US individuals aged 12 to 25 years, and assessed whether they varied based on age and sex.

Method:

Suicide deaths (N = 113,512) from the 2000–2019 National Vital Statistics System Multiple Cause of Death files for age groups 12 to 13, 14 to 16, 17 to 19, 20 to 22, and 23 to 25 years were examined in relation to time-varying cannabis law status using a staggered adoption difference-in-difference (DiD) approach with a negative binomial regression to determine associations between MML, RML, and suicide rates, controlling for individual- and state-level covariates and accounting for the varying effective dates of MML and RML by state.

Results:

The overall unadjusted annual suicide rate was 10.93/100,000, varying from 9.76 (states without marijuana laws (ML)) to 12.78 (MML states) to 16.68 (RML states). In multivariable analysis, both MML (incidence rate ratio [IRR] = 1.10, 95% CI: 1.05–1.15) and RML (IRR = 1.16, 95% CI: 1.06–1.27) were associated with higher suicide rates among female youth compared to those in states without ML. Youth aged 14 to 16 years had higher rates of suicide in states with RML compared to states with MML (IRR = 1.14, 95% CI: 1.00–1.30) and states without ML (IRR = 1.09, 95% CI: 1.00–1.20). Findings were consistent across sensitivity analyses.

Conclusion:

MML and RML were associated with increased suicide-related mortality in female youth and 14- to- 16-year-old individuals of both sexes. Mechanisms through which cannabis policies are related to increased youth suicide warrant further study and should inform legislative reform." Hammond et al. (2024)

If we consider the incidence rate ratio in states that have legalized the recreational use of marijuana in comparison with states that have not legalized marijuana or have legalized its medical use—a medical use that I believe is necessary to avoid some forms of physical and psychological suffering—we find that there are more deaths among young women and very young minors (14–16), with ratios such as 3.8:100,000.

The incidence rate ratio of young women committing suicide in RMM by comparison with MML is 1:16, which means 16.68:14.3 = 2.3:100,000. The incidence rate ratio of suicide among minors aged 14–16 in RML by comparison with ML is 1.09, which means 16.68:15.2 − 1.5:100,000.

Past-year consumers of marijuana among persons aged 12 or older in 2019 were 48,242,000: this was about 17.5% of the overall population; the percentage was 18% for persons aged 18 or older and about 35.4% for persons aged 18–25. Therefore, 3.8 more suicide deaths for every 100,000 people means 10,792 more suicide deaths associated with legalized recreational use of cannabis if cannabis use were to be legalized across the United States population (the United States has a population of about 284,000,000 people 12 aged or older), in comparison with 48,242,000, which is the total number of consumers of marijuana in the United States. We then have a percentage or mortality rate of 0.0223, or a mortality rate of 0.090, that is, 10,792 for every 11,900,000 cannabis consumers aged 18–25, 35% of a population of 34,000,000 between 18 to 25. Or we can amount to a more likely mortality rate of 0.06461, that means 10,792 for every 16,700,760 cannabis consumers aged 14 to 34, if we assume, we don't know exactly, a reasonable consumption of 18% over a population of 92,782,000 aged between 14 and 34. Even if we consider 10,792 suicides for every 4,836,000, the mortality rate for past-year consumers of marijuana with a substance use disorder is about 0.2239%.

The total number of suicide deaths if recreational cannabis use were legalized in all of the United States (with 284,000,000 people aged 12 or older) would amount to 47,371. The total mortality rate would therefore be 0.098194 out of a total of 48,242,000 cannabis users in the United States.

That mortality rate is much lower than the mortality rate associated with tobacco and heavy alcohol use.

What about deaths associated with tobacco smoking and heavy consumption of alcohol? According to different surveys and studies, annual deaths associated with tobacco smoking in the United States from 2005 to 2009 ranged from 450,000 to 480,000. "The often-cited Centers for Disease Control and Prevention (CDC) estimate of 480,000 annual U.S. smoking-attributable deaths (SADs), including 439,000 first-hand smoke deaths, derives from 2005 to 2009 data. Since then, adult smoking prevalence has decreased by 40%, while the population has grown and the smoking population aged. An updated estimate is presented to determine whether the CDC figure remains accurate or has changed substantially. In addition, the likely annual smoking-related mortality toll is projected through 2035.

Methods

A well-established model of smoking prevalence and health effects is employed to estimate annual SADs among individuals exposed to first-hand smoke in the U.S. for two distinct periods: 2005–2009 and 2020–2035. The estimate for 2005–2009 serves as a benchmark to evaluate the reliability of the model's estimate in comparison to CDC's. The projections for 2020–2035 provide up-to-date figures for SADs, predicting how annual SADs are likely to change in the coming years. Data were collected between 2005 and 2020. The analysis was conducted in 2023.

Results

This study's estimate of 420,000 first-hand smoke deaths over 2005–2009 is 95.7% of CDC's estimate during the same period. The model projections indicate that SADs among individuals who currently smoke or formerly smoked have increased modestly since 2005–2009. Beginning in 2020, annual SADs will remain relatively stable at approximately 450,000 before starting to decline around 2030.

Conclusions

These findings suggest that the CDC estimate of the annual mortality burden of smoking remains valid. Despite U.S. population growth and the aging of the smoking population, substantial reductions in smoking will finally produce a steady, if gradual, decline in SADs beginning around 2030." Thuy et al. (2024).

In the United States in particular, there were 46 million tobacco smokers in 2021, with a mortality rate of 1.010% for an average of 465,000 annual deaths. The percentage of adults who ever smoked cigarettes who reported having quit was 66.5% over a population 18 aged and older of 246,000,000, that means 163,590,000 million of past smokers. If we consider all the past smokers and the current smokers who started smoking many years ago, because lung cancer develops years or decades after tobacco consumption, we have approximately a mortality rate of. 0.2492 over a population of past and current smokers of 186,590,000. This rate however, is unrealistic, because we should only take into account tobacco users for decades of the last forty or fifty years. Therefore, a more realistic mortality rate of tobacco use is approximately, 0.44372 over a population of past smokers of about 81,795,000 (the half) and a population of current smokers who started smoking many years ago about 23,000,000 (the half), in total 104,795,000 00.

Source: https://www.cdc.gov/tobacco/data-statistics/mmwr/2023-mm7218a1.html.

The deaths related to excessive use of alcohol, typically associated with a substance use disorder, were 178,000. Source: https://www.cdc.gov/xalcohol/facts-stats/index.html. Past-year consumers of alcohol with a substance use disorder among persons aged 12 or older were 14,500,000 in 2019, about 8.1% of drinkers overall. Past-year consumers of alcohol among persons aged 12 or older in 2019 were 179,144,000 in all. The percentage of past-year consumers of alcohol with a substance use disorder among persons aged 12 or older in 2019 was about 5.3%. The mortality rate for excessive consumption of alcohol, typically associated with a substance use disorder, was about 1.22758%.

Does it make sense to argue that a young person's death by suicide associated with cannabis use is a graver loss than that of someone who dies of lung cancer at 50 or 60 because of tobacco smoking? It does not make any sense.

It is not clear how it is possible for there to have been an in increase in the number of suicides among very young people, aged 14 to 16, in countries that have legalized marijuana for recreational purposes, since minors are prohibited from buying marijuana. But it may be that people 21 or older pass cannabis illegally to minors.

There are three different possible explanations, not incompatible with each other, for the higher rates of suicide, suicide ideation, suicide attempts, and suicide plans in countries that have legalized recreational marijuana use. The fundamental empirical premise underlying these three explanations is that there has been an unimportant increase in marijuana consumption in countries that have legalized recreational marijuana use, approximately about 25–29%, but we can assume a greater increase, I do not know how much, among persons depressed or suffering from another personality disorder. The first is that among a small minority of consumers, as we have seen increased, daily or regular cannabis use increases depression because depressed individuals who consume cannabis to alleviate or heal the suffering of depression must accept the total failure of cannabis use, having to reckon with frustrated expectations about the soothing effects of cannabis. A second possibility is that in a small minority of cases, as we have seen increased, daily or regular cannabis consumption increases the degree of depression, and consequently the likelihood of suicide, attempted suicide, suicidal ideation, or suicide plans. The third possibility is that daily or regular cannabis consumption, as we have seen increased, increases the risk of depression among those who do not suffer from depression, and it therefore increases the risk of suicide, attempted suicide, or suicide plans.

Hashish and marijuana could be sold in licensed shops or in coffee shops to which people can gain access only if they can show they are authorized, to which end, under the scheme I am proposing, they would have to produce a special health card that is valid for ten years and is issued by a doctor working for a public or private hospital. To that end, the doctor would carry out a decision-making procedure designed to make sure that the person seeking authorization to consume marijuana is (a) aware of the facts of consumption, (b) sufficiently free from coercive pressures, and (c) rational, and that this person (d) has mental capacity and (e) desires that are stable over time. In this sense, the doctor will advise patients with depression not to consume cannabis—since that could worsen their situation—and will advise them, as well as individuals without depression, of the risks of marijuana consumption, and will advise them to immediately discontinue consumption of cannabis if they are having suicidal thoughts, making suicide plans, or engaging in suicidal ideation, since they are at risk of committing suicide. With such an interview with a physician, in which the person concerned is made aware of the relevant facts, the effect will be to reduce suicides and attempted suicides associated with cannabis use by two-thirds; the mortality suicide rate associated with cannabis use in countries that have legalized recreational marijuana use will then be lower than the suicide rate in countries that have not legalized recreational marijuana use, and it will also be lower than the overall suicide rate.

The same notice should be printed on the packaging of marijuana that is sold in the form of drinks, sweets, cakes, or cigarettes, as happens with tobacco. (Such a notice would read: "Cannabis use may cause depression and suicidal attempts.") We arrive at the same conclusion with empirical data on marijuana substance-use disorder. In the United States, the number of past-year consumers of marijuana with a substance-use disorder is 4,836,000 among people 12 or older (about 10% of consumers overall), and the number of consumers with a severe substance-use disorder is much lower: only a very small minority has symptoms such as addiction, mood swings, anxiety, and depression. That means that there are more cannabis users among depressed and suicidal individuals than depressed people among cannabis users.

The vast majority of people, even young people, makes a not dangerous recreational or occasional use of cannabis or a not dangerous compulsive use. It may be that suicide rates increased from 2002 to 2018 because of the Great Recession of 2008 and 2009.

7.5 Drugs Legalization and Increase in Drug Use

The data would show that there is no necessary correlation between de facto legalization or decriminalization and any significant increase in drug use.[19] On the other hand, historical analyses tell us that marijuana consumption in the Netherlands increased, with two significant peaks around 1970 and in the mid-1990s, especially among young people, and then stabilized. This is a consumption trend that follows the classic wave-like trend pattern. Is the increase in consumption due to or causally related to de facto legalization? It does not appear to be, because a similar wave-like trend, with some obvious peaks, can be found in other countries, for example, Germany or the United States.[20] Several studies, in particular, seem to support the view that in the Netherlands there has been an increase in first-time marijuana use, especially among young people, but not in habitual or continuous use over the medium to long term. In other words, legalization would lead more people to give marijuana a "try" once or several times, but in comparison with to other countries, it would not lead many more people to consume it occasionally or continuously over time.[21] Korf and Reudband's conclusion in this regard is unequivocal. Trends in

[19] See World Drug Report (2009) and (2022); Husak (1992), p. 55, 154. "However, antiprohibitionist experiences (such as the legal selling of hashish and marijuana in the Netherlands or production for personal use in Alaska), however limited they may be, demonstrate, however, that a regulated market expands less than a market free from any oversight, like those that develop under a prohibitionist system" (Taradash (1991), p. 160, my translation).

[20] Cf. Korf (2002), p. 858. "A first complication here is that marijuana use among youth in the US also evolved in waves, with a peak during the late 1970s, a decline in the 1980s, a rise in the 1990s, followed by stabilisation. Harrison concludes that such a wave-like development can be understood as a verification of Musto's (1987) more general model on trends in drug use. In addition, structural factors (post World War II baby boom) and drug education (health risk perception) might help to explain the development in marijuana use in the US. Also, in other European countries, the development in cannabis use has been interpreted as a wave-like trend (Kraus 1997). For example, cannabis use spread rapidly in Germany (West) toward the end of the 1960s, followed by a stabilisation and a decline in the early 1970s, and then an increase in the 1980s (Kraus 1997; Reuband 1992). The rising use of cannabis in Germany (West) continued in the 1990s; among 18–39-year-olds lifetime use increased from 16.7% to 21.0% in 1995 and last year use almost doubled from 4.9% to 8.8%" Korf (2002), pp. 859–860. The same ebb-and-flow trend, says Korf, can be found in Great Britain and Germany, with marijuana consumption among young people in the mid-1990s much higher than in the early 1980s. The same trends in cannabis consumption emerge from the Annual Report on the State of the Drugs Problem in Europe (EMCDDA (2009), p. 46). In general, marijuana consumption in the world from 1990 to 2004–2005 increased by 5.5% on average in Europe, 6.5% in the Americas.

[21] Several empirical data point in this direction. The average age at which people started to consume cannabis in Amsterdam from 1987 to 2001 was around 20 years old. Habitual consumption (last-month cannabis use), high in the 18–25 age group, collapses after the age of 25, and "the average age of habitual consumers of cannabis and other illicit substances is much lower than that of alcohol consumers and tobacco, and this suggests that people stop using these substances shortly after they start using them" Abraham et al. (2003), p. 41. The studies conducted by Abraham et al. (2003) and those conducted by MacCoun and Reuter (2004) both indicate, in particular, that in the Netherlands there has been a considerable increase (of up to 30–40%) in consumption in the

cannabis use in the Netherlands are quite similar to those in other European countries, including countries that have not decriminalized use. The evolution of cannabis use shows a wave-like trend in many countries, including the Netherlands, a trend that would evolve regardless of drug policies (cf. Reuband 1995; Korf 2002, p. 861).

Third, and this is the decisive argument, a thorough statistical study should take into account the reasons that people have for their consumption. The available empirical data tell us that, especially in metropolises or medium-sized European and North American cities, drugs of all kinds are sold rather freely. "There is no other market where money travels as fast as in the illegal drug market [...]. There is in Europe, as in the US, an extensive sales network, ranging from clandestine supply in the square or in a dark doorway to a highly efficient door-to-door system for the wealthy classes" (Taradash 1991, p. 196, my translation). In other words, if the purpose of prohibitionist policies is to halt or significantly limit the sale and consumption of drugs, they are largely ineffective (ibid.; cf. Alldridge (1996), p. 256).[22] Which means that adult individuals of average intelligence, if they want to buy narcotics, would take anywhere from two hours to no more than two days to locate an available pusher.[23] If they do not consume drugs, then, it is not because they cannot or do not know where to buy them, or because they fear criminal penalties from

---

youngest age group, 16–24 years old, at least since the mid-1980s, compared to Dutch consumption prior to 1970, the year in which the actual, de facto phase of decriminalization and legalization more or less began (meaning that the selling of these substances was tolerated in coffee shops), while the overall level of consumption, taking into account all age groups, has always remained no much higher than the threshold of other prohibitionist countries. Furthermore, according to MacCoun and Reuter, the increase in consumption among young people began above all in the mid-1980s, and so not with the decriminalization phase, which began in 1970, but with that of the increased selling of marijuana, i.e., the spread of such selling tolerated under certain conditions in coffee shops, which brought with it greater visibility, signs, advertising, postcards, and announcements. See MacCoun and Reuter (2004), p. 257ff. Against the thesis of a correlation between increases in consumption and the marketing of marijuana in the Netherlands, see Korf (2002).

[22] These data are even confirmed by government bodies: "Only through an appropriate ability to study, analyze, and evaluate the threat as a whole is it possible to develop an adequate strategy to fight criminal multinationals, whose main source of profit comes precisely from drug trafficking, so as to counteract, in an increasingly tight, effective, and intelligent manner, a supply side which, at the moment, does not appear to be contracting or reversing its trend. [...] The massive influx of heroin from Asia, cocaine from South America, cannabis from North Africa, and synthetic drugs from European bases is in fact continuously growing. In this context, the global trend in opium production is slightly upward, while the production of coca [...]—with a decrease in Colombia, the result of a strategic action plan called Plan Colombia—is seeing a slight overall increase, both in the production of coca leaves and in that of cocaine, due to production increases in Peru and Bolivia. The trend in cannabis production is decidedly upward, with an increase compared to previous years due to greater consumption worldwide" (Serpelloni et al. (2006), sec 1.3, my translation, italics added). The authors reach the same conclusions as Husak (1992), p. 52). Along the same lines, Husak (2002), p. 67ff., 71ff. reports different statistics according to which 56% of North American adolescents between the ages of 12 and 17 say that illicit drugs are easy to obtain, and 60% of high-school students have experimented with drug use.

[23] The same conclusions are reached by the survey on the consumption of cannabis carried out by Cohen and Kaal (2001), p. 109.

the state (which in many countries, unlike in the United States, are nonexistent), but because they simply do not want to—that for the moral, prudential, and social reasons analyzed above.

It is essential, first of all, to distinguish between those who simply have a *desire* to consume narcotics for recreational reasons (pleasure, enjoyment, mood control), or on an occasional basis, and others who have a *need* to consume because of some physical or psychological distress (or addiction in the strict sense), meaning that they have a high level of consumption or are chronic users.[24] Now it is reasonable to think that consumption for recreational reasons may increase as the health risks, the risks of "contact" with organized crime, decrease and the price of the drug decreases. In other words, it is likely that some people choose not to consume cannabis because they do not want to finance organized crime, or that others choose not consume cocaine because the price is very high. With reference to those who consume for recreational reasons, or occasionally, the demand for narcotics is more elastic, that is, more influenced by price and other risk factors. So, it could be argued, if narcotics were sold legally, if the price of some narcotics decreased significantly, it is likely that occasional or recreational consumption would increase.[25] In fact, this thesis conflicts with numerous arguments to the contrary. Dutch empirical data show an increase, likely caused by de facto legalization, especially among young people and in first-time consumption, but not in medium- to long-term consumption. Second, cocaine use even seems to have declined in the United States (particularly from 2005 onward), while in other European countries it has increased by 7%, despite the sharp decline in price, from 50–70% down, in the 1990s and 2000s. Finally, some studies on the Dutch situation speculate that increased consumption is owed not to greater availability or to tolerance for the selling and consumption of cannabis, but to the intensification of marketing in coffee shops.

If, on the other hand, cocaine and heroin were sold in pharmacies, hospitals, or licensed private establishments, and so in ways much more restrictive than with tobacco or alcohol, if no form of advertising, print or web, were allowed, then this increase in consumption might be much more reduced.[26] The idea that such restrictions on the sale of narcotics (only in pharmacies, hospitals, following a prescrip-

---

[24] Some authors distinguish three fundamental reasons in the use of drugs: recreational use (achieving a positive psychological state, such as euphoria or pleasure), medical or therapeutic use (use of cannabis or opiates to alleviate chronic pain or other forms of suffering), and compulsive-dependent (addictive) use. But see Husak (1992), p. 44ff.; Husak (2002), p. 33ff., who notes that it is not easy to distinguish recreational use from medical use. The distinction depends on the notion of disease/disorder used, which often has a conventional or ideological character. Increasing one's intellectual performance through the use of drugs that keep users awake is considered by many to be a recreational use, while increasing one's sexual performance (using Viagra) is considered a medical use.

[25] The data collected in the survey carried out on cannabis consumption by Cohen and Kaal (2001, p. 70) can be interpreted along the same lines.

[26] Cf. MacCoun and Reuter (2004), p. 98ff., chap. 8, which also points to the effects of aggressive advertising campaigns, direct or indirect (in films) promoted by the tobacco and alcohol industries. Cf. Rolles (2009), p. 48.

tion, as for legal psychotropic drugs, or better a particular ten-year health card) would reintroduce the rise of the black market with its disadvantages is a prediction as likely to come true as it is true that there is, today, a thriving black market, retail, for antibiotics or psychotropic drugs that can be sold only in pharmacies (with prescription).[27] In contrast, for those who consume because of some physical or psychological distress or serious addiction, or on a continuous basis over time, the demand for narcotics is likely to be more inelastic, that is, less influenced by significant price fluctuations or other factors (cf. Miron (2004), p. 35; Costa Storti and De Grauwe (2008), p. 13ff., 33; World Drug Report (2012), p. 68). Of course, the elasticity of demand for narcotics also depends on the type of narcotic. The greater the health damage that consumption brings, the more unlikely it is that consumption will occur only for recreational reasons.

So, in the worst-case scenario, consumption for recreational reasons, such as occasional consumption of marijuana, cocaine, or Ecstasy, might increase. By contrast, medium- or long-term users seeking to alleviate their suffering—especially users of drugs (such as cocaine or heroin) whose consumption carries with it greater risks (physical dependence, health damage), or users who have already acquired a significant dependence on a certain drug—would continue to consume, whether through a legal or an illegal market; therefore, they would probably not increase (although they might consume more). In short, in the worst-case scenario, despite empirical data going in the opposite direction with respect to elasticity of demand, consumption could reasonably be expected to increase, by 20%, for example.[28]

---

[27] On this argument see MacCoun and Reuter (2004), p. 327; World Drug Report (2009), pp. 1–2.

[28] There are many economic studies on the degree of price elasticity of demand for cocaine. Unfortunately, they all give quite different results, in part because they are projections based on different samples. Some are based on variations in consumption, as the price varies, among high school seniors in a certain state, others on the probability of emergency room treatment; others are differentiated by ethnic groups; others are based on the quantity of arrested people who tested positive for cocaine, others on the statistics of national institutes that monitor the phenomenon of drug use. (Monitoring the Future [MTF], National Household Surveys on Drug Abuse [NHSDA]). The elasticity rates estimated by the various authors are different and often lie within a fairly wide range, for example: −0.40, −0.40, −0.80, −0.50, −0.26, −0.90, −0.26. Same range (between −0.7 and −0.2) is estimated by the World Drug Report (2012), p. 96. It is difficult to draw conclusions. It can be said, with Costa Storti, that everyone agrees that the demand for cocaine would increase as the price decreases, and that this increase, taking an average between the different estimated rates, would not be high (it could be around −0.50). Which means that if the price of cocaine decreases by 50%, consumption increases by 25%. But it's difficult to make predictions. Based on data from the 2007 UNODOC Drug Report, it is estimated that the price of cocaine and heroin decreased by 50 to 70% from 1990 to 2004/2005, while consumption in many European Contres increased by 7%, and that in the United States it even decreased, as well as that global production increased (but not by much). With great persuasive force, Costa Storti argues that, even if the efforts at the international level (seizures, resources used) have greatly increased from 1990 to 2006, consumption has increased, as has production; while on the one hand the prices of cocaine and heroin plunges, on the other they the profit margins of traffickers and retail dealers shrank, as did the cultivated areas in the world and the available drugs (especially cocaine), as the increase in production did not fully compensate for the increase in seizures. The only possible explanation, according to the author, is the cumulative effect of globalization, fierce competitiveness at the

And from the point of view of the feared harm to others, recreational or leisure users are the more responsible consumers, that is, those who, all things being equal, exercise more control over themselves and their conduct, so as to avoid conduct that is dangerous to others (such as driving a car or operating a crane while impaired by drugs).[29] Indeed, the greater the state of substance dependence, and the greater the likelihood of withdrawal, the greater the likelihood of conduct harmful to third parties. So the probability of harmful conduct is higher, rather than lower, in the case of prohibition, where a consumer crisis is more likely to occur owing to the high price of illegal substances, the greater difficulty in obtaining them, and the lower quality of the substances. Nor is it worth arguing that occasional users, users for recreational or leisure reasons, cannot but turn, necessarily, into severely addicted users. The effects of narcotics on the individual, the state of dependence these narcotics eventually lead to, arise from various factors (genetic, psychological, environmental), and it is statistically proven that only a minority of users (of substances such as marijuana, cocaine, MDMA, or hallucinogens), 20–25%, develop a significant form of addiction.[30] Heroin and methamphetamine, in the National Survey on

---

international level, the entry of new criminal groups working with lower profit margins, the discovery of new routes to introduce drugs (from West Africa), and the use of technologically advanced communication and distribution systems. See Costa Storti and De Grauwe (2007, 2008); Dave (2004); Caulkins (1995); Abt Associates (2000); Saffer and Chaloupka (1999); Chaloupka et al. (1998).

[29] This is what MacCoun and Reuter (2004, p. 327) call the composition effect.

[30] "For example, one-third of subjects who smoke become chronic smokers, 23% of subjects who experiment with heroin become addicted to heroin, and 17% of those who experiment with cocaine become addicted to cocaine (Bricolo et al. 2006). This data is consistent with the Cocaine Project (1995, p. 28) and the 2009 Annual Report on the the State of the Drugs Problem in Europe (EMCDDA 2009), according to which those who out of curiosity experiment with cocaine use (one-off users) or those who use it occasionally represent by far the most common users (EMCDDA 2009, pp. 66, 68–70), while a smaller percentage uses it compulsively or intensively. Also similar is the empirical data cited by Husak (1992, p. 124). Likewise, the 2009 EMCDDA Report states that "a study conducted in the United States showed that approximately 5% of cocaine users can develop dependence during the first year of use, although no more than approximately 20% of consumers have developed long-term dependence" (EMCDDA 2009, p. 72). According to the 2021 National Survey on Drug Use and Health in the United States (NSDUH 2021), past-year consumers of illicit drugs among persons aged 12 or older in 2019 were in total 57,200,000, about 20.8%. Past-year consumers of cocaine among persons aged 12 or older in 2019 were 5,468,000, about 2.0%, 2.1% among people aged 18 or older. Past-year consumers of marijuana among persons aged 12 or older in 2019 were 48,242,000, about 17.5%, about 18% among persons aged 18 or older and about 35.4% among persons aged 18–25. Past-year consumers of crack among persons aged 12 or older in 2019 were 778,000, about 0.3%. Past-year consumers of heroin among persons aged 12 or older in 2019 were 745,000, about 0.3%. Past-year consumers of methamphetamine among persons aged 12 or older in 2019 were 1,999,000, about 0.7%. Past-year consumers of hallucinogens—ketamine, methoxetamine (MXE), phencyclidine (PCP), dextromethorphan (DXM), nitrous oxide, LSD, MDMA, or Ecstasy—among persons aged twelve or older in 2019 were 6,010,000, about 2.2%. Past-year consumers of illicit drugs among people aged 12 or older who have a substance use disorder were 8,313,000 and past-year cocaine consumers in past year among people aged 12 for older which have a substance use disorder were 1,011,000, about one-fifth, 18%. The percentage of the population 12 years or older who in 2019 were past-year consum-

Drug Use and Health in the United States (NSDUH 2021), shows a substance use disorder in about 50% of consumers. But only severe substance use disorder is defined as addiction in the literature. Substance use disorder (SUD) is the persistent use of drugs (including alcohol) despite substantial harm and adverse consequences as a result of their use. The National Institute of Mental Health (NIMH) states that "Substance use disorder (SUD) is a treatable mental disorder that affects a person's brain and behavior, leading to their inability to control their use of substances like legal or illegal drugs, alcohol, or medications. Symptoms can be moderate to severe, with addiction being the most severe form of SUD." Substance use disorders (SUD) are considered to be a serious mental illness that fluctuates with the age that symptoms first start appearing in an individual, the time during which it exists, and the type of substance that is used. It is not uncommon for those who have SUD to also have other mental health disorders. Substance use disorders are characterized by an array of mental/emotional, physical, and behavioral problems such as chronic guilt; an inability to reduce or stop consuming the substance(s) despite repeated attempts; operating vehicles while intoxicated; and physiological withdrawal symptoms. Drug classes that are commonly involved in SUD include alcohol (alcoholism); cannabis; opioids; stimulants such as nicotine (including tobacco), cocaine and amphetamines; benzodiazepines; barbiturates; and other or unknown substances. In the 5th edition of the Diagnostic and Statistical Manual of Mental Disorders (DSM-5 2013), the DSM diagnoses of substance abuse and substance dependence were merged into the category of substance use disorders. The severity of substance use disorders can vary widely; in the DSM-5 diagnosis of SUD, the severity of an individual's SUD is qualified as mild, moderate, or severe on the basis of how many of the 11 diagnostic criteria are met. The International Classification of Diseases, 11th revision (ICD-11), divides substance use disorders into two categories: (1) harmful pattern of substance use; and (2) substance dependence. The diagnostic criteria are as follows:

- addiction—a biopsychosocial disorder characterized by persistent use of drugs (including alcohol) despite substantial harm and adverse consequences

---

ers of cocaine with a substance use disorder was 0.4%, one-fifth of the total number of consumers of cocaine. Past-year consumers of heroin aged 12 years or older who had a substance use disorder was 438,000 in 2019, 0.2% of the population in the age bracket from 12 to 64, about 58% of consumers of heroin. Past-year consumers of hallucinogens with a substance use disorder among people aged 12 or older were 274,000 in 2019, about 4.5% of hallucinogen users. Past-year consumers of methamphetamine with a substance use disorder among people aged 12 or older were 1,048,000 in 2019 about 50% of methamphetamine users. Past-year consumers of marijuana with a substance use disorder among people aged 12 or older were 4,836,000, about 10% of total consumers. Past-year consumers of alcohol with a substance use disorder among persons aged 12 or older were 14,500,000 in 2019, about 8.10% of total consumers. Past-year consumers of alcohol among persons aged 12 or older were 179,144,000 in 2019. The percentage of past-year consumers of alcohol with a substance use disorder among persons aged 12 or older is about 5.3%, 5.6% among people aged 18 or older in 2019. The population in United States in 2020 among people aged 15 or older is about 271,464,000. The percentage of past-year consumers of illicit drugs with a substance use disorder among persons aged 12 or older was about 3% in 2019.

- addictive drug—psychoactive substances that with repeated use are associated with significantly higher rates of substance use disorders, due in large part to the drug's effect on brain reward systems
- dependence—an adaptive state associated with a withdrawal syndrome upon cessation of repeated exposure to a stimulus (e.g., drug intake)
- drug sensitization or reverse tolerance—the escalating effect of a drug resulting from repeated administration at a given dose
- drug withdrawal—symptoms that occur upon cessation of repeated drug use
- physical dependence—dependence that involves persistent physical–somatic withdrawal symptoms (e.g., fatigue and delirium tremens)
- psychological dependence—dependence socially seen as being extremely mild compared to physical dependence (e.g., with enough willpower it could be overcome)
- reinforcing stimuli—stimuli that increase the probability of repeating behaviors paired with them
- rewarding stimuli—stimuli that the brain interprets as intrinsically positive and desirable or as something to approach
- sensitization—an amplified response to a stimulus resulting from repeated exposure to it
- tolerance—the diminishing effect of a drug resulting from repeated administration at a given dose (see Nestler (2013); Nestler et al. (2009); Volkow et al. (2016)).

Symptoms for substance use disorder include behavioral, physical, and social changes. Changes in behavior include being absent from school or work, changes in appetite or sleep patterns, personality and attitude changes, mood swings, and anxiety. Signs include physical changes such as weight gain or loss, tremors, and bloodshot eyes. Different substances used can give different signs and symptoms. Substance use disorders can range widely in severity, and there are numerous methods to monitor and qualify the severity of an individual's SUD. The DSM-5 includes specifiers for the severity of a SUD. Individuals who meet only two or three criteria are often deemed to have mild SUD. Substance users who meet four or five criteria may have their SUD described as moderate, and persons meeting six or more criteria as severe. In DSM-5, the term *drug addiction* is synonymous with *severe substance use disorder*.

In the same vein, some studies on marijuana use in the Netherlands show that only a small number of regular cannabis users become heroin or cocaine users.[31] Similarly, widely exaggerated by the media and many politicians are the pharmacological effects of consumption, which would turn users into so many Mr. Hydes. There is no significant empirical evidence that heroin and marijuana use alone makes users more aggressive or violent, while the strong statistical link between cocaine use and violent crime does not explain the cause or the effect. That is, there

[31] See Cohen and Sas (1996), who cite studies that suggest otherwise, but only to criticize and refute them.

is evidence that many criminals use cocaine, but this does not mean that it was consumption that caused them to act as criminals. On the contrary, some statistical and motivational surveys conducted on incarcerated criminals show that, normally, crimes committed under the influence of cocaine would have been committed in any case, regardless of cocaine use, that many more people (seven times more) commit violent crimes under the influence of alcohol, and not cocaine, and that criminals take cocaine or alcohol before committing a crime they have already planned, to loosen their inhibitory brakes, increase their self-esteem, and feel physically stronger. Moreover, while it is statistically true that many criminals convicted of violent crimes use drugs, it is by contrast completely false, statistically, that many drug users are criminals. And yet there is evidence that cocaine abuse leads some individuals to a psychotic break that could make them violent (cf. Husak (1992), p. 195ff., 197–98; Husak (2002), p. 88ff., 105; Beltramini (2010)).

Fourth, if the sale and consumption of drugs were legalized, it is possible to predict, on the other hand, a decrease in the consumption of many drugs, as well as a decrease in many accidents on highways and in workplaces, due to the fact that users would be moving in the light of day, and thus would have

(a) greater knowledge of the relevant facts, i.e., the health harms attributable to drugs and the genetic and environmental risks of developing a form of addiction;
(b) easier access to treatment in case of infections and diseases (users would not be afraid of fines or penalties); and
(c) a greater possibility of being persuaded to take part in therapeutic and detoxification programs (a greater possibility that they would be offered a way out, e.g., psychotherapy and psychotropic drugs, to remove some of the causes of use, such as poverty and unemployment).
(d) In addition, the increased revenue from legalization could be used to (*i*) fund education programs in schools, as well as detoxification programs, to ensure greater protection of social rights and remove some of the causes (such as emotional suffering) that lead people to use drugs, (*ii*) increase roadside checks on young people driving cars, on Friday and Saturday nights, especially outside discos.
(e) In contrast to what happens in prohibitionist regimes, habitual users, who have developed a serious physical dependence on certain substances, could be temporarily inhibited from performing certain jobs (like ones involving the use of machinery that is dangerous to others), get help in finding jobs that do not involve risks to others (such as clerical or office work), and be prohibited from owning or using firearms.
(f) Finally, legalization would end the "prohibited fruit" effect that many authors say increases drug use in young people (see Husak (1992), p. 55; Husak (2002), p. 162; MacCoun and Reuter (2004), p. 89ff.).

So the legalization of drugs would not give rise to any epidemic of cocaine, marijuana or heroin use. The epidemic argument—the apocalyptic image where our children, friends, and relatives turn into zombies or violent gangsters, whose hunger for drugs and money prompts them to buy or resell the next dose—is falsely or specious,[32] while some paternalists, in good faith, fear more than anything else the consequences for the fate of their children, not taking into account that a democratic, liberal-egalitarian (not autocratic) state cannot significantly curb the phenomenon of drug use, which has deep cultural, psychological, historical, and socioeconomic roots, nor, consequently, can it, or should it, repair all the educational mistakes made by parents. The proof is in the facts, which can no longer be ignored. Despite the fact that efforts at the international level (seizures, resources used) have greatly increased from 1990 to 2006, and that DEA funding has probably doubled or even more than tripled in the US since 1980, drug consumption has increased worldwide and production has remained stable or has increased; while on the one hand cocaine and heroin prices have collapsed, on the other hand the profit margins of traffickers, wholesalers, and retail distributors have decreased in absolute value terms, as have cultivated areas around the world. According to Costa Storti, the cumulative effect of globalization, international competitiveness, the use of new communications systems, the lowering of some intermarket costs, the entry of new criminal groups working with lower profit margins, and the discovery of new

[32] Cf. Husak (1992), p. 126. For a justification of the drug epidemic (an increase in cocaine and heroin consumption close to 1000%) which is complex and detailed, but which on careful analysis lays bare the two or three deductive or inductive fallacies that make it fatal, see MacCoun and Reuter (2004), p. 333ff. In particular, MacCoun and Reuter do not underline and do not explain in depth the fact that in the Netherlands the levels of marijuana consumption are not much higher than in many prohibitionist countries despite de facto legalization; they do not explain the high levels of cocaine consumption in the United States despite the high level of enforcement compared to European countries, nor do they explain the relationship between the steep fall in the price of cocaine—which according to the World Drug Report 2007 was 70% in the United States (but 50% according to the 2009 World Drug Report), and at least 50% in Europe from 1990 to 2005 to 2006—and changes in cocaine consumption. In contrast to the predictions usually made by prohibitionists, consumption has in fact decreased according to the 2007–2009 World Drug Report in the United States (while in Europe it has increased by an average of 7% since 1990, but with profound differences between countries). Since the 1990s, but above all from 2000 onwards, in Spain, Italy, Germany, the United Kingdom, and Denmark, cocaine consumption has increased considerably, for example, which seems completely disproportionate, if there is a relationship between the two, with respect to the decrease in price (while in other European countries, despite the same decrease in price, consumption has remained stable). Furthermore, the two American authors overestimate the deterrence argument, and in general underestimate empirical investigations into the reasons why people do not consume drugs; the statistics on the high availability of drugs on the black market inexplicably do not take into account that the increase in consumption consequent on legalization would give rise to an increase in revenue that would cover healthcare in case of intoxication and other damage to the health of consumers, and they claim, without any plausible explanation, that a legalized but regulated drug market like that for other controlled substances (such as antibiotics or legal psychotropic drugs) would necessarily give rise to a thriving black market. As I was saying, the epidemic argument does not find justification in empirical studies on the consumption and sale of narcotic substances. In any case, it would always be possible to carry out pilot experiments on the effectiveness of legalization in certain cities or regions, or it would be possible to carefully monitor the phenomenon of drug consumption after legalization and possibly interrupt the experiment after two or five years if it proves to be unsuccessful.

routes for bringing in drugs (from West Africa) has trumped any prohibitionist policy.[33]

Generally speaking, the basic error of most prohibitionist discourse is to contrast prohibition and antiprohibition, as if the prohibition on the selling and consumption of drugs meant the absence of consumption (and related harms) and as if the permissibility of their sale and consumption meant the spread of consumption (and related harms). Which is completely false,[34] not to mention the incomprehensible inconsistency of taking into account the health harms and crimes related to drug use (harms such as traffic accidents, occupational accidents, or child and domestic abuse) rather than the health harms and crimes related to alcohol use and the health harms related to tobacco use, which harms and crimes are, according to many authors, significantly greater.[35]

---

[33] See Costa Storti and De Grauwe (2007), p. 19ff. "Since 1980 the number of worldwide seizures has increased by a factor of 10."

[34] Following this line of reasoning are, for example, Donini (2008, p. 86) and Romano (2010, p. 158).

[35] See Alldridge (1996), p. 246; Husak (1992), p. 95; Husak (2002), p. 105. Not just that, according to the Italian government (Ministero della Salute 2022) the number of grave diseases (such as tumors, lung disease, or cardiovascular disease) and deaths connected to the use of tobacco is 93,000 people in Italy every year, and alcohol is associated with even greater harms, not only in absolute but also in relative terms, in relation to the number of consumers. In Italy, there were 12.4 million tobacco consumers in 2020, about 24.2% of the Italian population and 7.7 million former smokers. If we calculate that lung cancer and other diseases associated with tobacco smoke develop after many years of consumption, we have to take into account former smokers and at least two-thirds of current smokers, i.e., 15,700,000 million smokers, the percentage of deaths is about 0.592%. But in the medium-to-long run the smokers who die are 50% (Pacifici 2022).

Overdose deaths, mainly from opiate use, were 373 in 2019, and over the course of forty years, from 1973 to 2020, those deaths were 25,780, i.e., 548 per year (from the annual report issued in 2020 by the Italian Drug Agency). About half of all overdose deaths are due to opiate consumption, an average of 274 deaths per year. According to the 2022 European Drug Report EMCDDA 2002), it is estimated that in Europe in 2021, 3.5 million adults consumed cocaine (1.2% of the population aged 15–65, about 291,666,000 million people), 2.6 million consumed MDMA (0.9% of the population aged 15–65), and 2 million consumed amphetamines (0.7% of the population aged 15–65). About 1 million Europeans were high-risk consumers of heroin or other illicit opiate in 2021. This means, on average, 786,857 Italian consumers of cocaine and opiate users out of an Italian population of about 51 million people (aged 15–65). We can estimate a percentage of 0.0696 overdose deaths. In Italy, we can estimate 174,857 consumers of opiates out of an Italian population of about 51 million people (aged 15–65). This means a percentage of overdose deaths for consumption of opiates of about 0.156%.

According to the 2022 European Drug Report (EMCDDA 2022), which shows different percentages, there were 5,800 overdose cases in 2020. About 75% (4350 people) was related to opiate use. In the European Union, we can estimate one million high-risk consumers of opiates out of a population (aged 15–65 years) of about 291,666,000 people. This means a percentage of overdose deaths for consumption of opiates of about 0.435%. According to the World Drug Report 2022, sects. 3 and 4), there were 2,350,000 opiate users in 2020 in North America and 14,000 overdose deaths involving sinthetic opioids in the United States, a percentage of 0.5957%. There is in the United States a population of about 340,950,000 people. Consumers of cocaine are about 2% (6,819,000 people); the number of overdose deaths for cocaine use is 6,000 people, equal to 0.087% of the population of cocaine users.

Even if there were no great increase in the consumption of certain drugs, which is possible in the worst-case scenario, wouldn't the greater harm resulting from greater consumption be offset by the greater revenue from greater consumption? In fact, the greater the consumption, the greater would be the revenue from indirect taxes on the purchase price of the good. Wouldn't the greater harms be offset by the higher revenue from the end of the war on drugs? Wouldn't they be offset by the sharp reduction in crime turnover, or even by the reduction in crimes committed by consumers, or even by the reduced health harms resulting from the existence of greater oversight and better drug quality? The answer is obviously yes. Antipaternalism and antiprohibition, in strictly economic terms, would still converge. Not to mention that the significant increase in checks on roads and highways, which would be possible because of the increased funds available, would decrease, rather than increase, traffic accidents, accidents in which individuals who have consumed alcohol and not other drugs are often involved.[36] Moreover, as some authors point out, it is rather problematic, as well as painful and in a way very sad, to calculate the medical and hospital costs of increased drug use. The reason is simple. While it is true that the effect of drug use is initially more medical and welfare expenses borne by the community, the reckless lifestyle of a small minority of users certainly makes them more susceptible to a premature death, one that, on the other hand, implies lower welfare expenses due to the endless ailments of old age.[37]

It could be argued that it does not matter much that antipaternalism and antiprohibition are "beneficial" from an economic point of view. It seems far more important to ask how beneficial they are from the point of view of harm to others. How far do increased tax revenues count if there is more harm to people's integrity and lives due to a (limited) increase in drug use? That is the point. Antipaternalism and antiprohibitionism would still converge, and would do so for the numerous reasons discussed: far fewer crimes committed by users; more revenue to fund education programs in schools, detoxification programs, and increased police checks on roads and highways; an eventual increase in consumption mainly for recreational purposes or for leisure; fewer serious crimes committed by organized crime; employment of severely addicted users in jobs with little risk to others; free supervised administration for severely dependent and low-income users; fewer withdrawal crises, overdose deaths, suicide deaths, suicide attempts and intoxication crises; and users' greater knowledge of the effects of drug use, of the risks of intoxication (and its effects), and of crashing (the exhaustion occurring hours after taking a drug) and craving (the more or less intense desire to seek another fix); notices printed on the packaging of marijuana, ecstacy or cocaine as happens with tobacco. (Such a notice would read: "Cannabis use may cause depression and suicidal attempts" or "Cocaine

[36] This is so as well because severely addicted drug addicts authorized to consume certain drugs could have their driving license temporarily suspended.

[37] In general, Miron (2004, p. 63) claims, the net result of unhealthy activities—such as smoking tobacco, drinking large amounts of alcohol, consuming only fast food, and becoming obese—is ambiguous because actions that make life shorter mean less social welfare and medical expenses in the future. For a similar line of argument, see Husak (1992), p. 159.

use may cause paranoid crisis or heart attack.") All that translates to less injury to the integrity and lives of others.

Finally, as I said, any risks or dangers to minors could be easily avoided by permitting the sale of narcotics only in pharmacies, hospitals, or private establishments (e.g., for cocaine and heroin) or in licensed shops or coffee shops (e.g., for hashish and marijuana), excluding forms of advertising, and prohibiting the consumption of cocaine and heroin in public places or in places open to the public (except possibly in restricted areas).

References

Abraham MD, Kaal HL, Cohen PDA (2003) Licit and Illicit Drug Use in Amsterdam, 1987 to 2001. Development of Drug Use in Amsterdam, as Measured in Five Population Surveys between 1987 and 2001. Amsterdam. CEDRO/Mets & Schilt (CEDRO: Centrum voor Drugsonderzoek)

ABT Associates (2000) Illicit drugs: price elasticity of demand and supply. Report Prepared for the National Institute of Justice. Cambridge

Alldridge P (1996) Dealing with drug dealing. In: Simester AP, Smith ATH (eds) Harm and culpability. Clarendon Press, Oxford, pp 239–258

Beltramini A (2010) La droga della violenza. Focus, May

Bricolo F, Aldegheri F, Serpelloni G (2006) Meccanismi di azione della cocaina e implicazioni per i trattamenti farmacologici. In: Serpelloni G, Macchia T, Gerra G (eds) Cocaina: Manuale di aggiornamento tecnico scientifico, http://cocaina.dronetplus.eu/manuale.html

Caulkins JP (1995) Estimating elasticities of Demand for Cocaine and Heroin with DUF data. Pittsburgh, Working Paper, Heinz School of Public Policy, Carnegie Mellon University

Caulkins JP, Reuter P (1998) What price data tell us about drug markets. J Drug Iss 28(3):593–612

Chaloupka FJ Grossman M, Tauras JA (1998) The Demand for Cocaine and Marijuana by Youth. NBER working paper no. 6411, February

Cocaine Project (1995) Report by the World Health Organization and the UN Inter-regional Crime and Justice Research Institute (UNICRI). https://wikileaks.org/wiki/World_Health_Organization_global_Cocaine_Project_Study_suppressed_by_the_United_States_for_13_years%2C_1995

Cohen P, Sas A (1996) Cannabis use: a stepping stone to other drugs? The case of Amsterdam. CEDRO, Amsterdam

Cohen PDA, Kaal HL (2001) The irrelevance of drug policy. CEDRO, Amsterdam

Costa Storti C, De Grauwe P (2007) Globalization and the Price Decline of Illicit Drugs. CESIFO working paper n. 1990

Costa Storti C, De Grauwe P (2008) Modelling the Cocaine and Heroin markets in the era of globalization and drug reduction policies. CESIFO Venice Summer Institute

D'Agostino F (1998) Bioetica: Nella prospettiva della filosofia del diritto. Giappichelli, Turin

Dave D (2004) The effects of Cocaine and Heroin prices on drug-related emergency department visits. NBER working paper n. 10619, July

David P, Ofria F (2017) Perché legalizzare la cannabis: Una analisi di costi e benefici. Economia e politica 9(14):1–6. http://www.economiaepolitica.it/politiche-economiche/perche-legalizzare-la-cannabis-una-analisi-di-costi-e-benefici/

Devlin P (1959) The enforcement of morals. Maccabaean Lecture in Jurisprudence of the British Academy. From The Proceedings of the British Academy, vol. XLV 3s., 6d.., 25 pp. (1965, London, Oxford University Press)

Donini M (2008) 'Danno' e 'offesa' nella tutela penale dei sentimenti: Note su morale e sicurezza come beni giuridici, a margine della categoria dell''offense' di Joel Feinberg. Rivista italiana di diritto e procedura penale.

EMCDDA (2009) Annual Report on the State of the Drugs Problem in Europe. European Monitoring Centre for Drugs and Drug Addiction. https://www.emcdda.europa.eu/publications/annual-report/2009_en

EMCDDA (2018) European Monitoring Centre for Drugs and Drug Addiction. Colorado Publishes Latest Statistics on Impact of Cannabis legalization Lisbon, 19 Dec. 2018. http://www.emcdda.europa.eu/news/2018/colorado-publishes-latest-statistics-on-impact-of-cannabis-legalisation_en

EMCDDA (2022) European Drug Report 2022: Trends and Developments. European Monitoring Centre for Drugs and Drug Addiction. https://www.emcdda.europa.eu/publications/edr/trends-developments/2022_en

Hammond et al (2024) Association between Marijuana laws and suicide among 12- to 25-year-olds in the United States from 2000 to 2019. J Am Acad Child Adolescent Psychiatry 63 3:345–354

Hart HLA (1963) Law, liberty and morality. Stanford University Press, Stanford

Husak DN (1992) Drugs and rights. Cambridge University Press, Cambridge

Husak DN (2002) Legalize this! The case for decriminalizing drugs. Verso, London

Johnston LD et al. (2022) Monitoring the future: National Survey Results on Drug Use 1975–2021. 2021 overview: key findings on adolescent drug use. Institute for Social Research, University of Michigan, Ann Arbor

Kahn GD et al (2022) Marijuana use is associated with suicidal ideation and behavior among US adolescents at rates similar to Tobacco and Alcohol. Arch Suicide Res., April-June

Korf DJ (2002) Dutch coffee shops and trends in cannabis use. Addict Behav 27:851–866

Lavezzi AM (2014) Organised crime and the economy: a framework for policy prescriptions. Global Crime

MacCoun RJ, Reuter P (2004) Drug war heresies. Cambridge University Press, Cambridge

Mackinnon C (1987) Feminism unmodified. Discourses on life and law. Harvard University Press, Cambridge

Mackinnon C (1989) Towards a feminist theory of state. Harvard University Press, Cambridge

Maniaci G (2016) Aporie e distorsioni del femminismo radicale. Diritto e questioni pubbliche 16(2):339–364

Mill JS (1971) On liberty (1859) In vol. 18 of collected works. In: Robson JM (ed) Routledge & Kegan Paul, London, pp 213–310

Ministero della Salute (2022) Tabagismo. https://www.salute.gov.it/portale/fumo/dettaglioContenutiFumo.jsp?id=5579&area=fumo&menu=vuoto

Miron JA (2004) Drug war crimes: the consequences of prohibition. The Independent Institute, Oakland

Miron JA, Earleywine M (2010) The Budgetary Implications of Marijuana Prohibition https://www.semanticscholar.org/paper/The-Budgetary-Implications-of-Marijuana-Prohibition-Miron-Earleywine/3a344f53e78a8226299debd033213ea37b6cd81d

Miron JA, Waldock K (2010) The budgetary impact of ending drug prohibition. Cato Institute, Washington. https://www.cato.org/white-paper/budgetary-impact-ending-drug-prohibition#

Molinaro S, Salvadori S, Mariani F (2006) Epidemiologia dell'uso e del consumo problematico di cocaina in Italia. In: Serpelloni G, Macchia T, Gerra G (eds) Cocaina: Manuale di aggiornamento tecnico scientifico. http://cocaina.dronetplus.eu/manuale.html

Nestler EJ (2013) Cellular basis of memory for addiction. Dialog Clin Neurosci 15(4):431–443. https://doi.org/10.31887/DCNS.2013.15.4/enestler

Nestler EJ, Hyman SE, Malenka RC (2009) Reinforcement and addictive disorders. In: Nestler EJ, Hyman SE (eds) Molecular neuropharmacology: a foundation for clinical neuroscience, 2nd edn. McGraw-Hill Medical, New York, Chap. 15, pp 364–375

NSDUH (2021) National Survey on Drug Use and Health in the United States. https://www.samhsa.gov/data/report/2021-nsduh-detailed-tables.

Pacifici R (2022) Annual report on tobacco consumption in Italy, 2022, drawn up by Roberta Pacifici, Director of the National Observatory for Addictions and Doping, Smoking, Alcohol, and Drugs (OSSFAD). Istituto Superiore di Sanità. https://www.salute.gov.it/portale/fumo/dettaglioContenutiFumo.jsp?id=5579&area=fumo&menu=vuoto

Reuband KH (1995) Drug use and drug policy in Western Europe: epidemiological findings in a comparative perspective. Eur Addict Res 1–2:61–62

Rolles S (2009) After the war on drugs: blueprint for regulation. Transform Drug Policy Foundation

Romano M (2010) Danno a sé stessi, paternalismo legale e limiti del diritto penale. In: Cadoppi A (ed) Laicità, valori e diritto penale: "The Moral Limits of the Criminal Law"; In ricordo di Joel Feinberg, Milan, Giuffrè

RUSSELL DEH (1993) Pornography and rape: a causal model. In: ID. (ed) Making violence sexy. Teachers College Press, New York

Saffer H, Chaloupka F (1999) The demand for illicit drugs. Econ Inq 37(3):401–411

SAMHSA (2020) United States substance abuse and Mental Health Services Administration. Results from the 2020 National Survey on drug use and health: detailed tables. Center for Behavioral Health Statistics and Quality, Rockville, MD

Serpelloni G, Macchia T, Gerra G (eds) (2006) Cocaina: Manuale di aggiornamento tecnico scientifico. Editrice La Grafica, Mori (TN). https://www.politicheantidroga.gov.it/it/attivita/attivita-e-progetti/le-pubblicazioni/cocaina-manuale-di-aggiornamento-tecnico-scientifico/

Taradash M (1991) Come riformare la politica sulla droga. In: Manconi L (ed) Legalizzare la droga: Una ragionevole proposta di sperimentazione. Feltrinelli

Thuy TT, Méndez K, Warner E (2024) New estimates of smoking-attributable mortality in the U.S. from 2020 through 2035. Am J Prev Med 66:877–882

Tincani P (2012) Perché l'antiproibizionismo è logico (e morale): Filosofia, diritto e libertà individuali. Sironi Editore, Milan

Volkow ND, Koob GF, Thomas McLellan A (2016) Neurobiologic advances from the brain disease model of addiction. New England J Med 374(4):363–371

Wikipedia (2023a) Substance use disorder. https://en.wikipedia.org/wiki/Substance_use_disorder#cite_note-Cellular_basis-30. Accessed December 2023

Wikipedia (2023b) War on Drugs https://en.wikipedia.org/wiki/War_on_drugs. Accessed October 2023

World Drug Report. 2008, 2009, 2010, 2011, 2012, 2013, 2018, 2022, 2023. United Nations Office on Drugs and Crime (UNODC), United Nations Publication. http://www.unodc.org/unodc/data-and-analysis/WDR.html

The manufacturer's authorised representative in the EU is Springer Nature Customer Service Centre GmbH, Europaplatz 3, 69115 Heidelberg, Germany. If you have any concerns regarding our products, please contact ProductSafety@springernature.com

Printed and bound by CPI Group (UK) Ltd, Croydon, CR0 4YY
01/10/2026
02225968-0011